Lecture Notes in Computer Science 5356

Commenced Publication in 1973
Founding and Former Series Editors:
Gerhard Goos, Juris Hartmanis, and Jan van Leeuwen

T0224100

G. Ramalingam (Ed.)

Programming Languages and Systems

6th Asian Symposium, APLAS 2008
Bangalore, India, December 9-11, 2008
Proceedings

 Springer

Volume Editor

G. Ramalingam
Microsoft Research India
196/36, 2nd Main, Sadashivnagar, Bangalore 560080, India
E-mail: grama@microsoft.com

Library of Congress Control Number: Applied for

CR Subject Classification (1998): D.3, D.2, F.3, D.4, D.1, F.4.1

LNCS Sublibrary: SL 2 – Programming and Software Engineering

ISSN   0302-9743
ISBN-10   3-540-89329-6 Springer Berlin Heidelberg New York
ISBN-13   978-3-540-89329-5 Springer Berlin Heidelberg New York

Springer is a part of Springer Science+Business Media

springer.com

© Springer-Verlag Berlin Heidelberg 2008
Printed in Germany

Typesetting: Camera-ready by author, data conversion by Scientific Publishing Services, Chennai, India
Printed on acid-free paper   SPIN: 12564330   06/3180   5 4 3 2 1 0

Preface

This volume contains the proceedings of the 6th Asian Symposium on Programming Languages and Systems (APLAS 2008), which took place in Bangalore, December 9 – December 11, 2008. The symposium was sponsored by the Asian Association for Foundation of Software (AAFS) and the Indian Institute of Science. It was held at the Indian Institute of Science, as part of the institute's centenary celebrations, and was co-located with FSTTCS (Foundations of Software Technology and Theoretical Computer Science) 2008, organized by the Indian Association for Research in Computer Science (IARCS).

In response to the call for papers, 41 full submissions were received. Each submission was reviewed by at least four Program Committee members with the help of external reviewers. The Program Committee meeting was conducted electronically over a 2-week period. After careful discussion, the Program Committee selected 20 papers. I would like to sincerely thank all the members of the APLAS 2008 Program Committee for their excellent job, and all the external reviewers for their invaluable contribution. The submission and review process was managed using the EasyChair system.

In addition to the 20 contributed papers, the symposium also featured three invited talks by Dino Distefano (Queen Mary, University of London, UK), Radha Jagadeesan (DePaul University, USA), and Simon Peyton-Jones (Microsoft Research Cambridge, UK).

Many people have helped to promote APLAS as a high-quality forum in Asia to serve programming language researchers worldwide. Following a series of well-attended workshops that were held in Singapore (2000), Daejeon (2001), and Shanghai (2002), the first five formal symposiums were held in Beijing (2003), Taipei (2004), Tsukuba (2005), Sydney (2006), and Singapore (2007).

I thank the General Chair, S. Ramesh, for his support and guidance. I am indebted to our Local Arrangements Chairs, Venkatesh-Prasad Ranganath and Prahlad Sampath, for their considerable efforts in planning and organizing the meeting itself. I am grateful to Komondoor V. Raghavan for serving as the Poster Chair. I would also like to thank the Program Chairs of the past APLAS symposiums, especially Zhong Shao and Naoki Kobayashi, and the members of the AAFS Executive Committee, especially Joxan Jaffar, for their advice. Last but not least, I would like to thank Deepak D'Souza and Madhavan Mukund for making it possible to colocate APLAS with FSTTCS and for their help in all aspects of organizing the conferences.

September 2008   G. Ramalingam

Organization

General Chair

S. Ramesh   India Science Lab, GM R&D

Program Chair

G. Ramalingam   Microsoft Research India

Program Committee

Tyng-Ruey Chuang	Institute of Information Science, Academia Sinica, Taiwan
Xinyu Feng	Toyota Technological Institute at Chicago, USA
Mathew Flatt	University of Utah, USA
Yuxi Fu	Shanghai Jiaotong University, China
Rajiv Gupta	University of California, Riverside, USA
Siau-Cheng Khoo	National University of Singapore, Singapore
Naoki Kobayashi	Tohoku University, Japan
P. Madhusudan	University of Illinois at Urbana-Champaign, USA
Soo-Mook Moon	Seoul National University, Korea
Komondoor V. Raghavan	Indian Institute of Science, Bangalore, India
G. Ramalingam	Microsoft Research India
Mooly Sagiv	Tel Aviv University, Israel
Koushik Sen	University of California, Berkeley, USA
Zhendong Su	University of California, Davis, USA
Martin Sulzmann	IT University of Copenhagen, Denmark
Hongseok Yang	Queen Mary, University of London, UK
Nobuko Yoshida	Imperial College, London, UK

Local Arrangements Chairs

Venkatesh-Prasad Ranganath	Microsoft Research India
Prahladavaradan Sampath	India Science Lab, GM R&D

Poster Chair

Komondoor V. Raghavan   Indian Institute of Science, Bangalore

External Referees

Vicki Allan
Zachary Anderson
Jim Apple
Martin Berger
Jacob Burnim
Florin Craciun
Marco Carbone
Marco Carbone
Chin-Lung Chang
Kung Chen
Taolue Chen
Wei-Ngan Chin
Hyung-Kyu Choi
Tiago Cogumbreiro
Derek Dreyer
Yahav Eran
Min Feng
Rodrigo Ferreira
Akihiro Fujiwara
Mark Gabel
Jacques Garrigue
Alexey Gotsman
Rajiv Gupta

Ryu Hasegawa
Martin Henz
Yoshinao Isobe
Dennis Jeffrey
Pallavi Joshi
Dong-Heon Jung
Sudeep Juvekar
Akash Lal
Martin Lange
Jaemok Lee
Seong-Won Lee
Tal Lev-Ami
David Lo
Louis Mandel
Leo Meyerovich
Samuel Mimram
Rasmus Mogelberg
Soo-Mook Moon
Shin-Cheng Mu
Vijay Nagarajan
Aleksandar Nanevski
Koki Nishizawa
Hyeong-Seok Oh

Chang-Seo Park
Mauro Piccolo
Corneliu Popeea
Francois Pottier
Venkatesh-Prasad
  Ranganath
Noam Rinetzky
Abhik Roychoudhury
Raluca Sauciuc
Max Schaefer
RK Shyamasundar
Konrad Slind
Kohei Suenaga
Tachio Terauchi
Chen Tian
Yih-Kuen Tsay
Dimitrios Vytiniotis
Bow-Yaw Wang
Meng Wang
Reinhard Wilhelm
Yinqi Xiao
Greta Yorsh
Frank de Boer

Sponsoring Institutions

Asian Association for Foundation of Software (AAFS)
Indian Institute of Science

Table of Contents

Abductive Inference for Reasoning about Heaps

Dino Distefano

Queen Mary, University of London

The driving force behind Space Invader [1,2,3] — an automatic tool aiming to perform accurate static analysis of programs using pointers — is the idea of local reasoning, which is enabled by the Frame Rule of separation logic [4]:

$$\frac{\{P\}\ C\ \{Q\}}{\{P * R\}\ C\ \{Q * R\}}$$

In this rule R is the *frame*, i.e., the part of the heap which is not touched by the execution of the command C. The Frame Rule allows pre and postconditions to concentrate on the footprint: the cells touched by command C.

In moving from by-hand to automatic verification the ability to deduce the frame becomes a central task. Computation of the frame is done by *frame inference*, which can be formally defined as:

> Given (separation logic) formulae H and H' compute a formula X such that $H \vdash H' * X$ holds.

An algorithm for inferring frames was introduced in [5]. Interestingly, crucial tasks necessary to perform automatic heap analysis — such as rearrangement (materialization) and abstraction — can be reduced to solving frame inference questions [6].

In our attempts to deal with incomplete code and increase automation in Space Invader, we discovered that the idea of *abductive inference* — introduced by Charles Peirce in the early 1900s in his writings on the scientific process [7] — is highly valuable. When reasoning about the heap, abductive inference, often known as inference of explanatory hypotheses, is a natural dual to the notion of frame inference, and can be defined as follows:

> Given (separation logic) formulae H and H' compute a formula X such that $H * X \vdash H'$ holds.

Here we call X the "anti-frame". Inference of frame and abduction of anti-frame together are the ingredients which allow for an analysis method where pre/post specs of procedures are inferred independently of their context. Abduction allows us to automatically compute (approximations of) *footprint* of commands and preconditions of procedures [8].

This talk, which describes joint work with Cristiano Calcagno, Peter O'Hearn, and Hongseok Yang, will introduce abductive inference and its use in reasoning about heap manipulating programs. Moreover, besides exploring the relation between abductive and frame inference, it will describe our experience in the application of abduction for designing compositional shape analyses [8].

G. Ramalingam (Ed.): APLAS 2008, LNCS 5356, pp. 1–2, 2008.
© Springer-Verlag Berlin Heidelberg 2008

References

1. Distefano, D., O'Hearn, P., Yang, H.: A local shape analysis based on separation logic. In: Hermanns, H., Palsberg, J. (eds.) TACAS 2006. LNCS, vol. 3920, pp. 287–302. Springer, Heidelberg (2006)
2. Berdine, J., Calcagno, C., Cook, B., Distefano, D., O'Hearn, P., Wies, T., Yang, H.: Shape analysis of composite data structures. In: Damm, W., Hermanns, H. (eds.) CAV 2007. LNCS, vol. 4590, pp. 178–192. Springer, Heidelberg (2007)
3. Yang, H., Lee, O., Berdine, J., Calcagno, C., Cook, B., Distefano, D., O'Hearn, P.: Scalable shape analysis for systems code. In: Gupta, A., Malik, S. (eds.) CAV 2008. LNCS, vol. 5123, pp. 385–398. Springer, Heidelberg (2008)
4. O'Hearn, P., Reynolds, J., Yang, H.: Local reasoning about programs that alter data structures. In: Fribourg, L. (ed.) CSL 2001 and EACSL 2001. LNCS, vol. 2142, p. 1. Springer, Heidelberg (2001)
5. Berdine, J., Calcagno, C., O'Hearn, P.W.: Symbolic execution with separation logic. In: Yi, K. (ed.) APLAS 2005. LNCS, vol. 3780, pp. 52–68. Springer, Heidelberg (2005)
6. Distefano, D., Parkinson, M.: jStar: Towards practical verification for java. In: OOPSLA 2008 (to appear, 2008)
7. Peirce, C.S.: Collected papers of Charles Sanders Peirce. Harvard University Press (1958)
8. Calcagno, C., Distefano, D., O'Hearn, P., Yang, H.: Compositional shape analysis. Technical Report 2008/12, Imperial College, London (July 2008)

A Sound Floating-Point Polyhedra Abstract Domain*

Liqian Chen[1,2], Antoine Miné[3], and Patrick Cousot[1]

[1] École Normale Supérieure, Paris, France
{chen,mine,cousot}@di.ens.fr
[2] National Laboratory for Parallel and Distributed Processing, Changsha, P.R.China
[3] CNRS, École Normale Supérieure, Paris, France

Abstract. The polyhedra abstract domain is one of the most powerful and commonly used numerical abstract domains in the field of static program analysis based on abstract interpretation. In this paper, we present an implementation of the polyhedra domain using floating-point arithmetic without sacrificing soundness. Floating-point arithmetic allows a compact memory representation and an efficient implementation on current hardware, at the cost of some loss of precision due to rounding. Our domain is based on a constraint-only representation and employs sound floating-point variants of Fourier-Motzkin elimination and linear programming. The preliminary experimental results of our prototype are encouraging. To our knowledge, this is the first time that the polyhedra domain is adapted to floating-point arithmetic in a sound way.

1 Introduction

Static analysis is a technique to automatically discover program properties at compile-time. One important application is to prove the absence of run-time errors in a program before actually running it. Since, in general, the exact behavior of a program cannot be computed statically, an analysis needs to use approximation. We only consider analyses that are *sound*, that is, compute an over-approximation of all possible behaviors including all real errors, but may fail to prove the correctness if the approximation is too coarse.

The abstract interpretation framework [6] allows devising static analyses that are sound by construction. A core concept in abstract interpretation is that of *an abstract domain*, that is, a set of computer-representable properties together with operators to model soundly the semantic actions of a program (assignments, tests, control-flow joins, loops, etc.). Specifically, we are interested in *numerical* abstract domains that represent properties of the numerical variables of a program.

Among them, one of the most famous is the *polyhedra* abstract domain introduced in 1978 by Cousot and Halbwachs [7] which can infer linear relationships between variables in a program. It has a wide range of applications in the field of the analysis and verification of hardware and software systems. A number of implementations for manipulating polyhedra are currently available. Recent ones include the Parma Polyhedra Library (PPL) [3] and the APRON library [1].

* This work is supported by the INRIA project-team Abstraction common to the CNRS and the École Normale Supérieure. This work is partially supported by the Fund of the China Scholarship Council and National Natural Science Foundation of China under Grant No.60725206.

G. Ramalingam (Ed.): APLAS 2008, LNCS 5356, pp. 3–18, 2008.
© Springer-Verlag Berlin Heidelberg 2008

However, most implementations suffer from scalability problems [20]. One reason is the use of arbitrary precision rationals which are slow and may lead to excessively large numbers even when analyzing simple programs involving only small integer values. Alternatively, one can use fast machine integers but then overflows can cause much precision loss. Floating-point numbers are not only fast but they also allow a *gradual* loss of precision. Unfortunately, the pervasive rounding errors make it difficult to guarantee soundness. This is the problem we tackle in this paper.

This paper presents a sound floating-point implementation of the polyhedra abstract domain. Our approach is based on three key points: a constraint-based representation using floating-point coefficients, a sound version of Fourier-Motzkin elimination using floating-point arithmetic, and a rigorous linear programming method proposed in [19]. The preliminary experimental results are promising when analyzing programs involving coefficients of large magnitude, e.g., floating-point programs.

The rest of the paper is organized as follows. Section 2 discusses some related work. In Section 3, we review the design of the polyhedra domain based on a constraint-only representation over the rationals. In Section 4, we adapt this framework to the floating-point world. Section 5 discusses precision and efficiency issues due to rounding and proposes some solutions. Section 6 presents our prototype implementation together with preliminary experimental results. Finally, conclusions as well as suggestions for future work are given in Section 7.

2   Related Work

The Polyhedra Abstract Domain. Common implementations of the polyhedra domain [1,3] are based on a dual representation [7]. A polyhedron can be described as the conjunction of a finite set of linear constraints. Dually, in the frame representation, it can be represented as a finite collection of generators, that is, vertices or rays. Some domain operations (e.g., meet and test) can be performed more efficiently on the constraint representation, while some others (e.g., projection and join) can be performed more efficiently on the frame representation. Thus, it is often necessary to convert from one representation to the other. The dual conversions are performed using the Chernikova algorithm [13] which can produce an output that is exponential in the size of the input.

Recently, as an alternative to the dual representation, Simon and King [23] have demonstrated that the polyhedra domain can be fully implemented using only constraints, with the aim to remove the complexity bottleneck caused by the frame representation. Our work is based on the same principle.

In order to reduce the complexity, it has also been proposed to abandon general polyhedra in favor of less expressive weakly relational domains which are polyhedra of restricted forms that benefit from specialized algorithms with improved complexity. Examples include the Octagon domain [17], the Two Variables Per Inequality (TVPI) domain [24], and the Template Constraint Matrix (TCM) domain [22].

Linear Programming. Linear Programming (LP) [2] is a method used to find the optimal value of some affine function (so-called objective function) subject to a finite system of linear constraints (defining the so-called feasible space) . It is a well-studied problem for which highly efficient algorithms have already been developed that scale up to hundreds of thousands of variables and constraints. Most state-of-the-art LP solvers use floating-point arithmetic and only give approximate solutions which may not be the actual optimum solution or may even lie outside the feasible space. It would be possible but costly in practice to compute the exact solution using exact arithmetic. Instead, we take advantage of recent progress that has been made on computing *rigorous* bounds for the objective value using floating-point arithmetic [19]. In particular, the ability to infer rigorous bounds provides a basis for soundly implementing some operations in our domain.

Note that using LP in a polyhedral analysis is not new. Sankaranarayanan et al. [22] use it in their TCM domain which is less expressive than general polyhedra. They use approximate floating-point LP but the result is then checked using exact arithmetic. Simon et al. [23] consider general polyhedra but use exact arithmetic. We will consider here general polyhedra and use only floating-point arithmetic.

Static Analysis of Floating-Point Programs. A related problem is that of analyzing programs featuring floating-point computations. In [8], Goubault analyzes the origin of the loss of precision in floating-point programs. ASTRÉE [5] computes the set of reachable values for floating-point variables in order to check for run-time errors. In this paper, we will also apply our abstract domain to the reachability problem in floating-point programs.

Note that the polyhedra abstract domain described in this paper abstracts sets of real numbers. As in ASTRÉE, we rely on the linearization technique of [15] to soundly abstract floating-point computations in the analyzed program into ones over the field of reals. The use of floating-point arithmetic in the abstraction becomes very important for efficiency when analyzing linearized floating-point programs as they involve coefficients of large magnitude.

Although sound implementations of floating-point interval arithmetic have been known for a long time [18], such adaptations to *relational* domains are recent and few [15]. To our knowledge, we are the first to tackle the case of general polyhedra.

3   Rational Polyhedra Domain Based on Constraints

In this section, we describe the design of a polyhedra domain based on a constraint-only representation using rational numbers, most of which has been previously known [23] except for the implementation of the standard widening (Sect. 3.7). Internally, a *rational polyhedron* P is described as an inequality system $Ax \leq b$, where A is a matrix and b is a vector of rational numbers. It represents the set $\gamma(P) = \{x \in \mathbb{Q}^n \mid Ax \leq b\}$ where each point x is a possible environment, i.e., an assignment of rational values to abstract variables. In practice, program variables have to be mapped to these abstract variables by a memory model (see, e.g., [16]). We will now briefly describe the implementation of the common domain operations.

3.1   Redundancy Removal

The constraint representation of a polyhedron is not unique. For efficiency reasons, it is desirable to have as few constraints as possible. An inequality $\varphi \in P$ is said to be redundant when φ can be entailed by the other constraints in P, that is, $P \setminus \{\varphi\} \models \varphi$. Given $\varphi = (\sum_i a_i x_i \leq b)$ in P, we can check whether φ is redundant by solving the LP problem: $\mu = \max \sum_i a_i x_i$ subject to $P \setminus \{\varphi\}$. If $\mu \leq b$, then φ is redundant and can be eliminated from P. This process is repeated until no more inequality can be removed.

3.2   Emptiness Test

A polyhedron is *empty* if and only if its constraint set is infeasible. The feasibility of a constraint system is implicitly checked by LP solvers when computing the maximum (minimum) of an objective function. During program analysis, constraints are often added one by one. Thus, the test for emptiness can also be done incrementally. When adding a new constraint $\sum_i a_i x_i \leq b$ to a nonempty polyhedron P, we solve the LP problem $\mu = \min \sum_i a_i x_i$ subject to P. If $b < \mu$, the new polyhedron is indeed empty.

3.3   Projection

An important operation on polyhedra is to remove all information pertaining to a variable x_i without affecting the relational information between other variables. To this end, we define the projection operator $\pi(P, x_i) \overset{\text{def}}{=} \{ x[x_i/y] \mid x \in \gamma(P), y \in \mathbb{Q} \}$, where $x[x_i/y]$ denotes the vector x in which the i-th element is replaced with y. It can be computed by eliminating all occurrences of x_i in the constraints defining P, using the classic Fourier-Motzkin algorithm:

$$Fourier(P, x_i) \overset{\text{def}}{=} \left\{ (-a_i^-)c^+ + a_i^+ c^- \left| \begin{array}{l} c^+ = (\sum_k a_k^+ x_k \leq b^+) \in P, a_i^+ > 0 \\ c^- = (\sum_k a_k^- x_k \leq b^-) \in P, a_i^- < 0 \end{array} \right. \right\}$$
$$\cup \{ (\sum_k a_k x_k \leq b) \in P \mid a_i = 0 \}.$$

The projection is useful to model the non-deterministic assignment of an unknown value to a variable x_i, namely by defining: $[\![x_i := random()]\!]^\#(P) \overset{\text{def}}{=} Fourier(P, x_i)$, where $[\![\cdot]\!]^\#(P)$ denotes the effect of a program statement on the polyhedron P.

3.4   Join

To abstract the control-flow join, we need to compute the union of environments of program variables. The smallest polyhedron enclosing this union is the topological closure of the convex hull. To compute it, we use the method proposed in [23]. Given $\gamma(P) = \{ x \in \mathbb{Q}^n \mid Ax \leq b \}$ and $\gamma(P') = \{ x \in \mathbb{Q}^n \mid A'x \leq b' \}$, the convex hull of P and P' is

$$\gamma(P_H) = \left\{ x \in \mathbb{Q}^n \left| \begin{array}{l} x = \sigma_1 z + \sigma_2 z' \wedge \sigma_1 + \sigma_2 = 1 \wedge \sigma_1 \geq 0 \wedge \\ Az \leq b \quad \wedge \quad A'z' \leq b' \wedge \sigma_2 \geq 0 \end{array} \right. \right\}$$

where $\sigma_1, \sigma_2 \in \mathbb{Q}$ and $x, z, z' \in \mathbb{Q}^n$. To avoid the non-linear equation $x = \sigma_1 z + \sigma_2 z'$, we introduce $y = \sigma_1 z$ as well as $y' = \sigma_2 z'$ and relax the system into

$$\gamma(P_{CH}) = \left\{ x \in \mathbb{Q}^n \left| \begin{array}{l} x = y + y' \wedge \sigma_1 + \sigma_2 = 1 \wedge \sigma_1 \geq 0 \wedge \\ Ay \leq \sigma_1 b \wedge A'y' \leq \sigma_2 b' \wedge \sigma_2 \geq 0 \end{array} \right. \right\} . \quad (1)$$

Projecting out $\sigma_1, \sigma_2, y, y'$ from (1) yields the closure of the convex hull of P and P'.

3.5   Transfer Functions

Test Transfer Function. An affine test with exact rational arithmetic can be converted to the form $\sum_i a_i x_i \leq c$. The result of such a test $[\![\sum_i a_i x_i \leq c]\!]^\#(P)$ is simply the polyhedron P with the constraint $\sum_i a_i x_i \leq c$ added. Note that a test may introduce redundancy or make the polyhedron infeasible. More complicated cases, such as tests involving floating-point or non-linear operations, can be soundly abstracted to the form $\sum_i a_i x_i \leq c$ following the method in [15]. In the worst case, we can always ignore the effect of a test, which is sound.

Assignment Transfer Function. The assignment of some expression e to x_j can be modeled using projection, test, and variable renaming as follows:

$$[\![x_j := e]\!]^\#(P) \stackrel{\mathrm{def}}{=} (Fourier([\![x'_j - e = 0]\!]^\#(P), x_j))[x'_j/x_j].$$

First, a fresh variable x'_j is introduced to hold the value of the expression. Then, we project out x_j by Fourier-Motzkin elimination and the final result system is obtained by renaming x'_j back to x_j. The temporary variable x'_j is necessary for invertible assignments such as $x := x + 1$.

3.6   Inclusion Test

Inclusion test between two polyhedra P_1 and P_2, denoted $P_1 \sqsubseteq P_2$, reduces to the problem of checking whether each inequality in P_2 is entailed by P_1, which can be implemented using LP. For each $\sum_i a_i x_i \leq b$ in P_2, compute $\mu = \max \sum_i a_i x_i$ subject to P_1. If $\mu > b$, the inclusion does not hold.

3.7   Widening

For loops, widening ensures an efficient analysis by accelerating the fixpoint computation [6]. The first widening operator on polyhedra was proposed in [7] using the dual representation. Its improvement, presented in [9], is now the standard widening:

Definition 1 (Standard widening). *Given two polyhedra $P_1 \sqsubseteq P_2$, represented by sets of linear inequalities, we define*

$$P_1 \triangledown P_2 \stackrel{\mathrm{def}}{=} S_1 \cup S_2$$

where

$$S_1 = \{ \varphi_1 \in P_1 \mid P_2 \models \varphi_1 \},$$
$$S_2 = \{ \varphi_2 \in P_2 \mid \exists \varphi_1 \in P_1, \gamma(P_1) = \gamma((P_1 \setminus \{ \varphi_1 \}) \cup \{ \varphi_2 \}) \}.$$

The key point of the standard widening is to keep not only the inequalities S_1 from P_1 satisfied by P_2, but also the inequalities S_2 from P_2 that are mutually redundant with an inequality of P_1 with respect to P_1. S_2 ensures that the result does not depend on the representation of P_1 and P_2. Note that S_1 can be computed using entailment checks. The following property shows that S_2 also reduces to entailment checks, which shows that the standard widening can be efficiently implemented using LP only.

Property 1. $\forall \varphi_1 \in P_1, \varphi_2 \in P_2, \gamma(P_1) = \gamma((P_1 \setminus \{\varphi_1\}) \cup \{\varphi_2\})$ *iff* $P_1 \models \varphi_2$ *and* $((P_1 \setminus \{\varphi_1\}) \cup \{\varphi_2\}) \models \varphi_1$.

4   Floating-Point Polyhedra Domain

In this section, we present a floating-point implementation of the polyhedra domain. A *floating-point* polyhedron is represented as an inequality system $Ax \leq b$ where coefficients in A and b are now floating-point numbers. Such a system still represents a set of environments with rational-valued variables, namely $\{x \in \mathbb{Q}^n \mid Ax \leq b\}$ where $Ax \leq b$ is interpreted mathematically (rather than in floating-point semantics).

In order to distinguish floating-point arithmetic operations from exact arithmetic ones, we introduce additional notations. As usual, $\{+, -, \times, /\}$ are used as exact rational arithmetic operations. The corresponding floating-point operations are denoted by $\{\oplus_r, \ominus_r, \otimes_r, \oslash_r\}$, tagged with a rounding mode $r \in \{-\infty, +\infty\}$ ($-\infty$: downward; $+\infty$: upward). The floating-point unary minus $\ominus$ is exact and does not incur rounding. For the sake of convenience, we occasionally use the command *roundup* (respectively *rounddown*) to change the current rounding mode to upward (respectively downward). All the algorithms in this section are implemented in floating-point arithmetic.

4.1   Linearization

We say that a point x satisfies some linear interval inequality $\varphi : \sum_k [a_k, b_k] \times x_k \leq c$, denoted by $x \in \gamma(\varphi)$, when for all k there is some $d_k \in [a_k, b_k]$ such that $\sum_k d_k \times x_k \leq c$ holds. This definition lifts to systems of inequalities straightforwardly and corresponds to the classic notion of *weak solution* in the field of linear interval optimization [21].

A linear inequality in the common sense is simply a linear interval inequality where all the coefficients are singletons (scalars). Our internal representation of a polyhedron supports only linear (non-interval) inequalities, while as we will see in the following sections, some operations of our domain naturally output linear interval inequalities. To convert a linear interval inequality φ to a linear inequality, we adapt the *linearization* technique from [15]. Our linearization operator $\zeta(\varphi, \mathbf{x})$ is defined with respect to a bounding box $\mathbf{x}$ of variables as follows:

Definition 2 (Linearization operator). *Let* $\varphi : \sum_k [a_k, b_k] \times x_k \leq c$ *be a linear interval inequality and* $\mathbf{x} := [\underline{x}, \overline{x}]$ *be the bounding box of x.*

$$\zeta(\varphi, \mathbf{x}) \stackrel{\text{def}}{=} \sum_k d_k \times x_k \leq c \oplus_{+\infty} \bigoplus_k {}_{+\infty} (\max\{b_k \ominus_{+\infty} d_k, d_k \ominus_{+\infty} a_k\} \otimes_{+\infty} |x_k|)$$

where d_k *can be any floating-point number inside* $[a_k, b_k]$ *and* $|x_k| = \max\{-\underline{x_k}, \overline{x_k}\}$.

In theory, d_k can be any floating-point number in $[a_k, b_k]$. In practice, we often choose the midpoint $d_k = (a_k \oplus_r b_k) \oslash_r 2$ which causes the least loss of precision. More strategies to choose a proper d_k will be discussed in Sect. 5.3.

Example 1. Consider the linear interval inequality $[0, 2]x + [1, 1]y \leq 2$ with respect to the bounding box $x, y \in [-10, 5]$. If we choose the midpoint of $[a_k, b_k]$ as d_k, the linearization result will be $x + y \leq 12$ (since $2 \oplus_{+\infty} \max\{2 \ominus_{+\infty} 1, 1 \ominus_{+\infty} 0\} \otimes_{+\infty} 10 \oplus_{+\infty} \max\{1 \ominus_{+\infty} 1, 1 \ominus_{+\infty} 1\} \otimes_{+\infty} 10 = 12$). Note that some loss of precision happens here, e.g., the point $(0, 12)$ satisfies the result inequality $x + y \leq 12$ but does not satisfy the original interval inequality $[0, 2]x + [1, 1]y \leq 2$.

Theorem 1 (Soundness of the linearization operator). *Given a linear interval inequality φ and a bounding box $\mathbf{x}$, $\zeta(\varphi, \mathbf{x})$ soundly over-approximates φ, that is, any point in $\mathbf{x}$ that also satisfies φ satisfies $\zeta(\varphi, \mathbf{x})$: $\forall x \in \mathbf{x}, x \in \gamma(\varphi) \Rightarrow x \in \gamma(\zeta(\varphi, \mathbf{x}))$.*

Proof. For any linear interval inequality $\varphi : \sum_k [a_k, b_k] \times x_k \leq c$,

$$\sum_k [a_k, b_k] \times x_k \leq c$$
$$\Longleftrightarrow \sum_k (d_k + [a_k - d_k, b_k - d_k]) \times x_k \leq c$$
$$\Longleftrightarrow \sum_k d_k \times x_k \leq c + \sum_k [d_k - b_k, d_k - a_k] \times x_k$$
$$\Longrightarrow \sum_k d_k \times x_k \leq (c \oplus_{+\infty} \bigoplus_k {}_{+\infty}(\max\{b_k \ominus_{+\infty} d_k, d_k \ominus_{+\infty} a_k\} \otimes_{+\infty} |x_k|) \qquad \square$$

Note that although the value of the right hand of $\zeta(\varphi, \mathbf{x})$ depends on the evaluation ordering of the summation $\bigoplus_{+\infty}$, the linearization operator is still sound because in fact every ordering gives an upper bound of $c + \sum_k [d_k - b_k, d_k - a_k] \times x_k$ in the real field.

4.2 Floating-Point Fourier-Motzkin Elimination

The key idea in building a sound floating-point Fourier-Motzkin elimination algorithm is to use interval arithmetic with outward rounding (i.e., rounding upper bounds up and lower bounds down). Then, using the linearization operator introduced in Sect. 4.1, the interval coefficients in the result can be linearized to scalars.

Assume we want to eliminate variable x_i from the following two inequalities

$$\begin{cases} a_i^+ x_i + \sum_{k \neq i} a_k^+ \times x_k \leq c^+, & \text{where } a_i^+ > 0 \\ a_i^- x_i + \sum_{k \neq i} a_k^- \times x_k \leq c^-, & \text{where } a_i^- < 0. \end{cases} \qquad (2)$$

After dividing (2) by the absolute value of the coefficient of x_i using interval arithmetic with outward rounding, we get

$$\begin{cases} x_i + \sum_{k \neq i} [a_k^+ \oslash_{-\infty} a_i^+, a_k^+ \oslash_{+\infty} a_i^+] \times x_k \leq c^+ \oslash_{+\infty} a_i^+, & \text{where } a_i^+ > 0 \\ -x_i + \sum_{k \neq i} [a_k^- \oslash_{-\infty} (\ominus a_i^-), a_k^- \oslash_{+\infty} (\ominus a_i^-)] \times x_k \leq c^- \oslash_{+\infty} (\ominus a_i^-), & \text{where } a_i^- < 0 \end{cases}$$

and by addition

$$\sum_{k \neq i} [(a_k^+ \oslash_{-\infty} a_i^+) \oplus_{-\infty} (a_k^- \oslash_{-\infty} (\ominus a_i^-)), (a_k^+ \oslash_{+\infty} a_i^+) \oplus_{+\infty} (a_k^- \oslash_{+\infty} (\ominus a_i^-))] \times x_k$$
$$\leq (c^+ \oslash_{+\infty} a_i^+) \oplus_{+\infty} (c^- \oslash_{+\infty} (\ominus a_i^-)). \qquad (3)$$

Then (3) can be abstracted into a linear (non-interval) form by the linearization operator ζ. We denote as $Fourier_f(P, x_i)$ the result system with x_i projected out from P this way.

Theorem 2 (Soundness of the floating-point Fourier-Motzkin elimination). *Given a polyhedron P, a variable x_i and a bounding box $\mathbf{x}$, any point in $\mathbf{x}$ that also satisfies $Fourier(P, x_i)$ satisfies $Fourier_f(P, x_i)$: $\forall x \in \mathbf{x}, x \in \gamma(Fourier(P, x_i)) \Rightarrow x \in \gamma(Fourier_f(P, x_i))$.*

The key point is that the coefficient of the variable to be eliminated can always be reduced exactly to 1 or -1 by division. In some cases, an alternative algorithm can be used. Suppose that $a_i^+ \otimes_{-\infty} (\ominus a_i^-) = a_i^+ \otimes_{+\infty} (\ominus a_i^-)$, i.e., the floating-point multiplication of a_i^+ and $\ominus a_i^-$ is exact. Then, the Fourier-Motzkin elimination can be done in a multiplicative way:

$$\sum_{k \neq i} [(a_k^+ \otimes_{-\infty} (\ominus a_i^-)) \oplus_{-\infty} (a_k^- \otimes_{-\infty} a_i^+), (a_k^+ \otimes_{+\infty} (\ominus a_i^-)) \oplus_{+\infty} (a_k^- \otimes_{+\infty} a_i^+)] \times x_k \quad (4)$$
$$\leq (c^+ \otimes_{+\infty} (\ominus a_i^-)) \oplus_{+\infty} (c^- \otimes_{+\infty} a_i^+) .$$

Note that the condition $a_i^+ \otimes_{-\infty} (\ominus a_i^-) = a_i^+ \otimes_{+\infty} (\ominus a_i^-)$ guarantees that the coefficient of x_i is exactly 0 in (4). When all the coefficients in (2) are small integers, (4) often gives an exact result, which is rarely the case of (3). In practice, the Fourier-Motzkin elimination by multiplication is very useful for producing constraints with regular co-efficients, especially for programs with only integer variables.

Example 2. Consider two inequalities $3x + y \leq 10$ and $-7x + y \leq 10$ with respect to the bounding box $x, y \in (-\infty, 10]$. After eliminating the variable x, (4) will result in $y \leq 10$ while (3) will result in $y \leq +\infty$.

4.3   Rigorous Linear Programming

The rigorous bounds for the objective function in floating-point linear programming can be derived by a cheap post-processing on the approximate result given by a standard floating-point LP solver [19].

Assume the linear program is given in the form

$$min \quad c^T x$$
$$s.t. \quad Ax \leq b$$

the dual of which is

$$max \quad b^T y$$
$$s.t. \quad A^T y = c, y \leq 0.$$

Suppose that y is an approximate solution of the dual program, then we calculate a rigorous interval $\mathbf{r}$ using interval arithmetic with outward rounding as follows:

$$r := A^T y - c \in \mathbf{r} = [\underline{r}, \overline{r}].$$

Recall that $y \leq 0$ and $Ax \leq b$, hence $y^T Ax \geq y^T b$. By introducing the interval vector $\mathbf{x} := [\underline{x}, \overline{x}]$, we get

$$c^T x = (A^T y - r)^T x = y^T Ax - r^T x \geq y^T b - r^T x \in y^T b - \mathbf{r}^T \mathbf{x}$$

and

$$\mu := \inf(y^T b - \mathbf{r}^T \mathbf{x}) \quad (5)$$

is the desired rigorous lower bound for $c^T x$. The value of (5) can be calculated as follows using floating-point arithmetic:

> rounddown;
> $\underline{r} = A^T y - c;$
> $t = y^T b;$
> roundup;
> $\overline{r} = A^T y - c;$
> $\mu = \max\{ \underline{r}^T \underline{x}, \underline{r}^T \overline{x}, \overline{r}^T \underline{x}, \overline{r}^T \overline{x} \} - t;$
> $\mu = -\mu;$

Note that the precision of such a rigorous bound depends on the range of the bounding box $\mathbf{x}$. Moreover, finding a rigorous upper bound for the maximum objective function can be reduced to the minimum case as $\max c^T x = -\min (-c)^T x$.

4.4 Soundness of the Floating-Point Polyhedra Domain

Observe that the rational domain of Sect. 3 relies on two primitives: Fourier-Motzkin elimination and linear programming. Substituting the two primitives with the floating-point Fourier-Motzkin elimination algorithm (Sect. 4.2) and rigorous linear programming (Sect. 4.3) yields the floating-point polyhedra domain. Note that both primitives may produce floating-point overflows or the value NaN (Not a Number). In these cases, a sound Fourier-Motzkin elimination can be obtained by discarding the constraint. With respect to the rigorous linear programming, we return $+\infty$ (respectively $-\infty$) as the maximum (respectively minimum) objective value.

The soundness of the whole floating-point polyhedra domain is guaranteed by the soundness of each domain operation, which means that each operation should result in a conservative answer with respect to the exact one. Due to the floating-point Fourier-Motzkin elimination algorithm of Sect. 4.2, the projection operator will always result in a sound over-approximated polyhedron compared to the exact one, which implies the soundness of both the join (convex hull) operator and the assignment transfer operator. The soundness of redundancy removal and the test transfer operator is obvious. For the entailment check of an inequality with respect to a polyhedron by rigorous LP, a positive answer indicates actual entailment while a negative answer is inconclusive. Indeed, if an inequality is entailed but is close to or touches the polyhedron, rigorous LP may give a too conservative objective value and fail to declare the entailment. As a consequence, our inclusion test actually outputs either "true" or "don't know". This kind of approximation does not alter the overall soundness of an analysis by abstract interpretation. A similar argument can be given for the incremental emptiness test. Another consequence is that our widening may keep fewer inequalities than an exact implementation would, but this is also sound.

5 Precision and Efficiency Issues

Each operation of the floating-point polyhedra domain outputs over-approximations of those of the rational domain, which indicates that some loss of precision may happen along with each operation. Also, the conservative results returned by rigorous LP cause efficiency degradations since redundancy removal may fail to remove many constraints generated during Fourier-Motzkin elimination, making the system larger and larger as the analysis proceeds. This section addresses these problems from a practical point of view. We propose some tactics to regain some precision and make the domain more efficient while still retaining soundness.

5.1 Bounds Tightening

The bounds of variables play a very important role in our domain, as they determine how much precision is lost in both the linearization and the rigorous LP. The bounds may change along with the operations on the polyhedra, especially when the polyhedron is restricted by adding new constraints. In this case, the bounds must be updated. Bounds tightening can be achieved using different strategies.

Rigorous Linear Programming. A simple way to tighten the bound information of a polyhedron P is to use the rigorous LP, to calculate max (min) x_k subject to P and get the upper (lower) bound of variable x_k. However, since the result given by rigorous LP itself depends on the range of the bounding box, the bounds found by rigorous LP may be too conservative, especially when the bounds of some variable are very large or even lost after widening. In addition, it is costly to run $2n$ linear programs after every operation on an n-dimensional polyhedron. Thus we need some alternative lightweight methods for bounds tightening.

Bound Propagation. Bound propagation is a kind of constraint propagation widely used in constraint programming. Each inequality in the linear constraints of the polyhedron can be used to tighten the bounds for those variables occurring in it. Given an inequality $\sum_i a_i x_i \leq b$, if $a_i > 0$, a new candidate upper bound v for x_i comes from: $x_i \leq v = (b - \sum_{j \neq i} a_j x_j)/a_i$. In practice, an over-approximation of v can be computed by interval arithmetic with outward rounding. If $a_i < 0$, we find a new candidate lower bound in the same way. If the new bounds are tighter, then x_i's bounds are updated. This process can be repeated with each variable in that inequality and with each inequality in the system.

Combining Strategies. In fact, the above two methods for bounds tightening are complementary with respect to each other. Each of them may find tighter bounds than the other one in some cases.

Example 3. Given $\{-x + 3y \leq 0, x - 6y \leq -3\}$ with the bounds $x, y \in (-\infty, +\infty)$, the bound propagation fails to find any tighter bounds while the rigorous LP will only find the tighter bounds $x \in [3, +\infty), y \in (-\infty, +\infty)$. Then, if we perform bound propagation on $\{-x + 3y \leq 0, x - 6y \leq -3\}$ with the bounds $x \in [3, +\infty)$ and $y \in (-\infty, +\infty)$, the exact bounds $x \in [3, +\infty)$ and $y \in [1, +\infty)$ can be found.

Therefore, we should combine the above strategies and strike a balance between cost and precision. For example, we can use rigorous LP to tighten only the bounds of those variables that appear with high frequency in the system, and then use bound propagation to tighten the other variables. Note that both rigorous LP and bound propagation are sensitive to the ordering of variables considered. More precision can be achieved, at greater cost, by iterating the process.

5.2 Convex Hull Tightening

The convex hull computation is the most complicated part of our domain and also where the most severe loss of precision may happen because it is internally implemented via Fourier-Motzkin elimination. In many cases, part of the precision can be recovered by applying certain heuristics, such as using the envelope [4] and bounds information.

Definition 3 (Envelope). *Given two polyhedra P_1 and P_2, represented by sets of linear inequalities, the envelope of P_1 and P_2 is defined as*

$$env(P_1, P_2) \stackrel{\text{def}}{=} S_1 \cup S_2$$

where

$$S_1 = \{ \varphi_1 \in P_1 \mid P_2 \models \varphi_1 \},$$
$$S_2 = \{ \varphi_2 \in P_2 \mid P_1 \models \varphi_2 \}.$$

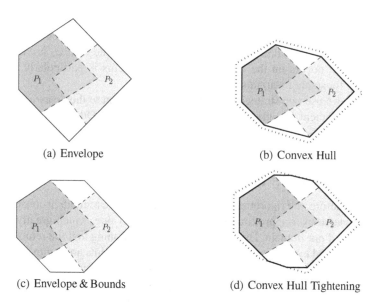

(a) Envelope

(b) Convex Hull

(c) Envelope & Bounds

(d) Convex Hull Tightening

Fig. 1. (a) the envelope $env(P_1, P_2)$ (solid lines), (b) the exact convex hull (solid bold lines) and a possible approximate floating-point convex hull (dotted lines), (c) the smallest polyhedron which can be determined by the envelope and bounding box (solid lines), (d) the floating-point convex hull (dotted lines) and the convex hull after tightening by the envelope and bounding box (solid bold lines)

It is easy to see that the envelope is an over-approximation of the convex hull and contains a subset of the constraints defining the convex hull. In other words, all the inequalities in the envelope can be safely added to the final convex hull. Using rigorous LP, most of the envelope constraints can be determined by entailment checking on the arguments, before the convex hull computation.

The bounding box of the convex hull can also be obtained exactly before the convex hull computation as it is the join, in the interval domain, of the bounding box of the arguments.

We add all constraints from the envelope and the bounding box to tighten the floating-point convex hull and retrieve some precision while still retaining soundness, as shown in Fig. 1. This is of practical importance because at the point of widening, such constraints often hold a large percentage of the stable ones.

5.3 Linearization Heuristics

In polyhedral analysis, new relationships between variables are often derived from the convex hull operation. Their actual coefficients depend greatly on the choices made during the linearization step, in particular the choice of $d_k \in [a_k, b_k]$. In Sect. 4.1, we advocated the use of the interval mid-point $d_k = (a_k \oplus_r b_k) \oslash_r 2$, a greedy choice as it minimizes the constant term of the result constraint. However, choosing a more regular value, such as an integer, will improve the efficiency and numerical stability of subsequent computations, such as LP solving. In addition, due to rounding errors, computations that give the same result in exact arithmetic may give different floating-point results in floating-point arithmetic. Thus, it is desirable that the same d_k is chosen when some slight shift occurs on the input interval $[a_k, b_k]$. This is particularly important when looking for stable invariants in loops.

In practice, we use two strategies: rounding the mid-point to the nearest integer and reusing the coefficient already chosen for another variable. Other strategies may be devised. In fact, it is even possible to choose d_k outside $[a_k, b_k]$, by slightly adapting the formula in Def. 2.

5.4   Efficient Redundancy Removal

As mentioned before, the rigorous LP may fail to detect some redundant constraints due to the conservative over-approximation of the objective value, which greatly weakens the tractability of our domain. However, it is worth mentioning that the removal operation is always sound even when some non-redundant constraints are removed, in which case, the result is merely a larger polyhedron. In order to remove as many redundant constraints as possible, we can use less conservative approaches which may remove constraints that are *likely* to be redundant, but may not be. One approach is to employ a standard LP solver instead of a rigorous one. We can even go further by removing inequalities $\varphi = \sum_i a_i x_i \le b$ in P when $\max \sum_i a_i x_i$ subject to $P \setminus \{\varphi\}$ is less than $(1 + \epsilon)b$, for some tolerance $\epsilon > 0$.

In order to remove constraints more efficiently, it is worth using lightweight redundancy removal methods first and resorting to the expensive LP-based method only when necessary. First, we use a syntactic check: given a pair of inequalities $\sum_i a_i x_i \le b$ and $\sum_i a'_i x_i \le b'$, if $\forall i. a'_i = a_i$, only the inequality with the smaller constant needs to be kept. Second, we first check an inequality against the bounding box of the polyhedron before the actual polyhedron. Finally, we employ methods proposed in [10,11] to tackle the combinatorial explosion problem of redundant constraints occurring during sequences of Fourier-Motzkin eliminations (e.g., in the join computations).

6   Implementation and Experimental Results

Our prototype domain, FPPol, is developed using only double precision floating-point numbers. It makes use of GLPK (GNU Linear programming kit) [14] which implements the simplex algorithm for linear programming. FPPol is interfaced to the APRON library [1] which provides a common interface for numerical abstract domains. Our experiments were conducted using the Interproc [12] static analyzer. In order to assess the precision and efficiency of FPPol, we compare the obtained invariants as well as the performance of FPPol with the NewPolka library which is implemented using exact arithmetic in APRON.

We tested FPPol on all examples from Interproc. Most of them are pure integer programs using exact arithmetic, except *numerical* which is a program involving both integer and real variables with floating-point arithmetic. We also analyzed the *ratelimiter* program presented in Fig.2, which is a more challenging example extracted from a real-life system and uses single precision floating-point numbers. In theory, any interval

```
Y ← [−M, M];
while random() {
        X ← [−128, 128];
        D ← [1, 16];
        S ← Y;
  ①    R ← X ⊖? S;
        Y ← X;
        if R ≤ ⊖D {  Y ← S ⊖? D  }  else
        if D ≤ R {  Y ← S ⊕? D  }
} ②
```

Fig. 2. Floating-point rate limiter program. Different values of the parameter M give different versions of the program (see Fig. 3). $\ominus_?$ denotes single precision floating-point semantics with arbitrary rounding mode ($? \in \{+\infty, -\infty\}$).

$[−M, M]$, where $M = 128 + \epsilon$ and $\epsilon > \epsilon_0$, is stable at ②, for some very small positive ϵ_0. Because this example requires relational invariants, the non-relational interval domain fails to find any stable interval for Y, while the weakly relational octagon domain, although better, can only find over-approximated stable intervals wherein $M > M_0$ and $M_0 \approx 144.00005$. The smallest stable interval that can be found using the polyhedra domain is the interval $[−M_1, M_1]$ wherein $M_1 \approx 128.000047684$. This example is interesting since abstracting floating-point expressions to linear interval expressions over reals [15] gives rise to rather complex expressions. For example, at ①, the assignment $R ← X \ominus_? S$ is abstracted into:

$$R ← [1 − p, 1 + p] \times X − [1 − p, 1 + p] \times S + [−mf, mf]$$

with $p = 2^{-23}$ and $mf = 2^{-149}$ (respectively corresponding to the relative error and the smallest non-zero positive value in the single precision floating-point format). Note that this expression contains numbers of large magnitude, which are costly to represent using exact rationals.

Fig. 3 shows the type of each benchmark program: "int" means the program involves only integer variables with exact arithmetic and "fp" means that the program involves real variables with floating-point arithmetic. The column "#∇ delay" specifies the value of the widening delay parameter for Interproc (i.e., the number of loop iterations performed before applying the widening operator). The column "#iterations" gives the number of loop iterations before a fixpoint is reached.

Invariants. The column "Result Invar." compares the invariants obtained. A "=" indicates that FPPol outputs exactly the same invariants as NewPolka. A "≈" means that FPPol finds the same invariants as NewPolka, up to slight variations in coefficients due to rounding. In this case, the polyhedra computed by FPPol are slightly larger than those computed by NewPolka. A ">" denotes that FPPol finds strictly stronger invariants than NewPolka. For the integer programs, all the invariants obtained by FPPol were the same as those produced by NewPolka. Indeed, such programs involve only small integer values. In these cases, we can often use the multiplicative version of the Fourier-Motzkin elimination, which incurs no precision loss.

Program		Analyzer	FPPol			NewPolka		Result
type	name	#∇delay	#iterations	#lp	$t(ms)$	#iterations	$t(ms)$	Invar.
int	ackerman	1	6	1476	35	6	7	=
int	bubblesort	1	8	675	24	8	8	=
int	fact	1	9	2106	65	9	15	=
int	heapsort	1	4	1968	76	4	15	=
int	maccarthy91	1	4	418	13	4	3	=
int	symmetricalstairs	1	6	480	18	6	6	=
fp	numerical	1	1	250	17	1	31	≈
fp	ratelimiter(M=128)	3	5	1777	125	5	394	≈
fp	ratelimiter(M=128)	4	5	2555	227	6	809	>
fp	ratelimiter(M=128.000047683)	6	9	4522	510	8	1889	≈
fp	ratelimiter(M=128.000047683)	7	8	3688	238	9	2435	>
fp	ratelimiter(M=128.000047684)	1	3	1068	57	3	116	≈

Fig. 3. Experimental results for benchmark examples

The *numerical* program involves floating-point arithmetic but without loops, so it provides no challenge. For *ratelimiter*, FPPol can find the invariant $-M_1 \leq x \leq M_1$ where $M_1 \approx 128.000047684$ if the widening delay parameter is set large enough: at least 4 when $M=128$, 7 when $M=128.000047683$, 1 when $M=128.000047684$, whereas NewPolka can only find the invariant when $M=128.00004\ 7684$. Interestingly, for *ratelimiter* with $M = 128.000047683$, NewPolka fails to find any invariant at ② even when delaying the widening for 100 iterations (413.2 seconds). In this case, the floating-point over-approximations within FPPol actually accelerate the fixpoint computation even before applying widening and help in reaching a fixpoint faster than when using New-Polka.

Performance. Fig. 3 presents the analysis times in milliseconds when the analyzer runs on a 2.4GHz PC with 2GB of RAM running Fedora Linux. For integer programs, NewPolka outperforms FPPol. Because such programs involve small integer values, the computation in NewPolka is very cheap while FPPol needs a number of expensive LP queries. However, for the floating-point programs, FPPol greatly outperforms New-Polka. Indeed, after floating-point abstractions, programs involve rational numbers of large magnitude which degrade the performance of NewPolka, while the floating-point number representation avoids such problems in our domain.

LP costs. Fig. 3 shows also statistics on the number of LP queries (#lp) in FPPol. In addition, we found that, for floating-point programs, more than 75% of the LP queries are used for redundancy removal, almost 80% of which come from the convex hull computation. The performance of our domain completely relies on the LP solver we use. During our experiments, we found that the time spent in the LP solver frequently takes more than 85% of the total analysis time for floating-point programs and 70% for integer programs. Note that a naive floating-point implementation of polyhedra, without any soundness guarantee, could not bypass these LP computations either. Thus, the soundness guarantee in our domain does not incur much overhead.

Numerical instability. During our experiments on floating-point programs, GLPK often encountered the "numerical instability" problem due to the simultaneous occurrence of tiny and large coefficients. Indeed, during the analysis, tiny floating-point numbers introduced due to rounding are propagated in the whole system and produce large coefficients by division. In our implementation, we solve the problem by shifting the tiny term or huge term into the constant term following the same idea as linearization in Sect. 4.1, e.g, choosing $d_k = 0$. We believe a faster, more robust LP solver with better scalability, such as the CPLEX LP solver, may greatly improve the precision, performance and scalability of our domain.

7   Conclusion

In this paper, we presented a sound implementation of the polyhedra domain using floating-point arithmetic. It is based on a constraint-only representation, together with a sound floating-point Fourier-Motzkin elimination algorithm and rigorous linear programming techniques. Moreover, we proposed advanced tactics to improve the precision and efficiency of our domain, which work well in practice. The benefit of our domain is its compact representation and the ability to leverage the power of state-of-the-art linear programming solvers. It remains for future work to examine the scalability of our domain for large realistic programs and to reduce the number of LP queries.

Acknowledgments

We would like to thank Axel Simon, Ji Wang and the anonymous reviewers for their helpful comments and suggestions.

References

1. APRON numerical abstract domain library, http://apron.cri.ensmp.fr/library/
2. Alexander, S.: Theory of Linear and Integer Programming. John Wiley & Sons, Chichester (1998)
3. Bagnara, R., Hill, P.M., Zaffanella, E.: The Parma Polyhedra Library: Toward a complete set of numerical abstractions for the analysis and verification of hardware and software systems. Quaderno 457, Dipartimento di Matematica, Università di Parma, Italy (2006)
4. Bemporad, A., Fukuda, K., Torrisi, F.D.: Convexity recognition of the union of polyhedra. Computational Geometry 18(3), 141–154 (2001)
5. Blanchet, B., Cousot, P., Cousot, R., Feret, J., Mauborgne, L., Miné, A., Monniaux, D., Rival, X.: A static analyzer for large safety-critical software. In: ACM PLDI 2003, San Diego, California, USA, June 2003, pp. 196–207. ACM Press, New York (2003)
6. Cousot, P., Cousot, R.: Abstract interpretation: a unified lattice model for static analysis of programs by construction or approximation of fixpoints. In: ACM POPL 1977, Los Angeles, California, pp. 238–252. ACM Press, New York (1977)
7. Cousot, P., Halbwachs, N.: Automatic discovery of linear restraints among variables of a program. In: ACM POPL 1978, pp. 84–96. ACM, New York (1978)
8. Goubault, E.: Static analyses of floating-point operations. In: Cousot, P. (ed.) SAS 2001. LNCS, vol. 2126, pp. 234–259. Springer, Heidelberg (2001)

9. Halbwachs, N.: Détermination automatique de relations linéaires vérifiées par les variables d'un programme. Ph.D thesis, Thèse de 3ème cycle d'informatique, Université scientifique et médicale de Grenoble, Grenoble, France (March 1979)

10. Huynh, T., Lassez, C., Lassez, J.-L.: Practical issues on the projection of polyhedral sets. Annals of Mathematics and Artificial Intelligence 6(4), 295–315 (1992)

11. Imbert, J.-L.: Fourier's elimination: Which to choose? In: PCPP 1993, pp. 117–129 (1993)

12. Lalire, G., Argoud, M., Jeannet, B.: Interproc,
http://pop-art.inrialpes.fr/people/bjeannet/bjeannet-forge/interproc/

13. LeVerge, H.: A note on Chernikova's algorithm. Technical Report 635, IRISA, France (1992)

14. Makhorin, A.: The GNU Linear Programming Kit (2000),
http://www.gnu.org/software/glpk/

15. Miné, A.: Relational abstract domains for the detection of floating-point run-time errors. In: Schmidt, D. (ed.) ESOP 2004. LNCS, vol. 2986, pp. 3–17. Springer, Heidelberg (2004)

16. Miné, A.: Field-sensitive value analysis of embedded C programs with union types and pointer arithmetics. In: LCTES 2006, Ottawa, Ontario, Canada, pp. 54–63. ACM Press, New York (2006)

17. Miné, A.: The octagon abstract domain. Higher-Order and Symbolic Computation 19(1), 31–100 (2006)

18. Moore, R.: Interval Analysis. Prentice-Hall, Englewood Cliffs (1966)

19. Neumaier, A., Shcherbina, O.: Safe bounds in linear and mixed-integer linear programming. Math. Program. 99(2), 283–296 (2004)

20. Que, D.N.: Robust and generic abstract domain for static program analysis: the polyhedral case. Technical report, École des Mines de Paris (July 2006)

21. Rohn, J.: Solvability of systems of interval linear equations and inequalities. In: Linear Optimization Problems with Inexact Data, pp. 35–77. Springer, Heidelberg (2006)

22. Sankaranarayanan, S., Sipma, H., Manna, Z.: Scalable analysis of linear systems using mathematical programming. In: Cousot, R. (ed.) VMCAI 2005. LNCS, vol. 3385, pp. 25–41. Springer, Heidelberg (2005)

23. Simon, A., King, A.: Exploiting sparsity in polyhedral analysis. In: Hankin, C. (ed.) SAS 2005. LNCS, vol. 3672, pp. 336–351. Springer, Heidelberg (2005)

24. Simon, A., King, A., Howe, J.M.: Two variables per linear inequality as an abstract domain. In: Leuschel, M.A. (ed.) LOPSTR 2002. LNCS, vol. 2664, pp. 71–89. Springer, Heidelberg (2003)

A Flow-Sensitive Region Inference for CLI

Alexandru Stefan[1], Florin Craciun[2], and Wei-Ngan Chin[1]

[1] Department of Computer Science, National University of Singapore
{alexandr,chinwn}@comp.nus.edu.sg
[2] Department of Computer Science, Durham University, UK
florin.craciun@durham.ac.uk

Abstract. Region-based memory management can offer improved time performance, relatively good memory locality and reuse, and also provide better adherence to real-time constraints during execution, when compared against traditional garbage collection. We have implemented a region-memory subsystem into the SSCLI 2.0 platform and then adapted an inference system to *region-enable* CIL programs, with the aid of newly introduced instructions. Initial results are promising, as the programs running with regions have considerably smaller interrupting delays, compared to those running with garbage collection. Regions can bring runtime improvement for some programs (up to 50%), depending on how complicated are the data structures used in execution.

1 Introduction

The Common Language Infrastructure (CLI) [16] is an ECMA standard that describes the core of the .NET Framework. The Microsoft *Shared Source CLI* [15] (SSCLI) is one of the implementations of the ECMA CLI standard, made publicly available for research purposes.

We modified the SSCLI memory system such that its default garbage collector can co-exist with our *region-based memory system*. This allowed us to study performance aspects and the typical problems related to introducing this kind of memory system at the bytecode level of .NET. The modified system is targeted for using a stack of lexically scoped regions in which the last region created is the first deleted. A region is used to give bounds to the lifetime of objects allocated within it. Deallocating a region deletes all its contents in one operation, resulting in better memory utilization at the cost of some predictable risks: the dangling references. Our solution to this problem is to statically prevent the run programs from creating any dangling references at all.

We also formalised and implemented a *flow-sensitive* region inference system for CIL (the language used in CLI). The region inference is developed using techniques from an earlier work [7], guaranteeing that low-level stack oriented CIL programs never create dangling references while running on our modified SSCLI platform. Notable contributions of the current work are:

- **Modified SSCLI Platform for using Regions:** We added region-based memory features to the existing SSCLI 2.0 memory system found in the execution engine, while also keeping the default garbage collector.

G. Ramalingam (Ed.): APLAS 2008, LNCS 5356, pp. 19–35, 2008.

- **Region Inference for CIL:** We have formalized and implemented a system that rewrites plain CLI-targeted programs for running with regions, using a type inference algorithmic approach. The inference is adapted for CIL, a stack-based object oriented language used in CLI. The prototype implementation covers essential parts of CIL program syntax and constructs, also dealing with features such as polymorphism and method recursion.

- **Improved Inference Techniques:** We tested our CLI region inference which lead to some new optimizations. We identified and studied different ways for how region instructions could be inserted by our inference, so as to achieve faster region management speed and better memory reuse.

- **Evaluation:** We evaluated our proposal on a set of benchmark programs. We note significant runtime improvement for some programs using more complex data structures.

2   Existing SSCLI Memory System

2.1   Garbage Collector

The default memory system in SSCLI is a generational garbage collector, managing two generations of objects. This GC is also a copying/mark-and-sweep collector depending on the generation being inspected. There is a distinction made between small objects (stored in the two generations) and large objects (with a size bigger than 85KB). Large objects are allocated in a *large object heap*, a special heap having the same age as the old generation.

A newly created object is usually placed in generation 0, and occupies memory (also after becoming dead) until garbage collection takes place. Garbage collection is triggered by memory scarcity and other runtime considerations. The simplified GC algorithm follows these lines:

- For generation 0, copy all live objects to generation 1
- For generation 1 and large heap, use mark-and-sweep (without compaction)
- Additional cleaning-up for both generations.

The GC follows the usual steps of a tracing collector for identifying live objects in its copy and mark-and-sweep phases ('tracing the roots', recursively scanning live references resulting in the transitive closure over the live objects set). The mark-and-sweep phase is optional, being performed as necessary, and contains no compaction of the live objects; that is, the objects from the old generation and large object heap are never moved.

2.2   CIL and Allocation Instructions

Whenever the Shared Source CLI execution environment runs compiled code (in the form of an .exe file), what it actually executes are CIL (Common Intermediate Language) instructions. Languages which target the CLI standard (C#, Visual Basic, managed C++ and other .NET languages) compile to CIL, which is assembled into bytecode. CIL resembles an object-oriented assembly language, and is entirely stack-based. The language is platform independent, being run by execution environments (virtual machines) such as the CLR (Common Language Runtime) or SSCLI's execution engine named CLIX. The following CIL opcodes have most direct relations with the GC of the Shared Source CLI:

newobj - Creates a new object instance, pushing its object reference onto the evaluation stack. Necessary arguments are popped from the stack and passed to the constructor for object creation.

newarr - Pushes an object reference to a new one-dimensional array whose elements are of a specific type onto the evaluation stack. The array length is popped from the stack before the array creation and must be a 32-bit integer.

```
class A {
    public int i = 3;
    public double j = 5.2;
    public A(int p, double q) { i = p; j = q; }
} class MainApp {
    public static void Main() { A a = new A(2, 3.5); }
}
```

Fig. 1. Example C# program

```
.class private auto ansi beforefieldinit MainApp
        extends [mscorlib]System.Object {
  .method public hidebysig static void  Main() cil managed {
   .entrypoint                      //execution starts with this method
   .maxstack  3                     //approximative stack slots needed
   .locals init (class A V_0)       //a local variable, V_0
   IL_0000:  nop                    //no effect, used for opcode patching
   IL_0001:  ldc.i4.2               //loads value 2 on stack (4-byte int)
   IL_0002:  ldc.r8    3.5          //loads 3.5 on stack (8-byte float)
   IL_000b:  newobj    instance void A::.ctor(int32, float64)
             //calls the A constructor using the two values on stack
   IL_0010:  stloc.0                //stores the new object's ref into V_0
   IL_0011:  ret                    //return from method
  } // end of method MainApp::Main
  ..
} // end of class MainApp
```

Fig. 2. CIL program corresponding to the Fig.1 example

Fig.1 presents a simple C# program, with its corresponding CIL program in Fig.2. Notice how the stack is used for passing parameters to newobj. The newobj and newarr opcodes request the allocation of a new object and an array respectively (represented as an object); the newly created entity will be allocated in either generation 0 or the large object heap and be taken into account by GC's management.

3   Regions for SSCLI

3.1   Modifying the Environment

We aimed at using the large object heap (from the existing GC) for allocating regions. This decision is accounted for by the usually broad sizes of regions and the fact that the memory address of a region should not be moved (no copying is made for the large object heap). So we modified the SSCLI code for the large object heap to also hold regions, and these in turn were made to hold objects. Allocating a region can correspond to allocating a large object of a special kind, not having any contents at creation, directed only at reserving memory for future allocations within it. Special care had to be taken regarding possible conflicts between GC and the new subsystem (concerns like the visibility of regions and region-contained objects to the GC).

3.2   New CIL Instructions

As new features are added into the SSCLI platform, the following new CIL instructions (opcodes) become necessary:

letreg - Allocates a region into the large object heap. Requires two int32 parameters from the stack: the region index and the initial space size. If this initial size is exceeded afterwards, an extension will be created.

freereg - Deallocates a region. Pops an index from the stack, denoting which region to deallocate.

newrobj - Creates an object (inside a region) in a similar way to newobj, but also requiring an extra parameter from the stack, designating a region index.

newrarr - Similar to newarr, but requiring an additional region index parameter from the stack.

A simple example program that creates a region and then allocates an object inside is shown in Fig.3. The runtime engine is modified to act appropriately when encountering these region opcodes, making full use of the new region subsystem added to the engine.

Manipulating regions directly at the CIL level is the only possible start for our approach to region-based memory for SSCLI, since CIL is the core language for any .NET execution engine. As these instructions are rather low level, we propose to insert them automatically with a region inference system.

4   Region Inference for CIL

We devised a modular region inference process for automating the translation of CLI (.NET) programs into the region-aware versions. The inference is performed at the CIL assembly level. One key difference from our previous (flow-insensitive) system [7] is the adoption of a *flow-sensitive* region inference system to better support the stack-based model of CIL programs.

```
.method public hidebysig static void  Main() cil managed {
 .entrypoint
 .maxstack   5
 .locals init (class A V_0)
 IL_0000:  nop
 IL_0001:  ldc.i4.1          // region's index
 IL_0002:  ldc.i4    8000  // initial size of 8K for the region
 IL_0003:  letreg           // create the region
 IL_0005:  nop
 IL_0006:  ldc.i4.2          // push an int
 IL_0007:  ldc.r8    3.5  // push a double
 IL_0008:  ldc.i4.1          // push an int used as region handle
 IL_000b:  newrobj    instance void A::.ctor(int32, float64)
           // the constructor takes the first two values from stack
           // the third value from stack denotes a region index
 IL_000c:  stloc.0           // store reference of new object in V_0
 ..
 IL_0010:  ret
} // end of method MainApp::Main
```

Fig. 3. CIL program with region opcodes

4.1   Lexically-Scoped Regions

Our region inference presumes programs will use a stack of memory regions during execution. We use fixed sizes for regions and region extensions (whenever overflow occurs for a region, it will be extended with a fixed size increment). We express the introduction and disposal of a region r with the pseudocode construct: letreg r in e, where the region r can only be used for allocating objects in the scope of the expression e. Although the new CIL instructions letreg and freereg are not strictly required to be lexically scoped, we still respect the lexical discipline because it is dictated by our type inference, which inserts them automatically.

Typically, a method definition will be translated as presented in Fig.4 (pseudocode). The escaping objects (like o2 and o3) are objects found by the inference to require living longer than the point when the method meth returns. All other objects that do not respect this condition are considered *localized* objects. The technique of localization remains unchanged from the previous work [7]. Object o2 cannot be localized because it is assigned to a parameter's field, and o3 because it is returned by the method, so they both escape. If any objects are localized (like o1), the method will be assigned a new local region (r) for holding them. This local region will be freed as soon as the method ends. Notice how the method has some new parameters in Fig 4(b), denoting region handles (such as r1 and r2, used also with the alternate notation meth<r1,r2>(..)). These external regions will be used for allocating escaping objects (o2, o3), while making sure they have suitable lifetimes.

```
                                     meth(r1, r2, p1, p2) {
                                       letreg r in {
  meth(p1, p2) {                         o1 = new A() in r; //local
    o1 = new A(); //local                o2 = new B() in r1; //escaping
    o2 = new B(); //escaping             o3 = new C() in r2; //escaping
    o3 = new C(); //escaping             p1.field = o2;
    p1.field = o2;                        ..
     ..                                 }
    return o3;                          return o3;
  }                                   }
```

        a) input code   b) translated code

Fig. 4. Typical method translation via region inference

The inference will gather detailed lifetime information for any region or object (or object field) that should go inside a region in the form of constraints, so that its localization stages can easily determine which objects should go in what regions and insert instructions like `letreg`, `freereg`, `newrobj` having appropriate parameters. Loop blocks can also have localized regions, if some of their objects do not live longer than the loop's scope.

4.2 Inference Details

We will present the inference mechanism formally, mainly listing the inference rules that are new or have changed considerably from those in our previous work [7]. The differences originate from the distinct designs of the previous Core-Java language (subset of Java) and now the more realistic CIL (assembly-like, OO).

When beginning the analysis, each CIL class definition is parameterized with one or more regions to form a *region type*. For instance, a region type $cn\langle r_1,...,r_n\rangle$ is a class name cn annotated with region parameters $r_1...r_n$. The first region parameter r_1 denotes the region in which the instance object of this class is allocated, while $r_2...r_n$ are regions corresponding to the fields of the object. Using the constraint $\bigwedge_{i=2}^{n}(r_i \succeq r_1)$ we are capturing the condition that field objects should not have shorter lifetimes than the region (r_1) of the parent object, thus forbidding dangling references. Constraints like $r_1 \succeq r_2$ indicate that the lifetime of region r_1 is not shorter than that of r_2; $r_1 = r_2$ denotes that r_1 and r_2 must be the same region. Sets of such constraints are gathered for each of the program's classes (expressing class invariants) and methods (method preconditions). Parameterization similar to the one for classes is also done for methods, indicating regions for the method's receiver object, arguments and return object. The primitive types do not require region parameters.

Region constraints are gathered from virtually every relevant program point inside every method (using a type inference based approach) and then grouped as method preconditions for each method analyzed. Whenever encountering instructions that deal with new objects or object declarations, fresh region variables are considered. These abstract region variables will be translated into actual region handles (or identifiers) in the final phases. Using a notation like below we express that having the type environment Γ, the currently analyzed method m and the operand stack S, the program expression e is translated (e.g. adding annotation) into e', resulting in a possibly modified stack S' and the region constraints φ:

$$\Gamma, m, S \vdash e \Rightarrow e', S', \varphi$$

If the expression e is not modified we simply use $\Gamma, m, S \vdash e, S', \varphi$. As an addition, the inference rules now make use of a stack for storing (region) information about any operands passed to method calls or to other operations.

Below is the sequence inference rule; this rule enforces the inference to be flow-sensitive. As the sequence of operations that update or read the stack is important, we need this flow-sensitive requirement to correctly keep track of the stack S.

$$[\text{SEQUENCE}]$$
$$\frac{\Gamma, m, S \vdash e_1 \Rightarrow e_1', S_1, \varphi_1 \qquad \Gamma, m, S_1 \vdash e_2 \Rightarrow e_2', S_2, \varphi_2}{\Gamma, m, S \vdash e_1\ e_2 \Rightarrow e_1'\ e_2', S_2, \varphi_1 \wedge \varphi_2}$$

The stack is a list of the form $S = [el_1, ..., el_n]$ with $el_i = (name : type \langle regions \rangle)$. We express with $ldprim$ any opcode that pushes a primitive value on the stack (`ldc.i4`, `ldc.i8`, `ldc.r4` ...). Pushing null value (`ldnull`) is a similar situation. The newly stored items will contain no region information in these cases.

$$[\text{PRIMITIVE}]$$
$$\frac{S' = [anonymous : prim\langle\rangle] {+}{+} S}{\Gamma, m, S \vdash ldprim, S', true}$$

$$[\text{NULL}]$$
$$\frac{S' = [null : t_\perp\langle\rangle] {+}{+} S}{\Gamma, m, S \vdash \text{ldnull}, S', true}$$

All CIL opcodes are used for their side-effects, none of them return a value. Following is a list of more opcodes with their description and rules. The subtyping relation $(t_1\langle \bar{r}_1 \rangle <: t_2\langle \bar{r}_2 \rangle, \varphi)$, that infers the constraints φ, as in [7].

The `pop` opcode removes the value currently on top of the evaluation stack. The `dup` opcode copies the current topmost value on the evaluation stack, and then pushes the copy onto the evaluation stack.

$$[\text{POP}]$$
$$\frac{S = [el_1, ..., el_m] \qquad S' = [el_2, ..., el_m]}{\Gamma, m, S \vdash \text{pop}, S', true}$$

$$[\text{DUPLICATE}]$$
$$\frac{S = [el_1, ..., el_m] \qquad S' = [el_1, el_1, ..., el_m]}{\Gamma, m, S \vdash \text{dup}, S', true}$$

`ldloc` loads the local variable having the specified index onto the stack.

`stloc` pops the current value from the top of the evaluation stack and stores it in the local variable list at the specified index. We use $localVar(m, i)$ for obtaining the i-th local variable of method m. We also mention that the type environment Γ contains all arguments and local variables of the analyzed method. Similarly, $argument(m, i)$ gets the i-th parameter name of the method m.

[LoadLocal]
$$\frac{\begin{array}{c} localVar(m, i) = v \\ (v : t\langle\overline{r}\rangle) \in \Gamma \\ S' = [v : t\langle\overline{r}\rangle]{+}{+}S \end{array}}{\Gamma, m, S \vdash \texttt{ldloc.i}, \, S', \, true}$$

[StoreLocal]
$$\frac{\begin{array}{c} S = [el_1, \dots, el_m] \qquad S' = [el_2, \dots, el_m] \\ localVar(m, i) = v \qquad (v : t\langle\overline{r}\rangle) \in \Gamma \\ el_1 = (v' : t\langle\overline{r}'\rangle) \qquad \vdash t\langle\overline{r}'\rangle <: t\langle\overline{r}\rangle, \, \varphi \end{array}}{\Gamma, m, S \vdash \texttt{stloc.i}, \, S', \, \varphi}$$

In CIL any assignment takes at least two instructions (something similar with a stack push, and then a store e.g. `stloc`, `stfld`). First we have to keep information of whatever could be coming from the stack: variable name, type and regions. When the actual assignment takes place only then will we have to consider subtyping checks.

`ldarg` loads an argument (referenced by a specified index value) onto the stack. If the method m is not static ($\neg isStatic(m)$) then, in CIL conventions, the *this* reference is considered argument 0. Thus the offset j could be 0 or 1.

[LoadArgument]
$$\frac{\begin{array}{c} j = (0 \lhd isStatic(m) \rhd 1) \\ (\neg isStatic(m) \wedge i = 0) \Rightarrow el = (this : t\langle\overline{r}\rangle), \, el \in \Gamma \\ (isStatic(m) \vee i \neq 0) \Rightarrow el = (v : t'\langle\overline{r}'\rangle), \, el \in \Gamma, \, argument(m, i - j) = v \end{array}}{\Gamma, m, S \vdash \texttt{ldarg.i}, \, (el{+}{+}S), \, true}$$

`ldfld` finds the value of a field in the object whose reference is currently on the evaluation stack, and pushes the result on the stack.

[LoadField]
$$\frac{\begin{array}{c} S = [el_1, \dots, el_m] \qquad el_1 = (v : t\langle\overline{r}\rangle) \\ \vdash (t_f\langle\overline{r}_f\rangle \ f) \in t\langle\overline{r}\rangle \qquad S' = [(v.f : t_f\langle\overline{r}_f\rangle), el_2, \dots, el_m] \end{array}}{\Gamma, m, S \vdash \texttt{ldfld} \ f, \, S', \, true}$$

`stfld` replaces the value stored in the field of an object reference with a new value. Takes two elements off the stack: the first (el_1) is the new value, the second (el_2) is the target parent object.

[StoreField]
$$\frac{\begin{array}{c} S = [el_1, el_2, \dots, el_m] \qquad S' = [el_3, \dots, el_m] \\ el_1 = (v_1 : t_f\langle\overline{r}_1\rangle) \qquad el_2 = (v_2 : t_2\langle\overline{r}_2\rangle) \\ \vdash (t_f\langle\overline{r}_f\rangle \ f) \in t_2\langle\overline{r}_2\rangle \qquad \vdash t_f\langle\overline{r}_1\rangle <: t_f\langle\overline{r}_f\rangle, \varphi \end{array}}{\Gamma, m, S \vdash \texttt{stfld} \ f, \, S', \, \varphi}$$

`ret` returns from the current method, pushing a return value (if present) from the callee's evaluation stack onto the caller's evaluation stack. Whatever is left on the callee stack is of no interest so we can consider it empty afterwards.

[Return]
$$\frac{\begin{array}{c} S = [el_1, \dots] \qquad (ret_m : t\langle\overline{r}\rangle) \in m \\ el_1 = (v : t\langle\overline{r}'\rangle) \qquad \vdash t\langle\overline{r}'\rangle <: t\langle\overline{r}\rangle, \varphi \end{array}}{\Gamma, m, S \vdash \texttt{ret}, \, [\,], \, \varphi}$$

`call` calls the method indicated by the passed method descriptor. The method's arguments are popped from the stack, and the return is pushed on the stack. For object creation, via `newobj`, the analysis process is similar.

[METHODCALL]

$$\frac{\begin{array}{c} S = [el_p, \ldots, el_1, el_{p+1}, \ldots, el_m] \qquad el_i = (v_i : t'_i \langle \overline{r}'_i \rangle) \;\; i = 1..p \\ \text{.method } t_0 \; mn_2 \langle \overline{r}_{this}, \overline{r}_{pars}, \overline{r}_{ret} \rangle (t_i \; v_i)_{i:2..p} \text{ where } \varphi \in P' \\ \vdash t_0 \Rightarrow t_0 \langle \overline{r}'_{ret} \rangle \qquad \rho = [\, \overline{r}_{this} \mapsto \overline{r}'_1, \, (\overline{r}_{pars}[i] \mapsto \overline{r}'_i)_{i:2..p}, \, \overline{r}_{ret} \mapsto \overline{r}'_{ret} \,] \\ S' = [\, (anonymous : t_0 \langle \overline{r}'_{ret} \rangle), \, el_{p+1}, \ldots, el_m] \end{array}}{\Gamma, m, S \vdash \text{call } cn :: mn_2(t_i)_{i:2..p} \Rightarrow \text{call } cn :: mn_2 \langle \overline{r}'_1, \overline{r}'_{2..p}, \overline{r}'_{ret} \rangle (t_i)_{i:2..p}, \, S', \rho \, \varphi}$$

`.method` $t_0 \; mn_2 \langle \overline{r}_{this}, \overline{r}_{pars}, \overline{r}_{ret} \rangle \ldots$ is an annotated method name, with regions corresponding to the receiver, parameters and return. It belongs to the partially region-annotated program P'. A substitution ρ is applied over the method's precondition constraints (φ) for them to be valid at the call site. This is an example of an inference rule that annotates the analyzed expression ($e \Rightarrow e'$). The region information annotated is needed later, when actual region handles (loads) will be written in the program, as required.

If-then(-else) branches do not present a special problem in the inference. Their effect is accomplished in CIL with the help of jump opcodes (specifying a label to where the execution should be transfered). Loops are also translated into labels and conditional jumps. When entering an if branch or a loop never information from the previous stack state is necessary, variables and values are freshly pushed on the stack before any operations - compiling to CIL assures this. It suffices when the opcodes are inferred in order ([**Sequence**]), ignoring labels and jump opcodes completely (for if branches and also loops, initially).

We are obliged to perform localization (briefly described below) only after we have analyzed an entire method body, as opposed to our previous algorithm. This is because all local variables have the scope of the entire method body, thus we cannot say anything about the (localization of) regions tied to a certain variable until all instructions of the method have been analyzed.

Localization is performed much like in the previous inference, with any region parameter that lives longer than an outside (of the method) region being made equal to a suitable outside region. The localized regions are made equal to a fresh region, that will be allocated via `letreg`, and discarded with a corresponding `freereg`, at each of the containing block's margins. `newrobj` will be used instead of `newobj` (likewise `newrarr`) and all other necessary inserts for region handle passing to methods will also be carried out.

To make the localization even more precise we also insert `letreg` and `freereg` also for loops. A loop block (not clearly marked in CIL) can be detected whenever encountering jump opcodes targeting labels placed higher in the CIL program sequence, thus implying recurrence. The method's local regions can be partitioned into sets corresponding to each of the (possibly nested) loops found in the method body, thus each one with it's own lexical region. In CIL all local variables are usually declared at the beginning of the method with no need for more variable declarations further down the program.

4.3   Special Techniques for Translation

To further improve memory management within our region memory system, we experimented with three new techniques, that can help us obtain faster runtime performance.

Region resetting. Instead of creating a new region everytime a loop block is entered, we allocate one region prior to the block and reuse the same region for all iterations by resetting it at the end of each iteration. This technique is adapted from [17], but is different as it does not require region liveness analysis. The approach is presented in Fig.5, using pseudocode. By resetting, we avoid repeated memory allocation/deallocation in the large heap. The region's extensions are also kept after resets, further reducing execution overhead (generated by repeated extending/deallocation). Keeping the extensions is acceptable as the memory space required for each iteration usually remains about the same.

Resetting should be used for each loop-local region in the program, as there is very little downside to this technique (maybe a risk of some cycles not filling the reserved memory completely).

```
                                letreg r in {
   while (flag) {                  while (flag) {
     letreg r in {                   ..
                                      reset r;
       ..                          }
     }                           }
   }
     a) loop region              b) loop resetting region
```

Fig. 5. Region resetting

Region relegation. This is used to prevent the excessive fragmentation of memory into regions. If the objects that should go inside a new region are too few or simply occupy too little memory, then we allocate them into an already existing region, instead of creating a new one. This brings reduced overhead of managing too many regions and a better memory usage (from filling up more unused region space).

In Fig.6, the B instance has been found to occupy too little space for it to require a separate region. Relegation should only be used when the new objects require just small amounts of memory; this is to avoid the risk of generating excessively large upper regions. An object can be considered *simple* (or *small*) if all its fields are primitive, thus implying small memory amounts required for its storage. This size estimation relies on the fact that an object's non-primitive fields have high chance of ending up in the same region as the object itself, thus taking up more space. Different criteria can be used too, e.g. a depth limit for inner references: depth 1 allows fields to be objects that have only primitive fields. If all the localized objects in a given scope are simple ones, then we use relegation at that site, allocating the objects in a suitable existing region.

```
void meth<r1>(A p, ..) {           void meth<r1>(A p, ..) {
   letreg r2 in {                     v = new B() in r1;
      v = new B() in r2;           }
   }
}
```

a) using a new lexical region   b) using an existing upper region

Fig. 6. Region relegation

Forced localization. Assigning a new region to some particular sequences of instructions that would not normally need their own lexical region. This is the opposite of relegation. Our experiments have shown that some code portions tend to fill unnecessary space (with dead objects) from the local block region. Our inference may sometimes fail to assign local regions to those spots, without this new adjustment.

For example, a method call could be creating a lot of temporary objects that have to be allocated in the outside region r1 (as listed in Fig.7). This will lead to the unnecessary storage of numerous dead objects inside r1 unless the method call is enclosed in its own new region.

```
                                    letreg r1 in {
                                       ..
   letreg r1 in {                      letreg r2 in {
      ..                                  meth<r2>(p);
      meth<r1>(p);                     }
      ..                               ..
   }                                }
```

a) using the same localized region   b) raising meth in a new region

Fig. 7. Forced region localization

Some of the situations generating unexpected temporary objects, requiring a (forced) enclosement in a new region, are:

- a method call whose returned object is not stored in a variable (the method was called for its effects and not for the returned object)
- simple allocations of soon-to-become-dead objects made at the beginning of a block of instructions, thus having to be unnecessarily kept in the local region until the block is exited
- cases of relegation (resulting in dead objects generated by a method call) when a method is used in multiple contexts.

Fig. 8. Pipeline of items and actions for the region-enabling process

The forced localization for code portions should be applied if the temporary objects resulting from that code use significant memory space. The reference depth criteria can help determine if objects will occupy enough memory. The soundness of the forced new region is assured with the verification that only temporary objects will be placed in this region.

4.4   Implementation

The implemented inference system was coded using F# [20], a mixed functional and object-oriented language for the .NET platform. F#'s functional features combined with .NET interoperability proved to be helpful in our application's design. The phases of the automated process we use are listed in Figure 8.

The last item (7.) is a program able to be run on our modified CLI runtime environment. The phases between 3. and 6. are performed by the F# system. In short, an Abstract Syntax Tree (AST) is built from the parsed CIL program, additional information is then decorated into the tree through elaborate inference, then the region program file is outputted at the end (translated from AST).

4.5   Experimental Evaluation

We measured performance aspects of test programs translated for running with regions via inference. They were adapted from the RegJava [9] and Olden benchmarks [4].

The initial small tests helped with isolating certain behaviors as for studying likely causes and effects. These tests included some features like region relegation

Table 1. Micro-benchmarks for comparing regions with GC

	Input size	R1 (ms)	R2 (ms)	R3 (ms)	GC (ms)	GC p x m (int x ms)	R m (kb)	GC m (kb)
1. Eratosthenes	n=5000	672	672	672	719	4 x 20	3,906K	3,765K
	n=10000	969	969	969	1453	15 x 87	12,757K	12,475K
2. Ackermann	n=3*10+8	4614	1299	1299	1452	18 x 38	47K(R1)	818K
	n=3*10+9	15645	2081	2081	3543	73 x 58	63K(R1)	819K
3. Merge Sort	n=20000	1405	1405	1405	1609	12 x 153	1,309K	2,710K
	n=25000	1499	1499	1499	2373	15 x 711	1,629K	3,360K
4. Mandelbrot	n=800*400	1671	1094	1046	1046	12 x 19	13K	814K
	n=1000*500	2343	1405	1343	1343	19 x 19	13K	814K
5. GC Trees	fixed	6090	6090	5965	7277	64 x 72	18,908K	15,091K

and resetting being enabled/disabled. The first four columns of Table 1 present millisecond timings for execution with region memory (R1 - no relegation, no resetting; R2 - relegation, no resetting; R3 - relegation and resetting) and execution with the SSCLI GC (GC - timings; GC p x m - number of pauses and maximum delay). We kept the GC's default settings (e.g. its heap size).

Eratosthenes works with linked lists (also tests some data locality), *Ackermann* has big call stacks (lots of recursive function calls) but large amounts of just temporary objects, and *Merge Sort* uses linked lists for its sorting, doing moderate amounts of recursive calls. GC has to traverse the call stacks and references at each collection session, thus losing some runtime speed. *Mandelbrot* creates a lot of temporary objects, so GC's tracing of live objects and also the copying phase is done instantly (nothing marked or copied); there is no time advantage to be gained by regions with this test, only a quicker memory recovery. The *GC Trees*[1] program builds tree structures in both top-down and bottom-up fashion, bringing over 1 second faster time performance for regions (because of the dense reference networks).

Notice how relegation (R2, R3 columns) plays a key role in the fourth and second test. With relegation disabled (R1), the programs create a very large number of regions that will host very few objects (as low as 1% of the regions' fixed size, causing much memory waste). The cost of managing another new region for just few simple objects looks very big when cumulated. Resetting of regions (R2 vs R3) can also bring a small improvement to the overall speed.

The last two columns in Table 1 indicate the highest values (kilobytes) for memory consumption for region and GC executions. We observe that regions offer favorable memory consumption peaks, reflecting an efficient recycling of memory. Only the Ackermann test presents two extremes: with relegation enabled regions are too big and holding unnecessary objects (with large, unacceptable memory demand), while disabling relegation brings good memory usage but slower execution.

Next, we tried the pointer-intensive Olden benchmark, rewritten for C#.

While not being particularly a memory benchmark, four out of ten programs from the Olden suite have notable speed advantage when run with regions (Table 2). The improvement is largely based on the regions' avoidance of the usual GC interruptions and scans. The other Olden programs, which did not show speed improvement, use simpler memory structures and have low memory demand. Nonetheless, we observed in our testing that region programs are usually at least as fast in execution as the ones running with GC.

Memory performance for regions is usually good, but has a tendency to require more memory. On the other hand, regions will be freed as soon as they become dead, which can bring better memory recycling than with GC, even if this doesn't guarantee short presence of dead objects inside regions.

What may slow region-memory down is *excessive region creation/destruction* (including region extension). Relegation avoids this shortcoming by storing more objects into the same region. Region resetting also prevents the same problem by reusing regions and all of their existing extensions. Otherwise allocating an

Table 2. Olden benchmarks - 4 out of 10 show speed improvement

Olden suite	Input size	GC (ms)	R (ms)	Improv.	GC p x m (int x ms)	GC m (kb)	R m (kb)
1. BH	200	5703	5609	1.6 %	12 x 16	1,316K	1,863K
	300	8984	8813	1.9 %	21 x 16	1,639K	2,772K
2. BiSort	100,000	9562	9531		1 x 18	1,337K	1,340K
	200,000	19187	19062		3 x 20	2,648K	2,652K
3. Em3d	50	1187	1187		-	498K	499K
	100	1297	1297		3 x 21	875K	887K
4. Health	100	2468	2422		2 x 17	1,171K	1,281K
	200	4094	4062		5 x 19	1,636K	2,470K
5. MST	500	5843	5453	6.7 %	10 x 40	8,296K	8,305K
	700	10609	9687	8.7 %	19 x 62	16,224K	16,238K
6. Perimeter	300	2828	2781	1.7 %	17 x 37	3,600K	3,600K
	400	8531	8078	5.3 %	17 x 60	14,521K	14,521K
7. Power	fixed	31515	32062		38 x 17	1,333K	3,736K
8. TreeAdd	20	2468	1609	34.8 %	25 x 107	20,999K	21,009K
	21	5250	2188	58.3 %	51 x 223	41,971K	41,991K
9. TSP	2000	1312	1312		1 x 15	813K	903K
	5000	2328	2328		5 x 16	1,099K	1,201K
10. Voronoi	1000	1109	1094		1 x 16	813K	826K
	2000	1344	1329		2 x 16	1,376K	1,759K

object inside a region takes the same amount of time as allocating it inside a GC generation. If the total time delay for regions' creation/disposal/reset is less than the summed garbage collection delays, then the region program will have better time performance (with good likelihood).

Table 3 presents some of the factors influencing the two systems' performance; (+) denotes a speeding effect and (-) a slowing effect. These evaluations confirm the previously stated cause for possible region memory speed loss (the two minus signs in last column). Table 3 also indicates that GC seems to have a higher bias towards runtime speed loss, as influenced by the factors presented.

To clarify the x86 processor optimizations: they comprise a way of executing object allocation sequences by directly using native code for the processor type. Our platform uses a batch of hand-written machine code for doing (within-region) allocations. This considerably improves execution speed.

Besides the time improvement and better memory recycling of regions, there is also another performance aspect, relating to response times, namely *real-time performance* [3]. Real-time constraints are operational deadlines from an event to system response. For example, if a critical portion of code needs to execute according to some real-time deadlines, then the GC constitutes a potential hindrance. Such code could be interrupted at runtime by an inopportune garbage collection, thus suffering unbounded delays in its time-sensitive computations (and possibly mission critical). Regions offer more predictability in programs, as region management uses less time-consuming pauses, moreover not

Table 3. Factors influencing running performance

	GC	R
processor-specific optimizations (x86)	(+) are used when allocating objects in generation 0 (-) not possible for large objects	(+) are used when allocating objects inside regions (-) not possible when allocating the regions (or disposing)
deallocation	(+) (non-large) objects are never explicitly deallocated, but copied or overwritten	(-) regions have to be explicitly deallocated (+) region reset brings some speed
tracing (with c or m&s)	(-) any main phase of garbage collection requires tracing	(+) never done for regions
environment suspension	(-) must be done during any garbage collection session	(+) never done for regions
data locality	(-) generations can eventually get fragmented, offering poor locality	(+) related objects usually grouped in common regions

necessitating environment (and program) suspension for garbage collection. In our experiments GC pauses may be frequent for garbage-collected programs, but hardly so (in fact never in our experiments) for those that are region-enabled.

5   Related Work and Conclusion

There are two main directions for related proposals in the area of compile-time memory management: stack allocation via escape analysis, and region allocation via region inference. The first approach, escape analysis, is based on distinguishing the objects that do not escape their static scopes in order to allocate them on the run-time stack instead of the heap, providing increased speed for memory reclamation. Existing work in this area has first targeted functional languages [10,13], and later on imperative languages [8,19] (dataflow analyses computing point-to graphs and escape information), [2] (flow-insensitive approach using constraints). The region inference approach, also advocated in this paper, groups heap objects into regions and then determines safe region deallocation points. Techniques using region inference have been initially formulated for functional languages [18] (lexically scoped regions), and more recently, they have been applied to imperative languages [9,11,5,7] (most of the proposals using lexical regions, except for [5] that supports unrestricted regions but requires a more complex analysis). Also, a new direction in static memory management is individual object deallocation, in which the compiler automatically inserts reclamation statements for single object instances. Some proposals using this approach rely on shape analysis in [14,6] and flow-insensitive points-to analysis in [12].

We built region-based memory support into the SSCLI 2.0 environment and added new instructions in the CIL opcode set for supporting region operations. We implemented a region inference system that automates the translation of initially garbage collected CLI (.NET) programs into the region-aware versions.

Some notable features of this CIL adaptation of our older algorithm have been presented in the paper. Then we measured performance aspects of executing programs obtained with the inference. Execution of region programs exhibits significant speed improvement for programs using more complex data structures. Because regions have bounded delays throughout execution (unlike GC's pauses), they also possess a better real-time performance.

Acknowledgments. This work is supported by A*STAR research grant R-252-000-233-305 and a gift from Microsoft.

References

1. Boehm, H.: http://www.hpl.hp.com/personal/Hans_Boehm/gc/
2. Bogda, J., Hölzle, U.: Removing Unnecessary Synchronization in Java. ACM SIG-PLAN Notices 34(10), 35–46 (1999)
3. Bollella, G., Brosgol, B., Dibble, P., Furr, S., Gosling, J., Hardin, D., Turnbull, M.: The Real-Time Specification for Java. Addison-Wesley, Reading (2000)
4. Carlisle, M.C., Rogers, A.: Software Caching and Computation Migration in Olden. In: ACM PPoPP, Santa Barbara, California, pp. 29–38. ACM Press, New York (1993)
5. Cherem, S., Rugina, R.: Region Analysis and Transformation for Java Programs. In: Proceedings of the International Symposium on Memory Management (ISMM 2004). ACM Press, New York (October 2004)
6. Cherem, S., Rugina, R.: Compile-Time Deallocation of Individual Objects. In: Proceedings of the 2006 International Symposium on Memory Management (ISMM 2006) (June 2006)
7. Chin, W.N., Craciun, F., Qin, S.C., Rinard, M.: Region Inference for an Object-Oriented Language. In: ACM PLDI, Washington, DC (2004)
8. Choi, J.D., Gupta, M., Serrano, M.J., Sreedhar, V.C., Midkiff, S.P.: Escape Analysis for Java. In: Proceedings of the Conference on Object-Oriented Programming Systems, Languages, and Applications (OOPSLA), pp. 1–19 (1999)
9. Christiansen, M.V., Velschow, P.: Region-Based Memory Management in Java. Master's Thesis, Department of Computer Science (DIKU), University of Copenhagen (1998)
10. Goldberg, B., Park, Y.G.: Higher Order Escape Analysis: Optimizing Stack Allocation in Functional Program Implementations. In: Proceedings of the 1990 European Symposium on Programming, pp. 152–160 (1990)
11. Grossman, D., Morrisett, G., Jim, T., Hicks, M., Wang, Y., Cheney, J.: Region-Based Memory Management in Cyclone. In: ACM PLDI. ACM Press, New York (2002)
12. Guyer, S.Z., McKinley, K.S., Frampton, D.: Free-Me: A Static Analysis for Automatic Individual Object Reclamation. In: Proceedings of the SIGPLAN 2006 Conference on Program Language Design and Implementation (June 2006)
13. Park, Y.G., Goldberg, B.: Escape Analysis on Lists. In: Proceedings of the ACM SIGPLAN 1992 conference on Programming language design and implementation, pp. 116–127 (1992)
14. Shaham, R., Yahav, E., Kolodner, E.K., Sagiv, M.: Establishing Local Temporal Heap Safety Properties with Application to Compile-Time Memory Management. In: Cousot, R. (ed.) SAS 2003. LNCS, vol. 2694, Springer, Heidelberg (2003)

15. Stutz, D., Neward, T., Shilling, G.: Shared Source CLI Essentials. O'Reilly, Sebastopol (2003)
16. ECMA-335 Standard: Common Language Infrastructure (CLI), 4th edition (2006)
17. Tofte, M., Birkedal, L., Elsman, M., Hallenberg, N., Olesen, T.H., Sestoft, P.: Programming with Regions in the ML Kit (for Version 4). The IT University of Copenhagen (September 2001)
18. Tofte, M., Talpin, J.: Implementing the Call-By-Value λ-calculus Using a Stack of Regions. In: ACM POPL. ACM Press, New York (1994)
19. Whaley, J., Rinard, M.: Compositional Pointer and Escape Analysis for Java Programs. In: ACM OOPSLA, Denver, CO. ACM Press, New York (1999)
20. F# Language, http://research.microsoft.com/fsharp/fsharp.aspx

Context-Sensitive Relevancy Analysis for Efficient Symbolic Execution*

Xin Li[1], Daryl Shannon[2], Indradeep Ghosh[3],
Mizuhito Ogawa[1], Sreeranga P. Rajan[3], and Sarfraz Khurshid[2]

[1] School of Information Science,
Japan Advanced Institute of Science and Technology, Nomi, Japan
[2] Department of Electrical and Computer Engineering,
University of Texas at Austin, Austin, TX, USA
[3] Trusted Systems Innovation Group,
Fujitsu laboratory of America, Sunnyvale, CA, USA

Abstract. Symbolic execution is a flexible and powerful, but computationally expensive technique to detect dynamic behaviors of a program. In this paper, we present a *context-sensitive relevancy analysis* algorithm based on weighted pushdown model checking, which pinpoints memory locations in the program where symbolic values can flow into. This information is then utilized by a code instrumenter to transform only relevant parts of the program with symbolic constructs, to help improve the efficiency of symbolic execution of Java programs. Our technique is evaluated on a generalized symbolic execution engine that is developed upon Java Path Finder with checking safety properties of Java applications. Our experiments indicate that this technique can effectively improve the performance of the symbolic execution engine with respect to the approach that blindly instruments the whole program.

1 Introduction

A recent trend of model checking is to combine with the power of dynamic execution, such as simulation and constraint solving. Remarkable progress on both hardware and efficient decision procedures, such as Presburger arithmetic, satisfiability check on various logic, equality with uninterpreted function symbols, and various constraint solving, has made such a combination of model checking and off-the-shelf decision procedures more practical. For instance, symbolic execution [1], a classic technique for test-input generation, has been integrated into such model checking frameworks, including Bogor/Kiasan [2] and various extensions of Java Path Finder (JPF) [3,4]. JPF has been combined with decision procedures such as first-order provers CVClite and Simplify, the SMT solver Yices, the Presburger arithmetic constraint solver OMEGA, and the constraint solver STP on bit-vectors and arrays, for correctness checking and automated test-input generation. Symbolic execution interprets the program over symbolic

---

* D.Shannon was an intern at Fujistu Labs. Sunnyvale during this work.

G. Ramalingam (Ed.): APLAS 2008, LNCS 5356, pp. 36–52, 2008.

```
0. public class Limit{
1.   int v = 0;
2.   Limit (int x){this.v = x;}
3.   int GetL(){return this.v;}
4.   int IncL(int t) {return this.v + t;}
5.   String CutExcess(String s){
6.   if(s.length() > v)
7.     return s.substring(0, v);
8.   else return s;
9.   }
10.}
11. public class Driver{
12.   public static void main(String[] args){
13.     String s = Symbolic.string();
14.     int i = 7;
15.     Limit limit = new Limit(i);
16.     limit.IncL(i);
17.     s = limit.CutExcess(s);
18.   }
19. }
```

```
public class Limit implements Symbolic{
  int v = 0;
  Limit (int x){this.v = x;}
  int GetL(){return this.v;}
  int IncL(int t) {return this.v + t;}
  String CutExcess(String s) {
  return ___CutExcess(StringExpr.
        _constant(s))._getValue();
  }
  StringExpr ___CutExcess(StringExpr s){
  if(Symbolic._GT(s.___length(), v))
  return s.___substring(Symbolic.IntConstant(0),
        Symbolic.IntConstant(v));
  else return s;
  }
}
```

```
public class Driver{
  public static void ___main(String args[]){
    StringExpr s = new Symbolic.string();
    int i = 7;
    Limit limit = new Limit(i);
    limit.IncL(i);
    s = limit.___CutExcess(s);
  }
  public static void main(String args[]){
    ___main(args);
  }
}
```

Fig. 1. A Java Example for Code Instrumentation of Symbolic Execution

values and allows model checking to reason variables with infinite data domain. Though such exhaustive checking is very powerful, it is computationally expensive. Further sophistication is needed to make it scale to industrial size software applications.

Fig. 1 shows an example of code instrumentation from the Java code fragment (the left-hand side) into its symbolic counterpart (the right-hand side) for symbolic execution. In the *Driver* class, the String *s* is designated as symbolic (by the assignment of *Symbolic.string()* to *s*). The methods of *IncL()*, *GetL()*, and the constructor *Limit(int x)* of the class *Limit* does not need a symbolic version as no symbolic values ever flow into these methods. However, in the symbolic execution of Java programs, most of existing approaches transform the entire program with regarding all program entities as symbolic. Blind instrumentation will incur unnecessary runtime overhead on symbolic execution along with the extra time required to instrument the entire program. Therefore, some program analysis is expected to help identify the part of program entities that are subject to symbolic execution at run-time.

This paper makes the following primary contributions:

– We present an interprocedural *relevancy analysis* (RA), formalized and implemented as weighted pushdown model checking [5] with PER-based abstraction [6]. Our RA is context-sensitive, field-sensitive, and flow-insensitive, and conservatively detects the set of memory locations (i.e., program variables of various kinds) where symbolic values can flow into. Then the instrumenter can use this information to instrument only the relevant parts of the program with symbolic constructs, thereby improving the performance of symbolic execution and code instrumentation itself.

- We perform experiments on the generalized symbolic execution engine [3], which is developed upon JPF, for checking safety properties on three Java applications. Relevancy analysis is used as the preprocessing step to detect program variables that may store symbolic values at run-time. Only these portions of the applications are later transformed using a code instrumenter. Experimental results indicate that our technique can effectively improve the performance of the symbolic execution engine with respect to the approach that blindly instruments the whole program.

The rest of the paper is organized as follows. In Section 2 the relevancy analysis based on weighted pushdown model checking techniques is presented. In Section 3 we describe in detail how Java programs are abstracted and modelled for relevancy analysis. Experimental results are presented and discussed in Section 4, and related work is surveyed in Section 5. Section 6 concludes the paper with a description of our future work.

2   Context-Sensitive Relevancy Analysis

2.1   Interprocedural Program Analysis by Weighted Pushdown Model Checking

Definition 1. *A **pushdown system** $P = (Q, \Gamma, \Delta, q_0, w_0)$ is a pushdown automaton regardless of input, where Q is a finite set of states called control locations, and Γ is a finite set of stack alphabet, and $\Delta \subseteq Q \times \Gamma \times Q \times \Gamma^*$ is a finite set of transition rules, and $q_0 \in Q$ and $w_0 \in \Gamma^*$ are the initial control location and stack contents respectively. We denote the transition rule $((q_1, w_1), (q_2, w_2)) \in \Delta$ by $\langle q_1, w_1 \rangle \hookrightarrow \langle q_2, w_2 \rangle$. A **configuration** of P is a pair $\langle q, w \rangle$, where $q \in Q$ and $w \in \Gamma^*$. Δ defines the transition relation $\Rightarrow$ between pushdown configurations such that if $\langle p, \gamma \rangle \hookrightarrow \langle q, \omega \rangle$, then $\langle p, \gamma \omega' \rangle \Rightarrow \langle q, \omega \omega' \rangle$, for all $\omega' \in \Gamma^*$.*

A pushdown system is a transition system with a finite set of control states and an unbounded stack. A weighted pushdown system extends a pushdown system by associating a weight to each transition rule. The weights come from a bounded idempotent semiring.

Definition 2. *A **bounded idempotent semiring** $S = (D, \oplus, \otimes, 0, 1)$ consists of a set D ($0, 1 \in D$) and two binary operations $\oplus$ and $\otimes$ on D such that*

1. *$(D, \oplus)$ is a commutative monoid with 0 as its neutral element, and $\oplus$ is idempotent, i.e., $a \oplus a = a$ for $a \in D$;*
2. *$(D, \otimes)$ is a monoid with 1 as the neutral element;*
3. *$\otimes$ distributes over $\oplus$. That is, $\forall a, b, c \in D$, $a \otimes (b \oplus c) = (a \otimes b) \oplus (a \otimes c)$ and $(a \oplus b) \otimes c = (a \otimes c) \oplus (b \otimes c)$;*
4. *$\forall a \in D, a \otimes 0 = 0 \otimes a = 0$;*

5. *The partial ordering $\sqsubseteq$ is defined on D such that $\forall a, b \in D, a \sqsubseteq b$ iff $a \oplus b = a$, and there are no infinite descending chains on D wrt $\sqsubseteq$.*

Remark 1. As stated in Section 4.4 in [5], the distributivity of $\oplus$ can be loosened to $a \otimes (b \oplus c) \sqsubseteq (a \otimes b) \oplus (a \otimes c)$ and $(a \oplus b) \otimes c \sqsubseteq (a \otimes c) \oplus (b \otimes c)$.

Definition 3. *A **weighted pushdown system** is a triple $W = (P, S, f)$, where $P = (Q, \Gamma, \Delta, q_0, w_0)$ is a pushdown system, $S = (D, \oplus, \otimes, 0, 1)$ is a bounded idempotent semiring, and $f : \Delta \rightarrow D$ is a function that assigns a value from D to each rule of P.*

Definition 4. *Consider a weighted pushdown system $W = (P, S, f)$, where $P = (Q, \Gamma, \Delta, q_0, w_0)$ is a pushdown system, and $S = (D, \oplus, \otimes, 0, 1)$ is a bounded idempotent semiring. Assume $\sigma = [r_0, ..., r_k]$ to be a sequence of pushdown transition rules, where $r_i \in \Delta (0 \leq i \leq k)$, and $v(\sigma) = f(r_0) \otimes ... \otimes f(r_k)$. Let $path(c,c')$ be the set of all rule sequences that transform configurations from c into c'. Let $C \subseteq Q \times \Gamma^*$ be a set of regular configurations. The **generalized pushdown reachability problem**(GPR) is to find for each $c \in Q \times \Gamma^*$:*

$$\delta(c) = \bigoplus \{v(\sigma) | \sigma \in path(c, c'), c' \in C\}$$

Efficient algorithms for solving GPR are developed based on the property that the regular set of pushdown configurations is closed under forward and backward reachability [5]. There are two off-the-shelf implementations of weighted pushdown model checking algorithms, Weighted PDS Library[1], and WPDS+[2]. We apply the former as the back-end analysis engine for relevancy analysis.

The GPR can be easily extended to answer the "meet-over-all-valid-paths" program analysis problem MOVP(EntryPoints, TargetPoints), which intends to conservatively approximate properties of memory configurations at given program execution points (represented as TargetPoints) induced by all possible execution paths leading from program entry points (represented as EntryPoints). A *valid* path here satisfies the requirement that a procedure always exactly returns to the most recent call site in the analysis. The encoding of a program into a weighted PDS in a (flow-sensitive) program analysis [5] typically models program variables as control locations and program execution points (equivalently, line numbers) as stack alphabet. The weighted domain is designed as follows:

- A weight function represents the data flow changes for each program execution step, such as transfer functions;
- $f \oplus g$ represents the merging of data flow at the meet of two control flows;
- $f \otimes g$ represents the composition of two sequential control flows;
- **1** implies that an execution step does not change each datum; and
- **0** implies that the program execution is interrupted by an error.

---

[1] http://www.fmi.uni-stuttgart.de/szs/tools/wpds/
[2] http://www.cs.wisc.edu/wpis/wpds++/

Moreover, assume a Galois connection (L, α, γ, M) between the concrete domain L and the abstract domain M, and a monotone function space $\mathcal{F}_l : L \to L$. Taking weight functions from the monotone function space $\mathcal{F}_m : M \to M$ defined as $\mathcal{F}_m = \{f_m \mid f_m \supseteq \alpha \circ f_l \circ \gamma, \ f_l \in \mathcal{F}_l\}$, a sound analysis based on weighted pushdown systems can be ensured according to abstract interpretation.

2.2   PER-Based Abstraction and Relevancy Analysis Infrastructure

For program verification at source code level, it is a well understood methodology that *program analysis can be regarded as model checking of abstract interpretation* [7] on an *intermediate representation* (IR) of the target program. Our RA is designed and implemented as weighted pushdown model checking following this methodology.

The infrastructure of our RA is shown in Figure 2, with a soot[3] compiler as the front-end preprocessor and the Weighted PDS Library as the back-end model checking engine. The analysis starts off preprocessing by soot from Java to Jimple [8], which is a typed three-address intermediate representation of Java. In the meantime, points-to Analysis (PTA) is performed and thus a call graph is constructed. After preprocessing, Jimple codes are abstracted and modeled into a weighted PDS, and the generated model is finally checked by calling the Weighted PDS Library. The set of symbolic variables is detected and output into an XML file for later use by the code instrumenter.

We choose Jimple as our target language since its language constructs are much simpler than those of either Java source code or Java Bytecode. Although the choice of PTA is independent of RA, the precision of RA depends on the precision of PTA, in that (i) call graph construction and PTA are mutually dependent due to dynamic method dispatch; and (ii) a precise modelling on instance fields (a.k.a., field-sensitivity [9]), array references, and containers (Section 4.3) depends on PTA to cast aliasing.

The objective of our relevancy analysis is to compute the set of program variables of interested type that are *relevant* to any designated variables that are meant to be symbolic. We mark a variable as *relevant* if it can store symbolic values at run-time. Our relevancy analysis is leveraged from an interprocedural irrelevant code elimination [10]. The idea is that, if the change of a value does not affect the value of outputs, we regard it as irrelevant, and relevant otherwise.

The weighted domain for this analysis is constructed on a 2-point abstract domain L (Definition 5) based on a partial equivalence relation (PER). A PER on a set S is a transitive and symmetric relation $S \times S$. It is easy to see that $\gamma\, l$ is a PER for all $l \in L$. Our relevancy analysis works with an interpretation on L as follows: ANY is interpreted as any values, and ID is interpreted as fixed values. Designating a seed variable x to be ANY in a program, a variable y is relevant to x if its value can be ANY at run-time.

Definition 5. *Define the 2-point abstract domain L as $L = \{$ANY, ID$\}$, with the ordering ANY $\supseteq$ ID. Taking the concrete domain D as integers or other data*

---

[3] http://www.sable.mcgill.ca/soot/

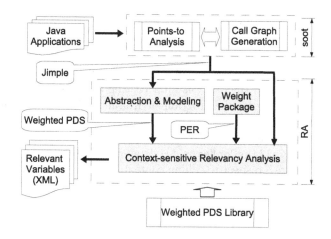

Fig. 2. The Analysis Infrastructure

sets of interest, the concretization γ of L is defined as γ ANY $= \{(x,y) \mid x,y \in D\}$, γ ID $= \{(x,x) \mid x \in D\}$.

Definition 6. *Define a set of transfer functions* $\mathcal{F} : L \to L$ *as*

$$\mathcal{F} = \{\lambda x.x, \lambda x.\text{ANY}, \lambda x.\text{ID} \mid x \in L\}$$

Let $f_0 = \lambda x.\text{ANY}$, $f_1 = \lambda x.x$, and $f_2 = \lambda x.\text{ID}$. We have $\forall x \in L$, $f_0\,x \supset f_1\,x$ and $f_1\,x \supset f_2\,x$. Thus, $\mathcal{F}$ is a monotone function space with the ordering $f_0 \sqsupseteq f_1 \sqsupseteq f_2$, where $f \sqsupseteq f'$ iff $\forall x \in L, f x \supset f'x$. The weighted domain in our analysis thus consists of $\mathcal{F}$ plus **0** element, and binary operations over weights are correspondingly induced by the ordering $\sqsupseteq$.

3   Modelling Java Programs

3.1   Building the Weighted Dependence Graph

Provided with a Java points-to analyzer, the analysis first builds a *weighted dependence graph* (WDG), a directed and labelled graph $G = (N, L, \rightsquigarrow)$. The WDG is then encoded as the underlying weighted pushdown system for model checking. Let `Var` denote the set of program variables of interested type which consist of local variables and field or array references, and let `ProS` denote the set of *method identifiers* which is identified as a pair of class names and method signatures. $N \subseteq$ `Var` $\times$ `ProS` is a set of nodes and each of them represents a program variable and the method where it resides. $L \subseteq \mathcal{F}$ is a set of labels, and $\rightsquigarrow\,\subseteq N \times L \times N$ is a set of directed and labelled edges that represent some dependence among variables regarding the changes of data flow. By $v_1 \overset{l}{\rightsquigarrow} v_2$, we mean that there is a data flow from v_1 to v_2 represented by a weight l. A WDG can be regarded as an instance of the exploded supergraph [11].

Let Stmt be the set of Jimple statements and let $\mathcal{P}$ be the powerset operator. An evaluation function $\mathcal{A}[\![\_]\!] : \text{Stmt} \to \mathcal{P}(\rightsquigarrow)$, which models Jimple statements (from a method $f \in \text{ProS}$) into edges in G, is given in Table 1, where

- GlobVar ($\subseteq$ Var) denotes the set of static fields and instance fields, as well as array references, in the analysis after casting aliasing;
- env ($\in$ GlobVar) denotes the program environment that allocates new memories; SymVal and ConstVal denotes symbolic values and program constants respectively; binop denotes binary operators;
- $\text{pta}(r, \text{cc})$ ($cc \in \text{CallingContexts}(f)$) denotes points-to analysis on a reference variable r with respect to calling contexts cc, and $\text{CallingContexts}(f)$ represents the calling contexts of a method f where r resides;
- $[\![o]\!]$ ($o \in \text{pta}(r)$) denotes the unique representative of array members $r[i]$ after calling points-to analysis on the base variable r;
- $\text{rp}(\in \text{RetP})$ is a return point associated with a method invocation. Return points denoted by RetP are introduced in addition to *method identifiers*, so that each method invocation is assigned with a unique return point;
- f'_{ret} (resp. f'_{arg_i}) is a variable that denotes a return value (resp. the i-th parameter) of the method $f' \in \text{ProS}$.

$\lambda x.\text{ANY}$ models that env assigns symbolic values to seed variables; $\lambda x.\text{ID}$ models that env assigns variables with program constants; $\lambda x.x$ models that a data flow is kept unchanged. For readability, the label $\lambda x.x$ (on $\rightsquigarrow$) is omitted in the table.

Our analysis is *context-sensitive* by encoding the program as a pushdown system, and thus calling contexts that can be infinite are approximated as regular pushdown configurations. A WDG G is encoded into a Weighted PDS as follows,

Table 1. Rules for Building the Weighted Dependence Graph

$\mathcal{A}[\![x = \text{SymVal}]\!] = \{(\text{env}, f) \overset{\lambda.\text{ANY}}{\rightsquigarrow} (x, f)\}$

$\mathcal{A}[\![x = \text{ConstVal}]\!] = \{(\text{env}, f) \overset{\lambda.\text{ID}}{\rightsquigarrow} (x, f)\}$

$\mathcal{A}[\![x = y]\!] = \{(y, f) \rightsquigarrow (x, f)\}$

$\mathcal{A}[\![z = x \text{ binop } y]\!] = \{(x, f) \rightsquigarrow (z, f), (y, f) \rightsquigarrow (z, f)\}$

$\mathcal{A}[\![x = r[n]]\!] = \{([\![o]\!], f) \rightsquigarrow (x, f) \mid o \in \text{pta}(r, \text{cc})\}$

$\mathcal{A}[\![r[n] = x]\!] = \{(x, f) \rightsquigarrow ([\![o]\!], f) \mid o \in \text{pta}(r, \text{cc})\}$

$\mathcal{A}[\![x = r.g]\!] = \{(o.g, f) \rightsquigarrow (x, f) \mid o \in \text{pta}(r, \text{cc})\}$

$\mathcal{A}[\![r.g = x]\!] = \{(x, f) \rightsquigarrow (o.g, f) \mid o \in \text{pta}(r, \text{cc})\}$

$\mathcal{A}[\![x = \text{lengthof } r]\!] = \{(o.len, f) \rightsquigarrow (x, f) \mid o \in \text{pta}(r, \text{cc})\}$

$\mathcal{A}[\![r = \text{newarray RefType } [x]]\!] = \{(x, f) \rightsquigarrow (o.len, f) \mid o \in \text{pta}(r, \text{cc})\}$

$\mathcal{A}[\![\text{return } x]\!] = \{(x, f) \rightsquigarrow (f_{\text{ret}}, f)\}$

$\mathcal{A}[\![x := @\text{parameter}_k : \text{Type}]\!] = \{(f_{\text{arg}_k}, f) \rightsquigarrow (x, f)\}$

$\mathcal{A}[\![x := (Type)y]\!] = \{(y, f) \rightsquigarrow (x, f)\}$

$\mathcal{A}[\![z = x.f'(m_1, ..., m_l, m_{l+1}, ...m_n)]\!] =$
$\quad \{(m_i, f) \rightsquigarrow (f'_{\text{arg}_i}, f') \mid 1 \leq i \leq l\} \cup \{(f'_{\text{ret}}, f') \rightsquigarrow (f'_{\text{ret}}, \text{rp})\}$
$\quad \cup \{(f'_{\text{ret}}, \text{rp}) \rightsquigarrow (z, f)\} \cup \{(v, f) \rightsquigarrow (v, f') \mid v \in \text{GlobVar}\}$
$\quad \cup \{(v, f') \rightsquigarrow (v, \text{rp}) \mid v \in \text{GlobVar}\} \cup \{(v, \text{rp}) \rightsquigarrow (v, f) \mid v \in \text{GlobVar}\}$

where $m_i (1 \leq i \leq l)$ are variables of interested type, and $cc \in \text{CallingContexts}(f)$.

- The set of control locations is the first projection of N ($\subseteq$ Var);
- The stack alphabet is ProS $\cup$ RetP;
- The weighted domain is the set of labels L;
- Let $(v_1, f_1) \overset{l}{\leadsto} (v_2, f_2) \in E$ for $l \in L$ such that

  • $\langle v_1, f_1 \rangle \hookrightarrow \langle v_2, f_2 \rangle$ if $f_1 = f_2$,
  • $\langle v_1, f_1 \rangle \hookrightarrow \langle v_2, f_2 f_r \rangle$ if the method f_1 calls f_2 with f_r designated as the return point, and
  • $\langle v_1, f_1 \rangle \hookrightarrow \langle v_2, \epsilon \rangle$ if $f_2 \in$ RetP.

Our analysis is also *field-sensitive*, so that not only different instance fields of an object are distinguished (otherwise called field-based analysis), but also are instance fields that belong to different objects (otherwise called field-insensitive analysis). Note that array references are treated similarly as instance fields. The abstraction we take is to ignore the indices of arrays, such that members of an array are not distinguished. Both field and array references can be nested, and we choose to avoid tracking such a nesting in the analysis by cast aliasing on their base variables with calling a points-to analysis.

Considering efficiency, we perform a *flow-insensitive* analysis, i.e., each method is regarded as a set of instructions by ignoring their execution order. Note that soot compiles Jimple in a SSA-like (Static Single Assignment) form. When a program is in the SSA-like form, a flow-insensitive analysis on it is expected to enjoy a similar precision of that of a flow-sensitive analysis [9], except that, in a flow-insensitive analysis, the return points of call sites also shrink to the nodes (i.e., methods) of the call graph. Thus, calling contexts of a method that is multiply invoked from one method are indistinguishable due to sharing the same return points. We remedy such a precession loss by associating a unique return point with each invocation site.

Definition 7. *Assume that the program under investigation starts with the entry point* ep $\in$ ProS. *Our relevancy analysis on a variable* $v \in$ Var *that resides in the method* $s \in$ ProS *computes* $\mathbf{ra}(v, m) = \text{MOVP}(\mathbf{S}, \mathbf{T})$, *where* $\mathbf{S} = \langle env, \text{ep} \rangle$ *and* $\mathbf{T} = \langle v, m.(\text{RetP})^* \rangle$. v *is marked as relevant if and only if* $\mathbf{ra}(v, m)$ *returns* $\lambda x.\text{ANY}$.

Remark 2. To compute MOVP$(\mathbf{S}, \mathbf{T})$, our analysis calls the Weighted PDS Library to (i) first construct a weighted automaton that recognizes all pushdown configurations reachable from $\mathbf{S}$; and (ii) then read out weights associated with pushdown configurations from $\mathbf{T}$ with respect to the variables of interest. The latter phase seems not to be a dominant factor in practice, and the time complexity of the former is $O(m \, n^2)$, where m is the number of variables and n is the program size (Lemma 1 in [12]).

Remark 3. We are interested in variables of primite type, strings, and the classes explicitly modelled (Appendix A) in the analysis. An array is regarded as symbolic if its unique representative is detected as symbolic by the analysis. Since

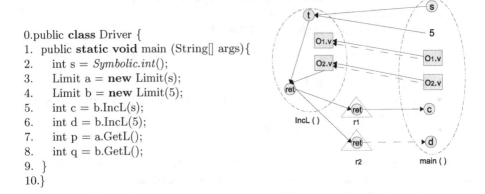

```
0.public class Driver {
1.  public static void main (String[] args){
2.    int s = Symbolic.int();
3.    Limit a = new Limit(s);
4.    Limit b = new Limit(5);
5.    int c = b.IncL(s);
6.    int d = b.IncL(5);
7.    int p = a.GetL();
8.    int q = b.GetL();
9.  }
10.}
```

Fig. 3. A Java Code Fragment   **Fig. 4.** The WDG for lines 3-4, 5-6

our analysis is field-sensitive, an instance field f of a class is regarded as symbolic, if it is detected as symbolic when belonging to any instance o of this class, i.e., when $o.f$ is detected as symbolic.

3.2   Precision Enhancement by Refined Modelling on Globals

A typical approach to perform context-sensitive analysis is based on *context-cloning*. In such methods, program entities, such as methods and local variables, typically have a separate copy for different calling contexts. Since possible calling contexts can be infinite due to recursions, this infinity is often bounded by limiting the call depth within which the precision is preserved (like k-CFA analysis [13]) or by performing context-insensitive analysis on all the procedure calls involved in any recursions [14]. In contrast, our approach to context-sensitivity is based on *context-stacking*. That is, the infinite program control structures are modelled by the pushdown stack with no limit on recursions and procedure calls. The context-stacking-based approach has an advantage over the context-cloning-based approach when there are deep procedure calls, or when a large number of procedures is involved in various recursions in the program. However, in some cases, it can be less precise than the context-cloning-based analysis.

Example 1. Suppose the int s is designated as symbolic (by the assignment of *Symbolic.int()*) in the Java code fragment in Fig. 3 that uses class Limit in Fig. 1. For the driver, variables c and p are symbolic, but variables d and q are not.

Assume the heap objects allocated at lines 3 and 4 are respectively O_1 and O_2. Fig. 4 shows part of the WDG corresponding to lines 3-4 and 5-6. Each dotted circle demarcates a method. There are two kinds of nodes identified by variable names: circles for local variables and rectangles for global variables, such as instance fields and array references. Dashed edges are induced by the method invocation at line 6, which is to be distinguished from the method invocation at line 5. Return points for method invocations at lines 5 and 6 are represented

Table 2. Refined Modelling on Globals

$$\mathcal{A}[\![x = r[n]]\!] = \{(([\![o]\!], \mathtt{cc}), f) \rightsquigarrow (x, f) \mid o \in \mathtt{pta}(r, \mathtt{cc}), \mathtt{cc} \in \mathtt{CallingContexts}(f)\}$$
$$\mathcal{A}[\![z = x.f'(m_1, ..., m_l, m_{l+1}, ...m_n)]\!] =$$
$$\{(m_i, f) \rightsquigarrow (f'_{\mathtt{arg}_i}, f') \mid 1 \leq i \leq l\} \cup \{(f'_{\mathtt{ret}}, f') \rightsquigarrow (f'_{\mathtt{ret}}, \mathtt{rp})\} \cup \{(f'_{\mathtt{ret}}, \mathtt{rp}) \rightsquigarrow (z, f)\}$$
$$\cup \{((v, \mathtt{cc}), f) \rightsquigarrow ((v, \mathtt{cc}'), f') \mid v \in \mathtt{GlobVar}, \mathtt{cc} \in \mathtt{CallingContexts}(f),$$
$$\mathtt{cc}' \in \mathtt{CallingContexts}(f')\}$$
$$\cup \{((v, \mathtt{cc}'), f') \rightsquigarrow ((v, \mathtt{rp}), \mathtt{rp}) \mid v \in \mathtt{GlobVar}, \mathtt{cc}' \in \mathtt{CallingContexts}(f')\}$$
$$\cup \{((v, \mathtt{rp}), \mathtt{rp}) \rightsquigarrow ((v, \mathtt{cc}), f) \mid v \in \mathtt{GlobVar}, \mathtt{cc} \in \mathtt{CallingContexts}(f)\}$$
where $m_i (1 \leq i \leq l)$ are variables of concerned type.

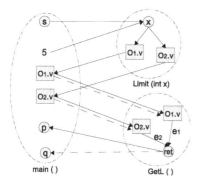

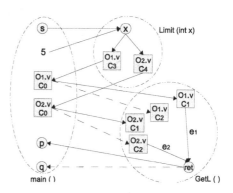

Fig. 5. The WDG for lines 2-4, 7-8   **Fig. 6.** Fig.5 with Refined Modeling

as triangles, and named r_1 and r_2 respectively. The variable ret represents the
return value of $IncL()$. Our analysis can precisely distinguish that c and d are
returned from two invocations on the same method, and only c is relevant to s.

However, the analysis cannot correctly conclude that q can only store concrete
values at run-time, whereas this case can be handled by the 1-CFA context-
sensitive approach based on context-cloning. Fig. 5 shows part of the WDG corresponding to lines 3-4 and 7-8, where dashed edges are induced by the method
invocation at line 6, and for readability, return points for line 7 and 8 are omitted
in the figure. $GetL()$ are invoked on objects O_1 and O_2 respectively from line 7
and 8, and instance fields of both $O_1.v$ and $O_2.v$ can flow to ret under two calling
contexts. However, since the pushdown transition only depends on the control
location (i.e., variable) and the topmost stack symbol (i.e., the method where
the variable presently resides), the pushdown transitions are incapable of distinguishing under which calling contexts a global variable ($\in \mathtt{GlobVar}$) flows into
a method. Therefore, pushdown transitions that model edges e_1 and e_2 cannot
distinguish invocations from lines 7 and 8.

To remedy a precision, our choice is to refine modelling on global variables
from $\mathtt{GlobVar}$ to avoid an invalid data flow. Such an extension is obtained by
modifying rules from Table 1 in which global variables are involved. Table 2 shows
some of the extensions on array references and method invocations. Assume that

the calling context of main() is C_0, the calling contexts of GetL() are C_1 and C_2, and that the calling contexts of Limit(int x) are C_3 and C_4. Fig. 6 shows the refined version of the WDG shown in Fig. 5. Note that the precision of refined modelling closely depends on that of the underlying context-sensitive points-to analysis.

4   Evaluations

4.1   Configuration of the Evaluation Steps

Our evaluation of checking safety properties of Java web applications through symbolic execution generally consists of the following steps:

- **Environment Generation:** Since model checking techniques require a closed system to run on, the first step is to convert a heterogeneous web application that uses various components into a closed Java program. This process is known as *environment generation* [15], which decomposes web applications into the *module* that is typically the middle tier of web applications, which comprises the business logic and the *environment* with which the module interacts with. The environment is further abstracted into *drivers* from Java classes that hold a thread of control and *stubs* from the rest of Java classes and components of the application. After this step, all the applications consist of a driver file that provides all input values to the application. Typically, these values are provided by a user using forms in a webpage. The back-end database is abstracted as a series of stubs that use a two-dimentional table structure, and also to store the input data if needed.

- **Property Specification:** Once the model is generated, some specific input values in the drivers are made to be symbolic quantities, such as values of integer, float, Boolean, or String. For example, if the requirement is that the shopping cart total must be the product of the item price and the item quantity specified by the user, then the item price, quantity, and cart-total are made to be symbolic entities. Sometimes this can be achieved using the input variables in the driver only. However, sometimes this also means changing the database stubs for inputs that were stored in the database (such as item price). The requirement is further inserted as an assertion comprising the symbolic entities and placed in an appropriate location in the program.

- **Code instrumentation:** The program is thus instrumented using a code instrumenter that replaces java codes that use concrete values with the counterparts that can handle symbolic values. For this purpose, extensive libraries have been developed that can handle symbolic integer, symbolic float, symbolic Boolean, *etc.*. The instrumenter uses the relevancy analysis to pinpoint the portions of the program that are required to tackle symbolic entities. The results of the relevancy analysis are conveyed as series of classes, methods, parameters, and variables to the instrumenter in an XML file.

 – **Symbolic program model checking:** Finally, once the instrumentation phase is completed, a state-based model checker is used to check safety properties of interest. The symbolic libraries create a system of equations with the symbolic variables, whenever those variables are manipulated. At each control point that consists of symbolic variables, an off-the-shelf decision procedure is invoked to check whether the system of equations is satisfiable. If not, the exploration is terminated along that path. An assertion containing symbolic variables is inserted into the program at an appropriate point to check for the negation of the property being checked. When the assertion is hit, a solution to the equations points to the existence of a counterexample or bug. If there are no solutions, then the requirement holds.

4.2   Experimental Results

Our experimental platform is built upon JPF at the University of Texas at Austin. The targets of our experiments are Java applications as shown in Table 3. Note that these numbers reflect the size of the generated Java model. The original application is usually much larger since it is heterogeneous and consists of HTML pages, JSP code, some database code, *etc.*. It is extremely difficult to estimate the exact size of the original application.

Table 3. Benchmark Statistics

Application	Description	#classes	#lines
WebStore	Simple Web E-store	6	410
DB-Merge	Database Application	26	706
Petstore	SUN's J2EE Sample App.	752	23,701

We now discuss the efficiency issues of this whole exercise. Table 4 shows the CPU times (in seconds) for various parts of the process by comparing symbolic execution with blind instrumentation and symbolic execution with RA-based instrumentation. The underlying points-to analysis of the relevancy analysis is provided by soot, which is 0-CFA context-insensitive analysis with call graph constructed on-the-fly. Since symbolic execution is computationally expensive, it was impractical to check all symbolic inputs in one pass for large-scale applications. As a result various symbolic execution instances of the same application were created based on the requirement that was being checked. As shown in the Table, multiple properties over symbolic variables are checked in separate passes. Therefore, although the soot PTA phase is one of the dominant factors in the execution time, it has been reused across all these requirements for a particular application as only some different set of variables are marked as symbolic in the program in each instance. Thus this analysis comprises of an one-time cost and is amortized across all the requirements that are checked. Typically hundreds of requirements need to be checked for a medium size application. Hence, this time has not been included in the overall CPU runtimes. Moreover, note that

Table 4. Performance of symbolic execution with instrumenter using static analysis

App. Program	Prop.	Blind Instrumentation			RA based Instrumentation					RT	CR
		Instr.	SECK	Total	PTA	RA	Instr.	SECK	Total		
WebStore	Prop.1	6.2	1.9	8.1	509	0.8	2.0	1.9	4.7	42%	43%
	Prop.2	6.2	2.9	9.1		0.9	2.0	2.8	5.7	37%	41%
DB-Merge	Prop.1	3.1	10.5	13.6	523	0.6	2.1	9.4	12.1	11%	19%
Petstore	Prop.1	36.9	259.2	296.1	575	1.2	4.8	109.4	115.4	61%	16%
	Prop.2	38.1	593.6	631.7		1.1	5.1	319.9	326.1	48%	16%
	Prop.3	39.2	2566.2	2605.4		1.2	5.4	1053.6	1060.2	59%	17%

Prop.: property being checked   Instr.: time for code instrumentation
PTA: time for points-to analysis   RA: time for relevancy analysis
Total: time for both Instr. and SECK   RT: percentage of runtime improvement
SECK: time for symbolic execution of requirement checking
CR: percentage of the reduction on the instrumented code size
All time above are measured in seconds

the Soot PTA time is relatively large even for small examples like *WebStore* and does not increase that much for the larger example. This is due to its analysis of many Java library classes used by the example which dominate the runtime. These library analysis results can be cached and reused not only across different requirements in the same application but across different applications that use the same libraries. This will reduce the PTA overhead even further. We can observe that there is an average gain in overall runtime as well as reduction in instrumented code size due to the static analysis phase. The CPU time improvement can be as high as 61% for larger examples. This can only grow as the number and influence of symbolic inputs become smaller compared to the overall application size. The CPU times are for a 1.8Ghz dual core Opteron machine running the Redhat Linux operating system and having a memory of 4GB.

5 Related Work

Symbolic execution for model checking of Java programs has been proposed in [3]. However, it is well known that symbolic execution is computationally expensive and efforts have been made to reduce its complexity by abstracting out library classes [16]. A framework for type inference and subsequent program transformation for symbolic execution is proposed in [17] which allows multiple user-defined abstractions. Execution of a transformed program for symbolic execution has been used in several approaches. In most of those approaches, the whole program is transformed akin to our blind instrumentation technique [18], [19]. In [20], the performance of symbolic execution is enhanced by randomly concretizing some symbolic variables at the cost of coverage. Instead of transforming the source code, an enhanced Java virtual machine is used to symbolically execute code in [2].

The approach in [21] is closely related to this work. However, the focus of that paper is precise instrumentation through static analysis whereas the focus of this work is on performance enhancements through the static analysis phase. Approaches adopted in [21] and this work consider two streams of performing context-sensitive program analysis, i.e., context-cloning vs. context-stacking. The analysis in [21] borrows ideas and algorithms from points-to analysis, e.g., the match of field read and write operations are formalized as a CFL (Context Free Language)-reachability problem. Their approach to context-sensitivity is based on context-cloning following [14] and the k-CFA approach to handle procedural calls, whereas our analysis based on pushdown system complemented with the refined modelling on globals can reach a higher precision due to the absence of restriction on recursions and call depth. Note that we cannot compare our work with [21] as neither the tool described in that work or the versions of the example programs used there are in the public domain. No performance statistics are mentioned in that paper.

6   Conclusions

We formalized a context-sensitive, field-sensitive and flow-insensitive relevancy analysis as weighted pushdown model checking, to help the symbolic execution technique scale to realistic Java applications. Our analysis was used as a pre-processing step of symbolic execution, which helps in identifying relevant sections of a program where symbolic values can flow into.

We evaluated the methodology on the generalized symbolic execution platform, built upon JPF at the Univieristy of Texas at Austin. Though the dominant overhead of this methodology is the PTA phase, the results of PTA can be cached and reused. Experimental results indicate that, as the program size increases,, the performance gains obtained from the symbolic execution phase far outweigh the overhead of analysis and thus produce a significant gain in overall performance. Moreover, the symbolic programs thus obtained are much smaller than the ones obtained by blind transformation, which avoids running out of memory during symbolic execution.

The precision and scalability of the relevancy analysis is closely related to that of the underlying points-to analysis. Currently, we performed a 0-CFA context-insensitive on-the-fly points-to analysis provided by Soot. In this work, we limit our focus to the performance improvement of symbolic execution. We are planning to apply a context-sensitive points-to analysis based on weighted pushdown model checking, to see the room of precision enhancement. Points-to analysis on Java web applications is expensive since, even for a small web application, the libraries of the web applications are huge and easily reach millions of lines. Thus, more sophisticated treatments for analyzing libraries are expected. Another interesting direction is that our relevancy analysis can be regarded as an instance of the traditional *taint-style analysis*, thus it is applicable to other application scenarios such as security vulnerability check on Java web applications [22].

References

1. King, J.C.: Symbolic execution and program testing. Commun. ACM 19(7), 385–394 (1976)
2. Deng, X., Lee, J., Robby: Bogor/Kiasan: A k-bounded symbolic execution for checking strong heap properties of open systems. In: The 21st IEEE International Conference on Automated Software Engineering (ASE 2006), pp. 157–166 (2006)
3. Khurshid, S., Pasareanu, C., Visser, W.: Generalized symbolic execution for model checking and testing. In: Garavel, H., Hatcliff, J. (eds.) TACAS 2003. LNCS, vol. 2619, pp. 553–568. Springer, Heidelberg (2003)
4. Anand, S., Pasareanu, C.S., Visser, W.: JPF-SE: A symbolic execution extension to Java PathFinder. In: Grumberg, O., Huth, M. (eds.) TACAS 2007. LNCS, vol. 4424, pp. 134–138. Springer, Heidelberg (2007)
5. Reps, T.W., Schwoon, S., Jha, S., Melski, D.: Weighted pushdown systems and their application to interprocedural dataflow analysis. Sci. Comput. Program. 58(1-2), 206–263 (2005)
6. Hunt, S.: PERs generalize projections for strictness analysis. In: Functional Programming. Proc. 1990 Glasgow Workshop, pp. 114–125. Springer, Heidelberg (1990)
7. Schmidt, D.A.: Data flow analysis is model checking of abstract interpretations. In: The 25th ACM SIGPLAN-SIGACT symposium on Principles of programming languages (POPL 1998), pp. 38–48 (1998)
8. Vallée-Rai, R., Co, P., Gagnon, E., Hendren, L.J., Lam, P., Sundaresan, V.: Soot - a Java bytecode optimization framework. In: Conference of the Centre for Advanced Studies on Collaborative Research, CASCON 1999 (1999)
9. Hasti, R., Horwitz, S.: Using static single assignment form to improve flow-insensitive pointer analysis. In: ACM SIGPLAN conference on Programming language design and implementation (PLDI 1998), pp. 97–105 (1998)
10. Li, X., Ogawa, M.: Interprocedural program analysis for Java based on weighted pushdown model checking. In: The 5th International Workshop on Automated Verification of Infinite-State Systems (AVIS 2006), ETAPS (April 2006)
11. Reps, T.W.: Program analysis via graph reachability. In: International Logic Programming Symposium (ILPS 1997), pp. 5–19. MIT Press, Cambridge (1997)
12. Reps, T.W., Lal, A., Kidd, N.: Program analysis using weighted pushdown systems. In: Arvind, V., Prasad, S. (eds.) FSTTCS 2007. LNCS, vol. 4855, pp. 23–51. Springer, Heidelberg (2007)
13. Shivers, O.: Control flow analysis in scheme. In: ACM SIGPLAN conference on Programming Language design and Implementation (PLDI 1988), pp. 164–174 (1988)
14. Whaley, J., Lam, M.S.: Cloning-based context-sensitive pointer alias analysis using binary decision diagrams. In: ACM SIGPLAN Conference on Programming Language Design and Implementation (PLDI 2004), pp. 131–144 (2004)
15. Tkachuk, O., Dwyer, M.B., Păsăreanu, C.: Automated environment generation for software model checking. In: The 18th IEEE International Conference on Automated Software Engineering (ASE 2003), pp. 116–129 (2003)
16. Khurshid, S., Suen, Y.L.: Generalizing symbolic execution to library classes. In: ACM SIGPLAN-SIGSOFT Workshop on Program Analysis For Software Tools and Engineering (PASTE 2005), pp. 103–110 (2005)

17. Dwyer, M., Hatcliff, J., Joehanes, R., Laubach, S., Pasareanu, C.S., Robby, Zheng, H., Visser, W.: Tool-supported program abstraction for finite-state verification. In: The 23rd International Conference on Software Engineering (ICSE 2001), pp. 177–187 (2001)
18. Cadar, C., Ganesh, V., Pawlowski, P.M., Dill, D.L., Engler, D.R.: EXE: Automatically generating inputs of death. In: ACM Conference on Computer and Communications Security 2006 (CCS 2006), pp. 322–335 (2006)
19. Schulte, W., Grieskamp, W., Tillmann, N.: XRT-exploring runtime for.NET architecture and applications. Electronic Notes in Theoretical Computer Science 144(3), 3–26 (2006)
20. Sen, K., Marinov, D., Agha, G.: CUTE: a concolic unit testing engine for C. In: ESEC/FSE-13: Proceedings of the 10th European software engineering conference held jointly with 13th ACM SIGSOFT international symposium on Foundations of software engineering, pp. 263–272. ACM, New York (2005)
21. Anand, S., Orso, A., Harrold, M.J.: Type-dependence analysis and program transformation for symbolic execution. In: Grumberg, O., Huth, M. (eds.) TACAS 2007. LNCS, vol. 4424, pp. 117–133. Springer, Heidelberg (2007)
22. Livshits, V.B., Lam, M.S.: Finding security vulnerabilities in Java applications with static analysis. In: The 14th conference on USENIX Security Symposium (SSYM 2005), p. 18. USENIX Association (2005)
23. Christensen, A., Møller, A., Schwartzbach, M.: Precise analysis of string expressions. In: Cousot, R. (ed.) SAS 2003. LNCS, vol. 2694, pp. 1–18. Springer, Heidelberg (2003)

A   Application-Oriented Modelling for Efficiency

It is often intractable and unnecessary to explore the whole Java libraries. We hence propose application-oriented explicit modelling on some popular Java libraries, such as containers and strings for better efficiency.

Container, such as HashMap, vectors and trees, is widely used in Java web applications, to store and fetch event attributes. A precise analysis on containers is nontrivial, since the capacity (or the index space) of containers can be unbounded. Our treatment on containers is inspired by the treatment on instance fields, based on the insight that *keys of containers can be regarded as fields of class instances.* Compared with modelling on instance fields, the modelling on containers differs in that keys of containers can be either string constants or more often reference variables. Therefore, both containers and keys need to be cast back to heap objects by calling points-to analysis. Table 5 gives rules of modelling Map containers. As shown in Table 5, the `key` of a `map` is bound with its corresponding `value` by the *put* and *get* methods. The pair of containers and keys are treated as variables from `GlobVar` when building the WDG. In particular, a Map container is marked as symbolic if there is any symbolic value put into or any symbolic key taken from it.

Strings. are also heavily used in Java web applications. For instance, the keys and values of containers are usually of type String. The space of string values is generally infinite, and to conduct a precise *string analysis* [23] will put too much

Table 5. Application-oriented Modelling

Map Container:

$\mathcal{A}[\![\texttt{map.put(key, value)}]\!]=\{(\texttt{value}, f) \rightsquigarrow (o_m.o_k, f) \mid o_m \in \texttt{pta(map)}, o_k \in \texttt{pta(key)}\}$

$\mathcal{A}[\![\texttt{value = map.get(key)}]\!]=\{(o_m.o_k, f) \rightsquigarrow (\texttt{value}, f) \mid o_m \in \texttt{pta(map)}, o_k \in \texttt{pta(key)}\}$

java.lang.String, java.lang.StringBuffer:

$\mathcal{A}[\![\texttt{str}.\text{getBytes}(m_0, m_1, m_2, m_3)]\!] = \mathcal{A}[\![\texttt{str}.\text{getChars}(m_0, m_1, m_2, m_3)]\!]$

$= \{(m_i, f) \rightsquigarrow (m_2, f) \mid 0 \leq i \leq 3 \text{ and } i \neq 2\} \cup \{(\texttt{str}, f) \rightsquigarrow (m_2, f)\}$

$\mathcal{A}[\![\texttt{strbuffer}.\text{getChars}(m_0, m_1, m_2, m_3)]\!]$

$= \{(m_i, f) \rightsquigarrow (m_2, f) \mid 0 \leq i \leq 3 \text{ and } i \neq 2\} \cup \{(\texttt{strbuffer}, f) \rightsquigarrow (m_2, f)\}$

---

overhead on the static analysis phase. However, we are only interested in the relevancy relationship among string variables. In our analysis, string constants that syntactically appear in the program (and are thus essentially bounded) are considered as distinguished string instances. Java library methods related to strings, i.e., `java.lang.String`, `java.lang.StringBuffer` are explicitly modelled. They fall into the following categories: (1) The receiver object is relevant to all arguments for a constructor; (2) The return value, if any, is relevant to all method arguments, as well as the receiver object, if any. Table 5 also shows a few of examples that require specific treatments.

Static Detection of Place Locality and Elimination of Runtime Checks

Shivali Agarwal, RajKishore Barik, V. Krishna Nandivada,
Rudrapatna K. Shyamasundar, and Pradeep Varma

IBM India Research Lab, New Delhi

Abstract. Harnessing parallelism particularly for high performance computing is a demanding topic of research. Limitations and complexities of automatic parallelization have led to programming language notations wherein a user programs parallelism explicitly and partitions a global address space for harnessing parallelism. X10 from IBM uses the notion of places to partition the global address space. The model of computation for such languages involves threads and data distributed over local and remote places. A computation is said to be *place local* if all the threads and data pertaining to it are at the same place. Analysis and optimizations targeting derivations of place-locality have recently gained ground with the advent of partitioned global address space (PGAS) languages like UPC and X10, wherein efficiency of place local accesses is performance critical.

In this paper, we present a novel framework for statically establishing place locality in X10. The analysis framework is based on a static abstraction of activities (threads) incorporating places and an extension to classical escape analysis to track the abstract-activities to which an object can escape. Using this framework, we describe an algorithm that eliminates runtime checks that are inserted by the X10 compiler to enforce place locality of data access. We also identify place locality checks that are guaranteed to fail. Our framework takes advantage of the high level abstraction of X10 distributions to reason about place locality of array accesses in loops as well. The underlying issues, the framework and its power are illustrated through a series of examples.

1 Introduction

As multi-core systems are gaining popularity, there is a definite need for languages and tools that can simplify programming high performance machines to exploit the hardware features to a significant level and achieve higher throughput. X10 [22] is an object-oriented explicitly parallel programming language being designed at IBM under the DARPA HPCS program that enables scalable, high-performance, and high-productivity programming for high-end computer systems.

X10 provides a notion of an activity as an independent execution sequence. An activity runs at a *place*. Multiple activities (zero or more) could be running at any one particular place at any point of time. Notion of activities and places becomes

G. Ramalingam (Ed.): APLAS 2008, LNCS 5356, pp. 53–74, 2008.

```
L0:   async (FirstPlace) {
L1:      final Y y = new Y();
L2:      ateach(AllPlaces) {
L3:         X x = new X();
L4:         ... = x.f;
L5:         final Z z = new Z();
L6:         async (FirstPlace) {
L7:            y.f = z;
L8:            ... = y.f.g; }}}
```

Fig. 1. X10 compiler inserts pcas before L4, L7 and L8

clear through the association of activities to threads of execution and places to processors in the program. Each place has a local memory and runs multiple activities. An object created at place p is considered local to p, and for any activity running at place $p'(\neq p)$ the location of the object is considered remote. X10 restricts accesses to remote memory and a runtime exception is thrown if an activity accesses remote data; note that X10 disallows migration of objects and activities. For any object o, the field $o.location$ yields the place at which the object was created. The current X10 compiler conservatively inserts a place check assertion (pca) to do a place check before every object dereference – leading to inefficient code. These checks, if they fail, throw a runtime exception called BadPlaceException. A pca preceding an object dereference gets translated to the following runtime code:

```
if (o.location != here) throw BadPlaceException
```

Each pca not only introduces additional code but also introduces additional control flow nodes. Since every object dereference needs to do a place check, the program is peppered with pc-assertions all around; this has a severe impact on the performance (execution time). The table below presents an experimental confirmation to this effect by presenting the runtime impact of pcas (execution time with and without the pcas being disabled) on two of the largest NAS [3] parallel benchmarks (note that this benchmark suite contains highly parallel applications).

Benchmark	Exec Time -pcas (seconds)	Exec Time +pcas (seconds)
CG	135	355
LU	22	60

It can be seen that the overhead of checking these assertions is significant. Besides the runtime impact of these pc-assertions, pervasive presence of *asserts* makes it hard to analyze and optimize programs. Also, certain constructs (for example, *atomic*) in the X10 language require that no pca is violated in the body of the statement. Our analysis can also be used by the compiler to enforce such a language guarantee.

We use the snippet of sample X10 program in Fig. 1 to motivate the problem further; we shall use this program as the running example throughout the paper. The program has been simplified in syntax for readability. Line L0 creates an *activity* at `FirstPlace` that executes the compound statement L1–L8. Line L1 allocates an object at the current place (`FirstPlace`). Line L2 creates an activity at each of the places in the set `AllPlaces`; each of these activities execute the compound statement L3–L8. At each place, we create a new local object at L3. This object is being dereferenced in L4. In L5, we create another local object, and assign it to a final variable. Another activity is created in L6. This activity runs at `FirstPlace` and dereferences objects pointed-to by y (in L7) and y.f (in L8). In this example, there are three object dereferences, and the current X10 compiler introduces pcas before each of the object dereferences L4, L7, and L8. However, it can be seen that variable y holds an object at place `FirstPlace` and hence, it's dereference in L7 that happens at place `FirstPlace` does not need a preceding pca. Similarly, variable x is local to each activity and holds an object local to the respective places. Again, there is no need of a preceding pca before L4. However, the one preceding L8 is needed, in particular, for dereferencing the field g of y.f.

In this paper, we present a static analysis framework to eliminate unnecessary pcas during compilation and/or identify assertions that will always fail. The analysis thus either leads to faster code or identifies illegal accesses or leads to programmer productivity (or both). In other place-based languages like UPC [5] and ParAlfl [10] where remote accesses are legal, such reasoning can be used to specialize accesses (local and remote). We have manually applied our analysis on several benchmarks and show that we can eliminate several pcas statically.

Our framework of eliminating pcas statically consists of the following steps:

1. Abstraction of activities: In order to reason about different object dereferences and their places of creation, it is important to be able to reason about all the possible activities and places statically. We define an abstraction for X10 places and use this to design a system for activity abstraction.

2. Extension to the classical escapes-to analysis: For guaranteeing that object dereferences do not violate pca, we need to guarantee that the object access happens at the place, where the object is created. This is done by tracking all the object creations and copying. For this purpose, we extend the traditional escape analysis to incorporate the target activity that the object can escape and present our escapes-to analysis by analyzing the heap using extensions to the connection graph [9].

3. Algorithm to detect place locality of programs with arrays: Besides objects, array accesses constitute the other source of pca insertions. In X10 a distributed array has its slots distributed across multiple places and each access of an array-slot is restricted to the place where the array slot resides. This is enforced by a compiler generated pca before the access of each array element. Reasoning about array accesses involves additional analysis about the values of the index expressions used for access. We use a constraint-based system to analyse the

values of the index expressions. Further,we extend the escapes-to analysis to reason about array accesses within X10 loops.

Our contributions are summarized below.

i. **Place Locality for Objects**: We define a notion of place-locality and present a framework to statically prove locality or non-locality of data. This allows us to identify pcas that are guaranteed to be either true or false; these identifications have special significance both to X10 and other PGAS languages.

ii. **Place Locality for Arrays**: We present a novel constraint based scheme for reasoning about place locality of X10 arrays distributed over multiple places as an extension to the algorithm described in (i). We present an optimized scheme for solving our generated constraints with regards to two popular X10 distributions *UNIQUE* and *CYCLIC*.

Rest of the paper is organized as follows. First, we present a brief overview of the relevant constructs of X10 in section 2. The activity abstraction is described in section 3 followed by the escapes-to analysis in section 4. Section 5 presents a place locality analysis and its' application to verify the need of pcas. In section 6, we describe a few case studies. This is followed by an analysis of distributed arrays and an illustrative example in section 7. Comparison of our work with related work is presented in section 8 followed by conclusions in section 9.

2   A Brief Overview of X10 Language

In this paper, we confine ourselves to simplified X10 programs that have only simple expressions (similar to the expressions in three-address-codes) and every statement has an associated label with it. Details about standard X10 can be found in the X10 reference manual [22].

Some of the constructs, we use are as follows. async (p) S creates a con-current activity to execute the statmenet S at place p. Every program can be considered as an async statement which recursively starts off all parallel computation. The place argument is optional, so async (here) S can be written more compactly as async S.

Any activity can reference only the final variables of its surrounding lexical environment. Attempt to reference other variables is a static error.

finish S is a structured barrier statement wherein S is executed with a surrounding barrier such that all activities created (recursively) inside S have to terminate before the barrier completes.

Parallel computation can be spawned with a future besides an async. The value of expr can be evaluated remotely and received using (future (p) expr). force(). A future is different from an async in terms of returning a value; force awaits for the value to become available before returning.

A *distribution* is a function from a set of points (called region) to a set of places. X10 has several pre-defined distributions, such as UNIQUE and CYCLIC. The former associates a set of points in one-to-one correspondence with the set of places; the latter wraps a set of points on a set of places in a cyclic fashion.

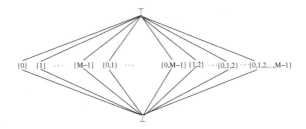

Fig. 2. Place Lattice

`ateach (point p: D) S` is a parallel, distributed loop wherein the statement S is evaluated for each point p, in the domain of a distribution D, at the place given by `D(p)`. An `ateach` can be written in terms of explicit `async` statements in a loop; however, our rules target `ateach`s explicitly for analysis. For this paper, we allow a shorthand for `ateach` statements over UNIQUE distributions by simply letting the user list the set of the distribution's places X as `ateach (X) S`.

A distributed array is described by its type and distribution `T[D]`. Construction of the array carries out a **new** operation over this specification e.g., `new T[UNIQUE]`.

3 Activity Representation

Efficient representation of parallel activities(threads) is critical to the complexity of static analysis of fine-grained parallel programs. At the same time, the precision of a static analysis would require enumeration of all instances of runtime activities during compile-time and track all of their interactions. In circumstances where parallel activities are created in loops, it is hard to estimate the upper bound of the loops during compile-time. To take into account precision and complexity of compile-time analysis, we describe an abstract activity representation that efficiently captures both single and multiple runtime activity instances. This work extends the previous work by Barik [4].

We use the following notation to define abstract-activities

L : Set of all labels in the program.

$\mathcal{P}$: Set of all abstract places in the program.

AA : Set of abstract-activities in the program.

We first present an abstract representation of the places to aid in the activity representation. In X10, places are represented by integer place identifiers that range from 0 to $\mathcal{M} - 1$, where $\mathcal{M}$ is the total number of places. We represent the place information of an abstract-activity using a place lattice shown in Fig. 2. The set of abstract places $\mathcal{P}$ is given by

$$\{\perp, \{0\}, \{1\} \cdots \{0,1\}, \cdots \{1,2\} \cdots \{0,1,2\} \cdots \{0,1 \ldots \mathcal{M} - 1\}\}$$

It consists of all the possible combinations of $\{0 \cdots \mathcal{M} - 1\}$, besides $\perp$, and $\top$. The special place $\perp$ indicates an undefined place. This captures the place information of an activity before its' creation. Singleton sets $\{0\}, \{1\} \cdots \{\mathcal{M}-1\}$ correspond to places $0, 1, \cdots \mathcal{M} - 1$ respectively. An abstract-activity might be created at multiple places. For example, if an activity is created in each iteration of a loop (iterating over a set of places S_p), then we say that there exists a single abstract-activity that represents all of the instances of the activity and this abstract-activity *must* run at an abstract place given by S_p. Non-singleton sets are used to represent the abstract places for such activities and they provide *must* information. Thus, the abstract place $\{0, 1, \cdots \mathcal{M} - 1\}$ is used to represent the place of an abstract-activity created at all the places. The element $\top$ indicates that the activity *may* be created at more than one place. Note that, unlike the *must*-information represented by the other elements of the lattice, $\top$ represents *may*-information; our place check analysis handles may-information conservatively.

An abstract-activity $at \in \mathsf{AA}$ is represented by a tuple $\langle Label, Places \rangle$, where $\mathsf{Label} \in \mathsf{L}$ and $Places \in \mathcal{P}$. The label uniquely identifies an abstract-activity. *Places* denote the abstract-place where the activity runs. Since, we use program labels to identify an activity, multiple activities (at different 'places') might be mapped to the same abstract-activity. We shall extend the notion of abstract-activities to suit our array analysis in section 7.

Consider the program shown in Fig. 1. The async statement in line L0 is represented in our abstract-activity representation by $\langle L0, \{0\} \rangle$, where 0 is the value of the place `FirstPlace`. However, the async statement in line L2 is represented by $\langle L2, \{0, 1, ..., \mathcal{M} - 1\} \rangle$. Looking at L6, it may be seen that the async statement is invoked at every place, but the activity is created only at `FirstPlace`. We represent the corresponding abstract-activity by $\langle L6, \{0\} \rangle$. [1]

Issues in Computing Abstract-Activities Set (AA) for X10

There are two components in the representation of an abstract-activity: label and place. Our simplified program representation helps us to compute unique labels for each statement and the expressions there in.

In X10, the target place for an activity can be specified as the return value of any arbitrary place expression [22]. That is, place expressions can be in terms of arrays, object dereferences and function calls. For analyzing such non-trivial place expressions we can use techniques similar to standard global value numbering mechanisms [17] or flow analysis [12]. Even though the escapes-to connection graph presented in section 4 can be extended to compute the values of the place expressions, we avoid doing that to keep the paper focused. We use a precomputed map

$$pV : \mathsf{L} \times V \to \mathcal{P},$$

where V is the set of all variables, and $pV(L, v)$ returns the abstract place value of variable v at the statement labeled L. Note that, our intermediate language

---

[1] In general, it may be useful to know if an abstract-activity represents an aggregation of actual activities, or not. And this can be made part of the activity representation. But for the scope of this paper we do not seek such detailed information.

only has simple expressions and hence, each expression will have an unique label associated with it.

We present an algorithm to compute the abstract-activity set AA in section 4 as part of the escapes-to analysis (See the rule to handle the *Async* statement).

4   Escapes to Analysis

Escape analysis in the context of Java like languages consists of determining whether an object (1) may escape a method - the object is not local to the method, and (2) may escape a thread - other threads access the object. Escape analysis results can be applied in various compiler optimizations: (1) determining if an object should be stack-allocatable, (2) determining if an object is thread-local (used for eliminating synchronization operations on an object). For an extensive study of escape analysis the reader is referred to [8,25].

In this section, we describe *escapes-to* analysis by extending the classical escape analysis that is needed for analyzing X10-like languages. The key difference lies in computing the set of threads (activities in the context of X10) to which an object escapes. To our knowledge, this is the first generalization of the escape analysis that takes into consideration the target activity to which an object escapes.

In X10, objects are created by activities at various places. Once created, the object is never migrated to another place during its entire lifetime. Objects created at a local place can be accessed by all the activities associated with that place.

Definition 1. *An object O is said to* escape-to *an activity A, if it is accessed by A but not created in A.*

We represent the escapes-to information by using a map

$$\text{nlEscTo} \in \text{Objs} \rightarrow \text{P}(\text{AA}),$$

where Objs is the set of abstract-objects (we create an unique abstract-object for each static allocation site). For each object in the program, nlEscTo returns a set consisting of abstract-activities that the object might escape to; $\text{P}(S)$ denotes the power set of S.

Prior escape analysis techniques track the 'escapement' of an object based on a lattice consisting of three values: (1) *NoEscape*: the object does not escape an activity; (2) *ArgEscape*: the object escapes a method via its argument; (3) *GlobalEscape*: the object is accessed by other activities and is globally accessible.

Escapes-to Connection Graph (ECG)

We present the escapes-to analysis by extending the connection graph of Choi et al. [8]. We define an abstract relationship between activities and objects through an *Escapes-To Connection Graph* (ECG). Apart from tracking points-to information, ECG also tracks abstract activities in which objects are created and accessed.

An ECG is a directed graph $G_e = (N, E)$, The set of nodes $N = N_O \cup N_v \cup N_a \cup \{O_\top, A_\top\}$ where N_O denotes the set of nodes corresponding to objects created in the program, N_v denotes the set of nodes corresponding to variables in the program, N_a is the set of nodes corresponding to different abstract-activities, $O_\top$ denotes a special node to summarize all the objects that we cannot reason about and $A_\top$ denotes a node corresponding to a special activity used to summarize all the activities that cannot be reasoned about.

The set of edges E comprises of four types of edges:

- *points-to edges*: E_p is the set of points-to edges resulting out of assignments of objects to variables. For $x \in N_v$ and $y \in N_O \cup \{O_\top\}$ $x \xrightarrow{\text{P}} y$ denotes a points-to edge from x to y.
- *field edges*: E_f is the set of field edges resulting from the assignment to the fields of different variables. For $x, y \in N_O \cup \{O_\top\}$, $x \xrightarrow{\text{f,g}} y$ denotes a field edge from x to y for field g in x.
- *created-by edges*: E_c: For each object O_i, created in an abstract-activity A_i, $(O_i, A_i) \in E_c$. For $x \in N_O \cup \{O_\top\}$ and $y \in N_a$, $x \xrightarrow{\text{c}} y$ denotes a created-by edge from x to y.
- *escapes-to edge*: E_e is the set of edges resulting from accessing of an object at a remote activity. For $x \in N_O \cup \{O_\top\}$ and $y \in N_a$, $x \xrightarrow{\text{e}} y$ denotes an escapes-to edge from x to y.

For simplification, we have omitted the *deferred edges* used by Choi et al. [8], which are used to invoke the *bypass* function in a lazy-manner. However, we invoke the *bypass* function eagerly.

Intraprocedural Flow-sensitive analysis

The goal of our escapes-to algorithm is to track the abstract-activities that any object is created or accesses in. We present an intra-procedural, flow sensitive, iterative data-flow analysis (standard abstract-interpretation), that maintains and updates G_e at each program point. The algorithm terminates when we reach a fix point.

Initialization. Our initial graph consists of nodes N_v, $O_\top$ and $A_\top$. Our intra-procedural analysis makes conservative assumptions about the function arguments (including *this* pointer). For each $v \in V_a$, where $V_a \subseteq N_v$ is the set of all the arguments to the current function:

- add $(v \xrightarrow{\text{P}} O_{a_i})$ to E. The special object O_{a_i} represents the object referenced by the ith argument passed to the function. Thus, we conservatively assume that each argument points to an object that is unknown, but not $O_\top$. This helps us reason about the activities created at the native place of these objects more precisely.
- add $(O_{a_i} \xrightarrow{\text{c}} A_{a_i})$ to E. For each argument i create a new activity A_{a_i} and use it to represent the activity that created the object referenced by the ith argument.
- for any field dereferenced from $O_\top$ and O_{a_i} add $(O_\top \xrightarrow{\text{f,*}} O_\top)$, and $(O_{a_i} \xrightarrow{\text{f,*}} O_\top)$ to E. The special edge $\xrightarrow{\text{f,*}}$ denotes all possible field access.

$(N, E) \overset{L:\texttt{async}(p)}{\Longrightarrow} (N \cup \{\langle L, pV(L, p)\rangle\}, E)$

$(N, E) \overset{L:a=\texttt{new } T}{\Longrightarrow} (N \cup \{O_L\}, E - \{(a \overset{P}{\to} y)|y \in N \wedge (a, y) \in E\} \cup \{(a \overset{P}{\to} O_L), (O_L \overset{c}{\to} A_c)\})$

$(N, E) \overset{L:a=b}{\Longrightarrow} (N, E - \{(a \overset{P}{\to} y)|y \in N \wedge (a, y) \in E\} \cup \{(a \overset{P}{\to} z)|z \in N \wedge (b \overset{P}{\to} z) \in E\})$

$(N, E) \overset{L:a=b.g}{\Longrightarrow} (N, E - \{(a \overset{P}{\to} y)|y \in N \wedge (a, y) \in E\}$
$$\cup \{(a \overset{P}{\to} z), (x \overset{e}{\to} A_c)|x, z \in N \wedge (b \overset{P}{\to} x) \in E \wedge (x \overset{\mathrm{f.g}}{\to} z) \in E \wedge (x \overset{c}{\to} A_c) \notin E\})$$

$(N, E) \overset{L:a.g=b}{\Longrightarrow} (N, E - \{(x \overset{\mathrm{f.g}}{\to} y)|x, y \in N \wedge (a \overset{P}{\to} x) \in E \wedge (x \overset{\mathrm{f.g}}{\to} y) \in E\}$
$$\cup \{(x \overset{\mathrm{f.g}}{\to} z), (x \overset{e}{\to} A_c)|x, z \in N \wedge (a \overset{P}{\to} x) \in E \wedge (b \overset{P}{\to} z) \in E \wedge (x \overset{c}{\to} A_c) \notin E\})$$
(Strong Update).

$(N, E) \overset{L:a.g=b}{\Longrightarrow} (N, E \cup \{(x \overset{\mathrm{f.g}}{\to} z), (x \overset{e}{\to} A_c)|x, z \in N \wedge (a \overset{P}{\to} x) \in E \wedge (b \overset{P}{\to} z) \in E \wedge (x \overset{c}{\to} A_c) \notin E\})$
(Weak Update).

$(N, E) \overset{L:a=f(b)}{\Longrightarrow} (N, E \cup \{(a \overset{P}{\to} O_T)\} \cup \{(x \overset{e}{\to} A_T)|(b \overset{P}{\to} z) \in E \wedge (z \overset{\mathrm{f,*}}{\to} x) \in E\})$

Fig. 3. Rules for different instructions

We distinguish objects O_{a_i} and O_T, and activities A_{a_i} and A_T, as we want to distinguish a field referenced from an argument to a field referenced from some unknown object.

Statements and Operations. Fig. 3 presents the effects of the relevant X10 instructions on our analysis. The transformations to the ECG with respect to the labeled construct L:S is denoted by

$$(N, E) \overset{L:S}{\Longrightarrow} (N', E')$$

where (N', E') denotes the updated graph as a result of the execution of statement S labelled L. The updates can include the addition of new nodes, addition of new edges, or updates to existing edges. ⬦

In X10, the statements that are of interest to us are: (a) async (p) S; (b) a = new T; (c) a=b; (d) a.f=b; (e) a=b.f; (f) a = f(b). We now discuss the effect of processing each of these statements.

Async: An async statement creates an abstract-activity node in the ECG. $pV(L, v)$ returns the place value of the variable p at the statement L (see section 3). The X10 construct ateach can be represented using a basic async statement inside a loop. The X10 construct future which also creates an activity is handled similar to async.

$a = \text{new } T()$: We create an object node O_L in the ECG. Since statements are executed within the scope of an activity, we add a created-by edge from O_L to current abstract-activity, given by A_c (O_L is 'local' to A_c). Each statement is in the syntactic scope of exactly one activity. If the current statement is in the syntactic scope of an async labeled L_1, then the current abstract-activity is of the form $\langle L_1, *\rangle$. Note that, for all those cases where we cannot reason about the current abstract-activity, A_c is set to $\bot$. We eliminate any existing points-to edges of the form $(a \overset{P}{\to} y) \in E$, for any $y \in N$. We introduce a new points-to edge $a \overset{P}{\to} O_L$.

$a = b$: We delete all the existing points-to edges starting at a, and for each points-to edge that b points to, we add a points-to edge from a.

$a = b.g$: We process this statement exactly like the copy statement $(a = b)$, above. For every dereference of an object, we add a new 'escape-to' edge from the object to the current abstract-activity, if the object is not created in the current activity.

$a.g = b$: Assignments to the fields is a bit more involved because we have to take into consideration possible *weak* and *strong* updates. If there can be multiple points-to edges from the node a, or if a has a single points-to edge to a node x but multiple activities could be updating the field g of x in parallel (See may happen analysis [1]) then $\forall y \in N : (a \xrightarrow{\text{P}} y) \in E$, we add a new edge $(y \xrightarrow{\text{f,g}} b)$ to the edge set E (weak update). Otherwise, we process the statement like the copy statement above - eliminate existing points-to edges and add new edge (strong update).

$a = f(b)$: Since we are doing intra procedural analysis, we can only make conservative assumptions about the arguments (that includes the receiver) and the return values of a function call. We add an escapes-to edge from objects pointed to by the arguments of the function to $A_\top$ and a points-to edge from a to $O_\top$.

Merge Operation. The meet/merge operation of the escapes-to analysis is the union of the two ECGs emanating from two different control flow paths: $\text{Merge}((N_1, E_1), (N_2, E_2)) = ((N_1 \cup N_2), (E_1 \cup E_2))$.

While processing all the above assignment statements and the merge operation, we ensure the following invariant: if a variable or a field of an object x has a points-to edge $(x \xrightarrow{\text{P}} O_\top)$ or $\exists i\ (x \xrightarrow{\text{P}} O_{a_i})$, then $\nexists y \in N - \{O_\top, \forall i\ O_{a_i}\}$ such that $(x \xrightarrow{\text{P}} y) \in E$. We ensure this property by checking for the special object $O_\top$ and O_{a_i} while editing the edges of the graph (not shown in the Fig. 3).

Termination. Our iterative data flow analysis follows the standard method of execution and stops only after reaching a fixed point. It can be seen that for any node the maximum number of edges (points-to or escapes-to) is bound by the number of nodes. And in every iteration at least one new edge is added to the set of edges, compared to any previous iteration. Hence, after a finite number of iterations we cannot add any more edges and the algorithm will terminate.

Compute nlEscTo map. Given an ECG at program point l, for each object O_i we populate nlEscTo (non local escape-to) and PtsTo (points-to) maps:

$$\text{nlEscTo}(l, O_i) = \{(\langle L, p \rangle | \langle L, p \rangle \in N_a \wedge (O_i \xrightarrow{\text{e}} \langle L, p \rangle) \in E \wedge \neg \exists L' \text{ such that } (O_i \xrightarrow{\text{c}} \langle L', p \rangle)\}$$
$$\text{PtsTo}(l, v_i) = \{(x | x \in N_o \wedge (v_i \xrightarrow{\text{P}} x) \in E\}$$

Analysis of the running example. Fig. 4 shows the ECG for the example shown in Fig. 1 after processing the last statement.

5 Place Locality

Traditionally, the notion of thread locality is used to denote the access of objects created in the same thread. In this section, we show that in languages like

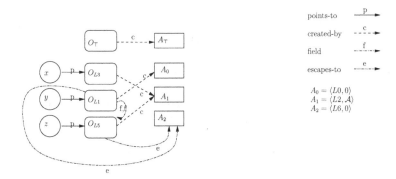

Fig. 4. ECG generated by our algorithm for the example shown in Fig. 1 (as seen after processing the last statement)

```
finish async (p) {                                    // th0
    S0: final global1 = new G();
    async      (p) {S1: global1.x = new Baz();} // th1
    async      (p) {S2: global1.x = new Baz();} // th2
    async      (p.next()) { ... }                // th3

    async      (p) {global1.x.f ++;}             // th4
}
```

Fig. 5. Place local $\Rightarrow$ Does not require PC assertion

X10, where each activity is associated with a place, activity locality provides insufficient information when we reason about locality of objects with respect to places. Later in the section, we extend the notion of locality to places.

Fig. 5 illustrates the distinctions between the notion of place locality and activity locality.

Traditional thread-local analysis would deduce that the object created in statement S0 is not activity (thread) local. Using this information to decide on the locality of the object being dereferenced would result in insertion of pcas before every dereference of global1 in th1, th2, and th4. Similar argument would follow for the dereference of global1.x in activity th4. However, say it is verified that in async th3, global1 is not accessed (that is, the object accessible by global1 does not escape place p and remains confined to the activities at place-p). Thus, we can conclude that we do not need a pca before statement S1. This is because although global1 is accessed in multiple activities, all of the activities execute at the place of creation (p). An important point to note is that none of these activities *escape* the object under consideration outside place p. That is, global1 holds a place local reference (local to place p) and hence, dereferencing of global1 does not require a preceding pca in th1, th2 and th4 (which execute at place p). Similarly, global.x can hold multiple references but all are local to place p. Hence, we do not require a `pca` in `th4` for accessing `global1.x.f`. In the following section, we propose an analysis that takes the abstraction of places into consideration while reasoning about the locality of an object.

Given an object O_a, we would like to know if dereference of O_a is done at the place of its allocation or not. Note that, multiple activities can run at the same place and hence, even if an object escapes to another activity running at the same place, we still will be accessing the object locally; thus no place check is required to dereference it. In essence, first we would like to know if object O_a escapes an activity and if so, to which activity. We get this information from the *escapes-to* analysis described in section 4. Further, for each of the dereferencing sites of object O_a, if we can deduce that the dereference happens at the same place as the place of allocation of O_a (say p) then we do not need a preceding `pca`. For each other activity that O_a can escape to, if we can guarantee that the activity executes only at place p, then we would not need a `pca` for any of the dereferences of O_a.

Traditional thread-local algorithms declare an object to be thread-non-local, if it gets assigned to a global (read static in Java/X10 context) variable or to a field of an object accessible via any global variable. In comparison, a place-local object can be assigned to a global g and/or be reachable via fields of objects accessible via a global g'. The constraint is that globals g and g' must only be accessible from activities running at only one place. That is, an object may escape to another activity running at the same place and still be place-local, as long as it does not escape to an activity running at a different place. Traditional notions of thread-locality caters to 'activity-locality' in X10.

In this section we present (i) the concept of place locality, (ii) an algorithm to deduce place local information, and (iii) a scheme to apply the place local information to eliminate useless `pcas`, and notify guaranteed `pca` failures.

Definition 1. An object is *native* to a place p, if it is created at place p.

Definition 2. An object is considered *local to place p*, if it is native to place p and is accessed only at place p.

Definition 3. Dereference of an object o at place p is considered *safe*, if o is local to p.

Remark. *Safe dereferences of an object p do not need a preceding* `pca`. Later, we present an algorithm to eliminate `pcas` for safe dereferences of objects.

Algorithm

Fig. 6 presents an algorithm to identify variables that point to only place-local objects. This algorithm is run after the escape-to analysis is run (i.e., `nlEscTo` map is populated. See section 4).

The algorithm presented in Fig. 6 populates the following map.

$$\wp : (L \times V) \rightarrow \langle \texttt{local}, \texttt{nonLocal}, \texttt{unknown} \rangle$$

```
 1  foreach lᵢ ∈ L, and vᵢ ∈ V do
 2  │ ℘[(lᵢ, vᵢ) ← unknown];

 3  foreach lᵢ ∈ L, and vᵢ ∈ V do
 4  │   Say lᵢ is part of the activity ⟨Lⱼ, pⱼ⟩;
 5  │   if pⱼ == ⊥ OR pⱼ == ⊤ then
 6  │   │ continue;

 7  │   boolean place-local = true ;
 8  │   boolean place-non-local = true;
 9  │   foreach oₖ ∈ PtsTo(lᵢ, vᵢ) do
10  │   │   if ⟨Lⱼ, pⱼ⟩ ∈ nlEscTo(lᵢ, oₖ) then
11  │   │   │ place-local=false;

12  │   │   if ⟨Lⱼ, pⱼ⟩ ∉ nlEscTo(lᵢ, oₖ) then
13  │   │   │ place-non-local=false;

14  │   if place-local then
15  │   │ ℘[(lᵢ, vᵢ) ← local];
16  │   if place-non-local then
17  │   │ ℘[(lᵢ, vᵢ) ← place-non-local];
```

Fig. 6. Algorithm to identify place local references

```
 1  foreach dereference of of x ∈ V at program point lᵢ in activity ⟨Lᵢ, pᵢ⟩ ∈ AA do
 2  │   if ℘(lᵢ, x) == local then
 3  │   │ eliminate pca before lᵢ.

 4  │   else if ℘(lᵢ, x) == nonLocal then
 5  │   │ report that pca before lᵢ will always fail.
```

Fig. 7. Algorithm to eliminate useless pcas and identify guaranteed pca failures

At a program point l, map $℘(l, v)$ returns `local` if all the objects pointed-to by variable v are place local, `nonLocal` if all the objects pointed-to by v are non-local, and `unknown` otherwise. The algorithm first initializes the $℘$ map conservatively to indicate that at all program points the locality of the set of objects pointed-to by all the variables is unknown (Line numbers 1-2). Lines 4-13 identify accesses of variables whose target objects are either guaranteed to be local or non-local. We update the $℘$ map at Lines 15 and 17.

In Fig. 7, we present a simple algorithm to apply place locality information to eliminate useless place-local-checks and report guaranteed place check failures. For each dereference (field access or method call) in activity a_i, the algorithm eliminates the preceding pca, if all the objects pointed-to by the variable are place local. Similarly, it reports cases where pca will always fail. This can be used to alert a user of the access error (in X10 context), or to specialize the memory access to remote access (in UPC context).

Analysis of the Running Example

Fig. 8 shows a run of the algorithms presented in this section.

It can be seen that out of the four pcas, our algorithm eliminates three of them. The remaining one assertion (before $L8$) must be present and cannot be eliminated.

Improvements to the Algorithm

It can be noted that the above presented algorithm does not take into account the possible control flow between two statements. For example, Fig. 9 presents a case where an object is created at place p1, and dereferenced at the same place. After that, the object escapes to an activity executing at place p2. Any dereferencing of the object at place p2 requires a preceding pca. However, our algorithm would declare object to be non-place-local and would eliminate neither of the pcas preceding S1 and S2. An analysis aware of may-happen-parallelism [19] can recognize such idioms and result in more precise results.

6   Examples

Here, we describe four examples that showcases the strengths and drawbacks of our algorithm.

Consider first the example shown in Fig. 5 of section 5. Our analysis identifies that reference O_{S0} is place local, and hence, its dereference at th1, th2 and th4 does not require a preceding pca.

Fig. 10(a) shows a snippet of a program for updating a dynamic linked list, as part of master-slave work paradigm. The master goes over the list and invokes the slave server if a boolean flag *done* is not set. The master also adds nodes regularly to the end of the list. The slave, when invoked, sets the flag *done* randomly. Our algorithm attaches a unique abstract object to each of the arguments and thus, is able to eliminate all the pcas.

Fig. 10(b) shows a snippet of a program of a postorder traversal of a tree. In this example, Tree is a *value* class. In X10, value classes have the property that after initialization the fields of the objects cannot be modified. After recognizing that a Tree object does not change, similar to the linked list example, we can

---

Objs=$\{O_{L1}, O_{L3}, O_{L5}\}$	nlEscTo=$\{((L8, O_{L5}), \langle L6, \{0\}\rangle))\}$

Compute Place Local Information
Iter 1: $\wp[(L4, \text{x}) \leftarrow \text{place-local}]$ Iter 2: $\wp[(L7, \text{y}) \leftarrow \text{place-local}]$
Iter 3: $\wp[(L8, \text{y.f}) \leftarrow \text{unknown}]$

Eliminate Place Local Assertion
Eliminate the pca before $L4$ Eliminate the pca before $L7$

Fig. 8. Eliminate pcas in the running example, shown in Fig. 1

```
finish {
    finish async (p1) {global1.x = new G();
                    S1:    ... = global1.x.y}// th0

    async (p2) { S2: ... = global1.x.y } // th1
}
```

Fig. 9. Limitations of of our Analysis: A smarter algorithm can eliminate the `pca` before S1

```
void master() {
    // Assert (head != null)
    i = 0;
    while (true) {
        nullable Node tmp = head;
        while (tmp != null) {
            // goto the end of the worklist.
            final node = tmp;
            tmp = getNext(node);
            boolean status=getStatus(node);
            if (status) slave(node); }
        final tail = tmp;
        i = (i + 1)%NumPlaces;
        addNewNode(tail,i); } }
void slave(Node n){
    if (random()%2 == 1)
        async (n) {n.done = true;} }
void getNext(Node n){
future (n) {n.next}.force();}
void getStatus(Node n){
future (n) {!n.done}.force();
void addNewNode(Node n, int i) {
finish async (i) {
        finish async (n) {
            n.next = future (i)
        {new Node()}.force();
        } } }
                (a)
```

```
value class Tree {
    int value;
    Tree left, right;

    public void postOrder() {
        if (left != null) {
        future (left)
            {left.postOrder() }.force();}
        if (right != null) {
        future (right)
            {right.postOrder()}.force();}
        print(value); } }

                (b)
```
```
async (p0) {
    final z = new Z();
    z.g = new G();
    async (p1) {
        final z1 = future (p0) z.g;
        ... = z1.h // escapes
    }
    async (p0) {
        ... = z.g.h.k; } }
                (c)
```

Fig. 10. Three example programs (a)Master slave update program. (b) PostOrder traversal : traverse a distributed binary tree (c) Dummy copies lead to non-elimination of `pca`.

infer that all the `pca`s in the function `postOrder` are redundant and can be eliminated.

Fig. 10(c) shows an example where an object created at place p0, is assigned to a final variable z. A field g of z is initialized in place p0. Now, two activities are created which can run in parallel. In one activity, running at place p1, the object referenced by `z.g` escapes to place p1. In the other activity, running at place p0, a field of the object referenced by `z.g` is dereferenced. Our algorithm identifies that the object referenced by z.g is created at place p0 and escapes to place p1. Hence, we declare it as place-non-local, and add pca before the dereference of z.g.h. However, the key point to note is that even though the object escapes to another place (p1), none of the fields are updated there. Hence, we do not require a pca for dereferencing the sub-fields, at p0. Our algorithm needs to be extended to recognize such idioms.

We have also applied our analysis on the LU NAS parallel benchmark. Our analysis could not remove most of the pcas as the program consisted of a large number of tiny helper functions that were invoked at many places. We attributed this to our conservative handling of function calls. Hence, we applied our analysis on another version of the source file after inlining these functions. As guessed, we could eliminate all the pcas in this version.

7   PCA Handling for Distributed Arrays

Arrays in X10 can be distributed over multiple places according to some prede-fined distributions provided as part of the language. X10 guarantees that any array slot located at place p can only be accessed by the activity running at p. Similar to object dereferences, the current X10 compiler inserts a pca before each array element access to maintain the above guarantee. In this section, we present a scheme to eliminate the useless pcas and report pcas that are guaranteed to fail for array accesses.

A distribution can be represented as a map $\mathcal{D} : X \to \mathcal{P}$, where X is the set of points (integers for one dimensional regions) over which the distribution is defined. For each point i, $\mathcal{D}(i)$ returns the place of the point i. Similarly, we define the inverse distribution function $\mathcal{D}^{-1} : \mathcal{P} \to \mathrm{P}(X)$ that maps each place to the corresponding set of points. For example, in a scenario with k places $p_0, \ldots p_{k-1}$, the cyclic distribution over n points can be defined as follows: $\forall i \in \{0..n-1\}$, $\mathcal{D}(i) = i \bmod k$. Similarly the inverse distribution function for cyclic distribution can be defined as $\forall i \in \{0..k-1\} \mathcal{D}^{-1}(p_i) = \{x | x = k \times j + i,\ x \in N,\ 0 \le j \le \frac{(n-1)}{k}\}$.

Fig. 11 presents some additions to the escapes-to analysis presented in sec-tion 4, to make it suitable for reasoning about array accesses. These rules are given to process only arrays and non-nested loops; these are to be used on top of the rules for non-array operations given in 3.

ateach(point x : A) *Stmt*: To model ateach loop bodies iterating over a distribution, we use a new type of abstract-activity of the form: $\langle Label, \mathcal{D} \rangle$, where *Label* is the label of the ateach statement and $\mathcal{D}$ is the distribution with respect to the ateach statement. We use a special abstract-activity $A'_{\top}$ to denote those activities where a specific distribution cannot be statically determined.

a = new [A] T: An array object distributed over A is considered to be created by an activity $\langle L, A \rangle$. We use ArrObjs to denote the set of all array objects, and map $\mathcal{D}_x$ returns the underlying distribution of the array object $x \in$ ArrObjs. Similarly, map $\mathcal{D}_x^{-1}$ returns the underlying inverse distribution map.

$$(N, E) \overset{L:\text{ateach}(\text{point } x : A) \ Stmt}{\Longrightarrow} (N \cup \{A_c\}, E)$$

$$(N, E) \overset{L:a=\text{new } [A]T}{\Longrightarrow} (N \cup \{O_L, A_c\}, E \cup \{(a \overset{\text{P}}{\to} O_L), (O_L \overset{\text{c}}{\to} A_c)\})$$

$$(N, E) \overset{L:a=b}{\Longrightarrow} (N, E - \{(a \overset{\text{P}}{\to} y) | y \in N \wedge (a, y) \in E\}$$
$$\cup \{(a \overset{\text{P}}{\to} z) | z \in N, \wedge(b \overset{\text{P}}{\to} z) \in E\})$$

$$(N, E) \overset{L:\text{ateach}(\text{point } x : A) \ \{..B[e]..\}}{\Longrightarrow} (N, E \cup \{(x \overset{\text{e}}{\to} A_c) | C1 \wedge (B \overset{\text{P}}{\to} x) \in E\})$$
$$\text{and } C1 = \forall(x, p_i) \in A, \forall(B \overset{\text{P}}{\to} z) \in E, \ [e/x] \in \mathcal{D}_z^{-1}(p_i)$$

$$(N, E) \overset{L:\text{ateach}(\text{point } x : A) \ \{..B[e]..\}}{\Longrightarrow} (N, E \cup \{(x \overset{\text{e}}{\to} A_f) | C2 \wedge (B \overset{\text{P}}{\to} x) \in E\})$$
$$\text{and } C2 = \forall(x, p_i) \in A, \forall(B \overset{\text{P}}{\to} z) \in E, \ [e/x] \notin \mathcal{D}_z^{-1}(p_i)$$

$$(N, E) \overset{L:a=f(b)}{\Longrightarrow} N, E \cup \{(a \overset{\text{P}}{\to} O_\top)\}$$

Fig. 11. Generate ECG for reasoning about pcas before array accesses. $A_c = \langle L, A \rangle$.

L: ateach(point x : A) {...B[e]...}: An array access in the body of an ateach loop introduces an escape-to edge from object pointed to by B to the activity corresponding to the loop provided the distribution of the array does not match the access pattern in the loop body (given by C1). The index expression e may be data/control dependent on the value of x. Constraint C1 ensures that for each point x located at place p_i in the distribution A, the array slot number e is located at place p_i. To reason about pcas that are guaranteed to fail, we use another special activity A_f, where all the pcas are guaranteed to fail. For such a scenario (given by C2), we add an escapes-to edge from the objects pointed to by B to A_f.

a = b: Assigning an array to another results in the removal of all the existing edges from a and points-to edges are created from a to all the nodes that b points-to. Note that, the rules specified for statements of the form a = b.f do not require any special treatment in the context of arrays.

a = f(b): It may be noted that any array object that is passed as argument doesn't get its' distribution modified. Thus, we need to add only a points-to edge from a to $O_\top$.

We generate constraints C1 and C2 for each array access in the given program and invoke a constraint solver (for example, [11]) to derive the ECGs at different program points and then invoke the algorithm shown in Fig. 12. Unlike scalar variables which may point to different objects at different program points, the array distribution is an immutable state of the array and thus, it simplifies our algorithm to remove pcas (compared to the algorithm presented in section 5).

We now present a optimized scheme for generating and evaluating constraints C1 and C2. The generation of constraints is illustrated through a subset of a priori defined array distributions in X10 : UNIQUE and CYCLIC. Note that the above distributions cover some of the most common idioms of X10 programs including the set of X10 benchmarks presented at the HPC Challenge in the fall of 2007 (and won the class II challenge). The presented techniques can be extended to other distributions as well. We first show that for the above distributions, the number of elements in the range of x is bounded by the number of places.

```
1  foreach access of the array variable v at program point lᵢ in activity aᵢ ∈ AA do
2  |   boolean local-access = true;
3  |   foreach oᵢ ∈ PtsTo(lᵢ, vᵢ) do
4  |   |   Say {cp} = nlEscTo(lᵢ, oᵢ) ; Say aᵢ = ⟨L, D⟩ ;
5  |   |   if 𝒟_cp ≠ D then
6  |   |   |   local-access=false;
7  |   boolean non-local-access = true;
8  |   foreach oᵢ ∈ PtsTo(lᵢ, vᵢ) do
9  |   |   if A_f ∉ nlEscTo(lᵢ, oᵢ) then
10 |   |   |   non-local-access = false;
11 |   if local-access then
12 |   |   eliminate pca.
13 |   else if non-local-access then
14 |   |   report guaranteed pca failure.
```

Fig. 12. Algorithm to eliminate useless pcas and identify guaranteed pca failures for array accesses

Lemma 1. $\forall (x, p_i)! \in \mathcal{D}_A \ [e/x] \in \mathcal{D}_B^{-1}(p_i)$ iff $\forall p_i \in \texttt{places}(A) \ \exists x \in \texttt{points}(p_i)$, $[e/x] \in \mathcal{D}_B^{-1}(p_i)$, where $\texttt{points}(p_i)$ returns the set of points mapped onto p_i.

Proof. Proof omitted for space.

The above lemma makes the constraint solving efficient by reducing the search space. We take advantage of the lemma and the nature of the distributions to present a simplification to constraints C1 and C2, for these distributions.

Let I denote the set of simplified (syntactic) index expressions (of the form $a \times i + b$) in the loop body (linear expressions over i), where i is a loop induction variable. Constraints C1 and C2 for the above two distributions can be reformulated as follows ('mod' is the modulo function) (say $\mathcal{M}$ = number of places in the ateach loop):

	UNIQUE	CYCLIC
C1	$\forall i \in \{0..\mathcal{M}-1\} \bigwedge_{e \in I}(|e - i| == 0)$	$\forall i \in \{0..\mathcal{M}-1\} \bigwedge_{e \in I}(\mathrm{mod}(|e - i|, \mathcal{M}) == 0)$
C2	$\forall i \in \{0..\mathcal{M}-1\}. \bigwedge_{e \in I}(|e - i| \neq 0)$	$\forall i \in \{0..\mathcal{M}-1\} \bigwedge_{e \in I}(\mathrm{mod}(|e - i|\mathcal{M}) \neq 0)$

Constraint C1 (constraint C2) for UNIQUE states that for each index expression, the absolute value of its difference from i must (must not) be zero. Constraint C1 (C2) for CYCLIC states that for each index expression, the absolute value of its' difference from i should (should not) be a multiple of $\mathcal{M}$.

Illustrative Example: Consider the scenario wherein one set of workers is directed to compute a function f on a test-space using the ateach loop on one half the set of machines and the second set of workers use the other half to compute the inverse of the result and check whether the function and its inverse compose to the identity function. The program snippet only shows the code to create the distributed array of jobs, and code to access the elements of the array in the two `ateach` loops.

```
final int N = NumPlaces/2 - 1;      int master() {
        // Assume NumPlaces > 1       finish ateach(i : unique([0..N]))
//Places 0..N reflect half the m/c      { job j = jobs[i]; ...f... }
final job[UNIQUE] jobs =            finish ateach(i : unique([N+1..2*N+1]))
    new (i:UNIQUE(AllPlaces))           { job j = jobs[id-N];
        {return new job(initNum(i));}      ...inv_f... } }
```

Our analysis would find that in the first `ateach` loop constraint C1 is satisfied, and the second loop satisfies C2. Thus, our analysis will eliminate the `pcas` before the array access in the first loop, and warn about the illegal array access in the second loop.

We have manually applied our analysis on two other NAS parallel benchmarks: RandomAccess, and CG. After inlining different utility functions, we could eliminate all the `pcas` in both the benchmarks.

8 Related Work

In this section, we place our work in the context of the existing literature.

Abstraction of runtime components: Abstraction of runtime components like objects have long been used to help in static analysis [18]. We have extended the thread abstraction techniques of Barik [4] to reason about the activities of X10 and also presented an abstraction of places, that is critical to our framework.

Locality of Context: The work that relates most closely to our addressed problem is that of Chandra et al. [7], who improve upon the works of Zhu and Hendren [26]. They present a dependent type system that can be used by the programmer to specify place locality information. They further present an inter-procedural type inference algorithm to infer the place locality information and use it to eliminate useless `pcas`. We have presented an intra-procedural data flow analysis based approach to infer place locality information, without depending on the programmer input. Their unification based approach would lead to conservative results compared to the results we obtain from the escapes-to-graph: our precise representation of places and activities lead to precise reasoning of activities and objects within loops. The following example clarifies the same.

```
ateach (p: A) { final X x = new X(); async (p) {... =x.f;}}
```

While our algorithm can detect that the dereference of x is place local, their unification based algorithm cannot detect so. Further, we have partially integrated may-happen-parallel analysis into our scheme to generate more precise results. Besides elimination of useless pcas our analysis reports guaranteed failures. It would be interesting to combine our algorithm with the techniques of Chandra et al. use for inter-procedural analysis.

Barton et al. [5] present memory affinity analysis, whereby local data accesses are statically identified and that is used to avoid overhead of routing the access through a machine-wide shared variable directory. Our language setting is more general as unlike in UPC multiple activities can share the same place. We have presented a scheme that tracks the heap statically to prove local, non-local properties.

Work involving inference of place information for programs without user specified places is extensive. For example, false-sharing identification tries to partition data so that a place does not have to deal with data not used by it and hence, does not pay for it through bus traffic and cache-coherency costs [13,15,23]. These approaches all differ from us since in our framework activities are explicitly programmed with places, which requires its own set of extensive static representations, analysis and optimizations.

There has been significant interest in proving the thread locality of data [14,24,25,9]. All of these approaches limit themselves to identifying if the object can be accessed in any thread besides the thread of creation. In this paper, we have extended the context of thread locality further to the 'place' of creation. An object whose reference is stored in a global variable and is accessed in another thread might still be 'place-local', provided that all the activities in which the object might be accessed are created at the same place.

Points-to and Escape Analysis: There has been a wide spread interest and good amount of research in the area of points-to and escape analysis [2,8,25,21]. They propose different applications to points-to analysis and different solutions there of. However, we are not aware of any work that tracks not only if an object escapes a context, but also the target context.

Our Escapes-to Connection Graph (ECG) is inspired from the connection graphs of Choi et al. [8]. Apart from tracking the points-to information, ECG also tracks abstract activities in which objects are created and accessed.

Exceptions and Performance: Safe programming languages like Java introduce a lot of runtime assertions, which may throw a runtime exception, in case the assertion fails. Some well known runtime exceptions are Null-pointer-exception, array-out-of-bounds exception and so on. Due to the nature of these assertions un-optimized code is littered with these exceptions. Researchers have shown that a majority of these can be eliminated statically [6,16]. Systems like CCured [20] have a notion of a dynamic (runtime verified) pointers which are expensive to use. They present a scheme to verify and thus, translate the dynamic pointers to static (statically, type safe) pointers. In our work, we have shown the elimination of pcas introduced in X10 (an explicitly parallel language) arising due to places.

9   Conclusion and Future Work

In this paper, we have presented a static analysis framework for conservatively computing the notion of place locality and have demonstrated the application of the framework for objects and arrays in the context of X10. Our representation of the abstract activities and places is general enough to allow us to extend our intra-procedural analysis to inter-procedural analysis.

Our framework supports reasoning about locality of activities, which can be useful for optimizing the invocation of the activities. We are working towards refining the analysis via may-happen-parallelism analysis and generalizations of the notion to other features of X10 and experimental validation of the concepts.

Acknowledgment. The results reported are based upon the work supported by the Defense Advanced Research Projects Agency under its agreement no. HR0011-07-9-0002. We thank Vivek Sarkar, Vijay Saraswat and the X10 team for valuable discussions. Thanks go to Raghavan Komondoor and Mangala Gowri for comments on an earlier draft.

References

1. Agarwal, S., Barik, R., Sarkar, V., Shyamasundar, R.K.: May-happen-in-parallel analysis of X10 programs. In: Proceedings of the 12th ACM SIGPLAN symposium on PPoPP, pp. 183–193 (2007)
2. Andersen, L.: Program Analysis and Specialization for the C Programming Language. PhD thesis, DIKU, University of Copenhagen (1994)
3. Bailey, D.H., Barszcz, E., Barton, J.T., Browning, D.S., Carter, R.L., Dagum, D., Fatoohi, R.A., Frederickson, P.O., Lasinski, T.A., Schreiber, R.S., Simon, H.D., Venkatakrishnan, V., Weeratunga, S.K.: The NAS Parallel Benchmarks. The International Journal of Supercomputer Applications 5(3), 63–73 (Fall 1991)
4. Barik, R.: Efficient computation of may-happen-in-parallel information for concurrent java programs. In: Ayguadé, E., Baumgartner, G., Ramanujam, J., Sadayappan, P. (eds.) LCPC 2005. LNCS, vol. 4339. Springer, Heidelberg (2006)
5. Barton, C., Cascaval, C., Almasi, G., Zheng, Y., Farreras, M., Chatterjee, S., Amaral, J.N.: Shared memory programming for large scale machines. In: Proceedings of the Conference on PLDI, pp. 108–117 (2006)
6. Bodík, R., Gupta, R., Sarkar, V.: ABCD: eliminating array bounds checks on demand. In: Proceedings of the ACM SIGPLAN 2000 conference on PLDI, pp. 321–333 (2000)
7. Chandra, S., Saraswat, V.A., Sarkar, V., Bodík, R.: Type inference for locality analysis of distributed data structures. In: Proceedings of the 13th ACM SIGPLAN symposium on PPoPP, pp. 11–22. ACM, New York (2008)
8. Choi, J.-D., Gupta, M., Serrano, M., Sreedhar, V.C., Midkiff, S.: Escape analysis for java. In: Proceedings of the ACM SIGPLAN conference on OOPSLA, pp. 1–19 (1999)
9. Choi, J.-D., Gupta, M., Serrano, M.J., Sreedhar, V.C., Midkiff, S.P.: Stack allocation and synchronization optimizations for java using escape analysis. ACM Transactions on Programming Languages and Systems 25(6), 876–910 (2003)

10. Hudak, P., Smith, L.: Para-functional programming: A paradigm for programming multiprocessor systems. In: Proc. of the ACM SIGPLAN Symposium on PoPP, pp. 243–254. ACM Press, New York (1986)

11. Huynh, T., Joskowicz, L., Lassez, C., Lassez, J.-L.: Reasoning about linear constraints using parametric queries. In: Veni Madhavan, C.E., Nori, K.V. (eds.) FSTTCS 1990. LNCS, vol. 472, pp. 1–20. Springer, Heidelberg (1990)

12. Jagannathan, S., Thiemann, P., Weeks, S., Wright, A.K.: Single and loving it: Must-alias analysis for higher-order languages. In: Proceedings of the 25th ACM SIGPLAN Symposium on POPL (January 1998)

13. Jeremiassen, T.E., Eggers, S.J.: Reducing false sharing on shared memory multiprocessors through compile time data transformations. In: Proceedings of the Symposium on PPoPP, pp. 179–188 (1995)

14. Jones, R., King, A.: A fast analysis for thread-local garbage collection with dynamic class loading. In: Fifth IEEE International Workshop on Source Code Analysis and Manipulation, September 2005, pp. 129–138 (2005)

15. Kandemir, M., Choudhary, A., Ramanujam, J., Banerjee, P.: On reducing false sharing while improving locality on shared memory multiprocessors. In: Malyshkin, V.E. (ed.) PaCT 1999. LNCS, vol. 1662, pp. 203–211. Springer, Heidelberg (1999)

16. Kawahito, M., Komatsu, H., Nakatani, T.: Effective null pointer check elimination utilizing hardware trap. SIGPLAN Notices 35(11), 139–149 (2000)

17. Muchnick, S.S.: Advanced Compiler Design and Implementation. Morgan Kaufmann, San Francisco (1997)

18. Nandivada, V.K., Detlefs, D.: Compile-time concurrent marking write barrier removal. In: Proceedings of the international symposium on CGO, pp. 37–48 (2005)

19. Naumovich, G., Avrunin, G.S.: A conservative data flow algorithm for detecting all pairs of statements that may happen in parallel. In: Proceedings of the ACM SIGSOFT International symposium on FSE, pp. 24–34 (1998)

20. Necula, G.C., McPeak, S., Weimer, W.: Ccured: type-safe retrofitting of legacy code. In: Proceedings of the 29th ACM SIGPLAN symposium on POPL, pp. 128–139. ACM, New York (2002)

21. Sagiv, M., Reps, T., Wilhelm, R.: Parametric shape analysis via 3-valued logic. ACM Transactions on Programming Languages and Systems 24(3), 217–298 (2002)

22. Saraswat, V.: Report on the experimental language X10, x10.sourceforge.net/docs/x10-101.pdf (2006)

23. Shuf, Y., Gupta, M., Franke, H., Appel, A., Singh, J.P.: Creating and preserving locality of java applications at allocation and garbage collection times. In: Proceedings of the conference on OOPSLA, pp. 13–25 (2002)

24. Steensgaard, B.: Thread-specific heaps for multi-threaded programs. In: Proceedings of the 2nd international symposium on Memory management, pp. 18–24 (2000)

25. Whaley, J., Rinard, M.: Compositional pointer and escape analysis for Java programs. In: Proceedings of the 14th ACM SIGPLAN conference OOPSLA, pp. 187–206 (1999)

26. Zhu, Y., Hendren, L.: Locality analysis for parallel C programs. IEEE Transactions on Parallel and Distributed Systems 10(2), 99–114 (1999)

Certified Reasoning in Memory Hierarchies[*]

Gilles Barthe[1,2], César Kunz[2], and Jorge Luis Sacchini[2]

[1] IMDEA Software
Gilles.Barthe@imdea.org
[2] INRIA Sophia Antipolis - Méditerranée
{Cesar.Kunz,Jorge-Luis.Sacchini}@inria.fr

Abstract. Parallel programming is rapidly gaining importance as a vector to develop high performance applications that exploit the improved capabilities of modern computer architectures. In consequence, there is a need to develop analysis and verification methods for parallel programs.

Sequoia is a language designed to program parallel divide-and-conquer programs over a hierarchical, tree-structured, and explicitly managed memory. Using abstract interpretation, we develop a compositional proof system to analyze Sequoia programs and reason about them. Then, we show that common program optimizations transform provably correct Sequoia programs into provably correct Sequoia programs.

1 Introduction

As modern computer architectures increasingly offer support for high performance parallel programming, there is a quest to invent adequate programming languages that exploit their capabilities. In order to reflect these new architectures accurately, parallel programming languages are gradually abandoning the traditional memory model, in which memory is viewed as a flat and uniform structure, in favor of a hierarchical memory model [1,7,11], which considers a tree of memories with different bandwidth and latency characteristics. Hierarchical memory is particularly appropriate for divide-and-conquer applications, in which computations are repeatedly fragmented into smaller computations that will be executed lower in the memory hierarchy, and programming languages based on this model perform well for such applications. Thus, programming languages for hierarchical memories are designed to exploit the memory hierarchy and are used for programs that require intensive computations on large amounts of data. Languages for hierarchical memories differ from general-purpose concurrent languages in their intent, and in their realization; in particular, such languages are geared towards deterministic programs and do not include explicit primitives for synchronization (typically programs will proceed by dividing computations between a number of cooperating subtasks, that operate on disjoints subsets of the memory).

As programming languages for high performance are gaining wide acceptance, there is an increasing need to provide analysis and verification methods to help

---

[*] This work is partially supported by the EU project MOBIUS.

G. Ramalingam (Ed.): APLAS 2008, LNCS 5356, pp. 75–90, 2008.
© Springer-Verlag Berlin Heidelberg 2008

developers write, maintain, and optimize their high-performance applications. However, verification methods have been seldom considered in the context of high-performance computing. The purpose of this paper is to show for a specific example that existing analysis and verification methods can be adapted to hierarchical languages and are tractable. We focus on the Sequoia programming language [8,12,10], which is designed to program efficient, portable, and reliable applications for hierarchical memories. We adopt the framework of abstract interpretation [5,6], and develop methods to prove and verify the correctness of Sequoia programs. Our methods encompass the usual automated and interactive verification techniques (static analyses and program logics) as well as methods to transform correctness proofs along program optimizations, which are of interest in the context of Proof Carrying Code [14]. In summary, the main technical contributions are: i) a generic, sound, compositional proof system to reason about Sequoia programs (Sect. 3.1); ii) a sound program logic derived as an instance of the generic proof system (Sect. 3.2); iii) algorithms that transform proofs of correctness along with program optimizations such as SPMD distribution or grouping of tasks [12] (Sect. 4).

2   A Primer on Sequoia

Sequoia [8,12,10] is a language for developing portable and efficient parallel programs for hierarchical memories. It is based on a small set of operations over a hierarchical memory, such as communication, memory movement and computation. Computations are organized into self-contained units, called tasks. Tasks can be executed in parallel at the same level of the memory hierarchy, on a dedicated address space, and may rely on subtasks that perform computations on a lower level (and in practice smaller and faster) fragment of the hierarchical memory (i.e., a subtree).

Hierarchical memory. A hierarchical memory is a tree of memory modules, i.e. of partial functions from a set $\mathcal{L}$ of locations to a set $\mathcal{V}$ of values. In our setting, values are either integers ($\mathbb{Z}$) or booleans ($\mathbb{B}$). Besides, locations are either scalar variables, or arrays elements of the form $A[i]$ where A is an array and i is an index. The set of scalar variables is denoted by $\mathcal{N}_S$ and the set of array variables is denoted by $\mathcal{N}_A$. The set of variable names is $\mathcal{N} = \mathcal{N}_S \cup \mathcal{N}_A$.

Definition 1 (States). *The set $\mathcal{M} = \mathcal{L} \rightharpoonup \mathcal{V}$ of memory modules is defined as the set of partial functions from locations to values. A memory hierarchy representing the machine structure is a memory tree defined as:*

$$\mathcal{T} ::= \langle \mu, \mathcal{T}_1, \ldots, \mathcal{T}_k \rangle \quad k \geq 0, \mu \in \mathcal{M} \ .$$

Intuitively, $\langle \mu, \vec{\tau} \rangle \in \mathcal{T}$ represents a memory tree with root memory μ and a possible empty sequence $\vec{\tau}$ of child subtrees.

The execution mechanism consists on splitting a task on smaller subtasks that operate on a dedicated copy of a memory subtree. Upon completion of each task, the initial memory tree is updated with the final state of each locally modified memory copy. However, inconsistencies may arise since, a priori, we cannot require subtasks to modify disjoint portions of the memory. Then, an auxiliary operator $+_\mu$ is defined to capture, as undefined, those portions of the state that are left with inconsistent values. The operator $+_\mu : \mathcal{M} \times \mathcal{M} \to \mathcal{M}$, indexed by a memory $\mu \in \mathcal{M}$, is formally defined as:

$$(\mu_1 +_\mu \mu_2)x = \begin{cases} \mu_1 x & \text{if } \mu_2 x = \mu x, \text{ else} \\ \mu_2 x & \text{if } \mu_1 x = \mu x \\ \text{undefined} & \text{otherwise .} \end{cases}$$

Note that the operator $+_\mu$ is partial, and the result is undefined if both μ_1 and μ_2 modify the same variable.

The operator $+_\mu$ is generalized over memory hierarchies in $\mathcal{T}$ and sequences $\vec{\mu} \in \mathcal{M}^\star$, where $\sum_{1 \le i \le n}^{\mu} \mu_i = (((\mu_1 +_\mu \mu_2) +_\mu \mu_3) +_\mu \cdots +_\mu \mu_n)$.

Syntax. Sequoia features usual constructions as well as specific constructs for parallel execution, for spawning new subtasks, and for grouping computations.

Definition 2 (Sequoia Programs). *The set of programs is defined by the following grammar:*

$$\begin{aligned} G ::= \; & \mathsf{Copy}^\uparrow(\vec{A}, \vec{B}) \; | \; \mathsf{Copy}^\downarrow(\vec{A}, \vec{B}) \; | \; \mathsf{Copy}(\vec{A}, \vec{B}) \\ & | \; \mathsf{Kernel}\langle A = f(B_1, \ldots, B_n)\rangle \; | \; \mathsf{Scalar}\langle a = f(b_1, \ldots, b_n)\rangle \\ & | \; \mathsf{Forall} \; i = m : n \; \mathsf{do} \; G \; | \; \mathsf{Group}(H) \; | \; \mathsf{Exec}_i(G) \\ & | \; \mathsf{If} \; cond \; \mathsf{then} \; G_1 \; \mathsf{else} \; G_2 \end{aligned}$$

where a, b are scalar variables, m, n are scalar constants, A, B are array variables, cond is a boolean expression, and H is a dependence graph of programs. We use the operators $\|$ and $;$ as a syntactic representation (respectively parallel and sequential composition) of the dependence graph composing a Group task.

Atomic statements, i.e. Copy, Kernel, and Scalar operations, are given a specific treatment in the proof system; we let atomStmt denote the set of atomic statements. A program G in the dependence graph H is maximal if G is not specified by H to depend on any other program in H.

Semantics. We now turn to the semantics of programs; in contrast to the original definition [12], our semantics is syntax-directed. We motivate this slight modification at the end of the paragraph.

The semantics of a program G is defined by a judgment $\sigma \vdash G \to \sigma'$ where $\sigma, \sigma' \in \mathcal{H}$, and $\mathcal{H} = \mathcal{M} \times \mathcal{T}$. Every $\sigma \in \mathcal{H}$ is a pair $\langle \mu_p, \tau \rangle$ where μ_p is the parent memory and τ is a child memory hierarchy. Abusing nomenclature, we refer to elements of $\mathcal{H}$ as memories. The meaning such a judgment is that the evaluation of G with initial memory σ terminates with final memory σ'. Note that for a specific architecture, the shape of the memory hierarchy (that is, the shape of the tree structure) is fixed and does not change with the execution of a program.

To manipulate elements in $\mathcal{H}$, we define two functions: $\pi_i : \mathcal{H} \to \mathcal{H}$ that returns the i-th child of a memory, and $\oplus_i : \mathcal{H} \times \mathcal{H} \to \mathcal{H}$ that, given two memories σ_1

$$\mu_p, \langle \mu, \vec{\tau} \rangle \vdash \mathsf{Copy}^\uparrow(\vec{A}, \vec{B}) \rightarrow \mu_p[B \mapsto \mu(A)], \langle \mu, \vec{\tau} \rangle$$

$$\mu_p, \langle \mu, \vec{\tau} \rangle \vdash \mathsf{Kernel}\langle A = f(B_1, \ldots, B_n) \rangle \rightarrow \mu_p, \langle \mu[A \mapsto f(B_1, \ldots, B_n)], \vec{\tau} \rangle$$

$$\mu_p, \langle \mu, \vec{\tau} \rangle \vdash \mathsf{Scalar}\langle a = f(b_1, \ldots, b_n) \rangle \rightarrow \mu_p, \langle \mu[a \mapsto f(b_1, \ldots, b_n)], \vec{\tau} \rangle$$

$$\frac{\begin{array}{c} X \text{ the subset of maximal elements of } H \text{ and } H' = H \setminus X \\ \forall g \in X, \ \mu, \tau \vdash g \rightarrow \mu_g, \tau_g \\ \sum_{g \in X}^{\mu, \tau}(\mu_g, \tau_g) \vdash \mathsf{Group}(H') \rightarrow \mu', \tau' \end{array}}{\mu, \tau \vdash \mathsf{Group}(H) \rightarrow \mu', \tau'}$$

$$\frac{\forall j \in [m, n] \neq \emptyset. \ \mu_p, \langle \mu[i \mapsto j], \vec{\tau} \rangle \vdash G \rightarrow \mu_p^j, \langle \mu^j, \vec{\tau}^j \rangle}{\mu_p, \langle \mu, \vec{\tau} \rangle \vdash \mathsf{Forall} \ i = m : n \ \mathsf{do} \ G \rightarrow \sum_{m \le j \le n}^{\mu_p, \langle \mu, \tau \rangle}(\mu_p^j, \langle \mu^j[i \mapsto \mu(i)], \vec{\tau}^j \rangle)}$$

$$\frac{\pi_i(\mu, \tau) \vdash G \rightarrow \mu', \tau'}{\mu, \tau \vdash \mathsf{Exec}_i(G) \rightarrow (\mu, \tau) \oplus_i (\mu', \tau')}$$

Fig. 1. Sequoia program semantics (excerpt)

and σ_2, replaces the i-th child of σ_1 with σ_2. Formally, they are defined as $\pi_i(\mu_p, \langle \mu, \vec{\tau} \rangle) = (\mu, \tau_i)$ and $(\mu_p, \langle \mu, \vec{\tau} \rangle) \oplus_i (\mu', \tau') = (\mu_p, \langle \mu', \vec{\tau_1} \rangle)$, where $\tau_{1i} = \tau'$ and $\tau_{1j} = \tau_j$ for $j \neq i$.

Definition 3 (Program semantics). *The semantics of a program G is defined by the rules given in Fig. 1.*

We briefly comment on the semantics—the omitted rules are either the usual ones (conditionals) or similar to other rules (copy).

The constructs $\mathsf{Copy}^\downarrow(\vec{A}, \vec{B})$ and $\mathsf{Copy}^\uparrow(\vec{A}, \vec{B})$ are primitives that enable data to migrate along the tree structure, from the parent memory to the root of the child memory hierarchy and conversely; and $\mathsf{Copy}(\vec{A}, \vec{B})$ represents an intra-memory copy in the root of the child memory hierarchy. Only the rule for $\mathsf{Copy}^\uparrow$ is shown in Fig. 1, since the others are similar.

The constructs $\mathsf{Kernel}\langle A = f(B_1, \ldots, B_n) \rangle$ and $\mathsf{Scalar}\langle a = f(b_1, \ldots, b_n) \rangle$ execute bulk and scalar computations. We implicitly assume in the rules that array accesses are in-bound. If this condition is not met then there is no applicable rule, and the program is stuck. The same happens if, in the rules for Group and Forall, the addition of memories is not defined; that is, the program gets stuck.

The construct $\mathsf{Forall} \ i = m : n \ \mathsf{do} \ G$ executes in parallel $n - m + 1$ instances of G with a different value of i, and merges the result. Progress is made only if the instances manipulate pairwise distinct parts of the memory, otherwise the memory after executing the Forall construct is undefined. The rule in Fig. 1 considers exclusively the case where $m \le n$, otherwise the memory hierarchy remains unchanged. The construct $\mathsf{Exec}_i(G)$ spawns a new computation on the i-th subtree of the current memory.

Finally, the construct $\mathsf{Group}(H)$ executes the set X of maximal elements of the dependence graph in parallel, and then merges the result before recursively executing $\mathsf{Group}(H \setminus X)$. A rule not shown in Fig. 1 states that if $H = \emptyset$ the state is left unchanged.

We conclude this section with a brief discussion of the difference between our semantics and the original semantics for Sequoia defined in [12]. First, we define the notion of safety. A Sequoia program is safe if its parallel subtasks are independent, i.e. if they modify disjoint regions of the memory hierarchy. [1]

The original semantics and our semantics differ in the rule for $\mathsf{Group}(H)$: whereas we require that X is the complete set of maximal elements, and is thus uniquely determined from the program syntax, the original semantics does not require X to be the complete set of maximal elements, but only a subset of it. Therefore, our semantics is a restriction of the original one. However, the semantics are equivalent in the sense that our semantics can simulate any run of the unrestricted semantics—provided the program is safe.

Checking that a program is safe can be achieved by an analysis that over-approximates the regions of the memory that each subtask reads and writes. A program is safe if, for parallel subtasks, these regions do not overlap. For lack of space, we do not give the complete definition the analysis.

For safe programs, the order of execution of parallel subtasks does not affect the final result and both semantics coincide. Note that the intention of Sequoia is to write safe programs; if a program is not safe, its execution might get stuck because of two (or more) subtasks writing to the same location.

3   Analyzing and Reasoning about Sequoia Programs

This section presents a proof system for reasoning about Sequoia programs. We start by generalizing the basics of abstract interpretation to our setting, using a sound, compositional proof system. Then, we define a program logic as an instance of our proof system, and show its soundness.

3.1   Program Analysis

We develop our work using a mild generalization of the framework of abstract interpretation, in which the lattice of abstract elements forms a preorder domain.[2] We also have specific operators over the abstract domain for each type of program, as shown below.

Definition 4. *An abstract interpretation is a tuple* $I = \langle A, T, +_A, \mathsf{weak}, \pi, \oplus, \rho \rangle$ *where:*

- $A = \langle A, \sqsubseteq, \sqsupseteq, \sqcup, \sqcap, \top, \bot \rangle$ *is a lattice of abstract states;*

---

[1] This notion of safety is similar to the notion of strict and-parallelism of logic programming [9].

[2] A preorder over A is a reflexive and transitive binary relation, whereas a partial order is an antisymmetric preorder. We prefer to use preorders instead of partial orders because one instance of an abstract interpretation is that of propositions; we do not want to view it as a partial order since it implies that logically equivalent formulae are equal, which is not appropriate in the setting of Proof Carrying Code.

- *for each $s \in$ atomStmt, a relation $T_s \subseteq A \times A$;*
- $+_A : A \times A \to A$;
- *for each $i \in \mathcal{N}_S$,* weak$_i : A \to A$;
- *for each $i \in \mathbb{N}$, $\pi_i^A : A \to A$ and $\oplus_i^A : A \times A \to A$;*
- $\rho : A \times$ Bool $\to A$, *where* Bool *is the set of boolean expressions.*

Intuitively, for each rule of the semantics, we have a corresponding operator that reflect the changes of the memory on the abstract domain. For each atomic statement s, the relation T_s characterizes the effect of the atomic semantic operation on the abstract domain. A particular instance of T that we usually consider is when s is a scalar assignment, i.e., $T_{i:=j}$, where $i \in \mathcal{N}_S$ and $j \in \mathbb{Z}$. Note that we don't use the common *transfer functions* to define the abstract operators regarding atomic statements. Instead, we use relations, which encompasses the use of the more typical *backward* or *forward* functions. We can consider backward transfer functions by defining $a \ T_s \ b$ as $a = f_s(b)$ for a suitable f_s (in fact, this is the case for our definition of the verification framework), and forward transfer functions by defining $a \ T_s \ b$ as $b = g_s(a)$ for a suitable g_s. Also, atomic statements include Kernel and Scalar operations that can be arbitrarily complex and whose behavior can be better abstracted in a relation. For instance, in the case of verification, we will require that these atomic statements be specified with pre and postconditions that define the relation.

The operator $+_A$ abstracts the operator $+$ for memories (we omit the reference to the domain when it is clear from the context).

Given an $i \in \mathcal{N}_S$ and $a \in A$, the function weak$_i(a)$ removes any condition on the scalar variable i from a. It is used when processing a Forall task, with i being the iteration variable, to show that after execution, the value of the iteration variable is not relevant. To give more intuition about this operator, consider, for instance, that A is the lattice of first-order formulae (as is the case of the verification framework of Sect. 3.2), then weak$_i(a)$ is defined as $\exists i.a$. If A has the form $\mathcal{N}_S \to D$, where D is a lattice, then weak$_i(a)$ can be defined as $a \sqcup \{i \to \top\}$, effectively removing any condition on i.

For each $i \in \mathbb{N}$, the operators $\{\pi_i^A\}_{i \in \mathbb{N}}$ and $\{\oplus_i^A\}_{i \in \mathbb{N}}$ abstract the operations π_i and $\oplus_i$ for memories (we omit the reference to the domain when it is clear from the context).

Finally, the function $\rho : A \times$ Bool $\to A$ is a transfer function used in an If task to update an abstract value depending on the test condition. It can be simply defined as $\rho(a, b) = a$, but this definition does not take advantage of knowing that b is true. If we have an expressive domain we can find a value that express this; for instance, in the lattice of logic formulae, we can define $\rho(a, b) = a \wedge b$.

To formalize the connection between the memory states and the abstract states, we assume a satisfaction relation $\models \subseteq \mathcal{H} \times A$ that is an approximation order, i.e., for all $\sigma \in \mathcal{H}$ and $a_1, a_2 \in A$, if $\sigma \models a_1$ and $a_1 \sqsubseteq a_2$ then $\sigma \models a_2$. The next definition formalizes the intuition given about the relation between the operators of an abstract interpretation and the semantics of programs. Basically, it states that satisfiability is preserved for each operator of the abstract interpretation. Note that we can also restate these lemmas and definitions in terms

$$X \text{ the set of maximal elements of } H \text{ and } H' = H \setminus X:$$

$$\frac{\forall g \in X, \ \langle a \rangle \vdash g \langle a_g \rangle \qquad \langle \sum_{g \in X} a_g \rangle \vdash \mathsf{Group}(H') \langle a' \rangle}{\langle a \rangle \vdash \mathsf{Group}(H) \langle a' \rangle} \quad [\mathbf{G}]$$

$$\frac{}{\langle a \rangle \vdash \mathsf{Group}(\emptyset) \langle a \rangle} \ [\mathbf{G_\emptyset}] \qquad \frac{s \in \mathsf{atomStmt} \quad a \ T_s \ a'}{\langle a \rangle \vdash s \langle a' \rangle} \ [\mathbf{A}] \qquad \frac{\langle \pi_i(a) \rangle \vdash G \langle a' \rangle}{\langle a \rangle \vdash \mathsf{Exec}_i(G) \langle a \oplus_i a' \rangle} \ [\mathbf{E}]$$

$$\frac{\forall j, \ m \leq j \leq n \qquad a \ T_{i:=j} \ a_j \qquad \langle a_j \rangle \vdash G \langle a'_j \rangle}{\langle a \rangle \vdash \mathsf{Forall} \ i = m : n \ \mathsf{do} \ G \ \langle \sum_{j=m}^{n} \mathsf{weak}_i(a'_j) \rangle} \ [\mathbf{F}]$$

$$\frac{b \sqsubseteq a \quad \langle a \rangle \vdash G \langle a' \rangle \quad a' \sqsubseteq b'}{\langle b \rangle \vdash G \langle b' \rangle} \ [\mathbf{SS}] \qquad \frac{\langle \rho(a, cond) \rangle \vdash G_1 \langle a' \rangle \quad \langle \rho(a, \neg cond) \rangle \vdash G_2 \langle a' \rangle}{\langle a \rangle \vdash \mathsf{If} \ cond \ \mathsf{then} \ G_1 \ \mathsf{else} \ G_2 \ \langle a' \rangle} \ [\mathbf{I}]$$

Fig. 2. Program analysis rules

of Galois connections, since we can define a Galois connection from the relation $\models$ by defining $\gamma : A \to \mathcal{H}$ as $\gamma(a) = \{\sigma \in \mathcal{H} : \sigma \models a\}$.

Definition 5. *The abstract interpretation* $I = \langle A, T, +, \mathsf{weak}, \pi, \oplus, \rho \rangle$ *is consistent if the following holds for every* $\sigma, \sigma' \in \mathcal{H}$, $a, a_1, a_2 \in A$, $\mu, \mu_p \in \mathcal{M}$, $\tau \in T$ *and* $cond \in \mathsf{Bool}$:

- *for every* $s \in \mathsf{atomStmt}$, *if* $\sigma \vdash s \to \sigma'$, $\sigma \models a$ *and* $a \ T_s \ a'$, *then* $\sigma' \models a'$;
- *if* $\sigma_1 \models a_1$ *and* $\sigma_2 \models a_2$ *then* $\sigma_1 +_\sigma \sigma_2 \models a_1 + a_2$;
- *if* $\mu_p, \langle \mu, \tau \rangle \models a$, *then for all* $k \in \mathbb{Z}$ *we have* $\mu_p, \langle \mu[i \mapsto k], \tau \rangle \models \mathsf{weak}_i(a)$;
- *if* $\sigma \models a$ *then* $\pi_i(\sigma) \models \pi_i(a)$;
- *if* $\sigma \models a$ *and* $\sigma' \models a'$, *then* $\sigma \oplus_i \sigma' \models a \oplus_i a'$;
- *if* $\sigma \models a$ *and* $\sigma \models_{\mathsf{Bool}} cond$, *then* $\sigma \models \rho(a, cond)$.[3]

Given an abstract interpretation I, a judgment is a tuple $\langle a \rangle \vdash_I G \langle a' \rangle$, where G is a program and $a, a' \in A$. We will omit the reference to I when it is clear from the context. A judgment is *valid* if it is the root of a derivation tree built using the rules in Fig. 2. The interpretation of a valid judgment $\langle a \rangle \vdash G \langle a' \rangle$ is that executing G in a memory that satisfies a, we end up in a memory satisfying a'. The following lemma claims that this is case, provided I is consistent.

Lemma 1 (Analysis Soundness). *Let* G *be a Sequoia program and assume that* $I = \langle A, T, +, \mathsf{weak}, \pi, \oplus, \rho \rangle$ *is a consistent abstract interpretation. For every* $a, a' \in A$ *and* $\sigma, \sigma' \in \mathcal{H}$, *if the judgment* $\langle a \rangle \vdash G \langle a' \rangle$ *is valid and* $\sigma \vdash G \to \sigma'$ *and* $\sigma \models a$ *then* $\sigma' \models a'$.

3.2 Program Verification

We now define a verification framework $I = \langle \mathsf{Prop}, T, +_{\mathsf{Prop}}, \mathsf{weak}, \pi, \oplus, \rho \rangle$ as an instance of the abstract interpretation, where Prop is the lattice of first-order formulae. Before defining I, we need some preliminary definitions.

---

[3] Given a memory σ and a boolean condition $cond$, the judgment $\sigma \models_{\mathsf{Bool}} cond$ states that the condition is valid in σ. The definition is standard so we omit it.

The extended set of scalar names, $\mathcal{N_S}^+$, is defined as

$$\mathcal{N_S}^+ = \mathcal{N_S} \cup \{x^\uparrow : x \in \mathcal{N_S}\} \cup \{x^{\downarrow^{i_1}\cdots\downarrow^{i_k}} : x \in \mathcal{N_S} \wedge k \in \mathbb{N} \wedge i_1,\ldots,i_k \in \mathbb{N}\} \ .$$

We define, in a similar way, the sets $\mathcal{N_A}^+$, $\mathcal{N}^+$, and $\mathcal{L}^+$ of extended locations. These sets allow us to refer to variables at all levels of a memory hierarchy, as is shown by the following definition. Given $\sigma \in \mathcal{H}$, with $\sigma = \mu_p, \langle \mu, \tau \rangle$, and $l \in \mathcal{L}^+$, we define $\sigma(l)$ with the following rules:

$$\sigma(l) = \begin{cases} \mu_p(x) & \text{if } l = x^\uparrow \\ \mu(x) & \text{if } l = x \\ (\mu, \tau_{i_1})(x^{\downarrow^{i_2}\cdots\downarrow^{i_k}}) & \text{if } l = x^{\downarrow^{i_1}\downarrow^{i_2}\cdots\downarrow^{i_k}} \end{cases} \ .$$

We also define the functions $\uparrow^i, \downarrow^i : \mathcal{N_S}^+ \to \mathcal{N_S}^+$ with the following rules:

$$\downarrow^i(x) = x^{\downarrow^i} \qquad\qquad \uparrow^i(x) = x^\uparrow$$
$$\downarrow^i(x^{\downarrow^{j_1}\cdots\downarrow^{j_n}}) = x^{\downarrow^i\downarrow^{j_1}\cdots\downarrow^{j_n}} \qquad \uparrow^i(x^{\downarrow^i\downarrow^{j_1}\cdots\downarrow^{j_k}}) = x^{\downarrow^{j_1}\cdots\downarrow^{j_k}}$$
$$\downarrow^i(x^\uparrow) = x \ .$$

Note that $\downarrow^i$ is a total function, while $\uparrow^i$ is undefined in $x^\uparrow$ and $x^{\downarrow^j\downarrow^{j_1}\cdots\downarrow^{j_k}}$ if $j \neq i$. These functions are defined likewise for $\mathcal{N_A}^+$, $\mathcal{N}^+$, and $\mathcal{L}^+$.

Given a formula ϕ, we obtain $\downarrow^i\phi$ by substituting every free variable $v \in \mathcal{N}^+$ of ϕ with $\downarrow^i v$. In the same way, the formula $\uparrow^i\phi$ is obtained by substituting every free variable $v \in \mathcal{N}^+$ of ϕ by $\uparrow^i v$; if $\uparrow^i v$ is not defined, we substitute v by a fresh variable, and quantify existentially over all the introduced fresh variables.

Definition of $+$. To define the operator $+$ we require that each subprogram comes annotated with the sets SW and AW specifying, respectively, the scalar variables and the array ranges that it may modify. Given two programs G_1 and G_2 annotated, respectively, with the modifiable regions SW_1, AW_1 and SW_2, AW_2, and the postconditions Q_1 and Q_2, we define $Q_1 + Q_2$ as $Q_1' \wedge Q_2'$, where Q_1' is the result of existentially quantifying in Q_1 the variables that may be modified by G_2. More precisely, $Q_1' = \exists X'. \ Q_1[^{X'}\!/x] \wedge \bigwedge_{A[m,n]\in AW_1} A'[m,n] = A[m,n]$, X representing the set of scalar and array variables in $SW_2 \cup AW_2$ and X' a set of fresh variables (and similarly with Q_2).

To explain the intuition behind this definition, assume two tasks G_1 and G_2 that execute in parallel with postconditions Q_1 and Q_2. After verifying that each G_i satisfies the postcondition Q_i, one may be tempted to conclude that after executing both tasks, the resulting state satisfies $Q_1 \wedge Q_2$. The reason for which we do not define $Q_1 + Q_2$ simply as $Q_1 \wedge Q_2$ is that while Q_1 may be true after executing G_1, Q_1 may state conditions over variables that are not modified by G_1 but are modified by G_2. Then, since from the definition of the operator $+$ in the semantic domain the value of a variable not modified by G_1 is overwritten with a new value if modified by G_2, Q_1 may be false in the final memory state after executing G_1 and G_2 in parallel.

For the definition of $Q_1 + Q_2$ to be sound we require the annotations SW_1, AW_1 and SW_2, AW_2 to be correct. For this, we can use a static analysis or generate additional proof obligations to validate the program annotations. However, for space constraints and since such analysis can be applied earlier and independently of the verification framework, we do not consider this issue. Certainly, the applicability of the logic is limited by the precision of such static analysis.

We generalize the operator $+$ for a set of postconditions $\{\phi_i\}_{i \in I}$ and a set of specifications of modified variables $\{SW_i\}_{i \in I}$ and $\{AW_i\}_{i \in I}$, by defining $\sum_{i \in I} \phi_i$ as $\bigwedge_{i \in I} \phi_i'$ where $\phi_i' = \exists X'. \; \phi_i[^{X'}\!/x] \wedge \bigwedge_{A[m,n] \in AW_i} A[m,n] = A'[m,n]$, s.t. X represents every scalar or array variable in $\{SW_j\}_{j \neq i \in I}$ or $\{AW_j\}_{j \neq i \in I}$, and X' a set of fresh variables. If an assertion ϕ_i refers only to scalar and array variables that are not declared as modifiable by other member $j \neq i$, we have $\phi_i' \Rightarrow \phi_i$.

Definition of other components of I. They are defined as follows:

- for each $s \in$ atomStmt, the relation T_s is defined from the weakest precondition transformer wp_s, as $\mathsf{wp}_s(\phi) \, T_s \, \phi$ for every logic formula ϕ. For Kernel and Scalar statements, we assume that we have a pre and postcondition specifying their behavior (the definition of $\{\mathsf{wp}_s\}_{s \in \text{atomStmt}}$ is standard);
- $\mathsf{weak}_i(\phi) = \exists i.\phi$, where $i \in \mathcal{N}_S{}^+$;
- $\pi_i(\phi) = \uparrow^i \phi$, where $i \in \mathbb{N}$;
- $\phi_1 \oplus_i \phi_2 = \overline{\phi_1}^i \wedge \downarrow^i \phi_2$, where $i \in \mathbb{N}$, and $\overline{\phi_1}^i$ is obtained from ϕ_1 by replacing every variable of the form x or $x^{\downarrow^i \downarrow^{j_1} \ldots \downarrow^{j_k}}$ with a fresh variable and then quantifying existentially all the introduced fresh variables;
- $\rho(\phi, cond) = \phi \wedge cond$.

The satisfaction relation $\sigma \models \phi$ is defined as the validity of $[\![\phi]\!]\sigma$, the interpretation of the formula ϕ in the memory state σ. To appropriately adapt a standard semantics $[\![.]\!]$ to a hierarchy of memories, it suffices to extend the interpretation for the extended set of variables $\mathcal{N}^+$, as $[\![n]\!]\sigma = \sigma(n)$ for $n \in \mathcal{N}^+$.

In the rest of the paper, we denote as $\{P\} \vdash G \; \{Q\}$ the judgments in the domain of logical formulae, and P and Q are said to be pre and postconditions of G respectively. If the judgment $\{P\} \vdash G \; \{Q\}$ is valid, and the program starts in a memory σ that satisfies P and finishes in a memory σ', then σ' satisfies Q. The proposition below formalizes this result.

Proposition 1 (Verification Soundness). *Assume that $\{P\} \vdash G \; \{Q\}$ is a valid judgment and that $\sigma \vdash G \to \sigma'$, where G is a program, P, Q are assertions, and $\sigma, \sigma' \in \mathcal{H}$. If $\sigma \models P$ then $\sigma' \models Q$.*

3.3   Example Program

We illustrate the verification with an example. Consider a program, G_{Add}, that add two input arrays (A and B) producing on output array C. The code of the program is given by the following definitions:

$G_{Add} := \mathsf{Exec}_0(\mathsf{Forall}\ i = 0 : n - 1\ \mathsf{do}\ \mathsf{Add})$

$\mathsf{Add} := \mathsf{Group}((\mathsf{CopyAX} \parallel \mathsf{CopyBY}); \mathsf{AddP}; \mathsf{CopyZC})$

$\mathsf{CopyAX} := \mathsf{Copy}^{\downarrow}(A[i.S, (i+1)S], X[i.S, (i+1)S])$

$\mathsf{CopyBY} := \mathsf{Copy}^{\downarrow}(B[i.S, (i+1)S], Y[i.S, (i+1)S])$

$\mathsf{AddP} := \mathsf{Kernel}\langle Z[i.S, (i+1)S] = \mathsf{VectAdd}(X[i.S, (i+1)S], Y[i.S, (i+1)S])\rangle$

$\mathsf{CopyZC} := \mathsf{Copy}^{\uparrow}(Z[i.S, (i+1)S], C[i.S, (i+1)S])$

Assume that the arrays have size $n.S$, and note that the program is divided in n parallel subtasks, each operating on different array fragments, of size S. The best value for S may depend on the underlying architecture.

It is easy to see that this program is safe, since each subtask writes on a different fragment of the arrays.

We show, using the verification framework, how to derive the judgment $\{\mathsf{true}\} \vdash G_{Add}\ \{\mathsf{Post}\}$, where $\mathsf{Post} = \forall k,\ 0 \leq k < n.S \Rightarrow C[k] = A[k] + B[k]$. Using the rules [A], [G] and [SS] we derive, for each $i \in [0 \ldots n - 1]$, the following:

$$\{\mathsf{true}\} \vdash \mathsf{Add}\ \{Q_i\}, \tag{1}$$

where $Q_i = \forall k,\ i.S \leq k < (i+1)S \Rightarrow C^{\uparrow}[k] = A^{\uparrow}[k] + B^{\uparrow}[k]$. Applying the rule [F] on (1) we obtain

$$\{\mathsf{true}\} \vdash \mathsf{Forall}\ i = 0 : n - 1\ \mathsf{do}\ \mathsf{Add}\ \left\{ \sum_{0 \leq j < n} Q_j \right\}. \tag{2}$$

Note that the postcondition of the i-th subtask only refers to variables that it modifies, therefore, it is not difficult to see that $\sum_{0 \leq j < n} Q_j \Rightarrow \bigwedge_{0 \leq j < n} Q_j$. Applying the subsumption rule to (2), we obtain

$$\{\mathsf{true}\} \vdash \mathsf{Forall}\ i = 0 : n - 1\ \mathsf{do}\ \mathsf{Add}\ \{Q\} \tag{3}$$

where $Q = \forall k,\ 0 \leq k < n.S \Rightarrow C^{\uparrow}[k] = A^{\uparrow}[k] + B^{\uparrow}[k]$. Finally, applying rule [E] to (3), we obtain the desired result, since $\mathsf{Post} = \downarrow^0 Q$.

4   Certificate Translation

In this section, we focus on the interplay between program optimization and program verification. To maximize the performance of applications, the Sequoia compiler performs program optimizations such as code hoisting, instruction scheduling, and SPMD distribution. We show, for common optimizations described in [12], that program optimizations transform provably correct programs into provably correct programs. More precisely, we provide an algorithm to transform a derivation for the original program into a derivation for the transformed program. The problem of transforming provably correct programs into provably correct programs is motivated by research in Proof Carrying Code (PCC) [15,14], and in particular by our earlier work on certificate translation [2,3].

We start by extending the analysis setting described in previous sections with a notion of certificates, to make it suitable for a PCC architecture. Then, we describe certificate translation in the presence of three optimizations: SPMD distribution, Exec Grouping and Copy grouping.

Certified setting. In a PCC setting, a program is distributed with a checkable certificate that the code complies with the specified policy. To extend the verification framework defined in Section 3.2 with a certificate infrastructure, we capture the notion of checkable proof with an abstract proof algebra.

Definition 6 (Certificate infrastructure). *A certificate infrastructure consists on a proof algebra* $\mathcal{P}$ *that assigns to every* $\phi \in$ Prop *a set of certificates* $\mathcal{P}(\vdash \phi)$. *We assume that* $\mathcal{P}$ *is sound, i.e. for every* $\phi \in$ Prop, *if* ϕ *is not valid, then* $\mathcal{P}(\phi) = \emptyset$. *In the sequel, we write* $c :\vdash \phi$ *instead of* $c \in \mathcal{P}(\phi)$.

We do not commit to an specific representation of certificates, since it is not relevant for this paper. To give an intuition, we can define them in terms of the Curry-Howard isomorphism by considering $\mathcal{P}(\phi) = \{e \in \mathcal{E} \mid \langle\rangle \vdash e : \phi\}$, where $\mathcal{E}$ is the set of expressions and $\vdash e : \phi$ a typing judgment in some λ-calculus.

In addition, we refine the notion of certified analysis judgment, to enable code consumers to check whether a judgment is a valid judgment. To this end, the definition of rule **[SS]** is extended to incorporate certificates attesting the validity of the (a priori undecidable) logical formulae required in rule **[SS]**.

Definition 7 (Certified Verification Judgment). *We say that the verification judgment* $\{\Phi\} \vdash G \{\Psi\}$ *is certified if it is the root of a derivation tree, built from the rules in Fig. 2, such that every application of the subsumption rule*

$$\frac{\phi \Rightarrow \phi' \quad \{\phi'\} \vdash G \{\psi'\} \quad \psi' \Rightarrow \psi}{\{\phi\} \vdash G \{\psi\}}\text{[SS]}$$

is accompanied with certificates c *and* c' *s.t.* c $:\vdash \phi \Rightarrow \phi'$ *and* c' $:\vdash \psi' \Rightarrow \psi$.

A *certificate* for the judgment $\{\Phi\} \vdash G \{\Psi\}$ is a derivation tree together with a tuple of certificates for each application of the subsumption rule.

A common characteristic of the optimizations considered in the following sections is that they are defined as a substitution of a subprogram g by another subprogram g' in a bigger program G. We denote with $G[\bullet]$ the fact that G is a program with a *hole*. Given a program g, we denote with $G[g]$ the program obtained by replacing the hole $\bullet$ with g. Then, optimizations are characterized by subprograms g and g', defining a transformation from a program $G[g]$ into a program $G[g']$. The following general result complements the results on certificate translators explained in the following sections.

Lemma 2. *Let* $G[\bullet]$ *be a program with a hole; g, g' programs and Φ, Ψ logic formulae. If the judgment $\{\Phi\} \vdash G[g] \{\Psi\}$ is certified, then the derivation of the latter contains a certificate for the judgment $\{\phi\} \vdash g \{\psi\}$, for some ϕ and ψ. If there is a certificate for the judgment $\{\phi\} \vdash g' \{\psi\}$, then we can construct a certificate for the judgment $\{\Phi\} \vdash G[g'] \{\Psi\}$.*

4.1   SPMD Distribution

Consider a program that executes multiple times a single piece of code represented by a subprogram g. If every execution of g involves and independent portion of data, the tasks can be performed in any sequential order or in parallel. SPMD distribution is a common parallelization technique that exploits this condition distributing the tasks among the available processing units.

Programs of the form $\mathsf{Forall}\ j = 0 : k.n - 1\ \mathsf{do}\ g$ are candidates for SPMD distribution, since $k.n$ instances of the single subprogram g are executed in parallel along the range of the iteration variable j. Furthermore, for each value of the iteration value j, the subprogram g operates over an independent partition of the data, as assumed for every program subject to verification.

G' is transformed from G by applying SPMD distribution if G' is the result of substituting every subprogram $\mathsf{Exec}_i(\mathsf{Forall}\ j = 0 : k.n - 1\ \mathsf{do}\ g)$ by the equivalent subprogram $\mathsf{Group}(G_1\ \|\ \ldots\ \|\ G_k)$, with G_i defined as the program $\mathsf{Exec}_i(\mathsf{Forall}\ j = i.n : (i+1)n - 1\ \mathsf{do}\ g)$ for all $i \in [0, k-1]$.

Normally, a real compiler will also consider whether it is convenient to span the computation of g over other child nodes. However, since orthogonal to the transformation of the verification judgment, we do not consider this issue.

Lemma 2 in combination with the following lemma that states that the local substitutions defining SPMD distribution preserve certified judgments, implies the feasibility of certificate translation.

Lemma 3. *Given a program* $G = \mathsf{Exec}_i(\mathsf{Forall}\ j = 0 : k.n - 1\ \mathsf{do}\ g)$, *and a certified judgment* $\{\Phi\} \vdash G\ \{\Psi\}$, *it is possible to generate a certified judgment* $\{\Phi\} \vdash \mathsf{Group}(G_1\ \|\ \ldots\ \|\ G_k)\ \{\Psi\}$, *where* G_i *is defined as* $\mathsf{Exec}_i(\mathsf{Forall}\ j = i.n : (i+1)n - 1\ \mathsf{do}\ g)$ *for any* $i \in [0, k-1]$.

Example: Consider again the program G_{Add} of Section 3.3. Assume that at the level of the memory hierarchy at which G_{Add} is executed there are k available child processing units, and that $n = k.m$ for some m. Then, we are interested in distributing the independent computations along the iteration range $[0, n-1]$ splitting them in k subsets of independent computations in ranges of length m. We obtain then, after applying SPMD distribution to program G_{Add}, the following transformed program:

$$G'_{\mathsf{Add}} := \mathsf{Exec}_0(\mathsf{Forall}\ i = 0 : m - 1\ \mathsf{do}\ \mathsf{Add})$$
$$\|\ \mathsf{Exec}_1(\mathsf{Forall}\ i = m : 2m - 1\ \mathsf{do}\ \mathsf{Add})$$
$$\ldots$$
$$\|\ \mathsf{Exec}_{k-1}(\mathsf{Forall}\ i = (k-1)m : k.m - 1\ \mathsf{do}\ \mathsf{Add})$$

Applying the result stated above, we can transform the derivation of the judgment $\{\mathsf{true}\} \vdash G_{\mathsf{Add}}\ \{\mathsf{Post}\}$ into a derivation of $\{\mathsf{true}\} \vdash G'_{\mathsf{Add}}\ \{\mathsf{Post}\}$, proving that the verification judgment is preserved. Recall that we can derive the judgment

$$\{\mathsf{true}\} \vdash \mathsf{Exec}_r(\mathsf{Forall}\ i = r.m : (r+1)m - 1\ \mathsf{do}\ \mathsf{Add})\ \left\{ \uparrow^r \left(\sum_{r.m \leq j < (r+1)m} Q_j \right) \right\}$$

for every $0 \leq r < k$. One more application of rule [**G**] allows us to derive the judgment $\{\text{true}\} \vdash G'_{\text{Add}} \left\{ \sum_{0 \leq r < k} \uparrow^r (\sum_{r.m \leq j < (r+1)m} Q_j) \right\}$. Finally, requiring a certificate of the distributivity of $\uparrow^r$ over the operator $+$, and a certificate for $\sum_{0 \leq r < k} \sum_{r.m \leq j < (r+1)m} Q_j \Rightarrow \sum_{0 \leq j < k.m} Q_j$ we get by rule [**SS**]

$$\{\text{true}\} \vdash G'_{\text{Add}} \left\{ (\sum_{0 \leq j < k.m} \uparrow^r Q_j) \right\} \ .$$

By the same reasoning in Section 3.3 we have $\sum_{0 \leq j < k.m} \uparrow^r Q_j \Rightarrow \bigwedge_{0 \leq j < n} \uparrow^r Q_j$, and finally by subsumption rule we get $\{\text{true}\} \vdash G'_{\text{Add}} \{\text{Post}\}$. Notice that judgment reconstruction entails the application of the [**SS**] rule and, thus, requires discharging extra proof obligations. These obligations include, for instance, proving commutativity of $+$, associativity of $+$ and distributivity of $\uparrow^r$ over $+$.

4.2 Exec Grouping

An Exec operation pushes the execution of a piece of code down to one of the memory subtrees. Since the cost of transferring code and data between different levels of the hierarchy is not negligible, there is an unnecessary overhead when several Exec operations contain code with short execution time. Hence, there is a motivation to reduce the cost of invoking code in child nodes, by grouping the computation defined inside a set of Exec operations into a single Exec operation.

We say that a program G' is the result of applying Exec grouping, if it is the result of replacing a set of Exec operations targeting the same child node, by an single and semantically equivalent Exec operation. More precisely, every subprogram $\text{Group}(\{\text{Exec}_i(G_1), \ldots, \text{Exec}_i(G_k)\} \cup H)$ such that $(\text{Exec}_i(G_j))_{j=1}^{k}$ are maximal in the dependence graph and mutually independent, is substituted by the equivalent subprogram $\text{Group}(\{\text{Exec}_i(\text{Group}(\{G_1, \ldots, G_k\}))\} \cup H)$. In addition, the dependence relation that defines the graph $\{\text{Exec}_i(\text{Group}(\{G_1, \ldots, G_k\}))\} \cup H$ must be accordingly updated. More precisely, if the subprogram $g \in H$ originally depends on G_i for some $i \in [1, k]$ then g depends on $\text{Exec}_i(\text{Group}(\{G_1, \ldots, G_k\}))$ in the modified dependence graph.

The following result expresses that a certified judgment corresponding to set of independent Exec operations can be translated to a certified judgment for the result of merging the Exec operations into a single one. This result, together with Lemma 2, implies the existence of a certificate translator for Exec grouping.

Lemma 4. *Consider a set of mutually independent tasks $G_1, \ldots, G_k$ and a dependence graph $\{\text{Exec}_i(G_1), \ldots, \text{Exec}_i(G_k)\} \cup H$ s.t. $(\text{Exec}_i(G_j))_{1 \leq j \leq k}$ are maximal elements. Assume that $\{\Phi\} \vdash \text{Group}(\{\text{Exec}_i(G_1), \ldots, \text{Exec}_i(G_k)\} \cup H) \{\Psi\}$ is a certified judgment. Then, it is possible to generate a certified judgment $\{\Phi\} \vdash \text{Group}(\{\text{Exec}_i(\text{Group}(\{G_1, \ldots, G_k\}))\} \cup H) \{\Psi\}$.*

4.3 Copy Grouping

Commonly, for the execution environments targeted by Sequoia programs, transferring several fragments of data to a different level of the memory hierarchy in a single copy operation is more efficient that transferring each fragment of data in a separate operation. For this reason, and since array copy operations are frequent in programs targeting data intensive applications, it is of interest to cluster a set of copy operations involving small and independent regions of the memory into a single transfer operation.

Naturally, this transformation may require an analysis to detect whether two copy operations referring to regions of the same array are indeed independent. However, for simplicity, we consider the case in which the original set of small copy operations are performed over different array variables.

Consider a subprogram $g = \mathsf{Group}(H \cup \{g_1, g_2\})$, where $g_1 = \mathsf{Copy}(A_1, B_1)$ and $g_2 = \mathsf{Copy}(A_2, B_2)$ are mutually independent and maximal in H. Copy propagation consists on substituting g by the equivalent program g' defined as $\mathsf{Group}(H \cup \{g_{1,2}\})$, where $g_{1,2}$ is a copy operation that merges atomic programs g_1 and g_2 into a single transfer operation. In addition, the dependence relation on $\mathsf{Group}(H \cup \{g_{1,2}\})$ must be updated accordingly, such that $g'' \in H$ depends on $g_{1,2}$ iff g'' depended on g_1 or g_2 in the original dependence graph.

Lemma 5. *Consider the programs g and g' as defined above. Then, from a certified judgment $\{\Phi\} \vdash g \{\Psi\}$ we can construct a certified derivation for the judgment $\{\Phi\} \vdash g' \{\Psi\}$.*

The program G' is the result of applying copy grouping to program G, if every subprogram of the form g in G is replaced by g', where g and g' are as characterized above. The existence of certificate translators follows from Lemma 2.

Example: Consider again the program G_{Add} of Section 3.3, that adds two arrays. From the definition of the subprogram Add, we can see that it is a candidate for a copy grouping transformation, since it can be replaced by the equivalent subprogram Add′ defined as $\mathsf{Group}(\mathsf{CopyAXBY}; \mathsf{AddP}; \mathsf{CopyZC})$, where CopyAXBY is defined as $\mathsf{Copy}^{\downarrow}(A[i.S, (i+1)S], B[i.S, (i+1)S], X[i.S, (i+1)S], Y[i.S, (i+1)S])$. Assume that judgment of for the example in Section 3.3 is certified. To translate this result after applying the transformation above, we must certify the judgment $\{\mathsf{true}\} \vdash \mathsf{CopyAXBY} \{Q_{AX} + Q_{BY}\}$. To this end, we reuse the certified judgments $\{\mathsf{true}\} \vdash \mathsf{CopyAX} \{Q_{AX}\}$ and $\{\mathsf{true}\} \vdash \mathsf{CopyBY} \{Q_{BY}\}$ that are included in the certificate for the judgment $\{\mathsf{true}\} \vdash G_{\mathsf{Add}} \{\mathsf{Post}\}$, where Q_{AX} is defined as $(\forall k, \ 0 \le k < S \Rightarrow X[k] = A^{\uparrow}[k + i.S])$ and Q_{BY} as $(\forall k, \ 0 \le k < S \Rightarrow Y[k] = B^{\uparrow}[k + i.S])$.

The fact that makes the translation through, is the validity of the formula $\mathsf{wp}_{\mathsf{CopyAX}}(\phi) \wedge \mathsf{wp}_{\mathsf{CopyBY}}(\psi) \Rightarrow \mathsf{wp}_{\mathsf{CopyAXBY}}(\phi + \psi)$.

5   Related Work

The present work follows the motivations on the framework introduced by some of the authors for certificate translation [2,3]. Certificate translation as originally proposed [2] targets low level unstructured code and a weakest precondition based verification, in contrast to the Hoare-like environment that we have defined to verify Sequoia programs. Another difference is that in previous work programs transformations consist on standard compiler optimizations on sequential code, whereas in this paper we deal with transformations that take advantage of the concurrent programming model of Sequoia. Extending certificate translation for Sequoia programs with transformations that optimize sequential components in isolation is feasible.

Recent work on concurrent separation logic [16] can be used to reason about Sequoia programs as well. Concurrent separation logic extends the standard Owicki-Gries logic [17] for concurrent programs to enable one to reason about heap operations. One key feature of separation logic is that it allows to express whether a concurrent component owns a specific resource. From the application of the logic rules, it is required that each resource is shared by at most one process (although ownership may change along program execution), and that a sequential component may only affect the resources it owns. Therefore, it is possible to show independence of parallel subtasks using the logic rules.

However, since interleaving, and hence interaction, in a Sequoia program occur only in specific program points, the disjointness conditions are simpler to check. Additionally, it is convenient that checking the disjointness conditions is performed systematically by compilers, in which case it is reasonable to rely on such information for proving properties of programs.

6   Conclusion

We have used the framework of abstract interpretation to develop a sound proof system to reason about Sequoia programs, and to provide sufficient conditions for the existence of certificate translators. Then, we have instantiated these results to common optimizations described in [12].

There are several directions for future work. First, it would be of interest to investigate whether our results hold for a relaxed semantics of Sequoia programs, allowing benign data races, where parallel subtasks are allowed to modify the same variables, with the condition that they do it in an identical manner. This notion of benign data races [13] is also closely related to non-strict and-parallelism, as studied in [9]. Second, we intend to investigate certificate translation in the context of parallelizing compilers. Finally, it would be interesting to see how separation logic compares with our work. In particular, if we can replace the region analysis with classical separation logic [18] or permission-accounting separation logic [4].

References

1. Alpern, B., Carter, L., Ferrante, J.: Modeling parallel computers as memory hierarchies. In: Proc. Programming Models for Massively Parallel Computers (1993)
2. Barthe, G., Grégoire, B., Kunz, C., Rezk, T.: Certificate translation for optimizing compilers. In: Yi, K. (ed.) SAS 2006. LNCS, vol. 4134, pp. 301–317. Springer, Heidelberg (2006)

3. Barthe, G., Kunz, C.: Certificate translation in abstract interpretation. In: Drossopoulou, S. (ed.) ESOP 2008. LNCS, vol. 4960, pp. 368–382. Springer, Heidelberg (2008)

4. Bornat, R., O'Hearn, P.W., Calcagno, C., Parkinson, M.: Permission accounting in separation logic. In: Principles of Programming Languages, pp. 259–270. ACM Press, New York (2005)

5. Cousot, P., Cousot, R.: Abstract interpretation: a unified lattice model for static analysis of programs by construction or approximation of fixpoints. In: Principles of Programming Languages, pp. 238–252 (1977)

6. Cousot, P., Cousot, R.: Systematic design of program analysis frameworks. In: Principles of Programming Languages, pp. 269–282 (1979)

7. Dally, W.J., Labonte, F., Das, A., Hanrahan, P., Ho Ahn, J., Gummaraju, J., Erez, M., Jayasena, N., Buck, I., Knight, T.J., Kapasi, U.J.: Merrimac: Supercomputing with streams. In: Conference on Supercomputing, p. 35. ACM, New York (2003)

8. Fatahalian, K., Horn, D.R., Knight, T.J., Leem, L., Houston, M., Park, J.Y., Erez, M., Ren, M., Aiken, A., Dally, W.J., Hanrahan, P.: Sequoia: programming the memory hierarchy. In: Conference on Supercomputing, p. 83. ACM Press, New York (2006)

9. Hermenegildo, M.V., Rossi, F.: Strict and nonstrict independent and-parallelism in logic programs: Correctness, efficiency, and compile-time conditions. J. Log. Program. 22(1), 1–45 (1995)

10. Houston, M., Young Park, J., Ren, M., Knight, T., Fatahalian, K., Aiken, A., Dally, W.J., Hanrahan, P.: A Portable Runtime Interface For Multi-Level Memory Hierarchies. In: Scott, M.L. (ed.) PPOPP, ACM, New York (2008)

11. Kapasi, U.J., Rixner, S., Dally, W.J., Khailany, B., Ho Ahn, J., Mattson, P.R., Owens, J.D.: Programmable stream processors. IEEE Computer 36(8), 54–62 (2003)

12. Knight, T.J., Young Park, J., Ren, M., Houston, M., Erez, M., Fatahalian, K., Aiken, A., Dally, W.J., Hanrahan, P.: Compilation for explicitly managed memory hierarchies. In: Yelick, K.A., Mellor-Crummey, J.M. (eds.) PPOPP, pp. 226–236. ACM, New York (2007)

13. Narayanasamy, S., Wang, Z., Tigani, J., Edwards, A., Calder, B.: Automatically classifying benign and harmful data races using replay analysis. In: Ferrante, J., McKinley, K.S. (eds.) PLDI, pp. 22–31. ACM, New York (2007)

14. Necula, G.C.: Proof-carrying code. In: Principles of Programming Languages, New York, NY, USA, pp. 106–119. ACM Press, New York (1997)

15. Necula, G.C., Lee, P.: Safe kernel extensions without run-time checking. In: Operating Systems Design and Implementation, Seattle, WA, October 1996, pp. 229–243. USENIX Assoc. (1996)

16. O'Hearn, P.W.: Resources, concurrency and local reasoning. Theoretical Computer Science 375(1-3), 271–307 (2007)

17. Owicki, S., Gries, D.: An axiomatic proof technique for parallel programs. Acta Informatica Journal 6, 319–340 (1975)

18. Reynolds, J.C.: Separation logic: A logic for shared mutable data structures. In: Logic in Computer Science, Copenhagen, Denmark, July 2002. IEEE Computer Society, Los Alamitos (2002)

The Complexity of Coverage*

Krishnendu Chatterjee[1], Luca de Alfaro[1], and Rupak Majumdar[2]

[1] CE, University of California, Santa Cruz, USA
[2] CS, University of California, Los Angeles, USA
c_krish@eecs.berkeley.edu, luca@soe.ucsc.edu, rupak@cs.ucla.edu

Abstract. We study the problem of generating a test sequence that achieves maximal coverage for a reactive system under test. We formulate the problem as a repeated game between the tester and the system, where the system state space is partitioned according to some coverage criterion and the objective of the tester is to maximize the set of partitions (or coverage goals) visited during the game. We show the complexity of the maximal coverage problem for non-deterministic systems is PSPACE-complete, but is NP-complete for deterministic systems. For the special case of non-deterministic systems with a re-initializing "reset" action, which represent running a new test input on a re-initialized system, we show that the complexity is coNP-complete. Our proof technique for reset games uses randomized testing strategies that circumvent the exponentially large memory requirement of deterministic testing strategies.

1 Introduction

Code coverage is a common metric in software and hardware testing that measures the degree to which an implementation has been tested with respect to some criterion. In its simplest form, one starts with a model of the program, and a partition of the behaviors of the model into *coverage goals* [3]. A *test* is a sequence of inputs that determines a behavior of the program. The aim of testing is to explore as many coverage goals as possible, ideally as quickly as possible. In this paper, we give complexity results for several coverage problems. The problems are very basic in nature: they consist in deciding whether a certain level of coverage can be attained in a given system.

Finite-state directed graphs have been used as program models for test generation of reactive systems for a long time (see [15,7] for surveys). A coverage goal is a partition of the states of the graph, and a test is a sequence of labels that determine a path in the graph. The maximal coverage test generation problem is to hit as many partitions as possible. In this paper, we show that the maximal coverage problem becomes NP-complete for graphs with partitions. We also distinguish between *system complexity* (the complexity of the problem in terms of the size of the graph) and the *coverage complexity* (the complexity of the problem in terms of the number of coverage goals). Then, the problem is NLOGSPACE in the size of the graph (but that algorithm uses space polynomial in the number of partitions).

We consider the special case where the graph has a special "reset" action that takes it back to the initial state. This corresponds in a testing setting to the case where the

---

* This research was supported in part by the NSF grants CCR-0132780 and CNS-0720884.

system can be re-initialized before running a test (we refer to this special class of graphs as *re-initializable graphs*). In this case, the maximal coverage problem can be solved in polynomial time for graphs with partitions.

Directed graphs form a convenient representation for deterministic systems, in which all the choices are under the control of the tester. Testing of non-deterministic systems in which certain actions are controllable (under the control of the tester) and other actions are uncontrollable lead to *game graphs* [14]. A game graph is a directed labeled graph where the nodes are partitioned into tester-nodes and system-nodes, and while the tester can choose the next input at a tester node, the system non-deterministically chooses the next state at a system node. Then, the test generation problem is to generate a test set that achieves maximal coverage no matter how the system moves. For general game graphs, we show the complexity of the maximal coverage problem is PSPACE-complete. However, there is an algorithm that runs in time linear in the size of the game graph but exponential in the number of coverage goals. Again, the re-initializability assumption reduces the complexity of coverage: in case there is a re-initialization strategy of the tester from any system state, the maximal coverage problem for games is coNP-complete. Dually, we show that the problem of whether it is possible to win a safety game while visiting fewer than a specified number of partitions is NP-complete.

Finally, we consider the coverage problem in bounded time, consisting in checking whether a specified number of partitions can be visited in a specified number of steps. We show that the problem is NP-complete for graphs and re-initializable graphs, and is PSPACE-complete for game graphs.

In summary, our main contributions can be enumerated as follows (Table 1 gives a summary of the complexity results).

1. *Graphs and re-initializable graphs.* We show the maximal coverage problem is NP-complete for graphs, and can be solved in polynomial time for re-initializable graphs. In contrast, the coverage problem in bounded time is NP-complete for both graphs and re-initializable graphs.
2. *Game graphs and re-initializable game graphs.* The maximal coverage problem is PSPACE-complete for game graphs, and for the special class of re-initializable game graphs the problem is coNP-complete. The coverage in bounded time problem is PSPACE-complete for game graphs, and for re-initializable game graphs the problem is both NP-hard and coNP-hard, and the problem can be solved in PSPACE.

Optimization problems arising out of test generation have been studied before in the context of both graphs and games [1,10,14,6]. However, to the best of our knowledge, the complexities of the coverage problems studied here have escaped attention so far.

While we develop our theory for the finite-state, discrete case, we can derive similar results for more general models, such as those incorporating incomplete information (the tester can only observe part of the system state) or timing. For timed systems modeled as timed automata, the maximal coverage problem is PSPACE-complete. For timed games as well as for (finite state) game graphs with incomplete information, the maximal coverage problem becomes EXPTIME-complete.

Table 1. The complexity of coverage

	Graphs	Recurrent Graphs	Game Graphs	Recurrent Game Graphs
Maximal Coverage	NP-complete	PTIME	PSPACE-complete	coNP-complete
Coverage in Bounded time	NP-complete	NP-complete	PSPACE-complete	NP-hard and coNP-hard in PSPACE

2 Definitions

In this section we define *labeled graphs* and *labeled games*, and then define the two decision problems of coverage, namely, *maximal coverage* problem and *coverage with bounded time* problem. We start with definition of graphs and games. To simplify the notation in subsequent arguments, it is convenient to define state-space partitions via labeling functions from states to predicates; the (single) predicate associated with a state indicates the partition to which the state belongs.

Definition 1 (Labeled graphs). *A labeled graph $\mathcal{G} = ((V, E), v_{in}, \mathsf{AP}, \mathcal{L})$ consists of the following component:*

1. *a finite directed graph with vertex set V and edge set E;*
2. *the initial vertex v_{in};*
3. *a finite set of atomic propositions AP; and*
4. *a labeling (or a partition) function $\mathcal{L} : V \to \mathsf{AP}$ that assigns to each vertex v, the atomic proposition $\mathcal{L}(v) \in \mathsf{AP}$ true at v.*

For technical convenience we will assume that for all vertices $v \in V$, there exists $u \in V$ such that $(v, u) \in E$, i.e., each vertex has at least one out-going edge.

Labeling and partition of vertex set. Given a labeled graph $\mathcal{G} = ((V, E), v_{in}, \mathsf{AP}, \mathcal{L})$, the atomic propositions and the labeling (or the partition) function gives a partition of the vertex set V. Let $\mathsf{AP} = \{p_1, p_2, \ldots, p_\ell\}$, and for $1 \le i \le \ell$, let $V^i = \{v \in V \mid \mathcal{L}(v) = p_i\}$. Then $(V^1, V^2, \ldots, V^\ell)$ gives a partition of the vertex set V.

Paths in graphs and reachability. Given a labeled graph $\mathcal{G}$, a *path* ω in $\mathcal{G}$ is an infinite sequence of vertices $\langle v_0, v_1, v_2 \ldots \rangle$ starting from the initial vertex v_{in} (i.e., $v_0 = v_{in}$) such that for all $i \ge 0$ we have $(v_i, v_{i+1}) \in E$. A vertex v_i is reachable from v_{in} if there is a path $\omega = \langle v_0, v_1, v_2 \ldots \rangle$ in $\mathcal{G}$ and $j \ge 0$ such that the vertex v_j in ω is the vertex v_i.

Definition 2 (Labeled game graphs). *A labeled game graph $\mathcal{G} = ((V, E), (V_1, V_2), v_{in}, \mathsf{AP}, \mathcal{L})$ consists of the components of a labeled graph along with a partition of the finite vertex set V into (V_1, V_2). The vertices in V_1 are player 1 vertices where player 1 chooses outgoing edges, and analogously, the vertices in V_2 are player 2 vertices where player 2 chooses outgoing edges. Again for technical convenience we will assume that for all vertices $v \in V$, there exists $u \in V$ such that $(v, u) \in E$, i.e., each vertex has at least one out-going edge.*

Plays and strategies in games. A *play* in a game graph is a path in the underlying graph of the game. A strategy for a player in a game is a recipe to specify how to extend the prefix of a play. Formally, a strategy π_1 for player 1 is a function $\pi_1 : V^* \cdot V_1 \to V$ that takes a finite sequence of vertices $w \cdot v \in V^* \cdot V_1$ ending in a player 1 vertex v ($w \cdot v$ represents the history of the play so far), and specifies the next vertex $\pi_1(w \cdot v)$ by choosing an out-going edge from v (i.e., $(v, \pi_1(w \cdot v)) \in E$). A strategy $\pi_2 : V^* \cdot V_2 \to V$ is defined analogously. We denote by Π_1 and Π_2 the set of all strategies for player 1 and player 2, respectively. Given strategies π_1 and π_2 for player 1 and player 2, there is a unique play (or a path) $\omega(v_{in}, \pi_1, \pi_2) = \langle v_0, v_1, v_2, \ldots \rangle$ such that (a) $v_0 = v_{in}$; (b) for all $i \geq 0$, if $v_i \in V_1$, then $\pi_1(v_0 \cdot v_1 \ldots \cdot v_i) = v_{i+1}$; and if $v_i \in V_2$, then $\pi_2(v_0 \cdot v_1 \ldots \cdot v_i) = v_{i+1}$.

Controllably recurrent graphs and games. Along with general labeled graphs and games, we will also consider graphs and games that are *controllably recurrent*. A labeled graph $\mathcal{G}$ is *controllably recurrent* if for every vertex v_i that is reachable from v_{in}, there is a path starting from v_i that reaches v_{in}. A labeled game graph $\mathcal{G}$ is *controllably recurrent* if for every vertex v_i that is reachable from v_{in} in the underlying graph, there is a strategy π_1 for player 1 such that against all player 2 strategies π_2, the path starting from v_i given the strategies π_1 and π_2 reaches v_{in}. Controllable recurrence models the natural requirement that systems under test are *re-initializable*, that is, from any reachable state of the system, there is always a way to bring the system back to its initial state no matter how the system behaves.

The maximal coverage problem. The *maximal coverage problem* asks whether at least m different propositions can be visited, in other words, it asks whether at least m different partitions of the vertex set (given by the proposition labeling) can be visited. We now define the problem formally for graphs and games. Given a path $\omega = \langle v_0, v_1, v_2, \ldots \rangle$, let $\mathcal{L}(\omega) = \bigcup_{i \geq 0} \mathcal{L}(v_i)$ be the set of propositions that appear in ω. Given a labeled graph $\mathcal{G}$ and $0 \leq m \leq |AP|$, the maximal coverage problem asks whether there is path ω such that $|\mathcal{L}(\omega)| \geq m$. Given a labeled game graph $\mathcal{G}$ and $0 \leq m \leq |AP|$, the maximal coverage problem asks whether player 1 can ensure that at least m propositions are visited, i.e., whether

$$\max_{\pi_1 \in \Pi_1} \min_{\pi_2 \in \Pi_2} |\mathcal{L}(\omega(v_{in}, \pi_1, \pi_2))| \geq m.$$

It may be noted that $\max_{\pi_1 \in \Pi_1} \min_{\pi_2 \in \Pi_2} |\mathcal{L}(\omega(v_{in}, \pi_1, \pi_2))| \geq m$ iff there exists a player 1 strategy π_1^* such that for all player 2 strategies π_2^* we have $|\mathcal{L}(\omega(v_{in}, \pi_1^*, \pi_2^*))| \geq m$.

The coverage with bounded time problem. The *coverage with bounded time problem* asks whether at least m different propositions can be visited within k-steps, that is, whether at least m different partitions of the vertex set can be visited within k-steps. We now define the problem formally for graphs and games. Given a path $\omega = \langle v_0, v_1, v_2, \ldots \rangle$ and $k \geq 0$, we denote by $\omega \upharpoonright k$ the prefix of the path of length $k + 1$, i.e., $\omega \upharpoonright k = \langle v_0, v_1, \ldots, v_k \rangle$. Given a path $\omega = \langle v_0, v_1, v_2, \ldots \rangle$ and $k \geq 0$, we denote by $\mathcal{L}(\omega \upharpoonright k) = \bigcup_{0 \leq i \leq k} \mathcal{L}(v_i)$. Given a labeled graph $\mathcal{G}$ and $0 \leq m \leq |AP|$ and $k \geq 0$, the coverage with bounded time problem asks whether there is path ω such that

$|\mathcal{L}(\omega \restriction k)| \geq m$. Given a labeled game graph $\mathcal{G}$ and $0 \leq m \leq |\mathsf{AP}|$, the maximal coverage problem asks whether player 1 can ensure that at least m propositions are visited within k-steps, i.e., whether

$$\max_{\pi_1 \in \Pi_1} \min_{\pi_2 \in \Pi_2} |\mathcal{L}(\omega(v_{in}, \pi_1, \pi_2) \restriction k)| \geq m.$$

It may be noted that $\max_{\pi_1 \in \Pi_1} \min_{\pi_2 \in \Pi_2} |\mathcal{L}(\omega(v_{in}, \pi_1, \pi_2) \restriction k)| \geq m$ iff there exists a player 1 strategy π_1^* such that for all player 2 strategies π_2^* we have $|\mathcal{L}(\omega(v_{in}, \pi_1^*, \pi_2^*) \restriction k)| \geq m$.

2.1 Examples

System-tester game. A *system* $\mathcal{S} = (Q, \Sigma, q_{in}, \Delta, \mathsf{AP}, \mathcal{L})$ consists of the following components:

- a finite set Q of states with the starting state q_{in};
- a finite alphabet Σ of input letters;
- a transition relation $\Delta \subseteq Q \times \Sigma \times Q$; and
- a finite set of atomic propositions AP and a labeling function $\mathcal{L}$ that assigns to each state q the atomic proposition $\mathcal{L}(q)$ true at q.

We consider *total* systems such that for all $q \in Q$ and $\sigma \in \Sigma$, there exists $q' \in Q$ such that $(q, \sigma, q') \in \Delta$. A system is *deterministic* if for all $q \in Q$ and $\sigma \in \Sigma$, there exists exactly one q' such that $(q, \sigma, q') \in \Delta$. The tester selects an input letter at every stage and the system resolves the non-determinism in transition to choose the successor state. The goal of the tester is to visit as many different propositions as possible. The interaction between the system and the tester can be reduced to a labeled game graph $\mathcal{G} = ((V, E), (V_1, V_2), v_{in}, \mathsf{AP}, \mathcal{L}')$ as follows:

- *Vertices and partition.* $V = Q \cup (Q \times \Sigma)$; $V_1 = Q$ and $V_2 = Q \times \Sigma$; and $v_{in} = q_{in}$.
- *Edges.* $E = \{(q, (q, \sigma)) \mid q \in Q, \sigma \in \Sigma\} \cup \{((q, \sigma), q') \mid (q, \sigma, q') \in \Delta\}$.
- *Labeling.* $\mathcal{L}'(q) = \mathcal{L}(q)$ and $\mathcal{L}'((q, \sigma)) = \mathcal{L}'(q)$.

The coverage question for game between tester and system can be answered by answering the question in the game graph. Also observe that if the system is deterministic, then for all player 2 vertices in the game graph, there is exactly one out-going edge, and hence the game can be reduced to a labeled graph. A system consists of a set of variables, and a state represents the valuation of variables. If a subset of variable valuations is of interest for the coverage criteria, then the partition of the state space of the system is obtained through the valuations of variables of interest, and the desired partition of the state space by the valuations of interest is captured by the labeling of the atomic propositions. In this paper we will present all the results for the labeled graph and game model. All the upper bounds we provide follow also for the game between tester and system. All the lower bounds we present can also be easily adapted to the model of the game between system and tester.

Graph Coverage Criteria. Graph-based coverage criteria, such as node or transition coverage on the control-flow graph or on a finite-state abstract model, are used commonly in software testing [3]. Such coverage criteria reduce to our notion of testing on labeled graphs. Intuitively, we define a *program state graph* where each node represents a program state (location as well as valuations to all variables) or an abstraction (e.g., a predicate abstraction [5]), and each edge (s, t) represents a program operation that takes a state s to the state t. For node coverage, we label a node with the value of the program location. The coverage goal is to maximize the number of visited locations. Other graph-based coverage criteria can be expressed by adding auxiliary state. For example, to capture def-use coverage (for each pair of definition point d and use point u of a variable, find a test such that the definition d is used at u), one can add auxiliary state variables that track the point of current definition of a variable, and label each node of the program state graph with a definition-use pair for each variable such that the current definition of the variable is used by the incoming operation to the node. The coverage goal is again to maximize the number of visited labels.

3 The Complexity of Maximal Coverage Problems

In this section we study the complexity of the maximal coverage problem. In subsection 3.1 we study the complexity for graphs, and in subsection 3.2 we study the complexity for game graphs.

3.1 Graphs

We first show that the maximal coverage problem for labeled graphs is NP-complete.

Theorem 1. *The maximal coverage problem for labeled graphs is NP-complete.*

Proof. The proof consists of two parts.

1. *In NP.* The maximal coverage problem is in NP can be proved as follows. Given a labeled game graph $\mathcal{G}$, let $n = |V|$. We show first that if there is a path ω in $\mathcal{G}$ such that $|\mathcal{L}(\omega)| \geq m$, then there is a path ω' in $\mathcal{G}$ such that $|\mathcal{L}(\omega' \upharpoonright (m \cdot n))| \geq m$, where $m \cdot n$ denotes the product of m and n. If ω visits at least m propositions, and there is a cycle in ω that does not visit a new proposition that is already visited in the prefix, then the cycle segment can be removed from ω and still the resulting path visits m propositions. Hence if the answer to the maximal coverage problem is "Yes", then there is a path ω' of length at most $m \cdot n$ that is a witness to the "Yes" answer. Since $m \leq |\mathsf{AP}|$, it follows that the problem is in NP.

2. *NP-hardness.* Now we show that the maximal coverage problem is NP-hard, and we present a reduction from the SAT-problem. Consider a SAT formula Φ, and let $X = \{x_1, x_2, \ldots, x_n\}$ be the set of variables and $C_1, C_2, \ldots, C_m$ be the set of clauses. For a variable $x_j \in X$, let

   (a) $\mathrm{T}(x_j) = \{\ell \mid x_j \in C_\ell\}$ be the set of indices of the set of clauses C_ℓ that is satisfied if x_j is set to be true; and

   (b) $\mathrm{F}(x_j) = \{\ell \mid \overline{x}_j \in C_\ell\}$ be the set of indices of the set of clauses C_ℓ that is satisfied if x_j is set to be false.

Without loss of generality, we assume that $\text{T}(x_j)$ and $\text{F}(x_j)$ are non-empty for all $1 \le j \le n$ (this is because, for example, if $\text{F}(x_j) = \emptyset$, then we can set x_j to be true and reduce the problem where the variable x_j is not present). For a finite set $F \subseteq \mathbb{N}$ of natural numbers, let $\max(F)$ and $\min(F)$ denote the maximum and minimum number of F, respectively. For an element $f \in F$ that is not the maximum element let $\text{next}(f, F)$ denote the next highest element to f that belongs to F; i.e., (a) $\text{next}(f, F) \in F$; (b) $f < \text{next}(f, F)$; and (c) if $j \in F$ and $f < j$, then $\text{next}(f, F) \le j$. We construct a labeled graph $\mathcal{G}^\Phi$ as follows. We first present an intuitive description: there are vertices named $x_1, x_2, \ldots, x_n, x_{n+1}$, and all of them are labeled by a single proposition. The vertex x_{n+1} is an absorbing vertex (vertex with a self-loop only), and all other x_i vertex has two successors. The starting vertex is x_1. In every vertex x_i given the right choice we visit in a line a set of vertices that are labeled by clauses that are true if x_i is true; and given the left choice we visit in a line a set of vertices that are labeled by clauses that are true if x_i is false; and then we move to vertex x_{i+1}. We now formally describe every component of the labeled graph $\mathcal{G}^\Phi = ((V^\Phi, E^\Phi), v_{in}^\Phi, \text{AP}^\Phi, \mathcal{L}^\Phi)$.

(a) The set of vertices is

$$V^\Phi = \{x_i \mid 1 \le i \le n+1\}$$
$$\cup \{x_{j,i} \mid 1 \le j \le n, i \in \text{T}(x_j)\} \cup \{\overline{x}_{j,i} \mid 1 \le j \le n, i \in \text{F}(x_j)\}.$$

There is a vertex for every variable, and a vertex x_{n+1}. There is a vertex $x_{j,i}$ iff $C_i \in \text{T}(x_j)$, and there is a vertex $\overline{x}_{j,i}$ iff $C_i \in \text{F}(x_j)$,

(b) The set of edges is

$$E^\Phi = \{(x_{n+1}, x_{n+1})\}$$
$$\cup \{(x_{j,\max(\text{T}(x_j))}, x_{j+1}), (\overline{x}_{j,\max(\text{F}(x_j))}, x_{j+1}) \mid 1 \le j \le n\}$$
$$\cup \{(x_j, x_{j,\min(\text{T}(x_j))}), (x_j, \overline{x}_{j,\min(\text{F}(x_j))}) \mid 1 \le j \le n\}$$
$$\cup \{(x_{j,i}, x_{j,\text{next}(i,\text{T}(x_j))}) \mid 1 \le j \le n, i < \max(\text{T}(x_j))\}$$
$$\cup \{(\overline{x}_{j,i}, \overline{x}_{j,\text{next}(i,\text{F}(x_j))}) \mid 1 \le j \le n, i < \max(\text{F}(x_j))\}.$$

We now explain the role if each set of edges. The first edge is the self-loop at x_{n+1}. The second set of edges specifies that from $x_{j,\max(\text{T}(x_j))}$ the next vertex is x_{j+1} and similarly, from $\overline{x}_{j,\max(\text{F}(x_j))}$ the next vertex is again x_{j+1}. The third set of edges specifies that from x_j there are two successors that are $x_{j,i}$ and $\overline{x}_{j,i'}$, where $i = \min(\text{T}(x_j))$ and $i' = \min(\text{F}(x_j))$. The final sets of edges specifies (a) to move in a line from $x_{j,\min(\text{T}(x_j))}$ to visit the clauses that are satisfied by setting x_j as true, and (b) to move in a line from $\overline{x}_{j,\min(\text{F}(x_j))}$ to visit the clauses that are satisfied by setting x_j as false. Fig 1 gives a pictorial view of the reduction.

(c) The initial vertex is $v_{in}^\Phi = x_1$.

(d) $\text{AP}^\Phi = \{C_1, C_2, \ldots, C_m, X\}$, i.e., there is a proposition C_i for each clause C_i and there is a proposition X for all variables;

(e) $\mathcal{L}^\Phi(x_j) = X$; i.e., every variable vertex is labeled by the proposition X; and we have $\mathcal{L}^\Phi(x_{j,i}) = C_i$ and $\mathcal{L}^\Phi(\overline{x}_{j,i}) = C_i$, i.e., each vertex $x_{j,i}$ and $\overline{x}_{j,i}$ is labeled by the corresponding clause that is indexed.

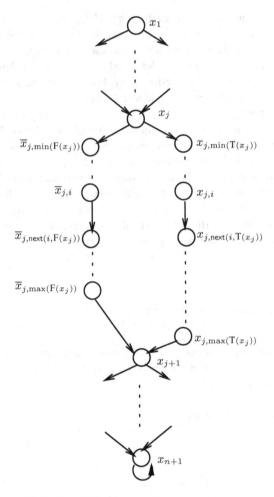

Fig. 1. The NP-hardness reduction in picture

The number of vertices in $\mathcal{G}^{\Phi}$ is $O(n \cdot m)$, and the reduction is polynomial in Φ. In this graph the maximal number of propositions visited is exactly equal to the maximal number of satisfiable clauses plus 1 (since along with the propositions for clauses, the proposition X for all variables is always visited). The proof of the above claim is as follows. Given a path ω in $\mathcal{G}^{\Phi}$ we construct an assignment A for the variables as follows: if the choice at a vertex x_j is $x_{j,\min(T(x_j))}$, then we set x_j as true in A, else we set x_j as false. Hence if a path in $\mathcal{G}^{\Phi}$ visits a set $P \subseteq AP^{\Phi}$ of r propositions, then the assignment A satisfies $r-1$ clauses (namely, $P \setminus \{X\}$). Conversely, given an assignment A of the variables, we construct a path ω^A in $\mathcal{G}^{\Phi}$ as follows: if x_j is true in the assignment A, then the path ω^A chooses $x_{j,\min(T(x_j))}$ at x_j, otherwise, it chooses $\overline{x}_{j,\min(F(x_j))}$ at x_j. If A satisfies a set Q of $r-1$ clauses, then ω^A visits $r+1$ propositions (namely, the set $Q \cup \{X\}$ of propositions). Hence

Φ is satisfiable iff the answer to the maximal coverage problem with input $\mathcal{G}^\Phi$ and $m + 1$ is true.

The desired result follows.   ∎

We note that from the proof of Theorem 1 it follows that the MAX-SAT problem (i.e., computing the maximal number of clauses satisfiable for a SAT formula) can be reduced to the problem of computing the exact number for the maximal coverage problem. From hardness of approximation of the MAX-SAT problem [4], it follows that the maximal coverage problem for labeled graphs is hard to approximate.

Theorem 2. *The maximal coverage problem for labeled graphs that are controllably recurrent can be decided in PTIME.*

Proof. To solve the maximal coverage problem for labeled graphs that are controllably recurrent, we compute the maximal strongly connected component C that v_{in} belongs to. Since the graph is controllably recurrent, all vertices that are reachable from v_{in} belong to C. Hence the answer to the maximal coverage problem is "Yes" iff $|\bigcup_{v \in C} \mathcal{L}(v)| \geq m$. The result follows.   ∎

3.2   Game Graphs

Theorem 3. *The maximal coverage problem for labeled game graphs is PSPACE-complete.*

Proof. The proof consists of two parts.

1. *In PSPACE.* We argue that the maximal coverage problem for labeled game graphs can be reduced to the coverage in bounded time problem. The reason is as follows: in a labeled game graph with n vertices, if player 1 can visit m propositions, then player 1 can visit m propositions within at most $m \cdot n$ steps; because player 1 can always play a strategy from the current position that visits a new proposition that is not visited and never needs to go through a cycle without visiting a new proposition unless the maximal coverage is achieved. Hence it follows that the maximal coverage problem for games reduces to the coverage in bounded time problem. The PSPACE inclusion will follow from the result of Theorem 7 where we show that the coverage in bounded time problem is in PSPACE.

2. *PSPACE-hardness.* The maximal coverage problem for game graphs is PSPACE-complete, even if the underlying graph is strongly connected. The proof is a reduction from QBF (truth of quantified boolean formulas) that is known to be PSPACE-complete [12], and it is a modification of the reduction of Theorem 1. Consider a QBF formula

$$\Phi = \exists x_1.\forall x_2.\exists x_3 \dots \exists x_n.C_1 \wedge C_2 \wedge \dots C_m;$$

defined on the set $X = \{x_1, x_2, \dots, x_n\}$ of variables, and $C_1, C_2, \dots, C_m$ are the clauses of the formula. We apply the reduction of Theorem 1 with the following modification to obtain the labeled game graph $\mathcal{G}^\Phi$: the partition (V_1^Φ, V_2^Φ) of V^Φ is as follows. For a variable x_j if the quantifier before x_j is existential, then $x_j \in V_1^\Phi$ (i.e., for existentially quantified variable, player 1 chooses the out-going edges denoting whether to set the variable true or false); and for a variable x_j if the quantifier before x_j is universal, then $x_j \in V_2^\Phi$ (i.e., for universally quantified variable, the opposing player 2 chooses the out-going edges denoting whether to set the variable true or false). The vertex x_{n+1} is a player 2 vertex, and all other vertex has an single out-going edges and can be player 1 vertex. Given this game graph we have Φ is true iff player 1 can ensure that all the propositions can be visited in $\mathcal{G}^\Phi$. Formally, let Π_1^Φ and Π_2^Φ denote the set of all strategies for player 1 and player 2, respectively, in $\mathcal{G}^\Phi$. Then Φ is true iff $\max_{\pi_1 \in \Pi_1^\Phi} \min_{\pi_2 \in \Pi_2^\Phi} |\mathcal{L}^\Phi(\omega(x_1, \pi_1, \pi_2))| \geq m + 1$. Observe that since x_{n+1} is a player 2 vertex if we add an edge from x_{n+1} to x_1, player 2 will never choose the edge x_{n+1} to x_1 (since the objective for player 2 is to minimize the coverage). However, adding the edge from x_{n+1} to x_1 makes the underlying graph strongly connected (i.e., the underlying graph of the game graph becomes controllably recurrent; but player 1 does not have a strategy to ensure that x_1 is reached, so the game is not controllably recurrent).

The desired result follows.   ∎

Complexity of maximal coverage in controllably recurrent games. We will now consider maximal coverage in controllably recurrent games. Our analysis will use fixing memoryless *randomized* strategy for player 1, and fixing a memoryless randomized strategy in labeled game graph we get a labeled Markov decision process (MDP). A labeled MDP consists of the same components as a labeled game graph, and for vertices in V_1 (which are randomized vertices in the MDP) the successors are chosen uniformly at random (i.e., player 1 does not have a proper choice of the successor but chooses all of them uniformly at random). Given a labeled game graph $\mathcal{G} = ((V, E), (V_1, V_2), v_{in}, \mathsf{AP}, \mathcal{L})$ we denote by $\mathsf{Unif}(\mathcal{G})$ the MDP interpretation of $\mathcal{G}$ where player 1 vertices chooses all successors uniformly at random. An *end-component* in $\mathsf{Unif}(G)$ is a set U of vertices such that (i) U is strongly connected and (ii) U is player 1 *closed*, i.e., for all $u \in U \cap V_1$, for all u' such that $(u, u') \in E$ we have $u' \in U$ (in other words, for all player 1 vertices, all the out-going edges are contained in U).

Lemma 1. *Let $\mathcal{G}$ be a labeled game graph that is controllably recurrent and let $\mathsf{Unif}(\mathcal{G})$ be the MDP interpretation of $\mathcal{G}$. Then the following assertions hold.*

1. *Let U be an end-component in $\mathsf{Unif}(\mathcal{G})$ with $v_{in} \in U$. Then $\max_{\pi_1 \in \Pi_1} \min_{\pi_2 \in \Pi_2} |\mathcal{L}(\omega(v_{in}, \pi_1, \pi_2))| \leq |\bigcup_{u \in U} \mathcal{L}(u)|$.*
2. *There exists an end-component $U \in \mathsf{Unif}(\mathcal{G})$ with $v_{in} \in U$ such that $|\bigcup_{u \in U} \mathcal{L}(u)| \leq \max_{\pi_1 \in \Pi_1} \min_{\pi_2 \in \Pi_2} |\mathcal{L}(\omega(v_{in}, \pi_1, \pi_2))|$.*

Proof. We prove both the claims below.

1. If U is an end-component in $\mathsf{Unif}(\mathcal{G})$, then consider a memoryless strategy π_2^* for player 2, that for all vertices $u \in U \cap V_2$, chooses a successor $u' \in U$ (such a successor exists since U is strongly connected). Since U is player 1 closed (i.e., for all player 1 out-going edges from U, the end-point is in U), it follows that for all strategies of player 1, given the strategy π_2^* for player 2, the vertices visited in a play is contained in U. The desired result follows.

2. An optimal strategy π_1^* for player 1 in $\mathcal{G}$ is as follows:

   (a) Let $Z_0 = \{v \in V \mid \mathcal{L}(v) = \mathcal{L}(v_{in})\}$ and $i = 0$;

   (b) At iteration i, let Z_i represent the vertices corresponding to the set of propositions already visited. At iteration i, player 1 plays a strategy to reach a vertex in $V \setminus Z_i$ (if such a strategy exists), and then reaches back v_{in} (a strategy to reach back v_{in} always exists since the game is controllably recurrent).

   (c) If a new proposition p_i is visited at iteration i, then let $Z_{i+1} = Z_i \cup \{v \in V \mid \mathcal{L}(v) = p_i\}$. Goto step (b) for $i + 1$ iteration with Z_{i+1}. If no vertex in $V \setminus Z_i$ can be reached, then stop.

   The strategy π_1^* is optimal, and let the above iteration stop with $Z_i = Z^*$. Let $X = V \setminus Z^*$, and let X^* be the set of vertices such that player 1 can reach X. Let $U^* = V \setminus X^*$. Then $v_{in} \in U^*$ and player 2 can ensure that from v_{in} the game can be confined to U^*. Hence the following conditions must hold: (a) for all $u \in U^* \cap V_2$, there exists $u' \in U^*$ such that $(u, u') \in E$; and (b) for all $u \in U^* \cap V_1$, for all $u' \in V$ such that $(u, u') \in E$ we have $u' \in U^*$. Consider the sub-graph $\mathcal{G}'$ where player 2 restricts itself to edges only in U^*. A bottom maximal strongly connected component $U \subseteq U^*$ in the sub-graph is an end-component in $\mathsf{Unif}(\mathcal{G})$, and we have

$$\left| \bigcup_{u \in U} \mathcal{L}(u) \right| \leq \left| \bigcup_{u \in U^*} \mathcal{L}(u) \right| \leq \left| \bigcup_{u \in Z^*} \mathcal{L}(u) \right|.$$

It follows that U is a witness end-component to prove the result.

The desired result follows. ∎

Theorem 4. *The maximal coverage problem for labeled game graphs that are controllably recurrent is coNP-complete.*

Proof. We prove the following two claims to establish the result.

1. *In coNP.* The fact that the problem is in coNP can be proved using Lemma 1. Given a labeled game graph $\mathcal{G}$, if the answer to the maximal coverage problem (i.e., whether $\max_{\pi_1 \in \Pi_1} \min_{\pi_2 \in \Pi_2} |\mathcal{L}(\omega(v_{in}, \pi_1, \pi_2))| \geq m$) is NO, then by Lemma 1, there exists an end-component U in $\mathsf{Unif}(\mathcal{G})$ such that $|\bigcup_{u \in U} \mathcal{L}(u)| < m$. The witness end-component U is a polynomial witness and it can be guessed and verified in polynomial time. The verification that U is the correct witness is as follows: we check (a) U is strongly connected; (b) for all $u \in U \cap V_1$ and for all $u' \in V$ such that $(u, u') \in E$ we have $u' \in U$; (c) $v_{in} \in U$; and (d) $|\bigcup_{u \in U} \mathcal{L}(u)| < m$. Hence the result follows.

2. *coNP hardness.* We prove hardness using a reduction from the complement of the *Vertex Cover* problem. Given a graph $G = (V, E)$, a set $U \subseteq V$ is a *vertex cover* if for all edges $e = (u_1, u_2) \in E$ we have either $u_1 \in U$ or $u_2 \in U$. Given a graph G whether there is a vertex cover U of size at most m (i.e., $|U| \leq m$) is NP-complete [8]. We now present a reduction of the complement of the vertex cover problem to the maximal coverage problem in controllably recurrent games. Given a graph $G = (V, E)$ we construct a labeled game graph $\overline{\mathcal{G}}$ as follows. Let the set E of edges be enumerated as $\{e_1, e_2, \ldots, e_\ell\}$, i.e., there are ℓ edges. The labeled game graph $\overline{\mathcal{G}} = ((\overline{V}, \overline{E}), (\overline{V}_1, \overline{V}_2), v_{in}, \mathsf{AP}, \mathcal{L})$ is as follows.

(a) *Vertex set and partition.* The vertex set $\overline{V}$ is as follows:

$$\overline{V} = \{v_{in}\} \cup E \cup \{e_i^j \mid 1 \le i \le \ell, 1 \le j \le 2\}.$$

All vertices in E are player 2 vertices, and the other vertices are player 1 vertices, i.e., $\overline{V}_2 = E$, and $\overline{V}_1 = \overline{V} \setminus \overline{V}_2$.

(b) *Edges.* The set $\overline{E}$ of edges are as follows:

$$\overline{E} = \{(v_{in}, e_j) \mid 1 \le j \le \ell\} \cup \{(e_i, e_i^j) \mid 1 \le i \le \ell, 1 \le j \le 2\}$$
$$\cup \{(e_i^j, v_{in}) \mid 1 \le i \le \ell, 1 \le j \le 2\}.$$

Intuitively, the edges in the game graph are as follows: from the initial vertex v_{in}, player 1 can choose any of the edges $e_i \in E$. For a vertex e_i in $\overline{V}$, player 2 can choose between two vertices e_i^1 and e_i^2 (which will eventually represent the two end-points of the edge e_i). From vertices of the form e_i^1 and e_i^2, for $1 \le i \le \ell$, the next vertex is the initial vertex v_{in}. It follows that from all vertices, the game always comes back to v_{in} and hence we have a controllably recurrent game.

(c) *Propositions and labelling.* AP $= V \cup \{\$ \mid \$ \notin V\}$, i.e., there is a proposition for every vertex in V and a special proposition $\$$. The vertex v_{in} and vertices in E are labeled by the special proposition $\$$, i.e., $\mathcal{L}(v_{in}) = \$$; and for all $e_i \in E$ we have $\mathcal{L}(e_i) = \$$. For a vertex e_i^j, let $e_i = (u_i^1, u_i^2)$, where u_i^1, u_i^2 are vertices in V, then $\mathcal{L}(e_i^1) = u_i^1$ and $\mathcal{L}(e_i^2) = u_i^2$. Note that the above proposition assignment ensures that at every vertex that represents an edge, player 2 has the choices of vertices that form the end-points of the edge.

The following case analysis completes the proof.

- Given a vertex cover U, consider a player 2 strategy, that at a vertex $e_i \in \overline{V}$, choose a successor e_i^j such that $\mathcal{L}(e_i^j) \in U$. The strategy for player 2 ensures that player 1 visits only propositions in $U \cup \{\$\}$, i.e., at most $|U| + 1$ propositions.
- Consider a strategy for player 1 that from v_{in} visits all vertices $e_1, e_2, \ldots, e_\ell$ in order. Consider any counter-strategy for player 2 and let $U \subseteq V$ be the set of propositions other than $\$$ visited. Since all the edges are chosen, it follows that U is a vertex cover. Hence if all vertex cover in G is of size at least m, then player 1 can visit at least $m + 1$ propositions.

Hence there is a vertex cover in G of size at most m if and only if the answer to the maximal coverage problem in $\mathcal{G}$ with $m + 1$ is NO. It follows that the maximal coverage problem in controllably recurrent games is coNP-hard.

The desired result follows. ∎

Complexity of minimal safety games. As a corollary of the proof of Theorem 4 we obtain a complexity result about *minimal safety games*. Given a labeled game graph $\mathcal{G}$ and m, the minimal safety game problem asks, whether there exists a set U such that a player can confine the game in U and U contains at most m propositions. An easy consequence of the hardness proof of Theorem 4 is minimal safety games are NP-hard, and also it is easy to argue that minimal safety games are in NP. Hence we obtain that the minimal safety game problem is NP-complete.

4   The Complexity of Coverage in Bounded Time Problem

In this section we study the complexity of the coverage in bounded time problem. In subsection 4.1 we study the complexity for graphs, and in subsection 4.2 we study the complexity for game graphs.

4.1   Graphs

Theorem 5. *The coverage in bounded time problem for both labeled graphs and controllably recurrent labeled graphs is NP-complete.*

Proof. We prove the completeness result in two parts below.

1. *In NP.* Given a labeled graph with n vertices, if there is a path ω such that $|\mathcal{L}(\omega \upharpoonright k)| \geq m$, then there is path ω' such that $|\mathcal{L}(\omega' \upharpoonright (m \cdot n))| \geq m$. The above claim follows since any cycle that does not visit any new proposition can be omitted. Hence a path of length $j = \min(k, m \cdot n)$ can be guessed and it can be then checked in polynomial time if the path of length j visits at least m propositions.
2. *In NP-hard.* We reduce the *Hamiltonian-path (HAM-PATH)* [8] problem to the coverage in bounded time problem for labeled graphs. Given a directed graph $G = (V, E)$ and an initial vertex v, we consider the labeled graph $\mathcal{G}$ with the directed graph G, with v as the initial vertex and $\mathsf{AP} = V$ and $\mathcal{L}(u) = u$ for all $u \in V$, i.e., each vertex is labeled with a unique proposition. The answer to the coverage in bounded time with $k = n$ and $m = n$, for $n = |V|$ is "YES" iff there is a HAM-PATH in G starting from v.

The desired result follows.   ∎

Complexity in size of the graph. We now argue that the maximal coverage and the coverage in bounded time problem on labeled graphs can be solved in non-deterministic log-space in the size of the graph, and polynomial space in the size of the atomic propositions. Given a labeled graph $\mathcal{G}$, with n vertices, we argued in Theorem 1 that if m propositions can be visited, then there is a path of length at most $m \cdot n$, that visits m propositions. The path of length $m \cdot n$, can be visited, storing the current vertex, and guessing the next vertex, and checking the set of propositions already visited. Hence this can be achieved in non-deterministic log-space in the size of the graph, and polynomial space in the size of the proposition set. A similar argument holds for the coverage in bounded time problem. This gives us the following result.

Theorem 6. *Given a labeled graph $\mathcal{G} = ((V, E), v_{in}, \mathsf{AP}, \mathcal{L})$, the maximal coverage problem and the coverage in bounded time problem can be decided in NLOGSPACE in $|V| + |E|$, and in PSPACE in $|\mathsf{AP}|$.*

4.2   Game Graphs

Theorem 7. *The coverage in bounded time problem for labeled game graphs is PSPACE-complete.*

Proof. We prove the following two cases to prove the result.

1. *PSPACE-hardness*. It follows from the proof of Theorem 3 that the maximal coverage problem for labeled game graphs reduces to the coverage in bounded time problem for labeled game graphs. Since the maximal coverage problem for labeled game graphs is PSPACE-hard (Theorem 3), the result follows.
2. *In PSPACE*. We say that an *exploration game tree* for a labeled game graph is a rooted, labeled tree which represents an unfolding of the graph. Every node α of the tree is labeled with a pair (v, b), where v is a node of the game graph, and $b \subseteq AP$ is the set of propositions that have been visited in a branch leading from the root of the tree to α. The root of the tree is labeled with $(v_{in}, \mathcal{L}(v_{in}))$. A tree with label (v, b) has one descendant for each u with $(v, u) \in E$; the label of the descendant is $(u, b \cup \mathcal{L}(u))$.

   In order to check if m different propositions can be visited within k-steps, the PSPACE algorithm traverses the game tree in depth first order. Each branch is explored up to one of the two following conditions is met: (i) depth k is reached, or (ii) a node is reached, which has the same label as an ancestor in the tree. The bottom nodes, where conditions (i) or (ii) are met, are thus the leaves of the tree. In the course of the traversal, the algorithm computes in bottom-up fashion the *value* of the tree nodes. The value of a leaf node labeled (v, b) is $|b|$. For player-1 nodes, the value is the maximum of the values of the successors; for player-2 nodes, the value is the minimum of the value of the successors. Thus, the value of a tree node α represents the minimum number of propositions that player 1 can ensure are visited, in the course of a play of the game that has followed a path from the root of the tree to α, and that can last at most k steps. The algorithm returns Yes if the value at the root is at least m, and no otherwise.

   To obtain the PSPACE bound, notice that if a node with label (v, b) is an ancestor of a node with label (v', b') in the tree, we have $b \subseteq b'$: thus, along a branch, the set of propositions appearing in the labels increases monotonically. Between two increases, there can be at most $|\mathcal{G}|$ nodes, due to the termination condition (ii). Thus, each branch needs to be traversed at most to depth $1 + |\mathcal{G}| \cdot (|AP| + 1)$, and the process requires only polynomial space.

The result follows.   ∎

Theorem 8. *The coverage in bounded time problem for labeled game graphs that are controllably recurrent is both NP-hard and coNP-hard, and can be decided in PSPACE.*

Proof. It follows from the (PSPACE-inclusion) argument of Theorem 3 that the maximal coverage problem for labeled game graphs that are controllably recurrent can be reduced to the coverage in bounded time problem for labeled game graphs that are controllably recurrent. Hence the coNP-hardness follows from Theorem 4, and the NP-hardness follows from hardness in labeled graphs that are controllably recurrent (Theorem 5). The PSPACE-inclusion follows from the general case of labeled game graphs (Theorem 7).   ∎

Theorem 8 shows that for controllably recurrent game graphs, the coverage in bounded time problem is both NP-hard and coNP-hard, and can be decided in PSPACE. A tight complexity bound remains an open problem.

Complexity in the size of the game. The maximal coverage problem can alternately be solved in time linear in the size of the game graph and exponential in the number of propositions. Given a game graph $\mathcal{G} = ((V, E), (V_1, V_2), v_{in}, \mathsf{AP}, \mathcal{L})$, construct the game graph $\mathcal{G}' = ((V', E'), (V_1', V_2'), v_{in}', \mathsf{AP}, \mathcal{L}')$ where $V' = V \times 2^{\mathsf{AP}}$, $((v, b), (v', b')) \in E'$ iff $(v, v') \in E$ and $b' = b \cup \mathcal{L}(v')$, $V_i' = \{(v, b) \mid v \in V_i\}$ for $i \in \{1, 2\}$, $v_{in}' = (v_{in}, \mathcal{L}(v_{in}))$, and $\mathcal{L}'(v, b) = \mathcal{L}'(v)$. Clearly, the size of the game graph $\mathcal{G}'$ is linear in $\mathcal{G}$ and exponential in AP. Now consider a reachability game on $\mathcal{G}'$ with the goal $\{(v, b) \mid v \in V \text{ and } |b| \geq m\}$. Player-1 wins this game iff the maximal coverage problem is true for $\mathcal{G}$ and m propositions. Since a reachability game can be solved in time linear in the game, the result follows. A similar construction, where we additionally track the length of the game so far, shows that the maximal coverage problem with bounded time can be solved in time linear in the size of the game graph and exponential in the number of propositions.

Theorem 9. *Given a labeled game graph* $\mathcal{G} = ((V, E), (V_1, V_2), v_{in}, \mathsf{AP}, \mathcal{L})$ *the maximal coverage and the coverage in bounded time problem can be solved in time linear in* $O(|V| + |E|)$ *and in time exponential in* $|\mathsf{AP}|$.

5 Extensions

The basic setting of this paper on graphs and games can be extended in various directions, enabling the modeling of other system features. For example, all our results hold even if every state is labeled with possibly multiple atomic propositions, instead of a single atomic proposition. We mention two important directions in which our results can be extended.

Incomplete Information. So far, we have assumed that at each step, the tester has complete information about the state of the system under test. In practice, this may not be true, and the tester might be able to observe only a part of the state. This leads to graphs and games of *imperfect information* [13]. The maximal coverage and the coverage in bounded time problem for games of imperfect information can be solved in EXPTIME. The algorithm first constructs a perfect-information game graph by subset construction [13], and then run the algorithm of Theorem 9, that is linear in the size game graph and exponential in the number of propositions, on the perfect-information game graph. Thus, the complexity of this algorithm is EXPTIME. The reachability problem for imperfect-information games is already EXPTIME-hard [13], hence we obtain an optimal EXPTIME-complete complexity.

Timed Systems. Second, while we have studied the problem in the discrete, finite-state setting, similar questions can be studied for timed systems modeled as timed automata [2] or timed game graphs [11]. Such problems would arise in the testing of real-time systems. We omit the standard definitions of timed automata and timed games. The maximal coverage problem for timed automata (respectively, timed games) takes as input a timed automaton T (respectively, a timed game T), with the locations labeled by a set AP of propositions, and a number m, and asks whether m different propositions can be visited. An algorithm for the maximal coverage problem for timed automata constructs the region graph of the automaton [2] and runs the algorithm of Theorem 6 on the labeled region graph. This gives us a PSPACE algorithm. Since the reachability problem for timed automata is PSPACE-hard, we obtain a PSPACE-complete complexity. Similar result holds for the coverage in bounded time problem for timed automata. Similarly, the maximal coverage and coverage in bounded time problem for timed games can be solved in exponential time by running the algorithm of Theorem 9 on the region game graph. This gives an exponential time algorithm. Again, since game reachability on timed games is EXPTIME-hard [9], we obtain that maximal coverage and coverage in bounded time in timed games is EXPTIME-complete.

References

1. Alur, R., Courcoubetis, C., Yannakakis, M.: Distinguishing tests for nondeterministic and probabilistic machines. In: Proc. 27th ACM Symp. Theory of Comp. (1995)
2. Alur, R., Dill, D.: The theory of timed automata. In: Huizing, C., de Bakker, J.W., Rozenberg, G., de Roever, W.-P. (eds.) REX 1991. LNCS, vol. 600, pp. 45–73. Springer, Heidelberg (1992)
3. Ammann, P., Offutt, J.: Introduction to software testing. Cambridge University Press, Cambridge (2008)
4. Arora, S., Lund, C., Motwani, R., Sudan, M., Szegedy, M.: Proof verification and the hardness of approximation problems. J. ACM 45(3), 501–555 (1998)
5. Ball, T.: A theory of predicate-complete test coverage and generation. In: de Boer, F.S., Bonsangue, M.M., Graf, S., de Roever, W.-P. (eds.) FMCO 2004. LNCS, vol. 3657, pp. 1–22. Springer, Heidelberg (2005)
6. Blass, A., Gurevich, Y., Nachmanson, L., Veanes, M.: Play to test. In: Grieskamp, W., Weise, C. (eds.) FATES 2005. LNCS, vol. 3997, pp. 32–46. Springer, Heidelberg (2006)
7. Brinksma, E., Tretmans, J.: Testing transition systems: An annotated bibliography. In: Cassez, F., Jard, C., Rozoy, B., Dermot, M. (eds.) MOVEP 2000. LNCS, vol. 2067, pp. 187–195. Springer, Heidelberg (2001)
8. Garey, M.R., Johnson, D.S.: Computers and Intractability: A Guide to the Theory of NP-Completeness. Freeman and Co., New York (1979)
9. Henzinger, T., Kopke, P.: Discrete-time control for rectangular hybrid automata. Theoretical Computer Science 221, 369–392 (1999)
10. Lee, D., Yannakakis, M.: Optimization problems from feature testing of communication protocols. In: ICNP: International Conference on Network Protocols, pp. 66–75. IEEE Computer Society, Los Alamitos (1996)
11. Maler, O., Pnueli, A., Sifakis, J.: On the synthesis of discrete controllers for timed systems. In: Mayr, E.W., Puech, C. (eds.) STACS 1995. LNCS, vol. 900, Springer, Heidelberg (1995)
12. Papadimitriou, C.H.: Computational Complexity. Addison-Wesley, Reading (1993)
13. Reif, J.H.: The complexity of two-player games of incomplete information. Journal of Computer and System Sciences 29, 274–301 (1984)
14. Yannakakis, M.: Testing, optimization, and games. In: LICS, pp. 78–88. IEEE Computer Society, Los Alamitos (2004)
15. Yannakakis, M., Lee, D.: Testing for finite state systems. In: Gottlob, G., Grandjean, E., Seyr, K. (eds.) CSL 1998. LNCS, vol. 1584, pp. 29–44. Springer, Heidelberg (1999)

Game Characterizations of Process Equivalences

Xin Chen* and Yuxin Deng**

Department of Computer Science and Engineering,
Shanghai Jiao Tong University, China

Abstract. In this paper we propose a hierarchy of games that allows us
to make a systematic comparison of process equivalences by characterizing process equivalences as games. The well-known linear/branching time
hierarchy of process equivalences can be embedded into the game hierarchy, which not only provides us with a refined analysis of process equivalences, but also offers a guidance to defining interesting new process
equivalences.

1   Introduction

A great amount of work in process algebra has centered around process equivalences as a basis for establishing system correctness. Usually both specifications
and implementations are written as process terms in the same algebra, where
a specification describes the expected high-level behaviour of the system under
consideration and an implementation gives the detailed procedure of achieving
the behaviour. An appropriate equivalence is then chosen to verify that the implementation conforms to the specification. In the last three decades, a lot of
process equivalences have been developed to capture various aspects of system
behaviour. They usually fit in the linear/branching time hierarchy [10]; see Figure 1 for some typical process equivalences.

Process equivalences can often be understood from different perspectives such
as logics and games. For example, bisimulation equivalence can be characterized
by Hennessy-Milner logic [1] and the modal mu-calculus [2]. Equivalences which
are weaker than bisimulation equivalence in the linear/branching time hierarchy
can be characterized by some sub-logics of Hennessy-Milner logic [3]. It is also
well-known that bisimulation equivalence can be characterized by bisimulation
games [6] between an attacker and a defender in an elegant way; two processes
are bisimilar if and only if the defender of a bisimulation game played on the
processes has a history free winning strategy. Bisimulation games came from
Ehrenfeucht-Fraïssé games that were originally introduced to determine expressive power of logics [9]. To some extent games can be considered as descriptive
languages like logics. In many cases we can design a game directly from the
semantics of a particular logic such that the game captures the logic. For example, the bisimulation game with infinite duration is an Ehrenfeucht-Fraïssé game

* Supported by the National 973 Project (2003CB317005) and the National Natural
Science Foundation of China (60573002).
** Supported by the National Natural Science Foundation of China (60703033).

G. Ramalingam (Ed.): APLAS 2008, LNCS 5356, pp. 107–121, 2008.

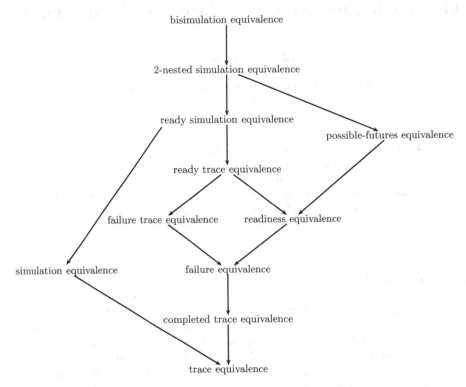

Fig. 1. The linear/branching time hierarchy [10]

that captures Hennessy-Milner logic [6], and the fixed point game that allows infinite fixed point and modal moves captures the modal mu-calculus [8]. Games indeed offer new sights into old problems, and sometimes let us understand these problems easier than before.

In this paper we provide a systematic comparison of different process equivalences from a game-theoretic point of view. More precisely, we present a game hierarchy (cf. Figure 4) which has a more refined structure than the process equivalence hierarchy in Figure 1. Viewing the hierarchies as partial orders, we can embed the process equivalence hierarchy into the game hierarchy because each process equivalence can be characterized by a corresponding class of games. Moreover, there are games that do not correspond to any existing process equivalences. This kind of games would be useful for guiding us to define interesting new process equivalences.

To define games, we make use of a game template that is basically an abstract two-player game leaving concrete moves unspecified. Then we define a few types of moves. Instantiating the game template by different combinations of moves generates different games. We compare the games using a preorder which says that $\mathcal{G}_1 \succeq \mathcal{G}_2$ if player II has a winning strategy in $\mathcal{G}_1$ implies she has a winning strategy in $\mathcal{G}_2$. The preorder provides us with a neat means to compare process equivalences. Suppose $\mathcal{G}_1$ and $\mathcal{G}_2$ characterize process equivalences $\sim_1$ and $\sim_2$, respectively. Then we have that $\mathcal{G}_1 \succeq \mathcal{G}_2$ if and only if $\sim_1 \subseteq \sim_2$, i.e. $\sim_2$ is a coarser relation than $\sim_1$.

The rest of the paper is organized as follows. Section 2 briefly recalls the definitions of labelled transition systems and bisimulations. In Section 3, we design several kinds of moves and a game template in order to define games. In Section 4, we present two game hierarchies, with or without considering alternations of moves, and we combine them into a final hierarchy. In Section 5, we show that the linear/branching time hierarchy can be embedded into our game hierarchy. Section 6 concludes and discusses some future work.

2 Preliminaries

We presuppose a countable set of actions $Act = \{a, b, \dots\}$.

Definition 1. *A labelled transition systems (LTS) is a triple* $(\mathcal{P}, A, \rightarrow)$, *where*

- $\mathcal{P}$ *is a set of states,*
- $A \subseteq Act$ *is a set of actions,*
- $\rightarrow \subseteq \mathcal{P} \times A \times \mathcal{P}$ *is a transition relation.*

As usual, we write $P \xrightarrow{a} Q$ for $(P, a, Q) \in \rightarrow$ and we extend the transition relation to traces in the standard way, e.g. $P_0 \xrightarrow{t} P_n$ if $P_0 \xrightarrow{a_1} P_1 \xrightarrow{a_2} P_2 \dots P_{n-1} \xrightarrow{a_n} P_n$, where $t = a_1 a_2 \dots a_n$. An LTS $(\mathcal{P}, A, \rightarrow)$ is *finitely branching* if for all $P \in \mathcal{P}$ and $a \in A$ the set $\{P' \mid s \xrightarrow{a} P'\}$ is finite. In this paper we only consider finitely branching LTSs. Instead of drawing LTSs as graphs, we use CCS processes to represent the LTSs generated by their operational semantics [4]. We say two processes are isomorphic if their LTSs are isomorphic.

Definition 2. *A binary relation* $\mathcal{R}$ *is a bisimulation if for all* $(P, Q) \in \mathcal{R}$ *and* $a \in Act$,

(1) whenever $P \xrightarrow{a} P'$, *there exists* $Q \xrightarrow{a} Q'$ *such that* $(P', Q') \in \mathcal{R}$, *and*
(2) whenever $Q \xrightarrow{a} Q'$, *there exists* $P \xrightarrow{a} P'$ *such that* $(P', Q') \in \mathcal{R}$.

We define the union of all bisimulations as bisimilarity, written $\sim$.

Bisimilarity can be approximated by a sequence of inductively defined relations. The following definition is taken from [4], except that $\sim_k$ is replaced by $\sim_k^r$. The meaning of the superscript r will be clear in Section 5.

Definition 3. *Let* $\mathcal{P}$ *be the set of all processes, we define*

- $\sim_0^r = \mathcal{P} \times \mathcal{P}$,
- $P \sim_{n+1}^r Q$, *for* $n \geq 0$, *if for all* $t \in Act^*$,
   (1) whenever $P \xrightarrow{t} P'$, *there exists* $Q \xrightarrow{t} Q'$ *such that* $P' \sim_n^r Q'$,
   (2) whenever $Q \xrightarrow{t} Q'$, *there exists* $P \xrightarrow{t} P'$ *such that* $P' \sim_n^r Q'$.

The definition of $\sim_k^a$ for $k \geq 0$ is similar to the previous one, except that we replace $\xrightarrow{t}$ with $\xrightarrow{a}$ where $a \in Act$. For finitely branching LTSs, it holds that $\sim \ = \ \bigcap_{n \geq 0} \sim_n^r \ = \ \bigcap_{n \geq 0} \sim_n^a$.

3   Game Template

We briefly review the bisimulation games [8]. A bisimulation game $\mathcal{G}_k(P,Q)$ starting from the pair of processes (P,Q) is a round-based game with two players. Player I, viewed as an attacker, attempts to show that the initial states are different whereas player II, viewed as a defender, wishes to establish that they are equivalent. A configuration is a pair of processes of the form (P_i, Q_i) examined in the i-th round, and (P,Q) is the configuration for the first round. Suppose we are in the i-th round. The next configuration (P_{i+1}, Q_{i+1}) is determined by one of the following two moves:

$\langle a \rangle$: Player I chooses a transition $P_i \xrightarrow{a} P_{i+1}$ and then player II chooses a transition with the same label $Q_i \xrightarrow{a} Q_{i+1}$.

$[a]$: Player I chooses a transition $Q_i \xrightarrow{a} Q_{i+1}$ and then player II chooses a transition with the same label $P_i \xrightarrow{a} P_{i+1}$.

Player I wins if she can choose a transition and player II is unable to match it within k rounds. Otherwise, Player II wins. If $k = \infty$ then there is no limitation on the number of rounds.

Below we define four other moves that will give rise to various games later on.

Definition 4 (Moves). *Suppose the current configuration is (P,Q), we define the following kinds (or sets, more precisely) of moves.*

$\langle t \rangle$: *Player I performs a nonempty action sequence $t = a_1 \cdots a_l \in Act^*$ from P, $P \xrightarrow{a_1} P_1 \xrightarrow{a_2} \cdots \xrightarrow{a_l} P_l$ and then player II performs the same action sequence from Q, $Q \xrightarrow{a_1} Q_1 \xrightarrow{a_2} \cdots \xrightarrow{a_l} Q_l$. Player I selects some $1 \leq j \leq l$ and sets the configuration for the next round to be (P_j, Q_j).*

$[t]$: *Player I performs a nonempty action sequence $t = a_1 \cdots a_l \in Act^*$ from Q, $Q \xrightarrow{a_1} Q_1 \xrightarrow{a_2} \cdots \xrightarrow{a_l} Q_l$ and then player II performs the same action sequence from P, $P \xrightarrow{a_1} P_1 \xrightarrow{a_2} \cdots \xrightarrow{a_l} P_l$. Player I selects some $1 \leq j \leq l$ and sets the configuration for the next round to be (P_j, Q_j).*

$r\text{-}\langle t \rangle$: *Player I performs a nonempty action sequence $t = a_1 \cdots a_l \in Act^*$ from P, $P \xrightarrow{a_1} P_1 \xrightarrow{a_2} \cdots \xrightarrow{a_l} P_l$ and then player II performs the same action sequence from Q, $Q \xrightarrow{a_1} Q_1 \xrightarrow{a_2} \cdots \xrightarrow{a_l} Q_l$. The configuration for the next round is (P_l, Q_l).*

$r\text{-}[t]$: *Player I performs a nonempty action sequence $t = a_1 \cdots a_l \in Act^*$ from Q, $Q \xrightarrow{a_1} Q_1 \xrightarrow{a_2} \cdots \xrightarrow{a_l} Q_l$ and then player II performs the same action sequence from P, $P \xrightarrow{a_1} P_1 \xrightarrow{a_2} \cdots \xrightarrow{a_l} P_l$. The configuration for the next round is (P_l, Q_l).*

For the sake of convenience, we define some unions of the moves above:

- *$t := \langle t \rangle \cup [t]$.*
- *$r := r\text{-}\langle t \rangle \cup r\text{-}[t]$.*
- *$a := \langle a \rangle \cup [a]$.*
- *$\mathfrak{M}$ is the set of all moves.*

Clearly, $\langle a \rangle$ moves are special $r\text{-}\langle t \rangle$ moves and $r\text{-}\langle t \rangle$ moves are special $\langle t \rangle$ moves. We have similar observation for box modalities.

- $\langle a \rangle \subsetneq r\text{-}\langle t \rangle \subsetneq \langle t \rangle$.
- $[a] \subsetneq r\text{-}[t] \subsetneq [t]$.

We now introduce the concept of alternation for games; it has an intimate relation with quantifier alternation in logics.

Definition 5 (Alternation). *An* alternation *consists of two successive moves such that one of them is in $\langle t \rangle$ and the other is in $[t]$. The number of alternations in a game is the number of occurrences of such successive moves in the game.*

Note that bisimulation games have no restriction on their alternation numbers.

Definition 6 (Extra conditions). *Given a round-based game and a set α which is the set of moves player I can make in the game, an extra condition can be one of the following, for some $m \subseteq \mathfrak{M}$,*

m: *The game is extended with one more round, where player I can only make a move in m. Moreover, player I can make a move in $m - \alpha$ in each round, but the game has to be finished regardless of the remaining rounds, which implies that if player I fails to make player II stuck by this move, she loses.*

−m: *Similar to the case for m, except that if player I makes a move in $m - \alpha$ to end the game, the last two moves must be an alternation. Therefore, this condition could not be applied to a 0-round game.*

c_0: *In the beginning of the game, all deadlock processes reachable from P_0 and Q_0 are colored C_0. In each round, the two processes in the related configuration should be in the same color (or neither of them is colored), otherwise player II loses.*

We now define a *game template* which is intuitively an abstract game in the sense that concrete games can be obtained from it by instantiating its moves.

Definition 7 (Game template). *The game template $n\text{-}\Gamma_k^{\alpha,\beta}(P,Q)$ with $n \geq 0$ denotes a k-round game between player I and player II with the starting configuration (P,Q) such that the following conditions are satisfied.*

1. *The number of alternations in the game is at most n; it is omitted when there is no restriction on the number of alternations.*
2. *β is an extra condition; it is omitted when there is no extra condition.*
3. *Player I can only make a move in $\alpha \subseteq \mathfrak{M}$ in each round if β is neither m nor $-m$. Otherwise, player I can also make a move in $m - \alpha$ in each round, but if she cannot make player II stuck by this move, she loses.*
4. *The players' winning conditions are similar to those in bisimulation games.*

Notice that k-round bisimulation games can be defined by Γ_k^a. Although a lot of games can be defined by various combinations of n, α and β; this paper mainly focuses on some typical ones. Given a game $\Gamma_k^{\alpha,\beta}(P,Q)$, we say player I (resp. player II) wins $\Gamma_k^{\alpha,\beta}(P,Q)$ if player I (resp. player II) has a winning strategy in it, and we abbreviate the game to $\Gamma_k^{\alpha,\beta}$ if the starting configuration is insignificant.

4   Game Hierarchy

To facilitate the presentation, we classify our games into two hierarchies with respect to a preorder relation between games; one hierarchy counts alternations of moves and the other does not count. We show that all the relations in the hierarchies are correct. Then we combine the two hierarchies into one, by introducing some new relations. At last, we prove that no more non-trivial relations can be added into the final hierarchy. We shall see in Section 5 that the hierarchy of process equivalences in Figure 1 can be embedded into this hierarchy of games.

The preorder relation between games is defined as follows.

Definition 8. *Given two games $\mathcal{G}_1$ and $\mathcal{G}_2$, we write $\mathcal{G}_1 \succeq \mathcal{G}_2$, if for any processes P and Q,*

$$\text{player II wins } \mathcal{G}_1(P,Q) \implies \text{player II wins } \mathcal{G}_2(P,Q).$$

Here $\succeq$ is indeed a preorder as this is inherited from logical implication. We write $\mathcal{G}_1 \succ \mathcal{G}_2$ if $\mathcal{G}_1 \succeq \mathcal{G}_2$ and $\mathcal{G}_2 \nsucceq \mathcal{G}_1$.

4.1   Game Hierarchy I

We propose the game hierarchy I in Figure 2. Its correctness is stated by the next theorem.

Theorem 1. *In Figure 1, if $\mathcal{G}_1 \to \mathcal{G}_2$ then $\mathcal{G}_1 \succeq \mathcal{G}_2$.*

The rest of this section is devoted to proving Theorem 1.

Let $\alpha, \alpha' \subseteq \mathfrak{M}$ and β be an extra condition. The following statements can be derived from Definition 7 immediately:

(1) $\Gamma_0^\alpha = \Gamma_0^{\alpha'}$.
(2) $\Gamma_0^{\alpha,\beta} = \Gamma_0^{\alpha',\beta}$.
(3) For $k \geq 0$, $\Gamma_k^{\alpha,\alpha} = \Gamma_{k+1}^\alpha$.
(4) For $k \geq 0$, $\Gamma_k^{\alpha,t} = \Gamma_k^{\alpha,r}$.

Since t contains r, r contains a, and if two processes P, Q do not have the same color, they can be distinguished in a round by a move in a, we get the following statement:

$$\Gamma_\infty^\alpha = \Gamma_\infty^{\alpha,co} = \Gamma_\infty^{\alpha,-a} = \Gamma_\infty^{\alpha,a}, \text{ for } \alpha \in \{a,r,t\}.$$

Lemma 1. *For any processes P and Q, the following statements are equivalent:*

(1) $P \sim Q$.
(2) player II wins $\Gamma_\infty^a(P,Q)$.
(3) player II wins $\Gamma_\infty^r(P,Q)$.
(4) player II wins $\Gamma_\infty^t(P,Q)$.

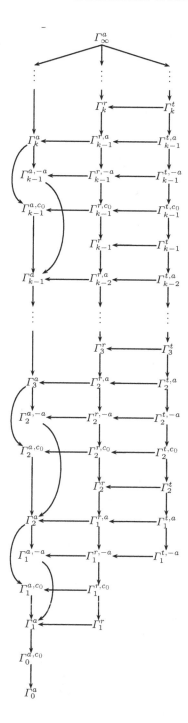

Fig. 2. Game hierarchy I

Proof. It is trivial that $\Gamma^a_\infty \preceq \Gamma^r_\infty \preceq \Gamma^t_\infty$, so we have (4)$\Rightarrow$(3)$\Rightarrow$(2). Observe that Γ^a_k is exactly the k-round bisimulation game, which means (1)$\Leftrightarrow$(2) (cf. [6]). We now show (1)$\Rightarrow$(4). Assume $P \sim Q$, we construct a winning strategy for player II for the game $\Gamma^t_\infty(P,Q)$: in any round, suppose the configuration is (P_i, Q_i). If player I performs $P_i \xrightarrow{a_1} P_{i1} \xrightarrow{a_2} \cdots \xrightarrow{a_l} P_{il}$, then player II can respond with $Q_i \xrightarrow{a_1} Q_{i1} \xrightarrow{a_2} \cdots \xrightarrow{a_l} Q_{il}$, such that $P_{ij} \sim Q_{ij}$ for all $1 \leq j \leq l$. Clearly, whatever configuration for the next round player I selects, she cannot win the game.

Lemma 1 yields the immediate corollary that $\Gamma^a_\infty = \Gamma^r_\infty = \Gamma^t_\infty$.

Lemma 2. *(1)* $\Gamma^a_{k+1} \preceq \Gamma^{r,a}_k \preceq \Gamma^{t,a}_k$ *for all* $k \geq 1$.
(2) $\Gamma^r_k \preceq \Gamma^t_k$ *for all* $k \geq 1$.

Proof. Since $a \subsetneq r \subsetneq t$, both (1) and (2) can be easily derived. $\quad\square$

Lemma 3. $\Gamma^r_k \preceq \Gamma^{r,c_0}_k \preceq \Gamma^{r,-a}_k \preceq \Gamma^{r,a}_k \preceq \Gamma^r_{k+1}$ *for all* $k \geq 1$.

Proof. It is easy to see that $\Gamma^r_k \preceq \Gamma^{r,c_0}_k \preceq \Gamma^{r,a}_k \preceq \Gamma^r_{k+1}$ and $\Gamma^r_k \preceq \Gamma^{r,-a}_k \preceq \Gamma^{r,a}_k \preceq \Gamma^r_{k+1}$. We now prove $\Gamma^{r,c_0}_k \preceq \Gamma^{r,-a}_k$ by induction on k. Given two processes P, Q, suppose player II wins $\Gamma^{r,-a}_k(P,Q)$. We show that player II wins $\Gamma^{r,c_0}_k(P,Q)$ as well.

- $k = 1$. From the assumption, player II wins $\Gamma^{r,-a}_1(P,Q)$. The game $\Gamma^{r,c_0}_1(P,Q)$ has just one round and all deadlock processes reachable from P and Q are colored C_0, and the other processes are uncolored. (Clearly both P and Q are colored C_0 or neither of them is colored.) We distinguish four cases.

  Case 1: Player I performs $P \xrightarrow{t} P'$, where $t \in Act^*$ is a nonempty action sequence and P' is colored. Player II can perform $Q \xrightarrow{t} Q'$ such that Q' is colored. Otherwise there is some $a \in Act$ and player I can make player II stuck by performing $P \xrightarrow{ta} P''$ for some P'' in the first round of $\Gamma^{r,-a}_1(P,Q)$, which contradicts the assumption.

  Case 2: Player I performs $P \xrightarrow{t} P'$, where $t \in Act^*$ is a nonempty action sequence and P' is uncolored C_0. Player II can perform $Q \xrightarrow{t} Q'$ such that Q' is uncolored C_0. Otherwise, in $\Gamma^{r,-a}_1(P,Q)$, player I can make player II stuck by making a move in $[a]$ in the second round, contradicting the assumption.

  Case 3: Player I performs $Q \xrightarrow{t} Q'$, where $t \in Act^*$ is a nonempty action sequence and Q' is colored. This case is similar to Case 1.

  Case 4: player I performs $Q \xrightarrow{t} Q'$, where $t \in Act^*$ is a nonempty action sequence and Q' is uncolored C_0. This case is similar to Case 2.

- $k > 1$. We know player II wins $\Gamma^{r,-a}_k(P,Q)$. In the first round of $\Gamma^{r,c_0}_k(P,Q)$, whenever player I performs some action sequence from P (resp. Q) to P' (resp. Q'), player II can always perform the same action sequence from Q (resp. P) to Q' (resp. P') such that both P' and Q' are colored C_0, or neither of them is colored. Otherwise, in $\Gamma^{r,-a}_k(P,Q)$, player I can make player II stuck in the second round. In the second round of $\Gamma^{r,c_0}_k(P,Q)$, the game becomes $\Gamma^{r,c_0}_{k-1}(P',Q')$ and by induction player II wins the $\Gamma^{r,c_0}_{k-1}(P',Q')$. $\quad\square$

Similar to Lemmas 2 and 3, all the other relations illustrated in Figure 2 can be proven, thus Theorem 1 is established.

4.2   Game Hierarchy II

The games in Section 4.1 do not count alternations of moves, which are taken into account in this section. For simplicity, we are not going to discuss all the games defined from those in Figure 2 by restricting the number of alternations. Instead, we focus on the games in which the players can only make moves in a. To further simplify the exposition, Figure 3 only illustrates a game hierarchy where the number of alternations n is restricted to 0 and 1. However, in the rest of the paper the lemmas cover all $n \geq 0$. From Definitions 6 and 7, the relations illustrated in Figure 3 are apparent, so we omit the proof of the theorem below.

Theorem 2. *In Figure 2, if $\mathcal{G}_1 \to \mathcal{G}_2$ then $\mathcal{G}_1 \succeq \mathcal{G}_2$.*   □

4.3   The Whole Game Hierarchy

We now combine game hierarchies I and II into a single hierarchy, as described in Figure 4. Similar to Figure 3, we have not drawn the games with alternations exceeding 1, but our lemmas below cover them.

In the combined game hierarchy, we have the new relations, $\Gamma^t_{n+1} \preceq n\text{-}\Gamma^a_\infty$, $\Gamma^{t,co}_{n+1} \preceq n\text{-}\Gamma^{a,co}_\infty$, $\Gamma^{t,a}_{n+1} \preceq n\text{-}\Gamma^{a,a}_\infty$ for $n \geq 0$. We give a proof of $\Gamma^t_{n+1} \preceq n\text{-}\Gamma^a_\infty$ in the lemma below; the others can be proven analogously.

Lemma 4. $\Gamma^t_{n+1} \preceq n\text{-}\Gamma^a_\infty$ *for all $n \geq 0$.*

Proof. We prove the statement by induction on n. Assume player II wins n-$\Gamma^a_\infty(P_0, Q_0)$ for some processes P_0 and Q_0.

- $n = 0$. Suppose player I performs $P_0 \xrightarrow{a_1} P_1 \xrightarrow{a_2} \ldots \xrightarrow{a_l} P_l$ (resp. $Q_0 \xrightarrow{a_1} Q_1 \xrightarrow{a_2} \cdots \xrightarrow{a_l} Q_l$). Since player II wins 0-$\Gamma^a_\infty(P_0, Q_0)$, she can respond with $Q_0 \xrightarrow{a_1} Q_1 \xrightarrow{a_2} \ldots \xrightarrow{a_l} Q_l$ (resp. $P_0 \xrightarrow{a_1} P_1 \xrightarrow{a_2} \cdots \xrightarrow{a_l} P_l$). Hence, player II wins $\Gamma^t_1(P_0, Q_0)$.
- $n > 0$. From the assumption, player II wins n-$\Gamma^a_\infty(P_0, Q_0)$. In the first round of $\Gamma^t_{n+1}(P_0, Q_0)$, if player I performs $P_0 \xrightarrow{a_1} P_1 \xrightarrow{a_2} \ldots \xrightarrow{a_l} P_l$ (resp. $Q_0 \xrightarrow{a_1} Q_1 \xrightarrow{a_2} \cdots \xrightarrow{a_l} Q_l$), player II can respond with $Q_0 \xrightarrow{a_1} Q_1 \xrightarrow{a_2} \ldots \xrightarrow{a_l} Q_l$ (resp. $P_0 \xrightarrow{a_1} P_1 \xrightarrow{a_2} \cdots \xrightarrow{a_l} P_l$), such that for each P_i and Q_i, where $1 \leq i \leq l$, player II wins $(n-1)$-$\Gamma^a_\infty(P_i, Q_i)$. By induction, $\Gamma^t_n \preceq (n-1)$-Γ^a_∞, player II wins $\Gamma^t_n(P_i, Q_i)$ for any $1 \leq i \leq l$. Hence, player II wins $\Gamma^t_{n+1}(P_0, Q_0)$.   □

We are in a position to state the main result of the paper.

Theorem 3. *(1) In Figure 4, if $\mathcal{G}_1 \to \mathcal{G}_2$ then $\mathcal{G}_1 \succ \mathcal{G}_2$.*
(2) No more relations can be added to the game hierarchy in Figure 4, except for those derived from the transitivity of $\succ$.   □

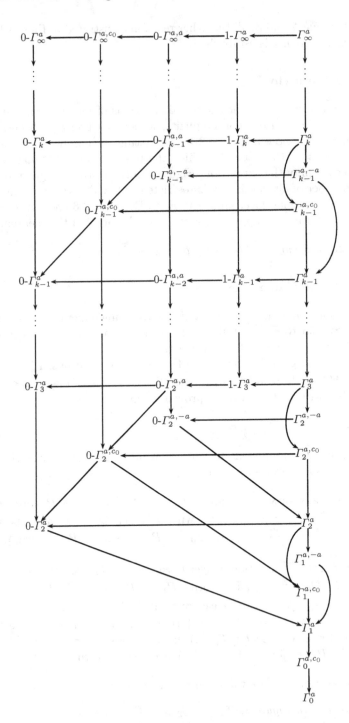

Fig. 3. Game hierarchy II

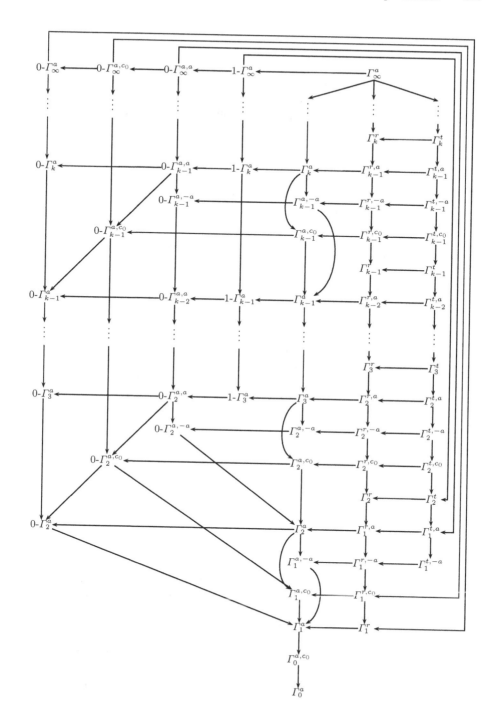

Fig. 4. The whole game hierarchy

The first statement follows from Theorems 1, 2 and Lemma 4 provided we could show that

$$(*) \qquad \text{In Figure 4, if } \mathcal{G}_1 \rightarrow \mathcal{G}_2 \text{ then } \mathcal{G}_2 \not\succeq \mathcal{G}_1.$$

The rest of this section is devoted to proving (*) and the second statement of Theorem 3 by providing counterexamples to prove the invalidities of some relations. For that purpose, it suffices to establish Lemmas 5 to 7 below.

Lemma 5. *For all $k \geq 1$,*

(1) $\Gamma_1^r \not\preceq \Gamma_k^a$.
(2) $\Gamma_1^{t,-a} \not\preceq \Gamma_k^r$.

Proof. (1) We define the processes below:

Example 1. $A \overset{def}{=} a.A$ and $A_i \overset{def}{=} \begin{cases} 0 & \text{if } i = 0 \\ a.A_{i-1} & \text{if } i > 0 \end{cases}$

Consider $\Gamma_k^a(A, A_k)$, in each round player I can only perform action a from one process, and player II can always respond properly, since both A and A_k can perform action a for k times. Then player II wins $\Gamma_k^a(A, A_k)$. But player I wins $\Gamma_1^r(A, A_k)$, she performs an action sequence $t = a^{k+1}$ from A in the first round, player II fails to respond to such sequence from A_k, since the process can only perform action a for k times.

(2) Consider the following processes.

Example 2.

$$P_0 \overset{def}{=} b.0, \quad Q_0 \overset{def}{=} c.0,$$

$$P_{i+1} \overset{def}{=} a.(P_i + d.0) + a.(Q_i + e.0),$$

$$Q_{i+1} \overset{def}{=} a.(P_i + e.0) + a.(Q_i + d.0).$$

It is not difficult to prove that player II wins $\Gamma_k^r(P_{k+1}, Q_{k+1})$ by induction on k.

- $k = 1$. This case is easy.
- $k > 1$. We distinguish five sub-cases.
  Case 1: Player I performs $P_{k+1} \overset{a}{\rightarrow} (P_k + d.0)$. Then player II can perform $Q_{k+1} \overset{a}{\rightarrow} (Q_k + d.0)$. By induction player II wins $\Gamma_{k-1}^r(P_k, Q_k)$ and thus she also wins $\Gamma_{k-1}^r(P_k + d.0, Q_k + d.0)$.
  Case 2: Player I performs $P_{k+1} \overset{a}{\rightarrow} (Q_k + e.0)$. Then player II can perform $Q_{k+1} \overset{a}{\rightarrow} (P_k + e.0)$. Similar to the previous case, player II wins $\Gamma_{k-1}^r(Q_k + e.0, P_k + e.0)$.
  Case 3: Player I performs $Q_{k+1} \overset{a}{\rightarrow} (Q_k + d.0)$. Then player II can perform $P_{k+1} \overset{a}{\rightarrow} (P_k + d.0)$. The rest is similar to Case 1.
  Case 4: Player I performs $Q_{k+1} \overset{a}{\rightarrow} (P_k + e.0)$. Then player II can perform $P_{k+1} \overset{a}{\rightarrow} (Q_k + e.0)$. The rest is similar to Case 2.

Case 5: If player I performs $P_{k+1} \xrightarrow{t} P'$ (resp. $Q_{k+1} \xrightarrow{t} Q'$) for some $t \in Act^*$ and $|t| > 1$, player II can always respond with $Q_{k+1} \xrightarrow{t} Q'$ (resp. $P_{k+1} \xrightarrow{t} P'$) such that P' and Q' are isomorphic.

On the other hand, player I wins $\Gamma_1^{t,-a}(P_{k+1}, Q_{k+1})$. A winning strategy is to perform $P_{k+1} \xrightarrow{a} (P_k + d.0) \xrightarrow{a} (P_{k-1} + d.0) \xrightarrow{a} \cdots \xrightarrow{a} (b.0 + d.0)$, where each process passed in the sequence can perform action d and the last process can perform action b. But player II fails to perform such an action sequence from Q_{k+1} and will become stuck in the second round.   □

Similar to Lemma 5, the next two lemmas can be proven by providing appropriate counterexamples.

Lemma 6. *For all $k \geq 1$,*

(1) $0\text{-}\Gamma_k^{a,c_0} \not\lesssim \Gamma_k^t$.
(2) $0\text{-}\Gamma_k^{a,-a} \not\lesssim \Gamma_k^{t,c_0}$.
(3) $0\text{-}\Gamma_{k+1}^{a} \not\lesssim \Gamma_k^{t,-a}$.
(4) $0\text{-}\Gamma_k^{a,c_0} \not\lesssim \Gamma_k^{a,-a}$.   □

Lemma 7. *For all $n \geq 0$,*

(1) $\Gamma_{n+1}^{a,c_0} \not\lesssim n\text{-}\Gamma_\infty^a$.
(2) $\Gamma_{n+1}^{a,-a} \not\lesssim n\text{-}\Gamma_\infty^{a,c_0}$.
(3) $(n+1)\text{-}\Gamma_{n+3}^{a} \not\lesssim n\text{-}\Gamma_\infty^{a,a}$.   □

5   Characterizing Process Equivalences

In this section we revisit some important process equivalences[1] in the linear/branching time hierarchy showed in Figure 1.

Definition 9. *Given a game $\mathcal{G}$ and a process equivalence $\approx$, we say $\approx$ is characterized by $\mathcal{G}$ if for any processes P, Q, it holds that $P \approx Q$ iff player II wins $\mathcal{G}(P, Q)$.*

Theorem 4. *(1) Trace equivalence is characterized by Γ_1^r.*
(2) Completed trace equivalence is characterized by Γ_1^{r,c_0}.
(3) Failures equivalence is characterized by $\Gamma_1^{r,-a}$.
(4) Failure trace equivalence is characterized by $\Gamma_1^{t,-a}$.
(5) Ready trace equivalence is characterized by $\Gamma_1^{t,a}$.
(6) Readiness equivalence is characterized by $\Gamma_1^{r,a}$.
(7) Possible-futures equivalence is characterized by Γ_2^r.

---

[1] Due to lack of space we do not list the definitions of those process equivalences; they can be found in [10].

Proof. We only prove (5) and the others can be proven analogously. Suppose P and Q are ready trace equivalent, written $P \sim_{RT} Q$, we prove that player II wins $\Gamma_1^{t,a}(P,Q)$. In the first round, if player I performs some trace t from P or Q, then player II considers t as a ready trace, since she has full knowledge of player I's move. Clearly, in the second round player I cannot make player II stuck. Conversely, suppose player II wins $\Gamma_1^{t,a}(P,Q)$. It is apparent that P, Q have the same ready traces, and then $P \sim_{RT} Q$.   □

Similar to the approximation of bisimilarity (cf. Definition 3), we can define similarity $\sim_S$, completed similarity $\sim_{CS}$, ready similarity $\sim_{RS}$, 2-nested similarity $\sim_{2S}$, and their approximants. We write $\sim_k^*$, where $k \geq 0$, for the approximants of $\sim^*$.

Lemma 8. *For all $k \geq 0$,*

(1) Γ_k^a characterizes $\sim_k^a$.
(2) Γ_k^r characterizes $\sim_k^r$.
(3) $0\text{-}\Gamma_k^a$ characterizes $\sim_k^S$.
(4) $0\text{-}\Gamma_k^{a,co}$ characterizes $\sim_k^{CS}$.
(5) $0\text{-}\Gamma_k^{a,a}$ characterizes $\sim_k^{RS}$.
(6) $1\text{-}\Gamma_k^a$ characterizes $\sim_k^{2S}$.

Proof. All the statements can be easily proven by induction on k, so we omit them.   □

Since we are dealing with finitely branching LTSs, the next theorem follows from Lemma 8.

Theorem 5. *(1) Simulation equivalence is characterized by $0\text{-}\Gamma_\infty^a$.*
(2) Completed simulation equivalence is characterized by $0\text{-}\Gamma_\infty^{a,co}$.
(3) Ready simulation equivalence is characterized by $0\text{-}\Gamma_\infty^{a,a}$.
(4) 2-nested simulation equivalence is characterized by $1\text{-}\Gamma_\infty^a$.   □

Furthermore, new equivalences can be defined using the games in Figure 4. For example, we can define a new equivalence using game Γ_2^t which is stronger than possible-futures equivalence and ready trace equivalence, but weaker than 2-nested simulation equivalence. In addition, from the game hierarchy, we learn the relationship between the approximants of bisimilarity, similarity, completed similarity etc. For example, possible-futures equivalence is stronger than $\sim_2^S$, but is incomparable with $\sim_3^S$. Hence, the game hierarchy is interesting in that it offers an intuitive way of comparing various process equivalences.

6   Concluding Remarks

We have presented a hierarchy of games that allows us to compare process equivalences systematically in a game-theoretic way by characterizing process equivalences as games. The hierarchy not only provides us with a refined analysis of process equivalences, but also offers a guidance to defining interesting new process equivalences.

The work closely related to ours is [5] which provides a Stirling class of games to characterize various process equivalences. The methodology adopted in the current work is different because we examine in a systematic way the theory of games that could characterize typical equivalences in the process equivalence hierarchy.

Paying our attention to the analysis of process equivalences is for the purpose of studying the complexity of equivalence checking. We know that model checking can be considered in a game-theoretic way [7], but the complexity depends on particular models. Similar phenomena exist for equivalence checking. However, equivalence checking is much harder than model checking, and sometimes it cannot be done in similar ways. Further investigation in this respect would be interesting.

Acknowledgement. We thank Enshao Shen, Yunfeng Tao and Chaodong He for interesting discussions. We also thank the anonymous referees for their constructive comments.

References

[1] Hennessy, M., Milner, R.: Algebraic laws for nondeterminism and concurrency. Journal of the ACM 32(1), 137–161 (1985)

[2] Kozen, D.: Results on the propositional mu-calculus. Theoretical Computer Science 27, 333–354 (1983)

[3] Kucera, A., Esparza, J.: A logical viewpoint on process-algebraic quotients. In: Flum, J., Rodríguez-Artalejo, M. (eds.) CSL 1999. LNCS, vol. 1683, pp. 499–514. Springer, Heidelberg (1999)

[4] Milner, R.: Communication and concurrency. Prentice-Hall, Inc., Englewood Cliffs (1989)

[5] Shukla, S.K., Hunt III, H.B., Rosenkrantz, D.J.: Hornsat, model checking, verification and games (extended abstract). In: Alur, R., Henzinger, T.A. (eds.) CAV 1996. LNCS, vol. 1102, pp. 99–110. Springer, Heidelberg (1996)

[6] Stirling, C.: Modal and temporal logics for processes. Notes for Summer School in Logic Methods in Concurrency (1993)

[7] Stirling, C.: Local model checking games. In: Lee, I., Smolka, S.A. (eds.) CONCUR 1995. LNCS, vol. 962, pp. 1–11. Springer, Heidelberg (1995)

[8] Stirling, C.: Games and modal mu-calculus. In: Margaria, T., Steffen, B. (eds.) TACAS 1996. LNCS, vol. 1055, pp. 298–312. Springer, Heidelberg (1996)

[9] Thomas, W.: On the Ehrenfeucht-Fraïssé game in theoretical computer science. In: Gaudel, M.-C., Jouannaud, J.-P. (eds.) CAAP / FASE 1993. LNCS, vol. 668, pp. 559–568. Springer, Heidelberg (1993)

[10] van Glabbeek, R.J.: The linear time-branching time spectrum (extended abstract). In: Baeten, J.C.M., Klop, J.W. (eds.) CONCUR 1990. LNCS, vol. 458, pp. 278–297. Springer, Heidelberg (1990)

Extensional Universal Types for Call-by-Value

Kazuyuki Asada

Research Institute for Mathematical Sciences, Kyoto University, Japan
asada@kurims.kyoto-u.ac.jp

Abstract. We propose $\lambda_c 2_\eta$-*calculus*, which is a second-order polymorphic call-by-value calculus with *extensional* universal types. Unlike product types or function types in call-by-value, extensional universal types are genuinely right adjoint to the weakening, i.e., β-equality and η-equality hold for not only values but all terms. We give monadic style categorical semantics, so that the results can be applied also to languages like Haskell. To demonstrate validity of the calculus, we construct concrete models for the calculus in a generic manner, exploiting "relevant" parametricity. On such models, we can obtain a reasonable class of monads consistent with extensional universal types. This class admits polynomial-like constructions, and includes non-termination, exception, global state, input/output, and list-non-determinism.

1 Introduction

Polymorphic lambda calculi like System F [11,30] have been widely studied and also used in some practical programing languages like ML and Haskell as their semantical background. With universal types in them, we can abstract terms defined uniformly for each type into one term, which improves usability, efficiency, readability and safety. Moreover in impredicative polymorphic lambda calculi, we can encode various datatypes like products, coproducts, initial algebras, and final coalgebras with universal types. These datatypes have merely *weak* universal properties in System F, but they are truly universal if we assume relational parametricity [31,34,29,1,16,7].

As well as purely functional calculi, extensions of polymorphic lambda calculi to call-by-name calculi/languages with some computational effects have been studied: with a fixed-point operator [28,4,5], and with first-class continuations [14].

While call-by-value is one of the most frequently used evaluation strategy in practical programing languages, extensions to call-by-value polymorphic languages raise a subtle problem on the treatment of universally typed *values*. Suppose that we have a type-abstracted term $\Lambda\alpha.M$. Then, is this a value at all? Or should we treat this as a value, only when M is a value? It corresponds to the choice whether we evaluate M under the type abstraction, or do not (as function closure). This problem does not occur in modern ML, because, due to *value restriction*, M must always be a value.

When we set $\Lambda\alpha.M$ as a value only when so is M, then we can obtain extensional universal types, i.e., "type" η-equality, for some reasonable class of effects.

G. Ramalingam (Ed.): APLAS 2008, LNCS 5356, pp. 122–137, 2008.

We call the η-equality $\Lambda\alpha.M\alpha = M$ ($\alpha \notin \mathrm{FTV}\,(M)$) for type abstraction *type η-equality*, and also the β-equality $(\Lambda\alpha.M)\,\sigma = M\,[\sigma/\alpha]$ for type abstraction *type β-equality*. Clearly, if we treat $\Lambda\alpha.M$ as a value for any term M, then type η-equality does not hold in general, as function types in call-by-value.

We expect that such type η-equality can be useful for program transformation to optimize programs. Also we can use it when reasoning with *parametricity for call-by-value*, for type η-equality is often used in parametric reasoning.

In the present paper we propose a second-order polymorphic call-by-value lambda calculus with extensional universal types. We give syntax and its sound and complete categorical semantics, and describe how we can construct concrete models with a variety of computational effects.

Our main contribution is to show that, for some parametric models or semantic setting, we can obtain a reasonable class of effects which are compatible with extensional universal types. The class includes non-termination, exception, global state, input/output, and list-non-determinism. We can not show at present whether (commutative) nondeterminism (like finite or infinite powersets, multisets and probabilistic non-determinism) and continuations belong to the class of models or not.

We use Moggi's monadic semantics [25,26,27,2] rather than direct-style semantics for call-by-value calculi [10,21]. One reason is that it is easier to represent the class of effects considered in the present paper. The monads modeling the effects mentioned above are respectively lifting monad $(-)+1$, exception monads $(-) + E$, global state monads $((-) \times S)^S$, input monads $\mu\beta.\,(-) + \beta^U$, output monads $\mu\beta.\,(-) + (U \times \beta)$, and the list monad $\mu\beta.1 + (-) \times \beta$. As these examples, this class is characterized as that of all "polynomial" monads constructed by constants, products, separated sum, powers, final coalgebras, and *linearly* initial algebras; the last construction is explained in Section 6.4.

One more reason to use monadic semantics is because we can apply the results to call-by-name (meta-)languages with monads like Haskell, as well as to call-by-value languages as object languages like ML. In (some simplified) Haskell, only fixed-point operators involving the non-termination effect exists in the call-by-name object language, and other effects are treated via monadic style translations with various monads. The semantics which we give with "relevant" parametricity and fixed-point operators in Section 6 is close to such subset of Haskell, with extensional universal types.

1.1   Related Work

Harper et al. studied two kinds of call-by-value (and two kinds of call-by-name) extensions of the higher order polymorphic lambda calculus System F_ω with first-class continuations [12]. The difference between the two call-by-value extensions is exactly as above, i.e., whether, for a type-abstracted term, we evaluate the inside of the body or not. They took an operational semantics-based approach, and noted there the failure of proving the preservation theorem which asserts that a closed answer-typed term is evaluated to a closed answer-typed term. Thus first-class continuations raise difficulty to obtain extensional universal types.

Recently in [22], Møgelberg studied polymorphic FPC, a call-by-value functional language with recursive types and hence a fixed-point operator. The universal types in this language are not designed to be extensional. However, it seems that we can make it extensional because the effect used there is non-termination, though the problems to adjust other features of the language like recursive types are not trivial.

An extension of System F with parametricity to call-by-push-value [20] was also studied [23]. The paradigm of call-by-push-value is similar to that of the monadic metalanguages, and it might be possible to express our results in terms of call-by-push-value. Call-by-push-value can be also used to translate call-by-name languages as done in [24].

1.2 Outline

In Section 2, we introduce two *second order* computational lambda calculi. One is $\lambda_c 2_\eta$-calculus which has extensionality on universal type, and the other is $\lambda_c 2$-calculus which does not.

Section 3 is devoted to preliminaries for semantics in later sections. In Section 4, we give categorical semantics for the calculi given in Section 2. These sections 3 and 4 may be skipped by readers who are not particularly interested in general semantic framework.

In Section 5, we start to look at concrete models for $\lambda_c 2_\eta$-calculus. First we describe a class of monads which admit extensional universal types, then we show in two sections that they indeed form concrete models. In Section 5, we treat parts which hold in relatively general, i.e., only by categorical property and by parametricity. In Section 6, we consider more specific models with fixed-point operators and "relevant" parametricity.

Lastly, we give some concluding remarks in Section 7.

2 Second Order Computational Lambda Calculi

In this section, we introduce two calculi: *second order computational λ-calculus* ($\lambda_c 2$-*calculus* for short) and *second order computational λ-calculus with extensional universal types* ($\lambda_c 2_\eta$-*calculus* for short). These are extensions of Moggi's computational lambda calculus (λ_c-calculus), listed in Figure 1, with universal types.

We give the $\lambda_c 2$-calculus in Figure 2, and the $\lambda_c 2_\eta$-calculus in Figure 3. Note that the classes of values include e.g. $\pi_1 \langle V, V' \rangle$. A "value" here means an "effect-free" term, rather than a canonical form.

The differences between the $\lambda_c 2$-calculus and the $\lambda_c 2_\eta$-calculus are not in the definitions of types or terms but only in equation theories, i.e., the values and the axioms. The universal types in the $\lambda_c 2$-calculus satisfy type β-equality for any term and type η-equality for only values, while those in the $\lambda_c 2_\eta$-calculus satisfy type β- and η-equality for any term. We call such universal types with full type η-equality *extensional* universal types. In the paper we put the focus on the $\lambda_c 2_\eta$-calculus, to demonstrate how many effects are consistent with extensional universal types.

$$\text{Types } \sigma ::= b \mid \sigma \to \sigma \mid 1 \mid \sigma \times \sigma$$
$$\text{Terms } M ::= x \mid c^\sigma \mid \lambda x^\sigma.M \mid MM \mid * \mid \langle M, M \rangle \mid \pi_0 M \mid \pi_1 M$$
$$\text{Values } V ::= x \mid c^\sigma \mid \lambda x^\sigma.M \mid * \mid \langle V, V \rangle \mid \pi_0 V \mid \pi_1 V$$
$$\text{Evaluation Contexts } E ::= [-] \mid EM \mid VE \mid \langle E, M \rangle \mid \langle V, E \rangle \mid \pi_0 E \mid \pi_1 E$$

where b ranges over base types, and c^σ ranges over constants of type σ

Typing Rules:

$$\frac{}{\Gamma \vdash x : \sigma}\,(x{:}\sigma \in \Gamma) \qquad \frac{}{\Gamma \vdash c^\sigma : \sigma} \qquad \frac{\Gamma, x{:}\sigma \vdash M : \tau}{\Gamma \vdash \lambda x^\sigma.M : \sigma \to \tau} \qquad \frac{\Gamma \vdash M : \sigma \to \tau \quad \Gamma \vdash N : \sigma}{\Gamma \vdash MN : \tau}$$

$$\frac{}{\Gamma \vdash * : 1} \qquad \frac{\Gamma \vdash M : \sigma \quad \Gamma \vdash N : \tau}{\Gamma \vdash \langle M, N \rangle : \sigma \times \tau} \qquad \frac{\Gamma \vdash M : \sigma \times \tau}{\Gamma \vdash \pi_0 M : \sigma} \qquad \frac{\Gamma \vdash M : \sigma \times \tau}{\Gamma \vdash \pi_1 M : \tau}$$

Axioms:

$$(\lambda x^\sigma.M)\, V = M\,[V/x] \qquad\qquad \pi_i \langle V_0, V_1 \rangle = V_i \quad (i = 0, 1)$$
$$\lambda x^\sigma.V x = V \quad (x \notin \mathrm{FV}\,(V)) \qquad\qquad \langle \pi_0 V, \pi_1 V \rangle = V$$
$$V = * \quad (V : 1) \qquad\qquad (\lambda x^\sigma.E\,[x])\, M = E\,[M] \quad (x \notin \mathrm{FV}\,(E))$$

Fig. 1. The λ_c-calculus

In Section 6, we give relevant parametric models with fixed-point operators as concrete models for the $\lambda_c 2_\eta$-calculus. And there is a reasonably wide class of monads on the models, including non-termination, exception, global state, input, output, and list-non-determinism.

Such fixed-point operators are not included in the syntax of the $\lambda_c 2_\eta$-calculus. Also, the $\lambda_c 2_\eta$-calculus includes no proper axioms which induce computational effects, as well as the λ_c-calculus. However, with such models, we will be able to extend the $\lambda_c 2_\eta$-calculus with suitable axioms and terms which induce such computational effects, and also with call-by-value fixed-point operators [15]. Alternatively, we will also be able to define "second order monadic metalanguages" which have call-by-name fixed-point operators [32] and in which we can simulate such extended $\lambda_c 2_\eta$-calculi by use of corresponding monads.

3 Preliminaries for Semantics

This section is devoted to preliminaries for some category theoretical notions.

Notation: '$\Rightarrow$' is used for exponentials in a CCC (cartesian closed category). An identity on A is written also as just A. For 2-cells, '$*$' and '$\circ$' mean horizontal and vertical compositions respectively.

For a functor p being a fibration, we say an object X is *over* an object I (resp. an arrow f is *over* an arrow u) if $pX = I$ (resp. $pf = u$). A functor $p : \mathbb{E} \longrightarrow \mathbb{B}$ is called a *fibration* if for any arrow $u : J \longrightarrow I$ in $\mathbb{B}$ and object X over I, there is an object u^*X over J and an arrow $\bar{u}X : u^*X \longrightarrow X$ over u which is *cartesian*: for any object Z over K, arrow $h : Z \longrightarrow X$ in $\mathbb{E}$ and arrow $v : K \longrightarrow J$ in $\mathbb{B}$ s.t. $ph = u \circ v$, there is unique arrow $g : Z \longrightarrow u^*X$ over v satisfying $h = \bar{u}X \circ g$.

Types $\sigma ::= \dots \mid \alpha \mid \forall \alpha . \sigma$ Values $V ::= \dots \mid \Lambda \alpha . M$

Terms $M ::= \dots \mid \Lambda \alpha . M \mid M \sigma$ Evaluation Contexts $E ::= \dots \mid E \sigma$

Typing Rules: All the rules in the λ_c-calculus in which a kind context Ξ is added to the all contexts, and:

$$\frac{\Xi , \alpha \mid \Gamma \vdash M : \sigma}{\Xi \mid \Gamma \vdash \Lambda \alpha . M : \forall \alpha . \sigma} \ (\alpha \notin \mathrm{FTV}(\Gamma)) \qquad \frac{\Xi \mid \Gamma \vdash M : \forall \alpha . \sigma}{\Xi \mid \Gamma \vdash M \tau : \sigma [\tau / \alpha]}$$

Axioms: All the axioms in the λ_c-calculus where the evaluation contexts are extended as above, and:

$$(\Lambda \alpha . M) \, \sigma = M \, [\sigma / \alpha] \qquad \Lambda \alpha . V \alpha = V \quad (\alpha \notin \mathrm{FTV}(V))$$

Fig. 2. The $\lambda_c 2$-calculus, extended from the λ_c-calculus

Types $\sigma ::= \dots \mid \alpha \mid \forall \alpha . \sigma$ Values $V ::= \dots \mid \Lambda \alpha . V \mid V \sigma$

Terms $M ::= \dots \mid \Lambda \alpha . M \mid M \sigma$ Evaluation Contexts $E ::= \dots \mid E \sigma$

Typing Rules are the same as those in the second order λ_c-calculus ($\lambda_c 2$-calculus). Axioms: All the axioms in the λ_c-calculus where the evaluation contexts are extended as above, and:

$$(\Lambda \alpha . M) \, \sigma = M \, [\sigma / \alpha] \qquad \Lambda \alpha . M \alpha = M \quad (\alpha \notin \mathrm{FTV}(M))$$

Fig. 3. The $\lambda_c 2_\eta$-calculus, extended from the λ_c-calculus

For most of basic fibred category theory in the context of categorical semantics, we refer to [19]. In the present paper we use fibred-category-theoretical notions only *with a fixed base category*. $\mathbf{Fib}_\mathbb{B}$ is the 2-category of all fibrations, fibred functors and fibred natural transformations over a fixed base category $\mathbb{B}$.

A *fibred monad* (over $\mathbb{B}$) is an *internal* monad *in* the 2-category $\mathbf{Fib}_\mathbb{B}$ [33]. For a fibred monad T, we can construct the Kleisli adjunction $U \vdash F : p \longrightarrow p_T$ in $\mathbf{Fib}_\mathbb{B}$ (cf. [17]). For a fibration $(p, \otimes, \mathrm{I}, \alpha, \lambda, \rho)$ with fibred products, for which we use the tensor notation, a *strong fibred monad* (T, η, μ, τ) over p is a fibred monad (T, η, μ) and fibred natural transformation $\tau : \otimes \circ (p \times T) \implies T \circ \otimes$ satisfying the four equations: $\lambda * T = (T * \lambda) \circ (\tau * \langle \mathrm{C_I}, p \rangle)$, $(\tau * (\otimes \times p)) \circ (\alpha * (p^2 \times T)) = (T * \alpha) \circ (\tau * (p \times \otimes)) \circ (\otimes * \tau)$, $\eta * \otimes = \tau \circ (\otimes * (p \times \eta))$, $\tau \circ (p \times \mu) = (\mu * \otimes) \circ (T * \tau) \circ (\tau * (p \times T))$, where $\mathrm{C_I} := \mathrm{I} \circ \, ! : p \longrightarrow 1 \longrightarrow p$ is the constant fibred functor of I.

4   Categorical Semantics for Second Order Computational Lambda Calculi

In this section, we give categorical semantics for the $\lambda_c 2$-calculus and the $\lambda_c 2_\eta$-calculus. As mentioned in the introduction, we use monadic style semantics rather than direct style semantics for call-by-value. They are equivalent [10], since we include into the definitions below the equalizing requirement, which asks each component η_A of the unit of a monad T is an equalizer of $T\eta_A$ and η_{TA}.

First we define a "λ_c-version of polymorphic fibration", which models the λ_c-calculus and type variables, but does not model universal types.

Definition 1. *A* polymorphic λ_c-model *consists of*

  (i) *a cartesian polymorphic fibration, i.e. a fibration $p : \mathbb{E} \longrightarrow \mathbb{B}$ which has products in the base category, generic object Ω and fibred products,*
 (ii) *a fibred strong monad T on p satisfying the equalizing requirement fiberwise, and*
(iii) *fibred Kleisli exponentials, i.e., a family of right adjoint functors $X \multimap (-)$ to the composite functors $F_I((-) \times X) : \mathbb{E}_I \xrightarrow{(-) \times X} \mathbb{E}_I \xrightarrow{F_I} (\mathbb{E}_T)_I$ where I is an object in $\mathbb{B}$ and X is over I in p, and which satisfies the Beck-Chevalley condition:*
       for any $u : J \longrightarrow I$ in $\mathbb{B}$ and X over I in p, the natural transformation from $u^* \circ (X \multimap (-))$ to $(u^* X \multimap (-)) \circ u^* T$ induced by the natural isomorphism from $F_J((-) \times u^* X) \circ u^*$ to $u^* T \circ F_I((-) \times X)$ is isomorphic. ☐

If we have the first and the second item in the above definition, and if the fibration is a fibred CCC, then we get the third item of polymorphic λ_c-model for free by composition of the Kleisli adjunction and the adjunction defining cartesian closedness. All the examples in the present paper are such models.

In the following, we use Ω for a generic object of a fibration, if it exists and there is no ambiguity.

Definition 2. *Let p be a polymorphic λ_c-model. By change-of-base of the Kleisli embedding $F : p \longrightarrow p_T$ along $(-) \times \Omega : \mathbb{B} \longrightarrow \mathbb{B}$, we have a fibred functor $F^\Omega : p^\Omega \longrightarrow p_T{}^\Omega$. In addition, the reindexing functors induced by the projections give a "weakening" fibred functor $\pi^*_{(-),\Omega} : p \longrightarrow p^\Omega$. Then,*

  - Kleisli simple Ω-products *is a fibred right adjoint functor to the composite of these two fibred functors, and*
  - a λ_c2-model *is a polymorphic λ_c-model p which has Kleisli simple Ω-products.* ☐

As the case of fibred Kleisli exponentials for a fibred CCC, if we have a polymorphic λ_c-model p which has simple Ω-products, then we obtain Kleisli simple Ω-products in a quite similar way, and hence a λ_c2-model for free. So any λ2-fibration [19] which has the second item in Definition 1 forms a λ_c2-model.

Definition 3. *A λ_c2$_\eta$-model is a polymorphic λ_c-model p whose Kleisli fibration p_T has simple Ω-products.* ☐

It is easily seen that all λ_c2$_\eta$-models are λ_c2-models.

An interpretation of the $\lambda_c 2_\eta$-calculus in a $\lambda_c 2_\eta$-model is defined by inductions on type formation and on typing rules. This can be done in a quite similar way to that of λ_c-calculus [25], with referring to that of System F [19], too.

On the type abstraction rule, $[\![\Xi \mid \Gamma \vdash \Lambda\alpha.M : \forall\alpha.\sigma]\!] : [\![\Gamma]\!] \longrightarrow [\![\forall\alpha.\sigma]\!] :=$ $\prod [\![\sigma]\!]$ in $(p_T)_{[\![\Xi]\!]}$ is defined as the transposition of the composite $[\![\Xi, \alpha \mid \Gamma \vdash M : \sigma]\!] \circ$ ("canonical isomorphism") $: \pi^*[\![\Gamma]\!] \cong [\![\Gamma]\!] \longrightarrow [\![\sigma]\!]$ in $(p_T)_{[\![\Xi,\alpha]\!]} = (p_T)_{[\![\Xi]\!]\times\Omega}$ under simple Ω-products adjointness.

On the type application rule, first we have an arrow $[\![\Xi \mid \Gamma \vdash M : \forall\alpha.\sigma]\!] : [\![\Gamma]\!] \longrightarrow [\![\forall\alpha.\sigma]\!] := \prod [\![\sigma]\!]$ in $(p_T)_{[\![\Xi]\!]}$ with its transposition $m : \pi^*[\![\Gamma]\!] \longrightarrow [\![\sigma]\!]$ in $(p_T)_{[\![\Xi]\!]\times\Omega}$, and also have an arrow $[\![\tau]\!]^\sharp : [\![\Xi]\!] \longrightarrow \Omega$ in $\mathbb{B}$, where $(-)^\sharp$ is the correspondence induced by the generic object. Then $[\![\Xi \mid \Gamma \vdash M\tau : \sigma\,[\tau/\alpha]]\!] : [\![\Gamma]\!] \longrightarrow [\![\sigma\,[\tau/\alpha]]\!]$ in $(p_T)_{[\![\Xi]\!]}$ is defined as the composite $[\![\Gamma]\!] \cong \left\langle \mathrm{id}_{[\![\Xi]\!]}, [\![\tau]\!]^\sharp \right\rangle^* \pi^*[\![\Gamma]\!] \longrightarrow \left\langle \mathrm{id}_{[\![\Xi]\!]}, [\![\tau]\!]^\sharp \right\rangle^* [\![\sigma]\!] \cong [\![\sigma\,[\tau/\alpha]]\!]$, where the last isomorphism is the canonical isomorphism from a semantic type substitution lemma proved routinely, and the middle arrow is the reindexing of m by $\left\langle \mathrm{id}_{[\![\Xi]\!]}, [\![\tau]\!]^\sharp \right\rangle$.

Theorem 4 *The class of all $\lambda_c 2_\eta$-models are sound and complete for the $\lambda_c 2_\eta$-calculus with respect to the above interpretation.*

Proof. 1 *Soundness follows routinely by induction. For completeness, a term model can be constructed in the same way as those for System F [19] and for the λ_c-calculus [10].* ∎

Now we shall introduce a subclass of the class of $\lambda_c 2_\eta$-models. All concrete models we give in the present paper belong to this class.

Definition 5. *A monadic $\lambda_c 2_\eta$-model is a polymorphic λ_c-model such that p and p_T has simple Ω-products and the Kleisli embedding $F : p \longrightarrow p_T$ preserves them.* □

The notion of monadic $\lambda_c 2_\eta$-models is natural for monadic style translation. The preservation of simple Ω-products by the identity-on-objects functor F means that we use the same universal types before and after the monadic style translation. If we are interested in extensional universal types only for call-by-value languages themselves, then we should expand the semantics to the class of $\lambda_c 2_\eta$-models. However, if we are also interested in monadic metalanguages, then it is very simple and hence important to use the same universal types between the value (non-effect) language (base category of a monad) and various effectful languages (Kleisli categories), since in a monadic metalanguage we may use more than one monad, as we do so in Haskell.

Proposition 6. *Let p be a polymorphic λ_c-model such that p has simple Ω-products.*

(1) If p_T has simple Ω-products, then the fibred right adjoint functor $U : p_T \longrightarrow p$ preserves simple Ω-products.

(2) p is a monadic $\lambda_c 2_\eta$-model, (i.e., p_T has simple Ω-products and the fibred functor $F : p \longrightarrow p_T$ preserves simple Ω-products,) if and only if the underlying fibred endofunctor T of the monad preserves simple Ω-products. □

By this proposition, it turns out that, in order to find a monadic $\lambda_c 2_\eta$-model, we only have to pay attention to the underlying endofunctor of a monad, without considering η nor μ. This is because the canonical arrow $T (\prod A) \longrightarrow \prod TA$ respects η and μ, since the reindexings preserve them. This simplification is very useful as we use in the next section.

5   Concrete Models

In this section, we start to study concrete monadic $\lambda_c 2_\eta$-models.

In order to obtain monadic $\lambda_c 2_\eta$-models, we use Proposition 6 (2). For a $\lambda 2$-fibration and a fibred strong monad on it satisfying the equalizing requirement, if the underlying fibred endofunctor of the monad preserves simple Ω-products, i.e., if $T (\prod A) \cong \prod TA$ holds, then they form a monadic $\lambda_c 2_\eta$-model. So we analyze what kind of fibred functors preserve simple Ω-products in $\lambda 2$-fibrations.

5.1   The Class of Monads

We describe here the class of monads considered in the present paper. For the sake of simplicity, we concentrate on the underlying endofunctors of monads.

First let us consider the following class of functors. In order to consider initial algebras and final coalgebras, we consider multi-ary functors as well as unary endofunctors.

$$T ::= \gamma \,|\, C \,|\, 1 \,|\, T \times T \,|\, T + T \,|\, T^C \,|\, \mu\gamma.T \,|\, \nu\gamma.T$$

This class is constructed inductively by projections, (i.e., variables γ,) constant functors, finite products, binary coproducts, powers, (i.e., exponentials whose domains are constants,) initial algebras, and final coalgebras. Basically we would like to consider something like the above class, but there is a problem.

All we need to show is that the underlying fibred endofunctors of fibred monads preserve simple Ω-products, so it is sufficient to prove that the constructions defining inductively the above class (in the fibred setting) preserve simple Ω-products. However, it is shown in Section 6.1 that coproducts do not necessarily commute with universal quantifier in System F even with parametricity, and so we need some special morphism in a $\lambda 2$-fibration considered here. In the paper, we use models having fixed-point operators to resolve it. So, in order to avoid well-known conflict between fixed-point operators and coproducts, we consider linear (more precisely, *relevant*) models by which we can relax relational parametricity inducing coproducts as in [28,5], and replace coproducts with separated sums and initial algebras with *linearly initial algebras*. Linearly initial algebras are, roughly, something which are initial algebras only in a linear model. These notions of separated sums and linearly initial algebras will be explained in Section 6.3 and 6.4 respectively.

Now let us describe the class of monads considered in the present paper. It is the class of all fibred monads whose underlying fibred endofunctors are included in the following class (1).

$$T ::= \gamma \mid 1 \mid T \times T \mid T^C \mid \nu\gamma.T \mid C \mid T \oplus T \mid \mu^\circ\gamma.T \qquad (1)$$

In the above, $\oplus$ is separated sum, and $\mu^\circ\gamma.T$ is linearly initial algebras. These constructions form fibred functors, see Sections 5.2, 6.3, and 6.4 for final coalgebras, separated sums, and linearly initial algebras respectively.

From now on we show that simple Ω-products are preserved by (i): products, powers, final coalgebras, (ii): constant fibred functors, (iii): separated sums, and linearly initial algebras.

On the constructions of (i), we can show that they preserve simple Ω-products by their categorical universal property, because they are right adjoint as well as simple Ω-products. For constants of (ii), however, we need more *property* like parametricity, and for separated sums and linearly initial algebras of (iii), we need additionally more *structures* like fixed-point operators. We consider products, powers, final coalgebras in the next subsection, constants are treated in the next, and separated sums and linearly initial algebras are postponed to the next section.

In the paper, we do not mind whether such constructions as above are available or not, and do only show that they preserve simple Ω-products if they exist. If we try to show existence of e.g. parameterized initial algebras for multi-ary functor, to treat the list monad and input monads, then we need to introduce the notion of "fibrations and fibred functors *enriched* over a monoidal *fibration*", and perhaps need to use *fibrations with indeterminates* [17]. For space reason we postpone such detailed work elsewhere, which is less problematic because the existence of the constructions represented in syntax is well known by polymorphic encoding with parametricity.

5.2   Products, Powers and Final Coalgebras

Here, we investigate constructions which preserve simple Ω-products by only universal property.

Lemma 7. *Let $\mathbb{B}$ be a cartesian category, and K be any object of $\mathbb{B}$.*

(1) The subcategory of $\mathbf{Fib}_\mathbb{B}$ consisting of all fibrations having simple K-products, and all fibred functors preserving simple K-products, is cartesian subcategory.

(2) Let p be a fibration having simple K-products and fibred finite products. Then the fibred functors $\times : p \times p \longrightarrow p$, and $1 : 1 \longrightarrow p$ preserve simple K-products.

(3) Moreover assume that p is a fibred CCC. Then for any X over 1 in p, the "power" fibred functor $X \Rightarrow (-) : p \longrightarrow p$ preserves simple K-products. □

We can also add final coalgebras into the above list, if they exist sufficiently in the sense described below. The same things hold from here to Definition 8 for both initial algebras and final coalgebras in the dual way, so we do with initial algebras, since more examples of effects use initial algebras.

Let p, q be fibrations with the same base category $\mathbb{B}$, and $F : q \times p \longrightarrow p$ be a fibred functor. We say that $F : q \times p \longrightarrow p$ *has initial algebras with parameters*, if for any X over I in q, the endofunctor $F(X, -) : \mathbb{E}_I \longrightarrow \mathbb{E}_I$ has initial algebra $(\mu FX, \alpha_X : F(X, \mu FX) \longrightarrow \mu FX)$, and if the reindexings preserve them, i.e., for any X over I in q and any arrow $u : J \longrightarrow I$ in $\mathbb{B}$, the unique algebra map from the initial algebra $\mu F(u^* X)$ to the algebra $F(u^* X, u^* (\mu FX)) \cong u^* F(X, \mu FX) \xrightarrow{u^* \alpha_X} u^* (\mu FX)$ is isomorphism.

If F is in the case, then the assignment which maps an object X over I in q to the object μFX over I in p extends to the unique fibred functor $\mu F : q \longrightarrow p$ such that the family of maps $(\alpha_X : F(X, \mu FX) \longrightarrow \mu FX)_X$ forms into a fibred natural transformation from $F(-, \mu F-)$ to μF.

Definition 8. *For a fibred functor $F : q \times p \longrightarrow p$ having initial algebras with parameters, there is the* initial algebras fibred functor $\mu F : q \longrightarrow p$ *as above.*

Similarly, if $F : q \times p \longrightarrow p$ has final coalgebras with parameters, which is defined in the dual way, then we have the final coalgebras fibred functor $\nu F : q \longrightarrow p$ *with the fibred natural transformation from νF to $F(-, \nu F-)$.* ☐

Lemma 9. *Let $\mathbb{B}$ be a cartesian category, K be an object of $\mathbb{B}$, p, q be fibrations having simple K-products, and $F : q \times p \longrightarrow p$ be a fibred functor having final coalgebras with parameters. Then, if F preserves simple K-products, the fibred functor $\nu F : q \longrightarrow p$ also preserves simple K-products.* ☐

Typical usage of the above is to get endofunctors with $q = p$ (or p^n), but we will use a coKleisli fibration for q with linear models in Section 6.4.

5.3   Constant

In this short subsection, the construction using constants is added.

For a $\lambda 2$-fibration p and any object X over 1, the fibred functor $X : 1 \longrightarrow p$ preserves simple Ω-products if p satisfies suitable parametricity, including relational parametricity, linear parametricity, and focal parametricity.

In this case of constants we do not need additional arrows differently from the case in the next section, because we can adopt the (unique) projection as the inverse arrow of the canonical (diagonal) arrow $X \longrightarrow \prod X$.

At this point, we can add global state monads $((-) \times S)^S$ and output monads $\mu^\circ \beta. (-) + (U \times \beta) \cong (-) \times (\mu^\circ \beta. 1 + (U \times \beta))$ to the class of monads which form monadic $\lambda_c 2_\eta$-models.

6   Separated Sums and Linearly Initial Algebras

We continue to show how we construct monads compatible with extensional universal types. In this section we consider separated sums and linearly initial algebras. For space reason, we give only a sketch.

6.1   Basic Ideas

First we describe basic ideas used in later, and also why we use separated sums and linearly initial algebras instead of coproducts and initial algebras. Contrary to the case of constants, for coproducts and initial algebras we have to use more limited class of models with additional arrows. First let us see the reason for coproducts in a syntactic way.

Naively thinking, to get the desired term of the type $\forall \alpha.\,(\sigma + \tau) \rightarrow \forall \alpha.\sigma + \forall \alpha.\tau$, we can think of a term like

$$\lambda u{:}\forall \alpha.\,(\sigma + \tau).\ \text{case } u1 \text{ of} \tag{2}$$

$$\text{in}_0\ a' \rightarrow \text{in}_0\ \big(\varLambda \alpha.\text{case } u\alpha \text{ of } (\text{in}_0\ a \rightarrow a)\ |\ (\text{in}_1\ b \rightarrow \text{``this case nothing''}) \big)$$

$$|\text{in}_1\ b' \rightarrow \text{in}_1\ \big(\varLambda \alpha.\text{case } u\alpha \text{ of } (\text{in}_0\ a \rightarrow \text{``this case nothing''})\ |\ (\text{in}_1\ b \rightarrow b) \big)$$

where "this case nothing"'s mean that the cases of the coproducts are not realized, if we assume parametricity. In fact, we can prove in the Plotkin-Abadi logic that, for any term u of a type $\forall \alpha.\,(\sigma + \tau)$, every type instantiation of u has the same index of the coproduct.

However, this is just a reasoning in logic, and there is no assurance to be able to construct such terms as "this case nothing". In fact, there is no term of the type $\forall \alpha.\,(\sigma + \tau) \rightarrow \forall \alpha.\sigma + \forall \alpha.\tau$ in System F for certain σ and τ: for the case when σ is α and τ is $\alpha \rightarrow 0$, the type $\forall \alpha.\,(\alpha + (\alpha \rightarrow 0)) \rightarrow \forall \alpha.\alpha + \forall \alpha.\,(\alpha \rightarrow 0)$ in System F corresponds to the proposition $\forall \alpha.\,(\alpha \vee \neg \alpha) \Rightarrow \forall \alpha.\alpha \vee \forall \alpha.\neg \alpha$ in second order intuitionistic logic, and the inhabitation contradicts the soundness of second order classical logic. So we have to add more terms to realize the above "this case nothing".

To solve this problem, we use non-termination effects, with which we can replace "this case nothing"'s with bottoms.

In the next place, let us think about initial algebras. For e.g. the list monad, we may think a desired term f of the type $\forall \alpha.\mu \beta.1 + \sigma \times \beta \longrightarrow \mu \beta.1 + (\forall \alpha.\sigma) \times \beta$ as the following.

$$\text{let } f = \lambda u{:}\,(\forall \alpha.\mu \beta.1 + \sigma \times \beta).\ \text{case } u1 \text{ of Nil} \rightarrow \text{Nil} \mid \text{Cons}(a', as') \rightarrow$$

$$\text{Cons} \big(\ \varLambda \alpha.\text{case } u\alpha \text{ of } (\text{Nil} \rightarrow \text{``this case nothing''})\ |\ (\text{Cons}(a, as) \rightarrow a),$$

$$f\big(\varLambda \alpha.\text{case } u\alpha \text{ of } (\text{Nil} \rightarrow \text{``this case nothing''})\ |\ (\text{Cons}(a, as) \rightarrow as) \big)\ \big)$$

The two "this case nothing"'s are the same as that in the case of coproducts, and this is just because we use coproducts in the definition of lists. The essential here is the occurrence of f in the definition of f. This is not induction which follows from the universality of initial algebras, but recursion by fixed-point operators.

For fixed-point operators, we employ separated sums and linearly initial algebras instead of coproducts and initial algebras respectively. These cause no problem to construct monads, as we use these in Haskell in fact, because these also have universal property, though limited into a linear model. In the following subsections, we show that separated sums and linearly initial algebras preserve simple $\varOmega$-products in relevant parametric models with fixed-point operators.

6.2   Linear Parametric Models

From now on, we consider domain theoretic models. Let us begin with describing what kind of models we use.

We consider a PILL$_Y$ *model*[6] l having fibred products. PILL$_Y$ models are $\lambda 2$-version of linear categories which can also model fixed-point operators, see loc. cit. for details. The requirement on fibred products is not strong at all, since they can be obtained for free if we assume linear parametricity [5], and in fact we assume a bit stronger one, i.e., relevant parametricity in the next subsection. For the linear exponential fibred comonad ! on l, let $U : l \rightleftarrows p : L$ be its coKleisli fibred adjunction, where U is the right, so fiberwise identity-on-objects.

Then p is a $\lambda 2$-fibration: It is well-known that the coKleisli category of a linear model with cartesian products is a CCC, see e.g. [3]. A generic object is shared with l, since U is fiberwise identity-on-objects and the base is shared. Simple Ω-products are for free like fibred products.

We take this $\lambda 2$-fibration p as the base fibration of monadic $\lambda_c 2_\eta$-models. Then, the fibred monads T on p studied below are what we described in Section 5.1.

Since U is a fibred right adjoint functor, it preserves simple Ω-products, which follow from just the universal property, and irrelevant to the fact that Ω is a generic object or that U preserves it.

On the other hand, we do assume that the left fibred adjoint functor L preserves simple Ω-products. The reason for assuming this is to show the compatibility of separated sums and of linearly initial algebras with simple Ω-products. Thanks to this assumption, we can add the non-termination lifting monad to the class of monads compatible with simple Ω-products, but this is just a (welcome) secondary product. This is a reasonable assumption, since lifting monads usually preserve simple Ω-products in a parametric setting, as opposed to powerset monads.

6.3   Relevant Parametricity for Separated Sum

The use of fixed-point operators involves two matters, i.e., we have to use separated sums instead of coproducts in p, and have to use linear parametricity.

In fact, the use of separated sums is less problematic. Assuming linear parametricity, there are fibred coproducts in l, so we have also fibred separated sums $\oplus$ in p as $U \circ (+) \circ L^2$. Here, $(+) \circ L^2$ has the same kind of universal property as Kleisli exponentials, and by this we can construct familiar monads like e.g. exception monads, the list monad, and input monads. When we use separated sums for exception monads, it can be viewed also in terms of *linearly used effects* [13].

Now we show that these separated sums commute with simple Ω-products. We basically use the idea of the above term (2). After replacing "this case nothing"'s with bottoms, still there remain two problems. The first is, in (2), we use weakening rules for a' and b', and the second is the use of a contraction rule for the two u's in $u1$ and $u\alpha$. (The two $u\alpha$'s are essentially the same, since this is from the distributivity of monoidal products over coproducts in l.)

The problem of weakening is resolved as the following. To prove that separated sums preserve simple Ω-products, it suffices to prove $\prod^\circ (!A+!B) \cong \prod^\circ !A + \prod^\circ !B$ in l, where $\prod^\circ$ is simple Ω-products in l. This is because, we can then show that $\prod (A \oplus B) \overset{\text{def}}{=} \prod U (LA+LB) \cong U \prod^\circ (LA+LB) = U \prod^\circ (!A+!B) \cong U (\prod^\circ !A + \prod^\circ !B) \cong U (L \prod U A + L \prod U B) = \prod A \oplus \prod B$, noting that U and L preserve simple Ω-products, and U is identity-on-objects. So, we can use weakening rules by virtue of these two !'s.

On the other hand, to use a contraction rule, we need to strengthen a type theory to allow contraction, i.e., to the "relevant" one. Fortunately, lifting monads are usually *relevant monads* as in [18]. *Relevant lambda calculi* are extension of linear lambda calculi with contraction term formation rules. Then *relevant Plotkin-Abadi Logic* is simply linear Plotkin-Abadi logic [5] on top of such the second order relevant lambda calculus. As a result of this extension of the class of linear terms, the class of *admissible relations* is also extended, for instance we can use graph relations of such "relevant terms".

Finally, we need one more rule for forming admissible relations: for an admissible relation ρ between σ and τ, and a term $\langle f, g \rangle : \sigma' \times \tau' \multimap \sigma \times \tau$ of linear function type, the "inverse-image" relation $(x : \sigma', y : \tau') . \rho (f \langle x, y \rangle, g \langle x, y \rangle)$ is also an admissible relation between σ' and τ'. This is modeled with the intuition that admissible relations between σ and τ are subalgebras of the product of σ and τ. This rule is used in the parametric reasoning to prove the equality between the identity on $\prod^\circ (!A+!B)$ and the composite term through $\prod^\circ !A + \prod^\circ !B$ involving the isomorphism $\prod^\circ (!A+!B) \cong \prod^\circ !A + \prod^\circ !B$.

We introduce some of models (l, p, ...) for such relevant parametricity which satisfy the assumptions thus far: the models (PFam $(AP(D)_\perp)$, PFam $(AP(D))$, ...) of linear Plotkin-Abadi logic constructed from domain theoretic PERs, which is described in [8]. Hence,

Proposition 10. *The separated sums in PFam $(AP(D))$ preserve simple Ω-products.* $\square$

6.4   Linearly Initial Algebras

In this last subsection, we consider about linearly initial algebras.

Once we determine to use fixed-point operators, there is an easier way than considering of such a complicate term as in Section 6.1. That is, we can use the fact that if both initial algebras and final coalgebras exist for sufficiently many endofunctors, then the initial algebras and final coalgebras are canonically isomorphic for such endofunctors if and only if fixed-point operators exists [9,5]. Then Lemma 9 is applicable.

All the remaining matter is that we have to use linearly initial algebras instead of initial algebras. Now let q be a fibration which has the same base category and generic object Ω as those of l and p, and has simple Ω-products. Then for a fibred functor $F : q \times p \longrightarrow p$ preserving simple Ω-products, the composite fibred functor $F' := L \circ F \circ (q \times U) : q \times l \longrightarrow q \times p \longrightarrow p \longrightarrow l$ also preserves simple Ω-products.

Now if F' has initial algebras with parameters and also final coalgebras with parameters in the sense of Section 5.2, then the $\mu F'$ and $\nu F'$ are naturally isomorphic thanks to the fixed-point operators as mentioned above. So by Lemma 9, $\mu F'$ preserves simple Ω-products. Hence the *linearly initial algebras* fibred functor $U \circ \mu F' : q \longrightarrow l \longrightarrow p$ also preserves simple Ω-products.

Proposition 11. *Let* $F : PFam(AP(D))^{n+1} \longrightarrow PFam(AP(D))$ *be a fibred functor such that* F' *defined as above has initial algebras with parameters and final coalgebras with parameters. If* F *preserves simple* Ω-products, *then the linearly initial algebras fibred functor* $U \circ \mu F' : PFam(AP(D))^n \longrightarrow PFam(AP(D))$ *also preserves simple* Ω-products.   □

Theorem 12 *Let* T *be a fibred strong monad on* $PFam(AP(D))$ *satisfying the equalizing requirement. If the underlying fibred endofunctor of* T *is included in the class (1) in Section 5.1, then* T *and the* $\lambda 2$-fibration $PFam(AP(D))$ *form a monadic* $\lambda_c 2_\eta$-model.   □

7   Concluding Remark

We have given the second order computational λ-calculus with extensional universal types, which is a call-by-value lambda calculus with universal types satisfying η-equality. Then we have formulated its sound and complete categorical semantics, and also reasonable characterization in terms of monadic metalanguages. Finally, we have seen concrete domain theoretic models, in a somewhat general way with relevant parametricity. Such models can accommodate many familiar effects constructed polynomially to extensional universal types.

In Section 6, we have taken the domain theoretic approach. On the other hand, we can also take a dependent type theoretic approach, by which we can avoid "this case nothing" in the term (2) in Section 6, using *strong* coproducts. Moreover, by *inductive* initial algebras in the sense of [19], we can deal with some kinds of initial algebras including the list monad and input monads. In this way, we can see that the typical models for parametricity constructed from recursion theoretic PERs (see e.g. loc. cit.) also have a similar class of monads which form $\lambda_c 2_\eta$-models. These will be treated in a separate paper.

It is interesting to clarify whether we can include powerset monads and/or continuations monads into the class of models, and whether all lifting monads commute with parametric simple Ω-products.

Also, it is an interesting challenge to investigate principles of parametric polymorphism in the two call-by-value calculi in the paper.

Acknowledgements

I would like to thank Masahito Hasegawa for many helpful discussions and comments on earlier drafts. I am also grateful to Shin-ya Katsumata, Ichiro Hasuo, and Naohiko Hoshino for useful comments and discussions. Also I thank anonymous reviewers for helpful comments.

References

1. Abadi, M., Cardelli, L., Curien, P.-L.: Formal parametric polymorphism. TCS: Theoretical Computer Science 121 (1993)
2. Benton, N., Hughes, J., Moggi, E.: Monads and effects. In: Barthe, G., Dybjer, P., Pinto, L., Saraiva, J. (eds.) APPSEM 2000. LNCS, vol. 2395, pp. 42–122. Springer, Heidelberg (2002)
3. Benton, P.N.: A mixed linear and non-linear logic: Proofs, terms and models (extended abstract). In: CSL, pp. 121–135 (1994)
4. Bierman, G.M., Pitts, A.M., Russo, C.V.: Operational properties of Lily, a polymorphic linear lambda calculus with recursion. Electr. Notes Theor. Comput. Sci. 41(3) (2000)
5. Birkedal, L., Møgelberg, R.E., Petersen, R.L.: Linear Abadi & Plotkin logic. Logical Methods in Computer Science 2(5) (November 2006)
6. Birkedal, L., Møgelberg, R.E., Petersen, R.L.: Category-theoretic models of linear Abadi and Plotkin logic. Theory and Applications of Categories 20(7), 116–151 (2008)
7. Birkedal, L., Møgelberg, R.E.: Categorical models for Abadi and Plotkin's logic for parametricity. Mathematical Structures in Computer Science 15(4), 709–772 (2005)
8. Birkedal, L., Møgelberg, R.E., Petersen, R.L.: Domain-theoretical models of parametric polymorphism. Theor. Comput. Sci. 388(1-3), 152–172 (2007)
9. Freyd, P.: Recursive types reduced to inductive types. In: Mitchell, J. (ed.) Proceedings of the Fifth Annual IEEE Symp. on Logic in Computer Science, LICS 1990, pp. 498–507. IEEE Computer Society Press, Los Alamitos (1990)
10. Führmann, C.: Direct models of the computational lambda calculus. Electr. Notes Theor. Comput. Sci. 20 (1999)
11. Girard, J.-Y.: Interpretation fonctionelle et elimination des coupures de l'arithmetique d'ordre superieur. These D'Etat, Universite Paris VII (1972)
12. Harper, R., Lillibridge, M.: Operational interpretations of an extension of F_ω with control operators. J. Funct. Program. 6(3), 393–417 (1996)
13. Hasegawa, M.: Linearly used effects: Monadic and CPS transformations into the linear lambda calculus. In: Hu, Z., Rodríguez-Artalejo, M. (eds.) FLOPS 2002. LNCS, vol. 2441, pp. 167–182. Springer, Heidelberg (2002)
14. Hasegawa, M.: Relational parametricity and control. Logical Methods in Computer Science 2(3) (2006)
15. Hasegawa, M., Kakutani, Y.: Axioms for recursion in call-by-value. Higher-Order and Symbolic Computation 15(2-3), 235–264 (2002)
16. Hasegawa, R.: Categorical data types in parametric polymorphism. Mathematical Structures in Computer Science 4(1), 71–109 (1994)
17. Hermida, C.A.: Fibrations, Logical Predicates and Indeterminates. Ph.D thesis, University of Edinburgh (1993)
18. Jacobs, B.: Semantics of weakening and contraction. Ann. Pure Appl. Logic 69(1), 73–106 (1994)
19. Jacobs, B.: Categorical Logic and Type Theory. In: Studies in Logic and the Foundations of Mathematics, vol. 141. Elsevier, Amsterdam (1999)
20. Levy, P.B.: Call-By-Push-Value: A Functional/Imperative Synthesis. Semantics Structures in Computation, vol. 2. Springer, Heidelberg (2004)
21. Levy, P.B., Power, J., Thielecke, H.: Modelling environments in call-by-value programming languages. INFCTRL: Information and Computation (formerly Information and Control) 185 (2003)

22. Møgelberg, R.E.: Interpreting polymorphic FPC into domain theoretic models of parametric polymorphism. In: Bugliesi, M., Preneel, B., Sassone, V., Wegener, I. (eds.) ICALP 2006. LNCS, vol. 4052, pp. 372–383. Springer, Heidelberg (2006)

23. Møgelberg, R.E., Simpson, A.: Relational parametricity for computational effects. In: LICS, pp. 346–355. IEEE Computer Society, Los Alamitos (2007)

24. Møgelberg, R.E., Simpson, A.: Relational parametricity for control considered as a computational effect. Electr. Notes Theor. Comput. Sci. 173, 295–312 (2007)

25. Moggi, E.: Computational lambda-calculus and monads. Technical Report ECS-LFCS-88-66, Laboratory for Foundations of Computer Science, University of Edinburgh (1988)

26. Moggi, E.: Computational lambda-calculus and monads. In: LICS, pp. 14–23. IEEE Computer Society, Los Alamitos (1989)

27. Moggi, E.: Notions of computation and monads. Information and Computation 93(1), 55–92 (1991)

28. Plotkin, G.D.: Type theory and recursion (extended abstract). In: LICS, p. 374. IEEE Computer Society, Los Alamitos (1993)

29. Plotkin, G.D., Abadi, M.: A logic for parametric polymorphism. In: Bezem, M., Groote, J.F. (eds.) TLCA 1993. LNCS, vol. 664, pp. 361–375. Springer, Heidelberg (1993)

30. Reynolds, J.C.: Towards a theory of type structure. In: Robinet, B. (ed.) Symposium on Programming. LNCS, vol. 19, pp. 408–423. Springer, Heidelberg (1974)

31. Reynolds, J.C.: Types, abstraction and parametric polymorphism. In: IFIP Congress, pp. 513–523 (1983)

32. Simpson, A.K., Plotkin, G.D.: Complete axioms for categorical fixed-point operators. In: LICS, pp. 30–41 (2000)

33. Street, R.: The formal theory of monads. Journal of Pure and Applied Algebra 2, 149–168 (1972)

34. Wadler, P.: Theorems for free! In: Functional Programming Languages and Computer Architecture. Springer, Heidelberg (1989)

Harnessing the Multicores:
Nested Data Parallelism in Haskell

Simon Peyton Jones

Microsoft Research, Cambridge, U.K

Abstract. If you want to program a parallel computer, a purely functional language like Haskell is a promising starting point. Since the language is pure, it is by-default safe for parallel evaluation, whereas imperative languages are by-default unsafe. But that doesn't make it easy! Indeed it has proved quite difficult to get robust, scalable performance increases through parallel functional programming, especially as the number of processors increases.

A particularly promising and well-studied approach to employing large numbers of processors is to use data parallelism. Blelloch's pioneering work on NESL showed that it was possible to combine a rather flexible programming model (nested data parallelism) with a fast, scalable execution model (flat data parallelism). In this talk I will describe Data Parallel Haskell, which embodies nested data parallelism in a modern, general-purpose language, implemented in a state-of-the-art compiler, GHC. I will focus particularly on the vectorisation transformation, which transforms nested to flat data parallelism, and I hope to present performance numbers.

G. Ramalingam (Ed.): APLAS 2008, LNCS 5356, p. 138, 2008.

Minimal Ownership for Active Objects[*]

Dave Clarke[1], Tobias Wrigstad[2], Johan Östlund[2], and Einar Broch Johnsen[3]

[1] CWI, Amsterdam, The Netherlands
[2] Purdue University, USA
[3] University of Oslo, Norway

Abstract. Active objects offer a structured approach to concurrency, encapsulating both *unshared* state and a thread of control. For efficient data transfer, data should be passed by reference whenever possible, but this introduces aliasing and undermines the validity of the active objects. This paper proposes a minimal variant of ownership types that preserves the required *race freedom* invariant yet enables data transfer by reference between active objects (that is, without copying) in many cases, and a cheap clone operation where copying is necessary. Our approach is general and should be adaptable to several existing active object systems.

1 Introduction

Active objects have been proposed as an approach to concurrency that blends naturally with object-oriented programming [37,61,1]. Several slightly differently flavoured active object systems exist for Java [8], Eiffel [46,17], C++ [43] et al. Active objects encapsulate not only their state and methods, but also a single (active) thread of control. Additional mechanisms, such as *asynchronous method calls* and *futures*, reduce the temporal coupling between the caller and callee of a method. Together, these mechanisms offer a large degree of potential concurrency for deployment on multi-core or distributed architectures.

Internal data structures of active objects, used to store or transfer local data, do not need independent threads of control. In contrast to the active objects, these *passive objects* resemble ordinary (Java) objects. An immediate benefit of distinguishing active and passive objects is that all the concurrency control is handled by the active objects, and locking (via synchronised methods) becomes redundant in the passive objects. This simplifies programming and enables the (re-)use of standard APIs without additional concurrency considerations.

Unfortunately, introducing passive objects into the model gives rise to aliasing problems whenever a passive object can be shared between more than one active object. This allows concurrent modification and/or observation of changes to the passive data objects. Specifically, two active objects can access the same passive data; if at least one thread modifies the data, then different access orders

---

[*] This work is in the context of the EU project IST-33826 CREDO: Modeling and analysis of evolutionary structures for distributed services (http://credo.cwi.nl).

G. Ramalingam (Ed.): APLAS 2008, LNCS 5356, pp. 139–154, 2008.

may produce different results unless we re-introduce locks into the programming model. The resulting system would be as difficult to reason about as unconstrained shared variable concurrency. This problem can be addressed several ways, neither of which we feel is entirely satisfactory:

Immutable Data Only. Active objects are mutable, but field values belong to immutable data types; e.g., integers or booleans, immutable objects such as Java-style strings or XML, or Erlang- and Haskell-style datatypes [5, 35].

Cloning. Locally, active objects can arbitrarily access passive objects, but when data is passed between active objects, the data must be deeply cloned. This approach is taken for distributed active objects (e.g., [8, 18]).

Unique References. Only one reference to any passive object is allowed at any time. Passive objects can be safely transferred between active objects.

Emerald [33, 51] partly addresses this problem using the first approach. Objects can be declared immutable to simplify sharing and for compiler optimisation, but immutability is an unchecked annotation which may be violated. Emerald's use of immutability is optional, as adopting pure immutability means that programs can no longer be implemented in an imperative object-oriented style.

ProActive [8] uses the second approach and copies all message parameters. The programmer gets a very simple and straightforward programming model, but the copying overhead is huge in message-intensive applications.

Last, using uniqueness requires a radical change in programming style and may result in fragile code in situations not easily modelled without aliasing.

This paper investigates the application of ownership types in the context of active object-based concurrency. We propose a combination of ownership-based techniques that can identify the boundaries of active objects and statically verify where reference semantics can be used in place of copy semantics for method arguments and returns.

In previous work, we combined ownership types with effects to facilitate reasoning about disjointness [20] and with uniqueness to enable ownership transfer [21]. Recently, we coalesced these to realise flexible forms of immutability and read-only references [49]. In this paper we tune these systems to the active objects concurrent setting and extend the resulting system with the *arg* reference mode from Flexible Alias Protection [48]. Furthermore, our specific choices of ownership defaults make the proposed language design very concise in terms of additional type annotations. The main contributions of this paper are:

- A synthesised minimal type system with little syntactic overhead that identifies active object boundaries. This type system enables expressing and *statically checking* (and subsequent compiler optimisations) safe practices that programmers do manually today (framework permitting), such as:
  * Statically guarantee total isolation of active objects;
  * In a local setting, replace deep copying of messages with reference passing for (parts of) immutable objects, or unique objects;
  * In a distributed setting replace remote references to immutable (parts of) objects with copying for more efficient local access; and

  * Immutability is per object and the same class can be used to instantiate both immutable and mutable objects.

  All necessary annotations are expressed in terms of ownership, plus a trivial effects system which makes the formalisation (see [22]) clean and simple.

– We present our system in the context of a Java-like language, Joëlle, however our results are applicable to any active object or actor based concurrency model. Active object systems such as ProActive [8], Emerald [33, 51], and Scoop [41] use unchecked immutability or active annotations. Integrating our type system with these approaches for static checking seems straightforward.

The formal description of the system, which is a synthesized model of a large body of previous work [20, 21, 59, 25, 49], can be found in [22].

Organisation. Section 2 surveys the alias control mechanisms upon which we build our proposal. Section 3 further details the problem and presents our solution. Section 4 compares our work with related work, and Section 5 concludes.

2   Building Blocks

We now survey the alias control mechanisms used to construct our synthesized system. They address the problem of reasoning about *shared mutable state* [31, 48], which is problematic as a shared object's state can change *unexpectedly*, potentially violating a sharer's invariants or a client's expectations. There are three main approaches to this problem:

ownership: encapsulate all references to an object within some *box*; such as another object, a stack frame, a thread, a package, a class, or an active object [48, 23, 19, 4, 30, 45, 3, 11, 13].

uniqueness: eliminate sharing so that there is only one active reference to an object [30, 21, 14, 42, 3, 11].

immutability: eliminate or restrict mutability so an object cannot change, or so that changes to it cannot be observed [10, 58, 48, 15, 55, 62].

2.1   Ownership

Ownership types [23] initially formalised the core of Flexible Alias Protection [48]; variants have later been devised for a range of applications [48, 23, 19, 45, 3, 11, 13]. In general, object graphs form an unstructured "soup" of objects. Ownership types impose structure on these graphs by first *putting objects into boxes* [27], then imposing a topology [19, 2] on the boxes, and finally restricting the way objects in different boxes can access each other, either prohibiting certain references or limiting how the references can be used [45, 44].

  Ownership types record the box in which an object resides, called the *owner*, in the object's type. The type system syntactically ensures that fields and methods with types containing the name of a private box are encapsulated (thus only accessible by this). This encapsulation ensures that the contents of private boxes cannot be exported outside their owner. For this to work, the owner information must be retained in the type. Consider the following code fragment:[1]

```
class Engine {} class Car { this::Engine e; }
```

In class Car, the owner of the Engine object is this, which indicates that the object in the field e is owned by the current instance of Car (or, in other words, that every car has its own engine). The type system ensures that the field e is accessible only by this, the owning object.

Ownership types enforce a constraint on the structure of object graphs called *owners-as-dominators*. This property ensures that access to an object's internal state goes through the object's interface: the only way for a client of a Car object to manipulate the Car's Engine is via some method exposed in the Car's public interface. Some ownership types proposals [12, 3, 2, 45] weaken this property.

All classes, such as Engine above, have an implicit parameter owner which refers to the owner of each instance of the class. Thus, arbitrary and extensible linked data structures may be encapsulated in an object. Contrast this with Eiffel's expanded types [40] and C++'s value objects [57], which enable an object to be encapsulated in another object, but require a fixed sized object. In the following class

```
class Link { owner::Link next; int data; }
```

the next object has the same owner as the present object. This is a common idiom, and we call such objects *siblings*. (The Universes system [45] uses the keyword peer instead of owner.)

2.2 External Uniqueness

Object sharing can be avoided using unique or linear references [30, 21, 14, 42, 3, 11]: at any point in the execution of a program, only one *accessible* reference to an object exists. Clarke and Wrigstad introduced the notion of *external uniqueness* [21, 59] which fits nicely with ownership types and permits unique references to aggregate objects that are inherently aliased, such as circularly linked lists. In external uniqueness, unique references must be (temporarily) made non-unique to access or call methods on fields. The single external reference is thus the only active reference making the aggregate effectively unique. External uniqueness enables ownership transfer in ownership types systems.

External uniqueness is effectively equivalent to introducing an owner for the field or variable holding a reference into the data structure, such that the only occurrence of that owner is in the type of the field or variable. In the code below, first holds the only pointer to the (sibling) link objects.

```
class List { unique::Link first; }
```

Uniqueness can be maintained with e.g., destructive reads or Alias Burying [14]. In summary, ownership deals with encapsulating an entire aggregate. Uniqueness concerns having a single (usable) reference to an object. External uniqueness combines them, resulting in a single (usable) reference to an entire aggregate.

---

[1] In this section, code uses syntax from Joe-like languages [20, 21, 49].

2.3   Immutability and 'Safe' Methods

Immutable objects can never change after they are created. An *immutable reference* prevents the holder from calling methods that mutate the target object. Furthermore, references to representation objects returned from a method call via an immutable reference are also immutable—or immutability would be lost. *Observational exposure* [15] occurs when an immutable reference can be used to observe changes to an object, which is possible if non-immutable aliases exist to the object or its representation. Fortunately, strong encapsulation, uniqueness, and read-only methods make the (staged[2]) creation of "truly immutable" objects straightforward [49]. This is similar to Fähndrich and Xia's Delayed Types [28].

In Flexible Alias Protection [48], *'arg'* or *safe references* (our preferred terminology) to an object may only access immutable parts of the object; i.e., the parts which do not change after initialisation. Thus, clients accessing an object via a safe reference can only depend on the object's immutable state, which is safe as it cannot change unexpectedly. Safe references can refer to *any* object, even one which is being mutated by a different active object, without any risk of observational exposure.

2.4   Owner-Polymorphic Methods

Owner-polymorphism is crucial for code reuse and flexibility in the ownership types setting [19,59]. *Owner-polymorphic methods* are parameterised with owners to give the receiver temporary permission to reference an argument object. For example, the following method accepts an owner parameter `foo` in order to enable a list owned by any other object to be passed as an argument:

```
<foo> int sum(foo::List values) { ... }
```

Clarke [19] established that owner-polymorphic methods can express a notion of *borrowing*: an object may be passed to another object, which does not own it, without the latter being able to capture a reference to the former. (For further details, see [59].) Owner-polymorphic methods are reminiscent of region-polymorphic procedures in Cyclone [29].

3   Active Ownership

In *Concurrent programming in Java* [38], Doug Lea writes that "To guarantee safety in a concurrent system, you must ensure that *all* objects accessible from multiple threads are either immutable or employ appropriate synchronisation, and also must ensure that *no* other object ever becomes concurrently accessible by leaking out of its ownership domain."

The simple ways to guarantee the above are the first two we listed on Page 140: making everything immutable or use deep copying semantics. While efficient, the

---

[2] In *staged object creation* an object is initialised though a series of method calls, potentially within different objects, rather than exclusively in its constructor [49].

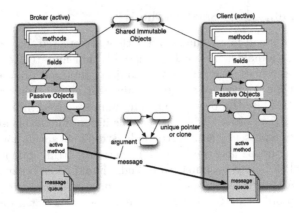

Fig. 1. Active Ownership. Safe references are not depicted. Broker and Client are active objects from the code example in Figure 2.

first is very restrictive and requires careful inspection of the code to determine that the messages are truly immutable. The second is easier to check (just clone all arguments) but has the downside of adding massive copying overhead.

We argue that the most effective approach is a pragmatic combination: using unique references or immutable objects where possible and deep copying only as a last resort. To enable this in a statically and modularly checkable fashion, we introduce a few extra annotations on interfaces of active object classes. We believe that requiring these extra annotations will be helpful for maintenance and possibly also refactoring. Most importantly, we believe that the static checking enabled by the annotations will save time, both programmer-time and run-time.

Our alias control mechanisms uphold the invariant that *no two 'threads' concurrently change or observe changes to an object,* which is the invariant obtained by the deep copying of message arguments in ProActive (with minor exceptions unimportant to us here). Note that our type system is agnostic of the thread model—it correctly infers the boundaries between active objects regardless.

3.1   Active and Passive Classes

Active and passive objects are instantiated from active and passive classes. Active classes are declared with the `active`. Passive is default.

Active objects encapsulate a *single* thread of control. They primarily interact via asynchronous method calls that return future values. A future is a placeholder for a value which need not be currently available [9]. For asynchronous calls, the future is the placeholder for the methods' actual return values. Thus, the caller need not wait for the call to complete. A future's value is accessed using its `get` method, which blocks until the future has a value, which is standard practise. Synchronous calls may be encoded by calling `get` directly after asynchronous method calls. Method calls to passive objects are always synchronous; i.e., they are similar to standard method calls as found in Java. Multiple asynchronous

```
active class Client {
    void run() {
        Request rm = ...; // formulate Request
        future Offer offer = myBroker!book(rm.clone()); // †
        ... // evaluate offer
        offer.getProvider()!accept(offer.clone()); // †
    }
}
active class Broker {
    void run() { ... } // go into reactive mode
    // book returns first Offer that responds to the request
    Offer book(Request request) { ... }
}
active class Provider {
    void run() { ... } // go into reactive mode
    Offer query(Request request) { ... }
    boolean accept(Offer offer) { ... }
}
class Request {
    Request(String desc) { ... }
    void markAccepted() { ... }
}
class Offer {
    Offer(Details d, Provider p, Request trackback) { ... }
    Provider getProvider() { ... }
}
```

Fig. 2. Example of active objects exchanging arguments by copying (shown at †). Here future Offer denotes a future of type Offer. For clarity, we use a !-notation on asynchronous method calls, e.g., myBroker!book(rm).

calls to an active object are put in an inbox and executed sequentially. Creol [25,34] uses release point to yield execution midway through a method, but this is irrelevant to the minimal ownership system.

Figures 1 and 2 show a use of active objects that deliberately copy arguments to avoid aliasing-induced data races. Figure 4 shows how we can annotate the code in our system to avoid the copying without comprising safety. For brevity, we focus simply on the interfaces, which suffices for the type annotations. The figure shows the following scenario:

1. Client sends request to broker
2. Broker forwards request to provider(s) and negotiates a deal
3. Broker returns resulting offer to client
4. If client accepts offer, client sends acceptance to provider

The client, the broker, and all providers are represented as active objects and execute concurrently. In contrast, requests and offers are passive objects, passed between active ones by copying to avoid data races between the active objects.

3.2 Putting It Together: Language Constructs for Active Ownership

This section describes our synthesised system leading up to an encoding of the example from Figure 2 that avoids copying. Figure 3 shows a few examples of code using our annotations. While our annotations are similar to capabilities, they are expressed as owners. This keeps the underlying formalism (see [22]) relatively simple. Our system has the following annotations:

`active`	globally accessible owner of all active objects
`owner`	the owner of the current object (in the scope of the annotation)
`this`	the owner denoting the current object (in the scope of the annotation)
`unique`	the owner denoting the current field or variable
`immutable`	globally accessible owner of all immutable objects
`safe`	globally accessible owner allowing safe access

The owners `active`, `immutable`, and `safe` are available in any context, and denote the global owner of active objects, immutable references, and safe references, respectively. `unique` is also available everywhere, but denotes field-as-owner, as explained in Section 2.2. Nested inside each active object is a collection of passive objects, owned by the active object with owner `this`. The owner `owner` is available only in passive classes for referring to the owner of the current instance, and is used to create data structures within an active object.

Note that the ownership hierarchy is very flat, as there is no owner `this` inside a passive class. Ownership encapsulates passive objects inside an active object. Consequently, there is no need to keep track of nesting or other relationships such as links between owners [2]. In addition, the classes in this system take no owner parameters, in contrast to the original ownership types system [23]. Therefore, no run-time representation of ownership is required [60].

Immutable and Safe References. Immutable types have owner `immutable`. In our system, only passive objects can have immutable type. Fields or variables containing immutable references are not final unless explicitly declared final or if the container enclosing the field is immutable. In order to preserve immutability, only *read-only* and *safe* methods (see below) can be called on immutable objects.

Safe references (called *argument* references in Flexible Alias Protection [48]) have owner `safe` and can be used only to access the final fields of an object, and the final fields of the values returned from methods, and so forth. These parts of an object cannot be changed underfoot. Methods that obey these conditions are called safe methods, denoted by a `safe` annotation. Any non-active type can be subsumed into a `safe` type.

Immutable references can only be created from unique references. The operation consumes the unique reference and thus guarantees the absence of any aliases to the object that allows mutation. This is powerful and flexible as it allows a single class to be used both as a template for both mutable and immutable objects (see [21]) and staged object construction. Effectively, immutability becomes a property of the object, rather than of the class or of references.

Safe references do not preclude the existence of mutable aliases, which is safe as it only allows access to the referenced object's immutable parts. Consequently, both safe and immutable references avoid observational exposure.

```
active class Foo { // active class
  this Bar f; // properly encapsulated field
  owner Bar b; // invalid -- owner is not legal in active classes
  active Bar k; // reference to (sibling) active object
}

class Bar { // passive class
  owner Bar f; // sibling field (same level of encapsulation)
  this Bar b; // invalid -- this is not legal in passive classes
}

unique Foo f = new Foo(); // new returns a unique reference
immutable Foo b = f--; // -- is destructive read, nullifies f

void foo() read { ... } // can only call read and safe methods
                        // on this, and not update fields

void foo() safe { ... } // can only call safe methods/read
safe Foo f;             // final immutable/safe fields on this/f

void foo() write { ... } // regular method, write can be omitted
```

Fig. 3. Examples of active and passive classes, unique, safe and immutable types, and read and safe methods

Read-only and Safe Methods. Following previous read-only proposals, e.g., [30,55,10,15], a read-only method preserves the immutability of objects, and does not return non-immutable references to otherwise immutable objects. Read-only methods cannot update any object with owner owner, which notably includes the receiver. They are not, however, purely functional: they can be used to modify unique references passed in as arguments or objects freshly created within the method itself and they can call mutating methods on active objects.

As immutability is encoded in the owners, a return value from a read-only method that has owner owner will (automatically) have the owner immutable when the read-only method is called on an immutable reference, and hence will not provide a means for violating the immutability of the original reference [49, 62]. To allow modular checking, read-only methods are annotated with read.

A safe method, annotated safe, is an additionally restricted read-only method that may only access immutable parts of the receiver's state, i.e., final fields containing safe or immutable references. Conceptually, a read-only method prevents mutation whereas a safe method also prevents the observation of mutation.

3.3   Data Transfer and Minimal Cloning

To ensure that the data race freedom invariant is preserved, care is needed when passing data between active objects. How data is passed, depends on its owner.

Active-owned objects are safe to pass by reference as external threads of control never enter them by virtue of asynchronous methods calls and futures. Immutable and safe-owned objects are obviously safe to pass by reference as their accessible parts cannot be changed. Last, unique objects are safe to pass by reference as they are effectively transferred to the target[3].

Other objects (owned by this, owner and owner-parameters to methods) must be cloned. Cloning returns a unique reference which can be transferred regardless of the owner of the expected parameter type. Cloning follows the above rules to determine whether an object's fields must be cloned or whether it is safe to simply copy the reference—the only difference is that clone clones fields holding unique references. A "minimal clone" operation can be trivially inferred statically from the owner annotations. This is similar to the *sheep clone* described for ownership types [47, 19] and Nienaltowski's object import [46].

Notably, our clone rightfully avoids cloning of active objects, something a naive clone would not do. This is necessary to allow returning a reference to a provider in our example and lets active objects behave like regular objects.

Reducing Syntactic Baggage. We adopt a number of reasonable defaults for owner annotations to reduce the amount of annotations required in a program, and to use legacy code immediately in a sensible way.

Passive Classes (including all library code) have one implicit owner parameter owner, which is the default owner of all fields and all method arguments. Note that this means that library code, in general, requires no annotations.
Active Classes have the implicit owner active. In an active class, the default owner is this for all fields and unique for all method arguments.

Together these defaults imply that all passive objects reachable from an active object's fields are encapsulated inside the active object, in the absence of immutable and safe references. By default, all method parameters in the public interface of active objects are unique. This is the only way to guarantee that *mutable* objects are not shared between active objects. References passed between active objects must be unique, either originally or as a result of performing a clone. Note that having unique as the default annotation does not apply to active class types appearing in the interface, as these can only be active. This choice of defaults is supported by the experimental results of Potanin and Noble [50] and Ma and Foster [39], which show that many arguments between objects could well be unique references.

3.4   Revisiting the Example

Figure 4 adds active ownership annotations to Figure 2. As a result, all copying is avoided. Only six annotations are needed to express the intended semantics of Figure 2. This might seem excessive for a 20-line program, but remember that we only focus on the parts of the program that needs annotations. Furthermore, no annotations are required for library code used by this program. But more importantly, we can now captures the programmer's intentions in statically checkable annotations.

---

[3] We currently do not support borrowing on asyncronous method calls. A unique object transferred to from active object A to B must be explicitly transferred back.

```
active class Client {
    void run() ‡ {
        †Request rm = ...; // formulate Request
        future immutable Offer offer = myBroker!book(rm); // (1)
        ... // evaluate offer
        offer.getProvider()!accept(offer); // (2)
    }
}
active class Broker {
    void run() ‡ { ... } // go into reactive mode
    // book returns first provider that responds to the request
    immutable Offer book(safe Request request) ‡ { ... } // (3)
}
active class Provider {
    immutable Offer query(safe Request request) ‡ { ... } // (4)
    boolean accept(immutable Offer offer) ‡ { ... } // (5)
}
class Request {
    Request(†String desc) ‡ { ... }
    void markAccepted() ‡ { ... }
}
class Offer {
    Offer(†Details d, †Provider p, safe Request r) ‡ ... // (6)
    Provider getProvider() read { ... } // (7)
}
```

Fig. 4. The active objects example with active ownership. † indicates an implicit use of a default, owner in passive classes and this in active. ‡ indicates an implicit use of the write default for methods. These are not part of the actual code.

The offer is made immutable (4), which allows it to be safely shared between concurrently executing clients, brokers and providers. The immutability requirement propagates to the type of the future variable (1) and formal parameter (5). The request is received as a safe reference (3), so the broker may only access its immutable parts which precludes both races and observational exposure. This constraint is reasonable, since changing crucial parts of a request under foot might lead to invalid offers. Parts of the request can still be updated by the client (but not by the broker or any provider), e.g., to store a handle to the accepted offer in it. The safe annotation propagates to (6). Read-only methods are annotated read (7). Reading the provider from an immutable offer (2) returns a reference to an active object, which is safe as it does not share any state with the outside world.

3.5   Other Relevant Features

For space reasons, we omit a discussion of exceptions, which is a straightforward addition (they would be immutable), and a discussion on how to deal with globals (see [22]) and focus on the issue of owner-polymorphic methods in the presence of asynchronous method calls.

Owner-polymorphic methods (and their problems). The previous discussion ignored owner-polymorphic methods. An owner-polymorphic method of an active object enables the active object to borrow passive objects from another active object, with the guarantee that it will not keep any references to the borrowed objects. Such methods require care, as they are problematic in the presence of asynchronous method calls. It is easy to see that an asynchronous call could easily lead to a situation where two active objects (`Client` and `Broker`) have access to the same passive objects (`Request`):

1. `Client` lends `Request` to `Broker` via an asynchronous method call.
2. `Client` continues executing on `Request`.
3. `Broker` concurrently operates on `Request`.

We choose the simplest solution to avoid this problem by banning asynchronous calls to owner-polymorphic methods. Alternative approaches would require preventing `Client` from accessing `Request`—or more precisely, objects with the same owner as `Request`—until the method call to `Broker` returned.

4   Related Work

4.1   Ownership Types

Several approaches using ownership types for concurrency control have been proposed. [7,11] introduce thread-local owners to avoid data races and deadlocks. Guava [7] is presented as an informal collection of rules which would require a significantly more complex ownership types system than the one we present here. Boyapati et al.'s PRFJ [11] encodes a lock ordering in class headers. The rigid structure imposed by this scheme along with explicit threads makes program evolution tedious and the system complex. Another related approach uses Universes instead of ownership types for race safety [24]. In each case the underlying concurrency model is threads and not active objects.

In X10 *place types* statically describe where data resides improving data locality [52], mainly for performance reasons. X10 also sports futures and a shared space of immutable data. Remote data is remotely accessed, and there are no unique references. However, due to the hierarchical memory model of X10, similar to a distributed system, pointer transfer might not be as effective as in a shared memory system.

STREAMFLEX [56] and its successor Flexotasks [6] are close in spirit to Joëlle. They use a minimal notion of ownership, with little need for annotations, to handle garbage collection issues in a real-time setting. Objects may be passed between concurrent components without copying (Singularity OS [32] allows this too). STREAMFLEX's notion of immutability is however more limited than ours and safe or unique references are not supported. In conclusion, the additional limitations of the stream programming approach (compared to our general-purpose approach) allows STREAMFLEX to use even less syntactic baggage than Joëlle.

4.2   Actors and Active objects

Erlang [5] is relevant as a purely functional language with immutable data. This is a bad fit for OO and encoding of data structures that rely on sharing or object identifiers is difficult or impossible. Carlsson et al. [16] present an under-approximate *message analysis* to detect when messages can be safely shared rather than copied for a mini-Erlang system with cubic worst-case time complexity. Our type-system based approach should fare better for the price of a few additional concepts and annotations.

Symbian OS [43] and the ProActive Java framework [8] use active objects for concurrency. Based on Eiffel, Eiffel// [17] is an active objects system with asynchronous method calls with futures, and SCOOP [41] uses preconditions for task scheduling. In SCOOP, active object boundaries are captured by `separate` annotations on variables, which, in contrast to our proposal, are not statically enforced. (This is partially improved by Nienaltowski [46].) In the original SCOOP proposal, method arguments across active objects have deep copying semantics, with the aforementioned associated pains. Object migration through uniqueness is not supported. Later versions of SCOOP [46] integrate an eager locking mechanism to enable pass-by-reference arguments for non-value objects. An integration of our approach with SCOOP seems fairly straightforward.

CoBoxes [53] impose a hierarchy structure on active objects to control the access to groups of objects. Our proposal permits only a flat collection of active objects. On the other hand, our system allows the transfer of objects between active objects and the sharing of immutable and safe objects.

Different components or active objects communicate data by cloning in, e.g., the coordination language ToolBus [26] and in ASP [18]. In a distributed setting this is vindicated, but, as ToolBus developers [26] observe, copying data is a major source of performance problems. This is exactly the problem our approach aims to address, without introducing data-races, in a statically checkable fashion.

4.3   Software Transactional Memory

Software Transactional Memory is a recent approach to avoiding data races [54]. Atomic blocks are executed optimistically without locking and versioning detects conflicting updates. STM could be used under the hood to implement Emerald's mutually exclusive object regions [33,51]. Ongoing work by Kotselidis et al. [36] adds software transactional memory to ProActive. Preliminary results are promising, but the system retains ProActive's deep-copying semantics even for inter-node computations.

5   Concluding Remarks

We have applied ownership types to a data sharing problem of active objects. Our solution involves a combination of ownership, external uniqueness, and immutability. Our minimal ownership system was defined so that default annotations can be chosen to give a low syntactic overhead. We expect few necessary changes to code for passive objects if our system was implemented in ProActive.

Our system is close in spirit to several existing systems that lack our static checking for things like immutability. No existing active objects system is powerful enough to use minimal safe cloning the way we outlined in Section 3.3. A prototype compiler for Joëlle is available from the authors.

References

1. Agha, G., Hewitt, C.: Actors: A conceptual foundation for concurrent object-oriented programming. In: Research Directions in Object-Oriented Programming, pp. 49–74. MIT Press, Cambridge (1987)
2. Aldrich, J., Chambers, C.: Ownership Domains: Separating Aliasing Policy from Mechanism. In: Odersky, M. (ed.) ECOOP 2004. LNCS, vol. 3086, pp. 1–25. Springer, Heidelberg (2004)
3. Aldrich, J., Kostadinov, V., Chambers, C.: Alias Annotations for Program Understanding. In: OOPSLA (November 2002)
4. Almeida, P.S.: Balloon Types: Controlling sharing of state in data types. In: Aksit, M., Matsuoka, S. (eds.) ECOOP 1997. LNCS, vol. 1241, pp. 32–59. Springer, Heidelberg (1997)
5. Armstrong, J.: Programming Erlang: Software for a Concurrent World. Pragmatic Bookshelf (2007)
6. Auerbach, J., Bacon, D., Guerraoui, R., Spring, J., Vitek, J.: Flexible task graphs: A unified restricted thread programming model for java. In: LCTES (2008)
7. Bacon, D.F., Strom, R.E., Tarafdar, A.: Guava: a dialect of Java without data races. In: OOPSLA (2000)
8. Baduel, L., Baude, F., Caromel, D., Contes, A., Huet, F., Morel, M., Quilici, R.: Grid Computing: Software Environments and Tools. In: Chapter Programming, Composing, Deploying, for the Grid. Springer, Heidelberg (2006)
9. Baker Jr., H.G., Hewitt, C.: The incremental garbage collection of processes. In: Proceeding of the Symposium on Artificial Intelligence Programming Languages, ACMSIGPLAN Notices, August 1977, vol. 12, p. 11 (1977)
10. Birka, A., Ernst, M.D.: A practical type system and language for reference immutability. In: OOPSLA, October 2004, pp. 35–49 (2004)
11. Boyapati, C., Lee, R., Rinard, M.: Ownership Types for Safe Programming: Preventing Data Races and Deadlocks. In: OOPSLA (2002)
12. Boyapati, C., Liskov, B., Shrira, L.: Ownership Types for Object Encapsulation. In: POPL (2003)
13. Boyapati, C., Rinard, M.: A Parameterized Type System for Race-Free Java Programs. In: OOPSLA (2001)
14. Boyland, J.: Alias burying: Unique variables without destructive reads. Software—Practice and Experience 31(6), 533–553 (2001)
15. Boyland, J.: Why we should not add readonly to Java (yet). Journal of Object Technology 5(5), 5–29 (June 2006) Special issue: ECOOP 2005 Workshop FTfJP.
16. Carlsson, R., Sagonas, K.F., Wilhelmsson, J.: Message analysis for concurrent programs using message passing. ACM TOPLAS 28(4), 715–746 (2006)
17. Caromel, D.: Service, Asynchrony, and Wait-By-Necessity. Journal of Object Orientated Programming (JOOP), 12–22 (November 1989)
18. Caromel, D., Henrio, L.: A Theory of Distributed Objects. Springer, Heidelberg (2005)

19. Clarke, D.: Object Ownership and Containment. Ph.D thesis, School of Computer Science and Engineering, University of New South Wales, Sydney, Australia (2001)
20. Clarke, D., Drossopolou, S.: Ownership, Encapsulation and the Disjointness of Type and Effect. In: OOPSLA (2002)
21. Clarke, D., Wrigstad, T.: External uniqueness is unique enough. In: Cardelli, L. (ed.) European Conference on Object-Oriented Programming. LNCS, vol. 2473, pp. 176–200. Springer, Heidelberg (2002)
22. Clarke, D., Wrigstad, T., Östlund, J., Johnsen, E.B.: Minimal Ownership for Active Objects. Technical Report SEN-R0803, CWI (June 2008), http://ftp.cwi.nl/CWIreports/SEN/SEN-R0803.pdf
23. Clarke, D.G., Potter, J., Noble, J.: Ownership types for flexible alias protection. In: OOPSLA, pp. 48–64 (1998)
24. Cunningham, D., Drossopoulou, S., Eisenbach, S.: Universe Types for Race Safety. In: VAMP 2007, September 2007, pp. 20–51 (2007)
25. de Boer, F.S., Clarke, D., Johnsen, E.B.: A complete guide to the future. In: de Nicola, R. (ed.) ESOP 2007. LNCS, vol. 4421, pp. 316–330. Springer, Heidelberg (2007)
26. de Jong, H.: Flexible Heterogeneous Software Systems. PhD thesis, Faculty of Natural Sciences, Math. and Computer Science, Uni. of Amsterdam (January 2007)
27. Drossopoulou, S., Clarke, D., Noble, J.: Types for hierarchic shapes. In: Sestoft, P. (ed.) ESOP 2006. LNCS, vol. 3924, pp. 1–6. Springer, Heidelberg (2006)
28. Fahndrich, M., Xia, S.: Establishing object invariants with delayed types. SIG-PLAN Not. 42(10), 337–350 (2007)
29. Grossman, D., Hicks, M., Jim, T., Morrisett, G.: Cyclone: A type-safe dialect of C. C/C++ Users Journal 23(1) (January 2005)
30. Hogg, J.: Islands: Aliasing protection in object-oriented languages. In: OOPSLA (November 1991)
31. Hogg, J., Lea, D., Wills, A., de Champeaux, D., Holt, R.: The Geneva Convention on the treatment of object aliasing. OOPS Messenger 3(2), 11–16 (1992)
32. Hunt, G., Larus, J.: Singularity: Rethinking the software stack. Operating Systems Review 40(2), 37–49 (2007)
33. Hutchinson, N.C., Raj, R.K., Black, A.P., Levy, H.M., Jul, E.: The Emerald programming language report. Technical Report 87-10-07, Seattle, WA (USA) (1987) (Revised 1997)
34. Johnsen, E.B., Owe, O.: An asynchronous communication model for distributed concurrent objects. Software and Systems Modeling 6(1), 35–58 (2007)
35. Jones, S.P., Hughes. J. (eds.): Haskell 98: A non-strict, purely functional language. Technical report (February 1999)
36. Kotselidis, C., Ansari, M., Jarvis, K., Luján, M., Kirkham, C., Watson, I.: Investigating software transactional memory on clusters. In: IWJPDC 2008. IEEE Computer Society Press, Los Alamitos (2008)
37. Lavender, R.G., Schmidt, D.C.: Active object: an object behavioral pattern for concurrent programming. In: Proc. Pattern Languages of Programs (1995)
38. Lea, D.: Concurrent Programming in Java, 2nd edn. Addison-Wesley, Reading (2000)
39. Ma, K.-K., Foster, J.S.: Inferring aliasing and encapsulation properties for Java. In: OOPSLA, pp. 423–440 (2007)
40. Meyer, B.: Eiffel: The Language. Prentice-Hall, Englewood Cliffs (1992)
41. Meyer, B.: Systematic concurrent object-oriented programming. CACM 36(9), 56–80 (1993)

42. Minsky, N.H.: Towards alias-free pointers. In: Cointe, P. (ed.) ECOOP 1996. LNCS, vol. 1098, pp. 189–209. Springer, Heidelberg (1996)
43. Morris, B.: CActive and Friends. Symbian Developer Network (November 2007), http://developer.symbian.com/main/downloads/papers/CActiveAndFriends/CActiveAndFriends.pdf
44. Müller, P.: Modular Specification and Verification of Object-Oriented Programs. LNCS, vol. 2262. Springer, Heidelberg (2002)
45. Müller, P., Poetzsch-Heffter, A.: Universes: A type system for controlling representation exposure. In: Poetzsch-Heffter, A., Meyer, J. (eds.), Programming Languages and Fundamentals of Programming, pp. 131–140. Technical Report 263, Fernuniversität Hagen (1999)
46. Nienaltowski, P.: Practical framework for contract-based concurrent object-oriented programming. Ph.D thesis, Department of Computer Science, ETH Zurich (2007)
47. Noble, J., Clarke, D., Potter, J.: Object ownership for dynamic alias protection. In: TOOLS Pacific, Melbourne, Australia (November 1999)
48. Noble, J., Vitek, J., Potter, J.: Flexible Alias Protection. In: Jul, E. (ed.) ECOOP 1998. LNCS, vol. 1445. Springer, Heidelberg (1998)
49. Östlund, J., Wrigstad, T., Clarke, D., Åkerblom, B.: Ownership, uniqueness and immutability. In: IWACO (2007)
50. Potanin, A., Noble, J.: Checking ownership and confinement properties. In: Formal Techniques for Java-like Programs (2002)
51. Raj, R.K., Tempero, E., Levy, H.M., Black, A.P., Hutchinson, N.C., Jul, E.: Emerald: A general-purpose programming language. Software: Practice and Experience 21(1), 91–118 (1991)
52. Saraswat, V.A., Sarkar, V., von Praun, C.: X10: concurrent programming for modern architectures. In: Yelick, K.A., Mellor-Crummey, J.M. (eds.) Principles and Practice of Parallel Programming (2007)
53. Schäfer, J., Poetzsch-Heffter, A.: CoBoxes: Unifying active objects and structured heaps. In: Barthe, G., de Boer, F.S. (eds.) FMOODS 2008. LNCS, vol. 5051, pp. 201–219. Springer, Heidelberg (2008)
54. Shavit, N., Touitou, D.: Software transactional memory. In: PODC 1995, pp. 204–213. ACM Press, New York (1995)
55. Skoglund, M., Wrigstad, T.: Alias control with read-only references. In: Sixth Conference on Computer Science and Informatics (March 2002)
56. Spring, J.H., Privat, J., Guerraoui, R., Vitek, J.: StreamFlex: High-throughput Stream Programming in Java. In: OOPSLA (October 2007)
57. Stroustrup, B.: The C++ Programming Language. Addison-Wesley, Reading (1986)
58. Tschantz, M.S., Ernst, M.D.: Javari: Adding reference immutability to Java. In: OOPSLA, pp. 211–230 (October 2005)
59. Wrigstad, T.: Ownership-Based Alias Management. PhD thesis, Royal Institute of Technology, Kista, Stockholm (May 2006)
60. Wrigstad, T., Clarke, D.: Existential owners for ownership types. Journal of Object Technology 4(6), 141–159 (2007)
61. Yonezawa, A., Briot, J.-P., Shibayama, E.: Object-oriented concurrent programming in ABCL/1. In: OOPSLA 1986. SIGPLAN Notices, vol. 21(11), pp. 258–268 (November 1986)
62. Zibin, Y., Potanin, A., Ali, M., Artzi, S., Kiezun, A., Ernst, M.D.: Object and reference immutability using Java generics. In: Crnkovic, I., Bertolino, A. (eds.) ESEC/SIGSOFT FSE, pp. 75–84. ACM Press, New York (2007)

Type-Based Deadlock-Freedom Verification for Non-Block-Structured Lock Primitives and Mutable References

Kohei Suenaga

Tohoku University

Abstract. We present a type-based deadlock-freedom verification for concurrent programs with non-block-structured lock primitives and mutable references. Though those two features are frequently used, they are not dealt with in a sufficient manner by previous verification methods. Our type system uses a novel combination of *lock levels*, *obligations* and *ownerships*. Lock levels are used to guarantee that locks are acquired in a specific order. Obligations and ownerships guarantee that an acquired lock is released exactly once.

1 Introduction

Concurrent programs are getting important as multi-processor machines and clusters are getting popular. Many programs including operating systems and various network servers are written as concurrent programs.

A problem with a concurrent program is the possibility of a deadlock: a state in which every thread is waiting for a lock to be released by other threads. A deadlock is considered to be a serious problem since a deadlock causes unintentional halt of a system.

This paper presents a type-based method for deadlock-freedom verification. Our verification framework supports *non-block-structured lock primitives* and *mutable references to locks*. Those two features are heavily used in real-world software. For example, non-block-structured lock primitives, whose locking operations do not syntactically correspond to unlocking operations, are used in, for example, C programs with POSIX thread library.

Figure 1 shows a program with non-block-structured lock primitives and mutable references to locks, which suffers from a deadlock. The example is based on an actual bug found in nss_ldap-226-20.rpm [5]. In that example, a function _nss_ldap_getgroups_dyn first calls _nss_ldap_enter and then executes two branches. The first branch calls _nss_ldap_leave before executing return , while the second branch does not call _nss_ldap_leave . Because _nss_ldap_enter acquires a global lock __lock and returns without unlocking it, __lock is kept acquired if the second branch is executed after _nss_ldap_getgroups_dyn returns. This causes a deadlock if _nss_ldap_getgroups_dyn is called twice with an environment under which the second branch is executed.

G. Ramalingam (Ed.): APLAS 2008, LNCS 5356, pp. 155–170, 2008.

```
static mutex_t __lock; void
_nss_ldap_enter() { ... mutex_lock(&__lock); ... } void
_nss_ldap_leave() { ... mutex_unlock(&__lock); ... } char
*_nss_ldap_getgroups_dyn(const char *user...) {
  ...
  _nss_ldap_enter ();
  if (...) { _nss_ldap_leave(); return NULL; }
  /* _nss_ldap_leave is not called in this branch. */
  if (...) { return NSS_STATUS_NOTFOUND; }
  ...
}
```

Fig. 1. A deadlock contained in nss_ldap-226-20.rpm

```
static mutex_t lockA, lockB;
                                        void thread1() {
void accessA() {                          mutex_lock(&lockB);
  mutex_lock(&lockA);                     accessA();
  ...                                     mutex_unlock(&lockB);
  mutex_unlock(&lockA);                 }
}                                       void thread2() {
void accessB() {                          mutex_lock(&lockA);
  mutex_lock(&lockB);                     accessB();
  ...                                     mutex_unlock(&lockA);
  mutex_unlock(&lockB);                 }
}
```

Fig. 2. An example of a deadlock caused by circular dependency between locks

Figure 2 shows another example of a deadlock, which is caused by circular dependency between locks. In the example, a function accessA acquires and releases a lock lockA , while accessB acquires and releases lockB . These two functions are called from two threads thread1 and thread2 . In those threads, accessA is called while lockB is acquired and accessB is called while lockA is acquired, so that the program may lead to a deadlock because of the lock order reversal between lockA and lockB .

The main idea of our type system is to guarantee that locks are acquired in a specific order, and that an acquired lock is released exactly once. The first property is guaranteed by *lock levels*, while the second property is guaranteed by *obligations* and *ownerships*.

So far, much effort has been paid for static deadlock-freedom verification [12,11,14,2,7,8,1]. However, non-block-structured lock primitives and mutable references to locks are not dealt with in a sufficient manner. For example, the analyses by Boyapati, Lee and Rinard [2] and by Flanagan and Abadi [8] consider only block-structured synchronization primitives (i.e., synchronized blocks in

$$x, y, z, f \ldots \in Var$$
$$lck ::= \mathbf{L} \mid \hat{\mathbf{L}}$$
$$P ::= \widetilde{D}s$$
$$D ::= x(\widetilde{y}) = s$$
$$v ::= \mathbf{true} \mid \mathbf{false}$$
$$s ::= \mathbf{skip} \mid x(\widetilde{y}) \mid (\mathbf{if}\ x\ \mathbf{then}\ s_1\ \mathbf{else}\ s_2) \mid \mathbf{putob}(x, y)$$
$$\mid\ \mathbf{let}\ x = v\ \mathbf{in}\ s \mid \mathbf{let}\ x = \mathbf{ref}\ y\ \mathbf{in}\ s \mid \mathbf{let}\ x\ =!y\ \mathbf{in}\ s \mid x := y$$
$$\mid\ \mathbf{spawn}\ s \mid \mathbf{let}\ x = \mathbf{newlock}\ ()\ \mathbf{in}\ s \mid \mathbf{lock}\ x \mid \mathbf{unlock}\ x \mid s_1; s_2$$
$$E ::= [] \mid E; s$$

Fig. 3. Syntax

the Java language.) Kobayashi et al. [12,11,14] proposed a deadlock-freedom analysis for the π-calculus. Although their analysis can, in principle, handle references by encoding them into channels, the resulting analysis is too imprecise.

The rest of this paper is organized as follows. Section 2 defines our target language. Section 3 introduces a type system for deadlock-freedom analysis. Section 4 states soundness of our type system. After discussing related work in Section 5, we conclude in Section 6.

2   Target Language

Figure 3 shows the syntax of our target language. A program P consists of mutually recursive function definitions $\widetilde{D}$ and a main statement s. A function definition D consists of the name of the function x, a sequence of arguments $\widetilde{y}$ and a function body s.

The meta-variable s ranges over the set of statements. The statement **skip** does nothing. The statement $x(\widetilde{y})$ is a function call. The conditional branch **if** x **then** s_1 **else** s_2 executes s_1 if x is **true** and s_2 otherwise. The statements **let** $x = \mathbf{ref}\ y\ \mathbf{in}\ s$, **let** $x\ =!y$ **in** s and $x := y$ are for generating, dereferencing and assignment to a reference. We write **let** $x = y$ **in** s for **let** $z = \mathbf{ref}\ y\ \mathbf{in}\ \mathbf{let}\ x\ =!z$ **in** s if the variable z does not freely appear in s. The statement **spawn** s spawns a new thread that executes s. $\mathbf{putob}(x, y)$, which is used for type soundness proof and operationally equivalent to **skip**, represents the end of scope of x in **let** $x\ =!y$ **in** s. $\mathbf{putob}(x, y)$ should not be included in a program. The statement **let** $x = \mathbf{newlock}\ ()$ **in** s generates a fresh lock, binds x to the lock and executes s. The statements **lock** x and **unlock** x are for acquiring and releasing a lock x. The statement $s_1; s_2$ is a sequential composition of s_1 and s_2. Figure 5 and 6 show how the programs in Figure 1 and 2 are encoded in our language. We omit the main statement of the program in Figure 1.

The operational semantics of our calculus is defined as a transition relation between configurations. Figure 4 presents an excerpt of the transition rules. A

$$\frac{x' \text{ is fresh}}{(\widetilde{D}, Env, H, L, \{\textbf{let } x = \textbf{ref } y \textbf{ in } s\} \uplus S) \to (\widetilde{D}, Env, H[x' \mapsto y], L, \{[x'/x]s\} \uplus S)} \text{ (E-Ref)}$$

$$(\widetilde{D}, Env, H[x \mapsto y'], L, \{x := y\} \uplus S) \to (\widetilde{D}, Env, H[x \mapsto y], L, \{\textbf{skip}\} \uplus S) \text{ (E-Assign)}$$

$$\begin{array}{l}(\widetilde{D}, Env, H[y \mapsto z], L, \{\textbf{let } x = !y \textbf{ in } s\} \uplus S) \to \\ (\widetilde{D}, Env, H[y \mapsto z], L, \{([z/x]s); \textbf{putob}(z, y)\} \uplus S)\end{array} \text{ (E-LetDeref)}$$

$$\frac{x' \text{ is fresh}}{\begin{array}{l}(\widetilde{D}, Env, H, L, \{\textbf{let } x = \textbf{newlock } () \textbf{ in } s\} \uplus S) \to \\ (\widetilde{D}, Env, H, L[x' \mapsto \hat{\textbf{L}}], \{[x'/x]s\} \uplus S)\end{array}} \text{ (E-LetNewlock)}$$

$$(\widetilde{D}, Env, H, L[x \mapsto \hat{\textbf{L}}], \{\textbf{lock } x\} \uplus S) \to (\widetilde{D}, Env, H, L[x \mapsto \textbf{L}], \{\textbf{skip}\} \uplus S) \text{ (E-Lock)}$$

$$(\widetilde{D}, Env, H, L[x \mapsto \textbf{L}], \{\textbf{unlock } x\} \uplus S) \to (\widetilde{D}, Env, H, L[x \mapsto \hat{\textbf{L}}], \{\textbf{skip}\} \uplus S) \text{ (E-Unlock)}$$

$$\frac{(\widetilde{D}, Env, H, L, \{s\} \uplus S) \to (\widetilde{D}', Env', H', L', \{s'\} \uplus S')}{(\widetilde{D}, Env, H, L, \{E[\textbf{spawn } s]\} \uplus S) \to (\widetilde{D}', Env', H', L', \{s, E[\textbf{skip}]\} \uplus S')} \text{ (E-Spawn)}$$

$$(\widetilde{D}, Env, H, L, \textbf{putob}(x, y)) \to (\widetilde{D}, Env, H, L, \textbf{skip}) \text{ (E-Putob)}$$

Fig. 4. Operational Semantics (excerpt)

$$\begin{array}{l}\textit{\_nss\_ldap\_enter}(\_lock) = \textbf{lock } \_lock \\ \textit{\_nss\_ldap\_leave}(\_lock) = \textbf{unlock } \_lock \\ \textit{\_nss\_ldap\_getgroups\_dyn}(ret, cond, \_lock) = \\ \quad \textit{\_nss\_ldap\_enter}(\_lock); \\ \quad \textbf{if } cond \textbf{ then } (\textit{\_nss\_ldap\_leave}(\_lock); ret := 0) \\ \quad \textbf{else } ret := 0\end{array}$$

Fig. 5. An encoding of the program in Figure 1 in our language

$$\begin{array}{l}\textit{accessA}(lockA) = \textbf{lock } lockA; \textbf{unlock } lockA \\ \textit{accessB}(lockB) = \textbf{lock } lockB; \textbf{unlock } lockB \\ \textit{thread1}(lockA, lockB) = \textbf{lock } lockB; \textit{accessA}(lockA); \textbf{unlock } lockB \\ \textit{thread2}(lockA, lockB) = \textbf{lock } lockA; \textit{accessB}(lockB); \textbf{unlock } lockA \\ \textbf{let } lockA = \textbf{newlock}() \textbf{ in let } lockB = \textbf{newlock}() \textbf{ in} \\ \quad \textbf{spawn } (\textit{thread1}(lockA, lockB)); \textbf{spawn } (\textit{thread2}(lockA, lockB))\end{array}$$

Fig. 6. An encoding of the program in Figure 2 in our language

$$f(x, y) = \textbf{unlock } x; \textbf{unlock } y$$
$$main() = \textbf{let } x = \textbf{newlock}() \textbf{ in}$$
$$\textbf{lock}(x); (\textbf{let } y = \textbf{ref } x \textbf{ in } f(x, !y))$$

Fig. 7. Programs that contain aliasing to a lock occurs

configuration in our semantics is a tuple of a set of function definitions $\tilde{D}$, an environment that maps a variable to a value Env, a heap H, a map from a lock variable to a state of the lock L and a multiset of running threads S. A state of a lock is either locked ($\textbf{L}$) or unlocked ($\hat{\textbf{L}}$.) In Figure 4, $S_1 \uplus S_2$ is the disjoint union of multisets S_1 and S_2.

3   Type System

3.1   Overview

We first present an overview of our type system. As mentioned in Section 1, our type system guarantees that locks are acquired in a specific order by using *lock levels* and that an acquired lock is released exactly once by using *obligations* and *ownerships*.

Lock levels. Each lock type in our type system is associated with a natural number called lock level. The type system prevents deadlocks by guaranteeing that locks are acquired in a strict increasing order of lock levels. For example, the statement **spawn** ($\textbf{lock } x; \textbf{lock } y; \textbf{unlock } y; \textbf{unlock } x$);
($\textbf{lock } y; \textbf{lock } x; \textbf{unlock } x; \textbf{unlock } y$) is rejected because the first thread requires the level of x to be less than that of y, while the second thread requires the level of y should be less than x.

Obligations. In order to guarantee that an acquired lock is released exactly once, each lock type in our type system has information on *obligation* to release the lock. A lock type $\textbf{lock}(lev, U)$ in our type system has a flow-sensitive component U called a usage, in addition to a lock level lev. A usage is either ob, which denotes an obligation to release the lock, or $\textbf{1}$, which shows there is no such obligation.

More precisely, the type system deals with obligations based on the following principles.

1. $\textbf{lock } x$ can be executed if and only if (1) x does not have an obligation and (2) the level of every lock with an obligation is less than the level of x. x has an obligation after $\textbf{lock } x$ is performed.
2. $\textbf{unlock } x$ can be performed if and only if x has an obligation. x does not have the obligation after $\textbf{unlock } x$ is performed.
3. An obligation is treated *linearly*, that is, if an alias to a lock with an obligation is generated, then exactly one of the lock or the alias inherits the obligation.

> let $x = $ **newlock**() in let $y = $ **newlock**() in
> let $z = $ **newlock**() in let $r = $ **ref** x in
>   **spawn** (**lock**(z); **lock**(!r); **unlock**(z); **lock**(z); **unlock**(!r); **unlock**(z));
>   (**lock**(z); $r := y$; **unlock**(z))

Fig. 8. A program in which a lock contained in a reference is not correctly released

For example, the type system rejects the program

$$f(x) = \text{\textbf{lock} } x$$
$$\text{let } x = \text{\textbf{newlock}}() \text{ in } f(x); \text{\textbf{lock} } x$$

because x has an obligation after the function call $f(x)$ returns, which is followed by **lock** x, so that (1) in the first condition above is violated. The program in Figure 7 is also rejected because, from the third condition above, only one of x or y inherits the obligation generated by **lock** x after the reference y is generated, while both x and y are required to have an obligation just before $f(x, !y)$.

Note the difference between our obligations and flow-sensitive type qualifiers in CQual [9]. Flow-sensitive type qualifiers in CQual represent *the current state of values*, while our obligations represent *how variables should be used afterwards*. This difference matters when we consider a program with aliasing. For example, consider the program (**lock** x; let $y = x$ in s). In our type system, x has the type **lock**(lev, ob) just after **lock** x, which means the lock should be released *through x afterwards*. After the alias y of x is created, the type environment may be either $x : \text{\textbf{lock}}(lev, ob), y : \text{\textbf{lock}}(lev, 1)$ or $x : \text{\textbf{lock}}(lev, 1), y : \text{\textbf{lock}}(lev, ob)$ depending on how x and y are used in s. On the other hand, in CQual, if x is put in an abstract location ρ, then the flow-sensitive type qualifier assigned to ρ just after **lock** x is locked, which means that x is *currently* locked. After the alias y is created, x and y have the same type as they are bound to the same lock.

Ownership. In order to guarantee deadlock-freedom of a program with thread creation and accesses to mutable references, obligations are still insufficient to guarantee that an acquired lock is released exactly once. For example, consider the program in Figure 8. That program consists of two threads. The first thread acquires and releases a lock contained in the reference r, while the second thread assigns another lock to the same reference. Then, the lock released by the first thread may be different from acquired one, so that the acquired lock may not be released.

The problem here can be described as follows: a write to a reference to a lock should not occur *while the lock is held*. Note that this property differs from race-freedom because race-freedom only guarantees that a write to a reference and another read or write to the reference do not occur at the same time. In fact, though the program in Figure 8 is race-free because each access to the reference r is guarded by a lock z, it still has a problem described above.

$$
\begin{aligned}
lev &\in \{0, 1, \ldots\} \cup \{\infty\} \\
U &::= ob \mid \mathbf{1} \\
r &\in [0, \infty) \\
\tau &::= \mathbf{bool} \mid \mathbf{lock}(lev, U) \mid \tau \ \mathbf{ref}^r \mid (\tau_1, \ldots, \tau_n) \xrightarrow{lev} (\tau'_1, \ldots, \tau'_n)
\end{aligned}
$$

Fig. 9. Syntax of types

To solve such problem, our type system uses *ownerships*, a thread's capability to access a reference. As in Boyland [3], Terauchi [17] and Kikuchi and Kobayashi [10] do, we use rational-numbered ownerships. A well-typed program obeys the following rules on ownerships in manipulating references.

1. An ownership less than or equal to 1 is assigned to a reference to a lock when the reference is generated.
2. A thread is required to have an ownership greater than 0 on a reference in order to read a lock from the reference.
3. A thread is required to have an ownership 1 on a reference in order to write a lock to the reference.
4. When a thread is spawned, an ownership of each reference is divided and distributed to each thread.

Based on those rules, a thread has to have an ownership greater than 0 to acquire a lock through a reference, which prevents other threads from overwriting the reference while the lock is acquired. For example, the program in Figure 8 is rejected because the total ownership required on the reference r exceeds 1: the first thread requires an ownership more than 0 while the second thread requires 1.

3.2   Syntax

Figure 9 shows the syntax of types. The set of *lock levels*, ranged over by a meta-variable lev, is the set of natural numbers with ∞. We extend the standard partial order $\leq$ on the set of natural numbers to that on lock levels by $lev \leq \infty$ for any lev. We write $lev_1 < lev_2$ for $lev_1 \leq lev_2 \wedge lev_1 \neq lev_2$.

Usage, ranged over by a meta-variable U, represents whether there is an obligation to release a lock. A usage ob represents an obligation to release a lock, while a usage $\mathbf{1}$ represents that there is not such obligation.

The meta variable τ ranges over types. A lock type $\mathbf{lock}(lev, U)$ is for locks that should be used according to lev and U. For example, if a variable x has the type $\mathbf{lock}(1, \mathbf{1})$, then the lock can be acquired through x if locks whose levels are more than 1 are not already acquired. If a variable x has the type $\mathbf{lock}(1, ob)$ then the lock should be released exactly once through the variable x.

The type $\tau \ \mathbf{ref}^r$ is for references, whose content should be used according to τ after it is read from the reference. The meta variable r, which is associated with a reference type, is a rational number in the set $[0, \infty)$ and represents a thread's capability to access the reference. An ownership being greater than 0

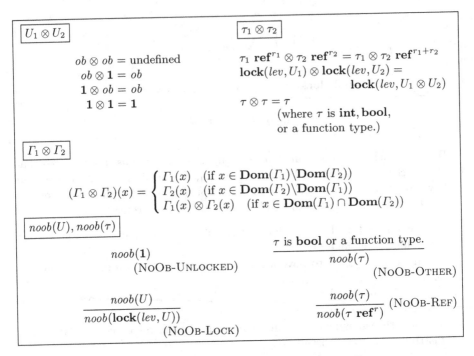

Fig. 10. Definition of auxiliary operators and predicates

means that one can read a value through the reference. An ownership 1 means that one can write a value to the reference. A function type $\tilde{\tau}\xrightarrow{lev}\tilde{\tau}'$ consists of the following components.

- $\tilde{\tau}$: the types of arguments before execution of the functions.
- $\tilde{\tau}'$: the types of arguments after execution of the functions.
- lev: the minimum level of locks that may be acquired by the functions.

3.3   Type Judgment

The type judgment for statements is $\Gamma \vdash s \Rightarrow \Gamma' \,\&\, lev$. Type environments Γ and Γ' describe the types of free variables in s before and after execution of s. A lock level lev is an effect of s, which is a minimum level of locks that may be acquired during execution of s.

The type judgment intuitively means that (1) locks are acquired in an strict increasing order of their levels, (2) an acquired lock is released exactly once and, (3) the levels of acquired locks are greater than or equal to lev if s is executed under an environment described by Γ and with a continuation that respects types in Γ'.

The type judgment is defined as the least relation that satisfies the typing rules in Figure 11. In those rules, we use the operation $\otimes$ defined in Figure 10. $U_1 \otimes U_2$

$$\emptyset \vdash \mathbf{skip} \Rightarrow \emptyset \ \& \ \infty \qquad \text{(T-Nop)}$$

$$\frac{\Gamma_1 \vdash s_1 \Rightarrow \Gamma_2 \ \& \ lev \qquad \Gamma_2 \vdash s_2 \Rightarrow \Gamma_3 \ \& \ lev}{\Gamma_1 \vdash s_1; s_2 \Rightarrow \Gamma_3 \ \& \ lev} \qquad \text{(T-Seq)}$$

$$\frac{x : \mathbf{bool}, \Gamma \vdash s \Rightarrow x : \mathbf{bool}, \Gamma' \ \& \ lev}{\Gamma \vdash \mathbf{let} \ x = v \ \mathbf{in} \ s \Rightarrow \Gamma' \ \& \ lev} \qquad \text{(T-LetBool)}$$

$$\frac{x : \mathbf{lock}(lev', 1), \Gamma \vdash s \Rightarrow x : \mathbf{lock}(lev', 1), \Gamma' \ \& \ lev}{\Gamma \vdash \mathbf{let} \ x = \mathbf{newlock} \ () \ \mathbf{in} \ s \Rightarrow \Gamma' \ \& \ lev} \qquad \text{(T-Newlock)}$$

$$x : \mathbf{lock}(lev, 1) \vdash \mathbf{lock} \ x \Rightarrow x : \mathbf{lock}(lev, ob) \ \& \ lev \qquad \text{(T-Lock)}$$

$$x : \mathbf{lock}(lev, ob) \vdash \mathbf{unlock} \ x \Rightarrow x : \mathbf{lock}(lev, 1) \ \& \ \infty \qquad \text{(T-Unlock)}$$

$$\frac{\tau = (\tau_1, \dots, \tau_n) \overset{lev}{\rightarrow} (\tau'_1, \dots, \tau'_n)}{y_1 : \tau_1 \otimes \cdots \otimes y_n : \tau_n \otimes x : \tau \vdash x(y_1, \dots, y_n) \Rightarrow y_1 : \tau'_1 \otimes \cdots \otimes y_n : \tau'_n \otimes x : \tau \ \& \ lev}$$
$$\text{(T-App)}$$

$$\frac{x : \mathbf{bool}, \Gamma \vdash s_1 \Rightarrow \Gamma' \ \& \ lev \qquad x : \mathbf{bool}, \Gamma \vdash s_2 \Rightarrow \Gamma' \ \& \ lev}{x : \mathbf{bool}, \Gamma \vdash \mathbf{if} \ x \ \mathbf{then} \ s_1 \ \mathbf{else} \ s_2 \Rightarrow \Gamma' \ \& \ lev} \qquad \text{(T-If)}$$

$$\frac{x : \tau_1 \ \mathbf{ref}^r, y : \tau_2, \Gamma \vdash s \Rightarrow x : \tau'_1 \ \mathbf{ref}^{r'}, y : \tau'_2, \Gamma' \ \& \ lev \qquad noob(\tau'_1)}{r \leq 1 \ \text{if} \ \neg nolock(\tau_1) \qquad \mathbf{wf}(\tau_1 \ \mathbf{ref}^r) \qquad \mathbf{wf}(\tau_2)}{y : \tau_1 \otimes \tau_2, \Gamma \vdash \mathbf{let} \ x = \mathbf{ref} \ y \ \mathbf{in} \ s \Rightarrow y : \tau'_2, \Gamma' \ \& \ lev}$$
$$\text{(T-Ref)}$$

$$\frac{x : \tau_1, y : \tau_2 \ \mathbf{ref}^r, \Gamma \vdash s \Rightarrow x : \tau'_1, y : \tau'_2 \ \mathbf{ref}^{r''}, \Gamma' \ \& \ lev \qquad r' > 0}{\mathbf{wf}(\tau_1) \qquad \mathbf{wf}(\tau_2 \ \mathbf{ref}^r)}{y : \tau_1 \otimes \tau_2 \ \mathbf{ref}^{r+r'}, \Gamma \vdash \mathbf{let} \ x =! y \ \mathbf{in} \ s \Rightarrow y : \tau'_1 \otimes \tau'_2 \ \mathbf{ref}^{r''}, \Gamma' \ \& \ lev}$$
$$\text{(T-Deref)}$$

$$\frac{noob(\tau_3) \qquad \mathbf{wf}(\tau_1) \qquad \mathbf{wf}(\tau_2)}{x : \tau_3 \ \mathbf{ref}^1, y : \tau_1 \otimes \tau_2 \vdash x := y \Rightarrow x : \tau_1 \ \mathbf{ref}^1, y : \tau_2 \ \& \ \infty} \qquad \text{(T-Assign)}$$

$$x : \tau_1 \otimes \tau_2, y : \tau_3 \ \mathbf{ref}^r \vdash \mathbf{putob}(x, y) \Rightarrow x : \tau_1, y : \tau_2 \otimes \tau_3 \ \mathbf{ref}^r \ \& \ \infty$$
$$\text{(T-Putob)}$$

$$\frac{\Gamma_1 \vdash s \Rightarrow \Gamma_3 \ \& \ lev \qquad noob(\Gamma_3) \qquad \mathbf{wf}(\Gamma_1) \qquad \mathbf{wf}(\Gamma_2)}{\Gamma_1 \otimes \Gamma_2 \vdash \mathbf{spawn} \ s \Rightarrow \Gamma_2 \ \& \ lev} \qquad \text{(T-Spawn)}$$

$$\frac{\Gamma \vdash s \Rightarrow \Gamma' \ \& \ lev \qquad lev' \leq lev \qquad \mathbf{max}(level_{ob}(\Gamma'')) < lev'}{\Gamma, \Gamma'' \vdash s \Rightarrow \Gamma', \Gamma'' \ \& \ lev'}$$
$$\text{(T-Weak)}$$

Fig. 11. Typing rules for statements

gives the usage that means *both* obligations in U_1 and U_2 have to be fulfilled. $ob \otimes ob$ is undefined because releasing an acquired lock twice is prohibited. The operator $\otimes$ on usages are naturally extended to types.

We also use the following definitions in Figure 11.

$$\widetilde{D} = \{f(x_{11}, \ldots, x_{1m_1}) = s_1, \ldots, f(x_{n1}, \ldots, x_{nm_n}) = s_m\}$$
$$\Gamma = f_1 : (\tau_{1,1}, \ldots, \tau_{1,m_1}) \overset{lev_1}{\to} (\tau'_{1,1}, \ldots, \tau'_{1,m_1}), \ldots,$$
$$f_n : (\tau_{n,1}, \ldots, \tau_{n,m_n}) \overset{lev_n}{\to} (\tau_{n,1}, \ldots, \tau_{n,m_n})$$
$$\frac{\Gamma, x_{i,1} : \tau_{i,1}, \ldots, x_{i,m_i} : \tau_{i,m_i} \vdash s_i \Rightarrow \Gamma, x_{i,1} : \tau'_{i,1}, \ldots, x_{i,m_i} : \tau'_{i,m_i} \ \& \ lev_i}{\vdash_{Def} \widetilde{D} : \Gamma}$$

(T-FUNDEF)

$$\frac{\vdash_{Def} \widetilde{D} : \Gamma \qquad \Gamma \vdash s \Rightarrow \Gamma' \ \& \ lev \qquad noob(\Gamma')}{\vdash_{Prog} \widetilde{D}s}$$

(T-PROG)

Fig. 12. Typing rules for programs

Definition 1 (No obligation). $noob(\tau)$ *is defined as the least predicate that satisfies the rules in Figure 10.*

The predicate $noob(\tau)$ asserts that τ does not have any obligation to fulfil.

Definition 2. $level_U$, *a function that takes a type and returns a set of lock levels, is defined as follows.*

$$level_U(\tau \ \mathbf{ref}^r) = level_U(\tau)$$
$$level_U(\mathbf{lock}(lev, U')) = \{lev\} \qquad (where \ U = U')$$
$$level_U(\tau) = \emptyset \qquad (otherwise)$$

$level_U(\Gamma)$ *is defined as* $\{lev | x : \tau \in \Gamma \wedge lev \in level_U(\tau)\}$.

The function $level_U$ collects levels of locks whose usages are equal to U.

Definition 3. *A predicate* **wf** *is defined as the least one that satisfies the following rules.*

$$\frac{\tau \ is \ \mathbf{bool}, \mathbf{lock}(lev, U) \ or \ a \ function \ type.}{\mathbf{wf}(\tau)} \qquad \frac{\mathbf{wf}(\tau) \quad \neg noob(\tau) \Rightarrow r > 0}{\mathbf{wf}(\tau \ \mathbf{ref}^r)} \qquad \frac{\forall x : \tau \in \Gamma.\mathbf{wf}(\tau)}{\mathbf{wf}(\Gamma)}$$

The predicate $\mathbf{wf}(\Gamma)$ asserts that ownerships of each reference type in Γ are consistent with its content type. Note that $\mathbf{wf}(\tau \ \mathbf{ref}^r)$ requires $r > 0$ if τ has an obligation to release a lock because one has to read the reference to release the lock.

We explain important rules in Figure 11. In the rule (T-NEWLOCK), $noob(U_1)$ means that the newly generated lock has no obligation. $noob(U_2)$ means that all the obligations in the type of x should be fulfilled at the end of s because x cannot be accessed after execution of s.

(T-LOCK) guarantees that there is no obligation before execution of **lock** x. After execution of **lock** x, x has an obligation to release the lock.

In the rule (T-REF), we use a predicate $nolock(\tau)$. This predicate holds if and only if τ does not contain lock types as its component. The rule (T-REF) states

$$\frac{\displaystyle \frac{\vdots}{\displaystyle \frac{\Gamma_3 \vdash \mathbf{unlock}\ z \Rightarrow \Gamma_4}{\Gamma_1 \vdash \mathbf{let}\ z = !x\ \mathbf{in}\ \mathbf{unlock}\ z \Rightarrow \Gamma_2}}\ noob(\mathbf{lock}(1,1))}{y : \mathbf{lock}(1, ob) \vdash \mathbf{let}\ x = \mathbf{ref}\ y\ \mathbf{in}\ \mathbf{let}\ z = !x\ \mathbf{in}\ \mathbf{unlock}\ z \Rightarrow y : \mathbf{lock}(1, 1)}$$

Fig. 13. A derivation tree of $\mathbf{let}\ x = \mathbf{ref}\ y\ \mathbf{in}\ \mathbf{unlock}\ x$ under the assumption $y : \mathbf{lock}(1, ob)$

that the ownership assigned to the new reference x in typing s is less than or equal to 1 if the type of x contains lock types as its component. At the end of s, x should not have any obligation because x cannot be accessed after execution of s.

In the rule (T-DEREF), if y has an obligation to release a lock, only one of x and y inherits that obligation during execution of s. The rule (T-DEREF) also states that the ownership assigned to the type of y should be greater than 0.

A derivation of a statement $\mathbf{let}\ x = \mathbf{ref}\ y\ \mathbf{in}\ \mathbf{let}\ z = !x\ \mathbf{in}\ \mathbf{unlock}\ z$ under the type environment $y : \mathbf{lock}(1, ob)$ in Figure 13 shows how (T-REF) and (T-DEREF) work. The type environments $\Gamma_1, \ldots, \Gamma_4$ in that figure are defined as follows.

$$\Gamma_1 = x : \mathbf{lock}(1, ob)\ \mathbf{ref}^1, y : \mathbf{lock}(1, 1)$$
$$\Gamma_2 = x : \mathbf{lock}(1, 1)\ \mathbf{ref}^1, y : \mathbf{lock}(1, 1)$$
$$\Gamma_3 = x : \mathbf{lock}(1, 1)\ \mathbf{ref}^{1-r}, y : \mathbf{lock}(1, 1), z : \mathbf{lock}(1, ob)$$
$$\Gamma_4 = x : \mathbf{lock}(1, 1)\ \mathbf{ref}^{1-r}, y : \mathbf{lock}(1, 1), z : \mathbf{lock}(1, 1).$$

Here, r is an arbitrary rational number in the set $(0, 1)$. Note that the obligation of y is passed to the newly generated reference x, delegated to z and fulfilled through z.

The rule (T-ASSIGN) guarantees that there is no obligation that must be fulfilled through the reference x because x is being overwritten. If y has an obligation, then either x or y inherits that obligation after execution of $x := y$. For example, both

$$x : \mathbf{lock}(0, 1)\ \mathbf{ref}^1, y : \mathbf{lock}(0, ob) \vdash x := y \Rightarrow x : \mathbf{lock}(0, 1)\ \mathbf{ref}^1, y : \mathbf{lock}(0, ob)$$
$$x : \mathbf{lock}(0, 1)\ \mathbf{ref}^1, y : \mathbf{lock}(0, ob) \vdash x := y \Rightarrow x : \mathbf{lock}(0, ob)\ \mathbf{ref}^1, y : \mathbf{lock}(0, 1)$$

hold. After the assignment, the obligation originally owned by y should be fulfilled through y in the first case, while it should be fulfilled through the reference x in the second case. However,

$$x : \mathbf{lock}(0, 1)\ \mathbf{ref}^1, y : \mathbf{lock}(0, ob) \vdash x := y \Rightarrow x : \mathbf{lock}(0, ob)\ \mathbf{ref}^1, y : \mathbf{lock}(0, ob)$$

does not hold.

In the rule (T-SPAWN), the pre type environment of the conclusion part is split into Γ_1 and Γ_2. The environment Γ_1 is for the newly generated thread s, while Γ_2 is for the continuation of **spawn** s. The condition $noob(\Gamma_3)$ imposes that all the obligations in Γ_1 should be fulfilled in the newly generated thread s.

The rule (T-WEAK) is for adding redundant variables to type environments. In that rule, the condition $\mathbf{max}(level_{ob}(\Gamma'')) < lev'$ guarantees that if newly added lock-typed variables have obligations, then the levels of those lock types $(level_{ob}(\Gamma''))$ should be less than the level of locks that may be acquired in s (lev'). With this condition, we can guarantee that locks are acquired in a strict increasing order of lock levels.

The type judgment for programs $\vdash_{Prog} \widetilde{D}s$ is defined as the least relation that satisfies the rules in Figure 12. The rule (T-PROG) states that a program $\widetilde{D}s$ is well-typed if (1) the defined functions have the types described in a type environment Γ and (2) the main statement s is well-typed under Γ and (3) all the obligations generated during execution of the program are fulfilled after execution of s. The rule (T-FUNDEF), which is a rule for function definitions, guarantees that each function has the type described in Γ.

Example. In the program in Figure 5, the function $\_nss\_ldap\_leave$ has type $\mathbf{lock}(lev, ob) \xrightarrow{lev} \mathbf{lock}(lev, \mathbf{1})$ where lev is an arbitrary natural number. Thus, $\_\_lock$ in the body of $\_nss\_ldap\_getgroups\_dyn$ has type $\mathbf{lock}(lev, \mathbf{1})$ at the end of the first branch and $\mathbf{lock}(lev, ob)$ at the end of the second branch, which violates the condition of (T-IF) that type environments at the end of two branches have to agree. In the example in Figure 6, the condition $\mathbf{max}(level_{ob}(\Gamma'')) < lev'$ in (T-WEAK) imposes that the level of $lockB$ has to be less than that of $lockA$ in the body of $thread1$. For the same reason, the level of $lockA$ has to be less than that of $lockB$ in the body of $thread2$, so that the program is ill-typed.

3.4   Type Inference

We informally describe a type inference algorithm in this section. Our algorithm is a standard constraint-based one; the algorithm takes a program as input, generates a constraint set based on the typing rules in Figure 11 and reduces those constraints.

We omit an explanation on the constraint generation phase which is done in a standard manner. A generated constraint is either (1) $lexp_1 \leq lexp_2$, (2) $\rho = ob \Rightarrow lexp_1 \leq lexp_2$, (3) $\rho = Uexp_1 \otimes \cdots \otimes Uexp_n$ or (4) a linear inequality on ownerships. Here, $lexp$ and $Uexp$ are defined by the following syntax.

$$lexp ::= \phi \text{ (lock level variables)} \mid \infty \mid lexp + 1$$
$$Uexp ::= \rho \text{ (usage variables)} \mid ob \mid \mathbf{1}.$$

Generated constraints are reduced as follows. First, linear inequalities on ownerships are solved using an external solver. Then, constraints of the form $\rho = Uexp_1 \otimes \cdots \otimes Uexp_n$ are reduced to a substitution on usage variables. This is done by applying a standard constraint reduction algorithm for linear type systems (e.g., one presented in [13].) By applying the obtained substitution to constraints of the form $\rho = ob \Rightarrow lexp_1 \leq lexp_2$, we obtain a constraint set of the

$$\frac{\vdash_{Def} \widetilde{D} : \Gamma_{fun} \qquad \Gamma_{fun}(x) = \tau}{\vdash (\widetilde{D} \uplus \{x(\widetilde{y}) = s\}, Env, H, L, x) : \tau, \emptyset, \emptyset} \quad \text{(TC-FUNDEF)}$$

$$\vdash (\widetilde{D}, Env \uplus \{x \mapsto v\}, H, L, x) : \textbf{bool}, \emptyset, \emptyset \qquad \text{(TC-ENV)}$$

$$\frac{\vdash (\widetilde{D}, Env, H \uplus \{x \mapsto x'\}, L, x') : \tau, P, O}{\vdash (\widetilde{D}, Env, H \uplus \{x \mapsto x'\}, L, x) : \tau \ \textbf{ref}^r, P, O \otimes \{x \mapsto r\}} \quad \text{(TC-HEAP)}$$

$$\vdash (\widetilde{D}, Env, H, L \uplus \{x \mapsto lck\}, x) : \textbf{lock}(lev, U), \{x \mapsto U\}, \emptyset$$
$$\text{(TC-LOCKSTATE)}$$

$$\forall x \in \textbf{Dom}(\widetilde{D} \cup Env \cup H \cup L). \vdash (\widetilde{D}, Env, H, L, x) : \Gamma(x), P_x, O_x$$
$$P = \bigotimes_{x \in \textbf{Dom}(\widetilde{D} \cup Env \cup H \cup L)} P_x \qquad O = \bigotimes_{x \in \textbf{Dom}(\widetilde{D} \cup Env \cup H \cup L)} O_x$$
$$\forall x \in \textbf{Dom}(L). \text{ if } L(x) = \hat{\textbf{L}} \text{ then } P(x) = \textbf{1} \text{ else } P(x) = ob$$
$$\frac{\forall y \in \textbf{Dom}(H).\neg nolock(\Gamma(y)) \Longrightarrow O(y) \leq 1}{\vdash_E (\widetilde{D}, Env, H, L) : \Gamma}$$
$$\text{(T-ENV)}$$

$$\vdash_E (\widetilde{D}, Env, H, L) : (\Gamma_1 \otimes \cdots \otimes \Gamma_n) \qquad \Gamma_i \vdash s_i \Rightarrow \Gamma_i' \ \& \ lev_i$$
$$\frac{\textbf{wf}(\Gamma_i) \qquad noob(\Gamma_i') \quad (s_i \in S)}{\vdash_{Conf} (\widetilde{D}, Env, H, L, S)}$$
$$\text{(T-CONFIG)}$$

Fig. 14. Typing rules for configurations

form $\{lexp_1 \leq lexp_1', \ldots, lexp_1 \leq lexp_n'\}$. This constraint set on lock levels can be solved in the same way as Kobayashi's deadlock-freedom analysis [11].

4   Type Soundness

This section states soundness of the type system introduced in the previous section. The proof of the soundness statement will appear in the full version of the current paper.

Because a deadlock is expressed as a stuck state in our language, soundness of the type system introduced in the previous section is stated as follows.

Theorem 1 (Type soundness). *If* $\vdash_{Prog} \widetilde{D}s$ *and* $(\widetilde{D}, \emptyset, \emptyset, \emptyset, \{s\}) \rightarrow^* (\widetilde{D}', Env', H', L', S')$, *then* $S = \emptyset$ *or there exists a configuration* $(\widetilde{D}'', Env'', H'', L'', S'')$ *that satisfies* $(\widetilde{D}', Env', H', L', S') \rightarrow (\widetilde{D}'', Env'', H'', L'', S'')$.

To state lemmas that are used in the proof of the theorem above, we first introduce a type judgment for configurations. Type judgments $\vdash_{Conf} (\widetilde{D}, Env, H, L, S)$, $\vdash_E (\widetilde{D}, Env, H, L) : \Gamma$ and $\vdash (\widetilde{D}, Env, H, L, x) : \tau, P$ are defined as the least relation that satisfies the rules in Figure 14. Here, the meta-variable P represents a map from lock-typed variables to usages and is used to describe which variable has an obligation to release each lock. The meta-variable O is a map from reference-typed variables to ownerships and used for calculating the sum of ownerships assigned to each reference. Operators $P_1 \otimes P_2$ and $O_1 \otimes O_2$ are defined as follows.

$$(P_1 \otimes P_2)(x) = \begin{cases} P_1(x) & (x \in \mathbf{Dom}(P_1) \backslash \mathbf{Dom}(P_2)) \\ P_2(x) & (x \in \mathbf{Dom}(P_2) \backslash \mathbf{Dom}(P_1)) \\ P_1(x) \otimes P_2(x) & (x \in \mathbf{Dom}(P_1) \cap \mathbf{Dom}(P_2)) \end{cases}$$

$$(O_1 \otimes O_2)(x) = \begin{cases} O_1(x) & (x \in \mathbf{Dom}(O_1) \backslash \mathbf{Dom}(O_2)) \\ O_2(x) & (x \in \mathbf{Dom}(O_2) \backslash \mathbf{Dom}(O_1)) \\ O_1(x) + O_2(x) & (x \in \mathbf{Dom}(O_1) \cap \mathbf{Dom}(O_2)) \end{cases}$$

The judgment $\vdash (\widetilde{D}, Env, H, L, x) : \tau, P, O$ means that (1) x has a type τ under $\widetilde{D}, Env, H$ and L, (2) x or a value reachable from x through H has obligations to release a lock y if $P(y) = ob$ and (3) references reachable from x are assigned ownerships as in O. By using this judgment, the rule (T-ENV) guarantees that, for each held lock, there exists exactly one variable that is reachable to the lock and that has the obligation to release the lock. The rule (T-CONFIG) guarantees that each obligation is fulfilled by exactly one thread.

The theorem above is proved using the following three lemmas.

Lemma 1. $\vdash_{Prog} \widetilde{D}s$ *implies* $\vdash_{Conf} (\widetilde{D}, \emptyset, \emptyset, \emptyset, \{s\})$.

Lemma 2 (Preservation). *If* $\vdash_{Conf} (\widetilde{D}, Env, H, L, S)$ *and* $(\widetilde{D}, Env, H, L, S)$ $\rightarrow (\widetilde{D}', Env', H', L', S')$, *then* $\vdash_{Conf} (\widetilde{D}', Env', H', L', S')$.

Lemma 3 (Progress). *If* $\vdash_{Conf} (\widetilde{D}, Env, H, L, S)$ *then* $S = \emptyset$ *or there exists a configuration* $(\widetilde{D}', Env', H', L', S')$ *such that* $(\widetilde{D}, Env, H, L, S) \rightarrow (\widetilde{D}', Env', H', L', S')$.

5   Related Work

Kobayashi et al. [12,11,14] proposed type systems for deadlock-freedom of π-calculus processes. Their idea is (1) to express how each channel is used by a *usage expression* and (2) to add *capability levels* and *obligation levels* to the inferred usage expressions in order to detect circular dependency among input/output operations to channels. Our usages can be seen as a simplified form of their usage expressions; following their encoding [11], **lock**(lev, ob) corresponds to $()/ * I^\infty_{lev}.O^{lev}_\infty$ and **lock**$(lev, 1)$ to $()/O^{lev}_\infty | * I^\infty_{lev}.O^{lev}_\infty$. Their verification method is applicable to programs which use various synchronization primitives other than mutexes because they use π-calculus as their target language. However, their framework does not have references as primitives and cannot deal with references encoded using channels accurately.

Boyapati, Lee and Rinard [2] proposed a type-based deadlock- and race-freedom verification of Java programs. In our previous work [16], we have proposed a type-based deadlock-freedom analysis for concurrent programs with block-structured lock primitives, references and interrupts. The main difference between those type systems and our type system is that our type system deals with non-block-structured lock primitives, while their type system only deals with block-structured lock primitives.

Foster, Terauchi and Aiken [9] proposed a type system with flow-sensitive type qualifiers [9] and applied their type system to an analysis which checks locks are not doubly acquired nor released. Their type system adds a flow-sensitive type qualifier (`locked` or `unlocked` in their lock usage analysis) to each abstract memory location which contains locks, and checks whether qualifiers are in an expected state. They check that each locking operation is followed by an unlocking operation but do not guarantee deadlock-freedom. They do not deal with concurrency, either. As discussed in Section 3.1, the meaning of our obligations differs from that of their flow-sensitive type qualifiers.

6   Conclusion

We have proposed a type-based deadlock-freedom verification method for concurrent programs with non-block-structured lock primitives and references. Our type system verifies deadlock-freedom by guaranteeing that locks are acquired in a specific order by using lock levels and that an acquired lock is released exactly once by using obligations and ownerships.

Future work includes conducting deadlock-freedom verification experiments of practical software. We have implemented a prototype of a verifier based on our framework and have successfully verified deadlock-freedom of a network device driver. We are trying to apply our verifier to larger software such as network servers.

Another future work is to extend our framework with several practical features such as interrupts, recursive types and synchronization primitives other than mutexes. We are especially interested in dealing with interrupts which are essential in verifying low-level software such as operating system kernels as pointed out in several papers [16,15,4,6]. We consider extending usages with information on whether the lock may be held while interrupts are enabled.

Acknowledgement. We thank Naoki Kobayashi for his fruitful comments on our research. We also thank the members of Kobayashi-Sumii group in Tohoku University and anonymous reviewers for their comments. This research is partially supported by Grant-in-Aid for JSPS Fellows (19·1504) and JSPS Research Fellowships for Young Scientists.

References

1. Abadi, M., Flanagan, C., Freund, S.N.: Types for safe locking: Static race detection for Java. ACM Transactions on Programming Languages and Systems 28(2), 207–255 (2006)
2. Boyapati, C., Lee, R., Rinard, M.: Ownership types for safe programming: Preventing data races and deadlocks. In: Proceedings of the 2002 ACM SIGPLAN Conference on Object-Oriented Programming Systems, Languages and Applications (OOPSLA 2002), SIGPLAN Notices, November 2002. vol. 37, pp. 211–230 (2002)

3. Boyland, J.: Checking interference with fractional permissions. In: Cousot, R. (ed.) SAS 2003. LNCS, vol. 2694, pp. 55–72. Springer, Heidelberg (2003)

4. Chatterjee, K., Ma, D., Majumdar, R., Zhao, T., Henzinger, T.A., Palsberg, J.: Stack size analysis for interrupt-driven programs. Information and Computation 194(2), 144–174 (2004)

5. Dahyabhai, N.: Bugzilla Bug 439215: dbus-daemon-1 hangs when using the option nss_initgroups_ignoreusers in /etc/ldap.conf. with the user root. Red Hat, Inc (accessed on June 19, 2008) (March 2008),
https://bugzilla.redhat.com/show_bug.cgi?id=439215

6. Feng, X., Shao, Z., Dong, Y., Guo, Y.: Certifying low-level programs with hardware interrupts and preemptive threads. In: Programming Language Design and Implementation (PLDI) (June 2008)

7. Flanagan, C., Abadi, M.: Object types against races. In: Baeten, J.C.M., Mauw, S. (eds.) CONCUR 1999. LNCS, vol. 1664, pp. 288–303. Springer, Heidelberg (1999)

8. Flanagan, C., Abadi, M.: Types for safe locking. In: Swierstra, S.D. (ed.) ESOP 1999. LNCS, vol. 1576, pp. 91–108. Springer, Heidelberg (1999)

9. Foster, J.S., Terauchi, T., Aiken, A.: Flow-sensitive type qualifiers. In: Proceedings of ACM SIGPLAN Conference on Programming Language Design and Implementation, pp. 1–12 (2002)

10. Kikuchi, D., Kobayashi, N.: Type-based verification of correspondence assertions for communication protocols. In: Proceedings of the Fifth ASIAN Symposium on Programming Languages and Systems (November 2007)

11. Kobayashi, N.: Type-based information flow analysis for the pi-calculus. Acta Informatica 42(4-5), 291–347 (2005)

12. Kobayashi, N.: A new type system for deadlock-free processes. In: Baier, C., Hermanns, H. (eds.) CONCUR 2006. LNCS, vol. 4137, pp. 233–247. Springer, Heidelberg (2006)

13. Kobayashi, N.: Substructural type systems for program analysis. In: Garrigue, J., Hermenegildo, M.V. (eds.) FLOPS 2008. LNCS, vol. 4989, p. 14. Springer, Heidelberg (2008), http://www.kb.ecei.tohoku.ac.jp/~koba/slides/FLOPS2008.pdf

14. Kobayashi, N., Saito, S., Sumii, E.: An implicitly-typed deadlock-free process calculus. In: Palamidessi, C. (ed.) CONCUR 2000. LNCS, vol. 1877, pp. 489–503. Springer, Heidelberg (2000)

15. Palsberg, J., Ma, D.: A typed interrupt calculus. In: Damm, W., Olderog, E.-R. (eds.) FTRTFT 2002. LNCS, vol. 2469, pp. 291–310. Springer, Heidelberg (2002)

16. Suenaga, K., Kobayashi, N.: Type-based analysis of deadlock for a concurrent calculus with interrupts. In: De Nicola, R. (ed.) ESOP 2007. LNCS, vol. 4421, pp. 490–504. Springer, Heidelberg (2007)

17. Terauchi, T.: Types for Deterministic Concurrency. PhD thesis, Electrical Engineering and Computer Sciences, University of California at Berkeley (August 2006)

Reasoning about Java's Reentrant Locks

Christian Haack[1,*], Marieke Huisman[2,*,†,‡], and Clément Hurlin[3,*,†]

[1] Radboud Universiteit Nijmegen, The Netherlands
[2] University of Twente, The Netherlands
[3] INRIA Sophia Antipolis - Méditerranée, France

Abstract. This paper presents a verification technique for a concurrent Java-like language with reentrant locks. The verification technique is based on permission-accounting separation logic. As usual, each lock is associated with a resource invariant, i.e., when acquiring the lock the resources are obtained by the thread holding the lock, and when releasing the lock, the resources are released. To accommodate for reentrancy, the notion of lockset is introduced: a multiset of locks held by a thread. Keeping track of the lockset enables the logic to ensure that resources are not re-acquired upon reentrancy, thus avoiding the introduction of new resources in the system. To be able to express flexible locking policies, we combine the verification logic with value-parameterized classes. Verified programs satisfy the following properties: data race freedom, absence of null-dereferencing and partial correctness. The verification technique is illustrated on several examples, including a challenging lock-coupling algorithm.

1 Introduction

Writing correct concurrent programs, let alone verifying their correctness, is a highly complex task. The complexity is caused by potential thread interference at every program point, which makes this task inherently non-local. To reduce this complexity, concurrent programming languages provide high-level synchronization primitives. The main synchronization primitive of today's most popular modern object-oriented languages — Java and C# — are reentrant locks. While reentrant locks ease concurrent programming, using them correctly remains difficult and their incorrect usage can result in nasty concurrency errors like data races or deadlocks. Multithreaded Java-like languages do not offer enough support to prevent such errors, and are thus an important target for lightweight verification techniques.

An attractive verification technique, based on the regulation of heap space access, is O'Hearn's concurrent separation logic (CSL) [18]. In CSL, the programmer formally associates locks with pieces of heap space, and the verification system ensures that a piece of heap space is only accessed when the associated lock is held. This, of course, is an old idea in verification of shared variable concurrent programs [2]. The novelty of CSL is that it generalizes these old ideas in an elegant way to languages with unstructured heaps, thus paving the way from textbook toy languages to realistic programming languages. This path has been further explored by Gotsman et al. [10] and Hobor et

---

* Supported in part by IST-FET-2005-015905 Mobius project.
† Supported in part by ANR-06-SETIN-010 ParSec project.
‡ Research done while at INRIA Sophia Antipolis - Méditerranée.

G. Ramalingam (Ed.): APLAS 2008, LNCS 5356, pp. 171–187, 2008.

al. [13], who adapt CSL from O'Hearn's simple concurrent language (with a static set of locks and threads) to languages with dynamic lock and thread creation and concurrency primitives that resemble POSIX threads. However, in these variants of CSL, locks are single-entrant; this paper adapts CSL to a Java-like language with *reentrant* locks.

Unfortunately, reentrant locks are inherently problematic for separation-logic reasoning, which tries to completely replace "negative" reasoning about the absence of aliasing by "positive" reasoning about the possession of access permissions. The problem is that a verification system for reentrant locks has to distinguish between initial lock entries and reentries, because only after initial entries is it sound to assume a lock's resource invariant. This means that initial lock entries need a precondition requiring that the current thread does *not* already hold the acquired lock. Establishing this precondition boils down to proving that the acquired lock does not alias a currently held lock, i.e., to proving absence of aliasing.

This does not mean, however, that permission-based reasoning has to be abandoned altogether for reentrant locks. It merely means that permission-based reasoning alone is insufficient. To illustrate this, we modularly specify and verify a fine-grained lock-coupling list (where lock reentrancy complicates verification) that has previously been verified with separation logic rules for single-entrant locks [10]. This example crucially uses that our verification system includes *value-parameterized types*. Value-parameterized types are generally useful for modularity, and are similar to type-parameterized types in Java Generics [17]. In the lock-coupling example, we use that value-parameterized types can express type-based ownership [7,5], which is a common technique to relieve the aliasing problem in OO verification systems based on classical logic [16].

Another challenge for reasoning about Java-like languages is the handling of inheritance. In Java, each object has an associated reentrant lock, its *object lock*. Naturally, the resource invariant that is associated with an object lock is specified in the object's class. For subclassing, we need to provide a mechanism for extending resource invariants in subclasses in order to account for extended object state. To this end, we represent resource invariants as abstract predicates [21]. We support modular verification of predicate extensions, by axiomatizing the so-called "stack of class frames" [9,3] in separation logic, as described in our previous work [12].

This paper is structured as follows. First, Section 2 describes the Java-like language that we use for our theoretical development. Next, Section 3 provides some background on separation logic and sketches the axiomatization of the stack of class frames. Section 4 presents Hoare rules for reentrant locking. The rules are illustrated by several examples in Section 5. Last, Section 6 sketches the soundness proof for the verification system, and Section 7 discusses related work and concludes.

2   A Java-Like Language with Contracts

This section presents the Java-like language that is used to write programs and specifications. The language distinguishes between read-only variables $\imath$, read-write variables ℓ, and logical variables α. The distinction between read-only and read-write variables is not essential, but often avoids the need for syntactical side conditions in the proof rules (see Section 4 and [12]). Method parameters (including this) are read-only; read-write variables can occur everywhere else, while logical variables can only occur in specifications and types. Apart from this distinction, the *identifier domains* are standard:

$$C, D \in \mathsf{ClassId} \quad I \in \mathsf{IntId} \quad s, t \in \mathsf{TypeId} = \mathsf{ClassId} \cup \mathsf{IntId} \quad o, p, q, r \in \mathsf{ObjId} \quad f \in \mathsf{FieldId}$$
$$m \in \mathsf{MethId} \quad P \in \mathsf{PredId} \quad \iota \in \mathsf{RdVar} \quad \ell \in \mathsf{RdWrVar} \quad \alpha \in \mathsf{LogVar}$$
$$x, y, z \in \mathsf{Var} = \mathsf{RdVar} \cup \mathsf{RdWrVar} \cup \mathsf{LogVar}$$

Values are integers, booleans, object identifiers and `null`. For convenience, read-only variables can be used as values directly. Read-only and read-write variables can only contain these basic values, while logical variables range over *specification values* that include both values and *fractional permissions* [6]. Fractional permissions are fractions $\frac{1}{2^n}$ in the interval $(0, 1]$. They are represented symbolically: 1 represents itself, and if symbolic fraction π represents concrete fraction fr then $\mathtt{split}(\pi)$ represents $\frac{1}{2} \cdot fr$. The full fraction 1 grants *read-write* access right to an associated heap location, while split fractions grant *read-only* access rights. The verification system ensures that the sum of all fractional permissions for the same heap location is always at most 1. As a result, the system prevents read-write and write-write conflicts, while permitting concurrent reads. Formally, the syntactic domain of *values* is defined as follows:

$$n \in \mathsf{Int} \qquad\qquad v, w \in \mathsf{Val} ::= \mathtt{null} \mid n \mid b \mid o \mid \iota$$
$$b \in \mathsf{Bool} = \{\mathtt{true}, \mathtt{false}\} \qquad \pi \in \mathsf{SpecVal} ::= \alpha \mid v \mid 1 \mid \mathtt{split}(\pi)$$

Now we define the *types* used in our language. Since interfaces and classes (defined next) can be parameterized with specification values, object types are of the form $t\texttt{<}\bar{\pi}\texttt{>}$. Further, we define special types `perm` (for fractional permissions) and `lockset` (for sets of objects).

$$T, U, V, W \in \mathsf{Type} ::= \mathtt{void} \mid \mathtt{int} \mid \mathtt{bool} \mid t\texttt{<}\bar{\pi}\texttt{>} \mid \mathtt{perm} \mid \mathtt{lockset}$$

Next, *class declarations* are defined. Classes declare *fields*, *abstract predicates* (as introduced by Parkinson and Bierman [21]), and *methods*. Following [21], predicates are always implicitly parameterized by the receiver parameter `this`, and can explicitly list additional parameters. Methods have pre/postcondition specifications, parameterized by logical variables. The meaning of a specification is defined via a universal quantification over these parameters. In examples, we usually leave the parameterization implicit, but it is treated explicitly in the formal language.

$F \in \mathsf{Formula}$	specification formulas (see Sec. 3 and 4)
$spec ::= \mathtt{req}\, F; \mathtt{ens}\, F;$	pre/postconditions
$fd ::= T\, f;$	field declarations
$pd ::= \mathtt{pred}\, P\texttt{<}\bar{T}\, \bar{\alpha}\texttt{>} = F;$	predicate definitions
$md ::= \texttt{<}\bar{T}\, \bar{\alpha}\texttt{>}\, spec\, U\, m\, (\bar{V}\, \bar{\iota})\, \{c\}$	methods (scope of $\bar{\alpha}, \bar{\iota}$ is $\bar{T}, spec, U, \bar{V}, c$)
$cl \in \mathsf{Class} ::=$	classes
$\quad \mathtt{class}\, C\texttt{<}\bar{T}\, \bar{\alpha}\texttt{>}\, \mathtt{ext}\, U\, \mathtt{impl}\, \bar{V}\, \{fd^*\, pd^*\, md^*\}$	(scope of $\bar{\alpha}$ is $\bar{T}, U, \bar{V}, fd^*, pd^*, md^*$)

In a similar way, *interfaces* are defined formally as follows:

$$int \in \mathsf{Interface} ::= \mathtt{interface}\, I\texttt{<}\bar{T}\, \bar{\alpha}\texttt{>}\, \mathtt{ext}\, \bar{U}\, \{pt^*\, mt^*\}$$

where pt^* are predicate types and mt^* are method types including specifications (see [11] for a formal definition). Class and interface declarations allow to define *class tables*: $ct \subseteq \mathsf{Interface} \cup \mathsf{Class}$. We assume that class tables contain the classes `Object` and

Thread. The Thread class declares a run() and a start() method. The run() method is meant to be overridden, whereas the start() method is implemented natively and must not be overridden. For thread objects o, calling o.start() forks a new thread (whose thread id is o) that will execute o.run(). The start()-method has no specification. Instead, our verification system uses run()'s precondition as start()'s precondition, and true as its postcondition.

We impose the following *syntactic restrictions* on interface and class declarations: *(1)* the types perm and lockset may only occur inside angle brackets or formulas; *(2)* cyclic predicate definitions in *ct* must be positive. The first restriction ensures that permissions and locksets do not spill into the executable part of the language, while the second ensures that predicate definitions (which can be recursive) are well-founded.

Subtyping, denoted $<:$, is defined as usual. Commands are sequences of head commands *hc* and local variable declarations, terminated by a return value:

$$c \in \text{Cmd} ::= v \mid T\,\ell;\,c \mid \text{final } T\,\iota = \ell;\,c \mid hc;\,c$$
$$hc \in \text{HeadCmd} ::= \ell = v \mid \ell = op(\bar{v}) \mid \ell = v.f \mid v.f = v \mid \ell = \text{new } C < \bar{\pi}> \mid \ell = v.m(\bar{v}) \mid$$
$$\qquad\qquad\qquad \text{if}\,(v)\{c\}\text{else}\{c\} \mid v.\text{lock}() \mid v.\text{unlock}() \mid sc$$
$$sc \in \text{SpecCmd} ::= \text{assert}(F) \mid \pi.\text{commit}$$

To simplify the proof rules, we assume that programs have been "normalized" prior to verification, so that every intermediate result is assigned to a local variable, and the right hand sides of assignments contain no read-write variables. *Specification commands sc* are used by the proof system, but are ignored at runtime. The specification command assert(F) makes the proof system check that F holds at this program point, while π.commit makes it check that π's resource invariant is initialized (see Section 4).

3   A Variant of Intuitionistic Separation Logic

We now sketch the version of intuitionistic separation logic that we use [12]. *Intuitionistic* separation logic [14,22,21] is suitable for reasoning about properties that are invariant under heap extensions, and is appropriate for garbage-collected languages.

Specification formulas are defined by the following grammar:

$$lop \in \{*, -*, \&, |\} \qquad qt \in \{\text{ex}, \text{fa}\} \qquad \kappa \in \text{Pred} ::= P \mid P@C$$
$$F \in \text{Formula} ::= e \mid \text{PointsTo}(e.f, \pi, e) \mid \pi.\kappa < \bar{\pi}> \mid F\;lop\;F \mid (qt\,T\,\alpha)\,(F)$$

We now briefly explain these formulas:

Expressions e are built from values and variables using arithmetic and logical operators, and the operators e instanceof T and C classof e. (The latter holds if C is e's dynamic class.) Expressions of type bool are included in the domain of formulas.

The *points-to predicate* PointsTo($e.f, \pi, v$) is ASCII for $e.f \xrightarrow{\pi} v$ [4]. Superscript π must be of type perm (i.e., a fraction). Points-to has a dual meaning: firstly, it asserts that field $e.f$ contains value v and, secondly, it represents access right π to $e.f$. As explained above, $\pi = 1$ grants write access, and any π grants read access.

The *resource conjunction F * G* expresses that resources F and G are independently available: using either of these resources leaves the other one intact. Resource conjunction is not idempotent: F does *not* imply $F * F$. Because Java is a garbage-collected language, we allow dropping assertions: $F * G$ implies F.

The *resource implication* $F -\!\!* G$ (a.k.a. *separating implication* or *magic wand*) means "consume F yielding G". Resource $F -\!\!* G$ permits to trade resource F to receive resource G in return. Resource conjunction and implication are related by the modus ponens: $F * (F -\!\!* G)$ implies G.

We remark that the logical consequence judgment of our Hoare logic is based on the natural deduction calculus of *(affine) linear logic* [23], which coincides with BI's natural deduction calculus [19] on our restricted set of logical operators. To avoid a proof theory with bunched contexts, we omit the $\Rightarrow$-implication between heap formulas (and did not need it in our examples). However, this design decision is not essential.

The *predicate application* $\pi.\kappa<\bar{\pi}>$ applies abstract predicate κ to its receiver parameter π and the additional parameters $\bar{\pi}$. As explained above, predicate definitions in classes map abstract predicates to concrete definitions. Predicate definitions can be extended in subclasses to account for extended object state. Semantically, P's predicate extension in class C gets $*$-conjoined with P's predicate extensions in C's superclasses. The *qualified predicate* $\pi.P@C<\bar{\pi}>$ represents the $*$-conjunction of P's predicate extensions in C's superclasses, up to and including C. The *unqualified predicate* $\pi.P<\bar{\pi}>$ is equivalent to $\pi.P@C<\bar{\pi}>$, where C is π's dynamic class.

The following *derived forms* are convenient:

$$\texttt{PointsTo}(e.f, \pi, T) \overset{\Delta}{=} (\texttt{ex } T\ \alpha)\,(\texttt{PointsTo}(e.f, \pi, \alpha))$$
$$F *\!\!-\!\!* G \overset{\Delta}{=} (F -\!\!* G)\ \&\ (G -\!\!* F) \qquad F \texttt{ ispartof } G \overset{\Delta}{=} G -\!\!* (F * (F -\!\!* G))$$

Intuitively, F `ispartof` G says that F is a physical part of G: one can take G apart into F and its complement $F -\!\!* G$, and can put the two parts together to obtain G back.

The logical consequence of our Hoare logic is based on the standard natural deduction rules of (affine) linear logic. Sound *axioms* capture additional properties of our model. We now present some selected axioms[1]:

The following axiom regulates permission accounting ($\frac{\pi}{2}$ abbreviates $\texttt{split}(\pi)$):

$$\Gamma \vdash \texttt{PointsTo}(e.f, \pi, e') *\!\!-\!\!* (\texttt{PointsTo}(e.f, \tfrac{\pi}{2}, e') * \texttt{PointsTo}(e.f, \tfrac{\pi}{2}, e'))$$

The next axiom allows predicate receivers to toggle between predicate names and predicate definitions. The axiom has the following side conditions: $\Gamma \vdash \texttt{this} : C<\bar{\pi}''>$, the extension of $P<\bar{\pi}, \bar{\pi}'>$ in class $C<\bar{\pi}''>$ is F, and $C<\bar{\pi}''>$'s direct supertype is $D<\_>$:

$$\Gamma \vdash \texttt{this}.P@C<\bar{\pi}, \bar{\pi}'> *\!\!-\!\!* (F * \texttt{this}.P@D<\bar{\pi}>) \qquad \text{(Open/Close)}$$

Note that $P@C$ may have more parameters than $P@D$: following Parkinson and Bierman [21] we allow subclasses to extend predicate arities. Missing predicate parameters are existentially quantified, as expressed by the following axiom:

$$\Gamma \vdash \pi.P<\bar{\pi}> *\!\!-\!\!* (\texttt{ex } \bar{T}\ \bar{\alpha})\,(\pi.P<\bar{\pi}, \bar{\alpha}>) \qquad \text{(Missing Parameters)}$$

Finally, the following axiom says that a predicate at a receiver's dynamic type (i.e., without @-selector) is stronger than the predicate at its static type. In combination with (Open/Close), this allows to open and close predicates at the receiver's static type:

$$\Gamma \vdash \pi.P@C<\bar{\pi}> \texttt{ ispartof } \pi.P<\bar{\pi}> \qquad \text{(Dynamic Type)}$$

---

[1] Throughout this paper, Γ ranges over *type environments* assigning types to free variables and object identifiers.

We note that our axioms for abstract predicates formalize the so-called "stack of class frames" [9,3] using separation logic.

Our Hoare rules combine typing judgment with Hoare triples. In a Java-like language, such a combination is needed because method specifications are looked up based on receiver types. As common in separation logic, we use local Hoare rules combined with a frame rule [22]. Except from the rules for reentrant locks, the Hoare rules are pretty standard and we omit them. We point out that we do not admit the structural rule of conjunction. As a result, we do not need to require that resource invariants associated with locks (as presented in Section 4) are precise or supported formulas[2].

4   Proof Rules for Reentrant Locks

We now present the proof rules for reentrant locks: as usual [18], we assign to each lock a *resource invariant*. In our system, resource invariants are distinguished abstract predicates named inv. They have a default definition in the Object class and are meant to be extended in subclasses:

```
class Object { ... pred inv = true; ... }
```

The resource invariant o.inv can be assumed when o's lock is acquired non-reentrantly and must be established when o's lock is released with its reentrancy level dropping to 0. Regarding the interaction with subclassing, there is nothing special about inv. It is treated just like other abstract predicates.

In CSL for single-entrant locks [18], locks can be acquired without precondition. For reentrant locks, on the other hand, it seems unavoidable that the proof rule for acquiring a lock distinguishes between initial acquires and re-acquires. This is needed because it is quite obviously unsound to simply assume the resource invariant after a re-acquire. Thus, a proof system for reentrant locks must keep track of the locks that the current thread holds. To this end, we enrich our specification language:

$$\pi \in \mathsf{SpecVal} ::= \ldots \mid \mathtt{nil} \mid \pi \cdot \pi$$
$$F \in \mathsf{Formula} ::= \ldots \mid \mathtt{Lockset}(\pi) \mid \pi \mathtt{\ contains\ } e$$

Here is the informal semantics of the new expressions and formulas:

- nil: the empty multiset.
- $\pi \cdot \pi'$: the multiset union of multisets π and π'.
- Lockset(π): π is the multiset of locks held by the current thread. Multiplicities record the current reentrancy level. *(non-copyable)*
- π contains e: multiset π contains object e. *(copyable)*

We classify the new formulas (of which there will be two more) into *copyable* and *non-copyable* ones. Copyable formulas represent *persistent state properties* (i.e., properties that hold forever, once established), whereas non-copyable formulas represent *transient state properties* (i.e., properties that hold temporarily). For copyable F, we postulate the axiom $(G \mathbin{\&} F) \mathbin{-\!\!*} (G * F)$, whereas for non-copyable formulas we postulate no such axiom. Note that this axiom implies $F \mathbin{-\!\!*} (F * F)$, hence the term "copyable". As indicated above, π contains e is copyable, whereas Lockset(π) is not.

---

[2] See O'Hearn [18] for definitions of precise and supported formulas, and why they are needed.

Initial locksets. When verifying the body of `Thread.run()`, we assume `Lockset(nil)` as a precondition.

Initializing resource invariants. Like class invariants must be initialized before method calls, resource invariants must be initialized before the associated locks can be acquired. In O'Hearn's simple concurrent language [18], the set of locks is static and initialization of resource invariants is achieved in a global initialization phase. This is not possible when locks are created dynamically. Conceivably, we could tie the initialization of resource invariants to the end of object constructors. However, this is problematic because Java's object constructors are free to leak references to partially constructed objects (e.g., by passing `this` to other methods). Thus, in practice we have to distinguish between initialized and uninitialized objects semantically. Furthermore, a semantic distinction enables late initialization of resource invariants, which can be useful for objects that remain thread-local for some time before getting shared among threads. To support flexible initialization of resource invariants, we introduce two more formulas:

$$F \in \mathsf{Formula} ::= \dots \mid e.\mathsf{fresh} \mid e.\mathtt{initialized}$$
Restriction: $e.\mathtt{initialized}$ must not occur in negative positions.

- $e.\mathsf{fresh}$: e's resource invariant is not yet initialized. *(non-copyable)*
- $e.\mathtt{initialized}$: e's resource invariant has been initialized. *(copyable)*

The `fresh`-predicate is introduced as a postcondition of `new`:

$$\frac{C{<}\bar{T}\,\bar{\alpha}{>} \in ct \quad \Gamma \vdash \bar{\pi}:\bar{T}[\bar{\pi}/\alpha] \quad C{<}\bar{\pi}{>} <: \Gamma(\ell)}{\Gamma \vdash \{\mathtt{true}\}\ell = \mathtt{new}\ C{<}\bar{\pi}{>}\{\ell.\mathtt{init} * C\ \mathtt{classof}\ \ell * \circledast_{\Gamma(u)<:\mathtt{0bject}}\ \ell\,!{=}u * \ell.\mathsf{fresh}\}} \; (\text{New})$$

In addition, the postcondition grants access to all fields of the newly created object ℓ (by the special abstract predicate $\ell.\mathtt{init}$), and records that ℓ's dynamic class is known to be C. Furthermore, the postcondition records that the newly created object is distinct from all other objects that are in scope. This postcondition is usually omitted in separation logic, because separation logic gets around explicit reasoning about the absence of aliasing. Unfortunately, we cannot entirely avoid this kind of reasoning when establishing the precondition for the rule (Lock) below, which requires that the lock is *not* already held by the current thread.

The specification command $\pi.\mathtt{commit}$ triggers π's transition from the `fresh` to the `initialized` state, provided π's resource invariant is established:

$$\frac{\Gamma \vdash \pi : \mathtt{Object} \quad \Gamma \vdash \pi' : \mathtt{lockset}}{\Gamma \vdash \{\mathtt{Lockset}(\pi') * \pi.\mathtt{inv} * \pi.\mathsf{fresh}\}} \; (\text{Commit})$$
$$\pi.\mathtt{commit}$$
$$\{\mathtt{Lockset}(\pi') *\;!\,(\pi'\ \mathtt{contains}\ \pi) * \pi.\mathtt{initialized}\}$$

Locking and unlocking. There are two rules each for locking and unlocking, depending on whether or not the `lock/unlock` is associated with an initial entry or a reentry:

$$\frac{\Gamma \vdash v : \mathtt{Object} \quad \Gamma \vdash \pi : \mathtt{lockset}}{\Gamma \vdash \{\mathtt{Lockset}(\pi) *\;!\,(\pi\ \mathtt{contains}\ v) * v.\mathtt{initialized}\}} \; (\text{Lock})$$
$$v.\mathtt{lock}()$$
$$\{\mathtt{Lockset}(v \cdot \pi) * v.\mathtt{inv}\}$$

$$\frac{\Gamma \vdash v : \mathtt{Object} \quad \Gamma \vdash \pi : \mathtt{lockset}}{\Gamma \vdash \{\mathtt{Lockset}(v \cdot \pi)\}v.\mathtt{lock}()\{\mathtt{Lockset}(v \cdot v \cdot \pi)\}} \; (\text{Re-Lock})$$

The rule (Lock) applies when lock v is acquired non-reentrantly, as expressed by the precondition $\text{Lockset}(\pi) * !(\pi \text{ contains } v)$. The precondition $v.\text{initialized}$ makes sure that *(1)* threads only acquire locks whose resource invariant is initialized, and *(2)* no null-error can happen (because initialized values are non-null). The postcondition adds v to the current thread's lockset, and assumes v's resource invariant. The rule (Re-Lock) applies when a lock is acquired reentrantly.

$$\frac{\Gamma \vdash v:\text{Object} \quad \Gamma \vdash \pi:\text{lockset}}{\Gamma \vdash \{\text{Lockset}(v \cdot v \cdot \pi)\}v.\text{unlock}()\{\text{Lockset}(v \cdot \pi)\}} \text{ (Re-Unlock)}$$

$$\frac{\Gamma \vdash v:\text{Object} \quad \Gamma \vdash \pi:\text{lockset}}{\Gamma \vdash \{\text{Lockset}(v \cdot \pi) * v.\text{inv}\}v.\text{unlock}()\{\text{Lockset}(\pi)\}} \text{ (Unlock)}$$

The rule (Re-Unlock) applies when v's current reentrancy level is at least 2, and (Unlock) applies when v's resource invariant gets established in the precondition.

Some non-solutions. One might wish to avoid the disequalities in (New)'s postcondition. Several approaches for this come to mind. First, one could drop the disequalities in (New)'s postcondition, and rely on (Commit)'s postcondition $!(\pi' \text{ contains } \pi)$ to establish (Lock)'s precondition. While this would be sound, in general it is too weak, as we are not be able to lock π if we first lock some other object x (because from $!(\pi' \text{ contains } \pi)$ we cannot derive $!(x \cdot \pi' \text{ contains } \pi)$ unless we know $\pi \mathbin{!=} x$). Second, the Lockset predicate could be abandoned altogether, using a predicate $\pi.\text{Held}(n)$ instead, that says that the current thread holds lock π with reentrancy level n. In particular, $\pi.\text{Held}(0)$ means that the current thread does not hold π's lock at all. We could reformulate the rules for locking and unlocking using the Held-predicate, and introduce $\ell.\text{Held}(0)$ as the postcondition of (New), replacing the disequalities. However, this approach does not work, because it grants only the object creator permission to lock the created object! While it is conceivable that a clever program logic could somehow introduce $\pi.\text{Held}(0)$-predicates in other ways (besides introducing it in the postcondition of (New)), we have not been able to come up with a workable solution along these lines.

5   Examples

In this section, we illustrate our proof rules by several examples. We use the following convenient abbreviations:

$$\pi.\text{locked}(\pi') \triangleq \text{Lockset}(\pi \cdot \pi') \qquad \pi.\text{unlocked}(\pi') \triangleq \text{Lockset}(\pi') * !(\pi' \text{ contains } \pi)$$

The formula $\pi.\text{locked}(\pi')$ says that the current thread's lockset $\pi \cdot \pi'$ contains lock π, and $\pi.\text{unlocked}(\pi')$ that the current thread's lockset π' does not contain lock π.

Example 1: A Method with Callee-side Locking. We begin with a very simple example of a race free implementation of a bank account. The account lock guards access to the account balance, as expressed by inv's definition below.

```
class Account extends Object {
    private int balance;
    pred inv = PointsTo(this.balance, 1, int);
```

```
req this.initialized * this.unlocked(s); ens Lockset(s);
int deposit(int x) {
     { this.initialized * this.unlocked(s) }  (expanding unlocked)
     { this.initialized * Lockset(s) * !(s contains this) }
   lock();
     { Lockset(this·s) * this.inv }
     (opening inv)
     { Lockset(this·s) * PointsTo(this.balance, 1, int) * (this.inv@Account -* this.inv) }
   balance = balance + x;
     { Lockset(this·s) * PointsTo(this.balance, 1, int) * (this.inv@Account -* this.inv) }
     (closing inv)
     { Lockset(this·s) * this.inv }
   unlock();
     { Lockset(s) } } }
```

The precondition of `deposit()` requires that prior to calling `acc.deposit()` the account's resource invariant must be initialized and the current thread must not hold the account lock already. The postcondition ensures that the current thread's lockset after the call equals its lockset before the call. We have annotated `deposit()`'s body with a proof outline and invite the reader to match the outline to our proof rules. Note that when opening `inv`, we use the axioms (Dynamic Type) and (Open/Close). When closing `inv`, we use (Open/Close) and the modus ponens.

Example 2: A Method with Caller-side Locking. In the previous example, `deposit()`'s contract does not say that this method updates the account balance. In fact, because our program logic ties the `balance` field to the account's resource invariant, it prohibits the contract to refer to this field unless the account lock is held before and after calling `deposit()`. Note that this is not a shortcoming of our program logic but, on the contrary, is exactly what is needed to ensure sound method contracts: pre/postconditions that refer to the `balance` field when the account object is unlocked are subject to thread interference and thus lead to unsoundness.

However, we can also express a contract for a `deposit()`-method that enforces that callers have acquired the lock prior to calling `deposit()`, and furthermore expresses that `deposit()` updates the `balance` field. To this end, we make use of the feature that the arity of abstract predicates can be extended in subclasses. Thus, we can extend the arity of the `inv`-predicate (which has arity 0 in the `Object` class) to have an additional integer parameter in the `Account` class:

```
class Account extends Object {
  private int balance;
  pred inv<int balance> = PointsTo(this.balance, 1, balance);
  req inv<balance>; ens inv<balance + x>;
  void deposit(int x){ balance = balance + x; } }
```

Here, `deposit()`'s contract is implicitly quantified by the variable `balance`. When a caller establishes the precondition, the `balance` variable gets bound to a concrete integer, namely the current content of the `balance` field. Note that `acc.deposit()` can only be called when `acc` is locked (as locking `acc` is the only way to establish the precondition `acc.inv<_>`). Furthermore, `deposit()`'s contract forces `deposit()`'s implementation to hold the receiver lock on method exit.

Example 3: A Method Designed for Reentry. The implementations of the `deposit()` method in the previous examples differ. Because Java's locks are reentrant, a single implementation of `deposit()` actually satisfies both contracts:

```
class Account extends Object {
  private int balance;
  pred inv<int balance> = PointsTo(this.balance, 1, balance);
  req unlocked(s) * initialized; ens Lockset(s);
  also
  req locked(s) * inv<balance>; ens locked(s) * inv<balance + x>;
  void deposit(int x) { lock(); balance = balance + x; unlock(); } }
```

This example makes use of *contract conjunction*. Intuitively, a method with two contracts joined by "`also`" satisfies both these contracts. Technically, contract conjunction is a derived form [20]:

$$\text{req } F_1; \text{ens } G_1; \text{ also req } F_2; \text{ens } G_2;$$
$$\triangleq \text{ req } (F_1 \,\&\, \alpha == 1) \mid (F_2 \,\&\, \alpha == 2); \text{ ens } (G_1 \,\&\, \alpha == 1) \mid (G_2 \,\&\, \alpha == 2);$$

In the example, the first clause of the contract conjunction applies when the caller does not yet hold the object lock, and the second clause applies when he already holds it. The precondition `locked(s)` in the second clause is needed as a pre-condition for re-acquiring the lock, see the rule (Re-Lock). In Example 2, this precondition was not needed because there `deposit()`'s implementation does not acquire the account lock.

Example 4: A Fine-grained Locking Policy. To illustrate that our solution also supports fine-grained locking policies, we show how we can implement lock coupling. Suppose we want to implement a sorted linked list with repetitions. For simplicity, assume that the list has only two methods: `insert()` and `size()`. The former inserts an integer into the list, and the latter returns the current size of the list. To support a constant-time `size()`-method, each node stores the size of its tail in a `count`-field.

In order to allow multiple threads inserting simultaneously, we want to avoid using a single lock for the whole list. We have to be careful, though: a naive locking policy that simply locks one node at a time would be unsafe, because several threads trying to simultaneously insert the same integer can cause a semantic data race, so that some integers get lost and the `count`-fields get out of sync with the list size. The lock coupling technique avoids this by simultaneously holding locks of two neighboring nodes at critical times.

Lock coupling has been used as an example by Gotsman et al. [10] for single-entrant locks. The additional problem with reentrant locks is that `insert()`'s precondition must require that none of the list nodes is in the lockset of the current thread. This is necessary to ensure that on method entry the current thread is capable of acquiring all nodes's resource invariants:

```
class LockCouplingList implements SortedIntList {
    Node<this> head;
    pred inv<int c> = (ex Node<this> n)(
       PointsTo(head, 1, n) * n.initialized * PointsTo(n.count, 1/2, c) );
    req this.inv<c>; ens this.inv<c> * result==c;
    int size() { return head.count; }
    req Lockset(s) * !(s contains this) * this.traversable(s); ens Lockset(s);
    void insert(int x) {
       lock(); Node<this> n = head;
       if (n!=null) {
         n.lock();
         if (x <= n.val) {
           n.unlock(); head = new Node<this>(x,head); head.commit; unlock();
         } else { unlock(); n.count++; n.insert(x); }
       } else { head = new Node<this>(x,null); unlock(); } } }

class Node<Object owner> implements Owned<owner> {
    int count; int val; Node<owner> next;
    spec_public pred couple<int count_this, int count_next> =
       (ex Node<owner> n)(
           PointsTo(this.count, 1/2, count_this) * PointsTo(this.val, 1, int)
         * PointsTo(this.next, 1, n) * n!=this * n.initialized
         * ( n!=null -* PointsTo(n.count, 1/2, count_next) )
         * ( n==null -* count_this==1 ) );
    spec_public pred inv<int c> = couple<c,c-1>;
    req PointsTo(next.count, 1/2, c);
    ens PointsTo(next.count, 1/2, c)
      * ( next!=null -* PointsTo(this.count, 1, c+1) )
      * ( next==null -* PointsTo(this.count, 1, 1) )
      * PointsTo(this.val, 1, val) * PointsTo(this.next, 1, next);
    Node(int val, Node<owner> next) {
       if (next!=null) { this.count = next.count+1; } else { this.count = 1; }
       this.val = val; this.next = next; }
    req Lockset(this·s) * owner.traversable(s) * this.couple<c+1,c-1>;
    ens Lockset(s);
    void insert(int x) {
      Node<owner> n = next;
      if (n!=null) {
        n.lock();
        if (x <= n.val) {
          n.unlock(); next = new Node<owner>(x,n); next.commit; unlock();
        } else { unlock(); n.count++; n.insert(x); }
      } else { next = new Node<owner>(x, null); unlock(); } } }
```

Fig. 1. A lock-coupling list

```
req this.unlocked(s) * no list node is in s ; ens Lockset(s);
void insert(int x);
```

The question is how to formally represent the informal condition. Our solution makes use of class parameters. We require that nodes of a lock-coupled list are *statically owned* by the list object, i.e., they have type Node<o>, where o is the list object. Then we can approximate the above contract as follows:

```
req this.unlocked(s) * no this-owned object is in s ; ens Lockset(s);
void insert(int x);
```

To express this formally, we define a marker interface for owned objects:

```
interface Owned<Object owner> { /* a marker interface */ }
```

Next we define an auxiliary predicate π.traversable(π') (read as "if the current thread's lockset is π', then the aggregate owned by object π is traversable"). Concretely, this predicate says that no object owned by π is contained in π':

$$\pi.\text{traversable}(\pi') \;\overset{\triangle}{=}\;$$
```
        (fa Object owner, Owned<owner> x)(!(π' contains x) | owner !=π)
```

Note that in our definition of π.traversable(π'), we quantify over a type parameter (namely the owner-parameter of the Owned-type). Here we are taking advantage of the fact that program logic and type system are inter-dependent.

Now, we can formally define an interface for sorted integer lists:

```
interface SortedIntList {
    pred inv<int c>;     // c is the number of list nodes
    req this.inv<c>; ens this.inv<c> * result==c;
    int size();
    req this.unlocked(s) * this.traversable(s); ens Lockset(s);
    void insert(int x); }
```

Figure 1 shows a tail-recursive lock-coupling implementation of `SortedIntList`. It makes use of the predicate modifier `spec_public`, which exports the predicate definition to object clients[3]. The auxiliary predicate n.couple<c,c'>, as defined in the Node class, holds in states where `n.count == c` and `n.next.count == c'`.

But how can clients of lock-coupling lists establish `insert()`'s precondition? The answer is that client code needs to track the types of locks held by the current thread. For instance, if C is not a subclass of `Owned`, then `list.insert()`'s precondition is implied by the following assertion, which is satisfied when the current thread has locked only objects of types C and Owned<ℓ>.

```
list.unlocked(s) * ℓ!=list *
(fa Object z)(!(s contains z) | z instanceof C | z instanceof Owned<ℓ>)
```

6 Semantics and Soundness

6.1 Runtime Structures

We model dynamics by a small-step operational semantics that operates on states, consisting of a heap, a lock table and a thread pool. As usual, *heaps* map each object identifier to its dynamic type and to a mapping from fields to closed values:

$$h \in \text{Heap} = \text{ObjId} \rightharpoonup \text{Type} \times (\text{FieldId} \rightharpoonup \text{ClVal}) \qquad \text{ClVal} = \text{Val} \setminus \text{RdVar}$$

Stacks map read/write variables to closed values. Their domains do not include read-only variables, because our operational semantics instantiates those by substitution:

$$s \in \text{Stack} = \text{RdWrVar} \rightharpoonup \text{ClVal}$$

---

[3] `spec_public` can be defined in terms of class axioms, see [12].

A *thread* is a pair of a stack and a command. A *thread pool* maps object identifiers (representing Thread objects) to threads. For better readability, we use syntax-like notation and write "s in c" for threads $t = (s,c)$, and "o_1 is $t_1 \mid \cdots \mid o_n$ is t_n" for thread pools $ts = \{o_1 \mapsto t_1, \ldots, o_n \mapsto t_n\}$:

$$t \in \text{Thread} = \text{Stack} \times \text{Cmd} \quad ::= s \text{ in } c$$
$$ts \in \text{ThreadPool} = \text{ObjId} \rightharpoonup \text{Thread} ::= o_1 \text{ is } t_1 \mid \cdots \mid o_n \text{ is } t_n$$

Lock tables map objects o to either the symbol free, or to the thread object that currently holds o's lock and a number that counts how often it currently holds this lock:

$$l \in \text{LockTable} = \text{ObjId} \rightharpoonup \{\text{free}\} \uplus (\text{ObjId} \times \mathbb{N})$$

Finally, a *state* consists of a heap, a lock table, and a thread pool:

$$st \in \text{State} = \text{Heap} \times \text{LockTable} \times \text{ThreadPool}$$

We omit the (pretty standard) rules for our small-step relation $st \rightarrow_{ct} st'$. The relation depends on the underlying class table (for looking up methods), hence the subscript ct.

6.2   Kripke Resource Semantics

We define a forcing relation of the form $\Gamma \vdash \mathcal{E}; \mathcal{R}; s \models F$, where Γ is a *type environment*, $\mathcal{E}$ is a *predicate environment*, $\mathcal{R}$ is a *resource*, and s is a *stack*. We assume that the stack s, the formula F, and the resource $\mathcal{R}$ are well-typed in Γ, i.e., the semantic relation is defined on well-typed tuples. The predicate environment $\mathcal{E}$ maps predicate identifiers to concrete heap predicates that satisfy the predicate definitions from the class table. Our well-foundedness restriction on predicate definitions ensures that such a predicate environment exists.

Resources $\mathcal{R}$ range over the set Resource with a binary relation $\# \subseteq \text{Resource} \times \text{Resource}$ (the *compatibility relation*) and a partial binary operator $* : \# \rightarrow \text{Resource}$ (the *resource joining operator*) that is associative and commutative. Concretely, resources are 5-tuples $\mathcal{R} = (h, \mathcal{P}, \mathcal{L}, \mathcal{F}, \mathcal{I})$: a *heap* h, a *permission table* $\mathcal{P} \in \text{ObjId} \times \text{FieldId} \rightarrow [0,1]$, an *abstract lock table* $\mathcal{L} \in \text{ObjId} \rightharpoonup \text{Bag(ObjId)}^4$, a *fresh set* $\mathcal{F} \subseteq \text{ObjId}$, and an *initialized set* $\mathcal{I} \subseteq \text{ObjId}$. We require that resources satisfy the following axioms: *(1)* $\mathcal{P}(o,f) > 0$ iff $o \in \text{dom}(h)$ and $f \in \text{dom}(h(o)_2)$, *(2)* $\mathcal{F} \cap \mathcal{I} = \emptyset$, and *(3)* if $o \in \mathcal{L}(p)$ then $o \in \mathcal{I}$. Each of the five resource components carries itself a resource structure $(\#, *)$. These structures are lifted to 5-tuples componentwise. We now define $\#$ and $*$ for the five components.

Heaps are compatible if they agree on object types and memory content:

$$h \# h' \text{ iff } \begin{cases} (\forall o \in \text{dom}(h) \cap \text{dom}(h'))(\\ h(o)_1 = h'(o)_1 \text{ and } (\forall f \in \text{dom}(h(o)_2) \cap \text{dom}(h'(o)_2))(\, h(o)_2(f) = h'(o)_2(f)\,)\,) \end{cases}$$

To define heap joining, we lift set union to deal with undefinedness: $f \vee g = f \cup g$, $f \vee \text{undef} = \text{undef} \vee f = f$. Similarly for types: $T \vee \text{undef} = \text{undef} \vee T = T \vee T = T$.

$$(h * h')(o)_1 \stackrel{\Delta}{=} h(o)_1 \vee h'(o)_1 \qquad (h * h')(o)_2 \stackrel{\Delta}{=} h(o)_2 \vee h'(o)_2$$

Joining *permission tables* is pointwise addition:

---

[4] Where we use $\sqcap$ to denote bag intersection, $\sqcup$ for bag union, and $[]$ for the empty bag.

$$\mathcal{P}\#\mathcal{P}' \text{ iff } (\forall o)(\mathcal{P}(o) + \mathcal{P}'(o) \le 1) \qquad (\mathcal{P}*\mathcal{P}')(o) \triangleq \mathcal{P}(o) + \mathcal{P}'(o)$$

Abstract lock tables map thread identifiers to locksets. The compatibility relation captures that distinct threads cannot hold the same lock.

$$\mathcal{L}\#\mathcal{L}' \text{ iff } \begin{cases} \text{dom}(\mathcal{L}) \cap \text{dom}(\mathcal{L}') = \emptyset \\ (\forall o \in \text{dom}(\mathcal{L}), p \in \text{dom}(\mathcal{L}'))(\mathcal{L}(o) \sqcap \mathcal{L}'(p) = []) \end{cases} \qquad \mathcal{L}*\mathcal{L}' \triangleq \mathcal{L} \cup \mathcal{L}'$$

Fresh sets $\mathcal{F}$ keep track of allocated but not yet initialized objects, while *initialized sets* $\mathcal{I}$ keep track of initialized objects. We define # for fresh sets as disjointness in order to mirror that $o.\texttt{fresh}$ is non-copyable, and for initialized sets as equality in order to mirror that $o.\texttt{initialized}$ is copyable:

$$\mathcal{F}\#\mathcal{F}' \text{ iff } \mathcal{F} \cap \mathcal{F}' = \emptyset \qquad \mathcal{F}*\mathcal{F}' \triangleq \mathcal{F} \cup \mathcal{F}'$$
$$\mathcal{I}\#\mathcal{I}' \text{ iff } \mathcal{I} = \mathcal{I}' \qquad \mathcal{I}*\mathcal{I}' \triangleq \mathcal{I} \ (= \mathcal{I}')$$

This completes the description of the semantic domains. We continue with the formal semantics of expressions and formulas. Expressions of type `lockset` are interpreted as multisets in the obvious way: $[\![\texttt{nil}]\!]_s^h = []$ and $[\![e \cdot e']\!]_s^h = [\![e]\!]_s^h \sqcup [\![e']\!]_s^h$. Here are the semantic clauses for our new formulas for reentrant locking:

$$\Gamma \vdash \mathcal{E}; (h, \mathcal{P}, \mathcal{L}, \mathcal{F}, \mathcal{I}); s \models \texttt{Lockset}(\pi) \qquad \text{iff} \quad \mathcal{L}(o) = [\![\pi]\!] \text{ for some } o$$
$$\Gamma \vdash \mathcal{E}; (h, \mathcal{P}, \mathcal{L}, \mathcal{F}, \mathcal{I}); s \models \pi \texttt{ contains } e \qquad \text{iff} \quad [\![e]\!]_s^h \in [\![\pi]\!]$$
$$\Gamma \vdash \mathcal{E}; (h, \mathcal{P}, \mathcal{L}, \mathcal{F}, \mathcal{I}); s \models e.\texttt{fresh} \qquad \text{iff} \quad [\![e]\!]_s^h \in \mathcal{F}$$
$$\Gamma \vdash \mathcal{E}; (h, \mathcal{P}, \mathcal{L}, \mathcal{F}, \mathcal{I}); s \models e.\texttt{initialized} \qquad \text{iff} \quad [\![e]\!]_s^h \in \mathcal{I}$$

These clauses are self-explanatory, except perhaps the existential quantification in the clause for $\texttt{Lockset}(\pi)$. Intuitively, this clause says that there exists a thread identifier o in the domain of $\mathcal{L}$ such that π denotes the current lockset associated with o. We omit the (standard) clauses for the other logical operators, see e.g., [11].

6.3   Soundness

In this section, we extend our verification rules to runtime states. The extended rules are never used in verification, but instead define a global state invariant, $st : \diamond$, that is preserved by the small-step rules of our operational semantics.

We need a few definitions: For $\mathcal{R} = (h, \mathcal{P}, \mathcal{L}, \mathcal{F}, \mathcal{I})$, let $\mathcal{R}_{\text{hp}} = h$, $\mathcal{R}_{\text{perm}} = \mathcal{P}$, $\mathcal{R}_{\text{lock}} = \mathcal{L}$, $\mathcal{R}_{\text{fresh}} = \mathcal{F}$ and $\mathcal{R}_{\text{init}} = \mathcal{I}$. Our forcing relation $\models$ from the last section assumes formulas without logical variables: we deal with those by substitution, ranged over by $\sigma \in \text{LogVar} \rightharpoonup \text{SpecVal}$. We state $(\Gamma \vdash \sigma : \Gamma')$ whenever $\text{dom}(\sigma) = \text{dom}(\Gamma')$ and $(\Gamma[\sigma] \vdash \sigma(\alpha) : \Gamma'(\alpha)[\sigma])$ for all α in $\text{dom}(\sigma)$. Furthermore, we define $\text{cfv}(c) = \{x \in \text{fv}(c) \mid x \text{ occurs in an object creation command } \ell = \texttt{new } C<\bar{\pi}> \}$.

Now, we extend the Hoare triple judgment to threads:

$$\frac{\begin{array}{cccc} \Gamma_{\text{hp}} = \text{fst} \circ \mathcal{R}_{\text{hp}} & \Gamma \vdash \sigma : \Gamma' & \text{dom}(\Gamma') \cap \text{cfv}(c) = \emptyset & \Gamma, \Gamma' \vdash s : \diamond \\ \text{dom}(\mathcal{R}_{\text{lock}}) \subseteq \{o\} & \Gamma[\sigma] \vdash \mathcal{E}; \mathcal{R}; s \models F[\sigma] & \Gamma, \Gamma'; r \vdash \{F\}c : \texttt{void}\{G\} \end{array}}{\mathcal{R} \vdash o \text{ is } (s \text{ in } c) : \diamond} \text{ (Thread)}$$

The object identifier r in the Hoare triple (last premise) is the current receiver, needed to determine the scope of abstract predicates. We have omitted the receiver parameter from our Hoare rules in Section 4, because for source code verification the receiver parameter is always this.

We straightforwardly extend this judgment to thread pools:

$$\frac{}{\mathscr{R} \vdash \mathbf{0} : \diamond} \text{ (Empty Pool)} \qquad \frac{\mathscr{R} \vdash t : \diamond \qquad \mathscr{R}' \vdash ts : \diamond}{\mathscr{R} * \mathscr{R}' \vdash t \mid ts : \diamond} \text{ (Cons Pool)}$$

To further extend the judgment to states, we define the set $\text{ready}(\mathscr{R})$ of all initialized objects whose locks are not held, and the function conc that maps abstract lock tables to concrete lock tables:

$$\text{ready}(\mathscr{R}) \stackrel{\Delta}{=} \mathscr{R}_{\text{init}} \setminus \{ o \mid (\exists p)(o \in \mathscr{L}(p)) \}$$

$$\text{conc}(\mathscr{L})(o) \stackrel{\Delta}{=} (p, \mathscr{L}(p)(o)), \text{ if } o \in \mathscr{L}(p) \qquad \text{conc}(\mathscr{L})(o) \stackrel{\Delta}{=} \text{free, otherwise}$$

In conc's definition, we let $\mathscr{L}(p)(o)$ stand for the multiplicity of o in $\mathscr{L}(p)$. Note that conc is well-defined, by axiom (2) for resources. The rule for states ensures that there exists a resource $\mathscr{R}$ to satisfy the thread pool ts, and a resource $\mathscr{R}'$ to satisfy the resource invariants of the locks that are ready to be acquired:

$$\frac{\mathscr{R} \# \mathscr{R}' \quad \mathscr{R}'_{\text{lock}} = \mathbf{0} \quad \text{fst} \circ \mathscr{R}'_{\text{hp}} \subseteq \text{fst} \circ h = \Gamma \quad \Gamma \vdash \mathscr{E}; \mathscr{R}'; \mathbf{0} \models \circledast_{o \in \text{ready}(\mathscr{R})} o.\text{inv}}{\langle h, l, ts \rangle : \diamond} \text{ (State)}$$

with $h = (\mathscr{R} * \mathscr{R}')_{\text{hp}}$, $l = \text{conc}(\mathscr{R}_{\text{lock}})$, $\mathscr{R} \vdash ts : \diamond$.

The judgment $(ct : \diamond)$ is the top-level judgment of our source code verification system, to be read as "class table ct is verified". We have shown the following theorem:

Theorem 1 (Preservation). *If $(ct : \diamond)$, $(st : \diamond)$ and $st \rightarrow_{ct} st'$, then $(st' : \diamond)$.*

From the preservation theorem, we can draw the following corollaries: verified programs are data race free, verified programs never dereference null, and if a verified program contains assert(F), then F holds whenever the assertion is reached.

7 Comparison to Related Work and Conclusion

Related work. There are a number of similarities between our work and Gotsman et al. [10], for instance the treatment of initialization of dynamically created locks. Our initialized predicate corresponds to what Gotsman calls lock handles (with his lock handle parameters corresponding to our class parameters). Since Gotsman's language supports deallocation of locks, he scales lock handles by fractional permissions in order to keep track of sharing. This is not necessary in a garbage-collected language. In addition to single-entrant locks, Gotsman also treats thread joining. We have covered joining in a recent paper [12] for Java threads (joining Java threads has a slightly different operational semantics than joining POSIX threads as modeled in [10]). The essential differences between Gotsman's and our paper are *(1)* that we treat reentrant locks, which are a different synchronization primitive than single-entrant locks, and *(2)* that we treat subclassing and extension of resource invariants in subclasses. Hobor et al.'s work [13] is very similar to [10].

Another related line of work is by Jacobs et al. [15] who extend the Boogie methodology for reasoning about object invariants [3] to a multithreaded Java-like language.

While their system is based on classical logic (without operators like * and -*), it includes built-in notions of ownership and access control. Their system deliberately enforces a certain programming discipline (like CSL and our variant of it also do) rather than aiming for a complete program logic. The object life cycle imposed by their discipline is essentially identical to ours. For instance, their shared objects (objects that are shared between threads) directly correspond to our initialized objects (objects whose resource invariants are initialized). Their system prevents deadlocks, which our system does not. They achieve deadlock prevention by imposing a partial order on locks. As a consequence of their order-based deadlock prevention, their programming discipline statically prevents reentrancy, although it may not be too hard to relax this at the cost of additional complexity.

In a more traditional approach, Ábrahám, De Boer et al. [1,8] apply assume-guarantee reasoning to a multithreaded Java-like language.

Conclusion. We have adapted concurrent separation logic to a Java-like language. Resource invariants are specified as abstract predicates in classes, and can be modularly extended in subclasses by a separation-logic axiomatization of the "stack of class frames" [9,3]. The main difficulty was dealing with reentrant locks. These complicate the proof rules, and some reasoning about the absence of aliasing is needed. However, permission-based reasoning is still largely applicable, as illustrated by a verification of a lock-coupling list in spite of reentrancy. In this example, a rich dependent type system with value-parameterized classes proved useful. Because we needed to extend CSL's proof rules to support reasoning about the absence of aliasing (e.g., by adding an additional postcondition to the object creation rule), it does not seem possible to derive our proof rules from CSL's standard proof rules through an encoding of reentrant locks in terms of single-entrant locks. We have omitted wait/notify (conditional synchronization) in this paper, but we have treated it in our technical report [11]. Whereas reentrancy slightly complicates the operational semantics of wait/notify (because the runtime has to remember the reentrancy level of a waiting thread), the proof rules for wait/notify are unproblematic.

References

1. Ábrahám, E., de Boer, F.S., de Roever, W.-P., Steffen, M.: Tool-supported proof system for multithreaded Java. In: de Boer, F.S., Bonsangue, M.M., Graf, S., de Roever, W.-P. (eds.) FMCO 2002. LNCS, vol. 2852, pp. 1–32. Springer, Heidelberg (2003)
2. Andrews, G.: Concurrent Programming: Principles and Practice. Benjamin/Cummings (1991)
3. Barnett, M., DeLine, R., Fähndrich, M., Leino, K.R.M., Schulte, W.: Verification of object-oriented programs with invariants. Journal of Object Technology 3(6) (2004)
4. Bornat, R., O'Hearn, P.W., Calcagno, C., Parkinson, M.: Permission accounting in separation logic. In: Principles of Programming Languages. ACM Press, New York (2005)
5. Boyapati, C., Lee, R., Rinard, M.: Ownership types for safe programming: Preventing data races and deadlocks. In: ACM Conference on Object-Oriented Programming Systems, Languages, and Applications (2002)
6. Boyland, J.: Checking interference with fractional permissions. In: Cousot, R. (ed.) SAS 2003. LNCS, vol. 2694, Springer, Heidelberg (2003)

7. Clarke, D.G., Potter, J.M., Noble, J.: Ownership types for flexible alias protection. In: ACM Conference on Object-Oriented Programming Systems, Languages, and Applications. ACM SIGPLAN Notices, vol. 33(10). ACM Press, New York (1998)
8. de Boer, F.S.: A sound and complete shared-variable concurrency model for multi-threaded Java programs. In: International Conference on Formal Methods for Open Object-based Distributed Systems (2007)
9. DeLine, R., Fähndrich, M.: Typestates for objects. In: European Conference on Object-Oriented Programming (2004)
10. Gotsman, A., Berdine, J., Cook, B., Rinetzky, N., Sagiv, M.: Local reasoning for storable locks and threads. In: Asian Programming Languages and Systems Symposium (2007)
11. Haack, C., Huisman, M., Hurlin, C.: Reasoning about Java's reentrant locks. Technical Report ICIS-R08014, Radboud University Nijmegen (2008)
12. Haack, C., Hurlin, C.: Separation logic contracts for a Java-like language with fork/join. In: Meseguer, J., Roşu, G. (eds.) AMAST 2008. LNCS, vol. 5140, pp. 199–215. Springer, Heidelberg (2008)
13. Hobor, A., Appel, A., Nardelli, F.: Oracle semantics for concurrent separation logic. In: Drossopoulou, S. (ed.) ESOP 2008. LNCS, vol. 4960, pp. 353–367. Springer, Heidelberg (2008)
14. Ishtiaq, S., O'Hearn, P.W.: BI as an assertion language for mutable data structures. In: Principles of Programming Languages (2001)
15. Jacobs, B., Smans, J., Piessens, F., Schulte, W.: A statically verifiable programming model for concurrent object-oriented programs. In: International Conference on Formal Engineering Methods (2006)
16. Müller, P. (ed.): Modular Specification and Verification of Object-Oriented Programs. LNCS, vol. 2262, p. 195. Springer, Heidelberg (2002)
17. Naftalin, M., Wadler, P.: Java Generics. O'Reilly, Sebastopol (2006)
18. O'Hearn, P.W.: Resources, concurrency and local reasoning. Theoretical Computer Science 375(1–3), 271–307 (2007)
19. O'Hearn, P.W., Pym, D.J.: The logic of bunched implications. Bulletin of Symbolic Logic 5(2) (1999)
20. Parkinson, M.: Local Reasoning for Java. Ph.D thesis, University of Cambridge (2005)
21. Parkinson, M., Bierman, G.: Separation logic and abstraction. In: Principles of Programming Languages (2005)
22. Reynolds, J.C.: Separation logic: A logic for shared mutable data structures. In: Logic in Computer Science, Copenhagen, Denmark. IEEE Press, Los Alamitos (2002)
23. Wadler, P.: A taste of linear logic. In: Mathematical Foundations of Computer Science (1993)

ML Modules and Haskell Type Classes:
A Constructive Comparison

Stefan Wehr[1] and Manuel M.T. Chakravarty[2]

[1] Institut für Informatik, Universität Freiburg, Georges-Köhler-Allee 079, 79110
Freiburg i. Br., Germany
wehr@informatik.uni-freiburg.de
[2] School of Computer Science and Engineering, The University of New South Wales,
UNSW SYDNEY NSW 2052, Australia
chak@cse.unsw.edu.au

Abstract. Researchers repeatedly observed that the module system of
ML and the type class mechanism of Haskell are related. So far, this
relationship has received little formal investigation. The work at hand
fills this gap: It introduces type-preserving translations from modules to
type classes and vice versa, which enable a thorough comparison of the
two concepts.

1 Introduction

On first glance, module systems and type classes appear to be unrelated program-
ming-language concepts: Module systems allow large programs to be decomposed
into smaller, relatively independent units, whereas type classes [1,2] provide a
means for introducing ad-hoc polymorphism; that is, they give programmers
the ability to define multiple functions or operators with the same name but
different types. However, it has been repeatedly observed [3,4,5,6,7,8] that there
is some overlap in functionality between the module system of the programming
language ML [9], one of the most powerful module systems in widespread use,
and the type class mechanism of the language Haskell [10], which constitutes a
sophisticated approach to ad-hoc polymorphism.

It is natural to ask whether these observations rest on a solid foundation, or
whether the overlap is only superficial. The standard approach to answer such
a question is to devise two formal translations from modules to type classes and
vice versa. The translations then pinpoint exactly the features that are easy,
hard, or impossible to translate; thereby showing very clearly the differences
and similarities between the two concepts.

Such a constructive comparison between ML modules and Haskell type classes
is particularly interesting because the strength of one language is a weak point
of the other: ML has only very limited support for ad-hoc polymorphism, so
translating Haskell type classes to ML modules could give new insights on how to
program with this kind of polymorphism in ML. Conversely, the Haskell module
system is weak, so an encoding of ML's powerful module system with type classes
could open up new possibilities for modular programming in Haskell.

G. Ramalingam (Ed.): APLAS 2008, LNCS 5356, pp. 188–204, 2008.

Contributions. Following the path just described, we make four contributions:

- We devise two formal translations from ML modules to Haskell type classes and vice versa, prove that the translations preserve type correctness, and provide implementations for both.
- We use the insights obtained from the translations to compare ML modules with Haskell type classes thoroughly.
- We investigate if and how the techniques used to encode ML modules in terms of Haskell type classes and vice versa can be exploited for modular programming in Haskell and for programming with ad-hoc polymorphism in ML, respectively.
- We suggest a lightweight extension of Haskell's type class system that enables type abstraction.

Outline. We start with examples that motivate the key ideas behind the translations from ML modules to Haskell type classes (Sec. 2) and from Haskell type classes to ML modules (Sec. 3). We then sketch the formalization and implementation of the translations (Sec. 4). Next, we discuss similarities and differences between ML modules and Haskell type classes (Sec. 5). Finally, we compare with related work (Sec. 6) and conclude (Sec. 7).

2   From Modules to Classes

The idea of the translation from ML modules to Haskell type classes is the following: signatures are modeled as type class declarations, structures and functors are translated into instance declarations, and type and value components of signatures and structures are mapped to associated type synonyms [6] and type class methods, respectively. We now substantiate the idea by presenting example translations of signatures and structures (Sec. 2.1), of abstract types (Sec. 2.2), and of functors (Sec. 2.3). Next, we provide a summary (Sec. 2.4). Finally, we elaborate on alternative translation techniques (Sec. 2.5).[1]

2.1   Translating Signatures and Structures

Our first example is shown in Fig. 1. The ML code defines a structure `IntSet`, which implements sets of integers in terms of lists. The signature of `IntSet` is inferred implicitly in ML; however, we represent it explicitly as a type class `SetSig` in Haskell. The **type** declarations in this class introduce two associated type synonyms `Elem a` and `Set a`. The identities of such type synonyms depend

---

[1] We use Standard ML in this section; the Haskell code runs under GHC's [11] latest development version (after replacing **abstype** with **type**). Throughout the paper, we assume an ML function `any : ('a -> bool) -> 'a list -> bool` corresponding to Haskell's standard function `any :: (a -> bool) -> [a] -> Bool`. Moreover, we rely on functions `intEq`, `intLt`, and `stringEq` for comparing integers and strings.

```
                                                                      ML
structure IntSet = struct type elem = int   type set = elem list
                          val empty = []   fun member i s = any (intEq i) s
                          fun insert i s = if member i s then s else (i::s)
              end
```

```
                                                                   Haskell
class SetSig a where
    type Elem  a;            type Set   a
    empty ::  a -> Set a;  member ::  a -> Elem a -> Set a -> Bool
    insert ::  a -> Elem a -> Set a -> Set a
data IntSet = IntSet
instance SetSig IntSet where
    type Elem IntSet = Int;  type Set  IntSet = [Int]
    empty _ = [];            member _ i s    = any (intEq i) s
    insert _ i s = if member IntSet i s then s else (i : s)
```

Fig. 1. ML structure for integer sets and its translation to Haskell

```
                                                                      ML
structure IntSet' = IntSet :> sig type elem = int   type set
                                  val empty : set
                                  val member : elem -> set -> bool
                                  val insert : elem -> set -> set   end
```

```
                                                                   Haskell
data IntSet' = IntSet'
instance SetSig IntSet' where
    type Elem IntSet' = Elem IntSet;  abstype Set  IntSet' = Set IntSet
    empty _ = empty IntSet;           member _ = member IntSet
    insert _ = insert IntSet
```

Fig. 2. Sealed ML structure for integer sets and its translation to Haskell

on a particular instantiation of the class variable a. Hence, concrete definitions for Elem and Set are deferred to instance declarations of SetSig.

The data type IntSet corresponds to the name of the structure in ML. We translate the structure itself by defining an instance of SetSig for IntSet. The translation of the insert function shows that we encode access to the structure component member by indexing the method member with a value of type IntSet. We use the same technique to translate qualified access to structure components. For example, the ML expression IntSet.insert 1 IntSet.empty is written as insert IntSet 1 (empty IntSet) in Haskell.

2.2   Translating Abstract Types

The IntSet structure reveals to its clients that sets are implemented in terms of lists. This is not always desirable; often, the type set should be kept abstract outside of the structure. Our next example (Fig. 2) shows that we can achieve the desired effect in ML by sealing the `IntSet` structure with a signature that leaves the right-hand-side of `set` unspecified. Such signatures are called *translucent*, in contrast to *transparent* (all type components specified) and *opaque* (all type components unspecified) signatures.

Abstract types pose a problem to the translation because there is no obvious counterpart for them in Haskell's type class system. However, we can model them easily by slightly generalizing associated type synonyms to also support *abstract associated type synonyms*. (We discuss other possibilities for representing abstract types in Haskell in Sec. 2.5). The idea behind abstract associated type synonyms is to limit the scope of the right-hand side of an associated type synonym definition to the instance defining the synonym: Inside the instance, the right–hand side is visible, but outside it is hidden; that is, the associated type synonym is equated with some fresh type constructor.[2] The first author's diploma thesis [13] includes a formalization of this extension.

The Haskell code in Fig. 2 demonstrates how our extension is used to model abstract types in Haskell. The new keyword **abstype** introduces an abstract associated type synonym `Set` in the instance declaration for `IntSet'`. The effect of using **abstype** is that the type equality `Set IntSet' =[Int]` is visible from within the instance declaration, but not from outside.

Note that there is no explicit Haskell translation for the signature of the structure `IntSet'`. Instead, we reuse the type class `SetSig` from Fig. 1. Such a reuse is possible because type abstraction in Haskell is performed inside instance (and not class) declarations, which means that the signatures of the ML structures `IntSet` and `IntSet'`—differing only in whether the type component `set` is abstract or not—would be translated into equivalent type classes.

2.3   Translating Functors

So far, we only considered sets of integers. ML allows the definition of generic sets through functors, which act as functions from structures to structures. Fig. 3 shows such a functor. (We removed the `elem` type component from the functor body to demonstrate a particular detail of the translation to Haskell.)

The Haskell version defines two type classes `EqSig` and `MkSetSig` as translations of the anonymous argument and result signatures, respectively. The class `MkSetSig` is a multi-parameter type class [14], a well-known generalization of Haskell 98's single-parameter type classes. The first parameter `b` represents a possible implementation of the functor body, whereas the second parameter `a` corresponds to the functor argument; the constraint `EqSig a` allows us to access the associated type synonym `T` of the `EqSig` class in the body of `MkSetSig`. (Now it should become clear why we removed the `elem` type component from the functor body: If `E.t` did not appear in a value specification of the functor body, the

---

[2] Interestingly, this idea goes back to ML's **abstype** feature, which is nowadays essentially deprecated; the Haskell interpreter Hugs [12] implements a similar feature. In contrast to abstract associated type synonyms, these approaches require the programmer to specify the scope of the concrete identity of an abstract type explicitly.

```
functor MkSet (E : sig type t  val eq : t -> t -> bool  end)          ML
  = struct type set = E.t list  val empty = []
            fun member x s = any (E.eq x) s
            fun insert x s = if member x s then s else (x :: s)        end
   :> sig type set  val empty : set  val member : E.t -> set -> bool
            val insert : E.t -> set -> set                             end
```

```
class EqSig a where                                                   Haskell
    type T a;  eq :: a -> T a -> T a -> Bool
class EqSig a => MkSetSig b a where
    type Set' b a;  empty' :: b -> a -> Set' b a
    member' :: b -> a -> T a -> Set' b a -> Bool
    insert' :: b -> a -> T a -> Set' b a -> Set' b a
data MkSet = MkSet
instance EqSig a => MkSetSig MkSet a where
    abstype Set' MkSet a = [T a];  empty' _ _ = []
    member' _ a x s = any (eq a x) s
    insert' _ a x s = if member' MkSet a x s then s else (x : s)
```

Fig. 3. ML functor for generic sets and its translation to Haskell

```
                                                                       ML
structure StringSet = MkSet(struct type t = string  val  eq = stringEq end)
```

```
data StringEq = StringEq                                              Haskell
instance EqSig StringEq where
    type T StringEq = String;  eq _ = stringEq
```

Fig. 4. Functor invocation in ML and its translation to Haskell

necessity for the class parameter a would not occur.) Note that we cannot reuse the names Set, empty, member, and insert of class SetSig because type synonyms and class methods share a global namespace in Haskell.

The instance of MkSetSig for the fresh data type MkSet and some type variable a is the translation of the functor body. The constraint EqSig a in the instance context is necessary because we use the associated type synonym T and the method eq in the instance body.

Fig. 4 shows how we use the MkSet functor to construct a set implementation for strings. To translate the functor invocation to Haskell, we define an appropriate EqSig instance for type StringEq. The combination of the two types MkSetSig and StringEq now correspond to the ML structure StringSet: accessing a component of StringSet is encoded in Haskell as an application (either on the type or the term level) with arguments MkSet and StringEq. For example, StringSet.empty translates to empty' MkSet StringEq.

Table 1. Informal mapping from ML modules to Haskell type classes

ML	Haskell
structure signature	one-parameter type class
structure	instance of the corresponding type class
functor argument signature	single-parameter type class
functor result signature	two-parameter type class (subclass of the argument class)
functor	instance of the result class (argument class appears in the instance context)
structure/functor name	data type
type specification	associated type synonym declaration
type definition	associated type synonym definition
type occurrence	associated type synonym application
value specification	method signature
value definition	method implementation
value occurrence	method application

To demonstrate that our Haskell implementation for sets of strings fits the general set framework, we provide an instance declaration for `SetSig` (Fig. 1):[3]

```
data StringSet = StringSet
instance SetSig StringSet where
    type Elem StringSet = String
    abstype Set StringSet = Set' MkSet StringEq
    empty _ = empty' MkSet StringEq; member _ = member' MkSet StringEq
    insert _ = insert' MkSet StringEq
```

2.4   Summary

Table 1 summarizes the (informal) translation from ML modules to Haskell type classes developed so far. We use the notion "type occurrence" ("value occurrence") to denote an occurrence of a type identifier (value identifier) of some structure in a type expression (in an expression).

2.5   Design Decisions Motivated

While developing our translation from ML modules to Haskell type classes, we have made (at least) two critical design decisions: associated type synonyms represent type components of signatures and structures, and abstract associated type synonyms encode abstract types. In this section, we discuss and evaluate other options for translating these two features.

To encode abstract types, we see two alternative approaches. Firstly, we could use Haskell's module system. It enables abstract types by wrapping them in a

---

[3] The formal translation generates a class and an instance corresponding to the implicit signature of the ML structure **StringSet** and the structure itself, respectively.

Haskell

```haskell
data IntSetAbs = forall a. (SetSig a, Elem a ~ Int) => IntSetAbs a (Set a)
data IntSet'' = IntSet''
instance SetSig IntSet'' where
    type Elem IntSet'' = Int;  type Set IntSet'' = IntSetAbs
    empty _ = IntSetAbs IntSet (empty IntSet)
    member _ i (IntSetAbs a s) = member a i s
    insert _ i (IntSetAbs a s) = IntSetAbs a (insert a i s)
```

Fig. 5. Alternative encoding of abstract types with Haskell's existential types

newtype constructor and placing them in a separate module that hides the constructor. This solution is unsatisfactory for two reasons: (i) Explicit conversion code is necessary to turn a value of the concrete type into a value of the abstract type and vice versa. (ii) We do not want Haskell's module system to interfere with our comparison of ML modules and Haskell type classes.

Secondly, we could use existentials [15,16] to encode abstract types. Fig. 5 shows the translation of the ML structure IntSet' from Fig. 2 for this approach. The type IntSetAbs hides the concrete identity of Set a by existentially quantifying over a. The constraint Elem a ~ Int ensures that the types Elem a and Int are equal [17]. In the following instance declaration, we use IntSetAbs to define the Set type and implement the methods of the instance by delegating the calls to the SetSig instance hidden inside IntSetAbs.

There is, however, a major problem with the second approach: It is unclear how to translate functions whose type signatures contain multiple occurrences of the same abstract type in argument position. For example, suppose the signature of structure IntSet' (Fig. 2) contained an additional function union : set -> set ->set. The translation in Fig. 5 then also had to provide a method union of type IntSetAbs -> IntSetAbs -> IntSetAbs. But there is no sensible way to implement this method because the first and the second occurrence of IntSetAbs may hide *different* set representation types.[4]

An obvious alternative to associated type synonyms for representing ML's type components are multi-parameter type classes [14] together with functional dependencies [18]. In this setting, every type component of an ML signature would be encoded as an extra parameter of the corresponding Haskell type class, such that the first parameter uniquely determined the extra parameters. Nevertheless, there are good reasons for using associated type synonyms instead of extra type class parameters: (i) The extra parameters are referred to by position; however, ML type components (and associated type synonyms) are referred to by name. (ii) Functional dependencies provide no direct support for abstract types, whereas a simple and lightweight generalization of associated type synonyms enables them. (Using existential types with functional dependencies has the same problem as discussed in the preceding paragraph.) Moreover, associated type synonyms are becoming

---

[4] The situation is similar for Java-style interfaces: two occurrences of the same interface type may hide two different concrete class types.

increasingly popular and are already available in the development version of the most widely used Haskell compiler, GHC [11].

3   From Classes to Modules

The translation from Haskell type classes to ML modules encodes type classes as signatures and instances of type classes as functors that yield structures of these signatures. It makes use of two extensions to Standard ML, both of which are implemented in Moscow ML [19]: recursive functors [20,21] model recursive instance declarations, and first-class structures [22] serve as dictionaries providing runtime evidence for type-class constraints. We first explain how to use first-class structures as dictionaries (Sec. 3.1). Then we show ML encodings of type class declarations (Sec. 3.2), of overloaded functions (Sec. 3.3), and of instance declarations (Sec. 3.4). Finally, we summarize our results (Sec. 3.5).[5]

3.1   First-Class Structures as Dictionaries

Dictionary translation [2,23,24,25] is a technique frequently used to eliminate overloading introduced by type classes. Using this technique, type-class constraints are turned into extra parameters, so that evidence for these constraints can be passed explicitly at runtime. Evidence for a constraint comes as a dictionary that provides access to all methods of the constraint's type class.

The translation from Haskell type classes to ML modules is another application of dictionary translation. In our case, dictionaries are represented as first-class structures [22], an extension to Standard ML that allows structures to be manipulated on the term level. This article uses first-class structure as implemented in Moscow ML [19].

We need to explicitly convert a structure into a first-class structure and vice versa. Suppose S is a signature, and s is a structure of signature S. Then the construct [**structure** s **as** S] turns s into a first-class structure of type [S]. Such types are called *package types*. Conversely, the construct **let structure** X **as** S = e1 **in** e2 **end**, where the expression e1 is expected to have type [S], makes the structure contained in e1 available in e2 under the name X.

Clearly, there are alternative representations for dictionaries in ML; for example, we could use records with polymorphic fields, as featured by OCaml [26]. We are, however, interested in a comparison between Haskell-style type classes and ML's *module system*, so we do not pursue this approach any further.

3.2   Translating Type Class Declarations

Fig. 6 shows two Haskell type classes Eq and Ord, which provide overloaded functions eq and lt. We translate these classes into ML signatures of the same name. Thereby, the type variable a in the class head is mapped to an opaque type specification t, and the methods of the class are translated into value specifications.

---

[5] We use Haskell 98 [10] in this section; the ML code runs under Moscow ML [19].

```
class Eq a          where eq :: a -> a -> Bool                    Haskell
class Eq a => Ord a where lt :: a -> a -> Bool
```

```
signature Eq  = sig type t val eq : t -> t -> bool      end        ML
signature Ord = sig type t val lt : t -> t -> bool
                   val superEq : [Eq where type t = t] end
```

Fig. 6. Haskell type classes Eq and Ord and their translations to ML

```
elem :: Eq a => a -> [a] -> Bool                                 Haskell
elem x l = any (eq x) l
```

```
fun elem d (x:'a) l = let structure D as Eq where type t = 'a = d   ML
                      in any (D.eq x) l end
```

Fig. 7. Overloaded function in Haskell and its translation to ML

The signature Ord has an additional value specification superEq to account for the superclass Eq of Ord. Consequently, superEq has type [Eq **where type** t = t] which represents a dictionary for Eq at type t.

3.3 Translating Overloaded Functions

Fig. 7 shows the Haskell function elem, which uses the eq method of class Eq. Hence, the constraint Eq a needs to be added to the (optional) type annotation of elem to limit the types that can be substituted for a to instances of Eq.

As already noted in Sec. 3.1, such a constraint is represented in the ML version of elem as an additional parameter d which abstracts explicitly over the dictionary for the constraint Eq a. Hence, the type of elem in ML is [Eq **where type** t = 'a] -> 'a -> 'a list -> bool.

In the body of elem, we open the first-class structure d and bind the content to the structure variable D, so that we can access the equality comparison function as D.eq. Note that we cannot do without the type annotation (x:'a): It introduces the lexically scoped type variable 'a used in the signature required for opening d. (Lexically scoped type variables are part of Standard ML.)

3.4 Translating Instance Declarations

Finally, we turn to the translation of instance declarations. The Haskell code in Fig. 8 makes the type Int an instance of the type classes Eq and Ord. Furthermore, it specifies that lists can be compared for equality as long as the list elements can be compared for equality. This requirement is expressed by the constraint Eq a in the context of the instance declaration for Eq [a]. (The constraints to

```
instance Eq Int where eq = intEq                                    Haskell
instance Ord Int where lt = intLt
instance Eq a => Eq [a] where eq []      []     = True
                             eq (x:xs) (y:ys) = eq x y && eq xs ys
                             eq _      _      = False
```

```
functor EqInt()  = struct type t = int  val eq = intEq end          ML
functor OrdInt() = struct type t = int  val lt = intLt
                          val superEq = [structure EqInt()
                                        as Eq where type t = t] end
structure R = rec
  (R' : sig functor F : functor (X: Eq) -> Eq where type t = X.t list end)
struct functor F(X: Eq) =
          struct type t = X.t list
                fun eq []      []     = true
                  | eq (x::xs) (y::ys) =
                      let structure Y as Eq where type t = t
                          = [structure R'.F(X) as Eq where type t = t ]
                      in X.eq x y andalso Y.eq xs ys end
                  | eq _      _      = false
          end
end
functor EqList(X: Eq) = R.F(X)
```

Fig. 8. Instance declarations in Haskell and their translations to ML

the left of the double arrow => are called the *context*; the part to the right is called the *head*. The double arrow is omitted if the context is empty.)

The functors EqInt and OrdInt are translations of the instances Eq Int and Ord Int, respectively. These two functors do not take any arguments because the contexts of the corresponding instance declarations are empty. (We could use structures instead of functors in such cases; however, for reasons of consistency we decided to use functors even if the instance context is empty.) The definition of the superEq component in OrdInt demonstrates that dictionaries are created by coercing structures into first-class structures.

The translation of the instance declaration for Eq [a] is more interesting because the Haskell version is recursive (through the expression eq xs ys in the second equation of eq) and has a non-empty context. Consequently, the functor EqList for this instance has to be defined recursively and takes an argument of signature Eq corresponding to the constraint Eq a in the instance context.

To encode recursive functors, we use Moscow ML's recursive structures [20,21]. We first define an auxiliary structure R that contains a definition of the desired functor F. The keyword **rec** together with the forward declaration (R' : ...) makes the content of R available inside its own body. In the definition of eq, we use R'.F to invoke the functor recursively, pack the result as a first-class structure, immediately open this structure again, and bind the result to the

Table 2. Informal mapping from Haskell type classes to ML modules

Haskell	ML
type class declaration	signature
class method	value component
superclass	superclass dictionary
dictionary	first-class structure
(recursive) instance declaration	(recursive) functor
constraint in instance context	argument to the corresponding instance functor
overloaded function	function with additional dictionary parameter(s)

variable Y. Now we can use Y.eq to compare xs and ys. The combination of pack and open operations is necessary to interleave computations on the term level with computations on the module level; it is not possible to invoke R'.F(X).eq directly. After the definition of R, we define EqList by invoking R.F.

It may seem awkward to use recursive functors in ML to encode recursive Haskell functions. Indeed, for the example just discussed, a recursive ML function would be sufficient. In general, however, it is possible to write polymorphic recursive functions [27] with Haskell type classes. For such cases, we definitely need to encode recursion in terms of recursive functors because polymorphic recursion is not available on the term level of Standard ML.[6]

3.5 Summary

We summarize the (informal) translation from Haskell type classes to ML modules in Table 2. Note that dictionaries are not part of Haskell's surface syntax; they only become manifest when evidence for constraints is made explicit by our translation technique.

4 Formalization and Implementation

So far, all we did was apply the translations between ML modules and Haskell type classes to some examples. How do we know that the translations work in general and not only for our examples? To answer this question, we have formalized the two translations, proved that they preserve types, and provided implementations for them. For space reasons, we only describe the source and target languages of the formalized translations. All the other details, all proofs, and the implementations are part of the first author's diploma thesis [13].

The source language of the formalized translation from modules to classes is a subset of Standard ML [9], featuring all important module language constructs except nested structures. The target language of the translation is Haskell 98 [10]

---

[6] Extending Standard ML's term language with polymorphic recursion is an alternative option. For Haskell type classes, polymorphic recursion comes "for free" because class declarations provide explicit type information.

extended with multi-parameter type classes [14], associated type synonyms [6], and abstract associated type synonyms (a contribution of the work at hand).

The translation from classes to modules uses a source language that supports type classes in the style of Haskell 98, but without constructor classes, class methods with constraints, and default definitions for methods. The target language of this translation is a subset of Standard ML extended with first-class structures [22] and recursive functors [20,21].

5   Discussion

Having developed translations from ML modules to Haskell type classes and vice versa, we now present a thorough comparison between the two concepts. Sec. 5.1 discusses how Haskell type classes perform as a replacement for ML modules. Sec. 5.2 changes the standpoint and evaluates how ML modules behave as an alternative to Haskell type classes.

5.1   Classes as Modules

Namespace management. ML modules provide proper namespace management, whereas Haskell type classes do not: It is not possible that two different type classes (in the same Haskell module) declare members of the same name.

Signature and structure components. Signatures and structures in ML may contain all sorts of language constructs, including substructures. Type classes and instances in Haskell 98 may contain only methods; extensions to Haskell 98 also allow type synonyms [6] and data types [5]. However, there exists no extension that allows nested type classes and instances.

Sequential vs. recursive definitions. Definitions in ML are type checked and evaluated sequentially, with special support for recursive data types and recursive functions. In particular, cyclic type abbreviations are disallowed. In Haskell, all top-level definitions are mutually recursive, so associated type synonyms must impose extra conditions to prevent the type checker from diverging while expanding their definitions. For our purpose, the original termination conditions [6] are too restrictive. Nevertheless, no program in the image of our translation from modules to type classes causes the type checker to diverge because the sequential nature of type abbreviations carries over to associated type synonym definitions.

Implicit vs. explicit signatures. In ML, signatures of structures are inferred implicitly. In Haskell, the type class to which an instance declaration belongs has to be stated explicitly. However, once recursive modules are introduced, ML also requires explicit signatures, so the difference between implicit and explicit signatures interplays with the preceding point of our comparison.

Anonymous vs. named signatures. Signatures in ML are essentially anonymous because named signatures can be removed from the language without losing expressiveness. Haskell type classes cannot be anonymous.

Structural vs. nominal signature matching. The difference between anonymous and named signatures becomes relevant when we compare signature matching in ML with its Haskell counterpart. In ML, matching a structure against a signature is performed by comparing the structure and the signature component-wise; the names of the structure and the signature—if present at all—do not matter. This sort of signature matching is often called *structural* matching. Our Haskell analog of signature matching is verifying whether the type representing a structure is an instance of the type class representing the signature. The name of a class is crucial for this decision. Therefore, we characterize our Haskell analog of signature matching as *nominal.*

Abstraction. In ML, abstraction is performed by sealing a structure with a translucent or opaque signature. In Haskell, we perform abstraction inside instance declarations through abstract associated type synonyms.

Unsealed and sealed view. A sealed structure in ML may look different depending on whether we view its body from inside or outside the signature seal: Inside, more values and types may be visible, some types may be concrete, and some values may have a more polymorphic type than outside. For our Haskell analog, the same set of types and values is visible and a value has the same type, regardless of whether we view the instance from inside or outside.

Translucent vs. opaque signatures Translucent signatures (signatures with both concrete and abstract type components) are a key feature of ML's module system. Signatures in Haskell (*i.e.*, type classes) may be classified as opaque because they do not provide definitions for type components (*i.e.*, associated type synonyms).[7]

First-class structures. First-class structures are a nontrivial extension to Standard ML [22]. In our representation of structures as data types and instance declarations, we get first-class structures for free, provided we only use top-level structures as first-class entities. This restriction is necessary because instance declarations in Haskell have to be top-level. All examples given by Russo [22,21] meet this restriction.

5.2   Modules as Classes

Implicit vs. explicit overloading resolution. Overloading in Haskell is resolved implicitly by the compiler. When type classes are simulated with ML modules, overloading has to be resolved explicitly by the programmer, which leads to awkward and verbose code.

Constructor classes. Our current translation scheme is unable to handle constructor classes because there is not direct counterpart of Haskell's higher-oder types in ML. We consider it as interesting future work to investigate whether an encoding of higher-order types as functors would enable a translation of constructor classes to ML modules.

---

[7] Default definitions for associated type synonyms do not help here because they may change in instance declarations.

Recursive classes. Type classes in Haskell may be recursive in the sense that a class can be used in a constraint for a method of the same class. We cannot translate such recursive classes to ML because signatures cannot be recursive.

Default definitions for methods. Haskell type classes may contain default definitions for methods. With our approach, such default definitions cannot be translated properly to ML because signatures specify only the types of value components and cannot contain implementations of value components.

Associated type synonyms. Type components in ML are similar to associated type synonyms in Haskell, but it is unclear whether they have the same expressivity as their Haskell counterpart. For example, consider Chakravarty and colleagues' use of associated type synonyms to implement a string formatting function. Their function `sprintf` has type `Format fmt => fmt -> Sprintf fmt`, where `Format` is a type class with an associated type synonym `Sprintf`. Given the translation presented in this article, we would use a first-class structure to encode the constraint `Format fmt` in ML. The translation of the result type `Sprintf fmt` would then require access to the type component of this structure that corresponds to the associated type synonym `Sprintf`. It is not clear how this can be realized.

6   Related Work

There is only little work on connecting modules with type classes. None of these works meet our goal of comparing ML modules with Haskell type classes based on formal translations.

The work closest to ours is Dreyer and colleagues' modular reconstruction of type classes [8]. This work, which strictly speaking came after our own [13], extends Harper & Stone's type-theoretic interpretation of modules [28] to include ad-hoc polymorphism in the style of Haskell type classes. Instead of adding an explicit notion of type classes to ML, certain forms of module signatures take the role of class declarations and matching modules may be nominated as being canonical for the purpose of overload resolution. The presented elaboration relation mirrors Haskell's notion of an evidence translation and is related to our translation of Haskell classes into ML modules. Dreyer and colleagues do not consider the converse direction of modeling modules by type classes.

Kahl and Scheffczyk [4] propose named instances for Haskell type classes. Named instances allow the definition of more than one instance for the same type; the instances are then distinguished by their name. Such named instances are not used automatically in resolving overloading; however, the programmer can customize overloading resolution by supplying them explicitly. Kahl and Scheffczyk motivate and explain their extension in terms of OCaml's module system [29,26]; they do not consider any kind of translation from ML modules to Haskell type classes or vice versa.

Shan [30] presents a formal translation from a sophisticated ML module calculus [31] into System F_ω [32]. The source ML module calculus is a unified formalism that covers a large part of the design space of ML modules. The target language System F_ω of Shan's translation can be encoded in Haskell extended with higher-rank types [33]; however, this encoding is orthogonal to the type class system. Kiselyov builds on Shan's work and translates a particular applicative functor into Haskell with type classes [34]. However, he does not give a formal translation, so it is unclear whether his approach works in general. Neither Shan nor Kiselyov consider translations from type classes to modules.

Schneider [3] adds Haskell-style type classes to ML. His solution is conservative in the sense that type classes and modules remain two separate concepts. In particular, he does not encode type classes as modules. Translations in the opposite direction are not addressed in his work.

Jones [35] suggests record types with polymorphic fields for modular programming. These record types do not support type components but explicit type parameterization. Jones then uses parametric polymorphism to express ML's sharing constraints and to abstract over concrete implementation types. His system supports first-class structures and higher-order modules.

Nicklisch and Peyton Jones [36] compare ML's with Haskell's module system. They report that the simple namespace mechanism offered by Haskell can compete with the module system offered by ML in many real–world applications. Moreover, they integrate Jones approach [35] into Haskell to find that the resulting system exceeds ML's module system in some cases.

7   Conclusion

This article demonstrates how to translate essential features of ML modules to Haskell type classes and vice versa. Both translations come with a formalization, a proof of type preservation, and an implementation. Based on the two translations, the article presents a thorough comparison between ML modules and Haskell type classes.

Acknowledgments. We thank the reviewers of FLOPS 2008 and APLAS 2008 for their detailed comments.

References

1. Kaes, S.: Parametric overloading in polymorphic programming languages. In: Ganzinger, H. (ed.) ESOP 1988. LNCS, vol. 300, pp. 131–144. Springer, Heidelberg (1988)
2. Wadler, P., Blott, S.: How to make ad-hoc polymorphism less ad-hoc. In: Proc. 16th ACM Symp. POPL, Austin, Texas, pp. 60–76. ACM Press, New York (1989)
3. Schneider, G.: ML mit Typklassen. Master's thesis, Universität des Saarlandes (2000), http://www.ps.uni-sb.de/Papers/abstracts/Schneider2000.html
4. Kahl, W., Scheffczyk, J.: Named instances for Haskell type classes. In: Hinze, R. (ed.) Proceedings of the 2001 Haskell Workshop (2001)
5. Chakravarty, M., Keller, G., Peyton Jones, S., Marlow, S.: Associated types with class. In: Abadi, M. (ed.) Proc. 32nd ACM Symp. POPL, Long Beach, CA, USA, pp. 1–13. ACM Press, New York (2005)

6. Chakravarty, M., Keller, G., Peyton Jones, S.: Associated type synonyms. In: Pierce, B.C. (ed.) Proc. ICFP 2005, Tallinn, Estonia, pp. 241–253. ACM Press, New York (2005)
7. Rossberg, A.: Post to the alice-users mailing list (May 2005), http://www.ps.uni-sb.de/pipermail/alice-users/2005/000466.html
8. Dreyer, D., Harper, R., Chakravarty, M.: Modular type classes. In: Felleisen, M. (ed.) Proc. 34th ACM Symp. POPL, Nice, France, pp. 63–70. ACM Press, New York (2007)
9. Milner, R., Tofte, M., Harper, R., MacQueen, D.: The Definition of Standard ML (Revised). MIT Press, Cambridge (1997)
10. Peyton Jones, S. (ed.): Haskell 98 Language and Libraries, The Revised Report. Cambridge University Press, Cambridge (2003)
11. GHC: The Glasgow Haskell compiler (2008), http://www.haskell.org/ghc/
12. Jones, M.P., Peterson, J.: The Hugs 98 user manual (1999), http://www.haskell.org/hugs/
13. Wehr, S.: ML modules and Haskell type classes: A constructive comparison. Master's thesis, Albert-Ludwigs-Universität Freiburg (November 2005), http://www.informatik.uni-freiburg.de/~wehr/publications/Wehr2005.html
14. Peyton Jones, S., Jones, M., Meijer, E.: Type classes: An exploration of the design space. In: Launchbury, J. (ed.) Proc. of the Haskell Workshop, Amsterdam, The Netherlands (June 1997)
15. Mitchell, J.C., Plotkin, G.D.: Abstract types have existential types. ACM Trans. Prog. Lang. and Systems 10(3), 470–502 (1988)
16. Läufer, K.: Type classes with existential types. J. Funct. Program 6(3), 485–517 (1996)
17. Chakravarty, M.M.T., Keller, G., Peyton Jones, S.: Associated type synonyms. In: Pierce, B.C. (ed.) Proc. ICFP 2005, Tallinn, Estonia, pp. 241–253. ACM Press, New York (2005)
18. Jones, M.P.: Type classes with functional dependencies. In: Smolka, G. (ed.) ESOP 2000. LNCS, vol. 1782, pp. 230–244. Springer, Heidelberg (2000)
19. Romanenko, S., Russo, C., Kokholm, N., Larsen, K.F., Sestoft, P.: Moscow ML homepage (2007), http://www.dina.dk/~sestoft/mosml.html
20. Crary, K., Harper, R., Puri, S.: What is a recursive module? In: Proc. 1999 PLDI, Atlanta, Georgia, USA, May 1999. SIGPLAN Notices, vol. 34(5), pp. 50–63 (1999)
21. Russo, C.V.: Recursive structures for Standard ML. In: Leroy, X. (ed.) Proc. 2001 ICFP, Florence, Italy, September 2001, pp. 50–61. ACM Press, New York (2001)
22. Russo, C.V.: First-class structures for Standard ML. In: Smolka, G. (ed.) ESOP 2000. LNCS, vol. 1782, pp. 336–350. Springer, Heidelberg (2000)
23. Jones, M.P.: Qualified Types: Theory and Practice. Cambridge University Press, Cambridge (1994)
24. Hall, C.V., Hammond, K., Peyton Jones, S.L., Wadler, P.L.: Type classes in Haskell. ACM Trans. Prog. Lang. and Systems 18(2), 109–138 (1996)
25. Faxén, K.F.: A static semantics for Haskell. J. Funct. Program 12(4&5), 295–357 (2002)
26. OCaml: Objective Caml (2007), http://caml.inria.fr/ocaml/index.en.html
27. Henglein, F.: Type inference with polymorphic recursion. ACM Trans. Prog. Lang. and Systems 15(2), 253–289 (1993)
28. Harper, R., Stone, C.: A type-theoretic interpretation of Standard ML. In: Plotkin, G., Stirling, C., Tofte, M. (eds.) Proof, Language, and Interaction: Essays in Honor of Robin Milner. MIT Press, Cambridge (2000)

29. Leroy, X.: Applicative functors and fully transparent higher-order modules. In: Proc. 1995 ACM Symp. POPL, San Francisco, CA, USA, pp. 142–153. ACM Press, New York (1995)
30. Shan, C.: Higher-order modules in System F_ω and Haskell (July 2004), http://www.eecs.harvard.edu/~ccshan/xlate/
31. Dreyer, D., Crary, K., Harper, R.: A type system for higher-order modules. In: Morrisett, G. (ed.) Proc. 30th ACM Symp. POPL, New Orleans, LA, USA, January 2003, pp. 236–249. ACM Press, New York (2003); ACM SIGPLAN Notices (38)1
32. Girard, J.Y.: Interpretation Fonctionnelle et Elimination des Coupures dans l'Arithmetique d'Ordre Superieur. Ph.D thesis, University of Paris VII (1972)
33. Peyton Jones, S., Vytiniotis, D., Weirich, S., Shields, M.: Practical type inference for arbitrary-rank types. J. Funct. Program 17(1), 1–82 (2007)
34. Kiselyov, O.: Applicative translucent functors in Haskell. Post to the Haskell mailing list (August 2004), http://www.haskell.org/pipermail/haskell/2004-August/014463.html
35. Jones, M.P.: Using parameterized signatures to express modular structure. In: Proc. 1996 ACM Symp. POPL, St. Petersburg, FL, USA. ACM Press, New York (1996)
36. Nicklisch, J., Peyton Jones, S.: An exploration of modular programs. In: Proc. 1996 Glasgow Workshop on Functional Programming (July 1996), http://www.dcs.gla.ac.uk/fp/workshops/fpw96/Nicklisch.pdf

The Essence of Form Abstraction*

Ezra Cooper, Sam Lindley, Philip Wadler, and Jeremy Yallop

School of Informatics, University of Edinburgh

Abstract. Abstraction is the cornerstone of high-level programming; HTML forms are the principal medium of web interaction. However, most web programming environments do not support abstraction of form components, leading to a lack of compositionality. Using a semantics based on idioms, we show how to support compositional form construction and give a convenient syntax.

1 Introduction

Say you want to present users with an HTML form for entering a pair of dates (such as an arrival and departure date for booking a hotel). In your initial design, a date is represented just as a single text field. Later, you choose to replace each date by a pair of pulldown menus, one to select a month and one to select a day.

In typical web frameworks, such a change will require widespread modifications to the code. Under the first design, the HTML form will contain *two text fields*, and the code that handles the response will need to extract and parse the text entered in each field to yield a pair of values of an appropriate type, say, an abstract date type. Under the second design, however, the HTML will contain *four menus*, and the code that handles the response will need to extract the choices for each menu and combine them in pairs to yield each date.

How can we structure a program so that it is isolated from this choice? We want to capture the notion of *a part of a form*, specifically a part for collecting values of a given type or purpose; we call such an abstraction a *formlet*. The designer of the formlet should choose the HTML presentation, and decide how to process the input into a date value. Clients of the formlet should be insulated from the choice of HTML presentation, and also from the calculation that yields the abstract value. And, of course, we should be able to compose formlets to build larger formlets.

Once described, this sort of abstraction seems obvious and necessary. But remarkably few web frameworks support it. Three existing web programming frameworks that do support some degree of abstraction over form components are WASH [28], iData [23] and WUI [11,12], each having distinctive features and limitations. (We discuss these further in Section 6.)

Our contribution is to reduce form abstraction to its essence. We use *idioms* [19] (also known as *applicative functors*), a notion of effectful computation,

---

* Supported by EPSRC grant number EP/D046769/1.

G. Ramalingam (Ed.): APLAS 2008, LNCS 5356, pp. 205–220, 2008.

related to both monads [20] and arrows [14]. We define a semantics for formlets by composing standard idioms, show how to support compositional form
construction, and give a convenient syntax. Furthermore, we illustrate how the
semantics can be extended to support additional features (such as checking form
input for validity), either by composing with additional standard idioms or by
generalising to indexed and parameterised idioms.

We originally developed formlets as part of our work on Links [6], a programming language for the web. Like many other systems the original design of Links
exposed programmers to the low-level details of HTML/CGI. We introduced
formlets as a means to abstract away from such details.

In this paper we present a complete implementation of formlets in OCaml.
We take advantage of the extensible Camlp4 preprocessor to provide syntactic
sugar, without which formlets are usable but more difficult to read and write.
Both the library and the syntax extension are available from

`http://groups.inf.ed.ac.uk/links/formlets/`

The Links implementation of formlets also provides the syntax presented here.
The complete Links system includes many features, such as a full suite of HTML
controls (textareas, pop-up menus, radio buttons, etc.), which are not described
here. Steve Strugnell has ported a commercial web-based project-management
application originally implemented in PHP to the Links version of formlets [26].
He gives an in-depth comparison between Links formlets and forms implemented
in PHP. Chris Eidhof has released a Haskell implementation of formlets [8].

The remainder of this paper is organised as follows. Section 2 presents formlets, as they appear to the programmer, through examples. Section 3 gives
a semantics for formlets as the composition of the three idiom instances that
capture the effects needed for form abstraction. Section 4 defines formally the
formlet syntax used throughout the paper and relates it to the formlet idiom.
Section 5 shows how to extend the basic abstraction with additional features:
static XHTML validation, user-input validation, and an optimised representation based on multi-holed contexts. Section 6 examines the relationship with
existing form-abstraction features in high-level web frameworks.

2 Formlets by Example

Now we illustrate formlets, as they might appear to the programmer, with an
example (Fig. 1). We assume familiarity with HTML and OCaml. This section
covers our OCaml implementation, and so has features that may vary in another
implementation of formlets. We use a special syntax (defined formally in Section 4) for programming with formlets; this syntax is part of the implementation,
and makes formlets easier to use, but not an essential part of the abstraction.

The formlet *date_formlet* has two text input fields, labelled "Month" and
"Day." Upon submission, this formlet will yield a *date* value representing the
date entered. The user-defined *make_date* function translates the day and month
into a suitable representation.

```
let date_formlet : date formlet = formlet
  <div>
    Month: {input_int ⇒ month}
    Day: {input_int ⇒ day}
  </div>
yields  make_date month day

let travel_formlet : (string × date × date) formlet =
formlet
  <#>
    Name: {input ⇒ name}
    <div>
      Arrive: {date_formlet ⇒ arrive}
      Depart: {date_formlet ⇒ depart}
    </div>
    {submit "Submit"}
  </#>
yields  (name, arrive, depart)

let display_itinerary : (string × date × date) → xml =
fun (name, arrive, depart) →
  <html>
    <head><title>Itinerary</title></head>
    <body>
      Itinerary for: {xml_text name}
      Arriving: {xml_of_date arrive}
      Departing: {xml_of_date depart}
    </body>
  </html>

handle travel_formlet display_itinerary
```

Fig. 1. Date example

```
let date_formlet : date formlet =
  pure (fun ((), month, (), day, ()) → make_date month day)
  ⊗ (tag "div" []
      (pure (fun () month () day () → ((), month, (), day, ()))
       ⊗ text "Month: " ⊗ input_int
       ⊗ text "Day: " ⊗ input_int ⊗ text "\n "))

let travel_formlet : (string × date × date) formlet =
  pure (fun ((), name, ((), arrive, (), depart), ()) →
        (name, arrive, depart))
  ⊗ (pure (fun () name ((), arrive, (), depart) () →
           ((), name, ((), arrive, (), depart), ()))
     ⊗ text "Name: " ⊗ input
     ⊗ (tag "div" []
        (pure (fun () arrive () depart → ((), arrive, (), depart))
         ⊗ text "Arrive: " ⊗ date_formlet
         ⊗ text "Depart: " ⊗ date_formlet))
     ⊗ xml (submit "Submit"))

let display_itinerary : (string × date × date) → xml =
fun (name, arrive, depart) →
  xml_tag "html" []
    ((xml_tag "head" []
      (xml_tag "title" [] (xml_text "Itinerary"))) @
     (xml_tag "body" []
      ((xml_text "Itinerary for: ") @ (xml_text name) @
       (xml_text "Arriving: ") @ (xml_of_date arrive) @
       (xml_text "Departing: ") @ (xml_of_date depart))))

handle travel_formlet display_itinerary
```

Fig. 2. Date example (desugared)

A formlet expression consists of a *body* and a *yields clause*. The body of *date_formlet* is

```
<div>
  Month: {input_int ⇒ month}
  Day: {input_int ⇒ day}
</div>
```

and its yields clause is

$$make\_date\ month\ day$$

The body of a formlet expression is a *formlet quasiquote*. This is like an XML literal expression but with embedded *formlet bindings*. A formlet binding $\{f \Rightarrow p\}$ binds the value yielded by f to the pattern p for the scope of the yields clause. Here f is an expression that evaluates to a formlet and the type yielded by the formlet must be the same as the type accepted by the pattern. Thus the variables *month* and *day* will be bound to the values yielded by the two instances of the *input_int* formlet. The bound formlet f will render some HTML which will take the place of the formlet binding when the outer formlet is rendered.

The value *input_int : int formlet* is a formlet that renders as an HTML text input element, and parses the submission as type *int*. It is built from the primitive formlet *input* which presents an input element and yields the entered string. Although *input_int* is used here twice, the system prevents any field name clashes.

It is important to realize that any given formlet defines behavior at two distinct points in the program's runtime: first when the form structure is built up, and much later (if at all) when the form is submitted by the user, when the outcome is processed. The first corresponds to the body and the second to the yields clause.

Next we illustrate how user-defined formlets can be usefully combined to create larger formlets. Continuing Fig. 2, *travel_formlet* asks for a name, an arrival date, and a departure date. The library function *submit* returns the HTML for a submit button; its string argument provides the label for the button. (This covers the common case where there is a single button on a form. A similar function *submit_button : string → bool formlet* constructs a submit button formlet, whose result indicates whether this button was the one that submitted the form.)

(The syntax <#> ··· </#> enters the XML parsing mode without introducing a root XML node; its result is an XML forest, with the same type as XML values introduced by a proper XML tag. We borrow this notation from WASH.)

Having created a formlet, how do we use it? For a formlet to become a form, we need to connect it with a *handler*, which will consume the form input and perform the rest of the user interaction. The function *handle* attaches a handler to a formlet.

Continuing the above example, we render *travel_formlet* onto a full web page, and attach a handler (*display_itinerary*) that displays the chosen itinerary back to the user. (The abstract type *xml* is given in Fig. 3; we construct XML using special syntax, which is defined in terms of the *xml_tag* and *xml_text* functions, as shown formally in Section 4.)

```
type xml = xml_item list              val xml_tag : tag → attrs → xml → xml
and tag = string                      val xml_text : string → xml
and attrs = (string × string) list
and xml_item
```

Fig. 3. The *xml* abstract type

This is a simple example; a more interesting application might render another form on the *display_itinerary* page, one which allows the user to confirm the itinerary and purchase tickets; it might then take actions such as logging the purchase in a database, and so on.

This example demonstrates the key characteristics of the formlet abstraction: static binding (we cannot fetch the value of a form field that is not in scope), structured results (the month and day fields are packaged into an abstract *date* type, which is all the formlet consumer sees), and composition (we reuse the date formlet twice in *travel_formlet*, without fear of field-name clashes).

2.1   Syntactic Sugar

Fig. 2 shows the desugared version of the date example. XML values are constructed using the *xml_tag* and *xml_text* functions and the standard list concatenation operator, @. Formlet values are slightly more complicated. The *xml_tag* and *xml_text* functions have formlet counterparts *tag* and *text*; composition of formlets makes use of the standard idiom operations *pure* and ⊗. The formlet primitives are covered in detail in Section 3.

The sugar makes it easier to freely mix static XML with formlets. Without the sugar, dummy bindings are needed to bind formlets consisting just of XML (see the calls to *pure* in Fig. 2), and formlets nested inside XML have to be rebound (see the second call to *pure* in the body of *travel_formlet* in Fig. 2). A desugaring algorithm is described in Section 4.

2.2   Life without Formlets

Now consider implementing the above example using the standard HTML/CGI interface. We would face the following difficulties with the standard interface:

- There is no static association between a form definition and the code that handles it, so the interface is fragile. This means the form and the handling code need to be kept manually in sync.
- Field values are always received individually and always as strings: the interface provides no facility for processing data or giving it structure.
- Given two forms, there is generally no easy way to combine them into a new form without fear of name clashes amongst the fields—thus it is not easy to write a form that abstractly uses subcomponents. In particular, it's difficult to use a form twice within a larger form.

```
module type Idiom = sig
  type α t
  val pure : α → α t
  val (⊗) : (α → β) t → α t → β t
end
```

```
module type FORMLET = sig
  include Idiom
  val xml : xml → unit t
  val text : string → unit t
  val tag  : tag → attrs → α t → α t
  val input : string t
  val run : α t → xml × (env → α)
end
```

Fig. 4. The idiom and formlet interfaces

Conventional web programming frameworks such as PHP [22] and Ruby on Rails [25] facilitate abstraction only through templating or textual substitution, hence there is no automatic way to generate fresh field names, and any form "abstraction" (such as a template) still exposes the programmer to the concrete field names used in the form. Even advanced systems such as PLT Scheme [10], JWIG [5], scriptlets [9], Ocsigen [2], Lift [15] and the original design for Links [6] all fall short in the same way.

Formlets address all of the above problems: they provide a static association between a form and its handler (ensuring that fields referenced actually exist and are of the right type), they allow processing raw form data into structured values, and they allow composition, in part by generating fresh field names at runtime.

3   Semantics

We wish to give a semantics of formlets using a well-understood formalism. We shall show that formlets turn out to be *idioms* [19], a notion of computation closely related to monads [3,20,29]. We begin with a concrete implementation in OCaml, which we then factor using standard idioms to give a formal semantics.

3.1   A Concrete Implementation

Figs. 4 and 5 give a concrete implementation of formlets in OCaml.

The type $\alpha\ t$ is the type of formlets that return values of type α (the library exposes this type at the top-level as α *formlet*). Concretely $\alpha\ t$ is defined as a function that takes a *name source* (integer) and returns a triple of a *rendering* (XML), a *collector* (function of type $env \to \alpha$) and an updated name source. The formlet operations ensure that the names generated in the rendering are the names expected (in the environment) by the collector.

The *pure* operation is used to create constant formlets whose renderings are empty and whose collector always returns the same value irrespective of the environment. The $\otimes$ operation applies an $A \to B$ formlet to an A formlet. The name source is threaded through each formlet in turn. The resulting renderings are concatenated and the collectors composed. Together *pure* and $\otimes$ constitute the fundamental idiom operations. (To be an idiom, they must also satisfy some laws, shown in Section 3.2.)

```
module Formlet : FORMLET = struct
  type α t = int → (xml × (env → α) × int)

  let pure x i = ([], const x, i)
  let (⊗) f p i = let (x₁, g, i) = f i in
                  let (x₂, q, i) = p i in
                  (x₁ @ x₂, (fun env → g env (q env)), i)

  let xml x i = (x, const (), i)
  let text t i = xml (xml_text t) i
  let tag t attrs fmlt i = let (x, f, i) = fmlt i in (xml_tag t attrs x, f, i)

  let next_name i = ("input_" ^ string_of_int i, i + 1)
  let input i = let (w, i) = next_name i in
                (xml_tag "input" [("name", w)] [], List.assoc w, i)

  let run c = let (x, f, _) = c 0 in (x, f)
end
```

Fig. 5. The formlet idiom

As before, the *xml* and *text* operations create unit formlets from the given XML or text, and the *tag* operation wraps the given formlet's rendering in a new element with the specified tag name and attributes.

The primitive formlet *input* generates HTML input elements. A single name is generated from the name source, and this name is used both in the rendering and the collector. The full implementation includes a range of other primitive formlets for generating the other HTML form elements (e.g. textarea, option, etc.).

The *run* operation "runs" a formlet by supplying it with a name source (we use 0); this produces a rendering and a collector function.

3.2   Idioms

Idioms were introduced by McBride [18] to capture a common pattern in functional programming.[1] An *idiom* is a type constructor I together with operations:

$$pure : \alpha \to I\,\alpha \qquad\qquad \otimes : I\,(\alpha \to \beta) \to I\,\alpha \to I\,\beta$$

that satisfy the following laws:

$$pure\ id \otimes u = u \qquad\qquad pure\ f \otimes pure\ x = pure\ (f\ x)$$
$$pure\ (\circ) \otimes u \otimes v \otimes w = u \otimes (v \otimes w) \qquad u \otimes pure\ x = pure\ (\lambda f.f\ x) \otimes u$$

where *id* is the identity function and ∘ denotes function composition.

---

[1] Subsequently McBride and Paterson [19] changed the name to *applicative functor* to emphasise the view of idioms as an "abstract characterisation of an applicative style of effectful programming". We stick with McBride's original "idiom" for brevity.

The *pure* operation lifts a value into an idiom. Like standard function application, idiom application $\otimes$ is left-associative. The idiom laws guarantee that pure computations can be reordered. However, an effectful computation cannot depend on the result of a pure computation, and any expression built from *pure* and $\otimes$ can be rewritten in the canonical form

$$pure\ f \otimes u_1 \otimes \cdots \otimes u_k$$

where f is the pure part of the computation and $u_1, \ldots, u_k$ are the effectful parts of the computation. This form captures the essence of idioms as a tool for modelling computation.

The intuition is that an idiomatic computation consists of a series of side-effecting computations, each of which returns a value. The order in which computations are performed is significant, but a computation cannot depend on values returned by prior computations. The final return value is obtained by aggregating the values returned by each of the side-effecting computations, using a pure function. As Lindley and others [17] put it: *idioms are oblivious*.

Formlets fit this pattern: the sub-formlets cannot depend on one another, and the final value yielded by a formlet is a pure function of the values yielded by the sub-formlets.

3.3   Factoring Formlets

Now we introduce the three idioms into which the formlet idiom factors (Fig. 6). Besides the standard idiom operations in the interface, each idiom comes with operations corresponding to primitive effects and a *run* operation for executing the effects and extracting the final result. A computation in the *Namer* idiom has type $int \rightarrow \alpha \times int$; it is a function from a counter to a value and a possibly-updated counter. The *next_name* operation uses this counter to construct a fresh name, updating the counter. A computation in the *Environment* idiom has type $env \rightarrow \alpha$; it receives an environment and yields a value. The *lookup* operation retrieves values from the environment by name. A computation in the *XmlWriter* idiom (also known as a monoid-accumulator) has type $xml \times \alpha$ and so yields both XML and a value; the XML is generated by the primitive *xml*, *text* and *tag* operations and concatenated using $\otimes$. Each of these idioms corresponds directly to a standard monad [19].

The formlet idiom is just the composition of these three idioms (see Fig. 8). The *Compose* module composes any two idioms (Fig. 7).

To work with a composed idiom, we need to be able to lift the primitive operations from the component idioms into the composed idiom. Given idioms F and G, we can lift any idiomatic computation of type $\alpha\ G.t$ to an idiomatic computation of type $(\alpha\ G.t)\ F.t$ using $F.pure$, or lift one of type $\alpha\ F.t$ to one of type $(\alpha\ G.t)\ F.t$ using $Compose\,(F)\,(G).refine$.

```
module Namer : sig
  include Idiom
  val next_name : string t
  val run : α t → α
end = struct
  type α t = int → α × int
  let pure v i = (v, i)
  let (⊗) f p i = let (f', i) = f i in
                  let (p', i) = p i in
                             (f' p', i)
  let next_name i =
    ("input_"^string_of_int i, i+1)
  let run v = fst (v 0)
end
```

```
module Environment : sig
  include Idiom
  type env = (string × string) list
  val lookup : string → string t
  val run : α t → env → α
end = struct
  type α t = env → α
  and env = (string × string) list
  let pure v e = v
  let (⊗) f p e = f e (p e)
  let lookup = List.assoc
  let run v = v
end
```

```
module XmlWriter : sig
  include Idiom
  val text : string → unit t
  val xml : xml → unit t
  val tag : tag → attrs → α t → α t
  val run : α t → xml × α
end = struct
  type α t = xml × α
  let pure v = ([], v)
  let (⊗) (x, f) (y, p) = (x @ y, f p)
  let text x = (xml_text x, ())
  let xml x = (x, ())
  let tag t a (x,v) = (xml_tag t a x, v)
  let run v = v
end
```

Fig. 6. Standard idioms

```
module Compose (F : Idiom) (G : Idiom) : sig
  include Idiom with type α t = (α G.t) F.t
  val refine : α F.t → (α G.t) F.t
end = struct
  type α t = (α G.t) F.t
  let pure x = F.pure (G.pure x)
  let (⊗) f x = F.pure (⊗_G) ⊗_F f ⊗_F x
  let refine v = (F.pure G.pure) ⊗_F v
end
```

Fig. 7. Idiom composition

```
module Formlet : FORMLET = struct
  module AE = Compose (XmlWriter) (Environment)
  include Compose (Namer) (AE)
  module N = Namer module A = XmlWriter module E = Environment
  let xml x = N.pure (AE.refine (A.xml x))
  let text s = N.pure (AE.refine (A.text s))
  let tag t ats f = N.pure (A.tag t ats) ⊗_N f
  let input = N.pure (fun n → A.tag "input" [("name", n)]
              (A.pure (E.lookup n))) ⊗_N N.next_name
  let run v = let xml, collector = A.run (N.run v) in (xml, E.run collector)
end
```

Fig. 8. The formlet idiom (factored)

In defining the composed formlet idiom, a combination of $N.pure$ and $AE.refine$ is used to lift the results of the $A.xml$ and $A.text$ operations. The tag operation is lifted differently as its third argument is a formlet: here we apply the $A.tag\ t\ ats$ operation to it. The run operation simply runs each of the primitive run operations in turn. The $input$ operation is the most interesting. It generates a fresh name and uses it both to name an input element and, in the collector, for lookup in the environment.

3.4   A Note on Monads

Monads [3,20,29] are a more standard semantic tool for reasoning about side-effects. However, it is not difficult to see that there is no monad corresponding to the formlet type. Intuitively, the problem is that a *bind* operation for formlets would have to read some of the input submitted by the user before the formlet had been rendered, which is clearly impossible. (Recall that the type of *bind* would be α *formlet* $\to$ $(\alpha \to \beta$ *formlet*$)$ $\to$ β *formlet* and to implement this would require extracting the α value from the first argument to pass it to the second argument; but the rendering of the β *formlet* should not depend on the α-type data submitted to the first formlet.)

Every monad is an idiom, though of course, being oblivious, the idiom interface is less powerful (see Lindley and others [17] on the relative expressive power of idioms, arrows and monads). Although the idioms in Fig. 6 are in fact also monads, their composition (the formlet idiom) is not a monad: although idioms are closed under composition, monads are not. Using monad transformers in place of functor composition recovers some compositionality, but there is no combination of monad transformers that layers these effects in the right order.

4   Syntax

The syntax presented in Section 2 can be defined as syntactic sugar, which desugars into uses of the basic formlet operations. Here we formally define the syntax and its translation. We add two new kinds of expression: XML quasiquotes, (or XML literals with embedded evaluable expressions), and formlet expressions, denoting formlet values. Fig. 9 gives the grammar for these expressions.

The desugaring transformations are shown in Fig. 10. The operation $\llbracket \cdot \rrbracket$ desugars the formlet expressions in a program; it is a homomorphism on all syntactic forms except XML quasiquotes and formlet expressions. The operation $(\cdot)^*$ desugars XML quasiquotes and nodes. The operation $z^\dagger$ denotes a pattern aggregating the sub-patterns of z where z ranges over formlet quasiquotes and nodes. In an abuse of notation, we also let $z^\dagger$ denote the expression that reconstructs the value matched by the pattern. (Of course, we need to be somewhat careful in the OCaml implementation to properly reconstruct the value from the matched pattern.) Finally, z° is a formlet that tuples the outcomes of sub-formlets of z.

Expressions

$$e ::= \cdots \mid r \qquad\qquad \text{(XML)}$$
$$\mid \text{formlet } q \text{ yields } e \quad \text{(formlet)}$$

XML quasiquotes

$$m ::= s \mid \{e\} \mid \texttt{<}t\ ats\texttt{>}m_1 \ldots m_k\texttt{</}t\texttt{>} \qquad\qquad \text{node}$$
$$r ::= \texttt{<}t\ ats\texttt{>}m_1 \ldots m_k\texttt{</}t\texttt{>} \mid \texttt{<\#>}m_1 \ldots m_k\texttt{</\#>} \quad \text{quasiquote}$$

Formlet quasiquotes

$$n ::= s \mid \{e\} \mid \{f \Rightarrow p\} \mid \texttt{<}t\ ats\texttt{>}n_1 \ldots n_k\texttt{</}t\texttt{>} \quad \text{node}$$
$$q ::= \texttt{<}t\ ats\texttt{>}n_1 \ldots n_k\texttt{</}t\texttt{>} \mid \texttt{<\#>}n_1 \ldots n_k\texttt{</\#>} \quad \text{quasiquote}$$

Meta variables

e	expression	f	formlet-type expression	t	tag
p	pattern	s	string	ats	attribute list

Fig. 9. Quasiquote syntax

As a simple example of desugaring, consider the definition of the *input_int* formlet used earlier:

let *input_int* : *int formlet* =
    formlet `<#>`{*input* $\Rightarrow$ *i*}`</#>` yields *int_of_string i*

Under the translation given in Fig. 10, the body becomes

$$pure\ (\text{fun } i \to int\_of\_string\ i) \otimes (pure\ (\text{fun } i \to i) \otimes input)$$

We can use the idiom laws (and η-reduction) to simplify the output a little, giving the following semantically-equivalent code:

$$pure\ int\_of\_string \otimes input$$

As a richer example, recall *date_formlet* from Fig. 1 and its desugaring in Fig. 2. We could easily optimise the desugared code by removing the extra units from the body of the inner *pure* and from the arguments to the function in the outer *pure*. One thing we cannot do is avoid the rebinding of *month* and *day*. Section 5.3 outlines an alternate desugaring that obviates this rebinding.

Completeness. Everything expressible with the formlet operations can be expressed directly in the syntax. For example, the $\otimes$ operator of the formlet idiom may be written as a function *ap* using syntactic sugar:

let *ap* : $(\alpha \to \beta)$ *formlet* $\to \alpha$ *formlet* $\to \beta$ *formlet* =
    fun *f p* $\to$ formlet `<#>`{*f* $\Rightarrow$ *g*}{*p* $\Rightarrow$ *q*}`</#>` yields *g q*

Under the desugaring transformation, the body becomes

$$(pure\ (\text{fun } (g,\ q) \to g\ q)) \otimes (pure\ (\text{fun } g\ q \to (g,\ q)) \otimes f \otimes p)$$

which, under the idiom laws, is equivalent to $f \otimes p$. And *pure*, too, can be defined in the sugar as fun $x \to$ formlet `<#></#>` yields x. This shows that the syntax is complete for the formlet operations.

$$[\![r]\!] = r^*$$
$$[\![\text{formlet } q \text{ yields } e]\!] = pure\,(\text{fun } q^\dagger \to [\![e]\!]) \;\otimes\; q^\circ$$

$$s^* = xml\_text\; s$$
$$\{e\}^* = [\![e]\!]$$
$$(\texttt{<}t\;ats\texttt{>}m_1 \ldots m_k\texttt{</}t\texttt{>})^* = xml\_tag\; t\; ats\; (\texttt{<\#>}m_1 \ldots m_k\texttt{</\#>})^*$$
$$(\texttt{<\#>}m_1 \ldots m_k\texttt{</\#>})^* = m_1^* @ \cdots @ m_k^*$$

$$s^\circ = text\; s$$
$$\{e\}^\circ = xml\; [\![e]\!]$$
$$\{f \Rightarrow p\}^\circ = [\![f]\!]$$
$$(\texttt{<}t\;ats\texttt{>}n_1 \ldots n_k\texttt{</}t\texttt{>})^\circ = tag\; t\; ats\; (\texttt{<\#>}n_1 \ldots n_k\texttt{</\#>})^\circ$$
$$(\texttt{<\#>}n_1 \ldots n_k\texttt{</\#>})^\circ = pure\,(\text{fun } n_1^\dagger \ldots n_k^\dagger \to (n_1^\dagger, \ldots, n_k^\dagger)) \otimes n_1^\circ \cdots \otimes n_k^\circ$$

$$s^\dagger = ()$$
$$\{e\}^\dagger = ()$$
$$\{f \Rightarrow p\}^\dagger = p$$
$$(\texttt{<}t\;ats\texttt{>}n_1 \ldots n_k\texttt{</}t\texttt{>})^\dagger = (n_1^\dagger, \ldots, n_k^\dagger)$$
$$(\texttt{<\#>}n_1 \ldots n_k\texttt{</\#>})^\dagger = (n_1^\dagger, \ldots, n_k^\dagger)$$

Fig. 10. Desugaring XML and formlets

5   Extensions

The formlet abstraction is robust, as we can show by extending it in several independent ways.

5.1   XHTML Validation

The problem of statically enforcing validity of HTML and indeed XML is well-studied [4,13,21,27]. Such schemes are essentially orthogonal to the work presented here: we can incorporate a type system for XML with little disturbance to the core formlet abstraction.

Of course, building static validity into the type system requires that we have a whole family of types for HTML rather than just one. For instance, we might have separate types for `block` and `inline` entities (as in Elsman and Larsen's system [9]), or even a different type for every tag (as in XDuce [13]).

Fortunately, it is easy to push the extra type parameters through our formlet construction. The key component that needs to change is the *XmlWriter* idiom. As well as the value type, this now needs to be parameterised over the XML type. The construction we need is what we call an *indexed idiom*. It is roughly analogous to an effect-indexed monad [30]. In OCaml, we define an indexed idiom as follows:

```
module type XIdiom = sig
  type (ψ, α) t
  val pure : α → (ψ, α) t
  val (⊗) : (ψ, α → β) t → (ψ, α) t → (ψ, β) t
end
```

(For the indexed XML writer idiom the parameter ψ is the XML type.) Like idioms, indexed idioms satisfy the four laws given in Section 3. They can be pre- and post-composed with other idioms to form new indexed idioms. Pre-composing the name generation idiom with the indexed XML writer idiom pre-composed with the environment idiom gives us an indexed formlet idiom.

As a proof of concept, we have implemented a prototype of formlets with XML typing in OCaml using Elsman and Larsen's encoding of a fragment of XHTML 1.0 [9]. It uses phantom types to capture XHTML validity constraints.

5.2 Input Validation

A common need in form processing is validating user input: on submission, we should ensure that the data is well-formed, and if not, re-display the form to the user (with error messages) until well-formed data is submitted.

Formlets extend to this need if we incorporate additional idioms for error-checking and accumulating error messages and add combinators *satisfies* and *err*, which add to a formlet, respectively, an assertion that the outcome must satisfy a given predicate and an error message to be used when it does not. Any time the continuation associated with a formlet is invoked, the outcome is sure to satisfy the validation predicate(s).

The need to re-display a page upon errors also requires additional mechanics. Instead of simply attaching a continuation to a formlet and rendering it to HTML, the formlet continuation now needs to have a complete page context available to it, in case it needs to redisplay the page. To facilitate this, we add a new syntactic form, which associates formlets with their continuations *in the context of* a larger page.

Extending with input validation adds some complexity to the implementation, so we omit details here. We have implemented it in the Links version of formlets and provide details in a technical report [7].

5.3 Multi-holed Contexts

The presentation of formlets we have given in this paper relies on lifting the *tag* constructor from the *XmlWriter* idiom into the *Formlet* idiom. As illustrated by the desugaring of the date example in Section 4 this makes it difficult to separate the raw XML from the semantic content of formlets and requires nested formlet values to be rebound.

Besides obfuscating the code, this rebinding is inefficient. By adapting the formlet datatype to accumulate a list of XML values rather than a single XML value, and replacing *tag* with a general operation for plugging the accumulated list into a multi-holed context *plug*, we obtain a more efficient formlet implementation that does provide a separation between the raw XML and the semantic content. Further, this leads to a much more direct desugaring transformation. For example, the desugared version of the date example becomes:

```
let date_formlet : (_, date) NFormlet.t =
  plug (tag "div" [] (text "Month: " @ hole @ text "Day: " @ hole))
    (pure (fun month day → make_date month day) ⊗ input_int ⊗ input_int)
```

Statically typing *plug* in OCaml requires some ingenuity. Using phantom types, we encode the number of holes in a context, or the number of elements in a list, as the difference between two type-level Peano numbers [16]. As with XHTML typing the key component that needs to change is the *XmlWriter* idiom. This now needs to be parameterised over the number of XML values in the list it accumulates. The construction we need is the what we call a *parameterised idiom*, the idiom analogue of a parameterised monad [1]. In OCaml, we define a parameterised idiom as follows:

```
module type PIdiom = sig
  type (μ, ν, α) t
  val pure : α → (μ, ν, α) t
  val (⊗) : (μ, ν, α → β) t → (σ, μ, α) t → (σ, ν, β) t
end
```

(For the parameterised XML writer idiom the parameters μ and ν encode the length of the list of XML values as $\nu - \mu$.) Like idioms, and indexed idioms, parameterised idioms satisfy the four laws given in Section 3. They can be pre- and post-composed with other idioms to form new parameterised idioms. Pre-composing the name generation idiom with the parameterised XML writer idiom pre-composed with the environment idiom gives a parameterised formlet idiom.

We have implemented a prototype of formlets with a multi-holed plugging operation in OCaml. Statically-typed multi-holed contexts can be combined with statically typed XHTML [16]. Lifting the result to idioms gives either an *indexed parameterised idiom*—that is, an idiom with an extra type parameter for the XML type and two extra type parameters for the number of XML values in the accumulated list—or, by attaching the XML type to both of the other type parameters, a parameterised idiom.

5.4   Other Extensions

These are by no means the only useful extensions to the basic formlet abstraction. For example, we might wish to translate validation code to JavaScript to run on the client [12], or enforce separation between those portions of the program that deal with presentation and those that treat application-specific computation, a common requirement in large web projects. Either of these may be combined with the formlet abstraction without injury to the core design presented here.

6   Related Work

The WASH, iData and WUI frameworks all support aspects of the form abstraction we have presented. WUI, in fact, meets all of the goals listed in the introduction. Underlying all these systems is the essential mode of form abstraction we describe, although they vary richly in their feature sets and limitations.

WASH. The WASH/CGI Haskell framework [28] supports a variety of web application needs, including forms with some abstraction. WASH supports user-defined types as the result of an individual form field, through defining a `Read` instance, which parses the type from a string. It also supports aggregating data from multiple fields using a suite of tupling constructors, but it does not allow arbitrary calculations from these multiple fields into other data types, such as our abstract *date* type. In particular, the tupling constructors still expose the structure of the form fields, preventing true abstraction. For example, given a one-field component, a programmer cannot modify it to consist of two fields without also changing all the uses of the component.

iData. The iData framework [23] supports a high degree of form abstraction, calling its abstractions *iData*. Underlying iData is an abstraction much like form-lets. Unlike formlets, where form abstraction is separated from control flow (the function *handle* attaches a handler to a formlet), iData have control flow baked in. An iData program defines a single web page consisting of a collection of interdependent iData. Whenever a form element is edited by the user, the form is submitted and then re-displayed to the user with any dependencies resolved. The iTasks library [24] builds on top of iData by enabling or disabling iData according to the state of the program.

WUI. The WUI (*Web User Interface*) library [11,12] implements form abstractions for the functional logic programming language Curry. Here the basic units are called WUIs. WUIs enforce an assumption that each WUI of type α should accept a value of type α as well as generate one; this input value models the default or current value for the component. Thus a *WUI* α is equivalent, in our setting, to a value of type $\alpha \to \alpha$ *formlet*.

References

1. Atkey, R.: Parameterised notions of computation. In: MSFP (2006)
2. Balat, V.: Ocsigen: typing web interaction with objective caml. In: ML Workshop 2006, pp. 84–94 (2006)
3. Benton, N., Hughes, J., Moggi, E.: Monads and effects. In: Barthe, G., Dybjer, P., Pinto, L., Saraiva, J. (eds.) APPSEM 2000. LNCS, vol. 2395, pp. 42–122. Springer, Heidelberg (2002)
4. Brabrand, C., Møller, A., Schwartzbach, M.I.: Static validation of dynamically generated HTML. In: PASTE, pp. 38–45 (2001)
5. Christensen, A.S., Møller, A., Schwartzbach, M.I.: Extending Java for high-level web service construction. TOPLAS 25(6), 814–875 (2003)
6. Cooper, E., Lindley, S., Wadler, P., Yallop, J.: Links: web programming without tiers. In: de Boer, F.S., Bonsangue, M.M., Graf, S., de Roever, W.-P. (eds.) FMCO 2006. LNCS, vol. 4709, pp. 266–296. Springer, Heidelberg (2007)
7. Cooper, E., Lindley, S., Wadler, P., Yallop, J.: An idiom's guide to formlets. Technical Report EDI-INF-RR-1263, University of Edinburgh (2008)
8. Eidhof, C.: Formlets in Haskell (2008),
   http://blog.tupil.com/formlets-in-haskell/
9. Elsman, M., Larsen, K.F.: Typing XHTML web applications in ML. In: Jayaraman, B. (ed.) PADL 2004. LNCS, vol. 3057, pp. 224–238. Springer, Heidelberg (2004)

10. Graunke, P.T., Krishnamurthi, S., Van Der Hoeven, S., Felleisen, M.: Programming the web with high-level programming languages. In: Sands, D. (ed.) ESOP 2001. LNCS, vol. 2028, pp. 122–136. Springer, Heidelberg (2001)
11. Hanus, M.: Type-oriented construction of web user interfaces. In: PPDP 2006, pp. 27–38 (2006)
12. Hanus, M.: Putting declarative programming into the web: Translating Curry to JavaScript. In: PPDP 2007, pp. 155–166 (2007)
13. Hosoya, H., Pierce, B.C.: XDuce: A statically typed XML processing language. ACM Trans. Internet Techn. 3(2), 117–148 (2003)
14. Hughes, J.: Generalising monads to arrows. Sci. Comput. Program. 37(1-3), 67–111 (2000)
15. Lift website (March 2008), http://liftweb.net/
16. Lindley, S.: Many holes in Hindley-Milner. In: ML Workshop 2008 (2008)
17. Lindley, S., Wadler, P., Yallop, J.: Idioms are oblivious, arrows are meticulous, monads are promiscuous. In: Capretta, V., McBride, C. (eds.) MSFP 2008, Reykjavik, Iceland (2008)
18. McBride, C.: Idioms, 2005. In: SPLS (June 2005),
    http://www.macs.hw.ac.uk/~trinder/spls05/McBride.html
19. McBride, C., Paterson, R.: Applicative programming with effects. Journal of Functional Programming 18(1) (2008)
20. Moggi, E.: Computational lambda-calculus and monads. In: LICS 1989, pp. 14–23 (1989)
21. Møller, A., Schwartzbach, M.I.: The design space of type checkers for XML transformation languages. In: Eiter, T., Libkin, L. (eds.) ICDT 2005. LNCS, vol. 3363, pp. 17–36. Springer, Heidelberg (2005)
22. PHP Hypertext Preprocessor (March 2008), http://www.php.net/
23. Plasmeijer, R., Achten, P.: iData for the world wide web: Programming interconnected web forms. In: Hagiya, M., Wadler, P. (eds.) FLOPS 2006. LNCS, vol. 3945, pp. 242–258. Springer, Heidelberg (2006)
24. Plasmeijer, R., Achten, P., Koopman, P.: iTasks: executable specifications of interactive work flow systems for the web. SIGPLAN Not. 42(9), 141–152 (2007)
25. Ruby on Rails website (March 2008), http://www.rubyonrails.org/
26. Strugnell, S.: Creating linksCollab: an assessment of Links as a web development language. B.Sc thesis, University of Edinburgh (2008),
    http://groups.inf.ed.ac.uk/links/papers/undergrads/steve.pdf
27. Thiemann, P.: A typed representation for HTML and XML documents in Haskell. J. Funct. Program. 12(4&5), 435–468 (2002)
28. Thiemann, P.: An embedded domain-specific language for type-safe server-side web scripting. ACM Trans. Inter. Tech. 5(1), 1–46 (2005)
29. Wadler, P.: Monads for functional programming. In: Jeuring, J., Meijer, E. (eds.) AFP 1995. LNCS, vol. 925, pp. 24–52. Springer, Heidelberg (1995)
30. Wadler, P., Thiemann, P.: The marriage of effects and monads. ACM Trans. Comput. Log. 4(1), 1–32 (2003)

On Affine Usages in Signal-Based Communication

Roberto M. Amadio and Mehdi Dogguy

Université Paris Diderot, PPS, UMR-7126

Abstract. We describe a type system for a *synchronous* π-calculus formalising the notion of *affine* usage in *signal-based* communication. In
particular, we identify a limited number of usages that preserve affinity
and that can be composed. As a main application of the resulting system,
we show that typable programs are *deterministic*.

1 Introduction

We are interested in *synchronous* systems. In these systems, there is a notion
of *instant* (or phase, or pulse, or round) and at each instant each component
of the system, *a thread*, performs some actions and synchronizes with all the
other threads. One may say that all threads proceed at the same speed and it is
in this specific sense that we shall refer to *synchrony* in this work. *Signal-based*
communication is often used as the basic interaction mechanism in synchronous
systems (see, *e.g.*, [6,7]). Signals play a role similar to *channels* in asynchronous
systems. Our goal in this paper is to study the notion of *affine usage* in this
context. In particular, we shall formalise our ideas in the context of a *synchronous*
π-calculus ($S\pi$-calculus) introduced in [2]. We assume that the reader is familiar
with the π-calculus and proceed to give a flavour of the language (the formal
definition of the $S\pi$-calculus is recalled in section 2).

The syntax of the $S\pi$-calculus is similar to the one of the π-calculus, however
there are some important *semantic* differences that we highlight in the following simple example. Assume $v_1 \neq v_2$ are two distinct values and consider the
following program in $S\pi$:

$$P = \nu\ s_1, s_2\ (\ \overline{s_1}v_1\ |\ \overline{s_1}v_2\ |\ s_1(x).\ (s_1(y).\ (s_2(z).\ A(x,y)\ \underline{,B(!s_1)}),0)\ \underline{,0}\ )$$

If we forget about the underlined parts and we regard s_1, s_2 as *channel names*
then P could also be viewed as a π-calculus process. In this case, P would reduce to $P_1 = \nu s_1, s_2\ (s_2(z).A(\theta(x), \theta(y))$ where θ is a substitution such that
$\theta(x), \theta(y) \in \{v_1, v_2\}$ and $\theta(x) \neq \theta(y)$. In $S\pi$, *signals persist within the in-*
stant and P reduces to $P_2 = \nu s_1, s_2\ (\overline{s_1}v_1\ |\ \overline{s_1}v_2\ |\ (s_2(z).A(\theta(x), \theta(y)), B(!s_1)))$
where again $\theta(x), \theta(y) \in \{v_1, v_2\}$ but possibly $\theta(x) = \theta(y)$. What happens
next? In the π-calculus, P_1 is *deadlocked* and no further computation is possible. In the $S\pi$-calculus, the fact that no further computation is possible in
P_2 is detected and marks the *end of the current instant*. Then an additional

G. Ramalingam (Ed.): APLAS 2008, LNCS 5356, pp. 221–236, 2008.

computation represented by the relation $\xrightarrow{N}$ moves P_2 to the following instant: $P_2 \xrightarrow{N} P_2' = \nu s_1, s_2\ B(v)$ where $v \in \{[v_1; v_2], [v_2; v_1]\}$. Thus at the end of the instant, a dereferenced signal such as $!s_1$ becomes a *list* (possibly empty) of (distinct) values emitted on s_1 during the instant and then all signals are reset.

We continue our informal discussion with an example of a 'server' handling a list of requests emitted in the previous instant on the signal s. For each request of the shape $\mathsf{req}(s', x)$, it provides an answer which is a function of x along the signal s' (the notation $x \trianglerighteq p$ is used to match a value x against a pattern p). The 'client' issues a request x on signal s and returns the reply on signal t.

$$
\begin{aligned}
Server(s) &= \mathsf{pause}.Handle(s, !s) \\
Handle(s, \ell) &= [\ell \trianglerighteq \mathsf{cons}(\mathsf{req}(s', x), \ell')](\overline{s'}f(x) \mid Handle(s, \ell')), Server(s) \\
Client(x, s, t) &= \nu s'\ (\overline{s}\mathsf{req}(s', x) \mid \mathsf{pause}.s'(x).\overline{t}x, 0)\ .
\end{aligned}
$$

Let us first notice that a request contains a 'pointer', namely the name of the signal on which to answer the request. Then the 'folklore solution' of transforming a list of values into one value via an associative and commutative function does not work here. Indeed there seems to be no reasonable way to define an associative and commutative function on pointers. Instead, we look at *Handle* as a function from (a signal and) a list of requests to behaviours which is invariant under permutations of the list of requests. Note that to express this invariance we need a notion of behavioural equivalence and that this equivalence must satisfy the usual associativity and commutativity laws of parallel composition and must be preserved by parallel composition.

These considerations are enough to argue that the *Server* is a 'deterministic' program. No matter how many clients will issue requests at each instant, the *Server* will provide an answer to each of them in the following instant in a way which is independent of the order of the requests. Let us now look at the *Client*. After issuing a request, the *Client* waits for a reply in the following instant. Clearly, if more than one reply comes, the outcome of the computation is not deterministic. For instance, we could have several 'Servers' running in parallel or a server could somehow duplicate the request. This means that the usage of the signal s must be such that many 'clients' may issue a request but at most one 'server' may handle them at the end of the instant in an 'affine' way. Further, on the client side, the return signal s' can only be used to read while on the server side it can only be used to emit.

This preliminary discussion suggests the need for a formal analysis of the principles that allow to establish the determinacy of a synchronous program. This analysis will be obviously inspired by previous work on the foundations of linear logic [8], on linear typing of functional programs (*e.g.*, [15]), and on linear usages of channels (*e.g.*, [11]). Following this line of works, the analysis presented in section 3 will take the form of a *typing system*. The previous section 2, will recall the formal definition of the $S\pi$-calculus. In the final section 4, first we shall introduce the properties of the typing system leading to a *subject reduction* theorem, and second we shall describe a suitable notion of typed bisimulation and show that with respect to this notion, typable programs can be regarded as *deterministic*.

2   Definition of the $S\pi$-Calculus

We recall the formal definition of the $S\pi$-calculus and its bisimulation based semantics while referring the reader to [2,4] for a deeper analysis. This section is rather technical but to understand the type system described in the following section 3 there are really just two points that the reader should keep in mind:

1. The semantics of the calculus is given by the labelled transition system presented in table 2. A reader familiar with a π-calculus with asynchronous communication can understand these rules rather quickly. The main differences are (a) the rule for emitting a signal formalises the fact that a signal, unlike a channel, persists within an instant and (b) the rules that describe the computation at the end of the instant.

2. The labelled transition system induces a rather standard notion of bisimulation equivalence (definition 1) which is preserved by *static* contexts (fact 1).[1] In section 4, we shall introduce a 'typed' definition of the bisimulation and show that with respect to this definition, typable programs are deterministic.

2.1   Programs

Programs $P, Q, \ldots$ in the $S\pi$-calculus are defined in table 1. We use the notation **m** for a vector $m_1, \ldots, m_n$, $n \geq 0$. The informal behaviour of programs follows. 0 is the terminated thread. $A(\mathbf{e})$ is a (tail) recursive call of a thread identifier A with a vector $\mathbf{e}$ of expressions as argument; as usual the thread identifier A is defined by a unique equation $A(\mathbf{x}) = P$ such that the free variables of P occur in $\mathbf{x}$. $\bar{s}e$ evaluates the expression e and emits its value on the signal s. $s(x).P, K$ is the *present* statement which is the fundamental operator of the model [1]. If the values $v_1, \ldots, v_n$ have been emitted on the signal s then $s(x).P, K$ evolves non-deterministically into $[v_i/x]P$ for some v_i ($[\_/\_]$ is our notation for substitution). On the other hand, if no value is emitted then the continuation K is evaluated at the end of the instant. $[s_1 = s_2]P_1, P_2$ is the usual matching function of the π-calculus that runs P_1 if s_1 equals s_2 and P_2, otherwise. Here both s_1 and s_2 are free. $[u \trianglerighteq p]P_1, P_2$, matches u against the pattern p. We assume u is either a variable x or a value v and p has the shape $\mathsf{c}(\mathbf{x})$, where c is a constructor and $\mathbf{x}$ is a vector of distinct variables. We also assume that if u is a variable x then x does not occur free in P_1. At run time, u is always a *value* and we run θP_1 if $\theta = match(u, p)$ is the substitution matching u against p, and P_2 if the substitution does not exist (written $match(u, p) \uparrow$). Note that as usual the variables occurring in the pattern p (including signal names) are bound in P_1. $\nu s\, P$ creates a new signal name s and runs P. $(P_1 \mid P_2)$ runs in parallel P_1 and P_2. A continuation K is simply a recursive call whose arguments are either expressions or values associated with signals at the end of the instant in a sense that we explain below. We shall also write $\mathsf{pause}.K$ for $\nu s\, s(x).0, K$ with s not free in K. This is the program that waits till the end of the instant and then evaluates K.

---

[1] As a matter of fact the labelled transition system is built so that the definition of bisimulation equivalence looks standard [4].

Table 1. Syntax of programs and expressions

$$
\begin{aligned}
P &::= 0 \mid A(\mathbf{e}) \mid \overline{s}e \mid s(x).P, K \mid & \text{(programs)} \\
&\quad [s_1 = s_2]P_1, P_2 \mid [u \trianglerighteq p]P_1, P_2 \mid \nu s\ P \mid P_1 \mid P_2 \\
K &::= A(\mathbf{r}) & \text{(continuation next instant)} \\
Sig &::= s \mid t \mid \cdots & \text{(signal names)} \\
Var &::= Sig \mid x \mid y \mid z \mid \cdots & \text{(variables)} \\
Cnst &::= * \mid \mathsf{nil} \mid \mathsf{cons} \mid \mathsf{c} \mid \mathsf{d} \mid \cdots & \text{(constructors)} \\
Val &::= Sig \mid Cnst(Val, \ldots, Val) & \text{(values } v, v', \ldots) \\
Pat &::= Cnst(Var, \ldots, Var) & \text{(patterns } p, p', \ldots) \\
Fun &::= f \mid g \mid \cdots & \text{(first-order function symbols)} \\
Exp &::= Var \mid Cnst(Exp, \ldots, Exp) \mid Fun(Exp, \ldots, Exp) & \text{(expressions } e, e', \ldots) \\
Rexp &::= !Sig \mid Var \mid Cnst(Rexp, \ldots, Rexp) \mid \\
&\quad Fun(Rexp, \ldots, Rexp) & \text{(exp. with deref. } r, r', \ldots)
\end{aligned}
$$

2.2 Expressions

Expressions are partitioned in several syntactic categories as specified in table 1. As in the π-calculus, signal names stand both for signal constants as generated by the ν operator and signal variables as in the formal parameter of the present operator. Variables Var include signal names as well as variables of other types. Constructors $Cnst$ include $*$, nil, and cons. Values Val are terms built out of constructors and signal names. Patterns Pat are terms built out of constructors and variables (including signal names). If P, p are a program and a pattern then we denote with $fn(P), fn(p)$ the set of free signal names occurring in them, respectively. We also use $FV(P), FV(p)$ to denote the set of free variables (including signal names). We assume first-order function symbols $f, g, \ldots$ and an evaluation relation $\Downarrow$ such that for every function symbol f and values $v_1, \ldots, v_n$ of suitable type there is a unique value v such that $f(v_1, \ldots, v_n) \Downarrow v$ and $fn(v) \subseteq \bigcup_{i=1,\ldots,n} fn(v_i)$. Expressions Exp are terms built out of variables, constructors, and function symbols. The evaluation relation $\Downarrow$ is extended in a standard way to expressions whose only free variables are signal names. Finally, $Rexp$ are expressions that may include the value associated with a signal s at the end of the instant (which is written $!s$, following the ML notation for dereferenciation). Intuitively, this value is a *list of values* representing the set of values emitted on the signal during the instant.

The definition of a *simple* type system for the $S\pi$-calculus can be extracted from the more elaborate type system presented in section 3 by confusing 'set-types' with 'list-types' and by neglecting all considerations on usages.

2.3 Actions

The syntactic category *act* of *actions* described in table 2 comprises relevant, auxiliary, and nested actions. The operations fn (free names), bn (bound names), and n (both free and bound names) are defined as in the π-calculus [14].

The *relevant actions* are those that are actually considered in the bisimulation game. They consist of: (i) an internal action τ, (ii) an emission action $\nu t\ \bar{s}v$ where it is assumed that the signal names t are distinct, occur in v, and differ from s, (iii) an input action sv, and (iv) an action N (for *Next*) that marks the move from the current to the next instant.

The *auxiliary actions* consist of an input action $s?v$ which is coupled with an emission action in order to compute a τ action and an action (E, V) which is just needed to compute an action N. The latter is an action that can occur *exactly* when the program cannot perform τ actions and it amounts to (i) collect in lists the set of values emitted on every signal, (ii) to reset all signals, and (iii) to initialise the continuation K for each present statement of the shape $s(x).P, K$.

In order to formalise these three steps we need to introduce some notation. Let E vary over functions from signal names to finite sets of values. Denote with $\emptyset$ the function that associates the empty set with every signal name, with $[M/s]$ the function that associates the set M with the signal name s and the empty set with all the other signal names, and with $\cup$ the union of functions defined point-wise.

We represent a set of values as a list of the values belonging to the set. More precisely, we write $v \parallel\!- M$ and say that v *represents* M if $M = \{v_1, \ldots, v_n\}$ and $v = [v_{\pi(1)}; \ldots; v_{\pi(n)}]$ for some permutation π over $\{1, \ldots, n\}$. Suppose V is a function from signal names to lists of values. We write $V \parallel\!- E$ if $V(s) \parallel\!- E(s)$ for every signal name s. We also write $dom(V)$ for $\{s \mid V(s) \neq [\,]\}$. If K is a continuation, *i.e.*, a recursive call $A(\mathbf{r})$, then $V(K)$ is obtained from K by replacing each occurrence $!s$ of a dereferenced signal with the associated value $V(s)$. We denote with $V[\ell/s]$ the function that behaves as V except on s where $V[\ell/s](s) = \ell$.

With these conventions, a transition $P \xrightarrow{(E,V)} P'$ intuitively means that (1) P is suspended, (2) P emits exactly the values specified by E, and (3) the behaviour of P in the following instant is P' and depends on V. It is convenient to compute these transitions on programs where all name generations are lifted at top level. We write $P \succeq Q$ if we can obtain Q from P by repeatedly transforming, for instance, a subprogram $\nu s P' \mid P''$ into $\nu s(P' \mid P'')$ where $s \notin fn(P'')$.

Finally, the *nested actions* $\mu, \mu', \ldots$ are certain actions (either relevant or auxiliary) that can be produced by a sub-program and that we need to propagate to the top level.

2.4   Labelled Transition System and Bisimulation

The labelled transition system is defined in table 2 where rules apply to programs whose only free variables are signal names and with standard conventions on the renaming of bound names. As usual, one can rename bound variables, and symmetric rules are omitted. The first 12 rules from (out) to (ν_{ex}) are quite close to those of a polyadic π-calculus with asynchronous communication (see [9,3]) with the following exception: rule (out) models the fact that the emission of a value on a signal *persists* within the instant. The last 5 rules from (0) to

Table 2. Labelled transition system

$$
\begin{aligned}
act &::= \alpha \mid aux & \text{(actions)} \\
\alpha &::= \tau \mid \nu t\ \bar{s}v \mid sv \mid N & \text{(relevant actions)} \\
aux &::= s?v \mid (E,V) & \text{(auxiliary actions)} \\
\mu &::= \tau \mid \nu t\ \bar{s}v \mid s?v & \text{(nested actions)}
\end{aligned}
$$

$$(out)\quad \dfrac{e \Downarrow v}{\bar{s}e \xrightarrow{\bar{s}v} \bar{s}e}$$

$$(in_{aux})\quad \dfrac{}{s(x).P, K \xrightarrow{s?v} [v/x]P}$$

$$(in)\quad \dfrac{}{P \xrightarrow{sv} (P \mid \bar{s}v)}$$

$$(rec)\quad \dfrac{A(\mathbf{x}) = P,\quad \mathbf{e} \Downarrow \mathbf{v}}{A(\mathbf{e}) \xrightarrow{\tau} [\mathbf{v}/\mathbf{x}]P}$$

$$(=_1^{sig})\quad \dfrac{}{[s = s]P_1, P_2 \xrightarrow{\tau} P_1}$$

$$(=_2^{sig})\quad \dfrac{s_1 \neq s_2}{[s_1 = s_2]P_1, P_2 \xrightarrow{\tau} P_2}$$

$$(=_1^{ind})\quad \dfrac{match(v,p) = \theta}{[v \unrhd p]P_1, P_2 \xrightarrow{\tau} \theta P_1}$$

$$(=_1^{ind})\quad \dfrac{match(v,p) = \uparrow}{[v \unrhd p]P_1, P_2 \xrightarrow{\tau} P_2}$$

$$(comp)\quad \dfrac{P_1 \xrightarrow{\mu} P_1'\quad bn(\mu) \cap fn(P_2) = \emptyset}{P_1 \mid P_2 \xrightarrow{\mu} P_1' \mid P_2}$$

$$(synch)\quad \dfrac{P_1 \xrightarrow{\nu t\ \bar{s}v} P_1'\quad P_2 \xrightarrow{s?v} P_2'}{\{t\} \cap fn(P_2) = \emptyset \over P_1 \mid P_2 \xrightarrow{\tau} \nu t\ (P_1' \mid P_2')}$$

$$(\nu)\quad \dfrac{P \xrightarrow{\mu} P'\quad t \notin n(\mu)}{\nu t\ P \xrightarrow{\mu} \nu t\ P'}$$

$$(\nu_{ex})\quad \dfrac{P \xrightarrow{\nu t\ \bar{s}v} P'\quad t' \neq s\quad t' \in n(v)\backslash\{t\}}{\nu t'\ P \xrightarrow{(\nu t',t)\bar{s}v} P'}$$

$$(0)\quad \dfrac{}{0 \xrightarrow{\emptyset,V} 0}$$

$$(reset)\quad \dfrac{e \Downarrow v\quad v \text{ occurs in } V(s)}{\bar{s}e \xrightarrow{[\{v\}/s],V} 0}$$

$$(cont)\quad \dfrac{s \notin dom(V)}{s(x).P, K \xrightarrow{\emptyset,V} V(K)}$$

$$(par)\quad \dfrac{P_i \xrightarrow{E_i,V} P_i'\quad i = 1,2}{(P_1 \mid P_2) \xrightarrow{E_1 \cup E_2,V} (P_1' \mid P_2')}$$

$$(next)\quad \dfrac{P \unrhd \nu s\ P'\quad V \Vdash E\quad P' \xrightarrow{E,V} P''}{P \xrightarrow{N} \nu s\ P''}$$

(next) are quite specific of the $S\pi$-calculus and determine how the computation is carried on at the end of the instant (cf. discussion in 2.3).

We derive from the labelled transition system a notion of (weak) labelled bisimulation. First define $\xRightarrow{\alpha}$ as $(\xrightarrow{\tau})^*$ if $\alpha = \tau$, $(\xRightarrow{\tau}) \circ (\xrightarrow{N})$ if $\alpha = N$, and $(\xRightarrow{\tau}) \circ (\xrightarrow{\alpha}) \circ (\xRightarrow{\tau})$ otherwise. This is the standard definition except that we insist on *not* having internal reductions after an N action. Intuitively, we assume that an observer can control the execution of programs so as to be able to test them at the very beginning of each instant. We write $P \xrightarrow{\alpha} \cdot$ for $\exists P'\ (P \xrightarrow{\alpha} P')$.

Definition 1 (labelled bisimulation). *A symmetric relation $\mathcal{R}$ on programs is a labelled bisimulation if $P\ \mathcal{R}\ Q$, $P \xrightarrow{\alpha} P'$, $bn(\alpha) \cap fn(Q) = \emptyset$ implies $\exists Q'\ (Q \overset{\alpha}{\Rightarrow} Q'$, $P'\ \mathcal{R}\ Q'$). We denote with $\approx$ the largest labelled bisimulation.*

Fact 1 ([4]). *Labelled bisimulation is preserved by parallel composition and name generation.*

3 An Affine Type System

An analysis of the notion of determinacy carried on in [4], along the lines of [13], suggests that there are basically two situations that need to be analysed in order to guarantee the determinacy of programs. (1) At least two distinct values compete to be received within an instant, for instance, consider: $\bar{s}v_1 \mid \bar{s}v_2 \mid s(x).P, K$. (2) At the end of the instant, at least two distinct values are available on a signal. For instance, consider: $\bar{s}v_1 \mid \bar{s}v_2 \mid \mathsf{pause}.A(!s)$. A sensible approach is to avoid completely the first situation and to allow the second provided the behaviour of the continuation A does not depend on the order in which the values are collected. Technically, we consider a notion of *affine signal usage* to guarantee the first condition and a notion of *set type* for the second one. While this is a good starting point, it falls short of providing a completely satisfying answer because the type constructions do *not* compose very well. Then our goal is to discover a collection of *signal usages* with better compositionality properties. The outcome of our analysis are three new kinds of usages (kinds $3 - 5$ in table 3).

3.1 Usages

In first approximation, we may regard a *usage* as an element of the set $L = \{0, 1, \infty\}$ with the intuition that 0 corresponds to no usage at all, 1 to at most one usage, and ∞ to any usage. We *add* usages with a *partial* operation $\oplus$ such that $0 \oplus a = a \oplus 0 = a$ and $\infty \oplus \infty = \infty$, and which is undefined otherwise (note in particular that $1 \oplus 1$ is undefined). The addition induces an *order* by $a \leq b$ if $\exists c\ a \oplus c = b$. With respect to this order, 0 is the least element while 1 and ∞ are *incomparable*. If $a \geq b$ then we define a *subtraction* operation $a \ominus b$ as the *largest* c such that $a = b \oplus c$. Therefore: $a \ominus 0 = a$, $1 \ominus 1 = 0$, and $\infty \ominus \infty = \infty$.

This classification of usages is adequate when handling purely functional data where the intuition is that data with usage 1 have at most one pointer to them [15]. However, when handling more complex entities such as references, channels, or signals it is convenient to take a more refined view. Specifically, a usage can be refined to include information about whether a signal is used: (i) to emit, (ii) to receive during the instant, or (iii) to receive at the end of the instant. Then a usage becomes an element of L^3. Among the 27 possible usages of the shape (a, b, c) for $a, b, c \in L$, we argue that there are 5 *main* ones as described in table 3 (left part). First of all, we must have $a \neq 0$ and $(b \neq 0 \vee c \neq 0)$ since a signal on which we cannot send or receive has no interest. Now if $a = \infty$ then we are forced to take $b = 0$ since we want to preserve the determinacy. Then for $c = \infty$ we have the usage e_1 and for $c = 1$ we have the usage e_3. Suppose now $a = 1$. One choice is to have $b = c = \infty$ and then we have the usage e_2. On the other hand if we want to preserve affinity then we should receive the emitted value at most once. Hence we have $b = 0, c = 1$ or $b = 1, c = 0$ which correspond to the usages e_4 and e_5, respectively. From these 5 *main* usages within an instant, we obtain the *derived ones* (see again table 3) by simply turning one or more 1's to 0's. We only add, subtract, compare usages in L^3 that are derived from the same main usage.

In a *synchronous* framework, it makes sense to consider how usages vary over *time*. The *simplest* solution would be to look at signal usages of the shape x^ω, $x \in L^3$, which are *invariant* under time. However, to reason effectively on programs, we are led to consider signal usages of the shape xy^ω where $x, y \in L^3$ are derived from the same main usage.

The reader may have noticed that in this discussion we have referred to increasingly complex 'usages' varying over L, L^3, and $(L^3)^\omega$. Henceforth a signal usage belongs to $(L^3)^\omega$. Usages are classified in 5 *kinds* as showed in table 3. [2]

We denote with U the set of all these usages and with $U(i)$ the set of usages of kind i, for $i = 1, \ldots, 5$. We consider that the addition operation $\oplus$ is defined only if $u, u' \in U(i)$ and $u \oplus u' \in U(i)$ for some $i \in \{1, \ldots, 5\}$. Similar conventions apply when comparing and subtracting usages. If $u \in U$ then $\uparrow u$, the *shift* of u, is the infinite word in U obtained from u by removing the first character. This operation is always defined. If u is a signal usage, then $u(i)$ for $i \geq 0$ denotes its ith character and $u(i)_j$ for $j \in \{1, 2, 3\}$ the jth component of $u(i)$.

Table 3. Usages and their classification

main usages	derived usages	$xy^\omega \in U(i)$ is	affine	uniform	aff. preserving
$e_1 = (\infty, 0, \infty)$	-	$i = 1$	*no*	*yes*	*no*
$e_2 = (1, \infty, \infty)$	$(0, \infty, \infty)$	$i = 2$	*yes/no*	*yes/no*	*no*
$e_3 = (\infty, 0, 1)$	$(\infty, 0, 0)$	$i = 3$	*yes/no*	*yes/no*	*yes*
$e_4 = (1, 0, 1)$	$(1, 0, 0), (0, 0, 1), (0, 0, 0)$	$i = 4$	*yes/no*	*yes/no*	*yes*
$e_5 = (1, 1, 0)$	$(1, 0, 0), (0, 1, 0), (0, 0, 0)$	$i = 5$	*yes/no*	*yes/no*	*yes*

We classify the usages according to 3 properties: affinity, uniformity, and preservation of affinity. We say that a usage is *affine* if it contains a '1' and *non-affine* otherwise. We also say that it is *uniform* if it is of the shape x^ω and that it is *neutral* if it is the neutral element with respect to the addition $\oplus$ on the set of usages $U(i)$ to which it belongs. It turns out that the non-affine signal usages are always uniform and moreover they coincide with the neutral ones. Finally, by definition, the usages in the sets $U(i)$ for $i = 3, 4, 5$ are *affine preserving* The classification is summarised in the table 3 (right part).

---

[2] The fact that, *e.g.*, $(1, 0, 0)$ occurs both in the usages of kind 4 and 5 is a slight source of ambiguity which is resolved by assuming that the kind of the usage is made explicit.

3.2 Types

In first approximation, types are either *inductive types* or *signal* types. As usual, an inductive type such as the type $List(\sigma)$ of lists of elements of type σ is defined by an equation $List(\sigma) = $ nil $|$ cons *of* $\sigma, List(\sigma)$ specifying the ways in which an element of this type can be built.

In our context, inductive types come with a *usage x* which belongs to the set $\{1, \infty\}$ and which intuitively specifies whether the values of this type can be used at most once or arbitrarily many times (once more we recall that 1 and ∞ are incomparable). To summarise, if $\sigma_1, \ldots, \sigma_k$ are types already defined then an inductive type $C_x(\sigma_1, \ldots, \sigma_k)$ is defined by case on constructors of the shape c *of* $\sigma'_1, \ldots, \sigma'_m$ where the types σ'_j, $j = 1, \ldots, m$ are either one of the types σ_i, $i = 1, \ldots, n$ or the inductive type $C_x(\ldots)$ being defined. There is a further constraint that has to be respected, namely that if one of the types σ_i is 'affine' then the usage x must be affine preserving, *i.e.*, $x = 1$. An affine type is simply a type which contains an affine usage. The grammar in table 4 will provide a precise definition of the affine types.

When collecting the values at the end of the instant we shall also need to consider *set types*. They are described by an equation $Set_x(\sigma) = $ nil $|$ cons *of* σ, $Set_x(\sigma)$ which is quite similar to the one for lists. Note that set types too come with a usage $x \in \{1, \infty\}$ and that if σ is an affine type then the usage x must be affine preserving. The reader might have noticed that we take the freedom of using the constructor nil both with the types $List_u(\sigma)$ and $Set_u(\sigma)$, $u \in \{1, \infty\}$, and the constructor cons both with the types $(\sigma, List_u(\sigma)) \rightarrow List_u(\sigma)$ and $(\sigma, Set_u(\sigma)) \rightarrow Set_u(\sigma)$. However, one should assume that a suitable label on the constructors will allow to disambiguate the situation.

Finally, we denote with $Sig_u(\sigma)$ the type of signals carrying values of type σ according to the signal usage u. As for inductive and set types, if σ is an affine type then the signal usage u must be affine preserving. To formalise these distinctions, we are lead to use several names for types as specified in table 4. We denote with κ non-affine (or classical) types, *i.e.*, types that carry *no* affine information. These types have a uniform usage. We denote with λ affine and uniform types. The types $\sigma, \sigma', \ldots$ stand for types with uniform usage (either non-affine or affine). Finally, the types $\rho, \rho', \ldots$ include all the previous ones plus types that have a non-uniform usage. We notice that classical uniform types can be nested in an arbitrary way, while affine uniform types can only be nested under type constructors that preserve affinity. Moreover, types with non-uniform usages (either classical or affine) cannot be nested at all.[3]

The partial operation of addition $\oplus$ is extended to types so that: $Op_{u_1}(\sigma) \oplus Op_{u_2}(\sigma) = Op_{u_1 \oplus u_2}(\sigma)$, where Op can be C, Set, or Sig, and provided that $u_1 \oplus u_2$ is defined. For instance, $List_1(\lambda) \oplus List_1(\lambda)$ is undefined because $1 \oplus 1$ is not defined.

---

[3] What's the meaning of sending a data structure containing informations whose usage is time-dependent? Is the time information relative to the instant where the data structure is sent or used? We leave open the problem of developing a type theory with usages more complex than the ones of the shape xy^ω considered here.

A type context (or simply a context) Γ is a partial function with finite domain $dom(\Gamma)$ from variables to types. An addition operation $\Gamma_1 \oplus \Gamma_2$ on contexts is defined, written $(\Gamma_1 \oplus \Gamma_2) \downarrow$, if and only if for all x such that $\Gamma_1(x) = \rho_1$ and $\Gamma_2(x) = \rho_2$, the type $\rho_1 \oplus \rho_2$ is defined. The shift operation is extended to contexts so that $(\uparrow \Gamma)(x) = Sig_{(\uparrow u)}(\sigma)$ if $\Gamma(x) = Sig_u(\sigma)$ and $(\uparrow \Gamma)(x) = \Gamma(x)$ otherwise. We also denote with $\Gamma, x : \sigma$ the context Γ *extended* with the pair $x : \sigma$ (so $x \notin dom(\Gamma)$). We say that a context is *neutral (uniform)* if it assigns to variables neutral (uniform) types.

3.3 Semantic Instrumentation

As we have seen, each signal belongs to exactly one of 5 kinds of usages. Let us consider in particular the kind 5 whose main usage is e_5. The forthcoming type system is supposed to guarantee that a value emitted on a signal of kind 5 is received at most once during an instant. Now, consider the program $\bar{s}t \mid s(x).\bar{x}, 0$ and attribute a usage e_5^ω to the signals s and t. According to this usage this program should be well typed. However, if we apply the labelled transition system in table 2, this program reduces to $(\bar{s}t \mid \bar{t})$ which fails to be well-typed because the double occurrence of t is not compatible with an affine usage of t. Intuitively, after the signal s has been read once no other synchronisation should arise during the instant either within the program or with the environment. To express this fact we proceed as follows. First, we instrument the semantics so that it marks (underlines) the emissions on signals of kind 5 that have been used at least once during the instant. The emission has no effect on the labelled transition system in the sense that $\underline{\bar{s}e}$ behaves exactly as $\bar{s}e$.

$$(out) \quad \frac{e \Downarrow v}{\bar{s}e \xrightarrow{\bar{s}v} \underline{\bar{s}e}} \qquad (\underline{out}) \quad \frac{e \Downarrow v}{\underline{\bar{s}e} \xrightarrow{\bar{s}v} \underline{\bar{s}e}} \qquad (\underline{reset}) \quad \frac{e \Downarrow v \quad v \text{ occurs in } V(s)}{\underline{\bar{s}e} \xrightarrow{[\{v\}/s],V} 0}$$

On the other hand, we introduce a special rule $(\underline{out})$ to type $\underline{\bar{s}e}$ which requires at least a usage $(1,1,0) \cdot (0,0,0)^\omega$ for the signal s while neglecting the expression e. By doing this, we make sure that a second attempt to receive on s will produce a type error. In other terms, if typing is preserved by 'compatible' transitions, then we can be sure that a value emitted on a signal of kind 5 is received at most once within an instant.

3.4 Type System

The type system is built around few basic ideas. (1) Usages including both input and output capabilities can be decomposed in simpler ones. For instance, $(1,1,0)^\omega = (1,0,0)(0,1,0)^\omega \oplus (0,1,0)(1,0,0)^\omega$. (2) A rely-guarantee kind of reasoning: when we emit a value we *guarantee* certain resources while when we receive a value we *rely* on certain resources. (3) Every affine usage can be consumed at most once in the typing judgement (and in the computation).

When formalising the typing judgements we need to distinguish the typing of an expression e from the typing of an expression with dereferenciation r and the typing of a recursive call $A(e_1, \ldots, e_n)$ from the typing of a recursive call at the end of the instant $A(r_1, \ldots, r_n)$. To do this we shall write $[r]$ rather than r and $[A(r_1, \ldots, r_n)]$ rather than $A(r_1, \ldots, r_n)$.

We shall consider *four typing judgements*: $\Gamma \vdash e : \rho$, $\Gamma \vdash [r] : \rho$, $\Gamma \vdash P$, and $\Gamma \vdash [A(r_1, \ldots, r_n)]$, and we wish to refer to them with a *uniform* notation $\Gamma \vdash U : T$. To this end, we introduce a fictious type Pr of programs and regard the judgements $\Gamma \vdash P : Pr$ and $\Gamma \vdash [A(r_1, \ldots, r_n)] : Pr$ as an expansion of $\Gamma \vdash P$ and $\Gamma \vdash [A(r_1, \ldots, r_n)]$, respectively. Then we let U stand for one of e, $[r]$, P, $[A(r_1, \ldots, r_n)]$, and T for one of ρ, Pr.

We assume that function symbols are given non-affine types of the shape $(\kappa_1, \ldots, \kappa_n) \rightarrow \kappa$. We denote with k either a constructor or a function symbol and we assume that its type is explicitly given.

The typing rules are given in table 4. We comment first on the typing rules for the expressions. We notice that the arguments and the result of a constructor or a function symbol have always a uniform type. The rules $(!_{Set})$ and $(!_{List})$ describe the type of a dereferenced signal following its usage. If the usage is of kind 1 then the list of values associated with the signal at the end of the instant must be treated as a set, if the usage is of kind 2 then we know that the list of values contains at most one element and therefore its processing will certainly be 'order-independent', if the usage is of kind 3 then the list may contain several values and it must be processed as an *affine* set, finally if the usage is of kind 4 (the usage of kind 5 forbids reception at the end of the instant) then again the list of values will contain at most one element so we can rely on an *affine* list type.

Notice the special form of the rule $[var_{sig}]$. The point here is that in a recursive call $K = A(!s, s)$ at the end of instant, we need to distinguish the resources needed to type $!s$ which should relate to the *current* instant from the resources needed to type s which should relate to the *following instants*. For instance, we want to type K in a context $s : Sig_u(\sigma)$ where $u = (0, 0, 1)^\omega$. This is possible because we can decompose u in $u_1 \oplus u_2$, where $u_1 = (0, 0, 1)(0, 0, 0)^\omega$ and $u_2 = (0, 0, 0)(0, 0, 1)^\omega$, and we can rely on u_1 to type $[!s]$ and on u_2 to type $[s]$ (by $[var_{sig}]$).

A set-type is a particular case of quotient type and therefore its definition goes through the definition of an equivalence relation $\sim_\rho$ on values. This is defined as the least equivalence relation such that $s \sim_{Sig_u(\sigma)} s$, $\mathsf{c} \sim_{C(\sigma)} \mathsf{c}$, if c is a constant of type $C(\sigma)$, and

$$\mathsf{c}(v_1, \ldots, v_n) \sim_{C_u(\sigma_1, \ldots, \sigma_n)} \mathsf{c}(u_1, \ldots, u_n) \quad \text{if } v_i \sim_{\sigma_i} u_i \text{ for } i = 1, \ldots, n$$
$$[v_1; \ldots; v_n] \sim_{Set_u(\sigma)} [u_1; \ldots; u_m] \quad \text{if } \{v_1, \ldots, v_n\} \sim_{Set_u(\sigma)} \{u_1, \ldots, u_m\},$$
$$\text{where: } \{v_1, \ldots, v_n\} \sim_{Set_u(\sigma)} \{u_1, \ldots, u_m\} \text{ if for a permutation } \pi, v_i \sim_\sigma u_{\pi(i)} .$$

Furthermore, we assume that each function symbol f, coming with a (classical) type $(\kappa_1, \ldots, \kappa_n) \rightarrow \kappa$, *respects* the typing in the following sense: (1) if $v_i \sim_{\kappa_i} u_i$, $i = 1, \ldots, n$, $f(v_1, \ldots, v_n) \Downarrow v$ and $f(u_1, \ldots, u_n) \Downarrow u$ then $v \sim_\kappa u$. (2) If $\Gamma \vdash f(v_1, \ldots, v_n) : \kappa$ and $f(v_1, \ldots, v_n) \Downarrow v$ then $\Gamma \vdash v : \kappa$.

Finally, we turn to the typing of programs. We assume that each thread identifier A, defined by an equation $A(x_1, \ldots, x_n) = P$, comes with a type $(\sigma_1, \ldots, \sigma_n)$.

Table 4. Affine type system

$$
\begin{aligned}
\kappa &::= C_\infty(\kappa) \mid Set_\infty(\kappa) \mid Sig_u(\kappa) &&(u \text{ neutral}) \\
\lambda &::= C_1(\sigma) \mid Set_1(\sigma) \mid Sig_u(\kappa) \mid Sig_v(\lambda) &&(u \text{ affine and uniform}, v \text{ aff.-pres.} \\
&&&\text{and uniform}) \\
\sigma &::= \kappa \mid \lambda &&(\text{uniform types}) \\
\rho &::= \sigma \mid Sig_u(\kappa) \mid Sig_v(\lambda) &&(v \text{ affine-preserving})
\end{aligned}
$$

(var)
$$\frac{u \geq u' \quad Op \in \{Sig, Set, C\}}{\Gamma, x : Op_u(\sigma) \vdash x : Op_{u'}(\sigma)}$$

(k)
$$\frac{\Gamma_i \vdash e_i : \sigma_i \quad i = 1, \ldots, n \quad k : (\sigma_1, \ldots, \sigma_n) \to \sigma \quad k = f \text{ or } k = \mathsf{c}}{\Gamma_0 \oplus \Gamma_1 \oplus \cdots \oplus \Gamma_n \vdash k(e_1, \ldots, e_n) : \sigma}$$

$[var_C]$
$$\frac{Op = C \quad Op = Set}{\Gamma, x : Op_u(\sigma) \vdash [x] : Op_u(\sigma)}$$

$[var_{sig}]$
$$\frac{y^\omega \geq u}{\Gamma, s : Sig_{xy^\omega}(\sigma) \vdash [s] : Sig_u(\sigma)}$$

$[k]$
$$\frac{\Gamma_i \vdash [r_i] : \sigma_i \quad i = 1, \ldots, n \quad k : (\sigma_1, \ldots, \sigma_n) \to \sigma \quad k = f \text{ or } k = \mathsf{c}}{\Gamma_0 \oplus \Gamma_1 \oplus \cdots \oplus \Gamma_n \vdash [k(r_1, \ldots, r_n)] : \sigma}$$

$[!_{Set}]$
$$\frac{(u(0) \geq (\infty, 0, \infty) \;\wedge\; x = \infty)\; \vee\; (u(0) \geq (\infty, 0, 1) \;\wedge\; x = 1)}{\Gamma, s : Sig_u(\sigma) \vdash [!s] : Set_x(\sigma)}$$

$[!_{List}]$
$$\frac{(u(0) \geq (0, \infty, \infty) \;\wedge\; x = \infty)\; \vee\; (u(0) \geq (0, 0, 1) \;\wedge\; x = 1)}{\Gamma, s : Sig_u(\sigma) \vdash [!s] : List_x(\sigma)}$$

(0)
$$\frac{}{\Gamma \vdash 0}$$

(out)
$$\frac{\Gamma_1 \vdash s : Sig_u(\sigma) \quad u(0)_1 \neq 0 \quad \Gamma_2 \vdash e : \sigma}{\Gamma_1 \oplus \Gamma_2 \vdash \bar{s}e}$$

(ν)
$$\frac{\Gamma, s : Sig_u(\sigma) \vdash P}{\Gamma \vdash \nu s : Sig_u(\sigma)\, P}$$

(in)
$$\frac{\Gamma_1 \vdash s : Sig_u(\sigma) \quad u(0)_2 \neq 0 \quad \Gamma_2, x : \sigma \vdash P \quad (\Gamma_1 \oplus \Gamma_2) \vdash [A(\mathbf{r})]}{(\Gamma_1 \oplus \Gamma_2) \vdash s(x).P, A(\mathbf{r})}$$

(m_s)
$$\frac{s_1, s_2 \in dom(\Gamma) \quad \Gamma \vdash P_i \quad i = 1, 2}{\Gamma \vdash [s_1 = s_2]P_1, P_2}$$

(m_{c})
$$\frac{\mathsf{c} : (\sigma_1, \ldots, \sigma_n) \to \sigma \quad \Gamma_1 \vdash u : \sigma \quad \Gamma_2, x_1 : \sigma_1, \ldots, x_n : \sigma_n \vdash P_1 \quad (\Gamma_1 \oplus \Gamma_2) \vdash P_2}{\Gamma_1 \oplus \Gamma_2 \vdash [u \unrhd \mathsf{c}(x_1, \ldots, x_n)]P_1, P_2}$$

(par)
$$\frac{\Gamma_i \vdash P_i \quad i = 1, 2}{\Gamma_1 \oplus \Gamma_2 \vdash P_1 \mid P_2}$$

(rec)
$$\frac{A : (\sigma_1, \ldots, \sigma_n), \quad \Gamma_i \vdash e_i : \sigma_i \quad i = 1, \ldots, n}{\Gamma_1 \oplus \cdots \oplus \Gamma_n \vdash A(e_1, \ldots, e_n)}$$

$(\underline{out})$
$$\frac{\Gamma \vdash s : Sig_u(\sigma) \quad u(0) = (1, 1, 0)}{\Gamma \vdash \underline{\bar{s}e}}$$

$[rec]$
$$\frac{A : (\sigma_1, \ldots, \sigma_n), \quad \Gamma_i \vdash [r_i] : \sigma_i \quad i = 1, \ldots, n}{\Gamma_1 \oplus \cdots \oplus \Gamma_n \vdash [A(r_1, \ldots, r_n)]}$$

Hence we require these types to be uniform. We also require that A has the property that: (i) if $v_i \sim_{\sigma_i} u_i$ for $i = 1, \ldots, n$ then $A(v_1, \ldots, v_n) \approx A(u_1, \ldots, u_n)$ and (ii) $x_1 : \sigma_1, \ldots, x_n : \sigma_n \vdash P$ is derivable.

We also suppose that generated signals names are *explicitly* labelled with their types as in $\nu s : \rho\ P$. The labelled transition system in table 2 is adapted so that the output action carries the information on the types of the extruded names. This type is lifted by the rule $(next)$ so that, e.g., $\nu s : \rho\ s.0, A(s) \xrightarrow{N} \nu s : \uparrow \rho\ A(s)$.

Example 1. With reference to the example of client-server in section 1, assume an inductive (non-affine) type D of data. Let $\sigma_1 = Sig_{u_1}(D)$ where $u_1 = (1, 0, 0)^\omega$ be the type of the signals on which the server will eventually provide an answer. Let $Req_1(\sigma_1, D) = \mathsf{req}\ of\ \sigma_r, D$ be the type of requests which are pairs composed of a signal and a datum. Let $\sigma_{set} = Set_1(Req_1(\sigma_1, D))$ be the type of the set of requests issued by the clients. Let $\sigma = Sig_u(Req_1(\sigma_1, D))$ with $u = (\infty, 0, 1)^\omega$ be the type of the signal on which the server gets the requests and $\sigma' = Sig_{u'}(Req_1(\sigma_1, D))$, with $u' = (\infty, 0, 0)^\omega$, the related type of the signal on which the clients send the requests. Finally, let $\sigma_t = Sig_u(D)$ be the type of the signal on which the client sends the received answer (with a suitable usage u). Then we can type *Server* and *Client* as follows: *Server* : (σ), *Handle* : (σ, σ_{set}), and *Client* : (D, σ', σ_t).

Remark 1. In a practical implementation of the type system, one can expect the programmer to assign a kind $(1 - 5)$ to each signal and let the system infer a *minimum* usage which is compatible with the operations performed by the program.

4   Results

We start by stating the expected *weakening* and *substitution* properties of the type system.

Lemma 1 (weakening). *If $\Gamma \vdash U : T$ and $(\Gamma \oplus \Gamma') \downarrow$ then $(\Gamma \oplus \Gamma') \vdash U : T$.*

Lemma 2 (substitution). *If $\Gamma, x : \rho \vdash U : T$, $\Gamma' \vdash v : \rho$, and $(\Gamma \oplus \Gamma') \downarrow$ then $(\Gamma \oplus \Gamma') \vdash [v/x]U : T$.*

Next we specify when a context Γ is *compatible* with an action act, written $(\Gamma, act) \downarrow$. Recall that V and E denote a function from signals to finite lists of distinct values and finite sets of values, respectively. If $V(s) = [v_1; \ldots; v_n]$ then let $(V \backslash E)(s) = \{v_1, \ldots, v_n\} \backslash E(s)$. Then define a program $P_{(V \backslash E)}$ as the parallel composition of emissions $\bar{s}v$ such that $v \in (V \backslash E)(s)$. Intuitively, this is the emission on an appropriate signal of all the values which are in V but not in E. We also let P_V stand for $P_{(V \backslash \emptyset)}$ where $\emptyset(s) = \emptyset$ for every signal s.

Definition 2. *With each action act, we associate a* minimal *program P_{act} that allows the action to take place:*

$$P_{act} = \begin{cases} 0 & \text{if } act = \tau \text{ or } act = N \\ \bar{s}v & \text{if } act = sv \text{ or } act = s?v \\ s(x).0,0 & \text{if } act = \bar{s}v \\ P_{V \setminus E} & \text{if } act = (E,V) \end{cases}$$

Definition 3 (compatibility context and action). *A context Γ is compatible with an action act, written $(\Gamma, act) \downarrow$, if $\exists \Gamma'$ $(\Gamma \oplus \Gamma') \downarrow$ and $\Gamma' \vdash P_{act}$.*

We can now introduce the concept of *typed* transition which is a transition labelled with an action *act* of a program typable in a context Γ such that Γ and *act* are compatible.

Definition 4 (typed transition). *We write $P \xrightarrow[\Gamma]{act} Q$ $(P \overset{act}{\underset{\Gamma}{\Rightarrow}} Q)$ if: (1) $\Gamma \vdash P$, (2) $(\Gamma, act) \downarrow$, and (3) $P \xrightarrow{act} Q$ $(P \overset{act}{\Rightarrow} Q$, respectively).*

Next, we introduce the notion of *residual context* which is intuitively the context left after a typed transition. (the definition for the auxiliary actions is available in [5]). First, we notice that given a (uniform) type σ and a value v we can define the minimum context $\Delta(v, \sigma)$ such that $\Delta(v, \sigma) \vdash v : \sigma$. Namely, we set $\Delta(s, \sigma) = s : \sigma$ and $\Delta(c(v_1, \ldots, v_n)) = \Delta(v_1, \sigma_1) \oplus \cdots \oplus \Delta(v_n, \sigma_n)$ if $c : (\sigma_1, \ldots, \sigma_n) \to \sigma$. Notice that $\Delta(v, \sigma)$ is the empty context if $fn(v) = \emptyset$ and it is a neutral context if σ is non-affine.

Definition 5 (residual context). *Given a context Γ and a compatible and relevant action α, the residual context $\Gamma(\alpha)$ is defined as follows:*

$$\Gamma(\alpha) = \begin{cases} \Gamma & \text{if } \alpha = \tau \\ \uparrow \Gamma & \text{if } \alpha = N \\ (\Gamma, \mathbf{t} : \sigma') \ominus \Delta(v : \sigma') \oplus \{s : Sig_{u_5}(\sigma')\} & \text{if } \Gamma(s) = Sig_u(\sigma'), \alpha = \nu\mathbf{t} : \sigma'\bar{s}v, (1) \\ \Gamma \oplus \Delta(v, \sigma') \oplus \{s : Sig_{u_{out}}(\sigma')\} & \text{if } \Gamma(s) = Sig_u(\sigma'), \alpha = sv, (2) \end{cases}$$

(1) $u_5 = (0,1,0) \cdot (0,0,0)^\omega$ if $u \in U(5)$ and it is neutral otherwise (i.e., $u \in U(2)$). (2) u_{out} is the least usage of the same kind as u which allows to perform an output within the instant (always defined).

The notion of residual context is instrumental to a precise statement of the way transitions affect the typing. First we notice that the type of expressions is preserved by the evaluation relation.

Lemma 3 (expression evaluation). *If $\Gamma \vdash e : \rho$ and $e \Downarrow v$ then $\Gamma \vdash v : \rho$.*

The following lemma records the effect of the substitution at the end of the instant.

Lemma 4 (substitution, end of instant). *(1) If $\Gamma \vdash [A(\mathbf{r})]$, $\Gamma' \vdash P_V$, and $(\Gamma \oplus \Gamma') \downarrow$ then $\uparrow (\Gamma \oplus \Gamma') \vdash V(A(\mathbf{r}))$.*
(2) If moreover there are V', E such that $V, V' \Vdash E$ then $V(A(\mathbf{r})) \approx V'(A(\mathbf{r}))$.

Finally, the subject reduction theorem states that the residual of a typed transition is typable in the residual context (again, the residual context on auxiliary actions is defined in [5]).

Theorem 2 (subject reduction). *If* $P \xrightarrow[\Gamma]{act} Q$ *then* $\Gamma(act) \vdash Q$.

Next we introduce a notion of *typed bisimulation* which refines the one given in definition 1 by focusing on typed processes and typed transitions. Let Cxt be the set of contexts and if $\Gamma \in Cxt$ let $Pr(\Gamma)$ be the set of programs typable in the context Γ.

Definition 6 (typed bisimulation). *A typed bisimulation is a function* $\mathcal{R}$ *indexed on* Cxt *such that for every context* Γ, $\mathcal{R}_\Gamma$ *is a symmetric relation on* $Pr(\Gamma)$ *such that:* $P \; \mathcal{R}_\Gamma \; Q$, $P \xrightarrow[\Gamma]{\alpha} P'$, $bn(\alpha) \cap fn(Q) = \emptyset$ *implies* $\exists Q'$ ($Q \xRightarrow[\Gamma]{\alpha} Q'$, $P' \; \mathcal{R}_{\Gamma(\alpha)} \; Q'$). *We denote with* $\approx^t$ *the largest typed labelled bisimulation.*

An expected property of typed bisimulation is that it is a weaker property than untyped bisimulation: if we cannot distinguish two processes by doing arbitrary actions we cannot distinguish them when doing actions which are compatible with the typing.

Proposition 1. *If* $P, Q \in Pr(\Gamma)$ *and* $P \approx Q$ *then* $P \approx^t_\Gamma Q$.

We write $P \xrightarrow[\Gamma]{\tau} Q$ if $P \xrightarrow[\Gamma]{\tau} Q$ or $P = Q$. The following lemma states a strong commutation property of typed τ actions and it entails that typed bisimulation is invariant under τ-actions.

Lemma 5. (1) *If* $P \xrightarrow[\Gamma]{\tau} P_i$ *for* $i = 1, 2$ *then there is a* Q *such* $P_i \xrightarrow[\Gamma]{\tau} Q$ *for* $i = 1, 2$.
(2) *If* $P \xRightarrow[\Gamma]{\tau} Q$ *then* $P \approx^t_\Gamma Q$.

The second key property is that the computation at the end of the instant is deterministic and combining the two lemmas, we derive that typable programs are deterministic.

Lemma 6. *If* $P \xrightarrow[\Gamma]{N} P_i$ *for* $i = 1, 2$ *then* $P_1 \approx^t_{\uparrow(\Gamma)} P_2$.

Theorem 3 (determinacy). *If* $P \xRightarrow[\Gamma]{N} \cdot \xRightarrow[\Gamma']{N} \cdots \xRightarrow[\Gamma']{N} P_i, i = 1, 2, \Gamma' =\uparrow \Gamma$ *then* $P_1 \approx^t_{\Gamma'} P_2$.

5   Conclusion

The main contribution of this work is the identification of 5 kinds of usages in signal-based communication and of the rules that allow their *composition* while preserving determinacy. This goes well-beyond previous analyses for ESTEREL-like languages we are aware of that are essentially 'first-order' in the sense that signals are not treated as first-class values. Technically, we have shown that a typable process P is *deterministic*. This result builds on previous work by the authors [2,4] on a mathematical framework to reason about the equivalence of programs which is comparable to the one available for the π-calculus.

References

1. Amadio, R.: The SL synchronous language, revisited. Journal of Logic and Algebraic Programming 70, 121–150 (2007)
2. Amadio, R.: A synchronous π-calculus. Information and Computation 205(9), 1470–1490 (2007)
3. Amadio, R., Castellani, I., Sangiorgi, D.: On bisimulations for the asynchronous π-calculus. Theoretical Computer Science 195, 291–324 (1998)
4. Amadio, R., Dogguy, M.: Determinacy in a synchronous π-calculus. Technical Report, Université Paris 7, Laboratoire PPS (July 2007); From semantics to computer science: essays in honor of Kahn, G., Bertot, Y., et al. (eds.) CUP (to appear)
5. Amadio, R., Dogguy, M.: On affine usages in signal based communication. Technical Report, Université Paris 7, Laboratoire PPS (April 2008)
6. Berry, G., Gonthier, G.: The Esterel synchronous programming language. Science of computer programming 19(2), 87–152 (1992)
7. Boussinot, F., De Simone, R.: The SL synchronous language. IEEE Trans. on Software Engineering 22(4), 256–266 (1996)
8. Girard, J.-Y.: Linear Logic. Theoretical Computer Science 50(1), 1–102 (1987)
9. Honda, K., Yoshida, N.: On reduction-based process semantics. Theoretical Computer Science 151(2), 437–486 (1995)
10. Kobayashi, N.: Type systems for concurrent programs. In: Aichernig, B.K., Maibaum, T. (eds.) Formal Methods at the Crossroads. From Panacea to Foundational Support. LNCS, vol. 2757, pp. 439–453. Springer, Heidelberg (2003)
11. Kobayashi, N., Pierce, B., Turner, D.: Linearity and the pi-calculus. ACM Transactions on Programming Languages and Systems (TOPLAS) 21(5) (1999)
12. Mandel, L., Pouzet, M.: ReactiveML, a reactive extension to ML. In: Proc. ACM Principles and Practice of Declarative Programming, pp. 82–93 (2005)
13. Milner, R.: Communication and concurrency. Prentice-Hall, Englewood Cliffs (1989)
14. Milner, R., Parrow, J., Walker, D.: A calculus of mobile processes, parts 1-2. Information and Computation 100(1), 1–77 (1992)
15. Wadler, P.: A Taste of Linear Logic. In: Proc. Mathematical Foundations of Computer Science, SLNCS, vol. 711, pp. 185-210 (1993)

Abstraction of Clocks
in Synchronous Data-Flow Systems*

Albert Cohen[1], Louis Mandel[2], Florence Plateau[2], and Marc Pouzet[2,3]

[1] INRIA Saclay - Ile-de-France, Orsay, France
[2] LRI, Univ. Paris-Sud 11, Orsay, France and INRIA Saclay
[3] Institut Universitaire de France

Abstract. Synchronous data-flow languages such as LUSTRE manage infinite sequences or *streams* as basic values. Each stream is associated to a *clock* which defines the instants where the current value of the stream is present. This clock is a type information and a dedicated type system — the so-called clock-calculus — statically rejects programs which cannot be executed synchronously. In existing synchronous languages, it amounts at asking whether two streams have the same clocks and thus relies on clock equality only. Recent works have shown the interest of introducing some relaxed notion of synchrony, where two streams can be composed as soon as they can be synchronized through the introduction of a finite buffer (as done in the SDF model of Edward Lee). This technically consists in replacing typing by subtyping. The present paper introduces a simple way to achieve this relaxed model through the use of *clock envelopes*. These clock envelopes are sets of concrete clocks which are not necessarily periodic. This allows to model various features in real-time embedded software such as bounded jitter as found in video-systems, execution time of real-time processes and scheduling resources or the communication through buffers. We present the algebra of clock envelopes and its main theoretical properties.

Keywords: Real-time systems; Synchronous languages; Kahn Process Networks; Compilation; Semantics; Type-systems.

1 Introduction

Synchronous data-flow languages such as LUSTRE [1] have been introduced in the 80's for the implementation of real-time critical software. Since then, they have been used in various industrial applications such as the fly-by-wire commands in Airbus planes. They were based on the objective to build a programming language close to the mathematical models used in embedded systems such as data-flow equations or the composition of finite-state machines. In these languages, synchrony finds a very practical justification: at a certain level of observation, time is considered *logically* as a sequence of instantaneous steps (or atomic reactions) of the system to external events and when processes are composed in

---

* This work was partially supported by the INRIA research project Synchronics.

G. Ramalingam (Ed.): APLAS 2008, LNCS 5356, pp. 237–254, 2008.

parallel, they agree on those steps [2]. This also coincides with Milner's interpretation of synchrony in SCCS [3] or the synchronized product of automata [4]. In a data-flow language such as LUSTRE, synchrony is essentially the one of control-theory and can be interpreted as a typing constraint on the domain of sequences: when combining two sequences $(x_i)_{i \in D_1}$ and $(y_i)_{i \in D_2}$ as in $(x_i)_{i \in D_1} + (y_i)_{i \in D_2}$, their time-domain D_1 and D_2 must be compatible in some ways. This static checking is done by a specific type system, the so-called clock-calculus [5,6] which imposes D_1 and D_2 to be equal. Such analysis appears not to be bound to synchronous languages and are of a much wider interest. For example, clock analysis is done in modeling tools such as SIMULINK [7] or SCICOS [8].

The clock-calculus essentially consists in asking whether two streams have the same clock. For that, those clock information are abstracted by types. Consider the following type language (taken from [5]):

$$\sigma ::= \forall \alpha. \forall X_1, ..., X_m.ct$$
$$ct ::= ct \rightarrow ct \mid ct * ct \mid ck \mid (X : ck)$$
$$ck ::= ck \text{ on } c \mid ck \text{ on } not \ c \mid \alpha$$
$$c ::= X \mid n \text{ where } n \text{ is a numerable set of names}$$

As in the Hindley-Milner type system [9], types are separated into clock schemes (σ) and clock types (ct). A clock scheme is quantified over clock variables (α) or boolean variables (X). Then, the clock type of $(+)$ is $\forall \alpha. \alpha \times \alpha \rightarrow \alpha$ stating that if x and y are two integer streams with the same clock α then $x + y$ have also the clock α. Said differently, the addition expects its two arguments to be synchronous and produces a third stream with the same clock. An other example of a synchronous primitive is the unitary delay which shifts its input. If x and y are two sequences $x_0 \, x_1 \, x_2 ...$ and $y_0 \, y_1 \, y_2 ...$ then $x \, \text{fby} \, y$ stands for $x_0 \, y_0 \, y_1 \, y_2 ....$ x and y must have the same clock as well as $x \, \text{fby} \, y$ and we can give to fby the clock signature: $\forall \alpha. \alpha \times \alpha \rightarrow \alpha$.

Things become more interesting when sampling occurs. Two typical programming constructs are the sampler and the merge operator:

when : $\forall \alpha. \forall X. \alpha \rightarrow (X : \alpha) \rightarrow \alpha \text{ on } X$
merge : $\forall \alpha. \forall X.(X : \alpha) \rightarrow \alpha \text{ on } X \rightarrow \alpha \text{ on } not \ X \rightarrow \alpha$

$x \, \text{when} \, y$ is well clocked when x and y have the same clock α. In that case, the result has a slower clock corresponding to the instant where y is true and we write it $\alpha \text{ on } y$ (the meta-variable X is substituted with the actual one y). For example, if $half$ is an alternating boolean sequence 10101010101... and x is a sequence $x_0 \, x_1 \, x_2 ...$ then $x \, \text{when} \, half$ is a half frequency sampling of x, that is, $x_0 \, x_2 \, x_4 ....$ If x has some clock type ck, then $x \, \text{when} \, half$ has clock type $ck \text{ on } half$. Then, the expression $x + (x \, \text{when} \, half)$ which would compute the sequence $(x_i + x_{2i})_{i \in \mathbb{N}}$ is not well clocked since ck is not equal to $ck \text{ on } half$ and is statically rejected by the compiler. The merge operator is symmetric: it expects two streams with complementary clocks and combines them to build a longer stream.

When comparing clocks, most implementations restrict the comparison to the equality of names: $ck \text{ on } n_1$ and $ck \text{ on } n_2$ can be unified only when $n_1 = n_2$. This strong restriction is justified by the graphical aspect of these languages. Two

streams can be composed when they are sampled by the same condition coming from the very same source block, that is, the same wire. This restriction is
reasonable when n_1 is the result of a complex computation (for which equality
is non-decidable). This is nonetheless overly restrictive for an important variety
of applications where clocks are periodic and it forbids to take their properties
into account. In particular, recent works have shown the interest of a more *relaxed*
model of synchrony allowing to compose streams as soon as they can be synchronized through the introduction of bounded buffers. This model is called the N-
synchronous Kahn model [10] and pursues the foundational work of Edward Lee
on Synchronous Data-Flow graphs (SDF) [11,12]. Data-flow equations in SDF are
not statically constrained with any notion of synchronous clock, yet *the existence
of* a static synchronous schedule is guaranteed by periodicity constraints on pro-
duction/consumption rates. From the typing point of view, N-synchrony amounts
at turning the clock calculus into a type-system with a subtyping rule:

$$(\text{SUB}) \; \frac{H \vdash e : ck \quad ck <: ck'}{H \vdash e : ck'}$$

Intuitively, $ck <: ck'$ means that the $1s$ of ck arrive before the $1s$ of ck' and
that ck and ck' have in average the same proportion of $1s$. In the particular case
of *ultimately periodic clocks* [13], subtyping is decidable. For example, the clock
half is written (10) whereas $0000(10)$ is the same clock with a prefix of four false
values. Thus, α on $(10) <: \alpha$ on $0000(10)$. Algebraic properties allow to compare
more clocks, e.g., α on (10) on (10) equals α on (1000). Note that those clocks
correspond to simple linear circuits (and automata). The technical details shall
be reminded in Section 2.

In the present paper, we adopt a slightly different and simpler point of view
than in [10]. Instead of focusing on periodic clocks, we give the ability to reason on sets of clocks or *clock envelopes* as abstractions of concrete clocks. Indeed, in various applications, exact synchrony with precise periodic clocks is
not mandatory and it is sufficient to reason on clock intervals where bounds
are nonetheless periodic. This is typically the case in three kind of applications, (1) video applications with bounded jitter, (2) the description of execution times when modeling physical resources, and (3) the communication
through buffers (or cyclic arrays). For example, a stream x which is present
in average 3 times over 7 according to a base clock ck and with a possible
jitter of 4 will be given a clock type ck on$^\sim$ $[-2, 2](7/3)$ as a shortcut for
$\exists n \in [-2, 2](7/3)$. ck on n. The existential quantifier hides the exact instant
where the element is present but gives a bound on it. The intuition behind
the notation $[-2, 2](7/3)$ is to account for all clocks whose $(j + 1)^{\text{th}}$ 1 is between
positions $(7/3) \times j - 2$ and $(7/3) \times j + 2$. Said differently, we consider all clocks
ck' such that ck on $1(1010100) <: ck' <: ck$ on (0010101). If f is of the form
$\lambda x.x$ when e for some complex boolean expression e but for which it can be proved
that its value belongs to the envelope $[-2, 2](7/3)$ then a valid abstraction for f
is $\forall \alpha.\alpha \to \alpha$ on$^\sim$ $[-2, 2](7/3)$.

Another example appears when modeling the execution time of processes
[14,15,16]. To state that a function f must be executed every ten cycles and

that its computation takes between two and four cycles, we can give it the clock signature: $\forall \alpha.\alpha$ on$^\sim$ $[0,0](10/1) \rightarrow \alpha$ on$^\sim$ $[2,4](10/1)$. When composed twice, we get: $f \circ f : \forall \alpha.(\alpha$ on$^\sim$ $[0,0](10/1)) \rightarrow \alpha$ on$^\sim$ $[4,8](10/1)$.

Another typical example can be taken from *elastic circuits* [17]. For example, an elastic adder is a stream function which takes two streams which are not synchronous but are in the same envelope up to one delay, that is, they belong to some envelope $(ck$ on $c)$ on$^\sim$ $[0,1](1/1)$ for some unknown boolean sequence c (not necessarily periodic).

Finally, it is also possible to mimic a common feature found in a video application: to read several inputs (or write several output) at once. Consider, for example a stream function f whose input has clock type α on$^\sim$ $[0,4](1/1)$ connected to a stream x with clock type ck on$^\sim$ $[0,0](1/1)$. Then, at each instant, x produces a value whereas f can wait four instants before to start consuming the values. At the fifth instant, f can consume the first five values and then continue to read arrays by slides of five elements every five instants.

The main contribution of this paper is thus to introduce those clock envelopes and to study their algebraic properties. The paper is organized as follows. In Section 2, we remind the basic properties of infinite binary words. In Section 3, we introduce the clock envelopes as sets of clocks. Section 4 presents related work and we conclude in Section 5.

For lack of space, proofs are not given or only sketched. Proofs and complements are available at www.lri.fr/~plateau/aplas08.

2   Clocks as Infinite Binary Words

A subtyping relation can be checked only if clock types are expressed with respect to the same clock variable. Intuitively, this is because sampling is always relative to a clock $(ck$ on c is relative to $ck)$. In that case the subtyping relation corresponds to a relation on boolean sequences: α on $c <: \alpha$ on $c' \Leftrightarrow c <: c'$.

In this section, we present infinite binary words and a boolean operation *on* for them such that $(ck$ on $c_1)$ on $c_2 = ck$ on $(c_1$ on $c_2)$. We then present the subtyping relation on these words. As we mainly manipulate the boolean stream part c of a clock type we will also call it clock.

2.1   Definitions

A clock can be an infinite binary word or a composition of those. Identifying names to their values, clocks have the following grammar:

$$c ::= w \mid \textit{not } w \mid c \textit{ on } c$$
$$w ::= 0.w \mid 1.w$$

not w is the negation of w, c_1 *on* c_2 is the sampled clock and w an infinite binary word. In infinite binary words, a 1 denotes the presence of a value on the flow, and a 0 the absence of value.

Remark 1. We will consider that in the clocks we manipulate, the maximal distance between two successive 1s is bounded (in particular, every word contains

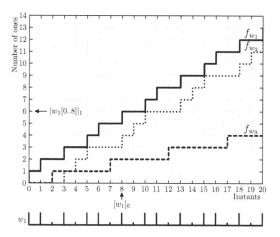

In the 2D-chronograms, the discrete function $f_w(i) = |w[0..i]|_1$ associates to each instant i the number of 1s seen in w since the beginning. The function $f_w^{-1}(j) = \min i$ s.t. $f(i) = j$ gives the index of the jth 1. A rising edge at instant i means that the element at index i of w is a 1 (i.e. $w[i] = 1$). In the contrary case (i.e. $f_w(i) = f_w(i-1)$), it is a 0 (i.e. $w[i] = 0$). The word w_1 is represented on the 1D-chronogram, which is a projection of f_{w_1}.

Fig. 1. Chronograms representing words $w_1 = (11010)$, $w_2 = 0(00111)$, $w_3 = (00100)$

an infinity of 1s). So, the **not** operator cannot be applied on a clock that does not contain an infinity of 0s.

Notations: The concatenation of a finite binary word u and a binary word w is written $u.w$. We will sometimes note 0^n the concatenation of n values 0 and 1^n of n values 1. $w[i]$ is the element at index i of w, $w[0..i]$ is the prefix of w of length $i + 1$, and $[w]_j$ the position of the jth 1 in w. It is defined by: $[1.w]_1 = 0$, $[1.w]_{j+1} = 1 + [w]_j$, $[0^d.w]_j = d + [w]_j$, with $d \in \mathbb{N}, j \in \mathbb{N}^*$.[1][2] Note that $\forall j \geq 1$, $[w]_j < [w]_{j+1}$. Finally, the number of 1s contained in a finite binary word v is denoted by $|v|_1$.

We will call *periodic binary words* and we will write $u(v)$, the words consisting of a finite prefix u, followed by the infinite repetition of a finite binary word v.

Fig. 1 shows some examples of infinite binary words, represented by chronograms. The discrete function $f_w(i) = |w[0..i]|_1$ associates to each instant i the number of 1 seen in w since the beginning. A rising edge at instant i means that $w[i] = 1$. If a flow is produced (resp. consumed) at clock w, then a token is produced (resp. consumed) at each rising edge of the chronogram.

Formally, the **on** operator is defined by:

$$1.w_1 \text{ \emph{on} } 1.w_2 = 1.(w_1 \text{ \emph{on} } w_2)$$
$$1.w_1 \text{ \emph{on} } 0.w_2 = 0.(w_1 \text{ \emph{on} } w_2)$$
$$0.w_1 \text{ \emph{on} } w_2 = 0.(w_1 \text{ \emph{on} } w_2)$$

The elements of w_1 **on** w_2 correspond to the elements of w_2, when w_2 is traversed at the rhythm of the 1s of w_1. So if the jth 1 of w_2 is the ith element of w_2, we know that the jth 1 of w_1 **on** w_2 is at the index of the ith 1 in w_1.

Proposition 1. $[w_1 \text{ \emph{on} } w_2]_j = [w_1]_{[w_2]_j+1}$

Corollary 1 (on associativity). $(w_1 \text{ \emph{on} } w_2) \text{ \emph{on} } w_3 = w_1 \text{ \emph{on} } (w_2 \text{ \emph{on} } w_3)$

---

[1] $\mathbb{N}$ is the set of natural numbers and $\mathbb{N}^*$ is the set of positive natural numbers.

[2] Note that for readability reasons and contrary to previous works, indexes of elements of w begin at 0. It involves a shift in some formulas, w.r.t those of [10].

2.2   Buffer Size

The minimal buffer size needed to communicate from an output with clock type α on w to an input with clock type α on w' is the maximum amount of data produced and not yet consumed in the course of the execution:

$$size(w, w') = \max_{i \in \mathbb{N}}(|w[0..i]|_1 - |w'[0..i]|_1)$$

Note that if the minimum of this difference is negative, then there will be at least one read in an empty buffer. Indeed, when a negative value is reached, more data have been consumed than produced.

In chronograms, the buffer size to communicate from α on w to α on w' is equal to the maximal difference $f_w(i) - f_{w'}(i)$. For example, in Fig. 1, the maximal amount of data produced and not yet consumed during the communication from α on w_1 to α on w_2 is 2, reached for the first time at instant 1. The amount of data to store during the communication from α on w_1 to α on w_3 grows infinitely.

2.3   Subtyping Relation

The subtyping relation is verified if the tokens are always produced before they are expected (precedence relation), and at a bounded distance of the instant they are consumed (synchronizability relation).

Definition 1 (precedence).

We say that w_1 precedes w_2 and we write $w_1 \preceq w_2$ iff $\forall j \geq 1$, $[w_1]_j \leq [w_2]_j$.

A word w_1 precedes a word w_2 if the jth 1 of w_1 always comes before (or at the same time as) the jth 1 of w_2. It permits to verify that the causality relation between flows is preserved, i.e. that the producer writes its outputs in the buffer before the consumer needs it.

In Fig. 1, the edges of the chronogram of w_1 occur earlier than the corresponding ones of w_2 and w_3, so $w_1 \preceq w_2$ and $w_1 \preceq w_3$ but chronograms of w_2 and w_3 are interleaved, so $w_2 \npreceq w_3$ and $w_3 \npreceq w_2$.

We can define the supremum $\sqcup$ and the infimum $\sqcap$ of a set of infinite binary words $W = \{w_1, ..., w_n\}$ for the $\preceq$ relation:
$\forall j \geq 1$, $[\sqcup W]_j = \max([w_1]_j, ..., [w_n]_j)$ and $[\sqcap W]_j = \min([w_1]_j, ..., [w_n]_j)$.
For instance, in Fig. 1, $w_2 \sqcup w_3$ is equal to w_2 until instant 3 and then equal to w_3.
For all $w \in W$, $\sqcap W \preceq w \preceq \sqcup W$.

Definition 2 (synchronizability). *We say that two words w_1 and w_2 are synchronizable and we write $w_1 \bowtie w_2$ iff there exists $d_1, d_2 \in \mathbb{N}$ such that $w_1 \preceq 0^{d_2}.w_2$ and $w_2 \preceq 0^{d_1}.w_1$.*

By definition of $\preceq$, it ensures that the jth 1 of w_1 is at a bounded distance of the jth 1 of w_2:

Proposition 2. $w_1 \bowtie w_2 \Leftrightarrow \exists d_1, d_2 \in \mathbb{N}, \forall j \geq 1, -d_1 \leq [w_1]_j - [w_2]_j \leq d_2$

For instance, in Fig. 1, $w_1 \bowtie w_2$, but $w_1 \not\bowtie w_3$ and $w_2 \not\bowtie w_3$. When the producer of a flow communicates with the consumer through a buffer, it allows to verify that there exists a correct size for this buffer such that there will never be an overflow. Indeed, if $-d_1 \leq [w_1]_j - [w_2]_j \leq d_2$, the jth 1 of w_2 occurs at worst d_1 instants after the jth 1 of w_1. So when it occurs in w_2, at worst d_1 supplementary 1s have occurred in w_1, and the size $\max_i |w_1[0..i]|_1 - |w_2[0..i]|_1$ is lower or equal to d_1.

Definition 3 (subtyping). *The subtyping relation, written* $<:$ *is the conjunction of precedence and synchronizability:* $w_1 <: w_2 \overset{def}{=} w_1 \preceq w_2 \wedge w_1 \bowtie w_2$.

In fact, if the tokens are always produced before they are needed, and at a bounded distance of the time they are consumed, then the communication can be made synchronous by the insertion of a bounded size buffer. For instance, in Fig. 1, $w_1 <: w_2$.

Remark 2. By Def. of $\preceq$ and $\bowtie$, $w_1 <: w_2 \Leftrightarrow \exists d \in \mathbb{N}, \forall j \geq 1, 0 \leq [w_2]_j - [w_1]_j \leq d$

The *on* operator is monotonous with respect to the $<:$ relation:

Proposition 3 (*on* monotonicity).

$$w_1 <: w_2 \wedge w_1' <: w_2' \Rightarrow w_1 \text{ on } w_1' <: w_2 \text{ on } w_2'$$

All definitions of this section can be lifted to clocks (c) by computation of *not* and *on* operators.

3   Abstraction of Clocks

Abstracting an infinite binary word w consists in keeping only (1) the average distance T between two 1s in w (the asymptotic rate of 1s of w is $\frac{1}{T}$) and (2) two phases d and D that bound indexes of 1s in w, with respect to the perfect repartition of one 1 every T instants. We note this abstraction $[d, D]\,(T)$ and we call it *envelope.*

Abstract clocks can be envelopes or compositions of those. They are defined by the following grammar:[3]

$$ac ::= a \mid \mathbf{not}^\sim a \mid ac \ \mathbf{on}^\sim ac$$
$$a \ ::= [d, D]\,(T) \text{ with } d, D, T \in \mathbb{Q}, D \geq 0 \text{ and } T \geq 1$$

In this section, we explain what set of words is represented by an envelope and we show that this language is recognizable by a finite automaton. Then we define *on*$^\sim$ and *not*$^\sim$ operators that can be computed efficiently, allowing to always reduce an abstract clock to an envelope. Finally, we show that relations presented in Sec. 2 can be easily checked, and that buffer size can be efficiently computed.

---

[3] $\mathbb{Q}$ is the set of rational numbers.

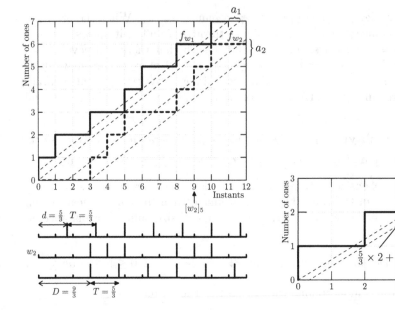

Fig. 2. If the rising edges of a word w all start between the lines of equation $\frac{i-d}{T}$ and $\frac{i-D}{T}$, then w is in the envelope $[d, D]\,(T)$, because for all $j \geq 0$, $T \times j + d \leq [w]_{j+1} \leq T \times j + D$. Thus w_1 is in $a_1 = \left[-\frac{2}{3}, 0\right]\left(\frac{5}{3}\right)$ and w_2 is in $a_2 = \left[\frac{5}{3}, \frac{9}{3}\right]\left(\frac{5}{3}\right)$. For instance, $\frac{5}{3} \times 4 + \frac{5}{3} \leq [w_2]_5 \leq \frac{5}{3} \times 4 + \frac{9}{3}$.

Fig. 3. The concretization set of $[0, \frac{1}{3}]\left(\frac{5}{3}\right)$ is empty: there is no valid discrete index for the third 1

3.1 Abstraction of Infinite Binary Words

An envelope $[d, D]\,(T)$, with $d, D, T \in \mathbb{Q}$, $D \geq 0$, $T \geq 1$, represents the following set of infinite binary words:

Definition 4 (concretization).

$$concr\left([d, D]\,(T)\right) \stackrel{def}{=} \{w, \ \forall j \geq 0, \ T \times j + d \leq [w]_{j+1} \leq T \times j + D\}$$

D will always be positive or null, otherwise we would have $[w]_1 < 0$. A $T < 1$ would represent words that have in average more that one 1 per instant, which are not considered (as mentioned in Sec. 2.1 $\forall j \geq 1$, $[w]_j < [w]_{j+1}$).

In 2D-chronograms, the envelope $[d, D]\,(T)$ can be represented by two lines that bound the rising edges starting points of the words it contains. The equations of these lines are $\frac{i-d}{T}$ and $\frac{i-D}{T}$. For instance, in Fig. 2 we can see the word $w_2 = 0(00111)$ and $a_2 = \left[\frac{5}{3}, \frac{9}{3}\right]\left(\frac{5}{3}\right)$, which is an abstraction of w_2.

The lines can be interpreted as "ideal clocks" such that from instant $\frac{5}{3}$ (resp. $\frac{9}{3}$), a tick occurs every $\frac{5}{3}$ of instant (i.e. each time the line crosses a y-axis discrete value). The word w_2 is bounded by these two ideal clocks (see the 1D-chronograms of Fig. 2).

Notice that every word staying at a bounded distance of its asymptotic rate can be abstracted by an envelope.

An envelope can always be normalized into the form $\left[\frac{k}{n}, \frac{K}{n}\right]\left(\frac{l}{n}\right)$ with $gcd(l, n) = 1$ without changing the concretization set:

Proposition 4 (normal form).
$\forall a = [d, D]\left(\frac{l'}{n'}\right),\ \exists k \in \mathbb{Z},\ K \in \mathbb{N},\ l \in \mathbb{N}, n \in \mathbb{N}^*\ with\ gcd(l, n) = 1$
such that $concr\left(\left[\frac{k}{n}, \frac{K}{n}\right]\left(\frac{l}{n}\right)\right) = concr(a)$.
$l = \frac{l'}{gcd(l',n')},\ n = \frac{n'}{gcd(l',n')},\ k = \lceil d \times n \rceil\ and\ K = \lfloor D \times n \rfloor.$[4]

The concretization set is empty if there exists a $j \geq 0$ such that there is no natural number between the bounds of the $(j+1)^{\text{th}}$ 1. Actually, in this case, there is no valid index for the $(j+1)^{\text{th}}$ 1.

Proposition 5 (empty concretization set).
Let $a = [d, D]\,(T)$ be an envelope.
$concr(a) = \varnothing \Leftrightarrow \exists j \geq 0,\ \{m \in \mathbb{N},\ T \times j + d \leq m \leq T \times j + D\} = \varnothing$
$ \Leftrightarrow \exists j \geq 0,\ \lceil T \times j + d \rceil > \lfloor T \times j + D \rfloor$

For instance, the concretization set of $\left[0, \frac{1}{3}\right]\left(\frac{5}{3}\right)$ is empty. Indeed, we can see in Fig. 3 that there is no valid index for the third 1, that must occur between the instants $\frac{5}{3} \times 2 + 0$ and $\frac{5}{3} \times 2 + \frac{1}{3}$.

The following proposition gives a sufficient condition on an envelope a, to ensure that its concretization set is not empty. If a is in normal form, this condition is necessary.

Proposition 6 (non-emptiness test).
Let $a = \left[\frac{k}{n}, \frac{K}{n}\right]\left(\frac{l}{n}\right)$ be an envelope. $\frac{K}{n} - \frac{k}{n} \geq 1 - \frac{1}{n} \Rightarrow concr(a) \neq \varnothing$
Additionally, if a is in normal form (i.e. $gcd(l, n) = 1$), then the converse holds.

A length $1 - \frac{1}{n}$ for the interval $\left[\frac{k}{n}, \frac{K}{n}\right]$ ensures that for all i, there is a natural number between the bounds of the jth 1 index. If furthermore the envelope is in normal form, then this length is the minimal length such that the concretization set is not empty.

The concretization set contains one and only one element iff for all j there is exactly one natural number between the lower bound and the upper bound, i.e. iff $\forall j, \lceil T \times j + d \rceil = \lfloor T \times j + D \rfloor$. Indeed, in that case there is only one choice for the index of each 1 of the binary word. This occurs when $D - d = 1 - \frac{1}{n}$, and only when this condition is verified in the case of abstract clocks in normal form. For instance, in Fig. 2, w_1 is the unique element in the concretization set of a_1. Indeed, $a_1 = \left[-\frac{2}{3}, 0\right]\left(\frac{5}{3}\right)$ and $0 - \left(-\frac{2}{3}\right) = 1 - \frac{1}{3}$. We can check on the 2D-chronogram that for each j on the y-axis, there is exactly one valid index i in the envelope.

Otherwise, the concretization set is infinite. In fact, in that case there are several integers between the bounds of certain indexes, thus several choices for them. Then, it is the case for an infinity of indexes. This occurs iff $\forall j \geq 0, \lceil T \times j + d \rceil \leq \lfloor T \times j + D \rfloor$ (non-emptiness condition) and $\exists j \geq 0, \lceil T \times j + d \rceil < \lfloor T \times j + D \rfloor$ (several choices for at most one index). This occurs when $D - d > 1 - \frac{1}{n}$, and

---

[4] $\lceil x \rceil$ (resp. $\lfloor x \rfloor$) is the notation for the ceiling (resp. floor) function.

only when this condition is verified in the case of envelopes in normal form. For instance in Fig. 2, if we consider the concretization set of a_2, we note that the fourth edge can occur at index 8 (as in w_2) or 7.

Remark 3. The chronogram never passes on the right of the envelope. Indeed, passing on the right of it leads to no more allow rising edges in the word, and thus to have clocks with a finite number of presence instants, which are not considered in this work.

Let us consider the concretization set of a simpler example: $a_4 = [2, 3]\,(2)$. $concr(a_4) = \{0^2(10), 0^2(1001), 0^2(0110), 0^2(01), 0^2(011001), 0010(01), \ldots\}$
To simplify the presentation, we only give here some periodic elements of the concretization set, but it contains an infinity of periodic and non-periodic infinite binary words, all of the form $00(10 + 01)^*$. We show in Sec. 3.2 a complete representation of the concretization sets.

The infimum and supremum of the concretization set (with respect to the $\preceq$ relation) are periodic binary words:

Proposition 7 ($\sqcap$, $\sqcup$). *Let $a = [d, D]\,(T)$ with $concr(a) \neq \varnothing$.*
$$w_{\inf} = \sqcap(concr(a)) \Leftrightarrow \forall j \geq 0, [w_{\inf}]_{j+1} = \lceil T \times j + d \rceil$$
$$w_{\sup} = \sqcup(concr(a)) \Leftrightarrow \forall j \geq 0, [w_{\sup}]_{j+1} = \lfloor T \times j + D \rfloor$$
If $T = \frac{l}{n}$, then the periodic pattern will be of length l and will contain n ones.

Proof. The formulas come from the definitions of $\sqcap$ and $\sqcup$. Let $T = \frac{l}{n}$. The word $w_{\inf}$ is periodic because for all $j \geq 0$, $[w_{\inf}]_{j+n+1} = \lceil \frac{l}{n} \times (j+n) + d \rceil = \lceil \frac{l}{n} \times j + d \rceil + l$, so $\forall j \geq n, [w_{\inf}]_{j+1} = [w_{\inf}]_{j+1-n} + l$. $\square$

For instance in Fig. 2, $w_2' = 00(10110)$ is the infimum of the concretization set of a_2, the rising edges occur as soon as possible, and $w_2'' = 00(01101)$ is the supremum, the rising edges occur as late as possible. As we illustrate in Sec. 3.2, these two particular clocks can be efficiently computed with a synchronous circuit with linear size (w.r.t $max(d, D, T)$) instead of the size of the period and they are perfectly balanced.

We have a partial order relation on abstract clocks:

Definition 5 (order relation $\sqsubseteq^\sim$). $ac_1 \sqsubseteq^\sim ac_2 \stackrel{def}{=} concr(ac_1) \subseteq concr(ac_2)$

It can be tested efficiently:

Proposition 8 ($\sqsubseteq^\sim$ **test**). *Let $a_1 = [d_1, D_1]\,(T_1)$ and $a_2 = [d_2, D_2]\,(T_2)$ be envelopes such that $concr(a_1) \neq \varnothing$ and $concr(a_2) \neq \varnothing$. Then,*
$$T_1 = T_2 \text{ and } [d_1, D_1] \subseteq [d_2, D_2] \Rightarrow a_1 \sqsubseteq^\sim a_2$$
Additionally, if a_1 and a_2 are in normal form, then the converse holds.

If we interpret this on the 2D-chronograms, $a_1 \sqsubseteq^\sim a_2$ if the lines representing the envelope of a_1 are between the ones of a_2.

Proof (Intuition). To stay between the lines of a_2, the lines of a_1 must have the same slope as the ones of a_2, thus $\frac{1}{T_2} = \frac{1}{T_1}$. Concerning the delays, the proof that the converse holds relies on the fact that a_1 and a_2 are in normal form. $\square$

We will write $abs(w)$ any function such that $abs(w) = a \Rightarrow w \in concr(a)$.

3.2   Abstract Clocks as Automata

We have seen that the concretization set of an abstract clock can be empty, contain a unique element or an infinity of elements. It can be represented by a deterministic finite automaton recognizing all binary words of the set, and only them. We first define an infinite automaton such that the language recognized is the concretization set, then we show that it is equivalent to a finite automaton.

Definition 6 (automaton associated to an envelope).
Let $a = [d, D] (T)$ be an envelope. The infinite automaton associated to a is $I_a = \langle Q, \Sigma, \delta, q_o \rangle$ with:
- *The set of states Q is a set of pairs $(i, j) \in \mathbb{N}^2$*
- *The initial state q_o is $(0, 0)$*
- *The alphabet Σ is $\{0, 1\}$*
- *The transition function δ is defined by:*
  $\delta(1, (i, j)) = (i + 1, j + 1)$ *if* $T \times j + d \leq i \leq T \times j + D$
  $\delta(0, (i, j)) = (i + 1, j)$ *if* $i + 1 \leq T \times j + D$
  It is undefined otherwise.

Proposition 9. *Let $a = [d, D] (T)$ be an envelope, and I_a its associated infinite automaton. The language recognized by I_a is $concr(a)$.*

The labels of the states correspond to coordinates in 2D-chronograms. The value i is the index of the current instant, and j is the number of 1s seen before the current instant. A transition from (i, j) to $(i + 1, j + 1)$ corresponds to a rising edge starting at (i, j), i.e. to the occurrence of the $(j + 1)^{\text{th}}$ 1 at index i. It can be taken if (i, j) is between the bounding lines, i.e. if $T \times j + d \leq i \leq T \times j + D$. A transition from (i, j) to $(i+1, j)$ corresponds to a flat edge in the chronogram. It can be taken if the destination state $(i + 1, j)$ is not on the right-side of the bounding lines (see Rem. 3), i.e. if $i + 1 \leq T \times j + D$ (it ensures that i is not the last valid index for the $(j + 1)^{\text{th}}$ 1).

Let us now define the set of reachable states. A state (i, j) is reachable if the two following conditions are verified: (1) if $j > 0$, it is possible that the jth 1 has occurred before i, i.e. the earliest possible index for the jth 1 ($T \times (j - 1) + d$) is smaller or equal to $i - 1$, and (2) it is still possible for the $(j + 1)^{\text{th}}$ 1 to occur, i.e. i is less or equal to the latest possible index for the $(j + 1)^{\text{th}}$ 1 ($T \times j + D$). So we can restrict the set of states to the set of reachable states which is

$$Q = \{(i, j) \in \mathbb{N}^2, (j = 0 \text{ or } d - T + 1 \leq i - T \times j) \text{ and } (i - T \times j \leq D)\}.$$

This infinite automaton can be transformed into a finite one, by noticing that the transition function only depends on the value of $i - T \times j$. We thus identify all states (i, j), (i', j') such that $i - T \times j = i' - T \times j'$. As states are such that $j = 0$ and $i \leq D$, or $d - T + 1 \leq i - T \times j \leq D$, the set of states obtained is finite. The transition function of the finite automaton A_a equivalent to the infinite automaton I_a is:

$\delta(1, (i, j)) = nf(i + 1, j + 1)$ if $T \times j + d \leq i \leq T \times j + D$
$\delta(0, (i, j)) = nf(i + 1, j)$ if $i + 1 \leq T \times j + D$
with $T = \frac{l}{n}$, $nf(i, j) = (i - x \times l, j - x \times n)$, $x = \max\{x \in \mathbb{N}, (x \times l \leq i) \wedge (x \times n \leq j)\}$

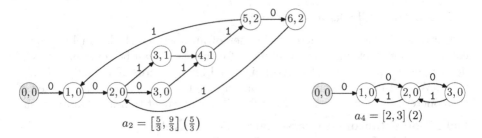

Fig. 4. Automata recognizing the clocks of $concr(a_2)$ and $concr(a_4)$

We thus are able to represent infinite concretization sets by finite automata. Fig. 4 shows the automaton associated to $a_2 = \left[\frac{5}{3}, \frac{9}{3}\right] \left(\frac{5}{3}\right)$ of Fig. 2, and to $a_4 = [2, 3]\, (2)$.

The infimum of the concretization set (with respect to $\preceq$) corresponds to the path taking in priority the 1-transitions, and the supremum corresponds to the path taking in priority the 0-transitions. All paths have the same asymptotic rate of 1s (e.g. choosing 1-transitions first only delays the corresponding 0-transitions).

It is interesting because it allows to check dynamically or statically (with model checking) that a clock is in the envelope specified by the user, and throw an error message if it's not the case. Note that it is not necessary to build explicitly the automaton. Here is a Lustre program that checks that a clock clk is in an envelope $\left[\frac{k}{n}, \frac{K}{n}\right] \left(\frac{l}{n}\right)$.

```
node norm(const l, n: int; i, j: int) returns (ni, nj: int);
let
    (ni, nj) = if i >= l and j >= n then (i - l, j - n) else (i,j);
tel
node check(const k, K, l, n: int; clk: bool) returns (ok: bool);
var i, j, v: int;
let
    (i,j) = (0,0) -> pre norm(l, n, i+1, if clk then j + 1 else j);
    v = i * n - j * l;
    ok = if clk then (k <= v and v <= K) else v <= K - n;
tel
```

The function **norm** incrementally computes the normal form of the state (i,j) using l and n. The function **check** maintains the value of the current state. It is initialized to (0,0), then at each instant, i is incremented, and j is incremented if the clock clk was true at the preceding instant. The normalization function is applied to the new state. Then, if the current value of clk is true, we check that a 1-transition is allowed, and in the contrary case, we check that a 0-transition is allowed.

The same principle allows to generate clocks within a certain abstraction, for simulation purposes. To generate the earliest clock we take a 1-transition each time it is allowed.

```
node early(const k, K, l, n: int) returns (clk: bool);
var i, j, v: int;
let
   (i, j) = (0,0) -> pre norm(l, n, i+1, if clk then j + 1 else j);
   v = i * n - j * l;
   clk = (k <= v and v <= K);
tel
```

Similarly, to generate the latest clock we take a 1-transition each time a 0-transition is not allowed.

3.3   Abstract Operators

We define in this section operators on envelopes, corresponding to operators on words defined in Sec. 2. Computing these operators in the abstract domain is in constant time and memory. Moreover, they are correct, i.e. the result of the operation in the abstract domain contains the result of the operation in the concrete one.

Definition 7 ($on^\sim$ operator).
We define an abstract on operator, written $on^\sim$:

$$[d_1, D_1] (T_1) \; on^\sim \; [d_2, D_2] (T_2) = [d_{12}, D_{12}] (T_{12})$$

with: $T_{12} = T_1 \times T_2, \quad d_{12} = d_1 + d_2 \times T_1, \quad D_{12} = D_1 + D_2 \times T_1.$

We have seen in Sec. 2 that the elements of $w_1 \; on \; w_2$ are the elements of w_2, traversed at the pace of the $1s$ of w_1. So if the distance between the $1s$ of w_2 is on average equal to T_2, and the distance between those of w_1 is on average equal to T_1, then the distance between the $1s$ of $w_1 \; on \; w_2$ is on average equal to $T_2 \times T_1$. Sampling w_1 with w_2 keeps intact the delays of w_1, and adds to it the delay of w_2 multiplied by T_1, because w_2 is traversed at the pace T_1.

Thus, this abstract operator has the expected property: for all words of the respective concretization sets, the result of the concrete on operation is in the concretization set of the result of the abstract operation.

Proposition 10.
$\forall w_1 \in concr(a_1), \; \forall w_2 \in concr(a_2), \; w_1 \; on \; w_2 \in concr(a_1 \; on^\sim \; a_2)$

Remark 4. The fact that a_1 and a_2 are in normal form does not necessary lead to a result $a_3 = a_1 \; on^\sim \; a_2$ in normal form.

Definition 8 ($not^\sim$ operator).
We define an abstract not operator, written $not^\sim$:

$$not^\sim \; ([d, D] (T)) = \left[\frac{-D+1}{T-1}, \max\left(0, 1 - \frac{d}{T-1} \right) \right] \left(\frac{T}{T-1} \right)$$

with $T > 1$.

The intuition behind this formula is the following. Let $a = [d, D] \left(\frac{l}{n} \right)$ and $w \in concr(a)$. It means that over l elements of the word, there are on average n $1s$ in w. So over l instants, there are on average $(l-n)$ $0s$ in w, thus $(l-n)$ $1s$ in $not \; w$.

The average distance between two $1s$ in $not\ w$ is $\frac{l}{l-n}$, i.e. $\frac{T}{T-1}$. Concerning the delays, the maximal amount of $0s$ that appear before the first 1 in w is defined by D, and the maximal amount of $1s$ that appear before the first 0 in w is function of d. Thus it is not surprising that in the negation of w, the lower bound of the interval is function of D, and the upper bound of the interval is function of d.

This abstract operator is correct:

Proposition 11. $\forall w \in concr(a),\ not\ w \in concr(not^{\sim} a)$

Remark 5. If a is in normal form, then by definition of the $not^{\sim}$ operator, $a' = not^{\sim} a$ is also in normal form.

Remark 6. Applying the abstract negation looses some information about the abstracted word: $a \sqsubseteq^{\sim} not^{\sim} not^{\sim} a$. It is due to the fact that the abstraction can represent words that will eventually begin with d $0s$, by setting the minimum of the interval to d, but cannot represent their negation without loss of information, i.e. words that will eventually begin with d $1s$ (D cannot be negative).

In fact, only the first negation looses information: $not^{\sim} a = not^{\sim} not^{\sim} not^{\sim} a$. For example, if $a = [2,3] \left(\frac{5}{3}\right)$ then $not^{\sim} a = [-3,0] \left(\frac{5}{2}\right)$, $not^{\sim} not^{\sim} a = \left[\frac{2}{3},3\right] \left(\frac{5}{3}\right)$ and $not^{\sim} not^{\sim} not^{\sim} a = [-3,0] \left(\frac{5}{2}\right) = not^{\sim} a$.

3.4   Abstraction of a Clock

Given an abstraction of words ($abs(w)$), we can compute the abstraction of clocks composed by these words. It is recursively defined as follows:

Definition 9 (clocks abstraction function).

$$abs(not\ w) \stackrel{def}{=} not^{\sim} abs(w)$$
$$abs(c_1\ on\ c_2) \stackrel{def}{=} abs(c_1)\ on^{\sim} abs(c_2)$$

This abstraction of clocks is correct:

Proposition 12. $c \in concr(abs(c))$

3.5   Abstract Relations

We now define the relations on envelopes, corresponding to the relations on words defined in Sec. 2. A relation is verified in the abstract domain if it is verified for all couple of words in the respective concretization sets.

Definition 10 (abstract synchronizability).
$$ac_1 \bowtie^{\sim} ac_2 \stackrel{def}{=} \forall w_1 \in concr(ac_1), w_2 \in concr(ac_2),\ w_1 \bowtie w_2$$

We are able to check the synchronizability on envelopes:

Proposition 13 (synchronizability test).
$$[d_1, D_1](T_1) \bowtie^{\sim} [d_2, D_2](T_2) \Leftrightarrow T_1 = T_2$$

Indeed, if two clocks stay at a bounded distance of there asymptotic rate, then the $1s$ of the first clock stay at a bounded distance of the $1s$ of the second clock iff their rates are equal.

Remark 7. A corollary of this proposition is that $\bowtie^\sim$ is reflexive, so every abstract clock is synchronizable with itself. That means that in a concretization set, all couple of words are synchronizable.

The abstraction contains all necessary information to exactly check the synchronizability of two clocks on their abstraction:

Proposition 14. $abs(c_1) \bowtie^\sim abs(c_2) \Leftrightarrow c_1 \bowtie c_2$

Proof. From Rem. 7 and by transitivity of $\bowtie$. □

Definition 11 (abstract precedence).
$$ac_1 \preceq^\sim ac_2 \overset{def}{=} \forall w_1 \in concr(ac_1), w_2 \in concr(ac_2), \ w_1 \preceq w_2$$

The precedence on abstract clocks is verified iff the $1s$ of the latest concrete clock in the first envelope arrive before or at the same instant as the $1s$ of the earliest concrete clock in the second envelope:

Proposition 15.
Let $a_1 = [d_1, D_1](T_1)$ and $a_2 = [d_2, D_2](T_2)$.
$$
\begin{aligned}
a_1 \preceq^\sim a_2 \ &\Leftrightarrow\ \sqcup(concr(a_1)) \preceq \sqcap(concr(a_2)) \\
&\Leftrightarrow\ \forall j \geq 0, [\sqcup(concr(a_1))]_{j+1} \leq [\sqcap(concr(a_2))]_{j+1} \\
&\Leftrightarrow\ \forall j \geq 0, \lfloor T_1 \times j + D_1 \rfloor \leq \lceil T_2 \times j + d_2 \rceil
\end{aligned}
$$

When abstract clocks are synchronizable, Prop. 15 can be checked by a sufficient condition. If abstract clocks are in normal form, this condition is also necessary.

Proposition 16 (precedence test).
Let $a_1 = \left[\frac{k_1}{n}, \frac{K_1}{n}\right]\left(\frac{l}{n}\right)$ and $a_2 = \left[\frac{k_2}{n}, \frac{K_2}{n}\right]\left(\frac{l}{n}\right)$ be two envelopes. Then:
$$\frac{K_1}{n} - \frac{k_2}{n} \leq 1 - \frac{1}{n} \Rightarrow a_1 \preceq^\sim a_2$$
Additionally, the converse holds if a_1 and a_2 are in normal form (i.e. here $gcd(l, n) = 1$).

Proof (Intuition). An overlap of less than $1 - \frac{1}{n}$ between $\left[\frac{k_1}{n}, \frac{K_1}{n}\right]$ and $\left[\frac{k_2}{n}, \frac{K_2}{n}\right]$ ensures that $\forall j \geq 0, \lfloor \frac{l}{n} \times j + \frac{K_1}{n} \rfloor \leq \lceil \frac{l}{n} \times j + \frac{k_2}{n} \rceil$. If furthermore a_1 and a_2 are in normal form, then this length is the maximal overlap such that this property is verified. □

To check the precedence relation between clocks on their abstraction, the lack of information about the positions of the $1s$ enforces us to consider the worst case of concretization. This verification on the abstraction is thus correct, but not complete with respect to the verification on the concrete clocks:

Proposition 17. $abs(c_1) \preceq^\sim abs(c_2) \Rightarrow c_1 \preceq c_2$

We now define the subtyping relation on envelopes:

Definition 12 (abstract subtyping relation).
$$ac_1 <:^\sim ac_2 \overset{def}{=} \forall w_1 \in concr(ac_1), \ w_2 \in concr(ac_2), \ w_1 <: w_2$$

Proposition 18. $a_1 <:^\sim a_2 \Leftrightarrow a_1 \bowtie^\sim a_2 \wedge a_1 \preceq^\sim a_2$

3.6   Computing Buffers Size

To synchronize producers and consumers, buffers are inserted. The question addressed here is the buffer size needed to store a flow produced on a clock of abstraction ac_1, and consumed on a clock of abstraction ac_2, with $ac_1 <:^\sim ac_2$.

Proposition 19. *Let* $a_1 = \left[\frac{k_1}{n}, \frac{K_1}{n}\right]\left(\frac{l}{n}\right)$ *and* $a_2 = \left[\frac{k_2}{n}, \frac{K_2}{n}\right]\left(\frac{l}{n}\right)$ *be two envelopes such that* $a_1 <:^\sim a_2$. *The minimal buffer needed to be able to communicate from any clock of abstraction* a_1 *to any clock of abstraction* a_2 *is of size:*

$$size(a_1, a_2) = \left\lceil \frac{K_2 - (n-1) - k_1}{l} \right\rceil$$

Proof (Intuition). The size of buffer needed to communicate from any clock of a_1 to any clock of a_2 is the size needed to communicate from the earliest clock of a_1 ($\sqcap(concr(a_1))$) to the latest clock of a_2 ($\sqcup(concr(a_2))$). The formula comes from the definition of the calculus of $size$ on concrete clocks and the formulas of $|w[0..i]|_1$ for the infimum and supremum of the concretization sets.   □

4   Discussion and Related Work

Back to Periodic Clocks. To be able to check the subtyping relation and compute buffer sizes, the exclusive use of periodic binary words has been proposed in [10].[5]

The periodic behavior of those words allows to statically compute the **on** and **not** operators (definitions become algorithms). In the same way, it allows to check the precedence relation (if it is verified until a certain rank, it will be verified forever) and the synchronizability relation which is equivalent to the equality of rates of $1s$ in the periodic behavior. Finally, the definition of the minimal buffers size also becomes an algorithm.

However, it can be interesting to avoid exact computations on periodic words because of their cost: for instance, the **on** operation needs a complete traversal of elements of the periods we compose. Moreover if operands have not a compatible size, the result is much longer that the operands. In contexts like video applications, this cost is a problem because the periods length can be huge: in the example cited in [10], a classical downscaler, the output clock has a periodic behavior of length 17280. Adding vertical blanking periods leads to a periodic behavior of size 2073600 (the size of a high definition frame). Computing on abstract values gives a solution to this drawback.

Notice that when periodic clocks are used, the abstraction of words can be automatically computed:

Proposition 20 (periodic binary words abstraction function).
Let $w = u(v)$ *be an infinite binary word.* $abs(w) = [d, D](T)$ *with* $T = \frac{|v|}{|v|_1}$, $d = \min_{j=0..(|u|_1+|v|_1-1)}([w]_{j+1} - T \times j)$, $D = \max_{j=0..(|u|_1+|v|_1-1)}([w]_{j+1} - T \times j)$.

---

[5] Those periodic binary words have been used since then to specify statically computed periodic schedules for Latency Insensitive Design [18].

For example, the abstraction of the downscaler's output clock is:

$$abs((10100100) \; on \; 0^{3600}(1) \; on \; (1^{720}0^{720}1^{720}0^{720}0^{720}1^{720}0^{720}0^{720}1^{720}))$$
$$= \left[-\tfrac{2}{3}, 0\right] \left(\tfrac{8}{3}\right) \; on^{\sim} \; [3600, 3600] \, (1) \; on^{\sim} \; \left[\tfrac{-4315}{4}, \tfrac{3600}{4}\right] \left(\tfrac{9}{4}\right) = [6723, 12000] \, (6)$$

A Particular Case of Periodic Clocks. Affine clocks, presented in [19,20], are a subset of periodic clocks of the form $0^{\phi}(10^{l-1})$. They have been used to extend the clock calculus of the synchronous data-flow language SIGNAL [21], in the context of hardware/software co-design. Thanks to the simple regular form of those clocks, the extended clock calculus of SIGNAL has a more powerful unification algorithm.

In the case of affine clocks, the abstraction mechanism presented in Sec. 3 is correct and complete. Abstracting a word is trivial: $abs(0^{\phi}(10^{l-1})) = [\phi, \phi] \, (l)$ and doesn't loose any information. Indeed, the concretization set contains only one element (as specified in Sec. 3, $\phi - \phi = 1 - \tfrac{1}{1}$). Moreover, $abs(c) \; on^{\sim} \; abs(c')$ has a singleton concretization set: $c \; on \; c'$, and is in normal form. Clocks being in normal form and concretization sets being singletons, testing precedence relations on the abstraction is equivalent to testing them on the concrete clocks. As it is also the case for the synchronizability relation, we have $abs(c) <:^{\sim} abs(c') \Leftrightarrow c <: c'$.

5   Conclusion

This paper generalizes the classical notion of clocks in synchronous data-flow languages by allowing to deal with sets of clocks. This is based on the introduction of *clock envelopes* which define intervals of clocks up to bounded buffering. We have focused on the algebraic properties of those clocks and illustrated their expressive power. The motivation behind them is essentially pragmatic and gives some answer to the need to model jittering phenomena, execution time and more generally communication through bounded buffering. The real novelty is to deal with quantitative properties during the clock calculus instead of simply strict synchrony as done usually. We have experimented the use of these clocks on several examples (e.g., video picture-and-picture or filters in software defined radio). The extension of the existing clock calculus of LUCID SYNCHRONE [22] compiler is under way.

Acknowledgements. Pascal Raymond showed us an unexpected (and very elegant) use of the Lustre compiler to generate clocks within an envelope. We also thank the anonymous reviewers for their helpful comments. The figures have been programmed in Mlpost, we acknowledge Johannes Kanig and Stéphane Lescuyer for their help.

References

1. Benveniste, A., Caspi, P., Edwards, S., Halbwachs, N., Le Guernic, P., de Simone, R.: The synchronous languages 12 years later. Proceedings of the IEEE 91(1) (January 2003)
2. Benveniste, A., Berry, G.: The synchronous approach to reactive and real-time systems, pp. 147–159. Kluwer Academic Publishers, Norwell (2002)

3. Milner, R.: Calculi for synchrony and asynchrony. Theoretical Computer Science 25(3), 267–310 (1983)
4. Arnold, A.: Systèmes de transitions et sémantique des processus communicants. Masson (1992)
5. Colaço, J.L., Pouzet, M.: Clocks as First Class Abstract Types. In: Third International Conference on Embedded Software, Philadelphia, USA (2003)
6. Amagbegnon, T., Besnard, L., Guernic, P.L.: Implementation of the data-flow synchronous language signal. In: Programming Languages Design and Implementation, pp. 163–173. ACM, New York (1995)
7. Caspi, P., Curic, A., Maignan, A., Sofronis, C., Tripakis, S.: Translating Discrete-Time Simulink to Lustre. ACM Transactions on Embedded Computing Systems (2005); Special Issue on Embedded Software
8. Scicos, http://www-rocq.inria.fr/scicos
9. Milner, R.: A theory of type polymorphism in programming. Journal of Computer and System Sciences 17(3), 348–375 (1978)
10. Cohen, A., Duranton, M., Eisenbeis, C., Pagetti, C., Plateau, F., Pouzet, M.: N-Synchronous Kahn Networks: a Relaxed Model of Synchrony for Real-Time Systems. In: ACM International Conference on Principles of Programming Languages (2006)
11. Lee, E., Messerschmitt, D.: Synchronous dataflow. IEEE Trans. Comput. 75(9) (1987)
12. Buck, J., Ha, S., Lee, E., Messerschmitt, D.: Ptolemy: A framework for simulating and prototyping heterogeneous systems. International Journal of computer Simulation (1994); special issue on Simulation Software Development
13. Vuillemin, J.: On Circuits and Numbers. Technical report, Digital, Paris Research Laboratory (1993)
14. Curic, A.: Implementing Lustre Programs on Distributed Platforms with Real-time Constraints. Ph.D thesis, Université Joseph Fourier (2005)
15. Sofronis, C.: Embedded Code Generation from High-level Heterogeneous Components. Ph.D thesis, Université Joseph Fourier (2006)
16. Halbwachs, N., Mandel, L.: Simulation and verification of asynchronous systems by means of a synchronous model. In: Sixth International Conference on Application of Concurrency to System Design, Turku, Finland (2006)
17. Krstic, S., Cortadella, J., Kishinevsky, M., O'Leary, J.: Synchronous elastic networks. In: Proceedings of the Formal Methods in Computer Aided Design, Washington, DC, USA, pp. 19–30. IEEE Computer Society, Los Alamitos (2006)
18. Boucaron, J., de Simone, R., Millo, J.V.: Formal methods for scheduling of latency-insensitive designs. EURASIP Journal on Embedded Systems (1), 8 (2007)
19. Smarandache, I.M., Guernic, P.L.: Affine transformations in SIGNAL and their application in the specification and validation of real-time systems. In: ARTS, pp. 233–247 (1997)
20. Smarandache, I.M., Gautier, T., Guernic, P.L.: Validation of mixed SIGNAL-ALPHA real-time systems through affine calculus on clock synchronisation constraints. In: World Congress on Formal Methods, vol. (2), pp. 1364–1383 (1999)
21. Benveniste, A., Guernic, P.L., Jacquemot, C.: Synchronous programming with events and relations: the SIGNAL language and its semantics. Sci. Comput. Program. 16(2), 103–149 (1991)
22. Pouzet, M.: Lucid Synchrone, version 3. Tutorial and reference manual. Université Paris-Sud, LRI (April 2006) Distribution,
http://www.lri.fr/~pouzet/lucid-synchrone

From Authorization Logics to Types for Authorization

Radha Jagadeesan

School of CTI, College of CDM, DePaul University, Chicago, IL 60604, USA

Abstract. Web services and mashups are collaborative distributed systems built by assembling components from multiple independent applications. Such composition and aggregation involves subtle combinations of authorization, delegation, and trust. Consequently, how to do so securely remains a topic of current research.

Authorization logics elegantly record the change of context from sender to receiver when messages are transmitted in distributed systems. Such logics are well suited to specify security policies since they satisfy a non-interference property: namely, that the dependencies between the statements of principals arise solely from the user-defined non-logical axioms. Building on the prior work of Abadi, Abadi and Garg, and Garg and Pfenning, we describe a semantic approach to such non-interference results.

Authorization logics constitute the logical foundations of our type-and-effect system for TAPIDO, a calculus of distributed objects. The effects are "object-centric" and record the rights associated with the object. Object effects are validated at the point of creation, ensuring that the security policy permits the creation of the object. When such an object is received, the associated rights, perhaps constrained by provenance information, are delegated as a benefit accrued to the recipient. A TAPIDO program is safe if every object creation at runtime is in conformance with the security policy of the system. Well-typed programs are safe even in the face of dishonest opponent processes that aim to subvert the global authorization policy by creating unauthorized objects.

This talk is based on joint work with Abramsky and joint work with Cirillo, Pitcher and Riely.

G. Ramalingam (Ed.): APLAS 2008, LNCS 5356, p. 255, 2008.
© Springer-Verlag Berlin Heidelberg 2008

Interface Types for Haskell

Peter Thiemann and Stefan Wehr

Institut für Informatik, Universität Freiburg, Germany
{thiemann,wehr}@informatik.uni-freiburg.de

Abstract. Interface types are a useful concept in object-oriented programming languages like Java or C#. A clean programming style advocates relying on interfaces without revealing their implementation.

Haskell's type classes provide a closely related facility for stating an interface separately from its implementation. However, there are situations in which no simple mechanism exists to hide the identity of the implementation type of a type class. This work provides such a mechanism through the integration of lightweight interface types into Haskell.

The extension is non-intrusive as no additional syntax is needed and no existing programs are affected. The implementation extends the treatment of higher-rank polymorphism in production Haskell compilers.

1 Introduction

Interfaces in object-oriented programming languages and type classes in Haskell are closely related: both define the types of certain operations without revealing their implementations. In Java, the name of an interface also acts as an *interface type*, whereas the name of a type class can only be used to constrain types. Interface types are a proven tool for ensuring data abstraction and information hiding. In many cases, Haskell type classes can serve the same purpose, but there are situations for which the solutions available in Haskell have severe drawbacks.

Interface types provide a simple and elegant solution in these situations. A modest extension to Haskell provides the simplicity and elegance of interface types: simply allow programmers to use the name of a type class as a first-class type. The compiler then translates such interface types into existentially quantified data types [11] (available in several Haskell compilers such as GHC [3] or Hugs [5]) and generates all the boilerplate code necessary for dealing with these existential types. To keep type inference manageable, we follow the same strategy as type inference algorithms for rank-n types [14] and require type annotations if interface types should be introduced.

Contributions and Outline. A *case study* (Section 2.1) compares several approaches to information hiding in Haskell. It demonstrates that interface types provide the simplest solution. Two further example applications (Section 2.2 and Section 2.3) underline the advantages of interface types.

In Section 3, we *formalize interface types* as an extension of a type system and inference algorithm for rank-n types introduced by Peyton Jones and others [14]. The resulting inference algorithm (explained in Section 4 in terms of a bidirectional type system) is close to the one used in GHC.

G. Ramalingam (Ed.): APLAS 2008, LNCS 5356, pp. 256–272, 2008.

A *prototype implementation* of the type inference algorithm is available.[1] We have developed it as an extension of Peyton Jones's implementation of rank-n type inference [14].

Section 5 sketches the translation to System F, the second component needed for implementing interface types in a compiler. Sections 6 and 7 discuss related work and conclude.

2   Motivation

To motivate the need for interface types, we present the results of a case study that compares different approaches to information hiding in the design of a library for database access (Section 2.1). In two additional examples, we show how interface types help in designing a library for sets and graphical user interfaces (Section 2.2 and Section 2.3, respectively).

2.1   Interface Types for Database Access

Consider a programmer designing a Haskell library for accessing databases. Ideally, the public interface of the library makes no commitment to a particular database system and users of the library should not be able to create dependencies on a particular database system (exception to both: opening new connections). Thus, all datatypes describing connections to the database, query results, cursors, and so on should be abstract, and the only way to manipulate them should be through operations provided in the library.

Record Types as Interface Types. As a concrete example, consider the HDBC package [4]. Up to version 1.0.1.2, HDBC provided database operations through a record type similar to the following:[2]

```
module Database.HDBC (Connection(..)) where
data Connection = Connection { dbQuery :: String -> IO [[String]] }
```

HDBC comes with a number of *drivers* that provide support for a specific database system through an operation to create a connection:

```
module Database.HDBC.PostgreSQL (connectPSQL) where
connectPSQL :: String -> IO Connection
```

```
module Database.HDBC.Sqlite3 (connectSqlite3) where
connectSqlite3    :: FilePath -> IO Connection
```

Once a connection is established, the `Connection` datatype ensures that application code works independently of the specific database system. Thus, the design just outlined fulfills the requirements at the beginning of this paragraph.

---

[1] http://www.informatik.uni-freiburg.de/~thiemann/haskell/IFACE/impl.tgz

[2] We only show those parts of the code relevant to our problem. Modules whose names start with `MyHDBC` are not part of HDBC.

There is, however, one major disadvantage: the set of database operations is fixed and cannot be extended easily. Suppose that we want to add support for PostgreSQL's [16] asynchronous events.[3] We cannot extend the existing `Connection` datatype because not all database systems support asynchronous events. Thus, we need to create a new datatype:

```
module MyHDBC (ConnectionAE(..)) where
data ConnectionAE = ConnectionAE { dbQuery' :: String -> IO [[String]],
                                   listen   :: String -> IO (),
                                   notify   :: String -> IO () }
```

But now functions operating on `Connection` do not work with `ConnectionAE`, although the latter type supports, in principle, all operations of the former.

Type Classes as Interface Predicates. For this reason, HDBC version 1.1.0.0 replaces the datatype `Connection` with a type class `IConnection`:

```
module Database.HDBC (IConnection(..)) where
class IConnection c where
  dbQuery :: c -> String -> IO [[String]]
```

Support for asynchronous events is now modeled through a subclass of `IConnection`:

```
module MyHDBC (IConnectionAE(..)) where
class IConnection c => IConnectionAE c where
  listen :: c -> String -> IO ()
  notify :: c -> String -> IO ()
```

This way, functions with signatures of the form `IConnection c => .. -> c -> ..` also work when passing an instance of `IConnectionAE` as the c argument.

The classes `Connection` and `IConnectionAE` are *not* types, but serve as predicates on type variables. Thus, the connect function provided by a database driver has to return the concrete connection type. For example:

```
module Database.HDBC.Sqlite3 (ConnectionSqlite3(), connectSqlite3) where
data ConnectionSqlite3 = ConnectionSqlite3 {
      sqlite3Query :: String -> IO [[String]] }
instance IConnection ConnectionSqlite3 where
  dbQuery = sqlite3Query
connectSqlite3 :: FilePath -> IO ConnectionSqlite3
```

A concrete return type violates our requirement that application code should not be able to create a dependency on a particular database system: The driver module `Database.HDBC.Sqlite3` exports the datatype `ConnectionSqlite3`. Application code may use this type in function signatures, data type declarations etc.

Is there a Haskell solution to this problem? Simply hiding the `ConnectionSqlite3` type inside the `Database.HDBC.Sqlite3` module is not enough, because a type name

---

[3] PostgreSQL provides a `listen` and a `notify` operation: `listen` allows processes to register for some event identified by a string, `notify` signals the occurrence of an event.

is useful for type specifications. There are at least two solutions to this problem, both of which involve advanced typing constructs.

Existential Types as Interface Types. The first solution uses algebraic datatypes with existential types [11].[4]

```
module Database.HDBC (IConnection(..), ExIConnection(..)) where
-- class IConnection as before
data ExIConnection =
    forall c . IConnection c => ExIConnection c
instance IConnection ExIConnection where
  dbQuery (ExIConnection c) = dbQuery c

module MyHDBC (IConnectionAE(..), ExIConnectionAE(..)) where
-- class IConnectionAE as before
data ExIConnectionAE = forall c . IConnectionAE c => ExIConnectionAE c
instance IConnection ExIConnectionAE where
  dbQuery (ExIConnectionAE c) = dbQuery c
instance IConnectionAE ExIConnectionAE where
  listen (ExIConnectionAE c) = listen c
  notify (ExIConnectionAE c) = notify c
```

With this solution, the module `Database.HDBC.Sqlite3` no longer exports the type `ConnectionSqlite3` and the return type of `connectSqlite3` becomes `ExIConnection`.

However, this solution has some drawbacks:

- A value of type `ExIConnectionAE` cannot be used where a value of type `ExIConnection` is expected. Instead, we have to unpack and re-pack the existential type.
- Writing and maintaining the boilerplate for the datatype declarations `ExIConnection` and `ExIConnectionAE`, as well as the corresponding instance declarations is tedious, especially when the class hierarchy becomes larger.

Rank-2 Types as Interface Types. The second solution is to provide a function that passes the newly created connection to a continuation. Thanks to higher-rank polymorphism [14], the continuation can be given a sensible type. With this approach, the driver for PostgreSQL would look like this:

```
module MyHDBC.PostgreSQL (runWithPSQL) where
data ConnectionPSQL = ConnectionPSQL { psqlQuery
:: String -> IO [[String]],
                                      psqlListen :: String -> IO (),
                                      psqlNotify :: String -> IO () }
instance IConnection ConnectionPSQL where
  dbQuery = psqlQuery
instance IConnectionAE ConnectionPSQL where
  listen = psqlListen
```

---

[4] GHC uses the keyword **forall** for existential quantifiers.

```
   notify = psqlNotify
connectPSQL :: String -> IO ConnectionPSQL
runWithPSQL :: String -> (forall c. IConnectionAE c => c -> IO t) -> IO t
runWithPSQL s f = do c <- connectPSQL s
                     f c
```

Thanks to the generic instantiation relation for types, this function allows for some unexpected flexibility. Clearly, a function of type

```
psqlWorker :: IConnectionAE c => c -> IO Result
```

can serve as a (second) parameter to `runWithPSQL`. But also

```
dbWorker :: IConnection c => c -> IO Result
```

is a type correct second argument to `runWithPSQL`. The flexibility of this approach is appealing, but writing the user code using continuations can be demanding and may obfuscate the code.

Which of the two solutions does HDBC choose? The answer is: *none*. It seems that the benefit of hiding the concrete connection type does not outweigh the complexity of the two solutions.

Type Classes as Interface Types. We propose an alternative solution that is lightweight and easy to use. We consider the name C of a type class as an *interface type* that denotes some unknown instance of the class. Thus, the interface type C stands for the bounded existential type $\exists c . C\, c \Rightarrow c$.

For example, the interface type `IConnection` represents some unknown instance of the type class `IConnection`. Here is some code for an Sqlite3 driver module following this approach:

```
module Database.HDBC.Sqlite3 (connectSqlite3) where
data ConnectionSqlite3 = ConnectionSqlite3 {
        sqlite3Query :: String -> IO [[String]] }
instance IConnection ConnectionSqlite3 where
  dbQuery = sqlite3Query
connectSqlite3 :: FilePath -> IO IConnection
connectSqlite3 = internConnectSqlite3
internConnectSqlite3 :: FilePath -> IO ConnectionSqlite3
```

Transferring the subclass hierarchy on type classes to a "more polymorphic than" relation on interface types allows values of type `IConnectionAE` to be passed to functions accepting a parameter of type `IConnection` without any explicit conversions. This approach yields the same flexibility with respect to parameter passing as with type classes and continuations using rank-2 types (but without requiring the use of continuations).

Thus, the solution combines the advantages of type classes approach (extensibility, flexibility with respect to parameter passing, ease to use) with the additional benefit that application code cannot directly refer to the implementation type of a connection. Moreover, there is no need to write boilerplate code as with existential types wrapped in data types and there is no need to use continuations as with the rank-2 types approach.

2.2   Interface Types for Sets

Consider a programmer designing a Haskell library for manipulating sets. The library should consist of a public interface for common set operations and various implementations of this interface. For simplicity, we consider only sets of integers with the operations `empty`, `insert`, `contains`, and `union`. We can easily encode the first three operations as methods of a type class `IntSet`:

```
class IntSet s where
  empty    :: s
  insert   :: s -> Int -> s
  contains :: s -> Int -> Bool
```

The signature of the `union` operation is not straightforward, because it should be possible to union two sets of *different* implementations. Thus, the second parameter of `union` should be an arbitrary `IntSet` instance, leading to the signature `union :: IntSet s' => s -> s' -> ?`. But what should the result type be?

When implementing sets using lists, we would like it to be `s'`:

```
instance IntSet [Int] where
  empty      = []
  insert l i = i:l
  contains l i = i 'elem' l
  union l s' = foldl insert s' l
```

When implementing sets using characteristic functions, we would like it to be `s`:

```
instance IntSet (Int -> Bool) where
  empty      = \i -> False
  insert f i = \j -> i == j || f j
  contains f i = f i
  union f s' = \i -> contains f i || contains s' i
```

In general, the result type of `union` is some unknown instance of `IntSet`, which is exactly the kind of interface type introduced in Section 2.1. This choice avoids the declaration of an extra algebraic data type with existential quantification, writing boilerplate instance definitions, and packing and unpacking the existential type. Instead, we simply define the signature of `union` as

```
-- inside type class IntSet
union :: s -> IntSet -> IntSet
```

and get the rest for free. Especially, the two instance declarations for `[Int]` and `Int -> Bool` now become valid.

2.3   Interface Types for Graphical User Interfaces

Consider a programmer designing a Haskell library for writing graphical user interfaces. The library should provide several different kinds of widgets: a text input widget, a button widget, a table widget, and so on. It is reasonable to abstract over the common operations of widgets with a type class:

```
class Widget w where
  draw    :: w -> IO ()
  minSize :: w -> (Int,Int)
  name    :: w -> String
```

Some widgets provide additional features. A typical example is focus handling:

```
class Widget w => FocusWidget w where
  setFocus   :: w -> IO ()
  unsetFocus :: w -> IO ()
```

As an example, let us write the representation of a table widget. A table widget is essentially a list of rows, where each row consists of a list of widgets. Additionally, a table stores a second list of all focusable widgets. Clearly, the list of widgets in a row and the list of focusable widgets are heterogeneous. The element types just happen to be instances of Widget or FocusWidget. Hence, we need some kind of existential type, again.

As in Section 2.1 and Section 2.2, algebraic datatypes with existential quantifiers are an option. Here is the code with a function that extracts all rows from a table containing at least one focusable widget.

```
data ExWidget      = forall w . Widget w => ExWidget w
data ExFocusWidget = forall w . FocusWidget w => ExFocusWidget w
instance Widget ExWidget where
  draw (ExWidget w)      = draw w
  minSize (ExWidget w) = minSize w
  name (ExWidget w)      = name w
instance Widget ExFocusWidget where
  draw (ExFocusWidget w)      = draw w
  minSize (ExFocusWidget w) = minSize w
  name (ExFocusWidget w)      = name w
instance FocusWidget ExFocusWidget where
  setFocus (ExFocusWidget w)   = setFocus w
  unsetFocus (ExFocusWidget w) = unsetFocus w

instance Eq ExWidget where
  w1 == w2 = name w1 == name w2
instance Eq ExFocusWidget where
  w1 == w2 = name w1 == name w2

data Table = Table { rows :: [[ExWidget]], focusable :: [ExFocusWidget] }

focusableRows :: Table -> [[ExWidget]]
focusableRows tab =
  filter (\row -> any (\w -> w 'elem' map asWidget (focusable tab)) row) (rows tab)
  where asWidget (ExFocusWidget w) = ExWidget w
```

With interface types all the boilerplate code vanishes:

```
instance Eq Widget where
  w1 == w2 = name w1 == name w2
instance Eq FocusWidget where
  w1 == w2 = name w1 == name w2
```

```
data Table = Table { rows      :: [[Widget]],
                     focusable :: [FocusWidget] }

focusableRows :: Table -> [[Widget]]
focusableRows tab =
  filter (\row -> any (\w -> w 'elem' (focusable tab)) row) (rows tab)
```

In the subexpression `w 'elem' (focusable tab)`, the compiler has to insert a coercion from `[FocusWidget]` to `[Widget]`. In general, such coercions are generated automatically if the corresponding datatype is an instance of `Functor`. In our concrete example, the datatype is `List`, which is already an instance of `Functor`.

2.4   Restrictions on Interface Types

Interface types are not a panacea. In the preceding section, we have seen that compound datatypes have to be instances of `Functor` if coercions should be generated automatically.

Moreover, not every type class makes for a sensible interface type. In particular, the "dispatch type" of the class must appear exactly once negatively in the signatures of the member functions. Without this restriction, it is not possible to derive the instance definition on the interface type automatically. The examples in this section all obey this restriction, but any type class with a "binary method" such as `(==)` `:: Eq a => a -> a -> Bool` does not.

3   A Language with Interface Types

This section defines a calculus with interface types in two steps. The first step recalls qualified types [6] and extends it with higher-rank polymorphism along the lines of Peyton Jones et al [14]. The second step adds interface types to that calculus and defines and investigates their induced subtyping relation.

The presentation relies on standard notions of free and bound variables, substitution for type variables in a syntactic object $s[a \mapsto m]$, as well as the notation $\bar{a}$ as a shorthand for the sequence $a_1, \ldots, a_n$, for some unspecified $n \geq 0$.

3.1   Qualified Types with Higher-Rank Polymorphism

Fig. 1 contains the syntax and the static semantics of λ^Q, the language of qualified types as considered by Jones [6]. There are expressions e, types t, monotypes m (types that only contain type variables and type constructors), and predicates P. Predicates are conjunctions of (at this point) unspecified atomic predicates A. The comma operator "," on predicates stands for conjunction and is assumed to be associative, commutative, and idempotent. Besides function types, the type language includes arbitrary covariant data type constructors T, which are introduced and eliminated with appropriate functions provided in the environment.[5]

---

[5] In Haskell, the covariance requirement boils down to require T to be an instance `Functor`.

Syntax

$$\textit{expressions } e, f ::= x \mid \lambda x.e \mid \lambda(x :: s).e \mid f\,e \mid \mathtt{let}\,x = e\,\mathtt{in}\,f \mid (e :: s)$$
$$\textit{types} \qquad\quad s, t ::= a \mid T\,\overline{t} \mid s \to t \mid \forall \overline{a}.P \Rightarrow t$$
$$\textit{monotypes } m \quad ::= a \mid T\,\overline{m} \mid m \to m$$
$$\textit{predicates } P, Q ::= \mathtt{true} \mid P, A$$

Typing rules

$$(\textit{E-var}) \; P \mid \Gamma(x : s) \vdash x : s \qquad\qquad (\textit{E-lam}) \; \frac{P \mid \Gamma(x : m) \vdash e : t}{P \mid \Gamma \vdash \lambda x.e : m \to t}$$

$$(\textit{E-alam}) \; \frac{P \mid \Gamma(x : s) \vdash e : t}{P \mid \Gamma \vdash \lambda(x :: s).e : s \to t} \qquad (\textit{E-app}) \; \frac{P \mid \Gamma \vdash f : s \to t \quad P \mid \Gamma \vdash e : s}{P \mid \Gamma \vdash f\,e : t}$$

$$(\textit{E-ann}) \; \frac{P \mid \Gamma \vdash e : s}{P \mid \Gamma \vdash (e :: s) : s} \qquad (\textit{E-let}) \; \frac{P \mid \Gamma \vdash e : s \quad P \mid \Gamma(x : s) \vdash f : t}{P \mid \Gamma \vdash \mathtt{let}\,x = e\,\mathtt{in}\,f : t}$$

$$(\textit{E-gen}) \; \frac{P, Q \mid \Gamma \vdash e : s \quad \overline{a} \cap \mathrm{free}(\Gamma) = \emptyset \quad \mathrm{free}(P) \subseteq \mathrm{free}(\Gamma)}{P \mid \Gamma \vdash e : \forall \overline{a}.Q \Rightarrow s}$$

$$(\textit{E-spec}) \; \frac{P \mid \Gamma \vdash e : s \quad P \vdash^{dsk} s \preceq t}{P \mid \Gamma \vdash e : t}$$

Fig. 1. Syntax and static semantics of λ^{Q}

The typing judgment and the rules defining its derivability are standard for a language with qualified types. The presentation extends Jones's by allowing arbitrary rank universally quantified types including type qualifications (cf. [10]). These higher-rank types are introduced through explicit type annotations following the initial lead of Odersky and Läufer [12]. Type inference for a language with these features is tricky and incomplete, but manageable [20, 14, 10]. In particular, this language is a core subset of the language implemented in bleeding edge Haskell compilers like GHC.

The rule *(E-spec)* relies on the generic instantiation relation $\preceq$ for types specified in Fig. 2. It generalizes the respective definition of Odersky and Läufer [12] (to qualified types) as well as Jones's ordering relation on constrained type schemes [6] (to higher-ranked types). Its particular formulation of $\preceq$ using deep skolemization is taken from Peyton Jones et al [14], extended with rule *(I-tycon)* that exploits the assumption that type constructors are covariant. A yet more general definition albeit without deep skolemization underlies the system of qualified types for MLF [10].

So far, the definition is independent of any particular choice of predicates. Thus, it remains to choose a language of atomic predicates and define the entailment relation $P \Vdash Q$. In our case, the atomic predicates are *type class constraints*. Their entailment relation $\Vdash$ relies on specifications of type classes **I** and

$$\text{Rho-types } r ::= m \mid s \to s$$

Weak prenex conversion $\text{pr}(s) = s'$

$$(N\text{-}poly) \quad \frac{\text{pr}(r_1) = \forall \bar{b}.Q \Rightarrow r_2 \quad \bar{a} \cap \bar{b} = \emptyset}{\text{pr}(\forall \bar{a}.P \Rightarrow r_1) = \forall \bar{a}\bar{b}.P, Q \Rightarrow r_2}$$

$$(N\text{-}fun) \quad \frac{\text{pr}(s_2) = \forall \bar{a}.P \Rightarrow r_2 \quad \bar{a} \cap \text{free}(s_1) = \emptyset}{\text{pr}(s_1 \to s_2) = \forall \bar{a}.P \Rightarrow s_1 \to r_2} \qquad\qquad (N\text{-}mono) \; \text{pr}(m) = m$$

Deep skolemization $P \vdash^{dsk} s \preceq r$

$$(I\text{-}dsk) \quad \frac{\text{pr}(s_2) = \forall \bar{a}.Q \Rightarrow r_2 \quad \bar{a} \cap \text{free}(s_1) = \emptyset \quad P, Q \vdash^{dsk^*} s_1 \preceq r_2}{P \vdash^{dsk^*} s_1 \preceq s_2}$$

$$(I\text{-}spec) \quad \frac{P \Vdash Q[\bar{a} \mapsto \bar{m}] \quad P \vdash^{dsk^*} r_1[\bar{a} \mapsto \bar{m}] \preceq r_2}{P \vdash^{dsk^*} \forall \bar{a}.Q \Rightarrow r_1 \preceq r_2}$$

$$(I\text{-}fun) \quad \frac{P \vdash^{dsk} s_3 \preceq s_1 \quad P \vdash^{dsk^*} s_2 \preceq r_4}{P \vdash^{dsk^*} s_1 \to s_2 \preceq s_3 \to r_4} \qquad (I\text{-}tycon) \quad \frac{P \vdash^{dsk^*} \bar{s} \preceq \bar{r}}{P \vdash^{dsk^*} T\,\bar{s} \preceq T\,\bar{r}}$$

$$(I\text{-}mono) \; P \vdash^{dsk^*} m \preceq m$$

Fig. 2. Instantiation rules for types

$$\textit{atomic predicates } A, B ::= \mathbf{I}\, m$$

$$(P\text{-}assume) \; P, A \Vdash A \qquad\qquad (P\text{-}collect) \quad \frac{P \Vdash Q \quad P \Vdash A}{P \Vdash Q, A}$$

$$(P\text{-}subcl) \quad \frac{P \Vdash \mathbf{I}\, m \quad \mathbf{I} \Rightarrow_C \mathbf{J}}{P \Vdash \mathbf{J}\, m} \qquad\qquad (P\text{-}inst) \quad \frac{m \in_I \mathbf{I}}{P \Vdash \mathbf{I}\, m}$$

Fig. 3. Entailment for predicates

of type class instances, *i.e.*, the subclass relation between two classes $\mathbf{I} \Rightarrow_C \mathbf{J}$ (read: $\mathbf{I}$ is a subclass of $\mathbf{J}$) and the instance relation $m \in_I \mathbf{I}$ between a monotype m and a class $\mathbf{I}$. Their syntactic details are of no concern for this work and we consider the relations as built into the entailment relation $\Vdash$ on predicates which obeys the rules in Fig. 3. To avoid clutter, Haskell's facility of recursively defining $\in_I$ from single instance definitions for type constructors is omitted.

3.2 Interface Types

The language λ^Q serves as a base language for the language λ^I, which augments λ^Q with the definitions in Fig. 4. The only extension of λ^I over λ^Q is the notion

Extended syntax of types

$$m ::= \cdots \mid \mathbf{I}$$

Additional type instantiation rules

$$(I\text{-}iface) \ \frac{P \Vdash \mathbf{I}\, m}{P \vdash^{dsk*} m \preceq \mathbf{I}}$$

Additional entailment rules

$$(P\text{-}subint) \ \frac{\mathbf{I} \Rightarrow_C \mathbf{J}}{P \Vdash \mathbf{J}\,\mathbf{I}}$$

Fig. 4. Extensions for λ^I with respect to Figures 1 and 2

$$(S\text{-}refl) \ t \leq t \qquad (S\text{-}trans) \ \frac{t_1 \leq t_2 \quad t_2 \leq t_3}{t_1 \leq t_3} \qquad (S\text{-}subclass) \ \frac{\mathbf{I} \Rightarrow_C \mathbf{J}}{\mathbf{I} \leq \mathbf{J}}$$

$$(S\text{-}instance) \ \frac{m \in_I \mathbf{J}}{m \leq \mathbf{J}} \qquad (S\text{-}tycon) \ \frac{\overline{s} \leq \overline{t}}{T\,\overline{s} \leq T\,\overline{t}} \qquad (S\text{-}fun) \ \frac{t_1 \leq s_1 \quad s_2 \leq t_2}{s_1 \to s_2 \leq t_1 \to t_2}$$

$$(S\text{-}qual) \ \frac{s \leq t}{\forall \overline{a}.Q \Rightarrow s \leq \forall \overline{a}.Q \Rightarrow t}$$

Fig. 5. Subtyping

of an *interface type* $\mathbf{I}$ and a slightly extended type instantiation relation. Each (single-parameter) type class $\mathbf{I}$ gives rise to an interface type of the same name. This interface type can be interpreted as the existential type $\exists a.\mathbf{I}\,a \Rightarrow a$ in that it stands for one particular element of the set of instances of $\mathbf{I}$. Furthermore, the interface type $\mathbf{I}$ is regarded an instance of $\mathbf{J}$ whenever $\mathbf{I} \Rightarrow_C \mathbf{J}$. This assumption is consistent with the observation that all instances of $\mathbf{I}$ are also instances of $\mathbf{J}$, hence the set of instances of $\mathbf{J}$ includes the instances of $\mathbf{I}$.

There is no explicit constructor for an element of interface type, but any suitable value can be coerced into one through a type annotation by way of the instantiation relation $\preceq$. This practice is analogous to the practice of casting to the interface type, which is the standard way of constructing values of interface type in, say, Java.[6] There is no explicit elimination form for a interface type $\mathbf{I}$, either. Rather, member functions of each class $\mathbf{J}$ where $\mathbf{I} \Rightarrow_C \mathbf{J}$ are directly applicable to a value of interface type $\mathbf{I}$ without explicitly unpacking the existential type.

Section 2 demonstrates that interface types are most useful if they enjoy a subtyping relation as they do in Java. Fig. 5 defines this subtyping relation in the obvious way. Each instance type of $\mathbf{J}$ is a subtype of $\mathbf{J}$ and the subclass

---

[6] An implementation can easily provide a cast-like operation to introduce interface types. However, type annotations are more flexible because they simplify the conversion of functions that involve interface types.

relation induces subtyping among the interface types. The remaining structural rules are standard.

Interestingly, the instantiation relation $\preceq$ already includes the desired subtyping relation $\leq$.

Lemma 1. *The instance relation* $P \vdash^{dsk} s \preceq t$ *is reflexive and transitive.*

Lemma 2. *1. If* $I \Rightarrow_C J$, *then* $P \Vdash I \preceq J$.
2. If $m \in_I J$, *then* $P \Vdash m \preceq J$.

Lemma 3. $s \leq t$ *implies* $P \Vdash s \preceq t$.

4   Inference

The type system presented in Section 2 is in logical form. It is a declarative specification for the acceptable type derivations, but gives no clue how to compute such a derivation, in particular because rules *(E-gen)* and *(E-spec)* allow us to generalize and specialize, respectively, everywhere. Thus, the logical system is suitable for investigating meta-theoretical properties of the system, such as type soundness, but unsuitable for inferring types.

This section introduces a bidirectional version of the system geared at type inference. As the development in this paper parallels the one in the "Practical Type Inference" paper [14, Fig. 8], we omit the intermediate step of forming a syntax-directed system, which would not yield further insight.

Fig. 6 displays the rules of the directional system. It relies on the same entailment relation as the logical system as well as on the weak prenex transformation and (extended) deep skolemization judgments from Figures 2 and 4. It extends the system of Peyton Jones et al [14] with the handling of predicates in general, one extra instantiation rule *(I-iface)*, and one extra generalization rule *(BE-gen3)*. This rule mimics *(I-iface)*, but it can only occur in a derivation in a place where full instantiation is not desired so that *(I-iface)* is not applicable.

It is straightforward to check that the directional system is sound with respect to the logical system. However, doing so requires extra type annotations because the directional system accepts more programs than the logical one.

Lemma 4. *Suppose that* $P \mid \Gamma \vdash^{poly}_{\delta} e : s$. *Then there exists some* e' *such that* $P \mid \Gamma \vdash e' : s$ *where* e' *differs from* e *only in additional type annotations on the bound variables of lambda abstractions.*

Here is an example for a term that type checks in the directional system (extended with integers and booleans), but not in the logical system:

$$\lambda(f :: ((\forall a.a \to a) \to \texttt{int} \times \texttt{bool}) \to (\forall a.a \to a) \to \texttt{int} \times \texttt{bool}).$$
$$f\,(\lambda id.(id\,5, id\,false))\,(\lambda x.x)$$

It works in the directional system because the rule *(BE-app)* infers a polymorphic type for f, checks its argument against the resulting polymorphic type, and

---

$$\text{Direction } \delta ::= \Uparrow \mid \Downarrow$$

Judgment $P \mid \Gamma \vdash_\delta e : r$

$$(BE\text{-}var) \quad \frac{P \vdash_\delta^{inst} s \preceq r}{P \mid \Gamma(x : s) \vdash_\delta x : r} \qquad\qquad (BE\text{-}lam1) \quad \frac{P \mid \Gamma(x : m) \vdash_\Uparrow e : r}{P \mid \Gamma \vdash_\Uparrow \lambda x.e : m \to r}$$

$$(BE\text{-}lam2) \quad \frac{P \mid \Gamma(x : s) \vdash_\Downarrow^{poly} e : s'}{P \mid \Gamma \vdash_\Downarrow \lambda x.e : s \to s'} \qquad (BE\text{-}alam1) \quad \frac{P \mid \Gamma(x : s) \vdash_\Uparrow e : r}{P \mid \Gamma \vdash_\Uparrow \lambda(x :: s).e : s \to r}$$

$$(BE\text{-}lam2) \quad \frac{P \mid \Gamma(x : s) \vdash_\Downarrow^{poly} e : s'' \quad P \vdash^{dsk} s' \preceq s}{P \mid \Gamma \vdash_\Downarrow \lambda(x :: s).e : s' \to s''}$$

$$(BE\text{-}app) \quad \frac{P \mid \Gamma \vdash_\Uparrow f : s' \to s'' \quad P \mid \Gamma \vdash_\Downarrow^{poly} e : s' \quad P \vdash_\delta^{inst} s'' \preceq r}{P \mid \Gamma \vdash_\delta f\, e : r}$$

$$(BE\text{-}ann) \quad \frac{P \mid \Gamma \vdash_\Downarrow^{poly} e : s \quad P \vdash_\delta^{inst} s \preceq r}{P \mid \Gamma \vdash_\delta (e :: s) : r}$$

$$(BE\text{-}let) \quad \frac{P \mid \Gamma \vdash_\Uparrow^{poly} e : s \quad P \mid \Gamma(x : s) \vdash_\delta f : r}{P \mid \Gamma \vdash_\delta \mathbf{let}\, x = e \,\mathbf{in}\, f : r}$$

Generalization judgment $P \mid \Gamma \vdash_\delta^{poly} e : s$

$$(BE\text{-}gen1) \quad \frac{P, Q \mid \Gamma \vdash_\Uparrow e : r \quad \bar{a} = \mathrm{free}(r) \setminus \mathrm{free}(\Gamma) \quad \mathrm{free}(P) \subseteq \mathrm{free}(\Gamma)}{P \mid \Gamma \vdash_\Uparrow^{poly} e : \forall \bar{a}.Q \Rightarrow r}$$

$$(BE\text{-}gen2) \quad \frac{P, Q \mid \Gamma \vdash_\Downarrow e : r \quad \mathrm{pr}(s) = \forall \bar{a}.Q \Rightarrow r \quad \bar{a} \cap \mathrm{free}(\Gamma) = \emptyset \quad \mathrm{free}(P) \subseteq \mathrm{free}(\Gamma)}{P \mid \Gamma \vdash_\Downarrow^{poly} e : s}$$

$$(BE\text{-}gen3) \quad \frac{P \Vdash \mathbf{I}\, m \quad P \mid \Gamma \vdash_\Downarrow e : m}{P \mid \Gamma \vdash_\Downarrow^{poly} e : \mathbf{I}}$$

Instantiation judgment $P \mid \Gamma \vdash_\delta^{inst} e : s \preceq r$

$$(BE\text{-}inst1) \quad \frac{P \Vdash Q[\bar{a} \mapsto \overline{m}]}{P \vdash_\Uparrow^{inst} \forall \bar{a}.Q \Rightarrow r \preceq r[\bar{a} \mapsto \overline{m}]} \qquad (BE\text{-}inst2) \quad \frac{P \vdash^{dsk} s \preceq r}{P \vdash_\Downarrow^{inst} s \preceq r}$$

Fig. 6. Bidirectional version of Odersky and Läufer, extended with qualified types and subtyping of interface types

then does the same for the second argument. However, in the logical system, the argument of the function $\lambda id.(id\, 5, id\, false)$ cannot receive a polymorphic type.

The directional system extends the logical one (viz. [14, Theorem 4.8]).

Lemma 5. *Suppose that $P \mid \Gamma \vdash e : s$. Then $P \mid \Gamma \vdash_\delta^{poly} e : s'$ and $P \vdash^{dsk} s' \preceq s$.*

Type translation

$$|a| = a \qquad |s \to t| = |s| \to |t| \qquad |\mathbf{I}| = W_{\mathbf{I}} \qquad |\forall \bar{a}.P \Rightarrow t| = \forall \bar{a}.|P| \to |t|$$

$$|\mathbf{true}| = * \qquad |P, Q| = |P| \times |Q| \qquad |\mathbf{I}\,m| = E_{\mathbf{I}}\{|m|\}$$

Term translation (excerpt)

$$(\textit{TS-tycon}) \quad \frac{P \vdash^{dsk^*} h : \overline{s} \preceq \overline{r}}{P \vdash^{dsk^*} map_T\ h : T\,\overline{s} \preceq T\,\overline{r}}$$

$$(\textit{TS-iface}) \quad \frac{P \Vdash y : \mathbf{I}\,m}{P \vdash^{dsk^*} \lambda(x :: |m|).K_{\mathbf{I}}\ y\,x : m \preceq \mathbf{I}}$$

$$(\textit{TE-gen3}) \quad \frac{\overline{v : A} \Vdash y : \mathbf{I}\,r \quad \overline{v : A} \mid \Gamma \vdash_{\Downarrow} e \rightsquigarrow e' : r}{\overline{v : A} \mid \Gamma \vdash_{\Downarrow}^{poly} e \rightsquigarrow K_{\mathbf{I}}\ y\,e' : \mathbf{I}}$$

Fig. 7. Translation from λ^I to System F. $E_{\mathbf{I}}\{t\}$ is the type of evidence values for class $\mathbf{I}$ at instance t. The type of a wrapper constructor is $K_{\mathbf{I}} : \forall a.E_{\mathbf{I}}\{a\} \to a \to W_{\mathbf{I}}$.

It is not clear whether the directional system retains the principal types property (viz. [14, Theorem 4.13]).

5 Translation to System F

The last step towards an implementation of interface types in a Haskell compiler is the translation to its internal language, System F, in Fig. 7. Peyton Jones et al [14] define most parts of this translation by extending their bidirectional system (without predicate handling), so the figure concentrates on the rules and types not present in that work.

This translation maps an atomic predicate $\mathbf{I}\,m$ into *evidence*, which is a variable binding $v : |\mathbf{I}\,m|$. The value of v is a suitable dictionary $D_{\mathbf{I}}\{|m|\} : E_{\mathbf{I}}\{|m|\}$ for the type class $\mathbf{I}$. A value with interface type $\mathbf{I}$ is represented as a System F term of type $W_{\mathbf{I}}$. This term wraps a dictionary of type $E_{\mathbf{I}}\{|m|\}$ and a witness of type $|m|$ using an automatically generated datatype constructor $K_{\mathbf{I}}$.

The translation rules for instantiation have the form $P \vdash h : s \preceq s'$ and yield a System F term h of type $|s| \to |s'|$. The rule *(TS-tycon)* demonstrates why the type constructors T have to be covariant: the translation of the instantiation judgment requires a map operation map_T for each such T.[7] The rule *(TS-iface)* shows the conversion of an instance type m of class $\mathbf{I}$ to its interface type $\mathbf{I}$ by applying the wrapper constructor $K_{\mathbf{I}}$ to the dictionary y yielded by the extended entailment judgment and the value x of type $|m|$.

The translation rules for expressions have the form $P \mid \Gamma \vdash e \rightsquigarrow e' : r$ where e is the source expression and e' its translation. The rule *(TE-gen3)* performs essentially the same task as *(TS-iface)*, but in a term context.

---

[7] In Haskell, T has to be an instance of **Functor**, so map_T becomes **fmap**.

The translation to System F preserves types:

Lemma 6. *Let $\vdash^F$ denote the System F typing judgment.*

- *Suppose that $\overline{(v :: A)} \mid \Gamma \vdash e \rightsquigarrow e' : r$. Then $\overline{(v :: |A|)}, |\Gamma| \vdash^F e' : |r|$.*
- *Suppose that $\overline{(v :: A)} \mid \Gamma \vdash^{poly} e \rightsquigarrow e' : s$. Then $\overline{(v :: |A|)}, |\Gamma| \vdash^F e' : |s|$.*

6   Related Work

There is a lot of work on type inference for first-class polymorphism [12, 7, 8, 18, 10, 20, 14, 9, 21]. Our inference algorithm directly extends the algorithm for predicative higher-rank types of Peyton Jones and others [14] with support for interface types. The interface type system is also predicative.

Läufer [11] extends algebraic data types with existential quantification constrained over type classes. In Läufer's system, programmers have to explicitly pack and unpack existential types through the standard introduction and elimination constructs of algebraic data types. Our approach translates interface types into algebraic data types with existential quantification. Type annotations serve as the pack operation for interface types. An explicit unpack operation for interface types is not required.

Diatchki and Jones [2] use type class names to provide a functional notation for functional dependencies. The name of a type class C with $n + 1$ parameters serves as a type operator that, when applied to n type arguments, represent the $(n + 1)$th class parameter, which must be uniquely determined by the other class parameters. Hence, the type $C\, t_1 \ldots t_n$ translates to a fresh type variable a subject to the constraint $C\, t_1 \ldots t_n\, a$. With interface types, the name of a single-parameter type class represents some unknown type that implements the type class. An interface type in argument position of some type signature could be handled by a local translation similar to the one used by Diatchki and Jones. An interface type in result position, however, requires a different treatment to cater for the existential nature of interface types.

Oliveira and Sulzmann [13] present a Haskell extension that unifies type classes and GADTs. Their extension also includes a feature that allows class names being used as types. Similar to our work, these types represent some unknown instance of the class. Different from our work, Oliveira and Sulzmann provide neither a type inference algorithm and nor an implementation.

The present authors [22] investigate a language design that extends Java's interface mechanism with the key features of Haskell's type class system. The resulting language generalizes interface types to bounded existential types, following an idea already present with LOOM's hash types [1].

Standard ML's module system [19] allows programmers to hide the implementation of a module behind an interface (*i.e.*, signature). For example, an ML implementation of the database library from Section 2.1 might provide several database-specific modules such that all implementation details are hidden behind a common signature. A programmer then chooses at *compile-time* which database should be used. In contrast, interface types allows this choice to be deferred until *runtime*. Providing this kind of flexibility to users of Standard ML's module system would require first-class structures [17].

7 Conclusion and Future Work

An interface type can be understood as an existential type representing an unknown instance of some type class. We demonstrated the usefulness of interface types through a case study from the real world and formalized a type system with support for interface types. Based on this type system, we implemented a prototype of a type inference algorithm that can be included easily in a production Haskell compiler.

Here are some items for future work:

- How about higher-order polymorphism? For higher-order classes such as Monad, the interface type would be parameterized and encapsulate a particular implementation of Monad.
- How about multi-parameter type classes? To support interface types for multi-parameter type classes, we would need explicit pack and unpack operations that coerce multiple values to/from an interface type.
- What if a type is coerced multiple times to an interface type? Each coercion results in the application of a wrapper, so that there might be a stack of wrappers. There is not much that can be done about it at the source level and it is not clear if it would have a significant performance impact on a realistic program. However, the implementation could be instrumented to have the application of a wrapper constructor check dynamically if it is applied to another wrapper and thus avoid the piling up of wrappers.

References

1. Bruce, K.B., Petersen, L., Fiech, A.: Subtyping is not a good "match" for object-oriented languages. In: Aksit, M., Matsuoka, S. (eds.) ECOOP 1997. LNCS, vol. 1241, pp. 104–127. Springer, Heidelberg (1997)
2. Diatchki, I.S., Jones, M.P.: Strongly typed memory areas programming systems-level data structures in a functional language. In: Löh, A. (ed.) Proceedings of the 2006 ACM SIGPLAN Haskell Workshop, Portland, Oregon, USA, pp. 72–83 (September 2006)
3. GHC. The Glasgow Haskell compiler (2008), http://www.haskell.org/ghc/
4. Goerzen, J.: Haskell database connectivity (2008), http://software.complete.org/software/projects/show/hdbc
5. Hugs 98 (2003), http://www.haskell.org/hugs/
6. Jones, M.P.: Qualified Types: Theory and Practice. Cambridge University Press, Cambridge (1994)
7. Jones, M.P.: First-class polymorphism with type inference. In: Jones, N. (ed.) Proc. 1997 ACM Symp. POPL, Paris, France, January 1997, pp. 483–496. ACM Press, New York (1997)

8. Le Botlan, D., Rémy, D.: MLF: raising ML to the power of System F. In: Shivers, O. (ed.) Proc. ICFP 2003, Uppsala, Sweden, August 2003, pp. 27–38. ACM Press, New York (2003)
9. Leijen, D.: HMF: Simple type inference for first-class polymorphism. In: ICFP, pp. 283–293. ACM Press, New York (2008)
10. Leijen, D., Lóh, A.: Qualified types for MLF. In: Pierce [15], pp. 144–155
11. Läufer, K.: Type classes with existential types. J. Funct. Program. 6(3), 485–517 (1996)
12. Odersky, M., Läufer, K.: Putting type annotations to work. In: Proc. 1996 ACM Symp. POPL, St. Petersburg, FL, USA, January 1996, pp. 54–67. ACM Press, New York (1996)
13. Oliveira, B., Sulzmann, M.: Objects to unify type classes and GADTs (April 2008), http://www.cs.mu.oz.au/~sulzmann/manuscript/objects-unify-type-classes-gadts.ps
14. Peyton Jones, S., Vytiniotis, D., Weirich, S., Shields, M.: Practical type inference for arbitrary-rank types. J. Funct. Program. 17(1), 1–82 (2007)
15. Pierce, B.C. (ed.): ICFP, Tallinn, Estonia. ACM Press, New York (2005)
16. PostgreSQL, the most advanced Open Source database system in the world (2008), http://www.postgresql.org
17. Russo, C.V.: First-class structures for Standard ML. In: Smolka, G. (ed.) ESOP 2000. LNCS, vol. 1782, pp. 336–350. Springer, Heidelberg (2000)
18. Rémy, D.: Simple, partial type-inference for System F based on type-containment. In: Pierce [15], pp. 130–143
19. Tofte, M.: Essentials of Standard ML Modules. In: Advanced Functional Programming, pp. 208–238. Springer, Heidelberg (1996)
20. Vytiniotis, D., Weirich, S., Peyton Jones, S.: Boxy types: Inference for higher-rank types and impredicativity. In: Lawall, J. (ed.) Proc. ICFP 2006, Portland, Oregon, USA, Sep. 2006, pp. 251–262. ACM Press, New York (2006)
21. Vytiniotis, D., Weirich, S., Peyton Jones, S.: FPH: First-class polymorphism for Haskell. In: ICFP (to appear, 2008), http://www.cis.upenn.edu/~dimitriv/fph/
22. Wehr, S., Lämmel, R., Thiemann, P.: JavaGI: Generalized interfaces for Java. In: Ernst, E. (ed.) ECOOP 2007. LNCS, vol. 4609, pp. 347–372. Springer, Heidelberg (2007)

Exception Handlers as Extensible Cases

Matthias Blume, Umut A. Acar, and Wonseok Chae

Toyota Technological Institute at Chicago
{blume,umut,wchae}@tti-c.org

Abstract. Exceptions are an indispensable part of modern programming languages. They are, however, handled poorly, especially by higher-order languages such as Standard ML and Haskell: in both languages a well-typed program can unexpectedly fail due to an uncaught exception. In this paper, we propose a technique for type-safe exception handling. Our approach relies on representing exceptions as sums and assigning exception handlers polymorphic, extensible row types. Based on this representation, we describe an implicitly typed external language EL where well-typed programs do not raise any unhandled exceptions. EL relies on sums, extensible records, and polymorphism to represent exception-handling, and its type system is no more complicated than that for existing languages with polymorphic extensible records.

EL is translated into an internal language IL that is a variant of System F extended with extensible records. The translation performs a CPS transformation to represent exception handlers as continuations. It also relies on duality to transform sums into records. (The details for this translation are given in an accompanying technical report.)

We describe the implementation of a compiler for a concrete language based on EL. The compiler performs full type inference and translates EL-style source code to machine code. Type inference relieves the programmer from having to provide explicit exception annotations. We believe that this is the first practical proposal for integrating exceptions into the type system of a higher-order language.

1 Introduction

Exceptions are widely used in many languages including functional, imperative, and object-oriented ones such as SML, Haskell, C++ and Java. The mechanism enables programs to *raise* an exception when an unexpected condition arises and to *handle* such exceptions at desired program points. Although uncaught exceptions—just like stuck states—constitute unrecoverable runtime errors, their presence or absence is usually not tracked by the type system and, thus, also not included in the definition of soundness. Even strongly typed languages such as ML and Haskell which claim that "well-typed programs do not go wrong" permit uncaught exceptions. This is unfortunate, since in practice an uncaught exception can be as dangerous as a stuck state. Critical software failing due to a divide-by-zero error is just as bad as it failing due to a segmentation fault. (Famously, the Ariane 5 disaster was in part caused by a runtime exception that was not appropriately handled by its flight-control software [15].)

G. Ramalingam (Ed.): APLAS 2008, LNCS 5356, pp. 273–289, 2008.
© Springer-Verlag Berlin Heidelberg 2008

There have been attempts at providing some form of exception checking. For example, CLU, Modula-3, and Java allow the programmer to declare the exceptions that each function may raise and have the compiler check that declared exceptions are caught properly [16,6,10]. If these languages were to be used only in the first-order setting, the approach would work well. But this assumption would preclude first-class use of objects and function closures. Functional languages like ML or Haskell, where higher-order features are used pervasively, do not even attempt to track exceptions statically.

In the higher-order setting, latent exceptions, before they get raised, can be carried around just like any other value inside closures and objects. To statically capture these highly dynamic aspects faithfully and precisely is challenging, which perhaps explains why existing language designs do not incorporate exceptions tracking. A practical design should have the following properties: (1) Exception types can be **inferred**[1] by the compiler, avoiding the need for prohibitively excessive programmer annotations. (2) **Exception polymorphism** makes it possible for commonly used higher-order functions such as `map` and `filter` to be used with functional arguments that have varying exception signatures. (3) Soundness implies that well-typed programs **handle all exceptions**. (4) The language is **practically implementable**. (5) Types **do not unduly burden** the programmer by being conceptually too complex.

In this paper we describe the design of a language that satisfies these criteria. We use *row types* to represent sets of exceptions and universal quantification over row type variables to provide the necessary polymorphism. As a result, our type system and the inference algorithm are no more complicated than those for extensible records and extensible cases. We implemented this design in our **MLPolyR** compiler.The proof of soundness and more implementation details can be found in the extended technical report [5].

The starting point for our work is **MLPolyR** [4], a language already featuring row polymorphism, polymorphic sum types, and extensible cases. To integrate exceptions into the type system, we consider an implicitly typed *external language* EL (Section 3) that extends λ-calculus with exceptions and extensible cases. Our syntax distinguishes between the act of establishing a new exception handler (**handle**) and that of overriding an existing one (**rehandle**). The latter can be viewed as a combination of **unhandle** (which removes an existing handler) and **handle**. As we will explain in Section 5, this design choice makes it possible to represent exception types as row types without need for additional complexity. From a usability perspective, the design makes overriding a handler explicit, reducing the likelihood of this happening by mistake.

In EL, the typing of an expression includes both a result type and an exception type. The latter describes the set of exceptions that might be raised by the expression. The typing of exception-handling constructs is analogous to that of

---

[1] There still will be a need for programmers to spell out types, including exception types, for example in module signatures. It is possible to avoid excessive notational overhead by choosing a syntax with good built-in defaults, e.g., shortcuts for common patterns and the ability to elide parts that can be filled in by the compiler. In our prototype, the pretty-printer for types employs such tricks (see footnote 4).

extensible first-class cases. Exception values themselves are sums, and those are also described by row types. To support exceptions, the dynamic semantics of EL evaluates every expression in an *exception context* that is an extensible record of individual evaluation contexts—one for each exception constructor.

Our implementation rests on a deterministic, type-sensitive semantics for EL based on elaboration (i.e., translation) into an explicitly typed internal language IL (Section 4). The elaboration process involves type inference for EL. IL is an extension of System F with extensible records and nearly coincides with the System F language we used in previous work on **MLPolyR**. The translation of exception constructs views an exception handler as an alternative continuation whose domain is the sum of all exceptions that could arise at a given program point. By duality, such a continuation is equivalent to a record of individual continuations, each responsible for a single exception constructor. Taking this view, establishing a handler for a new exception corresponds to functional extension of the exception handler record. Raising an exception simply projects out the appropriate continuation from the handler record and throws its payload to it. Since continuations are just functions, this is the same mechanism that underlies **MLPolyR**'s *first-class cases* feature; first-class cases are also extensible, and their dual representations are records of functions.

Previous work in this context focused on analysis tools for statically detecting uncaught exceptions [11,19,18,7,14,2]. We take advantage of our position as language designers and incorporate an exception analysis into the language and its compiler directly. The ability to adapt the language design to the analysis makes it possible to use a formalism that is simple and transparent to the programmer.

2 Motivating Examples

We will now visit a short sequence of simple program fragments, roughly ordered by increasing complexity. None of the examples exhibits uncaught exceptions. The rejection of any one of them by a compiler would constitute a false positive. The type system and the compiler that we describe accept them all.

Of course, baseline functionality consists of being able to match a manifest occurrence of a raised exception with a manifestly matching handler:

$$(\ldots \text{ \textbf{raise} 'Neg 10} \ldots) \text{ \textbf{handle} 'Neg i} \Rightarrow \ldots$$

The next example moves the site where the exception is raised into a separate function. To handle this in the type system, the function type constructor $\rightarrow$ acquires an additional argument ρ representing the set of exceptions that may be raised by an application, i.e., function types have the form $\tau_1 \xrightarrow{\rho} \tau_2$. This is about as far as existing static exception trackers that are built into programming languages (e.g., Java's **throws** declaration) go.

```
fun foo x = if x<0 then raise 'Neg x else ...
(... foo y ...) handle 'Neg i ⇒ ...
```

But we also want to be able to track exceptions through calls of higher-order functions such as **map**, which themselves do not raise exceptions while their functional arguments might:

```
fun map f [] = []    | map f (x :: xs) = f x :: map f xs
(... map foo l ...) handle 'Neg i ⇒ ...
```

Moreover, in the case of curried functions and partial applications, we want to be able to distinguish stages that do not raise exceptions from those that might. In the example of map, there is no possibility of any exception being raised when map is partially applied to the function argument; all exceptions are confined to the second stage when the list argument is supplied:

```
val mfoo = map foo
(... mfoo l ...) handle 'Neg i ⇒ ...
```

Here, the result mfoo of the partial application acts as a data structure that carries a latent exception. In the general case, exception values can occur in any data structure. For example, the SML/NJ Library [9] provides a constructor function for hash tables which accepts a programmer-specified exception value which becomes part of the table's representation from where it can be raised, for example when an attempt is made at looking up a non-existing key.

The following example shows a similar but simpler situation. Function check finds the first pair in the given list whose left component does not satisfy the predicate ok. If such a pair exists, its right component, which must be an exception value, is raised. To guarantee exception safety, the caller of check must be prepared to handle any exception that might be passed along in the argument of the call:

```
fun check ((x, e) :: rest) = if ok x then check rest else raise e
 | check [] = ()
(... check [(3, 'A 10), (4, 'B true)] ...) handle 'A i ⇒ ... | 'B b ⇒ ...
```

Finally, exception values can participate in complex data flow patterns. The following example illustrates this by showing an exception 'A that carries another exception 'B as its payload. The payload 'B 10 itself gets raised by the exception handler for 'A in function f2, so a handler for 'B on the call of f2 suffices to make this fragment exception-safe:

```
fun f1 () = ... raise 'A ('B 10) ...
fun f2 () = f1 () handle 'A x ⇒ raise x
(... f2 () ...) handle 'B i ⇒ ...
```

3   The External Language (EL)

We start by describing EL, our implicitly typed *external* language that facilitates sums, cases, and mechanisms for raising as well as handling exceptions.

Syntax of Terms

Figure 1 shows the definitions of expressions e and values v. EL is **MLPolyR** [4] extended with constructs for raising and handling exceptions. We have integer constants n, variables x, injection into sum types $l\ e$, applications $e_1\ e_2$, recursive functions **fun** $f\ x = e$, and *let*-bindings **let** $x = e_1$ **in** e_2. For the purpose of comparison, we also include first-class cases $\{\ l_1\ x_1 \Rightarrow e_1, \ldots, l_n\ x_n \Rightarrow e_n\ \}$ and with their elimination form **match** e_1 **with** e_2 as well as case extension

$e_1 \oplus \{l \; x \Rightarrow e_2\}$. The additions over **MLPolyR** consist of **raise** e for raising exceptions and several forms for managing exception handlers: The form e_1 **handle** $\{ l \; x \Rightarrow e_2 \}$ establishes a handler for the exception constructor l. The new exception context is used for evaluating e_1, while the old context is used for e_2 in case e_1 raises l. The old context cannot already have a handler for l. The form e_1 **rehandle** $\{ l \; x \Rightarrow e_2 \}$, on the other hand, overrides an existing handler for l. Again, the original exception context is restored before executing e_2. The form e_1 **handle** $\{ x \Rightarrow e_2 \}$ establishes a new context with handlers for *all* exceptions that e_1 might raise. As before, e_2 is evaluated in the original context. The form e **unhandle** l evaluates e in a context from which the handler for l has been removed. The original context must have a handler for l.

To simplify and shorten the presentation, we exclude features that are unrelated to exceptions. Therefore, EL does not have records or recursive types. Adding them back into the language would not cause technical difficulties.

Operational Semantics

We give an operational small-step semantics for EL as a context-sensitive rewrite system in a style inspired by Felleisen and Hieb [8]. An *evaluation context E* is essentially a term with one sub-term replaced by a hole (see Figure 2). Any closed expression e that is not a value has a unique decomposition $E[r]$ into an evaluation context E and a redex r that is placed into the hole within E.[2] Evaluation contexts in this style of semantics represent continuations. The rule for handling an exception could be written simply as $E[(E'[\textbf{raise} \; l \; v])$ **handle** $\{l \, x \Rightarrow e \}] \mapsto E[e[v/x]]$, but this requires an awkward side-condition stating that E' must not also contain a handler for l. We avoid this difficulty by maintaining the exception context separately and explicitly on a per-constructor basis. This choice makes it clear that exception contexts can be seen as extensible records of continuations. However, we now also need to be explicit about where a computation re-enters the scope of a previous context. This is the purpose of restore-frames of the form **restore** $_{E_{\textbf{exn}}}$ E that we added to the language, but which are assumed not to occur in source expressions.[3]

An *exception context $E_{\textbf{exn}}$* is a record $\{l_1 = E_1, \ldots, l_n = E_n\}$ of evaluation contexts $E_1, \ldots, E_n$ labeled $l_1, \ldots, l_n$. A *reducible configuration* $(E[r], E_{\textbf{exn}})$ pairs a redex r in context E with a corresponding exception context $E_{\textbf{exn}}$ that represents all exception handlers that are available when reducing r. A *final configuration* is a pair $(v, \{\})$ where v is a value. Given a reducible configuration $(E[r], E_{\textbf{exn}})$, we call the pair $(E, E_{\textbf{exn}})$ the *full context* of r.

The semantics is given as a set of single-step transition rules from reducible configurations to configurations. A program (i.e., a closed expression) e evaluates to a value v if $(e, \{\})$ can be reduced in the transitive closure of our step relation

---

[2] We omit the definition of redexes. All important redexes appear as part of our semantic rules. Non-value expressions that are not covered are stuck.

[3] There are real-world implementations of languages with exception handlers where restore-frames have a concrete manifestation. For example, SML/NJ [1] represents the exception handler as a global variable storing a continuation. When leaving the scope of a handler, this variable gets assigned the previous exception continuation.

Terms $e ::= n \mid x \mid l \mid e \mid e_1\,e_2 \mid \mathbf{fun}\ f\ x = e \mid \mathbf{let}\ x = e_1\ \mathbf{in}\ e_2 \mid \{l_i\ x_i \Rightarrow e_i\}_{i=1}^n \mid \mathbf{match}\ e_1\ \mathbf{with}\ e_2 \mid e_1 \oplus \{l\ x \Rightarrow e_2\} \mid$
$\qquad\ \ \mathbf{raise}\ e \mid e_1\ \mathbf{handle}\ \{l\ x \Rightarrow e_2\} \mid e\ \mathbf{unhandle}\ l \mid e_1\ \mathbf{rehandle}\ \{l\ x \Rightarrow e_2\} \mid e_1\ \mathbf{handle}\ \{x \Rightarrow e_2\}$

Values $v ::= n \mid \mathbf{fun}\ f\ x = e \mid l\ v \mid \{l_i\ x_i \Rightarrow e_i\}_{i=1}^n$

Types $\tau ::= \alpha \mid \mathbf{int} \mid \tau_1 \xrightarrow{\rho} \tau_2 \mid \langle \rho \rangle \mid \langle \rho_1 \rangle \xrightarrow{\rho_2} \tau$

Schemas $\sigma ::= \tau \mid \forall \alpha : \kappa.\sigma$

Label sets $L ::= \{l_1, \ldots, l_n\} \mid \varnothing$

Kinds $\kappa ::= \star \mid L$

$\rho ::= \alpha \mid \centerdot \mid l : \tau, \rho$

Typenv $\Gamma ::= \varnothing \mid \Gamma, x \mapsto \sigma$

Kindenv $\Delta ::= \varnothing \mid \Delta, \alpha \mapsto \kappa$

Fig. 1. External language (EL) syntax

$e ::= \ldots \mid \mathbf{restore}$

$E ::= [] \mid l\ E \mid E\ e \mid v\ E \mid \mathbf{let}\ x = E\ \mathbf{in}\ e \mid E \oplus \{l\ x \Rightarrow e\} \mid \mathbf{match}\ E\ \mathbf{with}\ e \mid \mathbf{match}\ v\ \mathbf{with}\ E \mid \mathbf{raise}\ E \mid \mathbf{restore}_{E_{exn}}\ E$

$E_{exn} ::= \{l_1 = E_1, \ldots, l_n = E_n\}$

Fig. 2. Evaluation contexts and exception contexts

$(E[\mathbf{fun}\ f\ x = e\ v], E_{exn}) \longmapsto (E[e[\mathbf{fun}\ f\ x = e/f, v/x]], E_{exn})$ (app)

$(E[\mathbf{let}\ x = v\ \mathbf{in}\ e], E_{exn}) \longmapsto (E[e[v/x]], E_{exn})$ (let)

$(E[\{l_i\ x_i \Rightarrow e'_i\}_{i=1}^n \oplus \{l\ x \Rightarrow e\}], E_{exn}) \longmapsto (E[\{l_i\ x_i \Rightarrow e'_i, \ldots, l_n\ x_n \Rightarrow e'_n, l\ x \Rightarrow e\}], E_{exn})$ (c/ext)

$(E[\mathbf{match}\ l_i\ v\ \mathbf{with}\ \{\ldots, l_i\ x_i \Rightarrow e_i, \ldots\}], E_{exn}) \longmapsto (E[e_i[v/x_i]], E_{exn})$ (match)

$(E[\mathbf{raise}\ l_i\ v], \{\ldots, l_i = E_i, \ldots\}) \longmapsto (E_i[v], \{\})$ (raise)

$(E[e_1\ \mathbf{handle}\ \{l\ x \Rightarrow e_2\}], E_{exn}) \longmapsto (E[\mathbf{restore}_{E_{exn}}\ e_1], E'_{exn})$ (handle)
$\qquad$ where $\quad E_{exn} = \{l_i = E_i\}_{i=1}^n$
$\qquad$ and $\qquad E'_{exn} = \{l_1 = E_1, \ldots, l_n = E_n, l = E[\mathbf{let}\ x = \mathbf{restore}_{E_{exn}}\ []\ \mathbf{in}\ e_2]\}$

$(E[e_1\ \mathbf{rehandle}\ \{l_j\ x \Rightarrow e_2\}], E_{exn}) \longmapsto$ (rehandle)
$\qquad$ where $\quad E_{exn} = \{l_i = E_i\}_{i=1}^n$ and $E'_{exn} = \{l_i = E'_i\}_{i=1}^n$ and $\forall i \neq j.E'_i = E_i$
$\qquad$ and $\qquad E'_j = E[\mathbf{let}\ x = \mathbf{restore}_{E_{exn}}\ []\ \mathbf{in}\ e_2]$

$(E[e\ \mathbf{unhandle}\ l_j], E_{exn}) \longmapsto (E[\mathbf{restore}_{E_{exn}}\ e], E'_{exn})$ (unhandle)
$\qquad$ where $\quad E_{exn} = \{l_i = E_i\}_{i=1}^n$ and $E'_{exn} = \{l_i = E_i\}_{i=1,i\neq j}^n$

$(E[e_1\ \mathbf{handle}\ \{x \Rightarrow e_2\}], E_{exn}) \longmapsto (E[\mathbf{restore}_{E_{exn}}\ e_1], E'_{exn})$ (handle all)
$\qquad$ where $\quad E'_{exn} = \{l_i = E[\mathbf{let}\ x = l_i(\mathbf{restore}_{E_{exn}}\ [])\ \mathbf{in}\ e_2]\}_{i=1}^n$ (for some n)

$(E[\mathbf{restore}_{E_{exn}}\ v], E_{exn}) \longmapsto (E[v], E'_{exn})$ (restore)

Fig. 3. Operational semantics for EL

to a final configuration $(v, \{\})$. Rules unrelated to exceptions are standard and leave the exception context unchanged. The rule for **raise** $l\ v$ selects field l of the exception context and places v into its hole. The result, paired with the empty exception context, is the new configuration which, by construction, will have the form $(E'[\textbf{restore}\ _{E'_{\textbf{exn}}}\ v], \{\})$ so that the next step will restore exception context $E'_{\textbf{exn}}$. The rules for e_1 **handle** $\{\ l\ x \Rightarrow e_2\ \}$ and e_1 **rehandle** $\{\ l\ x \Rightarrow e_2\ \}$ as well as e **unhandle** l are very similar to each other: one adds a new field to the exception context, another replaces an existing field, and the third drops a field. All exception-handling constructs augment the current evaluation context with a **restore**-form so that the original context is re-established if and when e_1 reduces to a value.

The rule for the "handle-all" construct e_1 **handle** $\{\ x \Rightarrow e_2\ \}$ stands out because it is non-deterministic. Since we represent each handled exception constructor separately, the rule must *guess* the relevant set of constructors $\{l_1, \ldots, l_n\}$. Introducing non-determinism here might seem worrisome, but we can justify it by observing that different guesses never lead to different outcomes:

Lemma 1. *If* $(e, \{\}) \mapsto^* (v, \{\})$ *and* $(e, \{\}) \mapsto^* (v', \{\})$, *then* $v = v'$.

The proof for this lemma uses a bi-simulation between configurations, where two configurations are related if they are identical up to records. Records may have different sets of labels, but common fields must themselves be related. It is easy to see that each step of the operational semantics preserves this relation.

However, guessing too few or too many labels can get the program stuck. Fortunately, for well-typed programs there always exists a good choice. The correct choice can be made deterministically by taking the result of type inference into account, giving rise to a type soundness theorem for EL. Type soundness is expressed in terms of a well-formedness condition $\vdash (E[e], E_{\textbf{exn}})$ wf on configurations. For details on its definition and the proof of soundness (progress and preservation) see the technical report [5]. Since uncaught exceptions are simply stuck configurations, the soundness theorem justifies our motto: *Well-typed* EL *programs do not have uncaught exceptions.*

Well-Formed Types

The type language for EL is also given in Figure 1. It contains type variables $(\alpha, \beta, \ldots)$, base types (e.g., int), constructors for function- and case types ($\to$ and $\hookrightarrow$), sum types ($\langle\rho\rangle$), the empty row type ($\cdot$), and row types with at least one typed label $(l : \tau, \rho)$. Notice that function- and case arrows take *three* type arguments: the domain, the co-domain, and a row type describing the exceptions that could be raised during an invocation. A type is either an ordinary type or a row type. Kinding judgments of the form $\Delta \vdash \tau : \kappa$ (stating that in the current kinding context Δ type τ has kind κ) are used to distinguish between these cases and to establish that types are well-formed. As a convention, wherever possible we will use meta-variables such as ρ for row types and τ for ordinary types. Where this distinction is not needed, for example for polymorphic instantiation (VAR), we will use the letter θ.

Ordinary types have kind $\star$. A row type ρ has kind L where L is a set of labels which are known not to occur in ρ. An unconstrained row variable has kind $\varnothing$. Inference rules can be found in the technical report [5]. The use of a kinding judgment in a typing rule constrains Δ and ultimately propagates kinding information back to the LET/VAL rule where type variables are bound and kinding information is used to form type schemas.

Typing

The type τ of a closed expression e characterizes the values that e can evaluate to. From a dual point of view it describes the values that the evaluation context E must be able to receive. In our operational semantics E is extended to a full context $(E, E_{\mathbf{exn}})$, so the goal is to develop a type system with judgments that describe the full context of a given expression. Our typing judgments have an additional component ρ that describes $E_{\mathbf{exn}}$ by individually characterizing the its constituent labels and evaluation contexts. General typing judgments have the form $\Delta; \Gamma \vdash e : \tau; \rho$, expressing that e has type τ and exception type ρ. The typing environment Γ is a finite map assigning types to the free variables of e. Similarly, the kinding environment Δ maps the free type variables of τ, ρ, and Γ to their kinds.

The **typing rules** for EL are given in Figure 4. Typing is syntax-directed; for most syntactic constructs there is precisely one rule, the only exceptions being the rules for **fun** and **let** which rely on the notion of *syntactic values* to distinguish between two sub-cases. As usual, in rules that introduce polymorphism we impose the *value restriction* by requiring certain expressions to be *valuable*. Valuable expressions do not have effects and, in particular, do not raise exceptions. We use a separate typing judgment of the form $\Delta; \Gamma \vdash_{\mathsf{v}} e : \tau$ for syntactic values (VAR, INT, FUN/VAL, FUN/NON-VAL, and C). Judgments for syntactic values are lifted to the level of judgments for general expressions by the VALUE rule. The VALUE rule leaves the exception type ρ unconstrained. Administrative rules TEQ and TEQ/V deal with type equivalences $\tau \approx \tau'$, especially the reordering of labels in row types. Rules for $\tau \approx \tau'$ were described in previous work [4].

Rules unrelated to exceptions simply propagate a single exception type without change. This is true even for expressions that have more than one sub-term, matching our intuition that the exception type characterizes the exception context. For example, consider function application $e\ e'$: The rules do not use any form of sub-typing to express that the set of exceptions is the union of the three sets corresponding to e, e', and the actual application. Like Pessaux and Leroy we rely on polymorphism to collect exception information across multiple sub-terms. As usual, polymorphism is introduced by the LET/VAL rule for expressions **let** $x = e_1$ **in** e_2 where e_1 is a syntactic value.

The rules for handling and raising exceptions establish bridges between ordinary types and handler types (i.e., types of exception handler contexts). Exceptions themselves are simply values of sum type; the **raise** expression passes such values to an appropriate handler. Notice that the corresponding rule equates the row type of the sum with the row type of the exception context; there is no implicit subsumption here. Instead, subsumption takes place where the exception payload is injected into the corresponding sum type (DCON).

Rule HANDLE-ALL is the inverse of RAISE. The form e_1 **handle** $\{\, x \Rightarrow e_2 \,\}$ establishes a handler that catches *any* exception emanating from e_1. The exception is made available to e_2 as a value of sum type bound to variable x. Operationally this corresponds to replacing the current exception handler context with a brand-new one, tailor-made to fit the needs of e_1. The other three constructs do not replace the exception handler context wholesale but adjust it incrementally: **handle** adds a new field to the context while retaining all other fields; **rehandle** replaces an existing handler at a specific label l with a new (potentially differently typed) handler at the same l; **unhandle** removes an existing handler. There are strong parallels between C/EXT (case extension) and HANDLE, although there are also some significant differences due to the fact that exception handlers constitute a hidden part of the context while cases are first-class values. As hinted in Section 4 and explained fully in the technical report [5], we can highlight the connection and de-emphasize the differences by translating both handlers and cases into the same representation, namely records of functions. The value-level counterpart to **rehandle** is functional case update, which we omitted for reasons of brevity. Similarly, **unhandle** corresponds to a form for narrowing cases or, dually, a form for widening a sums (not are shown here).

Whole programs are closed up to some initial basis environment Γ_0, raise no exceptions, and evaluate to int. This is expressed by a judgment $\Gamma_0 \vdash e$ program.

Polymorphic Recursion vs. Explicit Narrowing

Pessaux and Leroy explain that their exception analysis becomes more precise if they employ inference for polymorphic recursion. Since the problem of type inference in the presence of polymorphic recursion is generally undecidable [12], we chose not to base our language design on this idea. To see the problem, consider a scenario similar to the one described by Pessaux and Leroy:

```
fun f x = (if (... raise 'C() ...) then () else f x) handle 'C() ⇒ ()
```

Here f is called in a context that requires a handler for exception 'C, because 'C is raised in a different sub-expression. However, exception 'C will always be caught, and it would be nice to have this fact expressed in f's type. Since the Pessaux/Leroy system uses *presence types* (see Section 5), it can represent and (in some cases) infer this fact. But doing so requires type inference with polymorphic recursion because f's body has to be type-checked under the assumption of f being exception-free. Exception freedom is expressed via polymorphism.

In our language, the above example would be illegal even in the presence of polymorphic recursion. The body of f must be checked assuming that f's exception type can be instantiated with a row containing 'C. But the use of ... **handle** 'C() ⇒ ... within the same body ultimately invalidates this assumption. The problem can easily be understood in terms of the operational semantics: every recursive call of f wants to add another field 'C to the exception context. Since fields can only be added if they are not already present, this is impossible.

Fortunately, the programmer can work around such problems by explicitly removing 'C from the exception context at the site of the recursive call:

fun f x = (**if** (... **raise** 'C() ...) **then** () **else** (f x **unhandle** 'C))
          handle 'C() ⇒()

In the concrete language design implemented by our compiler we adopt an idea of Benton and Kennedy [3] and provide a variant of the **handle**-syntax that in some cases avoids the need for **unhandle**, since it provides an explicit success branch that is evaluated under the original context:

fun f x = **let val** tmp = ... **raise** 'C() ...
          handling 'C() ⇒()
          in if tmp **then** () **else** f x

Polymorphic Recursion and Curried Functions

There is one situation, however, where a limited form of type inference for polymorphic recursion is very helpful: curried functions, or—more generally— functions whose bodies are syntactic values. Our type system has a separate rule (FUN/VAL) that types the body of the function assuming unrestricted polymor- phism in its exception type. Since the body is a syntactic value, this assumption is guaranteed to be valid and leads to a decidable inference problem. The point of including the rule is improved precision. Consider our map example from Sec- tion 2. In the absence of FUN/VAL, i.e., if FUN/NON-VAL were to be used for all functions regardless of whether or not their bodies are syntactic values, we would infer the type of map (using Haskell-style notation for lists types $[\tau]$) as:

$$\textbf{val map} \ : \ \forall \alpha : \star. \forall \beta : \star. \forall \gamma : \varnothing.(\alpha \xrightarrow{\gamma} \beta) \xrightarrow{\gamma} ([\alpha] \xrightarrow{\gamma} [\beta])$$

Notice the use of the same row type variable γ on all three occurrences of $\rightarrow$. The type checker fails to notice that exceptions suspended within the first argument cannot be raised during the first stage (i.e., a partial application) of map. This violates one of the requirements that we spelled out when we motivated the need for an exception type system. The fix is the introduction of FUN/VAL. Consider map once again. Since it is curried, its body—when rendered in EL—is another **fun** expression, i.e., a syntactic value. Without having performed any type inference at all we know that map will not raise an exception at the time of a partial application, so we can use this as an assumption when type-checking the body. To express that a function cannot raise an exception we make its type polymorphic in the exception annotation on $\rightarrow$. Indeed, FUN/VAL binds f to $\forall \alpha : \varnothing. \tau_2 \xrightarrow{\alpha} \tau$ in the typing environment for the function body. With this rule in place, map's type is now inferred as we had hoped[4]:

$$\textbf{val map} \ : \ \forall \alpha : \star. \forall \beta : \star. \forall \gamma : \varnothing. \forall \delta : \varnothing.(\alpha \xrightarrow{\gamma} \beta) \xrightarrow{\delta} ([\alpha] \xrightarrow{\gamma} [\beta])$$

---

[4] As hinted in footnote 1, our compiler prints this type as $(\alpha \xrightarrow{\gamma} \beta) \rightarrow ([\alpha] \xrightarrow{\gamma} [\beta])$ since all elided parts (including δ) can be inferred from suitably chosen conventions.

4   CPS and Duality: The Internal Language (IL)

In previous work we used a type-directed translation of **MLPolyR** into a variant of System F with extensible polymorphic records. Sum types and extensible cases were eliminated by taking advantage of duality [4]. We then used an adaptation of Ohori's technique of compiling record polymorphism by passing sets of *indices* which serve as witnesses for row types [17].

It is possible to retain this general approach to compilation even in the presence of exceptions. For this we combine the original dual transformation—which eliminates sums and cases—with continuation-passing style (CPS). While a "double-barreled" CPS makes continuations explicit and represents exception handlers as alternative continuations, we take this idea one step further and split the exception context into a record of possibly many individual continuations—one for each exception constructor that is being handled. Such a "multi-barreled" CPS provides a manifest explanation for the claim contained in the title of this paper: after CPS- and dual translation both exception handlers and extensible cases are represented identically, namely as records of functions.

The type-sensitive translation from EL into the System F-like intermediate language IL is given as rules for an extended typing judgment. Such a judgment has the form:

$$\Delta; \Gamma \vdash e : \tau; \rho \rightsquigarrow \bar{c} : (\bar{\tau}, \bar{\rho}) \text{ comp}$$

Here Δ, Γ, e, τ, and ρ are EL-level environments, terms, and types which appear exactly as they do in Figure 4. The IL-term $\bar{c}$ is the result of the translation. Its type is that of a *computation* that either sends a result of type $\bar{\tau}$ (corresponding to τ) to its default continuation or invokes one of the handler continuations described by $\bar{\rho}$ (corresponding to ρ). The notation $(\bar{\tau}, \bar{\rho})$ comp is a type synonym for $\bar{\tau}$ cont $\rightarrow \bar{\rho}$ hdlr $\rightarrow$ ans, with $\bar{\tau}$ cont and $\bar{\rho}$ hdlr themselves being further type synonyms. The details of IL and the translation of EL-types to IL-types as well as all rules for deriving translation judgments are given in the extended technical report accompanying this paper [5].

Eliminating Non-determinism—reify

Recall that the **handle all** rule of the EL semantics had to guess the new exception record to be constructed. But guessing correctly is not that difficult: the constructed record merely needs to match the exception (row-) type inferred at this point. To provide runtime access to the necessary type information, we equipped IL with a special type-sensitive **reify** construct, whose role is to convert functions on (dually encoded) sums to their corresponding records of individual functions.

Since **reify** is type-sensitive, type-erasure cannot be applied to IL. This is not a problem in practice, since subsequent compilation into lower-level untyped languages via index-passing in the style of our previous work on **MLPolyR** [4] is still possible. Details can be found in our technical report [5].

The translation from EL into IL amounts to an alternative elaboration-based semantics for EL. IL is sound and the translation maps well-typed EL programs

$$\frac{\Gamma(x) = \forall \alpha_1 : \kappa_1 \ldots \forall \alpha_n : \kappa_n . \tau \qquad \forall i. \Delta \vdash \theta_i : \kappa_i}{\Delta; \Gamma \vdash_v x : \tau[\theta_1/\alpha_1, \ldots, \theta_n/\alpha_n]} \text{ (VAR)}$$

$$\frac{}{\Delta; \Gamma \vdash_v n : \mathbf{int}} \text{ (INT)}$$

$$\frac{\forall i. \Delta; \Gamma, x_i : \tau_i \vdash e_i : \tau; \rho \qquad \Delta \vdash (l_1 : \tau_1, \ldots, l_n : \tau_n, \bullet) : \varnothing}{\Delta; \Gamma \vdash_v \{l_i : x_i \Rightarrow e_i\}_{i=1}^n : \langle l_i : \tau_i \rangle_{i=1}^n \xrightarrow{\rho} \tau} \text{ (C)}$$

$$\frac{\Delta; \Gamma, f \mapsto (\forall \alpha : \varnothing . \tau_2 \xrightarrow{\alpha} \tau), x \mapsto \tau_2 \vdash_v e : \tau \qquad \Delta \vdash \rho : \varnothing}{\Delta; \Gamma \vdash_v \mathbf{fun}\, f\, x = e : \tau_2 \xrightarrow{\rho} \tau} \text{ (FUN/VAL)}$$

$$\frac{\Delta; \Gamma, f \mapsto \tau_2 \xrightarrow{\rho} \tau, x \mapsto \tau_2 \vdash e : \tau; \rho \qquad \Delta \vdash \rho : \varnothing \qquad \Delta \vdash \tau_2 : \star}{\Delta; \Gamma \vdash_v \mathbf{fun}\, f\, x = e : \tau_2 \xrightarrow{\rho} \tau} \text{ (FUN/NON-VAL)}$$

$$\frac{\Delta; \Gamma \vdash_v e : \tau \qquad \Delta \vdash \rho : \varnothing}{\Delta; \Gamma \vdash e : \tau; \rho} \text{ (VALUE)}$$

$$\frac{\Delta; \Gamma \vdash e : \tau; \rho \qquad \tau \approx \tau' \qquad \rho \approx \rho'}{\Delta; \Gamma \vdash e : \tau'; \rho'} \text{ (TEQ)}$$

$$\frac{\Delta; \Gamma \vdash_v e : \tau \qquad \tau \approx \tau'}{\Delta; \Gamma \vdash_v e : \tau'} \text{ (TEQ/V)}$$

$$\frac{\Delta; \Gamma \vdash e_1 : \tau_2 \xrightarrow{\rho} \tau; \rho \qquad \Delta; \Gamma \vdash e_2 : \tau_2; \rho}{\Delta; \Gamma \vdash e_1\, e_2 : \tau; \rho} \text{ (APP)}$$

$$\frac{\alpha_1, \ldots, \alpha_n = FTV(\tau_1) \setminus FTV(\Gamma) \quad \Delta, \alpha_1 \mapsto \kappa_1, \ldots, \alpha_n \mapsto \kappa_n; \Gamma \vdash_v e_1 : \tau_1 \quad \Delta; \Gamma, x \mapsto \forall \alpha_1 : \kappa_1 \ldots \forall \alpha_n : \kappa_n . \tau_1 \vdash e_2 : \tau_2; \rho}{\Delta; \Gamma \vdash \mathbf{let}\, x = e_1\, \mathbf{in}\, e_2 : \tau_2; \rho} \text{ (LET/VAL)}$$

$$\frac{\Delta; \Gamma \vdash e : \tau; \rho \qquad \Delta \vdash (l : \tau, \rho) : \varnothing}{\Delta; \Gamma \vdash l\, e : \langle l : \tau, \rho \rangle; \rho'} \text{ (DCON)}$$

$$\frac{\Delta; \Gamma \vdash e_1 : \tau_1; \rho \qquad \Delta; \Gamma, x \mapsto \tau_1 \vdash e_2 : \tau_2; \rho}{\Delta; \Gamma \vdash \mathbf{let}\, x = e_1\, \mathbf{in}\, e_2 : \tau_2; \rho} \text{ (LET/NON-VAL)}$$

$$\frac{\Delta; \Gamma \vdash e : \langle \rho \rangle; \rho \qquad \Delta \vdash \tau : \star}{\Delta; \Gamma \vdash \mathbf{raise}\, e : \tau; \rho} \text{ (RAISE)}$$

$$\frac{\Delta; \Gamma \vdash e_1 : \langle \rho \rangle; \rho' \qquad \Delta; \Gamma \vdash e_2 : \langle \rho \rangle \xrightarrow{\rho'} \tau; \rho'}{\Delta; \Gamma \vdash \mathbf{match}\, e_1\, \mathbf{with}\, e_2 : \tau; \rho'} \text{ (MATCH)}$$

$$\frac{\Delta; \Gamma \vdash e_1 : \langle \rho_1 \rangle \xrightarrow{\rho} \tau; \rho' \quad \Delta \vdash (l : \tau_1, \rho_1) : \varnothing \quad \Delta; \Gamma, x \mapsto \tau_1 \vdash e_2 : \tau; \rho}{\Delta; \Gamma \vdash e_1 \oplus \{l\, x \Rightarrow e_2\} : \langle l : \tau, \rho_1 \rangle \xrightarrow{\rho} \tau; \rho'} \text{ (C/EXT)}$$

$$\frac{\Delta; \Gamma \vdash e_1 : \tau; l : \tau', \rho \qquad \Delta; \Gamma, x \mapsto \tau' \vdash e_2 : \tau; \rho}{\Delta; \Gamma \vdash e_1\, \mathbf{handle}\, \{l\, x \Rightarrow e_2\} : \tau; \rho} \text{ (HANDLE)}$$

$$\frac{\Delta; \Gamma \vdash e_1 : \tau; l : \tau', \rho \qquad \Delta; \Gamma, x \mapsto \tau' \vdash e_2 : \tau; l : \tau'', \rho}{\Delta; \Gamma \vdash e_1\, \mathbf{rehandle}\, \{l\, x \Rightarrow e_2\} : \tau; l : \tau'', \rho} \text{ (REHANDLE)}$$

$$\frac{\Delta; \Gamma \vdash e : \tau; \rho \qquad \Delta \vdash (l : \tau', \rho) : \varnothing}{\Delta; \Gamma \vdash \mathbf{unhandle}\, l : \tau; l : \tau', \rho} \text{ (UNHANDLE)}$$

$$\frac{\Delta; \Gamma \vdash e_1 : \tau; \rho' \qquad \Delta; \Gamma, x \mapsto \langle \rho' \rangle \vdash e_2 : \tau; \rho}{\Delta; \Gamma \vdash e_1\, \mathbf{handle}\, \{x \Rightarrow e_2\} : \tau; \rho} \text{ (HANDLE-ALL)}$$

$$\boxed{\frac{\varnothing; \Gamma_0 \vdash e : \mathbf{int}; \cdot}{\Gamma_0 \vdash e\, \mathbf{program}} \text{ (PROGRAM)}}$$

Fig. 4. Typing rules for EL for syntactic values (top), type equivalence and lifting (2nd), basic computations (3rd), and computations involving cases or exceptions (bottom). The judgment for whole programs is shown in the framed box.

to well-typed IL programs. Since an uncaught EL exception would try to select from the top-level exception handler, which by definition is an empty record, this constitutes a proof for our motto that "well-typed programs do not have uncaught exceptions" in the setting of this alternative semantics.

5   Related Work

We know of no prior work that incorporates higher-order exception tracking into the design of a programming language and its type system. Previous work in this context focused on *analysis* for identifying uncaught exceptions without attempting to incorporate such analysis into the language design itself [11,19,18,7,14,2]. While most of these attempts use flow analysis for exception tracking, some are based on types. In particular, this is true for the analysis by Pessaux and Leroy [14]. Much like we do, they also encode exception types as row types and employ row polymorphism.

Since the technical details of the Pessaux-Leroy system are similar to our work, we will now discuss the differences in some detail.

5.1   The Pessaux-Leroy Type System

Pessaux and Leroy [14] describe an exception analysis based on a type system that is very similar to ours. However, there are a number of key differences which reflect the difference in purpose: The Pessaux-Leroy system is an exception *analyzer*, i.e., a separate tool that is used to fine-comb programs written in an existing language—in their case Ocaml [13]. In contrast, our exploration of the language design space itself leads us to different trade-offs. Perhaps most importantly, our type system is simpler but forces the programmer to choose among a variety of exception-handling constructs (**handle**, **rehandle**, **unhandle**).

In most dialects of ML, including Ocaml, there is only one **handle** construct which—depending on the current exception context—can act either like our **handle** or like our **rehandle**. To deal with this form of exception-handling, the Pessaux-Leroy type system uses a third kind of type called a *presence type*. In row types, labels are associated with presence types π rather than ordinary types. There are two forms of presence types: $\mathfrak{a}$ indicates that a field is absent; $\mathfrak{p}(\tau)$ expresses that the field is present and carries values of type τ. The key to the added expressive power of presence types is the fact that they can also be represented by type variables of *presence kind* ($\circ$), opening the possibility of functions being polymorphic in the presence of explicitly named fields.

Figure 5 shows the modified type language. Notice that this is an idealized version. Pessaux and Leroy use presence types only for nullary exception constructors (i.e., exceptions without "payload"). This is done in an attempt at

$$\rho ::= \alpha \mid \centerdot \mid l : \pi, \rho \qquad \pi ::= \alpha \mid \mathfrak{p}(\tau) \mid \mathfrak{a} \qquad \theta ::= \tau \mid \rho \mid \pi \qquad \kappa ::= \star \mid L \mid \circ$$

Fig. 5. Alternative type language with presence types (for τ see Figure 1)

$$\frac{\Delta; \Gamma \vdash e : \tau; \rho' \qquad \Delta \vdash (l : \mathfrak{p}(\tau), \rho) : \varnothing}{\Delta; \Gamma \vdash l\ e : \langle l : \mathfrak{p}(\tau), \rho \rangle; \rho'}\,(\text{DCON})$$

$$\frac{\Delta; \Gamma \vdash e_1 : \tau; l : \mathfrak{p}(\tau'), \rho \qquad \Delta; \Gamma, x : \tau' \vdash e_2 : \tau; \rho \qquad \Delta \vdash \pi : \circ}{\Delta; \Gamma \vdash e_1\ \textbf{handle}\ \{\, l\ x \Rightarrow e_2 \,\} : \tau; l : \pi, \rho}\,(\text{HANDLE})$$

$$\frac{\Delta \vdash (l_1 : \mathfrak{p}(\tau_1), \ldots, l_n : \mathfrak{p}(\tau_n), \bullet) : \varnothing \qquad \forall i.\Delta; \Gamma, x_i : \tau_i \vdash e_i : \tau; \rho}{\Delta; \Gamma \vdash_{\mathsf{v}} \{\, l_i\ x_i \Rightarrow e_i \,\}_{i=1\ldots n} : \langle\, l_i : \mathfrak{p}(\tau_i), l_j : \mathfrak{a}\, \rangle_{i=1\ldots n, j=n+1\ldots m} \overset{\rho}{\hookrightarrow} \tau}\,(\text{C})$$

$$\frac{\Delta; \Gamma \vdash e_1 : \langle l : \pi, \rho_1 \rangle \overset{\rho}{\hookrightarrow} \tau; \rho' \qquad \Delta \vdash (l : \mathfrak{p}(\tau_1), \rho_1) : \varnothing \qquad \Delta; \Gamma, x : \tau_1 \vdash e_2 : \tau; \rho}{\Delta; \Gamma \vdash e_1 \oplus \{\, l\ x \Rightarrow e_2 \,\} : \langle l : \mathfrak{p}(\tau_1), \rho_1 \rangle \overset{\rho}{\hookrightarrow} \tau; \rho'}\,(\text{C}/\text{EXT})$$

Fig. 6. Alternative typing rules for EL with presence types of kind $\circ$

dealing with *nested patterns*, a feature that is also absent from our language.[5] The new expression language is the same as the old one, except that we no longer need **rehandle** or **unhandle**.

New or modified typing rules are given in Figure 6. (For modified kinding see the technical report [5].) The addition of presence types results in a considerably more involved equational theory on types, since (assuming well-formedness) both ρ and $l : \mathfrak{a}, \rho$ are the same type. See rule C in Figure 6 for an example of how this formally manifests itself in the type system. To see the difference in expressiveness between the two systems—stemming from the fact that rule C/EXT can both extend and override cases—consider a function definition such as:

$$\textbf{fun}\ \texttt{f}\ \texttt{c} = \texttt{c} \oplus \{\text{`A}\ x \Rightarrow x + 1\}$$

In our type system, the most general type schema inferred for f is:

$$\textbf{val f} \ : \ \forall \alpha : \{\text{`A}\}. \forall \gamma : \varnothing. \forall \delta : \varnothing. ((\langle \alpha \rangle \overset{\gamma}{\hookrightarrow} \text{int}) \overset{\delta}{\hookrightarrow} ((\text{`A} : \text{int}, \alpha) \overset{\gamma}{\hookrightarrow} \text{int})$$

This type restricts the argument to cases that do not already handle the `A constructor. With presence types, the inferred schema is:

$$\textbf{val f} \ : \ \forall \alpha : \{\text{`A}\}. \forall \beta : \circ. \forall \gamma : \varnothing. \forall \delta : \varnothing. ((\text{`A} : \beta, \alpha) \overset{\gamma}{\hookrightarrow} \text{int}) \overset{\delta}{\hookrightarrow} ((\text{`A} : \mathfrak{p}(\text{int}), \alpha) \overset{\gamma}{\hookrightarrow} \text{int})$$

It does not restrict the argument, since all labels—including `A—are permitted to be present or absent, even though the type "talks" about label `A separately.

A low-level implementation technique based on index-passing is still possible. Presence type variables that in the IL are bound by a type abstraction turn into Boolean witness parameters. The calculation of indices itself becomes more complicated, since presence witnesses have to be taken into account.

The improved expressiveness of a type system with presence types comes at the expense of added conceptual complexity. Such complexity is perfectly acceptable when it is used internally by an analysis tool, but it may be undesirable in a type system that programmers confront directly in everyday use of the language.

---

[5] For some programs, not using presence types for non-constant constructors reduces the precision of the analysis. The fact that Pessaux and Leroy do not report on such a loss probably indicates that such exception constructors are rare in practice.

A more serious problem with presence types is the loss of a certain degree of functional abstraction. Let h be a polymorphic function of type $\forall \alpha : \varnothing.\forall \gamma : \varnothing.(\langle \alpha \rangle \overset{\gamma}{\hookrightarrow} \text{int}) \overset{\gamma}{\to} \text{int}$. Now consider the following two definitions:

```
fun f c = h c
fun g c = h (c ⊕ {'A x ⇒ x + 1})
```

Using presence types, the inferred signatures are:

$$\textbf{val } f \ : \ \forall \alpha : \varnothing.\forall \gamma : \varnothing.(\langle \alpha \rangle \overset{\gamma}{\hookrightarrow} \text{int}) \overset{\gamma}{\to} \text{int}$$

$$\textbf{val } g \ : \ \forall \alpha : \{`A\}.\forall \beta : \circ.\forall \gamma : \varnothing.(\langle `A : \beta, \alpha \rangle \overset{\gamma}{\hookrightarrow} \text{int}) \overset{\gamma}{\to} \text{int}$$

The type schemas for f and g look very different, yet their respective sets of instantiations coincide precisely. In traditional denotational models of types they *are* the same. Should we not consider the two schemas equivalent then? The obvious difference between them seems to be just an artifact of type inference. It arises due to the absence of case extension in f, while case extension is used in g. Clearly, an *implementation detail* has leaked into the inferred signature.

An obvious idea is to try and "normalize" g's type to make it equal to that of f. However, doing so would break index-passing compilation! Since g performs functional extension of a case, it needs to know the index of label $`A$. But the index-passing transformation—when working with the signature of f—would not generate such an index argument. Thus, not only has an implementation detail leaked into the signature, this leakage is actually essential to the compilation technology. Under the rules that we use for EL, function g is typed as:

$$\textbf{val } g \ : \ \forall \alpha : \{`A\}.\forall \gamma : \varnothing.(\langle \alpha \rangle \overset{\gamma}{\hookrightarrow} \text{int}) \overset{\gamma}{\to} \text{int}$$

Here g's type is not the same as that of f—neither syntactically nor denotationally. Indeed, f and g have different interfaces, since the latter does not accept arguments that already handle $`A$. While this seems like a restriction on where $g$ can be used, there is always an easy workaround when this becomes a problem: the programmer can explicitly narrow the intended argument by removing $`A$ at the call site. Applied to the problem of handling exceptions, the same reasoning inspired us to the inclusion of **rehandle** and **unhandle** in the language.

Forcing the programmer to be explicit about such things can be considered both burden and benefit. By being explicit about widening or narrowing, a program documents more clearly what is going on. We hope that practical experience with the language will tell whether or not this outweighs the disadvantages.

6 Conclusions

We have shown the design of a higher-order programming language that guarantees freedom from uncaught exceptions. Using a type system—as opposed to flow- or constraint-based approaches—for tracking exceptions provides a straightforward path for integration into a language design. Moreover, our type system is simpler than the one used by Pessaux and Leroy for exception analysis, because we are able to avoid presence types by trading them for language constructs that explicitly manipulate the shape of the exception handler context.

Our language is sound, and soundness includes freedom from uncaught exceptions. We formalized our language and also provided an elaboration semantics from the implicitly typed external language EL into an explicitly typed internal form IL that is based on System F. The elaboration performs CPS transformation as well as dual translation, eliminating exceptions, handlers, sums, as well as first-class cases. The translation supports our intuition that the act of establishing a new exception handler is closely related to the one of extending first-class cases. The latter had recently been described in the context of our work on **MLPolyR** [4]. Our new IL is almost the same as the original internal language, a fact that enabled us to reuse much of the existing implementation machinery. The only major addition to our IL is a type-sensitive **reify** construct that accounts for "catch-all" exception handlers.

We have adapted the existing index-passing translations into low-level code to work with our system. Our prototype compiler translates a concrete language modeled after EL into PowerPC machine code. It shares most of its type inference engine with the previous compiler for **MLPolyR**.

Index-passing, while providing motivation for this work, is not the driving force behind the actual language design. Instead, our distinction between **handle** and **rehandle** keeps the type system simpler and may have certain software-engineering benefits. The same considerations would apply even if the target language provided native support for, e.g., extensible sums. As we have explained in Section 5, based on the more complicated Pessaux-Leroy type system, witness-passing can also be used for implementing an ML-like dual-purpose **handle**-construct.

References

1. Appel, A.W., MacQueen, D.B.: Standard ML of New Jersey. In: Third International Symp. on Prog. Lang. Implementation and Logic Programming, pp. 1–13 (August 1991)
2. Benton, N., Buchlovsky, P.: Semantics of an effect analysis for exceptions. In: TLDI 2007, pp. 15–26. ACM, New York (2007)
3. Benton, N., Kennedy, A.: Exceptional syntax. J. Funct. Program. 11(4), 395–410 (2001)
4. Blume, M., Acar, U.A., Chae, W.: Extensible programming with first-class cases. In: ICFP 2006: Proceedings of the eleventh ACM SIGPLAN international conference on Functional programming, pp. 239–250. ACM, New York (2006)
5. Blume, M., Acar, U.A., Chae, W.: Exception handlers as extensible cases. U.Chicago, Computer Sci. Tech. Report TR-2008-03 (February 2008)
6. Cardelli, L., Donahue, J., Glassman, L., Jordan, M., Kalsow, B., Nelson, G.: Modula-3 report. Technical Report Research Report 31, DEC SRC (1988)
7. Fähndrich, M., Foster, J., Cu, J., Aiken, A.: Tracking down exceptions in Standard ML programs. Technical Report CSD-98-996, UC Berkeley (February 1998)
8. Felleisen, M., Hieb, R.: A revised report on the syntactic theories of sequential control and state. Theoretical Computer Science 103(2), 235–271 (1992)
9. Gansner, E.R., Reppy, J.H.: The Standard ML Basis Library. Cambridge University Press, Cambridge (2002)
10. Gosling, J., Joy, B., Steele, G., Bracha, G.: Java Language Specification, 2nd edn. The Java Series. Addison Wesley, Reading (2000)

11. Guzmán, J., Suárez, A.: An extended type system for exceptions. In: ACM SIG-PLAN Workshop on ML and its Applications (1994)
12. Henglein, F.: Type inference with polymorphic recursion. ACM Trans. Program. Lang. Syst. 15(2), 253–289 (1993)
13. Leroy, X.: The Objective Caml System (1996), http://caml.inria.fr/ocaml
14. Leroy, X., Pessaux, F.: Type-based analysis of uncaught exceptions. ACM Trans. Program. Lang. Syst. 22(2), 340–377 (2000)
15. Lions, J.L.: Ariane 5, flight 501 failure, report by the inquiry board (1996), http://sunnyday.mit.edu/accidents/Ariane5accidentreport.html
16. Liskov, B., Atkinson, R., Bloom, T., Moss, E., Schaffert, J.C., Scheifler, R., Snyder, A.: CLU Reference Manual. Springer, New York (1981)
17. Ohori, A.: A polymorphic record calculus and its compilation. ACM Trans. Program. Lang. Syst. 17(6), 844–895 (1995)
18. Yi, K.: An abstract interpretation for estimating uncaught exceptions in Standard ML programs. Sci. Comput. Program. 31(1) (1998)
19. Yi, K., Ryu, S.: Towards a cost-effective estimation of uncaught exceptions in sml programs. In: Van Hentenryck, P. (ed.) SAS 1997. LNCS, vol. 1302, pp. 98–113. Springer, Heidelberg (1997)

Sound and Complete Type Inference for a Systems Programming Language

Swaroop Sridhar, Jonathan S. Shapiro, and Scott F. Smith

Department of Computer Science, The Johns Hopkins University
swaroop@cs.jhu.edu, shap@cs.jhu.edu, scott@cs.jhu.edu

Abstract. This paper introduces a new type system designed for safe systems programming. The type system features a new mutability model that combines unboxed types with a consistent typing of mutability. The type system is provably sound, supports polymorphism, and eliminates the need for alias analysis to determine the immutability of a location. A sound and complete type inference algorithm for this system is presented.

1 Introduction

Recent advances in the theory and practice of programming languages have resulted in modern languages and tools that provide certain correctness guarantees regarding the execution of programs. However, these advances have not been effectively applied to the construction of *systems programs*, the core components of a computer system. One of the primary causes of this problem is the fact that existing languages do not simultaneously support modern language features — such as static type safety, type inference, higher order functions and polymorphism — as well as features that are critical to the correctness and performance of systems programs such as prescriptive data structure representation and mutability. In this paper, we endeavor to bridge this gap between modern language design and systems programming. We first discuss the support for these features in existing languages, identify the challenges in combining these feature sets and then describe our approach toward solving this problem.

Representation Control. A systems programming language must be expressive enough to specify details of representation including boxed/unboxed data-structure layout and stack/heap allocation. For systems programs, this is both a correctness as well as a performance requirement. Systems programs interact with the hardware through data structures such as page tables whose representation is dictated by the hardware. Conformance to these representation specifications is necessary for correctness. Languages like ML [16] intentionally omit details of representation from the language definition, since this greatly simplifies the mathematical description of the language. Compilers like TIL [24] implement unboxed representation as a discretionary optimization. However, in systems programs, statements about representation are *prescriptive*, not *descriptive*. Formal treatment of representation is required in systems programming languages.

G. Ramalingam (Ed.): APLAS 2008, LNCS 5356, pp. 290–306, 2008.

Systems programs also rely on representation control for performance since it affects cache locality and paging behavior. This expressiveness is also crucial for interfacing with external C [9] or assembly code and data. For example, a careful implementation of the TCP/IP protocol stack in Standard ML incurred a substantial overhead of up to 10x increase in system load and a 40x slowdown in accessing external memory relative to the equivalent C implementation [1,3]. This shows that representation control is as important as, or even more important than, high level algorithms for the performance of systems tasks.

Complete Mutability. One of the key features essential for systems programming is support for mutability. The support for mutability must be 'complete' in the sense that any location — whether on the stack, heap, or within other unboxed structures — can be mutated. Allocation of mutable cells on the stack boosts performance because (1) the top of the stack is typically accessible from the data cache (2) stack locations are directly addressable and therefore do not require the extra dereferencing involved in the case of heap locations (3) stack allocation does not involve garbage collection overhead. This is particularly important for high confidence and/or embedded kernels as they cannot tolerate unpredictable variance in overhead caused by heap allocation and collection. ML-like languages require all mutable (`ref`) cells to reside on the heap. In pure languages like Haskell [14], the support for mutability is even more restrictive than ML. These restricted models of mutability are insufficiently expressive from a systems programming perspective.

Consistent Mutability. The mutability support in a language is said to be 'consistent' if the (im)mutability of every location is invariant across all aliases over program execution. In this model, there is a sound notion of immutability of locations. This benefits tools that perform static analysis or model checking because conclusions drawn about the immutability of a location need never be conservative. It also increases the amount of optimization that a compiler can safely perform without complex alias analysis. Polymorphic type inference systems such as Hindley-Milner algorithm [15] also rely on a sound notion of immutability. ML supports consistent mutability since types are definitive about the (im)mutability of every location. In contrast, C does not support this feature. For example, in C it is legal to write:

```
const bool *cp = ...; bool *p = cp; *p = false; // OK!
```

The alleged "constness" of the location pointed to by `cp` is a local property (only) with respect to the alias `cp` and not a statement of true immutability of the target location. The analysis and optimization of critical systems programs can be improved by using a language with a consistent mutability model.

Type Inference and Polymorphism. Type inference achieves the advantages of static typing with a lower burden on the programmer, facilitating rapid prototyping and development. Polymorphic type inference (c.f. ML or Haskell) combines the advantages of static type safety with much of the convenience provided by dynamically typed languages like Python [18]. Automatic inference of polymorphism simplifies generic programming, and therefore increases the reuse and reliability of code. Safe languages like Java [17], C# [4], or Vault [2] do not support type inference. Cyclone [10] features partial type inference and supports polymorphism only for functions with explicit type annotations.

The following table summarizes the support available in existing languages for the above features and static type safety:

	C/Asm	Safe-C	CCured	Cyclone	Vault	Java	ML	Haskell
Representation	✓			✓	✓			
Complete Mutability	✓	✓	✓	✓	✓	✓		
Consistent Mutability							✓	✓
Static Type Safety				✓	✓	✓	✓	✓
Poly. Type Inference							✓	✓

In this paper, we present a new type system and formal foundations for a safe systems programming language that supports all of the above features.

The combination of mutability and unboxed representation presents several challenges for type inference. Mutability is an attribute of the *location* storing a value and not the value itself. Therefore, two expressions across a copy boundary (ex: arguments copied at a function call) can differ in their mutability. We refer to this notion of mutability compatibility of types as *copy compatibility*. Copy compatibility creates ramifications for syntax-directed type and mutability inference. Type inference is further complicated due to well known problems with the interaction of mutability and polymorphism [26]. This has forced a second-class treatment of mutability in ML-like languages and a lack of inferred polymorphism in others.

We present a sound and complete polymorphic type inference algorithm for a language that supports consistent and complete mutability. In order to overcome the challenges posed by copy compatibility, the underlying type system uses a system of constrained types that range over mutability and polymorphism. Safety of the type system as well as the soundness and completeness of the type inference algorithm have been proved.

2   Informal Overview

In this section, we give an informal description of our type system and inference algorithm. For purposes of presentation in this paper, we define $\mathbb{B}$, a core systems programming language calculus. $\mathbb{B}$ is a direct expression of lambda calculus with side effects, extended to be able to reflect the semantics of explicit representation.

Identifiers	$x ::= y \mid z \mid \dots$	Vars	$\alpha ::= \alpha \mid \beta \mid \gamma \mid \delta \mid \varepsilon \mid \dots$
Booleans	$b ::= true \mid false$		$\varsigma ::= \alpha \mid \Psi\alpha$
Indices	$i ::= 1 \mid 2 \mid !i$	Types	$\rho ::= \alpha \mid \mathbf{unit} \mid \mathbf{bool} \mid \tau \to \tau$
Values	$v ::= () \mid b \mid \lambda x.e \mid (v,v)$		$\mid \tau \times \tau \mid \Uparrow\tau \mid \Psi\rho$
Left Expr	$l ::= x \mid e\hat{} \mid l.i \mid l : \tau$		$\varrho ::= \rho \mid \alpha\vert\rho$
Expressions	$e ::= v \mid x \mid e\,e \mid l := e$		$\tau ::= \varrho \mid \varsigma{\downarrow}\rho$
	$\mid \mathbf{if}\ e\ \mathbf{then}\ e\ \mathbf{else}\ e \mid e : \tau$	Scheme	$\sigma ::= \tau \mid \forall\overline{\alpha}.\tau\backslash\mathcal{D}$
	$\mid \mathbf{dup}(e) \mid e\hat{} \mid (e,e) \mid e.i$	Ct. Set	$\mathcal{D} ::= \emptyset \mid \{\bigstar^{\varkappa}_{\overline{z}}(\tau)\} \mid \mathcal{D} \cup \mathcal{D}$
	$\mid \mathbf{let}\ x[:\tau] = e\ \mathbf{in}\ e$	Kinds	$\varkappa ::= \kappa \mid \psi \mid \forall$

The type $\Uparrow\tau$ represents a reference (pointer) type and $\Psi\rho$ represents a mutable type. The expression $\mathbf{dup}(e)$, where e has type τ, returns a reference of type $\Uparrow\tau$ to a heap-allocated *copy* of the value of e. The $\hat{}$ operator is used to dereference heap cells. Pairs (,) are *unboxed* structures whose constituent elements are contiguously allocated on the stack, or in their containing data-structure. $e.1$ and $e.2$ perform selection from pairs. We define $!1 = 2$ and $!2 = 1$. The $\mathbf{let}$ construct can be used for allocating (possibly mutable) stack variables and to create let-polymorphic bindings. $\mathbf{let}\ x[:\tau] = e$ represents optional type qualification of let-bound variables.

The Mutability Model. $\mathbb{B}$ supports consistent, complete mutability. The mutability support is complete since the $:=$ operator mutates both stack locations (let-bound locals, function parameters) and heap locations ($\mathbf{dup}$-ed values). It can also perform in-place updates to individual fields of unboxed pairs. The mutability support is consistent since we impose the "one location, one type" rule. For example, in the following expression,

$$\mathbf{let}\ cp : \Uparrow\mathbf{bool} = \mathbf{dup}(true)\ \mathbf{in}\ \mathbf{let}\ p : \Uparrow\Psi\mathbf{bool} = cp \quad (* \ \mathtt{Error}\ *)$$

cp has the type reference to bool ($\Uparrow\mathbf{bool}$), which is incompatible with that of p, reference to mutable-bool ($\Uparrow\Psi\mathbf{bool}$). Unlike ML, $:=$ does not dereference its target. The expressions that can appear on the left of an assignment $:=$ are restricted to left expressions (defined by the above grammar). This not only preserves the programmer's mental model of the relationship between locations storage, but also ensures that compiler transformations are semantics preserving.

Copy Compatibility. $\mathbb{B}$ is a call-by-value language, and supports copy compatibility, which permits locations across a copy boundary to differ in their mutability. For example, in the following expression:

$$\mathbf{let}\ fnxn = \lambda x.(x := false)\ \mathbf{in}\ \mathbf{let}\ y : \mathbf{bool} = true\ \mathbf{in}\ fnxn\ y$$

the type of $fnxn$ is $(\Psi\mathbf{bool}) \to \mathbf{unit}$, whereas that of the actual argument y is $\mathbf{bool}$. Since x is a *copy* of y and occupies a different location, this expression is type safe. Thus, we write $\mathbf{bool} \cong \Psi\mathbf{bool}$, where $\cong$ indicates copy compatibility.

Copy compatibility must not extend past a reference boundary in order to ensure that every location has a unique type. We define copy compatibility for $\mathbb{B}$ as:

$$\frac{}{\tau \cong \tau} \quad \frac{\tau_1 \cong \tau_2}{\tau_2 \cong \tau_1} \quad \frac{\tau_1 \cong \tau_2 \quad \tau_2 \cong \tau_3}{\tau_1 \cong \tau_3} \quad \frac{\tau \cong \rho}{\tau \cong \Psi\rho} \quad \frac{\tau_1 \cong \tau_1' \quad \tau_2 \cong \tau_2'}{\tau_1 \times \tau_2 \cong \tau_1' \times \tau_2'}$$

Copy compatibility is allowed at all positions where a copy is performed: at argument passing, new variable binding, assignment, and basically in all expressions where a left-expression is not expected or returned. For example, the expression $(x : \tau) : \Psi\tau$ is ill typed, but the branches of a conditional can have different but copy compatible types as in if *true* then $a : \tau$ else $b : \Psi\tau$.

2.1   Type Inference

We now consider the problem of designing a type inference algorithm for $\mathbb{B}$. Due to copy compatibility, it is no longer possible to infer a unique (simple) type for all expressions. For example, in the expression let $p = true$, we know that the type of the literal *true* is bool, but the type of p could either be bool or Ψbool. Therefore, unlike ML, we cannot use a straightforward syntax-directed type inference algorithm in $\mathbb{B}$.

It is natural to ask why mutability should be inferred at all. That is: why not require explicit annotation for all mutable values, and infer immutable types by default? Unfortunately, in a language with copy compatibility, this will result in a proliferation of type annotations. Constructor applications, polymorphic type instantiations, accessor functions, *etc.* will have to be explicitly annotated with their types. For example, if *fst* is an accessor function that returns the first element of a pair, and m is a variable of type Ψbool, we will have to write:

let xyz = dup(*fst* $(m,false)$: Ψbool $\times$ bool) : $\Uparrow\Psi$bool in ...

Therefore, if mutability is not inferred, it results in a substantial increase in the number of programmer annotations, and type inference becomes ineffective. It is desirable that the inference algorithm must automatically infer polymorphism (without any programmer annotations) as well, since this leads to better software engineering by maximizing code reuse.

Therefore, the desirable characteristics of a type inference algorithm for $\mathbb{B}$ are:

(1) It must be sound, complete, and decidable without programmer annotations.
(2) It must automatically infer both polymorphism and mutability.
(3) It must infer types that are intelligible to the programmer. That is, it must avoid the main drawback of many inference systems with subtyping, where the inferred principal type is presented as a set of equations and inequations.

In order to address the above requirements, we propose a variant of the Hindley-Milner algorithm [15]. This algorithm uses constrained types that range over mutability and polymorphism in order to infer principal types for $\mathbb{B}$ programs.

Polymorphism Over Mutability. In order to infer principal types in a language with copy compatibility, we define the following constrained types that allow us to infer types with variable mutability. Let $\simeq$ be a equivalence relation on types such that $\rho \simeq \Psi\rho$. Let $\tau \setminus \eta$ denote a constrained type where τ is constrained by the set of (in)equations η. We write :

$\alpha \mathord{\downarrow} \rho \equiv \alpha \setminus \{\alpha \simeq \rho\}$: any type equal to base type ρ except for top level mutability.
$\varsigma \mathord{\downarrow} \rho \equiv \varsigma \setminus \{\varsigma \cong \rho\}$: any type copy compatible with ρ, where $\varsigma = \alpha$ or $\Psi\alpha$.

Now, in the expression let $p = true$, we can give p the type $\alpha \mathord{\downarrow} \mathtt{bool}$. During inference, the type can later get resolved to either $\mathtt{bool}$ or $\Psi\mathtt{bool}$. The forms $\alpha \mathord{\downarrow} \rho$ and $\varsigma \mathord{\downarrow} \rho$ respectively provide fine grained and coarse grained control over expressing types with variable mutability. For example:

Type	Instances	Non-Instances
$\alpha \mathord{\downarrow}(\mathtt{bool} \times \mathtt{unit})$	$\mathtt{bool} \times \mathtt{unit}, \Psi(\mathtt{bool} \times \mathtt{unit})$	$\Psi\mathtt{bool} \times \mathtt{unit}$
$\alpha \mathord{\downarrow}(\mathtt{bool} \times \mathtt{unit})$	$\mathtt{bool} \times \mathtt{unit}, \Psi(\Psi\mathtt{bool} \times \Psi\mathtt{unit})$ $\Psi\mathtt{bool} \times \mathtt{unit}, \beta \mathord{\downarrow}(\mathtt{bool} \times \mathtt{unit})$	$\mathtt{unit} \times \mathtt{bool}$
$\Psi\alpha \mathord{\downarrow}(\mathtt{bool} \times \mathtt{unit})$	$\Psi(\mathtt{bool} \times \mathtt{unit}), \Psi(\mathtt{bool} \times \Psi\mathtt{unit})$	$\mathtt{bool} \times \mathtt{unit}, \beta \mathord{\downarrow}(\mathtt{bool} \times \mathtt{unit})$
$\alpha \mathord{\downarrow}\Uparrow\mathtt{bool}$	$\Uparrow\mathtt{bool}, \Psi\Uparrow\mathtt{bool}$	$\Uparrow\Psi\mathtt{bool}$

By embedding constraints within types, we obtain an elegant representation of constrained types that are self contained. The programmer is just presented a type, rather than a type associated with a set of unsolved inequations. Every type of the form $\varsigma \mathord{\downarrow} \rho$ can be realized through a canonical representation using $\alpha \mathord{\downarrow} \rho$ types. However, types of the form $\varsigma \mathord{\downarrow} \rho$ are critical for type inference. For example, the type $\alpha \mathord{\downarrow} \beta$ represents a type that is compatible with β, even if β later resolves to a more concrete (ex: pair) type.

Since we allow copy compatibility at function argument and return positions, two function types are equal regardless of the shallow mutability of the argument and return types. Therefore, we follow a convention of writing all function types with immutable types at copy compatible positions. The intuition here is that the type of a function must be described in the interface form, and must hide the "internal" mutability information. For example, the function $\lambda x.(x := true)$, has external type $\mathtt{bool} \to \mathtt{unit}$ even though the internal type is $\Psi\mathtt{bool} \to \mathtt{unit}$.

$\mathbb{B}$ is a let-polymorphic language. At a let boundary, we would like to quantify over variables that range over mutability, in order to achieve mutability polymorphism. The next sections discuss certain complications that arise during the inference of such types, present our solution to the problem.

Soundness implications. Like ML, $\mathbb{B}$ enforces the value restriction [26] to preserve soundness of polymorphic typing. This means that the type of x in let $x = e_1$ in e_2 can only be generalized if e_1 is an *immutable* syntactic value. For example, in the expression let $id = \lambda x.x$, the type of id before generalization is $\beta \mathord{\downarrow}(\alpha \to \alpha)$. However, giving id the generalized type $\forall\alpha\beta.\beta \mathord{\downarrow}(\alpha \to \alpha)$ is unsound, since it permits expressions such as let $id = \lambda x.x$ in ($id := \lambda x.true, id$ ()) to type check. We can give id either the polymorphic type $\forall\alpha.\alpha \to \alpha$, or the monomorphic type $\beta \mathord{\downarrow}(\alpha \to \alpha)$. However, neither is a principal type for id.

Overloading Polymorphism. Due to the above interaction of polymorphism and unboxed mutability, a traditional HM-style inference algorithm cannot defer decisions about the mutability of types past their generalization. Therefore, current algorithms fix the mutability of types before generalization based on certain heuristics — thus sacrificing completeness [22]. In order to alleviate this problem, we use a new form of constrained types that range over both mutability and polymorphism.

We introduce constraints $\bigstar_x^{\varkappa}(\tau)$ to enforce consistency restrictions on instantiations of generalized types. The constraint $\bigstar_x^{\varkappa}(\tau)$ requires that the identifier x only be instantiated according to the kind $\varkappa$, where $\varkappa = \psi$ or $\forall$. If $\varkappa = \psi$, the instantiation of x must be monomorphic. That is, all uses of x must instantiate τ to the same type τ'. Here, τ' is permitted to be a mutable type. If $\varkappa = \forall$, different uses of x can instantiate τ differently, but all such instantiations must be immutable. At the point of definition (let), if the exact instantiation kind of a variable is unknown, we add the constraint $\bigstar_x^{\kappa}(\tau)$, where κ ranges over ψ and $\forall$. The correct instantiation kind is determined later based on the uses of x, and consistency semantics are enforced accordingly. The variable x in $\bigstar_x^{\kappa}(\tau)$ represents the program point (let) at which this constraint is generated. We assume that there are no name collisions so that every such x names a unique program point.

In this approach, the definition of id will be given the principal constrained type:

$$\texttt{let } id = \lambda x.x \texttt{ in } e \qquad id : \forall\alpha\beta.\beta\!\downarrow\!(\alpha \to \alpha) \setminus \{\bigstar_{id}^{\kappa}(\beta\!\downarrow\!(\alpha \to \alpha))\}$$

Every time id is instantiated to type τ' in e, the constraints $\bigstar_{id}^{\kappa}(\tau')$ are collected. e is declared type correct only if the set of all instantiated constraints are consistent for some κ. Note that we do not quantify over κ.

Example of e	Constraint set	Kind assignment
$(id\ true, id\ ())$	$\{\bigstar_{id}^{\kappa}(\texttt{bool} \to \texttt{bool}),\ \bigstar_{id}^{\kappa}(\texttt{unit} \to \texttt{unit})\}$	$\kappa \mapsto \forall$
$id := \lambda x.x$	$\{\bigstar_{id}^{\kappa}(\Psi(\gamma \to \gamma))\}$	$\kappa \mapsto \psi$
$(id\ true, id := \lambda x.())$	$\{\bigstar_{id}^{\kappa}(\texttt{bool} \to \texttt{bool}),\ \bigstar_{id}^{\kappa}(\Psi(\texttt{unit} \to \texttt{unit}))\}$	Type Error
(id, id)	$\{\bigstar_{id}^{\kappa}(\beta_1\!\downarrow\!(\alpha_1 \to \alpha_1)),\ \bigstar_{id}^{\kappa}(\beta_2\!\downarrow\!(\alpha_2 \to \alpha_2))\}$	$\kappa \mapsto \psi$ or $\forall$

The final case type checks with either kind, under the type assignments ($\alpha_1 = \alpha_2$, $\beta_1 = \beta_2$) if $\kappa \mapsto \psi$ and ($\beta_1 = \alpha_1 \to \alpha_1$, $\beta_2 = \alpha_2 \to \alpha_2$) if $\kappa \mapsto \forall$. The intuition behind $\bigstar_x^{\kappa}(\tau)$ constraints is to achieve a form of *overloading* over polymorphism and mutability. We can think of $\bigstar_x^{\kappa}(\tau)$ as a type class [11] constraint that has exactly one possibly mutable instance $\bigstar_x^{\psi}(\tau_m)$, and an infinite number of $\bigstar_x^{\forall}(\tau_p)$ instances where all types $\overline{\tau_p}$ are immutable.

In practice, once the correct kind of instantiation is inferred, the type scheme can be presented in a simplified form to the programmer. For example, consider the expression $\texttt{let } f = \lambda x.\texttt{if } x\hat{} \texttt{ then } () \texttt{ else } () \texttt{ in } (f\ m, f\ n)$, where $m{:}{\Uparrow}\Psi$ bool and $n : {\Uparrow}\texttt{bool}$. Here, $f : \forall\alpha\beta.\beta\!\downarrow\!({\Uparrow}\alpha\!\downarrow\!\texttt{bool} \to \texttt{unit})\setminus\{\bigstar_f^{\kappa}(\beta\!\downarrow\!({\Uparrow}\alpha\!\downarrow\!\texttt{bool} \to \texttt{unit}))\}$. However, based on the polymorphic usage, we conclude that $\kappa \mapsto \forall$. We can now simplify the type scheme of f to obtain $f : \forall\alpha.{\Uparrow}\alpha\!\downarrow\!\texttt{bool} \to \texttt{unit}$. Since all function types are immutable, the mutability of the argument type need not be fixed, thus preserving mutability polymorphism. In order to ensure that type inference is modular, the $\bigstar_x^{\kappa}(\tau)$ constraints must not be exposed across a module boundary. For every top-level definition in a module, an arbitrary choice of $\kappa = \psi$ or $\kappa = \forall$ must be made for every surviving $\bigstar_x^\kappa(\tau)$ constraint.

In summary, we have used a system of constrained types to design a polymorphic type inference system that meets all of the design goals set at the beginning of this section. In the next section, we present a formal description of our type system and inference algorithm.

3   Formal Description

In order to formalize the semantics of $\mathbb{B}$, we extend the calculus with stack and heap locations (Fig. 1). Heap locations are first class values, but stack locations are not. Further, we annotate all `let` expressions with a kind — `let`$^\psi$: monomorphic, possibly mutable definition, and `let`$^\forall$: polymorphic definitions. The two kinds of `let` expressions have different execution semantics. We write `let`$^\kappa$ to range over the two kinds of `let` expressions. This distinction is similar to Smith and Volpano's Polymorphic-C [21]. However, unlike Polymorphic-C, let-kind is *meta syntax*, and is not a part of the input program. The correct kind of `let` is inferred from the static type information. We do not show the semantics for type-qualified expressions as they are trivial.

Locations	$L ::= 1 \mid \ell$	Stack	$S ::= \emptyset \mid S, 1 \mapsto v$
Stack Loc	$1 ::= 1_1 \mid 1_2 \mid \dots$	Heap	$H ::= \emptyset \mid H, \ell \mapsto v$
Heap Loc	$\ell ::= \ell_1 \mid \ell_2 \mid \dots$	Env.	$\Gamma ::= \emptyset \mid \Gamma, x \mapsto \sigma$
Sel Path	$p ::= i \mid p.p$	Store Typ	$\Sigma ::= \emptyset \mid \Sigma, L \mapsto \tau$
Values	$v ::= \dots \mid \ell$	Subst	$\theta ::= \langle \rangle \mid [\alpha \mapsto \tau] \mid [\kappa \mapsto \varkappa] \mid \theta \circ \theta$
Expr	$e ::= \dots \mid 1 \mid \ell$	Unf. Ctset	$\mathcal{C} ::= \mathcal{D} \mid \{\tau = \tau\} \mid \{\kappa = \varkappa\} \mid \mathcal{C} \cup \mathcal{C}$
Left Expr	$l ::= \dots \mid 1$	Redex	$\mathcal{R} ::= - \mid \mathcal{R} \; e \mid v \; \mathcal{R} \mid \mathcal{L} := \mathcal{R} \mid \mathrm{dup}(\mathcal{R})$
Syn. Val	$\upsilon ::= v \mid x \mid 1 \mid (\upsilon, \upsilon)$		$\mid \mathcal{R}\hat{\;} \mid$ if $\mathcal{R}$ then e else $e \mid (\mathcal{R}, e)$
lvalues	$\mathcal{L} ::= 1 \mid \ell\hat{\;} \mid 1.p \mid \ell\hat{\;}.p$		$\mid (v, \mathcal{R}) \mid \mathcal{R}.i \mid \mathtt{let}^\varkappa \; x = \mathcal{R}$ in e

Fig. 1. Extended $\mathbb{B}$ grammar

Dynamic Semantics. The system state is represented by the triple S; H; e consisting of the stack S, the heap H, and the expression e to be evaluated. Evaluation itself is a two place relation S; H; $e \Rightarrow$ S'; H'; e' that denotes a single step of execution. Fig. 2 shows the evaluation rules for our core language. We assume that the program is alpha-converted so that there are no name collisions due to inner bindings. Following the theoretical development of [6], we give separate execution semantics for left evaluation (execution of left expressions l on the LHS of an assignment, denoted by $\Rrightarrow$) and right evaluation ($\Rightarrow$) respectively.

Since the E-Dup and E-ˆ rules work only on the heap, we can only capture references to heap cells. Stack locations cannot escape beyond their scope since E-Rval rule performs implicit value extraction from stack locations in rvalue contexts. State updates can be performed either on the stack or on the heap (E-:=* rules). The stack is modeled as a pseudo-heap. This enables us to abstract away details such as closure-construction and garbage collection while illustrating the core semantics, as they can later be reified independently.

Rule	Pre-conditions	Evaluation Step
E-Rval	$S(l) = v$	$S; H; l \Rightarrow S; H; v$
E-#	$S; H; e \Rightarrow S'; H'; e'$	$S; H; \mathcal{R}[e] \Rightarrow S'; H'; \mathcal{R}[e']$
E-App	$l \notin dom(S)$	$S; H; \lambda x.e\ v \Rightarrow S, l \mapsto v; H; e[l/x]$
E-If	$b_1 = true \quad b_2 = false$	$S; H; \text{if } b_i \text{ then } e_1 \text{ else } e_2 \Rightarrow S; H; e_i$
E-.i		$S; H; (v_1, v_2).i \Rightarrow S; H; v_i$
E-Dup	$\ell \notin dom(H)$	$S; H; \mathsf{dup}(v) \Rightarrow S; H, \ell \mapsto v; \ell$
EL-^#	$S; H; e \Rightarrow S'; H'; e'$	$S; H; e^\smallfrown \Rightarrow S'; H'; e'^\smallfrown$
E-^	$H(\ell) = v$	$S; H; \ell^\smallfrown \Rightarrow S; H; v$
E-:=#	$S; H; l \Rightarrow S'; H'; l'$	$S; H; l := e \Rightarrow S'; H'; l' := e$
E-:=Stack		$S, l \mapsto v; H; l := v' \Rightarrow S, l \mapsto v'; H; ()$
E-:=Heap		$S, H, \ell \mapsto v; \ell^\smallfrown := v' \Rightarrow S; H, \ell \mapsto v'; ()$
E-:=S.p	$v'_{!i} = v_{!i} \quad S, l \mapsto v_i; H; l.p := v'_i \Rightarrow S, l \mapsto v'_i; H; ()$	$S, l \mapsto (v_1, v_2); H; l.p := v'_i \Rightarrow S, l \mapsto (v'_1, v'_2); H; ()$
E-:=H.p	$v'_{!i} = v_{!i} \quad S; H, \ell \mapsto v_i; \ell^\smallfrown.p := v'_i \Rightarrow S; H, \ell \mapsto v'_i; ()$	$S; H, \ell \mapsto (v_1, v_2); \ell^\smallfrown.i.p := v'_i \Rightarrow S; H, \ell \mapsto (v'_1, v'_2); ()$
E-Let-M	$l \notin dom(S)$	$S; H; \mathsf{let}^\psi\ x = v_1 \text{ in } e_2 \Rightarrow S, l \mapsto v_1; H; e_2[l/x]$
E-Let-P		$S; H; \mathsf{let}^\forall\ x = v_1 \text{ in } e_2 \Rightarrow S; H; e_2[v_1/x]$

Fig. 2. Small Step Operational Semantics

τ	$\triangle(\tau)$	$\triangledown(\tau)$	$\blacktriangle(\tau)$	$\blacktriangledown(\tau)$	$\mathfrak{I}(\tau)$	$\{\!|\tau|\!\}$
α	$\Psi\alpha$	α	$\Psi\alpha$	α	α	$\{\alpha\}$
unit	Ψunit	unit	Ψunit	unit	unit	$\emptyset$
bool	Ψbool	bool	Ψbool	bool	bool	$\emptyset$
$\tau_1 \to \tau_2$	$\Psi(\tau_1 \to \tau_2)$	$\tau_1 \to \tau_2$	$\Psi(\tau_1 \to \tau_2)$	$\tau_1 \to \tau_2$	$\tau_1 \to \tau_2$	$\{\!|\tau_1|\!\} \cup \{\!|\tau_2|\!\}$
$\Uparrow\tau$	$\Psi\Uparrow\tau$	$\Uparrow\tau$	$\Psi\Uparrow\tau$	$\Uparrow\tau$	$\Uparrow\mathfrak{I}(\tau)$	$\{\!|\tau|\!\}$
$\Psi\rho$	$\triangle(\rho)$	$\triangledown(\rho)$	$\blacktriangle(\rho)$	$\blacktriangledown(\rho)$	$\mathfrak{I}(\rho)$	$\{\!|\rho|\!\}$
$\tau_1 \times \tau_2$	$\Psi(\triangle(\tau_1) \times \triangle(\tau_2))$	$\triangledown(\tau_1) \times \triangledown(\tau_2)$	$\Psi(\tau_1 \times \tau_2)$	$\tau_1 \times \tau_2$	$\mathfrak{I}(\tau_1) \times \mathfrak{I}(\tau_2)$	$\{\!|\tau_1|\!\} \cup \{\!|\tau_2|\!\}$
$\alpha\!\downarrow\!\rho$	$\triangle(\rho)$	$\triangledown(\rho)$	$\blacktriangle(\rho)$	$\blacktriangledown(\rho)$	$\mathfrak{I}(\rho)$	$\{\alpha\!\downarrow\!\rho\} \cup \{\!|\rho|\!\}$
$\varsigma\!\downarrow\!\rho$	$\triangle(\rho)$	$\triangledown(\rho)$	$\blacktriangle(\varsigma)\!\downarrow\!\rho$	$\blacktriangledown(\varsigma)\!\downarrow\!\rho$	$\mathfrak{I}(\rho)$	$\{\varsigma\!\downarrow\!\rho\} \cup \{\!|\rho|\!\}$

τ	Immut(τ)	Mut(τ)	$\square(\tau)$	$\theta\langle\tau\rangle$
α	false	false	false	τ if $[\alpha \rightarrowtail \tau] \in \theta$, else α.
unit	true	false	true	unit
bool	true	false	true	bool
$\tau_1 \to \tau_2$	true	false	true	$\theta\langle\tau_1\rangle \to \theta\langle\tau_2\rangle$
$\Uparrow\tau$	Immut(τ)	Mut(τ)	$\square(\tau)$	$\Uparrow\theta\langle\tau\rangle$
$\Psi\rho$	false	true	$\square(\rho)$	$\Psi\theta\langle\rho\rangle$
$\tau_1 \times \tau_2$	Immut$(\tau_1) \wedge$ Immut(τ_2)	Mut$(\tau_1) \vee$ Mut(τ_2)	$\square(\tau_1) \wedge \square(\tau_2)$	$\theta\langle\tau_1\rangle \times \theta\langle\tau_2\rangle$
$\alpha\!\downarrow\!\rho$	false	Mut$(\blacktriangledown(\rho))$	$\square(\rho)$	$\alpha'\!\downarrow\!\theta\langle\rho\rangle$ if $\theta\langle\alpha\rangle = \alpha'$ ρ' if $\theta\langle\alpha\rangle = \rho' \neq \alpha'$
$\varsigma\!\downarrow\!\rho$	false	Mut$(\varsigma) \vee$ Mut$(\triangledown(\rho))$	$\square(\rho)$	$\varsigma'\!\downarrow\!\theta\langle\varsigma\rangle$ if $\theta\langle\varsigma\rangle = \varsigma'$ ϱ if $\theta\langle\varsigma\rangle = \varrho \neq \varsigma'$

Fig. 3. Operations and Predicates on Types

The execution semantics do not perform a copy operation in all cases where copy compatibility is permitted. For example, the E-If rule does not introduce a copy step in the branching expression. Since if-expressions are not lvalues, they cannot be the target of an assignment. Therefore, the value that either branch evaluates to, can itself be used in all cases where a copy of that value can be.

Static Semantics. Fig. 3 defines several operators and predicates on types that we use in this section. The operators $\blacktriangle$ and $\blacktriangledown$ respectively increase and decrease the shallow top-level mutability of a type. $\triangle$ and $\triangledown$ maximize / minimize the mutability of a type up to a reference or function boundary. $\mathfrak{I}$ removes all mutability in a type up to a function boundary. We write $\tau_1 \overset{\blacktriangledown}{=} \tau_2$ as shorthand for $\blacktriangledown(\tau_1) = \blacktriangledown(\tau_2)$ and $\tau_1 \stackrel{\triangledown}{=} \tau_2$ for $\triangledown(\tau_1) = \triangledown(\tau_2)$. In our algebra of types, the mutable type constructor is idempotent ($\Psi\Psi\tau \equiv \Psi\tau$). We also define the equivalences: $\alpha{\downarrow}\rho \equiv \alpha{\downarrow}\rho'$, where $\rho \stackrel{\blacktriangledown}{=} \rho'$ and $\varsigma{\downarrow}\rho \equiv \varsigma{\downarrow}\rho'$, where $\rho \stackrel{\triangledown}{=} \rho'$. The predicates Immut and Mut identify types that are observably immutable and mutable respectively. The $\Box(\tau)$ predicate tests if the type τ is concretizable by fixing variables that range over mutability.

$\theta\langle\tau\rangle$ denotes the application of a substitution θ on τ as defined in Fig. 3. $\theta\langle e\rangle$ performs substitutions for κ annotations in e. $\{\!|\tau|\!\}$ denotes the set of all constrained types and unconstrained type variables structurally present in τ. $\theta\langle\ \rangle$ and $\{\!|\ |\!\}$ are extended to σ, Γ, Σ, and $\{\overline{\tau}\}$ in the natural, capture-avoiding manner.

Definition 1 (Canonical Expressions). *An expression e is said to be canonical if all* `let` *expressions in e are annotated with one of the kinds ψ or $\forall$.*

Definition 2 (Consistency of Constrained types). *Let* $\mathrm{mtv}(\overline{\tau})$, $\mathrm{Mtv}(\overline{\tau})$, *and* $\mathrm{ntv}(\overline{\tau})$ *be the set of all type variables appearing in $\{\overline{\tau}\}$ constrained by $\alpha{\downarrow}\rho$, by $\varsigma{\downarrow}\rho$ and unconstrained respectively. We say that the set of types $\{\overline{\tau}\}$ is consistent, written* $\Vdash \{\overline{\tau}\}$*, if: (1) For all* $\{\alpha{\downarrow}\rho,\ \alpha{\downarrow}\rho'\} \subseteq \{\!|\overline{\tau}|\!\}$*, we have $\rho \stackrel{\blacktriangledown}{=} \rho'$.*
(2) For all $\{\varsigma{\downarrow}\rho,\ \varsigma'{\downarrow}\rho'\} \subseteq \{\!|\overline{\tau}|\!\}$ *such that $\varsigma \stackrel{\blacktriangledown}{=} \varsigma'$, we have $\rho \stackrel{\triangledown}{=} \rho'$.*
(3) $\mathrm{mtv}(\overline{\tau})$, $\mathrm{Mtv}(\overline{\tau})$, *and* $\mathrm{ntv}(\overline{\tau})$ *are mutually exclusive.*

Definition 3 (Consistency of substitutions). *A substitution θ is said to be consistent over a set of types $\{\overline{\tau}\}$, written $\theta \Vdash \{\overline{\tau}\}$ if: (1)* $\Vdash \theta\{\!|\overline{\tau}|\!\}$*.*
(2) For all $\alpha{\downarrow}\rho \in \{\!|\overline{\tau}|\!\}$*, we have $\theta\langle\alpha\rangle = \beta$, or $\theta\langle\alpha\rangle = \rho'$ such that $\rho' \stackrel{\blacktriangledown}{=} \theta\langle\rho\rangle$.*
(3) For all $\varsigma{\downarrow}\rho \in \{\!|\overline{\tau}|\!\}$*, we have $\theta\langle\varsigma\rangle = \varsigma'$, or $\theta\langle\varsigma\rangle = \varrho$ such that $\varrho \stackrel{\triangledown}{=} \theta\langle\rho\rangle$.*

Definition 4 (Consistency of $\bigstar$ constraints). *A set of $\bigstar$ constraints $\mathcal{D}$ is said to be consistent, written* $\models \mathcal{D}$ *if: (1) For all* $\bigstar_x^\forall(\tau) \in \mathcal{D}$*, we have* $\mathrm{Immut}(\tau)$*.*
(2) For all $\bigstar_x^\psi(\tau_1) \dots \bigstar_x^\psi(\tau_n) \in \mathcal{D}$*, we have $\tau_1 = \dots = \tau_n$.*
(3) For all $\bigstar_x^{\varkappa_1}(\tau_1) \in \mathcal{D}$ *and* $\bigstar_y^{\varkappa_2}(\tau_2) \in \mathcal{D}$*, $\varkappa_1 \neq \varkappa_2$ implies $x \neq y$.*

Declarative Type Rules. Fig. 4 presents a declarative definition of the type system of $\mathbb{B}$. In this type system, copy compatibility is realized through *copy coercion* ($\trianglelefteq:$) rules that are similar to subtyping rules (S-* rules in Fig. 4). Since reference types $\Uparrow\tau$ are handled only by S-Refl, types cannot coerced beyond a reference boundary. Also, two function types are coercible only if they are structurally identical. Here, the contravariance/covariance of argument/return types is unnecessary as we can follow a standard convention with respect to the mutability of argument/return types at copy positions. The rules for typing expressions (T-* rules) introduce these coercions at all copy-compatible positions.

The type judgment $\mathcal{D}; \Gamma; \Sigma \vdash e : \tau$ is understood as: given a binding environment Γ and store typing Σ, the expression e has type τ subject to the set of $\bigstar$ constraints $\mathcal{D}$. We write $e \trianglelefteq: \tau$ as a shorthand for $e : \tau'$ and $\tau' \trianglelefteq: \tau$, for some type τ'. The rule T-Lambda permits the interface type of a function be different from its internal type, as explained in Sec. 2.1. The rule T-App introduces copy-coercions at argument and return positions of an application. T-Let-M rule

$$\textbf{S-Refl} \quad \frac{}{\tau \trianglelefteq: \tau}$$

$$\textbf{S-Trans} \quad \frac{\tau_0 \trianglelefteq: \tau_1 \quad \tau_1 \trianglelefteq: \tau_2}{\tau_0 \trianglelefteq: \tau_2}$$

$$\textbf{S-Mut} \quad \frac{\rho \trianglelefteq: \rho'}{\Psi\rho \trianglelefteq: \Psi\rho'}$$

$$\textbf{S-Pair} \quad \frac{\tau_1 \trianglelefteq: \tau_1' \quad \tau_2 \trianglelefteq: \tau_2'}{\tau_1 \times \tau_2 \trianglelefteq: \tau_1' \times \tau_2'}$$

$$\textbf{S-Mt1} \quad \frac{\blacktriangledown(\rho) = \tau}{\alpha|\rho \trianglelefteq: \tau}$$

$$\textbf{S-Mt2} \quad \frac{\blacktriangle(\rho) = \tau}{\tau \trianglelefteq: \alpha|\rho}$$

$$\textbf{S-Mf1} \quad \frac{\triangledown(\rho) = \tau}{\alpha|\rho \trianglelefteq: \tau}$$

$$\textbf{S-Mf2} \quad \frac{\alpha|\rho \trianglelefteq: \rho'}{\Psi\alpha|\rho \trianglelefteq: \Psi\rho'}$$

$$\textbf{S-MF3} \quad \frac{\triangle(\rho) = \tau}{\tau \trianglelefteq: \varsigma|\rho}$$

$$\textbf{T-Unit} \quad \frac{}{\emptyset; \Gamma; \Sigma \vdash () : \texttt{unit}}$$

$$\textbf{T-Bool} \quad \frac{}{\emptyset; \Gamma; \Sigma \vdash b : \texttt{bool}}$$

$$\textbf{T-Id} \quad \frac{\Gamma(x) = \forall \overline{\alpha}.\tau \backslash \mathcal{D} \quad \theta \Vdash \{\tau, \mathcal{D}\} \quad dom(\theta) = \{\overline{\alpha}\}}{\theta\langle\mathcal{D}\rangle; \Gamma; \Sigma \vdash x : \theta\langle\tau\rangle}$$

$$\textbf{T-Hloc} \quad \frac{\Sigma(\ell) = \tau}{\emptyset; \Gamma; \Sigma \vdash \ell : \Uparrow\tau}$$

$$\textbf{T-Sloc} \quad \frac{\Sigma(l) = \tau}{\emptyset; \Gamma; \Sigma \vdash l : \tau}$$

$$\textbf{T-Lambda} \quad \frac{\mathcal{D}; \Gamma, x \mapsto \tau_1; \Sigma \vdash e : \tau_2 \quad \tau_1 \overset{\triangledown}{=} \tau_1' \quad \tau_2 \overset{\triangledown}{=} \tau_2'}{\mathcal{D}; \Gamma; \Sigma \vdash \lambda x.e : \tau_1' \rightarrow \tau_2'}$$

$$\textbf{T-App} \quad \frac{\mathcal{D}_1; \Gamma; \Sigma \vdash e_1 \trianglelefteq: \tau_a \rightarrow \tau_r \quad \mathcal{D}_2; \Gamma; \Sigma \vdash e_2 \trianglelefteq: \triangledown(\tau_a) \quad \triangle(\tau_r) \trianglelefteq: \tau}{\mathcal{D}_1 \cup \mathcal{D}_2; \Gamma; \Sigma \vdash e_1 e_2 : \tau}$$

$$\textbf{T-If} \quad \frac{\mathcal{D}_1; \Gamma; \Sigma \vdash e_1 \trianglelefteq: \texttt{bool} \quad \mathcal{D}_2; \Gamma; \Sigma \vdash e_2 \trianglelefteq: \tau \quad \mathcal{D}_3; \Gamma; \Sigma \vdash e_3 \trianglelefteq: \tau \quad \tau' \trianglelefteq: \tau}{\mathcal{D}_1 \cup \mathcal{D}_2 \cup \mathcal{D}_3; \Gamma; \Sigma \vdash \texttt{if } e_1 \texttt{ then } e_2 \texttt{ else } e_3 : \tau'}$$

$$\textbf{T-Pair} \quad \frac{\mathcal{D}_1; \Gamma; \Sigma \vdash e_1 \trianglelefteq: \tau_1 \quad \mathcal{D}_2; \Gamma; \Sigma \vdash e_2 \trianglelefteq: \tau_2 \quad \tau_1' \trianglelefteq: \tau_1 \quad \tau_2' \trianglelefteq: \tau_2}{\mathcal{D}_1 \cup \mathcal{D}_2; \Gamma; \Sigma \vdash (e_1, e_2) : \tau_1' \times \tau_2'}$$

$$\textbf{T-Sel} \quad \frac{\mathcal{D}; \Gamma; \Sigma \vdash e : \tau \quad \tau \overset{\blacktriangledown}{=} \tau_1 \times \tau_2}{\mathcal{D}; \Gamma; \Sigma \vdash e.i : \tau_i}$$

$$\textbf{T-Set} \quad \frac{\mathcal{D}_1; \Gamma; \Sigma \vdash l \trianglelefteq: \Psi\rho \quad \mathcal{D}_2; \Gamma; \Sigma \vdash e \trianglelefteq: \rho}{\mathcal{D}_1 \cup \mathcal{D}_2; \Gamma; \Sigma \vdash l := e : \texttt{unit}}$$

$$\textbf{T-Dup} \quad \frac{\mathcal{D}; \Gamma; \Sigma \vdash e \trianglelefteq: \tau \quad \tau' \trianglelefteq: \tau}{\mathcal{D}; \Gamma; \Sigma \vdash \texttt{dup}(e) : \Uparrow\tau'}$$

$$\textbf{T-Deref} \quad \frac{\mathcal{D}; \Gamma; \Sigma \vdash e \trianglelefteq: \Uparrow\tau}{\mathcal{D}; \Gamma; \Sigma \vdash e\hat{\ } : \tau}$$

$$\textbf{T-Let-M} \quad \frac{\mathcal{D}_1; \Gamma; \Sigma \vdash e_1 \trianglelefteq: \tau_1 \quad \tau \trianglelefteq: \tau_1 \quad \mathcal{D}_2; \Gamma, x \mapsto \tau; \Sigma \vdash e_2 : \tau_2}{\mathcal{D}_1 \cup \mathcal{D}_2; \Gamma; \Sigma \vdash (\texttt{let}^\psi x = e_1 \texttt{ in } e_2) : \tau_2}$$

$$\textbf{T-Let-MP} \quad \frac{\begin{array}{c}\mathcal{D}_1; \Gamma; \Sigma \vdash v \trianglelefteq: \tau_1 \quad \tau \trianglelefteq: \tau_1 \quad \mathcal{D} = \mathcal{D}_1 \cup \{\bigstar_x^{\varkappa}(\tau)\} \quad \{\overline{\alpha}\} = \text{ftv}(\tau, \mathcal{D}) \setminus \text{ftv}(\Gamma, \Sigma) \\ \mathcal{D}_2; \Gamma, x \mapsto \forall\overline{\alpha}.\tau \backslash \mathcal{D}; \Sigma \vdash e : \tau_2 \quad \models_{\overline{new}} \overline{\beta}\end{array}}{\mathcal{D}[\overline{\beta}/\overline{\alpha}] \cup \mathcal{D}_2; \Gamma; \Sigma \vdash (\texttt{let}^{\varkappa} x = v \texttt{ in } e) : \tau_2}$$

Fig. 4. Declarative Type Rules

types let expressions monomorphically, and thus requires a $\texttt{let}^\psi$ annotation. In this case, the expression e_1 is permitted to be expansive (i.e. need not be a syntactic value v). The T-Let-MP rule types let expressions where the expression being bound is a syntactic value. It assigns x a constrained type scheme along with the constraint $\bigstar_x^{\varkappa}(\tau)$. The T-Id rule instantiates types and constraints. The instantiated constraints are collected over the entire derivation, so that we can enforce instantiation consistency. $\models_{\overline{new}} \overline{\alpha}$ identifies fresh type variables.

We prove the soundness of our type system by demonstrating subject reduction. Here, we prove that the type of an expression is preserved exactly by left-execution, which ensures that the type of a location does not change during the execution of a program. We also show that right execution preserves types except for shallow mutability. The result of a right execution can only be used in copy compatible positions, or as the target of a dereference. In the former case, preservation of shallow mutability is unnecessary, and in the later, the type within the reference is preserved exactly.

The interesting case is the safety of polymorphic let expressions. The T-Let-MP rule does not require that the type τ being quantified over be immutable, but adds the $\bigstar_x^{\varkappa}(\tau)$ constraint. Now, if we have a derivation $\mathcal{D}; \Gamma; \Sigma \vdash e : \tau$

such that $\models \mathcal{D}$, then one of the two cases must follow. (1) If any instantiation of τ is mutable, then $\varkappa = \psi$. In this case, execution proceeds through the E-Let-M rule, which create a stack location for x. Therefore, x is permitted to be the target of an assignment. $\models \mathcal{D}$ guarantees that all instantiations of τ are identical, which ensures that the type of a location cannot change. (2) If τ is instantiated polymorphically, then $\varkappa = \forall$. Execution proceeds through the E-Let-P rule, which performs a value substitution. Here, $\models \mathcal{D}$ guarantees that all instantiations are deeply immutable. Therefore, x cannot be directly used (in the forms x or $x.\mathrm{p}$) as the target of an assignment, which ensures that the value substitution cannot lead to a stuck state.

Definition 5 (Consistent Type Derivation). *Let $\{\![\mathcal{D};\ \Gamma;\ \Sigma \vdash e : \tau]\!\}$ denote the extension $\{\![\ ]\!\}$ function to the set of all types used in the derivation of $\mathcal{D};\ \Gamma;\ \Sigma \vdash e : \tau$. We say that $\mathcal{D};\ \Gamma;\ \Sigma \vdash_{*} e : \tau$ is a consistent derivation if $\mathcal{D}';\ \Gamma;\ \Sigma \vdash e : \tau$ for some $\mathcal{D}' \subseteq \mathcal{D}$, and $\Vdash \{\![\mathcal{D}]\!\} \cup \{\![\mathcal{D}';\ \Gamma;\ \Sigma \vdash e : \tau]\!\}$.*

Definition 6 (Stack and Heap Typing) *A heap H and a stack S are said to be* well typed *with respect to Γ, Σ and $\mathcal{D}$, written $\mathcal{D};\ \Gamma;\ \Sigma \vdash_{*} H + S$, if:*
(1) $\mathrm{dom}(\Sigma) = \mathrm{dom}(H) \cup \mathrm{dom}(S)$
(2) $\forall \ell \in \mathrm{dom}(H),\ \mathcal{D};\ \Gamma;\ \Sigma \vdash_{*} H(\ell) : \tau$ such that $\Sigma(\ell) \overset{\triangledown}{=} \tau$
(3) $\forall l \in \mathrm{dom}(S),\ \mathcal{D};\ \Gamma;\ \Sigma \vdash_{*} S(l) : \tau$ such that $\Sigma(l) \overset{\triangledown}{=} \tau$

Definition 7 (Valid Lvalues). *We say that an lvalue $\mathcal{L}$ is valid with respect to a stack S and heap H, written $H + S \vdash_{v} \mathcal{L}$ if for some p, either (1) $\mathcal{L} = l$ or $\mathcal{L} = l.\mathrm{p}$ where $l \in \mathrm{dom}(S)$; or (2) $\mathcal{L} = \ell^{\wedge}$ or $\mathcal{L} = \ell^{\wedge}.\mathrm{p}$ where $\ell \in \mathrm{dom}(H)$.*

Lemma 1 (Progress). *If e is a closed canonical well typed expression, that is, $\mathcal{D};\ \emptyset;\ \Sigma \vdash_{*} e : \tau$ for some τ and Σ, given any heap and stack such that $\mathcal{D};\ \emptyset;\ \Sigma \vdash_{*} H + S$,*
(1) If e is a left expression ($e = l$), then e is either a valid lvalue (that is, $e = \mathcal{L}$ and $H + S \vdash_{v} \mathcal{L}$) or else $\exists\ e',\ S',\ H'$ such that $S;\ H;\ e \Rightarrow S';\ H';\ e'$.
(2) e is a value v or else $\exists\ e',\ S',\ H'$ such that $S;\ H;\ e \Rightarrow S';\ H';\ e'$.

Lemma 2 (Preservation). *For any canonical expression e, if $\mathcal{D};\ \Gamma;\ \Sigma \vdash_{*} e : \tau$, $\mathcal{D};\ \Gamma;\ \Sigma \vdash_{*} H + S$ and $\models \mathcal{D}$ then,*
(1) If $S;\ H;\ e \Rightarrow S';\ H';\ e'$, then, $\exists\ \Sigma' \supseteq \Sigma$ such that $\mathcal{D};\ \Gamma;\ \Sigma' \vdash_{*} e' : \tau$ and $\mathcal{D};\ \Gamma;\ \Sigma' \vdash_{*} H' + S'$.
(2) If $S;\ H;\ e \Rightarrow S';\ H';\ e'$, then, $\exists\ \Sigma' \supseteq \Sigma$ such that $\mathcal{D};\ \Gamma;\ \Sigma' \vdash_{*} e' : \tau'$, $\mathcal{D};\ \Gamma;\ \Sigma' \vdash_{*} H' + S'$ and $\tau \overset{\triangledown}{=} \tau'$.

Definition 8 (Stuck State). *A system state $S;\ H;\ e$ is said to be* stuck *if $e \neq v$ and there are no $S',\ H'$, and e' such that $S;\ H;\ e \Rightarrow S';\ H';\ e'$.*

Theorem 1 (Type Soundness). *Let $\overset{*}{\Rightarrow}$ denote the reflexive-transitive-closure of $\Rightarrow$. For any canonical expression e, if $\mathcal{D};\ \emptyset;\ \Sigma \vdash_{*} e : \tau$, $\mathcal{D};\ \emptyset;\ \Sigma \vdash_{*} H + S$, $\models \mathcal{D}$, and $S;\ H;\ e \overset{*}{\Rightarrow} S';\ H';\ e'$, then $S';\ H';\ e'$ is not stuck. That is, execution of a closed, canonical, well typed expression cannot lead to a stuck state.*

Type Inference Algorithm. Type inference is a program transformation that accepts a program in which `let` expressions are not annotated with their kinds,

I-Unit
$$\frac{}{\Gamma;\ \Sigma \vdash () : \text{unit} \mid \emptyset}$$

I-Bool
$$\frac{}{\Gamma;\ \Sigma \vdash b : \text{bool} \mid \emptyset}$$

I-Id
$$\frac{\Gamma(x) = \forall\overline{\alpha}.\tau \backslash \mathcal{D} \quad \theta = \overline{[\alpha \rightarrowtail \beta]} \quad \vDash_{\overline{new}} \overline{\beta}}{\Gamma;\ \Sigma \vdash x : \theta\langle\tau\rangle \mid \theta\langle\mathcal{D}\rangle}$$

I-Hloc
$$\frac{\Sigma(\ell) = \tau}{\Gamma;\ \Sigma \vdash \ell : \Uparrow\tau \mid \emptyset}$$

I-Sloc
$$\frac{\Sigma(l) = \tau}{\Gamma;\ \Sigma \vdash l : \tau \mid \emptyset}$$

I-Lambda
$$\frac{\Gamma, x \mapsto \beta\downarrow\alpha;\ \Sigma \vdash e : \tau \mid \mathcal{C} \quad \vDash_{\overline{new}} \alpha\beta\beta'\gamma\gamma'\delta}{\Gamma;\ \Sigma \vdash \lambda x.e : \beta'\downarrow\alpha \rightarrow \gamma'\downarrow\delta \mid \mathcal{C} \cup \{\tau = \gamma\downarrow\delta\}}$$

I-App
$$\frac{\Gamma;\ \Sigma \vdash e_1 : \tau_1 \mid \mathcal{C}_1 \quad \Gamma;\ \Sigma \vdash e_2 : \tau_2 \mid \mathcal{C}_2 \quad \vDash_{\overline{new}} \alpha\beta\beta'\gamma\gamma'\delta\varepsilon}{\Gamma;\ \Sigma \vdash e_1\ e_2 : \varepsilon\downarrow\gamma \mid \mathcal{C}_1 \cup \mathcal{C}_2 \cup \{\tau_1 = \alpha\downarrow(\beta'\downarrow\beta \rightarrow \gamma'\downarrow\gamma),\ \tau_2 = \delta\downarrow\beta\}}$$

I-If
$$\frac{\Gamma;\ \Sigma \vdash e_1 : \tau_1 \mid \mathcal{C}_1 \quad \Gamma;\ \Sigma \vdash e_2 : \tau_2 \mid \mathcal{C}_2 \quad \Gamma;\ \Sigma \vdash e_3 : \tau_3 \mid \mathcal{C}_3 \quad \vDash_{\overline{new}} \alpha\beta\gamma\delta\varepsilon}{\Gamma;\ \Sigma \vdash \text{if } e_1 \text{ then } e_2 \text{ else } e_3 : \varepsilon\downarrow\gamma \mid \mathcal{C}_1 \cup \mathcal{C}_2 \cup \mathcal{C}_3 \cup \{\tau_1 = \alpha\downarrow\text{bool},\ \tau_2 = \beta\downarrow\gamma,\ \tau_3 = \delta\downarrow\gamma\}}$$

I-Set
$$\frac{\Gamma;\ \Sigma \vdash l : \tau_1 \mid \mathcal{C}_1 \quad \Gamma;\ \Sigma \vdash e : \tau_2 \mid \mathcal{C}_2 \quad \vDash_{\overline{new}} \alpha\beta\gamma}{\Gamma;\ \Sigma \vdash l := e : \text{unit} \mid \mathcal{C}_1 \cup \mathcal{C}_2 \cup \{\tau_1 = (\Psi\alpha)\downarrow\beta,\ \tau_2 = \gamma\downarrow\beta\}}$$

I-Deref
$$\frac{\Gamma;\ \Sigma \vdash e : \tau \mid \mathcal{C} \quad \vDash_{\overline{new}} \alpha\beta}{\Gamma;\ \Sigma \vdash e\char`^ : \alpha \mid \mathcal{C} \cup \{\tau = \beta\downarrow\Uparrow\alpha\}}$$

I-Dup
$$\frac{\Gamma;\ \Sigma \vdash e : \tau \mid \mathcal{C} \quad \vDash_{\overline{new}} \alpha\beta\gamma}{\Gamma;\ \Sigma \vdash \text{dup}(e) : \Uparrow(\alpha\downarrow\beta) \mid \mathcal{C} \cup \{\tau = \gamma\downarrow\beta\}}$$

I-Sel
$$\frac{\Gamma;\ \Sigma \vdash e : \tau \mid \mathcal{C} \quad \tau_1 = \alpha\downarrow\beta \quad \tau_2 = \gamma\downarrow\delta \quad \vDash_{\overline{new}} \alpha\beta\gamma\delta\varepsilon}{\Gamma;\ \Sigma \vdash e.i : \tau_i \mid \mathcal{C} \cup \{\tau = \varepsilon\downarrow(\tau_1 \times \tau_2)\}}$$

I-Pair
$$\frac{\Gamma;\ \Sigma \vdash e_1 : \tau_1 \mid \mathcal{C}_1 \quad \Gamma;\ \Sigma \vdash e_2 : \tau_2 \mid \mathcal{C}_2 \quad \vDash_{\overline{new}} \alpha\alpha'\beta\beta'\gamma\delta}{\Gamma;\ \Sigma \vdash (e_1,e_2) : \alpha\downarrow\gamma \times \beta\downarrow\delta \mid \mathcal{C}_1 \cup \mathcal{C}_2 \cup \{\tau_1 = \alpha'\downarrow\gamma,\ \tau_2 = \beta'\downarrow\delta\}}$$

I-Let-Exp
$$\frac{\Gamma;\ \Sigma \vdash e_1 : \tau_1 \mid \mathcal{C}_1 \quad e_1 \neq v \quad \Gamma, x \mapsto \alpha\downarrow\beta;\ \Sigma \vdash e_2 : \tau_2 \mid \mathcal{C}_2 \quad \vDash_{\overline{new}} \alpha\beta\gamma\kappa}{\Gamma;\ \Sigma \vdash \text{let}^\kappa\ x = e_1 \text{ in } e_2 : \tau_2 \mid \mathcal{C}_1 \cup \{\tau_1 = \gamma\downarrow\beta,\ \kappa = \psi\} \cup \mathcal{C}_2}$$

I-Let-Val
$$\frac{\Gamma;\ \Sigma \vdash v : \tau_1 \mid \mathcal{C}_1 \quad \mathcal{C}'_1 = \mathcal{C}_1 \cup \{\tau_1 = \gamma\downarrow\beta\} \quad \mathcal{U}(\mathcal{C}'_1) = (\mathcal{D}',\theta) \quad \mathcal{D} = \mathcal{D}' \cup \{\bigstar^\kappa_x(\tau)\} \quad \tau = \theta\langle\delta\downarrow\beta\rangle}{\{\overline{\alpha}\} = \text{ftv}(\tau,\ \mathcal{D}) \setminus \text{ftv}(\theta\langle\Gamma\rangle,\ \theta\langle\Sigma\rangle) \quad \Gamma, x \mapsto \forall\overline{\alpha}.\tau\backslash\mathcal{D};\ \Sigma \vdash e : \tau_2 \mid \mathcal{C}_2 \quad \vDash_{\overline{new}} \beta\gamma\delta\overline{\varepsilon}\kappa}$$
$$\overline{\Gamma;\ \Sigma \vdash \text{let}^\kappa\ x = v \text{ in } e : \tau_2 \mid \mathcal{C}'_1[\overline{\varepsilon}/\overline{\alpha}] \cup \mathcal{C}_2}$$

Fig. 5. Type Inference Algorithm

and returns the same program with **let** expressions annotated with their kinds and all expressions annotated with their types. The type inference algorithm is shown in Fig. 5. The inference judgment $\Gamma;\ \Sigma \vdash e : \tau \mid \mathcal{C}$ is understood as: given a binding environment Γ and store typing Σ, the expression e has type τ subject to the constraints $\mathcal{C}$.

The inference algorithm introduces constrained types of the form $\varsigma\downarrow\rho$ at all copy compatible positions. For example, the I-App rule introduces copy compatibility for the function type itself, the argument and the return types. The I-Sel rule represents the pair type as $\varepsilon\downarrow(\alpha\downarrow\beta \times \gamma\downarrow\delta)$, which (1) permits top-level mutability of the pair type to be either mutable or immutable (2) ensures that the type of the selection is exactly same as the type of the field being selected (3) propagates full copy compatibility "one level down."

The unification algorithm is shown in Fig. 6. The unification of a constraint set $\mathcal{C}$ either fails with an error $\perp$, or produces the pair $(\mathcal{D},\theta)$. θ is a solution for all equality constraints and some of the $\bigstar$ constraints in $\mathcal{C}$. $\mathcal{D}$ is the set of $\bigstar$ constraints in $\mathcal{C}$ on which θ has been applied. $\uplus$ represents disjoint union of sets.

The U-Ct* rules perform unification of constrained types with other constrained or unconstrained types. First, immutable versions of the two types are unified to establish compatibility (through constraints involving $\overset{\blacktriangledown}{=}$ and $\overset{\triangledown}{=}$). Then, the constrained type is made to exactly equal the other type by unifying its variable part with the other type. The key observation here is that the copy

$$
\begin{array}{ll}
\textbf{U-Empty} & \mathcal{U}(\emptyset) = (\emptyset, \langle\rangle) \\
\textbf{U-Refl} & \mathcal{U}(\{\tau = \tau\} \uplus \mathcal{C}) = \mathcal{U}(\mathcal{C}) \\
\textbf{U-Sym} & \mathcal{U}(\{\tau_1 = \tau_2\} \uplus \mathcal{C}) = \mathcal{U}(\{\tau_2 = \tau_1\} \cup \mathcal{C}) \\
\textbf{U-Var} & \mathcal{U}(\{\alpha = \tau\} \uplus \mathcal{C}) \mid \alpha \notin \tau = (\mathcal{D}, \theta_a \circ \theta_u) \text{ where } \theta_a = [\alpha \rightarrowtail \tau] \text{ and} \\
& \qquad\qquad \mathcal{U}(\theta_a\langle\mathcal{C}\rangle) = (\mathcal{D}, \theta_u)
\end{array}
$$

$$
\begin{array}{ll}
\textbf{U-Fn} & \mathcal{U}(\{\tau_a \to \tau_r = \tau_a' \to \tau_r'\} \uplus \mathcal{C}) = \mathcal{U}(\mathcal{C} \cup \{\tau_a = \tau_a',\ \tau_r = \tau_r'\}) \\
\textbf{U-Ref} & \mathcal{U}(\{\Uparrow\tau_1 = \Uparrow\tau_2\} \uplus \mathcal{C}) = \mathcal{U}(\mathcal{C} \cup \{\tau_1 = \tau_2\}) \\
\textbf{U-Mut} & \mathcal{U}(\{\Psi\rho_1 = \Psi\rho_2\} \uplus \mathcal{C}) = \mathcal{U}(\mathcal{C} \cup \{\rho_1 = \rho_2\}) \\
\textbf{U-Pair} & \mathcal{U}(\{\tau_1 \times \tau_2 = \tau_1' \times \tau_2'\} \uplus \mathcal{C}) = \mathcal{U}(\mathcal{C} \cup \{\tau_1 = \tau_1',\ \tau_2 = \tau_2'\})
\end{array}
$$

$$
\begin{array}{ll}
\textbf{U-Ct1} & \mathcal{U}(\{\alpha\lfloor\rho_1 = \beta\lfloor\rho_2\} \uplus \mathcal{C}) = \mathcal{U}(\mathcal{C} \cup \{\rho_1 \overset{\blacktriangledown}{=} \rho_2,\ \alpha = \beta\}) \\
\textbf{U-Ct2} & \mathcal{U}(\{\alpha\lfloor\rho = \rho'\} \uplus \mathcal{C}) = \mathcal{U}(\mathcal{C} \cup \{\rho \overset{\blacktriangledown}{=} \rho',\ \alpha = \rho'\}) \\
\textbf{U-Ct3} & \mathcal{U}(\{\varsigma_1\lfloor\rho_1 = \varsigma_2\lfloor\rho_2\} \uplus \mathcal{C}) = \mathcal{U}(\mathcal{C} \cup \{\rho_1 \overset{\triangledown}{=} \rho_2,\ \varsigma_1 = \varsigma_2\}) \\
\textbf{U-Ct4} & \mathcal{U}(\{\varsigma\lfloor\rho = \varrho\} \uplus \mathcal{C}) = \mathcal{U}(\mathcal{C} \cup \{\rho \overset{\triangledown}{=} \varrho,\ \varsigma = \varrho\})
\end{array}
$$

$$
\begin{array}{ll}
\textbf{U-K} & \mathcal{U}(\{\kappa = \varkappa\} \uplus \mathcal{C}) = (\mathcal{D}, \theta_k \circ \theta_u) \text{ where } \theta_k = [\kappa \rightarrowtail \varkappa] \text{ and} \\
& \qquad\qquad \mathcal{U}(\theta_k\langle\mathcal{C}\rangle) = (\mathcal{D}, \theta_u) \\
\textbf{U-Om1} & \mathcal{U}(\{\bigstar_x^\psi(\tau_1),\ \bigstar_x^\psi(\tau_2)\} \uplus \mathcal{C}) = (\mathcal{D}, \theta\{\bigstar_x^\psi(\tau_1),\ \bigstar_x^\psi(\tau_2)\}, \theta) \text{ where} \\
& \qquad\qquad \mathcal{U}(\mathcal{C} \cup \{\tau_1 = \tau_2\}) = (\mathcal{D}, \theta) \\
\textbf{U-Op1} & \mathcal{U}(\{\bigstar_x^\vee(\tau)\} \uplus \mathcal{C}) \mid \Box(\tau) = (\mathcal{D} \cup \theta\{\bigstar_x^\vee(\tau)\}, \theta) \text{ where} \\
& \qquad\qquad \mathcal{U}(\mathcal{C} \cup \{\tau = \Im(\tau)\}) = (\mathcal{D}, \theta) \\
\textbf{U-Om2} & \mathcal{U}(\{\bigstar_x^\kappa(\tau)\} \uplus \mathcal{C}) \mid \mathrm{Mut}(\tau) = (\mathcal{D}, \theta_k \circ \theta_u) \text{ where } \theta_k = [\kappa \rightarrowtail \psi] \text{ and} \\
& \qquad\qquad \mathcal{U}(\theta_k\langle\{\bigstar_x^\kappa(\tau)\} \cup \mathcal{C}\rangle) = (\mathcal{D}, \theta_u) \\
\textbf{U-Op2} & \mathcal{U}(\{\bigstar_x^\kappa(\tau_1),\ \bigstar_x^\kappa(\tau_2)\} \uplus \mathcal{C}) = (\mathcal{D}, \theta_k \circ \theta_u) \text{ where } \theta_k = [\kappa \rightarrowtail \vee] \text{ and} \\
& \quad \text{where } \mathcal{U}(\{\tau_1 = \tau_2\} \cup \mathcal{C}) = \bot \quad \mathcal{U}(\theta_k\langle\{\bigstar_x^\kappa(\tau_1),\ \bigstar_x^\kappa(\tau_2)\} \cup \mathcal{C}\rangle) = (\mathcal{D}, \theta_u)
\end{array}
$$

$$
\begin{array}{ll}
\textbf{U-Error} & \mathcal{U}(c \uplus \mathcal{C}) \mid c \notin \mathcal{C}_v \cup \mathcal{C}_s \cup \mathcal{C}_p = \bot
\end{array}
$$

$$
\mathcal{C}_v = \forall\, \alpha, \varsigma, \rho, \tau, \tau' \mid \alpha \notin \tau' \,.\, \{\tau = \tau,\ \alpha = \tau',\ \tau' = \alpha,\ \alpha\lfloor\rho = \tau,\ \tau = \alpha\lfloor\rho,\ \varsigma\lfloor\rho = \tau,\ \tau = \varsigma\lfloor\rho\}
$$
$$
\mathcal{C}_s = \forall\, \rho, \rho', \tau, \tau', \tau_1, \tau_1' \,.\, \{\tau \to \tau_1 = \tau' \to \tau_1',\ \Uparrow\tau = \Uparrow\tau',\ \Psi\rho = \Psi\rho'\}
$$
$$
\mathcal{C}_p = \forall\, x, \kappa, \varkappa, \tau, \tau' \mid \neg\mathrm{Mut}(\tau') \,.\, \{\kappa = \varkappa,\ \bigstar_x^\psi(\tau),\ \bigstar_x^\varkappa(\tau'),\ \bigstar_x^\kappa(\tau)\}
$$

Fig. 6. Unification Algorithm

compatibility is a special restricted form of subtyping. Since the type of the copy can be anywhere in the lattice of copy compatible types, subtyping requirements are always with respect a local maxima (the most immutable compatible type). We exploit this behavior to design a simple unification algorithm that only uses equality constraints over constrained types.

The U-Om1 ensures that all instantiations of monomorphic kind are the same. U-Op1 rule forces any concretizable instantiation of polymorphic kind to be immutable. The U-Om2 rule infers monomorphic kind based on the mutability of the instantiated type, and U-Op2 infers polymorphic kind if a variable x is instantiated polymorphically to two types that do not inter-unify.

Definition 9 (Constraint Satisfaction). *The satisfaction of a constraint set $\mathcal{C}$ by a substitution θ is defined as follows.*

$$
\frac{\forall\, (\tau_1 = \tau_2) \in \mathcal{C},\ \theta\langle\tau_1\rangle = \theta\langle\tau_2\rangle \quad \forall\, (\kappa = \varkappa) \in \mathcal{C},\ \theta\langle\kappa\rangle = \theta\langle\varkappa\rangle \quad \mathcal{D} = \{\theta\langle\bigstar_x^\varkappa(\tau)\rangle \mid \bigstar_x^\varkappa(\tau) \in \mathcal{C}\}}{\theta \vdash_{sol} \mathcal{C} \rightsquigarrow \mathcal{D}}
$$

$$
\frac{\theta \vdash_{sol} \mathcal{C} \rightsquigarrow \mathcal{D} \quad \models \mathcal{D}}{\theta \vdash_{sat} \mathcal{C} \rightsquigarrow \mathcal{D}}
$$

Definition 10 (Notational Derivations). *We write:*

(1) $\theta; \Gamma; \Sigma \vdash_{\scriptscriptstyle\mp} e : \tau \mid \mathcal{D}$ if $\Gamma; \Sigma \vdash_{\scriptscriptstyle\mp} e : \tau \mid \mathcal{C}$, $\theta \vdash_{sol} \mathcal{C} \rightsquigarrow \mathcal{D}$, and $\theta \Vdash \{\Gamma, \Sigma, \tau, \mathcal{C}\}$

(2) $\theta; \mathcal{D}; \Gamma; \Sigma \vdash_{\scriptscriptstyle\ast} e : \tau$ if $\theta\langle\mathcal{D}\rangle; \theta\langle\Gamma\rangle; \theta\langle\Sigma\rangle \vdash_{\scriptscriptstyle\ast} \theta\langle e\rangle : \theta\langle\tau\rangle$

Lemma 3 (Correctness of Unification). *If $\mathcal{U}(C) = (\mathcal{D}, \theta)$, then $\theta \vdash_{sol} C \rightsquigarrow \mathcal{D}$*

Lemma 4 (Satisfiability of Unified Constraints). *If $\mathcal{U}(C) = (\mathcal{D}, \theta_u)$, then there exists a substitution θ_s such that $\theta_u \circ \theta_s \vdash_{sat} C \rightsquigarrow \mathcal{D}$.*

Lemma 5 (Principality of Unification). *If $\mathcal{U}(C) = (\mathcal{D}, \theta_u)$, where C is a set of constraints obtained from the type inference algorithm, then, for all θ_s such that $\theta_s \vdash_{sol} C \rightsquigarrow \mathcal{D}'$, we have $\theta_s \supseteq \theta_u$.*

Lemma 6 (Decidability of Unification). *The problem of computing a canonical derivation of $\mathcal{U}(C)$ for an arbitrary C, where no two applications of U-Sym rule happen consecutively is decidable.*

Theorem 2 (Soundness of Type Inference). *If $\theta; \Gamma; \Sigma \vdash_{\bar{i}} e : \tau \mid \mathcal{D}$, then $\theta; \mathcal{D}; \Gamma; \Sigma \vdash_{*} e : \tau$.*

Lemma 7 (Type Checkability). *If $\Gamma; \Sigma \vdash_{\bar{i}} e : \tau \mid C$ and $\mathcal{U}(C) = (\mathcal{D}, \theta)$, then $\exists \ \theta'$ such that $\models \theta'\langle \mathcal{D} \rangle$ and $\theta \circ \theta'\langle e \rangle$ is canonical, and $\theta \circ \theta'; \mathcal{D}; \Gamma; \Sigma \vdash_{*} e : \tau$.*

Theorem 3 (Completeness of Type Inference). *If $\theta; \mathcal{D}; \Gamma; \Sigma \vdash_{\bar{*}} e : \tau$, then there exists a $\theta' \supseteq \theta$ such that $\theta'; \Gamma; \Sigma \vdash_{\bar{i}} e : \tau \mid \mathcal{D}$.*

Proofs for safety of the type system and soundness and completeness of the inference algorithm can be found in [23].

4   Related Work

Grossman [6] provides a theory of using quantified types with imperative C style mutation for Cyclone. However, his formalization requires explicit annotation for all polymorphic definitions and instantiations. In contrast, we believe that the best way to integrate polymorphism into the systems programming paradigm is by automatic inference. A further contribution of our work (in comparison to [6]) is that we give a formal specification and proof of correctness of the inference algorithm, not just the type system. Cyclone [10] uses region analysis to provide safe support for the address & operator. This technique is complementary to our work, and can be used to incorporate & operator in $\mathbb{B}$.

C's **const** notion of immutability-by-alias offers localized checking of immutability properties, and encourages good programming practice by serving as documentation of programmers' intentions. Other systems have proposed immutability-by-name [2], referential immutability [19,25] (transitive immutability-by-reference), *etc.* These techniques are orthogonal and complementary to the immutability-by-location property in $\mathbb{B}$. For example, we could have types like (**const** $\Psi\tau$) that can express both global and local usage properties of a location.

A monadic model [13] of mutability is used in pure functional languages like Haskell [14]. In this model, the type system distinguishes side-effecting computations from pure ones (and not just mutable locations from immutable ones). Even though this model is beneficial for integration with verification systems, it is considerably removed from the idioms needed by systems programmers.

For example, Hughes argues that there is no satisfactory way of creating and using global mutable variables using monads [7]. There have been proposals for adding unboxed representation control to Haskell [12,8]. However, these systems are pure and therefore and do not consider the effects of mutability.

Cqual [5] provides a framework of type qualifiers, which can be used to infer maximal const qualifications for C programs. However, CQual does not deal with polymorphism of types. In a monomorphic language, we can infer types and qualifiers independently. Adding polymorphism to CQual would introduce substantial challenges, particularly if polymorphism should be automatically inferred. The inference of types and qualifiers (mutability) becomes co-dependent: we need base types to infer qualifiers; but, we also need the qualifiers to infer base types due to the value restriction. $\mathbb{B}$ supports a polymorphic language and performs simultaneous inference of base types and mutability.

5 Conclusion

In this paper, we have defined a language and type system for systems programming which integrates all of unboxed representation, consistent complete mutability support, and polymorphism. The mutability model is expressive enough to permit mutation of unboxed/stack locations, and at the same time guarantees that types are definitive about the mutability of every location across all aliases.

Complete support for mutability introduces challenges for type inference at copy boundaries. We have developed a novel algorithm that infers principal types using a system of constrained types. To our knowledge, this is the first sound and complete algorithm that infers both mutability and polymorphism in a systems programming language with copy compatibility.

The type inference algorithm is implemented as part of the BitC [20] language compiler. The core of the compiler involves 22,433 lines of C++ code, of which implementation of the type system accounts for about 7,816 lines. The source code can be obtained from http://bitc-lang.org.

References

1. Biagioni, E., Harper, R., Lee, P.: A network protocol stack in Standard ML. Higher Order and Symbolic Computation 14(4) (2001)
2. Deline, R., Fähndrich, M.: VAULT: a programming language for reliable systems (2001), http://research.microsoft.com/vault
3. Derby, H.: The performance of FoxNet 2.0. Technical Report CMU-CS-99-137 School of Computer Science, Carnegie Mellon University (June 1999)
4. ECMA International Standard ECMA-334 C# Language Specification, http://www.ecma-international.org/publications/standards/Ecma-334.htm
5. Foster, J.S., Johnson, R., Kodumal, J., Aiken, A.: Flow-Insensitive Type Qualifiers. Trans. on Programming Languages and Systems. 28(6), 1035–1087 (2006)
6. Grossman, D.: Quantified Types in an Imperative Language. ACM Transactions on Programming Languages and Systems (2006)

7. Hughes, J.: Global variables in Haskell. Journal of Functional Programming archive 14(5) (September 2004)
8. Diatchki, I.S., Jones, M.P., Leslie, R.: High- level Views on Low-level Representations. In: Proc. ACM Int. Conference on Functional Programming, pp. 168–179 (2005)
9. International Std. Organization ISO/IEC 9899:1999 (Prog. Languages - C) (1999)
10. Jim, T., Morrisett, G., Grossman, D., Hicks, M., Cheney, J., Wang, Y.: Cyclone: A safe dialect of C. In: Proc. of USENIX Annual Technical Conference, pp. 275–288 (2002)
11. Jones, M.P.: Qualified types: theory and practice.Cambridge Distinguished Dissertation in Computer Science (1995) ISBN:0-521-47253-9
12. Peyton Jones, S.L., Launchbury, J.: Unboxed values as first class citizens in a non-strict functional language. Functional Programming Languages and Computer Architecture (1991)
13. Peyton Jones, S.L., Wadler, P.: Imperative functional programming. In: Proc. ACM SIGPLAN Principles of Programming Languages (1993)
14. Peyton Jones, S.L. (ed.): Haskell 98 Language and Libraries: The Revised report. Cambridge University Press, Cambridge (2003)
15. Milner, R.: A theory of type polymorphism in programming. Journal of Computer and System Sciences, 348–375 (1978)
16. Milner, R., Tofte, M., Harper, R., MacQueen, D.: The Definition of Standard ML - Revised. The MIT Press, Cambridge (1997)
17. Gosling, J., Joy, B., Steele, G., Bracha, G.: The Java Language Specification, 3rd edn., http://java.sun.com/docs/books/jls
18. van Rossum, G.: Python Reference Manual. In: Drake Jr., F.L, ed. (2006), http://docs.python.org/ref/ref.html
19. Shapiro, J.S., Smith, J.M., Farber, D.J.: EROS: a fast capability system. In: ACM Symposium on Operating Systems Principles (December 1999)
20. Shapiro, J.S., Sridhar, S., Doerrie, M.S.: BitC Language Specification, http://www.bitc-lang.org/docs/bitc/spec.html
21. Smith, G., Volpano, D.: A sound polymorphic type system for a dialect of C. Science of Computer Programming 32(2–3), 49–72 (1998)
22. Sridhar, S., Shapiro, J.S.: Type Inference for Unboxed Types and First Class Mutability. In: Proc. 3rd Workshop on Prog. Languages and Operating Systems (2006)
23. Sridhar, S., Shapiro, J.S., Smith, S.F.: Sound and Complete Type Inference in BitC. Technical Report SRL-2008-02, Systems Research Laboratory, The Johns Hopkins University (2008)
24. Tarditi, D., Morrisett, G., Cheng, P., Stone, C., Harper, R., Lee, P.: TIL: A type-directed optimizing compiler for ML. In: Proc. ACM SIGPLAN PLDI (1996)
25. Tschantz, M.S., Ernst, M.D.: Javari: Adding reference immutability to Java. Object-Oriented Programming Systems, Languages, and Applications (October 2005)
26. Wright, A.: Simple Imperative Polymorphism. Lisp and Symbolic Comp. 8(4), 343–355 (1995)

An Operational Semantics for JavaScript

Sergio Maffeis[1], John C. Mitchell[2], and Ankur Taly[2]

[1] Department of Computing, Imperial College London
[2] Department of Computer Science, Stanford University

Abstract. We define a small-step operational semantics for the EC-MAScript standard language corresponding to JavaScript, as a basis for analyzing security properties of web applications and mashups. The semantics is based on the language standard and a number of experiments with different implementations and browsers. Some basic properties of the semantics are proved, including a soundness theorem and a characterization of the reachable portion of the heap.

1 Introduction

JavaScript [8,14,10] is widely used in Web programming and it is implemented in every major browser. As a programming language, JavaScript supports functional programming with anonymous functions, which are widely used to handle browser events such as mouse clicks. JavaScript also has objects that may be constructed as the result of function calls, without classes. The *properties* of an object, which may represent methods or fields, can be inherited from a prototype, or redefined or even removed after the object has been created. For these and other reasons, formalizing JavaScript and proving correctness or security properties of JavaScript mechanisms poses substantial challenges.

Although there have been scientific studies of limited subsets of the language [7,21,24], there appears to be no previous formal investigation of the full core language, on the scale defined by the informal ECMA specifications [14]. In order to later analyze the correctness of language-based isolation mechanisms for JavaScript, such as those that have arisen recently in connection with online advertising and social networking [1,2,6,20], we develop a small-step operational semantics for JavaScript that covers the language addressed in the ECMA-262 Standard, 3rd Edition [14]. This standard is intended to define the common core language implemented in all browsers and is roughly a subset of JavaScript 1.5. We provide a basis for further analysis by proving some properties of the semantics, such as a progress theorem and properties of heap reachability.

As part of our effort to make conformance to the informal standard evident, we define our semantics in a way that is faithful to the common explanations of JavaScript and the intuitions of JavaScript programmers. For example, JavaScript scope is normally discussed in relation to an object-based representation. We therefore define execution of a program with respect to a heap that contains a linked structure of objects instead of a separate stack. Thus entering a JavaScript scope creates an object on the heap, serving as an activation

G. Ramalingam (Ed.): APLAS 2008, LNCS 5356, pp. 307–325, 2008.

record for that scope but also subject to additional operations on JavaScript objects. Another unusual aspect of our semantics, reflecting the unusual nature of JavaScript, is that declarations within the body of a function are handled by a two-pass method. The body of a function is analyzed for declarations, which are then added to the scope before the function body is executed. This allows a declaration that appears after the first expression in the function body to be referenced in that expression.

While the ECMAScript language specification guided the development of our operational semantics, we performed many experiments to check our understanding of the specification and to determine differences between various implementations of JavaScript. The implementations that we considered include SpiderMonkey [17] (used by Firefox), the Rhino [4] implementation for Java, JScript [3] (used by Internet Explorer), and the implementations provided in Safari and Opera. In the process, we developed a set of programs that test implementations against the standard and reveal details of these implementations. Many of these program examples, a few of which appear further below, may be surprising to those familiar with more traditional programming languages. Because of the complexity of JavaScript and the number of language variations, our operational semantics (reported in full in [15]) is approximately 70 pages of rules and definitions, in ascii format. We therefore describe only a few of the features and implications of the semantics here. By design, our operational semantics is modular in a way that allows individual clauses to be varied to capture differences between implementations.

Since JavaScript is an unusual language, there is value and challenge in proving properties that might be more straightforward to verify for some other languages (or for simpler idealized subsets of JavaScript). We start by proving a form of soundness theorem, stating that evaluation progresses to an exception or a value of an expected form. Our second main theorem shows, in effect, that the behavior of a program depends only on a portion of the heap. A corollary is that certain forms of garbage collection, respecting the precise characterization of heap reachability used in the theorem, are sound for JavaScript. This is nontrivial because JavaScript provides a number of ways for an expression to access, for example, the parent of a parent of an object, or even its own scope object, increasing the set of potentially reachable objects. The precise statement of the theorem is that the operational semantics preserve a similarity relation on states (which include the heap).

There are several reasons why the reachability theorem is important for various forms of JavaScript analysis. For example, a web server may send untrusted code (such as an advertisement) as part of a trusted page (the page that contains third-party advertisement). We would therefore like to prove that untrusted code cannot access certain browser data structures associated with the trusted enclosing page, under specific conditions that could be enforced by web security mechanisms. This problem can be reduced to proving that a given well-formed JavaScript program cannot access certain portions of the heap, according to the operational semantics of the language. Another future application of heap bisimilarity (as shown in this paper) to security properties of JavaScript applications is that in the analysis of automated phishing defenses, we can reduce the question of whether JavaScript can distinguish between the original page and a phishing page to whether there exists a bisimulation between a certain good heap (corresponding to the original page) and a certain bad heap (corresponding to the phishing page). Thus the framework that we develop in this paper for proving basic progress and heap reachability theorems provides a useful starting point for JavaScript security mechanisms and their correctness proofs.

1.1 JavaScript Overview and Challenges

JavaScript was originally designed to be a simple HTML scripting language [8]. The main primitives are first-class and potentially higher-order functions, and a form of object that can be defined by an object expression, without the need for class declarations. Commonly, related objects are constructed by calling a function that creates objects and returns them as a result of the function call. Functions and objects have *properties,* which are accessed via the "dot" notation, as in x.p for property p of object x. Properties can be added to an object or reset by assignment. This makes it conceptually possible to represent activation records by objects, with assignable variables considered properties of the object corresponding to the current scope. Because it is possible to change the value of a property arbitrarily, or remove it from the object, static typing for full JavaScript is difficult. JavaScript also has eval, which can be used to parse and evaluate a string as an expression, and the ability to iterate over properties of an object or access them using string expressions instead of literals (as in x["p"]). Many online tutorials and books [10] are available.

One example feature of JavaScript that is different from other languages that have been formally analyzed is the way that declarations are processed in an initial pass before bytecode for a function or other construct is executed. Some details of this phenomenon are illustrated by the following code:

```
var f = function(){if (true) {function g() {return 1}}
                   else {function g() {return 2}};
                   function g() {return 3};
                   return g();
                   function g() {return 4}}
```

This code defines a function f whose behavior is given by one of the declarations of g inside the body of the anonymous function that returns g. However, different implementations disagree on which declaration determines the behavior of f. Specifically, a call f() should return 4 according to the ECMA specification. Spidermonkey (hence Firefox) returns 4, while Rhino and Safari return 1, and JScript and the ECMA4 reference implementation return 2. Intuitively, the function body is parsed to find and process all declarations before it is executed, so that reachability of second declarations is ignored. Given that, it is plausible that most implementations would pick either the first declaration or the last. However, this code is likely to be unintuitive to most programmers.

A number of features of JavaScript are particularly challenging for development of a formal semantics and proving properties of the language. Below, we just cite some. Global values such as undefined or Object can be redefined, so the semantics cannot depend on fixed meanings for these predefined parts of the language. Some JavaScript objects, such as Array.prototype, are implicitly reachable even without naming any variables in the global scope. The mutability of these objects allows apparently unrelated code to interact. Some properties of native JavaScript objects are constrained to be for example ReadOnly, but there is no mechanism to express these constraints in the (client) language. JavaScript's rules for binding this depend on whether a function is invoked as a constructor, as a method, as a normal function, etc.. If a function written to be called in one way is instead called in another way, its this property might be bound to an unexected object or even to the global environment.

1.2   Beyond this Paper

Our framework for studying the formal properties of JavaScript closely follows the specification document and models all the features of the language that we have considered necessary to represent faithfully its semantics. The semantics can be modularly extended to *user-defined getters and setters*, which are part of JavaScript 1.5 but not in the ECMA-262 standard. We believe it is similarly possible to extend the semantics to *DOM objects*, which are part of an independent specification, and are available only when JavaScript runs in a Web-browser. However, we leave development of these extensions to future work.

For simplicity, we do not model some features which are laborious but do not add new insight to the semantics, such as the switch and for construct (we do model the for−in), parsing (which is used at run time for example by the eval command), the native Date and Math objects, minor type conversions like ToUInt32, etc. and the details of standard procedures such as converting a string into the numerical value that it actually represents. For the same reason, we also do not model *regular expression matching*, which is used in string operations.

In Section 5 we summarize some directions for future work.

2   Operational Semantics

Our operational semantics consists of a set of rules written in a conventional meta-notation. The notation is not directly executable in any specific automated framework, but is designed to be humanly readable, insofar as is possible for a programming language whose syntax requires 16 pages of specification, and a suitable basis for rigorous but un-automated proofs. Given the space constraints of a conference paper, we describe only the main semantic functions and some representative axioms and rules; the full semantics is currently available online [15].

In order to keep the semantic rules concise, we assume that source programs are legal JavaScript programs, and that each expression is disambiguated (e.g. 5+(3∗4)). We also follow systematic conventions about the syntactic categories of metavariables, to give as much information as possible about the intended type of each operation. In addition to the source expressions and commands used by JavaScript programmers, our semantics uses auxiliary syntactic forms that conveniently represent intermediate steps in our small-step semantics.

In principle, for languages whose semantics are well understood, it may be possible to give a direct operational semantics for a core language subset, and then define the semantics of additional language constructs by showing how these additional constructs are expressible in the core language. Instead of assuming that we know how to correctly define some parts of JavaScript from others, we decided to follow the ECMA specification as closely as possible, defining the semantics of each construct directly as given in the ECMA specification. While giving us the greatest likelihood that the semantics is correct, this approach also did not allow us to factor the language into independent sublanguages. While our presentation is divided into sections for *Types*, *Expressions*, *Objects*, and so on, the execution of a program containing one kind of construct may rely on the semantics of other constructs. We consider it an important future task to streamline the operational semantics and prove that the result is equivalent to the form derived from the standard.

Syntactic Conventions. In the rest of the paper we abbreviate t1,..., tn with t˜ and t1 ... tn with t* (t+ in the nonempty case). In a grammar, [t] means that t is optional, t|s means either t or s, and in case of ambiguity we escape with apices, as in escaping [by "[". Internal values are prefixed with &, as in &NaN. For conciseness, we use short sequences of letters to denote metavariables of a specific type. For example, m ranges over strings, pv over primitive values, etc.. These conventions are summarized in Figure 1. In the examples, unless specified otherwise, JavaScript code prefixed by *js>* is verbatim code from the SpiderMonkey shell (release 1.7.0 2007-10-03).

2.1   Heap

Heaps and Values. Heaps map locations to objects, which are records of pure values va or functions fun(x,...){P}, indexed by strings m or internal identifiers @x (the symbol @ distinguishes internal from user identifiers). Values are standard.

As a convention, we append w to a syntactic category to denote that the corresponding term may belong to that category or be an exception. For example, lw denotes an address or an exception.

Heap Functions. We assume a standard set of functions to manipulate heaps. alloc(H,o) = H1,l allocates o in H returning a fresh address l for o in H1. H(l) = o retrieves o from l in H. o.i = va gets the value of property i of o. o−i = fun([x˜]){P} gets the function stored in property i of o. o:i = {[a˜]} gets the possibly empty set of attributes of property i of o. H(l.i=ov)=H1 sets the property i of l in H to the object value ov. del(H,l,i) = H1 deletes i from l in H. i !< o holds if o does not have property i. i < o holds if o has property i.

H ::= (l:o)˜ % heap
l ::= #x % object addresses
x ::= foo | bar | ... % identifiers (do not include reserved words)
o ::= "{"[(i:ov)˜]"}" % objects
i ::= m | @x % indexes
ov ::= va["{"a˜"}"] % object values
    | fun"("[x˜]"){"P"}" % function
a ::= ReadOnly| DontEnum | DontDelete % attributes

pv ::= m | n | b | null | &undefined % primitive values
m ::= "foo" | "bar" | ... % strings
n ::= −n | &NaN | &Infinity | 0 | 1 | ... % numbers
b ::= true | false % booleans
va ::= pv | l % pure values
r ::= ln"*"m % references
ln ::= l | null % nullable addresses
v ::= va | r % values
w ::= "<"va">" % exception

Fig. 1. Metavariables and Syntax for Values

2.2 Semantics Functions

We have three small-step semantic relations for expressions, statements and programs denoted respectively by $\xrightarrow{e}, \xrightarrow{s}, \xrightarrow{P}$. Each semantic function transforms a heap, a pointer in the heap to the current scope, and the current term being evaluated into a new heap-scope-term triple. The evaluation of expressions returns either a value or an exception, the evaluation of statements and programs terminates with a completion (explained below).

The semantic functions are recursive, and mutually dependent. The semantics of programs depends on the semantics of statements which in turn depends on the semantics of expressions which in turn, for example by evaluating a function, depends circularly on the semantics of programs. These dependencies are made explicit by contextual rules, that specify how a transition derived for a term can be used to derive a transition for a bigger term including the former as a sub-term. In general, the premises of each semantic rule are predicates that must hold in order for the rule to be applied, usually built of very simple mathematical conditions such as $t < S$ or $t != t'$ or $f(a) = b$ for set membership, inequality and function application.

Transitions axioms (rules that do not have transitions in the premises) specify the individual transitions for basic terms (the redexes). For example, the axiom H,l,(v) $\longrightarrow$ H,l,v describes that brackets can be removed when they surround a value (as opposed to an expression, where brackets are still meaningful).

Contextual rules propagate such atomic transitions. For example, if program H,l,P evaluates to H1,l1,P1 then H,l,@FunExe(l',P) (an internal expression used to evaluate the body of a function) reduces in one step to H1,l1,@FunExe(l',P1). The rule below show exactly that: @FunExe(l,−) is one of the contexts eCp for evaluating programs.

$$\frac{\text{H,l,P} \xrightarrow{P} \text{H1,l1,P1}}{\text{H,l,eCp[P]} \xrightarrow{e} \text{H1,l1,eCp[P1]}}$$

As another example, sub-expressions are evaluated inside outer expressions (rule on the left) using contexts eC ::= typeof eC | eCgv | ..., and exceptions propagated to the top level (axiom on the right).

$$\frac{\text{H,l,e} \xrightarrow{e} \text{H1,l1,e1}}{\text{H,l,eC[e]} \xrightarrow{e} \text{H1,l1,eC[e1]}} \qquad \text{H,l,eC[w]} \xrightarrow{e} \text{H,l,w}$$

Hence, if an expression throws an exception (H,l,e $\xrightarrow{e}$ H1,l,w) then so does say the typeof operator: H,l,typeof e $\xrightarrow{e}$ H1,l,typeof w $\xrightarrow{e}$ H1,l,w.

It is very convenient to nest contexts inside each other. For example, contexts for GetValue (the internal expression that returns the value of a reference), generated by the grammar for eCgv ::= −[e] | va[−] | eCto | eCts | ..., are expression contexts. Similarly, contexts for converting values to objects eCto ::= −[va] | ... or to strings eCts ::= l[−] | ... are get-value contexts.

$$\text{H,l,eCgv[ln∗m]} \xrightarrow{e} \text{H1,l,eCgv[@GetValue(ln∗m)]}$$

$$\frac{\text{Type(va)} \mathrel{!=} \text{Object} \quad \text{ToObject(H,va)} = \text{H1,lw}}{\text{H,l,eCto[va]} \xrightarrow{e} \text{H1,l,eCto[lw]}}$$

$$\frac{\text{Type(v)} \mathrel{!=} \text{String} \quad \text{ToString(v)} = \text{e}}{\text{H,l,eCts[v]} \xrightarrow{e} \text{H,l,eCts[e]}}$$

As a way to familiarize with these structures of nested contexts, we look in detail at the concrete example of member selection. The ECMA-262 specification states that in order to evaluate MemberExpression[Expression] one needs to:

```
MemberExpression : MemberExpression [ Expression ]
1. Evaluate MemberExpression.
2. Call GetValue(Result(1)).
3. Evaluate Expression.
4. Call GetValue(Result(3)).
5. Call ToObject(Result(2)).
6. Call ToString(Result(4)).
7. Return a value of type Reference whose base object is Result(5) and
whose property name is Result(6).
```

In our formalization, the rule for member selection is just H,l,l1[m] $\xrightarrow{e}$ H,l,l1∗m. As opposed to the textual specification, the formal rule is trivial, and makes it obvious that the operator takes an object and a string and returns the corresponding reference. All we had to do in order to model the intermediate steps was to insert the appropriate contexts in the evaluation contexts for expressions, values, objects and strings. In particular, $-[e]$ is value context, and value contexts are expression contexts, so we get for free steps 1 and 2, obtaining va$[e]$. Since va$[-]$ is also a value context, steps 3 and 4 also come for free, obtaining va$[va]$. Since $-[va]$ is an object context, and $I[-]$ a string context, steps 6 and 7 are also executed transparently. The return type of each of those contexts guarantees that the operations are executed in the correct order. If that was not the case, then the original specification would have been ambiguous. The rule for propagating exceptions takes care of any exception raised during these steps.

The full formal semantics [15] contains several other contextual rules to account for other mutual dependencies and for all the implicit type conversions. This substantial use of contextual rules greatly simplifies the semantics and will be very useful in Section 3 to prove its formal properties.

Scope and Prototype Lookup. The scope and prototype chains are two distinctive features of JavaScript. The stack is represented implicitly, by maintaining a chain of objects whose properties represent the binding of local variables in the scope. Since we are not concerned with performance, our semantics needs to know only a pointer to the head of the chain (the current scope object). Each scope object stores a pointer to its enclosing scope object in an internal @Scope property. This helps in dealing with constructs that modify the scope chain, such as function calls and the with statement.

JavaScript follows a prototype-based approach to inheritance. Each object stores in an internal property @Prototype a pointer to its prototype object, and inherits its properties. At the root of the prototype tree there is @Object.prototype, that has a null prototype. The rules below illustrate prototype chain lookup.

$$\mathsf{Prototype(H,null,m)=null}$$

$$\frac{m < H(l)}{\mathsf{Prototype(H,l,m)=l}} \qquad \frac{m! < H(l) \quad H(l).@Prototype=ln}{\mathsf{Prototype(H,l,m)=Prototype(H,ln,m)}}$$

Function Scope(H,l,m) returns the address of the scope object in H that first defines property m, starting from the current scope l. It is used to look up identifiers in the semantics of expressions. Its definition is similar to the one for prototype, except that the condition (H,l.@HasProperty(m)) (which navigates the prototype chain to check if l has property m) is used instead of the direct check $m < H(l)$.

Types. JavaScript values are dynamically typed. The internal types are:

T ::= Undefined | Null | Boolean | String | Number % *primitive types*
    | Object | Reference % *other types*

Types are used to determine conditions under which certain semantic rules can be evaluated. The semantics defines straightforward predicates and functions which perform useful checks on the type of values. For example, IsPrim(v) holds when v is a value of a primitive type, and GetType(H,v) returns a string corresponding to a more intuitive type for v in H. The user expression typeof e, which returns the type of its operand, uses internally GetType. Below, we show the case for function objects (i.e. objects which implement the internal @Call property).

$$\frac{\text{Type}(v)=\text{Object} \quad \text{@Call} < \text{H}(v)}{\text{GetType}(\text{H},v) = \textit{"function"}}$$

An important use of types is to convert the operands of typed operations and throw exceptions when the conversion fails. There are implicit conversions into strings, booleans, number, objects and primitive types, and some of them can lead to the execution of arbitrary code. For example, the member selection expression e1[e2] implicitly converts e2 to a string. If e2 denotes an object, its re-definable toString propery is invoked as a function.

js> var o={a:0}; o[{toString:function(){o.a++; return "a"}}] *% res: 1*

The case for ToPrimitive (invoked by ToNumber and ToString) is responsible for the side effects: the result of converting an object value into a primitive value is an expression l.@DefaultValue([T]) which may involve executing arbitrary code that a programmer can store in the valueOf or toString methods of said object.

$$\frac{\text{Type}(l)=\text{Object}}{\text{ToPrimitive}(l[,T]) = l.\text{@DefaultValue}([T])}$$

2.3   Expressions

We distinguish two classes of expressions: internal expressions, which correspond to specification artifacts needed to model the intended behavior of user expressions, and user expressions, which are part of the user syntax of JavaScript. Internal expressions include addresses, references, exceptions and functions such as @GetValue,@PutValue used to get or set object properties, and @Call,@Construct used to call functions or to construct new objects using constructor functions. For example, we give two rules of the specification of @Put, which is the internal interface (used also by @PutValue) to set properties of objects. The predicate H,l1.@CanPut(m) holds if m does not have a ReadOnly attribute.

$$\frac{\text{H,l1.@CanPut}(m) \quad m \,!{<}\, \text{H}(l1) \quad \text{H}(l1.m{=}va\{\}){=}\text{H1}}{\text{H,l,l1.@Put}(m,va) \xrightarrow{e} \text{H1,l,va}}$$

$$\frac{\text{H,l1.@CanPut}(m) \quad \text{H}(l1){:}m{=}\{[a^{\sim}]\} \quad \text{H}(l1.m{=}va\{[a^{\sim}]\}) = \text{H1}}{\text{H,l,l1.@Put}(m,va) \xrightarrow{e} \text{H1,l,va}}$$

These rules show that fresh properties are added with an empty set of attributes, whereas existing properties are replaced maintaining the same set of attributes.

Object Literal.   As an example of expressions semantics we present in detail the case of object literals. The semantics of the object literal expression {pn:e,...,pn':e'} uses an auxiliary internal construct AddProps to add the result of evaluating each e as a property with name pn to a newly created empty object. Rule (1) (with help from the contextual rules) creates a new empty object, and passes control to AddProps. Rule (2) converts identifiers to strings, and rule (3) adds a property to the object being initialized. It uses a sequential expression to perform the update and then return the pointer to the updated object l1, which rule (4) releases at the top level.

$$H,l,\{[(pn:e)^\sim]\} \xrightarrow{e} H,l,@AddProps(new\ Object()[,(pn:e)^\sim]) \quad (1)$$

$$H,l,@AddProps(l1,x:e[,(pn:e)^\sim]) \xrightarrow{e} H,l,@AddProps(l1,"x":e[,\ (pn:e)^\sim]) \quad (2)$$

$$H,l,@AddProps(l1,m:va[,(pn:e)^\sim]) \xrightarrow{e} H,l,@AddProps((l1.@Put(m,va),l1)[,(pn:e)^\sim])(3)$$

$$H,l,@AddProps(l1) \xrightarrow{e} H,l,l1 \quad (4)$$

Rule (1) is emblematic of a few other cases in which the specification requires to create a new object by evaluating a specific constructor expression whose definition can be changed during execution. For example,

js> var a = {}; a *% res: [object Object]*
ljs> Object = function(){return new Number()}; var b = {}; b *% res: 0*

where the second object literal returns a number object. That feature can be useful, but can also lead to undesired confusion.

2.4   Statements

Similarly to the case for expressions, the semantics of statements contains a certain number of internal statements, used to represent unobservable execution steps, and user statements that are part of the user syntax of JavaScript. A completion is the final result of evaluating a statement.

co ::= "("ct,vae,xe")" vae ::= &empty | va xe ::= &empty | x
ct ::= Normal | Break | Continue | Return | Throw

The completion type indicates whether the execution flow should continue normally, or be disrupted. The value of a completion is relevant when the completion type is Return (denoting the value to be returned), Throw (denoting the exception thrown), or Normal (propagating the value to be return during the execution of a function body). The identifier of a completion is relevant when the completion type is either Break or Continue, denoting the program point where the execution flow should be diverted to.

Expression and Throw. Evaluation contexts transform the expression operand of these constructs into a pure value. All the semantic rules specify is how such value is packaged into a completion. The rules for return,continue,break are similar.

$$H,l,va \xrightarrow{s} H,l,(Normal,va,\&empty) \qquad H,l,throw\ va; \xrightarrow{s} H,l,(Throw,va,\&empty)$$

2.5   Programs

Programs are sequences of statements and function declarations.

$$P ::= \mathsf{fd}\ [P]\ |\ \mathsf{s}\ [P] \qquad\qquad \mathsf{fd} ::= \mathsf{function}\ x\ ''(''[x\tilde{}]'')''\{''[P]''\}''$$

As usual, the execution of statements is taken care of by a contextual rule. If a statement evaluates to a break or continue outside of a control construct, an SyntaxError exception is thrown (rule (9)). The run-time semantics of a function declaration instead is equivalent to a no-op (rule (10)). Function (and variable) declarations should in fact be parsed once and for all, before starting to execute the program text. In the case of the main body of a JavaScript program, the parsing is triggered by rule (11) which adds to the initial heap NativeEnv first the variable and then the function declarations (functions VD,FD).

$$\frac{\begin{array}{c} \mathsf{ct} < \{\mathsf{Break},\mathsf{Continue}\} \\ \mathsf{o} = \mathsf{new\_SyntaxError}() \quad \mathsf{H1,l1} = \mathsf{alloc}(\mathsf{H,o}) \end{array}}{\mathsf{H,l,(ct,vae,xe)}\ [P] \xrightarrow{P} \mathsf{H1,l,(Throw,l1,\&empty)}} \quad (9)$$

$$\mathsf{H,l,function}\ x\ ([x\tilde{}])\{[P]\}\ [P1] \xrightarrow{P} \mathsf{H,l,(Normal,\&empty,\&empty)}\ [P1] \quad (10)$$

$$\frac{\begin{array}{c} \mathsf{VD}(\mathsf{NativeEnv},\#\mathsf{Global},\{\mathsf{DontDelete}\},P) = \mathsf{H1} \\ \mathsf{FD}(\mathsf{H1},\#\mathsf{Global},\{\mathsf{DontDelete}\},P) = \mathsf{H2} \end{array}}{P \xrightarrow{P} \mathsf{H2},\#\mathsf{Global},P} \quad (11)$$

2.6   Native Objects

The initial heap NativeEnv of core JavaScript contains native objects for representing predefined functions, constructors and prototypes, and the global object @Global that constitutes the initial scope, and is always the root of the scope chain. As an example, we describe the global object. The global object defines properties to store special values such as &NaN, &undefined etc., functions such as eval, toString etc. and constructors that can be used to build generic objects, functions, numbers, booleans and arrays. Since it is the root of the scope chain, its @Scope property points to null. Its @this property points to itself: @Global = {@Scope:null, @this:#Global, "eval":#GEval{DontEnum},...}. None of the non-internal properties are read-only or enumerable, and most of them can be deleted. By contrast, when a user variable or function is defined in the top level scope (i.e. the global object) it has only the DontDelete attribute. The lack of a ReadOnly attribute on "NaN","Number" for example forces programmers to use the expression $0/0$ to denote the real &NaN value, even though @Number.NaN stores &NaN and is a read only property.

Eval. The eval function takes a string and tries to parse it as a legal program text. If it fails, it throws a SyntaxError exception (rule (12)). If it succeeds, it parses the code for variable and function declarations (respectively VD,FD) and spawns the internal statement @cEval (rule (13)). In turn, @cEval is an execution context for programs, that returns the value computed by the last statement in P, or &undefined if it is empty.

$$\frac{\begin{array}{l} \mathsf{ParseProg(m)} = \&\mathsf{undefined} \\ \mathsf{H2,l2} = \mathsf{alloc(H,o)} \quad \mathsf{o} = \mathsf{new\_SyntaxError()} \end{array}}{\mathsf{H,l,\#GEval.@Exe(l1,m)} \xrightarrow{e} \mathsf{H2,l,<l2>}} \quad (12)$$

$$\frac{\begin{array}{l} \mathsf{l\ != \#Global} \quad \mathsf{ParseProg(m)} = \mathsf{P} \\ \mathsf{VD(H,l,\{\},P)} = \mathsf{H1} \quad \mathsf{FD(H1,l,\{\},P)} = \mathsf{H2} \end{array}}{\mathsf{H,l,\#GEval.@Exe(l1,m)} \xrightarrow{e} \mathsf{H2,l,@cEval(P)}} \quad (13)$$

$$\frac{\mathsf{va} = (\mathit{IF}\ \mathsf{vae}=\&\mathsf{empty}\ \mathit{THEN}\ \&\mathsf{undefined}\ \mathit{ELSE}\ \mathsf{vae})}{\mathsf{H,l,@cEval((ct,vae,xe))} \xrightarrow{e} \mathsf{H,l,va}} \quad (14)$$

As we are not interested in modeling the parsing phase, we just assume a parsing function ParseProg(m) which given string m returns a valid program P or else &undefined. Note how in rule (13) the program P is executed in the caller's scope l, effectively giving dynamic scope to P.

Object. The @Object constructor is used for creating new user objects and internally by constructs such as object literals. Its prototype @ObjectProt becomes the prototype of any object constructed in this way, so its properties are inherited by most JavaScript objects. Invoked as a function or as a constructor, @Object returns its argument if it is an object, a new empty object if its argument is undefined or not supplied, or converts its argument to an object if it is a string, a number or a boolean. If the argument is a host object (such as a DOM object) the behavior is implementation dependent.

$$\frac{\begin{array}{l} \mathsf{o} = \mathsf{new\_object}(\mathit{"Object"},\#\mathsf{ObjectProt}) \\ \mathsf{H1,lo} = \mathsf{Alloc(H,o)} \quad \mathsf{Type(pv)} < \{\mathsf{Null,Undefined}\} \end{array}}{\mathsf{H,l,\#Object.@Construct(pv)} \xrightarrow{e} \mathsf{H1,l,lo}}$$

$$\frac{\begin{array}{l} \mathsf{Type(pv)} < \{\mathsf{String, Boolean, Number}\} \\ \mathsf{H1,le} = \mathsf{ToObject(H,pv)} \end{array}}{\mathsf{H,l,\#Object.@Construct(pv)} \xrightarrow{e} \mathsf{H,l,le}} \qquad \frac{\mathsf{Type(l1)} = \mathsf{Object} \quad !\mathsf{IsHost(H,l1)}}{\mathsf{H,l,\#Object.@Construct(l1)} \xrightarrow{e} \mathsf{H,l,l1}}$$

The object @ObjectProt is the root of the scope prototype chain. For that reason, its internal prototype is null. Apart from *"constructor"*, which stores a pointer to @Object, the other public properties are native meta-functions such as toString or valueOf (which, like user function, always receive a value for @this as the first parameter).

2.7 Relation to Implementations

JavaScript is implemented within the major web browsers, or as standalone shells. In order to clarify several ambiguities present in the specification, we have run experiments inspired by our semantics rules on different implementations.

We have found that, besides resolving ambiguities in different and often incompatible ways, implementations sometimes openly diverge from the specification. In [15] we report several cases.

For example, in SpiderMonkey (the Mozilla implementation) the semantics of functions depends on the position, *within unreachable code* of statements which should have no semantic significance! The function call below returns 0, but if we move the var g; after the last definition of g, it returns 1.

(function(){if (true) function g(){return 0};return g();var g;function g(){return 1}})()

Apart from pathological examples such as this, Mozilla's JavaScript extends ECMA-262 in several ways, for example with *getters* and *setters*. A getter is a function that gets called when the corresponding property is accessed and a setter is a function that gets called when the property is assigned. While we can extend our semantics to deal with these further constructs, we leave for future work the full integration of this approach.

3 Formal Properties

In this section we give some preliminary definitions and set up a basic framework for formal analysis of well-formed JavaScript programs. We prove a progress theorem which shows that the semantics is sound and the execution of a well-formed term always progresses to an exception or an expected value. Next we prove a Heap reachability theorem which essentially justifies mark and sweep type garbage collection for JavaScript. Although the properties we prove are fairly standard for idealized languages used in formal studies, proving them for real (and unruly!) JavaScript is a much harder task.

Throughout this section, a program state S denotes a triple (H, l, t) where H is a heap, l is a current scope address and t is a term. Recall that a heap is a map from heap addresses to objects, and an object is a collection of properties that can contain heap addresses or primitive values.

3.1 Notation and Definitions

Expr, *Stmnt* and *Prog* denote respectively the sets of all possible expressions, statements and programs that can be written using the corresponding internal and user grammars. $\mathbb{L}$ denotes the set of all possible heap addresses. *Wf(S)* is a predicate denoting that a state S is well-formed. *prop(o)* is the set of property names present in object o. *dom(H)* gives the set of allocated addresses for the heap H.

For a heap address l and a term t, we say $l \in t$ iff the heap address l occurs in t. For a state $S = (H, l, t)$, we define $\Delta(S)$ as the set of heap addresses $\{l\} \cup \{l | l \in t\}$. This is also called the set of *roots* for the state S.

We define the well-formedness predicate of a state $S = (H, l, t)$ as the conjunction of the predicates $Wf_{Heap}(H)$, $Wf_{scope}(l)$ and $Wf_{term}(t)$. A term t is well-formed iff it can be derived using the grammar rules consisting of both the language constructs and the internal constructs, and all heap addresses contained in t are allocated ie $l \in t \Rightarrow l \in dom(H)$. A scope address $l \in dom(H)$ is well-formed iff the scope chain starting from l does not contain cycles, and $(@Scope \in prop(H(l))) \wedge (H(l).@Scope \neq null \Rightarrow \text{Wf}(H(l).@Scope))$. A heap H is well-formed iff it conforms to all the conditions on heap objects mentioned in the specification (see the long version [15] for a detailed list).

Definition 1 (Heap Reachability Graph). *Given a heap H, we define a labeled directed graph G_H with heap addresses $l \in dom(H)$ as the nodes, and an edge from address l_i to l_j with label p iff $(p \in prop(H(l_i)) \wedge H(l_i).p = l_j)$.*

Given a heap reachability graph G_H, we can define the view from a heap address l as the subgraph $G_{H,l}$ consisting only of nodes that are reachable from l in graph G_H. We use $view_H(l)$ to denote the set of heap addresses reachable from l: $view_H(l) = Nodes(G_{H,l})$. $view_H$ can be naturally extended to apply to a set of heap addresses. Observe that the graph G_H only captures those object properties that point to other heap objects and does not say anything about properties containing primitive values.

Definition 2 (l-Congruence of Heaps $\cong_l$). *We say that two heaps H_1 and H_2 are l-congruent (or congruent with respect to heap address l) iff they have the same views from heap address l and the corresponding objects at the heap addresses present in the views are also equal. Formally,*
$$H_1 \cong_l H_2 \Leftrightarrow (G_{H_1,l} = G_{H_2,l} \wedge \forall l' \in view_{H_1}(l) \; H_1(l') = H_2(l')).$$

Note that if $H_1 \cong_l H_2$ then $view_{H_1}(l) = view_{H_2}(l)$. It is easy to see that if two heaps H_1 and H_2 are congruent with respect to l then they are congruent with respect to all heap addresses $l' \in view_{H_1}(l)$.

Definition 3 (State congruence $\cong$). *We say that two states $S_1 = (H_1, l, t)$ and $S_2 = (H_2, l, t)$ are congruent iff the heaps are congruent with respect to all addresses in the roots set. Formally, $S_1 \cong S_2 \Leftrightarrow \forall l' \in \Delta(S_1) \; (H_1 \cong_{l'} H_2)$.*

Note that $\Delta(S_1) = \Delta(S_2)$ because the definition of Δ depends only on l and t. In the next section we will show that for a state $S = (H, l, t)$, $view_H(\Delta(S))$ forms the set of *live* heap addresses for the S because these are the only possible heap addresses that can be accessed during any transition from S.

Definition 4 (Heap Address Renaming). *For a given heap H, a heap address renaming function f is any one to one map from $dom(H)$ to $\mathbb{L}$.*

We denote the set of all possible heap renaming functions for a heap H by $\mathbb{F}_H$. We overload f so that $f(H)$ is the new heap obtained by renaming all heap addresses $l \in dom(H)$ by $f(l)$ and for a term t, $f(t)$ is the new term obtained by renaming all $l \in t$ by $f(l)$. Finally, for a state $S = (H, l, t)$ we define $f(S) = (f(H), f(l), f(t))$ as the new state obtained under the renaming.

Definition 5 (State similarity $\sim$). *Two states $S_1 = (H_1, l_1, t_1)$ and $S_2 = (H_2, l_2, t_2)$ are similar iff there exists a renaming function f for H_1 such that the new state $f(S_1)$ obtained under the renaming is congruent to S_2. Formally, $S_1 \sim S_2 \Leftrightarrow \exists f \in \mathbb{F}_{H_1} \, f(S_1) \cong S_2$.*

Property 1. Both $\cong$ and $\sim$ are equivalence relations. Moreover, $\cong \subsetneq \sim$.

3.2 Theorems and Formal Properties

We now present the main technical results. Our first result is a progress and preservation theorem, showing that evaluation of a well-formed term progresses to a value or an exception.

Lemma 1. *Let C denote the set of all valid contexts for expressions, statements and programs. For all terms t appropriate for the context C we have $Wf_{term}(C(t)) \Rightarrow Wf_{term}(t)$.*

Theorem 1 (Progress and Preservation). *For all states $S = (H, l, t)$ and $S' = (H', l', t')$:*

  - *$(Wf(S) \wedge S \to S') \Rightarrow Wf(S')$ (Preservation)*
  - *$Wf(S) \wedge t \notin v(t) \Rightarrow \exists S' \, (S \to S'))$ (Progress)*

where $v(t) = ve$ if $t \in Expr$ and $v(t) = co$ if $t \in Stmnt$ or $Prog$.

Our second result shows that similarity is preserved under reduction, which directly gives a construction for a simple mark-and-sweep-like garbage collector for JavaScript. The proofs for the theorems are given in the long version [15].

Lemma 2. *For all well-formed program states $S = (H, l, t)$, if $H, l, t \to H', l', t'$ then $H(l'') = H'(l'')$, for all $l'' \notin view_H(\Delta(H, l, t)) \cup view_{H'}(\Delta(H', l', t'))$.*

The above lemma formalizes the fact that the only heap addresses accessed during a reduction step are the ones present in the initial and final live address sets. We can formally prove this lemma by an induction over the rules.

Theorem 2 (Similarity preserved under reduction). *For all well-formed program states S_1, S_2 and S_1', $S_1 \sim S_2 \wedge S_1 \to S_1' \Rightarrow \exists S_2'. S_2 \to S_2' \wedge S_1' \sim S_2'$.*

We can intuitively understand this theorem by observing that if the reduction of a term does not involve allocation of any new heap addresses then the only addresses that can potentially be accessed during the reduction would be the ones present in the live heap address set. When the program states are similar, then under a certain renaming the two states would have the same live heap address sets . As a result the states obtained after reduction would also be congruent(under the same renaming function). On the other hand, if the reduction involves allocation of new heap addresses then we can simply extend the heap address renaming function by creating a map from the newly allocated addresses in the first heap (H_1') to the newly allocated addresses in the second heap (H_2'). Thus state similarity would be preserved in both cases.

A consequence of Theorem 2 is that we can build a simple mark and sweep type garbage collector for JavaScript. For any program state $S = (H, l, t)$, we mark all the heap addresses that are reachable from $\Delta(S)$. We modify the heap H to H' by freeing up all unmarked addresses and obtain the new program state $S' = (H', l, t)$. It is easy to show that $S' \sim S$. Hence by Theorem 2, a reduction trace starting from t, in a system with garbage collection, would be similar to the one obtained without garbage collection. In other words, garbage collection does not affect the semantics of programs.

4   Related Work

The JavaScript approach to objects is based on Self [23] and departs from the foundational object calculi proposed in the 1990s, e.g., [5,9,16]. Previous foundational studies include operational semantics for a subset of JavaScript [11] and formal properties of subsets of JavaScript [7,19,22,21]. Our aim is different from these previous efforts because we address the full ECMA Standard language (with provisions for variants introduced in different browsers). We believe a comprehensive treatment is important for analyzing existing code and code transformation methods [1,2]. In addition, when analyzing JavaScript security, it is important to consider attacks that could be created using arbitrary JavaScript, as opposed to some subset used to develop the trusted application. Some work on containing the effects of malicious JavaScript include [18,24]. Future versions of JavaScript and ECMAScript are documented in [13,12].

In the remainder of this section, we compare our work to the formalizations proposed by Thiemann [22] and Giannini [7] and comment on the extent to which formal properties they establish for subsets of JavaScript can be generalized to the full language.

Giannini et al. [7] formalize a small subset of JavaScript and give a static type system that prevents run-time typing errors. The subset is non-trivial, as it includes dynamic addition of properties to objects, and constructor functions to create objects. However the subset also lacks important features such as object prototyping, functions as objects, statements such as with, try−catch, for−in, and native functions and objects. This leads to substantial simplifications in their semantics, relative to ours. For example, function definitions are stored in a separate data structure rather than in the appropriate scope object, so there is no scope-chain-based resolution of global variables appearing inside a function body. Their simplification also makes it possible to define a sound type system that does not appear to extend to full JavaScript, as further discussed below.

Thiemann [22] proposes a type system for a larger subset of JavaScript than [7], as it also includes function expressions, function objects, and object literals. The type system associates type signatures with objects and functions and identifies suspicious type conversions. However, Thiemann's subset still does not allow object prototyping, the with and the try−catch statements, or subtle features of the language such as property attributes or arbitrary variable declarations in the body of a function. As we showed in section 2, these non-trivial (and non-intuitive) aspects of JavaScript make static analysis of arbitrary JavaScript code very difficult.

The substantial semantic difference between the subsets covered in [7,22] and full JavaScript is illustrated by the fact that: (i) Programs that are well-typed in the proposed subsets may lead to type errors when executed using the complete semantics, and (ii) Programs that do not lead to a type error when executed using the complete semantics may be considered ill-typed unnecessarily by the proposed type systems. The first point is demonstrated by var x = "a"; x.length = function(){ }; x.length(), which is allowed and well-typed by [22]. However it leads to a type error because although the type system considers implicit type conversion of the string x to a wrapped string object, it does not consider the prototyping mechanism and attributes for properties. Since property length of String.prototype has the ReadOnly attribute, the assignment in the second statement fails silently and thus the method call in the third statement leads to a type error. An example demonstrating the second point above is function f(){return o.g();}; result = f(), which is allowed by [7,22]. If method g is not present in the object o then both type systems consider the expression result = f() ill-typed. However g could be present as a method in the one of the ancestoral prototypes of o, in which case the expression will not lead to a type error. Because object prototyping is the main inheritance mechanism in JavaScript and it is pervasive in almost all real world JavaScript, we believe that a type system that does not consider the effects of prototypes will not be useful without further extension.

5   Conclusions

In this paper, we describe a structured operational semantics for the ECMA-262 standard [14] language. The semantics has two main parts: one-step evaluation relations for the three main syntactic categories of the language, and definitions for all of the native objects that are provided by an implementation. In the process of developing the semantics, we examined a number of perplexing (to us) JavaScript program situations and experimented with a number of implementations. To ensure accuracy of our semantics, we structured many clauses after the ECMA standard [14]. In a revision of our semantics, it would be possible to depart from the structure of the informal ECMA standard and make the semantics more concise, using many possible optimization to reduce its apparent complexity. As a validation of the semantics we proved a soundness theorem, a characterization of the reachable portion of the heap, and some equivalences between JavaScript programs.

In ongoing work, we are using this JavaScript semantics to analyze methods for determining isolation between embedded third-party JavaScript, such as embedded advertisements provided to web publishers through advertising networks, and the hosting content. In particular, we are studying at YAHOO!'s

ADsafe proposal [1] for safe online advertisements, the BeamAuth [6] authentication bookmarklet that relies on isolation between JavaScript on a page and JavaScript contained in a browser bookmark, Google's Caja effort [2] to provide code isloation by JavaScript rewriting, and FBJS [20], the subset of JavaScript used for writing FaceBook applications. While trying to formally prove properties of these mechanisms, we have already found violations of the intended security policies of two of them [15].

Acknowledgments. Sergio Maffeis is supported by EPSRC grant EP/E044956 /1. This work was done while the first author was visiting Stanford University, whose hospitality is gratefully acknowledged. Mitchell and Taly acknowledge the support of the National Science Foundation.

References

1. AdSafe: Making JavaScript safe for advertising, http://www.adsafe.org/
2. Google-Caja, A.: source-to-source translator for securing JavaScript-based Web, http://code.google.com/p/google-caja/
3. Jscript (Windows Script Technologies), http://msdn2.microsoft.com/en-us/library/hbxc2t98.aspx
4. Rhino: Javascript for Java, http://www.mozilla.org/rhino/
5. Abadi, M., Cardelli, L.: A Theory of Objects. Springer, Heidelberg (1996)
6. Adida, B.: BeamAuth: two-factor Web authentication with a bookmark. In: ACM Computer and Communications Security, pp. 48–57 (2007)
7. Anderson, C., Giannini, P., Drossopoulou, S.: Towards type inference for JavaScript. In: Black, A.P. (ed.) ECOOP 2005. LNCS, vol. 3586, pp. 428–452. Springer, Heidelberg (2005)
8. Eich, B.: Javascript at ten years, http://www.mozilla.org/js/language/ICFP-Keynote.ppt
9. Fisher, K., Honsell, F., Mitchell, J.C.: A lambda calculus of objects and method specialization. Nordic J. Computing (formerly BIT) 1, 3–37 (1994)
10. Flanagan, D.: JavaScript: The Definitive Guide. O'Reilly, Sebastopol (2006), http://proquest.safaribooksonline.com/0596101996
11. Herman, D.: Classic JavaScript, http://www.ccs.neu.edu/home/dherman/javascript/
12. Herman, D., Flanagan, C.: Status report: specifying JavaScript with ML. In: ML 2007: Proc. Workshop on ML, pp. 47–52 (2007)
13. ECMA International. ECMAScript 4, http://www.ecmascript.org
14. ECMA International. ECMAScript language specification. stardard ECMA-262, 3rd Edition (1999), http://www.ecma-international.org/publications/ECMA-ST/Ecma-262.pdf
15. Maffeis, S., Mitchell, J., Taly, A.: Complete ECMA 262-3 operational semantics and long version of present paper. Semantics: http://jssec.net/semantics/ Paper: http://jssec.net/semantics/
16. Mitchell, J.C.: Toward a typed foundation for method specialization and inheritance. In: POPL 1990, pp. 109–124 (1990)
17. Mozilla. Spidermonkey (javascript-c) engine, http://www.mozilla.org/js/spidermonkey/

18. Reis, C., Dunagan, J., Wang, H., Dubrovsky, O., Esmeir, S.: Browsershield: Vulnerability-driven filtering of dynamic HTML. ACM Transactions on the Web 1(3) (2007)
19. Siek, J., Taha, W.: Gradual typing for objects. In: Ernst, E. (ed.) ECOOP 2007. LNCS, vol. 4609, pp. 2–27. Springer, Heidelberg (2007)
20. The FaceBook Team. FBJS,
    http://wiki.developers.facebook.com/index.php/FBJS
21. Thiemann, P.: Towards a type system for analyzing JavaScript programs. In: Sagiv, M. (ed.) ESOP 2005, vol. 3444, pp. 408–422. Springer, Heidelberg (2005)
22. Thiemann, P.: A type safe DOM api. In: Bierman, G., Koch, C. (eds.) DBPL 2005. LNCS, vol. 3774, pp. 169–183. Springer, Heidelberg (2005)
23. Ungar, D., Smith, R.B.: Self: The power of simplicity. In: Proc. OOPSLA, vol. 22, pp. 227–242 (1987)
24. Yu, D., Chander, A., Islam, N., Serikov, I.: JavaScript instrumentation for browser security. In: ACM POPL, pp. 237–249 (2007)

JavaScript Instrumentation in Practice

Haruka Kikuchi[1], Dachuan Yu[2], Ajay Chander[2], Hiroshi Inamura[2],
and Igor Serikov[2]

[1] NTT DOCOMO, Inc.
[2] DOCOMO Communications Laboratories USA, Inc.

Abstract. JavaScript has been exploited to launch various browser-based attacks. Our previous work proposed a theoretical framework applying policy-based code instrumentation to JavaScript. This paper further reports our experience carrying out the theory in practice. Specifically, we discuss how the instrumentation is performed on various JavaScript and HTML syntactic constructs, present a new policy construction method for facilitating the creation and compilation of security policies, and document various practical difficulties arose during our prototyping. Our prototype currently works with several different web browsers, including Safari Mobile running on iPhones. We report our results based on experiments using representative real-world web applications.

1 Introduction

The success of the Web can be contributed partly to the use of client-side scripting languages, such as JavaScript [3]. Programs in JavaScript are deployed in HTML documents. They are interpreted by web browsers on the client machine, helping to make web pages richer, more dynamic, and more "intelligent."

As a form of mobile code, JavaScript programs are often provided by parties not trusted by web users, and their execution on the client systems raises security concerns. The extent of the problem [2,14] ranges from benign annoyances (*e.g.*, popping up advertisements, altering browser configurations) to serious attacks (*e.g.*, XSS, phishing).

In previous work [19], we formally studied the application of program instrumentation to enforcing security policies on JavaScript programs. Specifically, we clarified the execution model of JavaScript (particularly, higher-order script—script that generates other script at runtime), presented its instrumentation as a set of syntactic rewriting rules, and applied edit automata [12] as a framework of policy management. Focusing on articulating the generic instrumentation techniques and proving their correctness, the previous work is necessarily abstract on several implementation aspects, and can be realized differently when facing different tradeoffs. For example, among other possibilities, the instrumentation process can be carried out either by a browser on the client machine or by a proxy sitting on the network gateway.

In this paper, we discuss the practical application of the above theory to real-world scenarios. Specifically, we have completed a relatively mature prototype following a proxy-based architecture. In this prototype, both the instrumentation process and the policy input are managed by a proxy program, which is situated on the network gateway (or an enterprise firewall) and is maintained separately from the JavaScript programs of

G. Ramalingam (Ed.): APLAS 2008, LNCS 5356, pp. 326–341, 2008.

concern. The browser is set up to consult the proxy for all incoming traffic, and the proxy sends instrumented JavaScript programs (and HTML documents) to the browser.

Such an architecture provides centralized interposition and policy management through the proxy, thus enabling transparent policy creation and update for the end user. It requires no change to the browser implementation; therefore, it is naturally applicable to different browsers, modulo a few browser-specific implementation issues. As part of our experiments, we applied our proxy to the Safari Mobile browser on an iPhone [1]. The instrumentation and security protection worked painlessly, even though no software or browser plug-in can be installed on an iPhone. Furthermore, the proxy-based architecture poses minimal computation requirement on the client device for securely rendering web pages (as shown in our experiments, some popular web pages contain several hundred kilobytes of JavaScript code; their instrumentation takes a nontrivial amount of time). It is thus suitable for deployment with the use of mobile browsers.

We have successfully run our prototype with several browsers: Firefox, Konqueror, Opera, Safari, and Safari Mobile on an iPhone [1]. IE is currently only partially supported, because its behaviors on certain JavaScript code are significantly different than those of the other tested browsers. For the experiments, we applied a selected set of policies, which triggered the instrumentation of a variety of JavaScript constructs. We hand-picked some representative web pages as the instrumentation target. Measurements are made on both the proxy overhead and the client overhead. The initial numbers matched our expectations, noting that our prototype had not been optimized for performance.

2 Background

2.1 Previously: A Theoretical Framework

The generic theoretical framework for JavaScript instrumentation is illustrated in Figure 1 (reused from previous work [19]). Beyond the regular JavaScript interpreter provided in a browser, three modules are introduced to carry out the instrumentation and policy enforcement. A rewriting module ι serves as a proxy between the browser and the network traffic. Any incoming HTML document D, possibly with JavaScript code embedded, must go through the rewriting module first before reaching the browser.

The rewriting module identifies security-relevant actions A out of the document D and produces instrumented code $check(A)$ that monitors and confines the execution

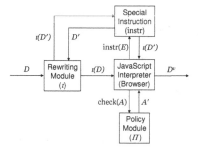

Fig. 1. JavaScript instrumentation for browser security

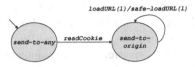

Fig. 2. Example edit automaton for a cookie policy

of A. This part is not fundamentally different from conventional instrumentation techniques [18,4]. However, this alone is not sufficient for securing JavaScript code, because of the existence of higher-order script (*e.g., document.write*(E), which evaluates E and use the result as part of the HTML document to be rendered by the browser)— some code fragments (*e.g.*, those embedded in the value of E) may not be available for inspection and instrumentation until at runtime. To address this, the rewriting module wraps higher-order script (*e.g.*, E) inside a special instruction (*e.g., instr*(E)), which essentially marks it to be instrumented on demand at runtime.

With the rewriting module as a proxy, the browser receives an instrumented document $\iota(D)$ for rendering. The rendering proceeds normally using a JavaScript interpreter, until either of the two special calls inserted by the rewriting module is encountered. Upon *check*(A), the browser consults the policy module Π, which is responsible for maintaining some internal state used for security monitoring, and for providing a replacement action A' (a secured version of A) for execution. Upon *instr*(E), the implementation of the special instruction *instr* will evaluate E to D' and invoke the rewriting module at runtime to perform the necessary rewriting on higher-order script. The instrumented $\iota(D')$ will then be sent back to the browser for rendering, possibly with further invocations of the policy module and special instruction as needed.

The policy module Π essentially manages an edit automaton [12] at runtime for security enforcement. A simple policy is illustrated in Figure 2, which restricts URL loading to prevent potential information leak after cookie is read. Following this, the policy module updates the automaton state based on the input actions A that it receives through the policy interface *check*(A), and produces output actions A' based on the replacement actions suggested by the automaton. For example, if the current state is `send-to-origin`, and the input action is `loadURL(1)`, then the current state remains unchanged, and the output action becomes `safe-loadURL(1)`, which performs necessary security checks and user promptings before loading a web page.

2.2 This Paper: A Proxy-Centric Realization

Focusing on the formal aspects and correctness of policy-based instrumentation on higher-order script, the previous work is largely abstract on the implementation aspects. Subsequently, we have conducted thorough prototyping and experiments on the practical realization of the formal theory. Several interesting topics were identified during the process, which we believe will serve as useful contributions to related studies.

Overall, we have opted for a proxy-centric realization for its browser independence and low computation overhead on client devices. This can be viewed as an instantiation of the framework in Figure 1 for a specific usage scenario—the use with multiple

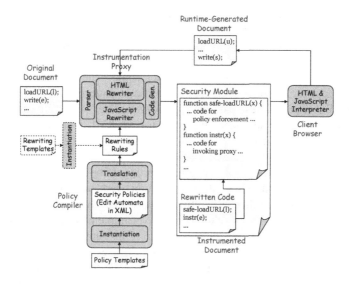

Fig. 3. A proxy-centric realization

mobile browsers. The instantiated architecture is more accurately depicted in Figure 3. The basic requirement here is that the proxy takes care of the rewriting and policy input, without changing the browser implementation. As a result, the tasks of the policy module Π and the special instruction $instr$ in Figure 1 have to be carried out in part by regular JavaScript code (the Security Module in Figure 3). Such JavaScript code is inserted into the HTML document by the proxy based on some policy input.

The rewriting process is carried out on the proxy using a parser, two rewriters, and a code generator. The rewriters work by manipulating abstract syntax trees (ASTs) produced by the parser. Transformed ASTs are converted into HTML and JavaScript by the code generator before fed to the browser that originally requested the web pages.

The rewriting rules direct the rewriters to put in different code for the security module when addressing different policies. On the one hand, the rewriters need to know what syntactic constructs to look for in the code and how to rewrite them. Therefore, they require low-level policies to work with syntactic patterns. On the other hand, human policy designers should think in terms of high-level actions and edit automata, not low-level syntactic details. We use a policy compiler to bridge this gap, which is a stand-alone program that can be implemented in any language.

We now summarize three major technical aspects of this proxy-centric realization. These will be expanded upon in the next three sections, respectively.

The first and foremost challenge is raised by the flexibility of the JavaScript language. Much effort is devoted to identifying security-relevant actions out of JavaScript code—there are many different ways of carrying out a certain action, hence many different syntactic constructs to inspect. We introduce a notion of *rewriting templates* to help managing this. Policy designers instantiate rewriting templates to rewriting rules, which in turn guides the instrumentation. This allows us to stick to the basic design without being distracted by syntactic details.

Next, the rewriting templates are still too low-level to manage. In contrast, the theoretical framework used edit automata for policy management. We support edit automata using an XML representation, and compile them into rewriting rules. As a result, we can handle all policies allowed by the theoretical framework. Nonetheless, edit automata are general-purpose, and browser-based policies could benefit further from domain-specific abstractions. We have identified some useful patterns of policies during our experiments. We organize these patterns as *policy templates*, which are essentially templates of specialized edit automata. We again use an XML representation for policy templates, which enables a natural composition of simple templates to form compound ones.

Finally, using a proxy, we avoid changing the browser implementation. This provides platform independence and reduces the computation overhead on the client devices. As a tradeoff, there are some other difficulties. In particular, the interfaces to the special instruction $instr$ and the policy module Π have to be implemented in regular JavaScript code and inserted into the HTML document during instrumentation. Such code must be able to call the proxy at runtime, interact with the user in friendly and meaningful ways, and be protected from malicious modifications. Furthermore, different browsers sometimes behave differently on the same JavaScript code, an incompatibility that we have to address carefully during instrumentation.

3   Rewriting JavaScript and HTML

We now describe the details of the instrumentation, which is carried out by transforming abstract syntax trees (ASTs). Specifically, the proxy identifies pieces of the AST to be rewritten, and replaces them with new ones that enforce the desired policies. Although a clean process in Figure 1, action replacement in the actual JavaScript language raises interesting issues due to the flexible and dynamic nature of the language. Specifically, actions A in Figure 1 exhibit themselves in JavaScript and HTML through various syntactic forms. Some common examples include property access, method calls, and event handlers. Therefore, upon different syntactic categories, the instrumentation should produce different target code, as opposed to the uniform $check(A)$. We specify what syntactic constructs to rewrite and how to rewrite them using rewriting rules.

We summarize commonly used rewriting rules for various syntactic constructs in Table 1 as *rewriting templates*. The first column shows the template names and parameters. The second shows the corresponding syntactic forms of the code pieces to be rewritten (which correspond to actions A). The third shows the target code pieces used to replace the original ones (which correspond to $check(A)$). These templates are to be instantiated using relevant JavaScript entities. Examples are given in the last column.

For example, the first row $(Get, obj, prop)$ specifies how to rewrite syntactic constructs of reading properties (both fields and methods). Get is the name of the template, and obj and $prop$ are parameters to be instantiated with the actual object and property. Two sample instantiations are given. The first is on the field access document.cookie. Based on (Get, document, cookie), the JavaScript rewriter will look for all AST pieces of property access (*i.e.*, those of the shape $obj.prop$ and $obj["prop"]$), and replace them with a call to a *redirector* function sec.GetProp. Here sec is a JavaScript

Table 1. Rewriting templates

Rewriting templates	Sample Code patterns	Rewritten code (redirectors)	Sample instantiation
$(\text{Get}, obj, prop)$	$obj.prop$ $obj[\text{``}prop\text{''}]$	$\text{sec.GetProp}(obj, prop)$	$(\text{Get}, \text{document}, \text{cookie})$ $(\text{Get}, \text{window}, \text{alert})$
$(\text{Call}, obj, meth)$	$obj.meth(E, \dots)$ $obj[\text{``}meth\text{''}](E, \dots)$	$\text{sec.CallMeth}(obj, meth, E_i, \dots)$	$(\text{Call}, \text{window}, \text{open})$
$(\text{GetD}, dprop)$	$dprop$	$\text{sec.GetDProp}(dprop)$	$(\text{GetD}, \text{location})$
$(\text{CallD}, dmeth)$	$dmeth(E, \dots)$	$\text{sec.isEval}(dmeth)\,?$ $\text{eval}(\text{sec.instrument}(E_i, \dots))\,:$ $\text{sec.CallDMeth}(dmeth, E_i, \dots)$	$(\text{CallD}, \text{open})$
$(\text{Set}, obj, prop)$	$obj.prop = E$ $obj[\text{``}prop\text{''}] = E$   $obj.prop \mathrel{+}= E$   $obj[\text{``}prop\text{''}] \mathrel{+}= E$	$\text{sec.SetProp}(obj, prop, E_i)$ $\text{sec.SetPropPlus}(obj, prop, E_i)$	$(\text{Set}, \text{document}, \text{cookie})$ $(\text{Set}, \text{window}, \text{alert})$
$(\text{SetD}, dprop)$	$dprop = E$ $dprop \mathrel{+}= E$	$\text{sec.SetDProp}(dprop, E_i)$ $\text{sec.SetDPropPlus}(dprop, E_i)$	$(\text{SetD}, \text{location})$ $(\text{SetD}, \text{open})$
$(\text{Event}, tag, attr)$	$<tag\ attr=\text{``}E\text{''}>$	$<tag\ attr=\text{``sec.Event}(\text{this}, E_i)\text{''}>$	$(\text{Event}, \text{button}, \text{onclick})$
(FSrc)	$<\text{img src}=\text{``}U\text{''}$   $\text{onerror}=\text{``}E\text{''}>$ $<\text{iframe src}=\text{``}U\text{''}$   $\text{onload}=\text{``}E\text{''}>$	$<\text{img src}=\text{``''}\ \text{onerror}=\text{``setAttribute}(\text{onerror}, \text{``}E_i\text{''});$   $\text{sec.FSimg}(\text{this}, U)\text{''}>$   $<\text{iframe src}=\text{``''}\ \text{onload}=\text{``setAttribute}(\text{onload}, \text{``}E_i\text{''});$ $\text{sec.FSiframe}(\text{this}, U)\text{''}>$	

object inserted by our proxy; it corresponds to the "Security Module" in Figure 3. Among other tasks, sec maintains a list of private references to relevant JavaScript entities, such as document.cookie. The body of the redirector above will inspect the parameters obj and $prop$ as needed to see if they represent document.cookie. If yes, the redirector proceeds to carry out a replacement action supplied during template instantiation.

The implementation of the replacement action is the topic of Section 4. For now, it suffices to understand the replacement action simply as JavaScript code. It can perform computation and analysis on the arguments of the redirector, provide helpful promptings to the user, and/or carry out other relevant tasks. One typical task that it carries out is to advance the monitoring state of the edit automaton used by the security policy.

The second example of the Get category is on accessing window.alert. Note that JavaScript allows a method to be accessed in the same way as a field. For example, var f = window.alert assigns the method window.alert to a variable f. This is handled during rewriting using the same Get category as described above, and the body of sec.GetProp can monitor such access and implement related policies (*e.g.*, to replace the access to window.alert with the access to an instrumented version sec.alert).

The remainder of the table follows the same intuition. $(\text{Call}, obj, meth)$ tells the rewriter to look for syntactic categories relevant to method calls (*e.g.*, $obj.prop(E, \dots)$, $obj[\text{"}prop\text{"}](E, \dots)$) and produce a call to a redirector sec.CallMeth. The argument E to the method invocation is rewritten to E_i following the same set of rewriting rules (the same also applies to other cases in the table). $(\text{GetD}, dprop)$ and $(\text{CallD}, dmeth)$ are for accessing default properties and calling default methods. $(\text{Set}, obj, prop)$ and $(\text{SetD}, dprop)$ are for setting object properties and default properties.

Sometimes relevant actions are coded as event handlers of certain HTML tags. For example, the code <button onclick = "alert()"> raises an alert window whenever the button is clicked. The template $(\text{Event}, tag, attr)$ captures such event handling constructs. The redirector sec.Event takes the instrumented expression E_i and the parent object this of the attribute as arguments. The exact implementation of the redirector depends on the security policy. Typically, the internal state of the policy edit automaton is updated while entering and exiting the corresponding event.

The last template (FSrc) is on the loading of external resources, such as those initiated by <img src="E"> and <iframe src="E">. Instead of directly loading such a resource, we use an event handler with a redirector for interposition. The src attribute is modified from the original URL U to a space character to trigger immediately a corresponding event (*e.g.*, onerror for img, onload for iframe). In the rewritten event handler, after binding the original event handler (rewritten from E to E_i) back to the event for execution later, we call a redirector function (*e.g.*, sec.FSimg, sec.FSiframe). The redirector implementation depends on the policy. For example, it may check the target domain of the URL U to identify where the HTTP request is sent, perform other URL filtering, and/or present user prompting. In general, this rule is also applicable to some other cases of HTTP requests (*e.g.*, <a href = "U">), except different event handlers (*e.g.*, onclick) and redirectors (*e.g.*, sec.FShref) are used accordingly.

Although designed mainly for rewriting actions (A), the rewriting templates are also applicable for handling higher-order script. For example, document.write(E) should be rewritten using sec.instrument (the realization of the instr of Figure 1). This can be represented using the Call template as (Call, document, write). In our prototype, however, the handling of higher-order script is directly coded in the rewriter for efficiency, since it is always performed regardless of what the security policy is.

There are some other cases where built-in rewriting rules are applied. Selected ones are given in the companion technical report [9]. Most of the cases are designed to handle script that is not available statically, but rather generated or loaded at runtime. Others are for facilitating error handling and instrumentation transparency.

In summary, the proxy performs rewriting by syntax-directed pattern matching on ASTs, and redirectors are used to implement appropriate interposition logic and security polices. Built-in rewriting rules are always applied, but a policy designer may customize action replacement using rewriting templates. If the same rewriting template is instantiated multiple times on different entities, a single rewriting rule with a merged function body for the redirector is produced. The proxy only rewrites cases described by the given rewriting rules. If a certain security policy only uses one rewriting template (*e.g.*, get, possibly with multiple instantiations), then only one rewriting rule is produced, and only the corresponding syntactic constructs (*e.g.*, obj.prop, obj["prop"]) are rewritten. This avoids unnecessary rewriting and execution overhead.

4   Policy Writing and Management

The rewriting templates and their redirector code in Section 3 serve as a low-level policy mechanism. It allows policy designers to focus on the abstract notion of "actions" without being distracted by the idiosyncrasies of JavaScript syntax. However, it provides little help on encoding edit automata. If used for construction, a policy designer needs to implement states and transitions of policy automata in the redirectors.

We now discuss a more manageable framework that directly accommodates the notion of edit automata, allowing policy designers to focus on implementing replacement actions (*e.g.*, insertion of runtime checks). The key of this framework is the policy compiler in Figure 3, a stand-alone program compiling policies into rewriting rules off-line.

(**Get**, *obj, prop*) / ... *filtering code...*

```
<template name = "ReadAccessFiltering">
  <object> obj </object>
  <property> prop </property>
  <states> some_state </states>
  <replacement>
    ... filtering code ...
  </replacement>
</template>
```

Fig. 4. Read access filtering

(**Call**, *obj, meth*) / ... *filtering code...*

```
<template name = "CallFiltering">
  <object> obj </object>
  <property> meth </property>
  <states> some_state </states>
  <replacement>
    ... filtering code ...
  </replacement>
</template>
```

Fig. 5. Call filtering

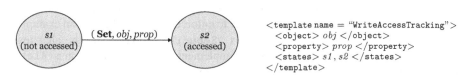

(**Set**, *obj, prop*)

```
<template name = "WriteAccessTracking">
  <object> obj </object>
  <property> prop </property>
  <states> s1, s2 </states>
</template>
```

Fig. 6. Write access tracking

In essence, an edit automaton concerns a set of states (with one as an initial state), a set of actions, and a set of state transitions. In any state, an input action determines which transition to take and which output action to produce. We use an XML file to describe all these aspects for an edit automaton as a security policy. Due to space constraints, we refer interested readers to the companion technical report [9] for the details of the XML representation and its compilation to rewriting rules.

During our policy experiments, we identified several commonly used patterns of edit automata. We organize these as *policy templates*. Instead of always describing an edit automaton from scratch, a policy designer may instantiate a relevant template to quickly obtain a useful policy. We illustrate this with examples.

One pattern is on filtering read access to object properties (both fields and methods). The (fragment of) edit automaton is shown in Figure 4, together with an XML representation. Note that this is essentially a template to be instantiated using a specific object, property, state, and filtering code. It captures a common pattern where the property access is filtered without applying any state transition.

One may also filter method calls in a similar pattern (Figure 5). This is typically used to insert security checks for method calls. Another pattern is on tracking write access (Figure 6). This tracks the execution of property writing by transitioning the state of the automaton. The replacement action is the same as the input action. The corresponding policy template specifies two states, but no replacement action.

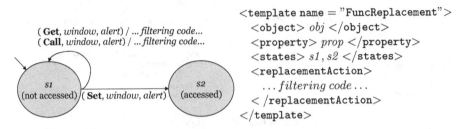

Fig. 7. Function replacement

We have implemented a total of 14 policy templates, including four on tracking property access (object and default properties; read and write access), four on filtering property access (object and default properties; read and write access), four on method calls (tracking and filtering; object and default methods), one on tracking inlined event handlers (e.g., `<body onunload="window.open();">`), and one on filtering implicit HTTP requests (e.g., images and inlined frames). The policy compiler expands instantiated policy templates into edit automata, and further compilation follows.

The above templates each describe a particular aspect of security issue. It is often the case that multiple templates are used together to enforce a useful policy. As an example, consider a simple policy of adding a prefix "Security Module : " to the alert text produced by `window.alert`. Naturally, we implement a replacement action `myAlert` as follows: `function myAlert(s) { window.alert("Security Module : " + s); }`.

This obviously requires some filtering on read access and calls to `window.alert`, as illustrated in Figures 4 and 5. For example, the former is applicable to rewriting code from `f = window.alert` to `f = myAlert`, and the latter is applicable to rewriting code from `window.alert("Hello")` to `myAlert("Hello")`.

An additional complication is that JavaScript code in the incoming document may choose to rewrite `window.alert` for other functionalities:

       `window.alert = function(s) {};`
       `window.alert("a debugging message to be ignored");`

Here, `window.alert` is redefined as an "ignore" function. It would be undesirable to perform the same filtering after the redefinition. Therefore, a more practical policy is to filter read access and calls to `window.alert` only if it has not been redefined.[1] This can be addressed using write access tracking as in Figure 6.

A compound edit automaton can be obtained by combining read access filtering, call filtering, and write access tracking, as shown on the left side of Figure 7. In our XML representation, this can be achieved using a direct combination of the three instantiated templates. This is a very common pattern, because any methods could be redefined in incoming JavaScript code. Therefore, we also support a compound template `FuncReplacement` (shown on the right side of Figure 7) to directly represent this pattern. The actual policy on `window.alert` can then be obtained by instantiating this compound template with the corresponding parameters.

---

[1] Readers might wonder if this could be exploited to circumvent the instrumentation. The answer is no, because the function body of the new definition would be instrumented as usual.

We have also implemented some other compound templates to represent common ways of template composition. Examples include one on filtering default function calls up to redefinition and one on tracking the invocation of global event handlers.

As a summary, instantiated policy templates are expanded into edit automata, which in turn are compiled into rewriting rules and redirectors. The XML-based representation supports arbitrary edit automata for expressiveness, and some domain-specific templates are introduced to ease the task of policy construction.

5 Runtime Interaction with Proxy and with Client

5.1 Structure of Instrumented Documents

We have described two stand-alone components—one is the proxy for the instrumentation of incoming contents at runtime, the other is a policy compiler compiling high-level security policies (edit automata) into low-level rewriting rules off-line. These two components collaborate to complete the instrumentation tasks.

The structure of an instrumented document is shown in Figure 8. Based on the rewriting rules, the proxy replaces relevant syntactic constructs in the incoming content with calls to redirectors. The proxy also inserts a *security module*, which contains the realization of the special instruction *instr* and policy module Π in Figure 1. Specifically, *instr* exhibits itself as a utility function sec.instrument (more in Section 5.2), and the policy module Π is interfaced through the redirectors. The redirectors call certain transition functions for maintaining edit automata at runtime, and invoke some replacement actions provided by policy designers. These functions may also refer to other utility functions as needed. We will discuss one such utility function on user notification in Section 5.3. Other commonly used utility functions include those for IP normalization, URL filtering, and policy object embedding and manipulation.

Since the security module is realized as regular JavaScript code, it resides in the same execution environment as incoming contents, and thus must be protected from malicious exploits. For example, malicious JavaScript code may modify the implementation of the security module by overwriting the functions of security checks. We organize the security module in a designated object named sec, and rename all other objects that could cause conflicts (*i.e.,* changing sec into _sec, _sec into __sec, and so on).

Although sec is usually inserted by the proxy during rewriting, sometimes a window could be created without going through the proxy at all. For example, the incoming

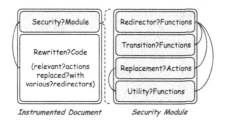

Fig. 8. Structure of an instrumented document

content may use window.open() to open up an empty new window without triggering the proxy. Once the window is open, its content could be updated by the JavaScript code in the parent window. In response, we explicitly load a sec object into the empty new window when needed, so as to correctly enforce its future behaviors.

Another potential concern is that the incoming code could modify the call sites to the redirectors through JavaScript's flexible reflection mechanisms. Suppose the rewritten document contains a node that calls sec.GetProp. Using features such as innerHTML, incoming script could attempt to overwrite the node with some different code, such as exploit. This is in fact one form of higher-order script, and it is correctly handled, provably [19], following the theoretical framework of Figure 1. In particular, the runtime-generated script exploit will be sent back to the proxy for further instrumentation before executed; therefore, it cannot circumvent the security policy. In essence, the effect of using the runtime-generated code exploit as above is not different from statically using exploit in the original content directly.

Finally, the proxy-centric architecture is browser-independent in theory, and the proxy should work for all browsers. In practice, however, different browsers sometimes behave differently when rendering the same content, due to either implementation flaws or ambiguity and incompleteness of the language specification [3] (*e.g.,* some behaviors are undefined). The companion technical report provides more details on this aspect.

5.2   Calling Proxy at Runtime

The utility function instrument needs to call the proxy at runtime to handle higher-order script. Therefore, we need to invoke the rewriters on the proxy from within the JavaScript code on the client. This is done with help of the XMLHttpRequest object [17] (or ActiveX in IE), which allows us to send runtime-generated JavaScript/HTML code to the proxy and receive their rewritten result.

An interesting subtlety is that XMLHttpRequest is restricted to communicate only with servers that reside in the same domain as the origin of the current document. We use a specially encoded HTTP request, targeting the host of the current document, as the argument to XMLHttpRequest. Since all HTTP requests go through the proxy, the proxy is able to intercept relevant requests based on the path encoding and respond with the instrumentation result. Some key code, simplified (*e.g.,* the handling of the scope chain is omitted) for ease of reading, is given below for illustration:

```
// This function sends str to the proxy for instrumentation.
// str is either HTML or JavaScript code, depending on type.
function instrument (type, str) {
    var xhr  = new XMLHttpRequest();
    var url = "http://" + location.hostname + "/?__proxy__/"
                       + type + "&url = " + escape(location.href);
    try{
        xhr.open("POST", url, false);   // false specifies synchronous communication.
        xhr.send(str);
    }catch(e){...}
    return xhr.responseXML;            // The result of the instrumentation is in XML.
}
```

5.3   User Interaction

Effective user interaction upon a policy violation is important for practical deployment. A simple notification mechanism such as a dialogue box may not appear sufficiently friendly or informative to some users. Upon most policy violations, we overlay the notification messages on top of the rendered content. This better attracts the user's attention, disables the user's access to the problematic content, and allows the user to better assess the situation by comparing the notification message with the rendered content.

This would be straightforward if we were to change the browser implementation. However, in the proxy architecture, we need to implement such notification in HTML. To enable the overlaying effect, we use a combination of JavaScript and Cascading Style Sheets (CSS) to provide the desired font, color, visibility, opacity and rendering areas. An interesting issue occurs, however, because such functionality works by directly manipulating the document tree. This manipulation happens after the entire document is loaded, *e.g.*, by using an `onload` event handler. Unfortunately, a policy violation may occur before the `onload` event. In this case, we fall back to use either dialogue boxes, silent suppression, or page redirection based on different code and error scenarios [9].

6   Experiments

We have run our proxy with several browsers: Firefox, Konqueror, Opera, Safari, Safari Mobile on iPhone, and (partially) IE. During experiments, we manually confirmed that appropriate error notifications were given upon policy violations. In this section, we report some performance measurements on well-behaved web pages to demonstrate the overhead. These measurements were made mainly using Firefox as the rendering browser, with help of the Firebug [7] add-on. Specifically, we profiled JavaScript execution in target web pages without counting in certain network-relevant activities, such as those due to the loading of inlined frames and external JavaScript sources, and the communication through `XMLHTTPRequest`. Two machines were used in the experiments—one as the proxy, the other as the client. Both machines have the same configuration: Intel Pentium 4, clock rate 3.2GHz, 1.5 GB of RAM, running FreeBSD 6.2. Micro-benchmarks are given in the companion technical report due to space constraints.

6.1   Macro-benchmarks

To learn how the instrumentation works under typical browsing behaviors, we run macro-benchmarks using a selected set of policies and some popular web applications.

Policy Set.3 We crafted a set of policies to serve together as the policy input to the proxy, as listed in Table 2. The policies are selected based on both relevance to security and coverage of rewriting rules. The Cookie policy warns against the loading of dynamic foreign links after a cookie access [10], helping preventing XSS. The IFrame policy warns against foreign links serving as iframe sources, helping preventing a form of phishing. The IP-URL policy disallows dynamic IP URLs so as to prevent incoming script from analysing the presence of hosts on the local network. The Pop-up policy sets a limit on the number of pop-up windows, and restricts the behaviors of unwieldy

Table 2. Policy set and coverage of rewriting cases

	Get	Call	GetD	CallD	Set	SetD	Event	FSrc
Cookie	X							
IFrame					X			X
IP-URL					X	X		X
Pop-up	X	X	X	X	X	X		
URL-Event					X	X	X	X

Table 3. Target applications and various performance measurements

	DoCoMo (corporate)	LinkedIn (social)	WaMu (bank)	MSN (portal)	YouTube (video)	MSNBC (news)	GMap (map)	GMail (email)
size before (B)	24,433	97,728	156,834	170,927	187,324	404,311	659,512	899,840
size after (B)	28,047	144,646	141,024	252,004	232,606	495,568	959,097	1,483,577
ratio	1.15	1.48	0.90	1.47	1.24	1.23	1.45	1.65
proxy time (ms)	614	1,724	2,453	3,933	4,423	7,290	10,570	14,570
time before (ms)	94	82	553	402	104	2,832	1,369	4,542
time after (ms)	143	143	688	695	167	3,719	1,783	7,390
time ratio	1.52	1.74	1.24	1.73	1.61	1.31	1.30	1.63
time diff (ms)	49	61	135	293	63	887	414	2,848

(*e.g.*, , very small/large, out-of-boundary, and respawning) pop-ups. Finally, the URL-Event policy inspects certain event handlers (*e.g.*, `onclick`) to prevent malicious code from updating target URLs unexpectedly (*e.g.*, redirection to a phishing site after a linked is clicked). These together cover all the rewriting cases of Table 1.

Target Applications and Overheads. We hand-picked a variety of web pages as the target applications. These applications and their "code" sizes (for contents that require rewriting, including JavaScript and various HTML constructs, but excluding images, etc) before and after the instrumentation are listed in the top portion of Table 3. A variety of sizes are included, ranging from about 24KB to nearly 900KB. Recall that the proxy produces rewritten code and inserts a security module. The sizes in Table 3 are about the rewritten code only. The security module is always the same once we fix the policy set. For our policy set, the security module is 16,202 bytes; it is automatically cached by the browser, thus reducing network cost.

The ratio row shows how much the code size grew after instrumentation. In most cases, the growth was less than 50%. The worst case was the inbox of GMail, where the nearly 900KB of code grew by 65%. Interestingly, the WaMu code reduced by about 10% after instrumentation. By inspection, we found out that there was a significant amount of code commented out in the WaMu page, which was removed by the proxy.

The middle row shows proxy rewriting time, calculated based on the average of 50 runs. The figures are roughly proportional to the code sizes. The proxy spent a few seconds for smaller applications but over ten seconds for bigger ones. Since there was usually multiple code chunks processed, the client side perceptual delay was alleviated, because part of the content had started rendering even before the rewriting was done.

The bottom portion is Firefox interpretation time of the code before and after rewriting. The ratio and diff columns show the proportional and absolute time increases for rendering the instrumented code. For most applications, the absolute increase is negligible with respect to user perception. For GMail, the increase is nearly three seconds.

6.2 Safari Mobile on iPhone

We briefly report our experience of web browsing using Safari Mobile on iPhone. Although there has been some fluctuation of traffic in the WLAN, the numbers we collected still seems useful in describing the perceptual overhead introduced by the proxy.

When directly loading the applications of Table 3 without using the proxy, almost all pages started showing within 7-12 seconds, and finished loading (as indicated by a blue progress bar) within 11-24 seconds. The only exception was the inbox of GMail, which took well over a minute to be rendered. When loading the applications through the proxy, almost all pages started showing within 9-14 seconds (with exceptions described below). The finish time of the loading varied from 15 seconds to over a minute.

A few special cases are worth noting. MSNBC used a special page for rendering on iPhones; it took on average about 11 seconds for the entire page to be loaded without the proxy, and 15 seconds with the proxy. For GMap, we further experimented with the address searching functionality. It took on average 17 seconds to render the resulting map without the proxy, and 34 seconds with the proxy. GMail inbox could not be rendered through the proxy, because the proxy does not currently support the CONNECT protocol [13] for tunnelling the SSL'ed login information. In contrast, our tested desktop browsers were set up to use direct connections for SSL'ed contents.

7   Related Work

There has been work applying code instrumentation to the security of machine code and Java bytecode. SFI [18] prevents access to memory locations outside of predefined regions. SASI [4] generalizes SFI to enforce security policies specified as security automata. Program Shepherding [11] restricts execution privileges on the basis of code origin, monitors control flow transfers to prevent the execution of data or modified code, and ensures that libraries are entered only through exported entry points. Naccio [6] enforces policies that place arbitrary constraints on resource manipulations as well as policies that alter how a program manipulates resources. PoET [5] applies inlined reference monitors to enforces EM policies [16] on Java bytecode. As pointed out by several studies [4,15,19], the above work is not directly applicable to JavaScript instrumentation for user-level security policies. Some notable problems include the pervasive use of reflection and higher-order script in JavaScript, the lack of flexible and usable policy management, and the difficulty of interpositioning a prototype-based object model.

A closely related work is BrowserShield [15], which applies runtime instrumentation to rewrite HTML and JavaScript. Designed mainly as a vulnerability-driven filtering mechanism to defend browser vulnerabilities prior to patch deployment, the policies of BrowserShield are mainly about vulnerability signatures, and are written directly as JavaScript functions. After initial rewriting at an enterprise firewall, rewriting logic is injected into the target web page and executed at browser rendering time. A browser plug-in is used to enable the parsing and rewriting on the client.

In contrast, we target general user-level policies, and much of our work has been on practical policy management. Specifically, domain-specific abstractions are used for policy construction, and a policy compiler is engaged to translate such constructed policies to syntactic rewriting rules. Different syntactic categories are rewritten based on different policies. For simple policies, only one or two kinds of syntactic constructs are rewritten, although a composite policy typically requires the rewriting of more. All the rewriting (both load-time and run-time) happens on a proxy. The rewritten page interacts with the proxy at runtime using `XMLHttpRequest`. No software or plug-in is required on the client. Therefore, our architecture is naturally applicable to work with multiple web browsers, even if software/plug-in installation is not allowed.

JavaScript instrumentation has also been applied to the monitoring of client-side behaviors of web applications. Specifically, AjaxScope [8] applies on-the-fly instrumentation of JavaScript code as it is sent to users' browsers, and provides facilities for reducing the client-side overhead and giving fine-grained visibility into the code-level behaviors of the web applications. Targeting the development and improvement of non-malicious code (*e.g.*, during debugging), AjaxScope does not instrument code that is generated at runtime (*i.e.*, higher-order script). Therefore, the rewriting is simpler and, as is, not suitable as a security protection mechanism against malicious code.

8   Conclusion and Future Work

We have presented a JavaScript instrumentation prototype for browser security. We reported experiences on instrumenting various JavaScript constructs, composing user-level policies, and using a proxy to enable runtime rewriting. Our proxy enables flexible deployment scenarios. It naturally works with multiple browsers, and does not require software installation on the client. It provides a centralized control point for policy management, and poses relatively small computation requirement on the client. Although not optimized, our prototype yields promising results on the feasibility of the approach.

In the future, we plan to conduct more experiments based on real-world web browsing patterns (*e.g.*, top URLs from web searches) and improve the support on popular browsers (most notably IE). We also plan to study the instrumentation of plug-in contents. For example, VBScript and Flash are both based on the ECMAScript standard [3], thus our instrumentation techniques are also applicable.

Our proxy-based architecture does not directly work with encrypted contents (*e.g.*, SSL). Some of our tested web pages (*e.g.*, GMail) uses SSL, but only for transmitting certain data, such as the login information. If the entire page was transmitted through SSL (as is the case of many banking sites), then the proxy cannot perform rewriting. This can be addressed by either decrypting on the proxy (if a trusted path between the proxy and the browser can be established), having the browser sending decrypted content back to the proxy, or directly implementing the instrumentation inside the browser.

Although the proxy-based architecture enables flexible deployment scenarios, a browser-based implementation may also be desirable. Some of our difficulties supporting multiple browsers have been due to their inconsistent treatment on undefined

JavaScript behaviors. If implemented inside the browser, the same parsing process would be applied to both the rendering and the instrumentation, thus avoiding extra parsing overhead and problems caused by specific semantic interpretations.

References

1. Apple Inc. Safari mobile on iphone, http://www.apple.com/iphone/internet/
2. Christey, S., Martin, R.A.: Vulnerability type distributions in CVE (2007), http://cve.mitre.org/
3. ECMA International. ECMAScript language specification. Standard ECMA-262, 3rd Edition (December 1999)
4. Erlingsson, U., Schneider, F.B.: SASI enforcement of security policies: A retrospective. In: Proc. 1999 New Security Paradigms Workshop, Caledon Hills, Ontario, Canada, pp. 87–95 (September 1999)
5. Erlingsson, U., Schneider, F.B.: IRM enforcement of Java stack inspection. In: Proc. IEEE S&P (2000)
6. Evans, D., Twyman, A.: Flexible policy-directed code safety. In: Proc. 20th IEEE S&P, pp. 32–47 (1999)
7. Hewitt, J.: Firebug—web development evolved, http://www.getfirebug.com/
8. Kiciman, E., Livshits, B.: AjaxScope: a platform for remotely monitoring the client-side behavior of web 2.0 applications. In: Proc. SOSP 2007, pp. 17–30 (2007)
9. Kikuchi, H., Yu, D., Chander, A., Inamura, H., Serikov, I.: Javascript instrumentation in practice. Technical Report DCL-TR-2008-0053, DoCoMo USA Labs (June 2008), http://www.docomolabsresearchers-usa.com/~dyu/jiip-tr.pdf
10. Kirda, E., Kruegel, C., Vigna, G., Jovanovic, N.: Noxes: a client-side solution for mitigating cross-site scripting attacks. In: Proc. 2006 ACM Symposium on Applied Computing, pp. 330–337 (2006)
11. Kiriansky, V., Bruening, D., Amarasinghe, S.P.: Secure execution via program shepherding. In: Proc. 11th USENIX Security Symposium, pp. 191–206 (2002)
12. Ligatti, J., Bauer, L., Walker, D.: Edit automata: Enforcement mechanisms for run-time security policies. International Journal of Information Security 4(2), 2–16 (2005)
13. Luotonen, A.: Tunneling TCP based protocols through web proxy servers. IETF RFC 2616 (1998)
14. OWASP Foundation. The ten most critical web application security vulnerabilities (2007), http://www.owasp.org/
15. Reis, C., Dunagan, J., Wang, H.J., Dubrovsky, O., Esmeir, S.: BrowserShield: Vulnerability-driven filtering of dynamic HTML. In: Proc. OSDI 2006, Seattle, WA (2006)
16. Schneider, F.B.: Enforceable security policies. Trans. on Information & System Security 3(1), 30–50 (2000)
17. van Kesteren, A., Jackson, D.: The XMLHttpRequest object. W3C working draft (2006), http://www.w3.org/TR/XMLHttpRequest/
18. Wahbe, R., Lucco, S., Anderson, T.E., Graham, S.L.: Efficient software-based fault isolation. In: Proc. SOSP 1993, Asheville, NC, pp. 203–216 (1993)
19. Yu, D., Chander, A., Islam, N., Serikov, I.: JavaScript instrumentation for browser security. In: Proc. POPL 2007, Nice, France, pp. 237–249 (January 2007)

Author Index

Lecture Notes in Computer Science

Sublibrary 2: Programming and Software Engineering

For information about Vols. 1– 4748
please contact your bookseller or Springer

Vol. 5052: D. Lea, G. Zavattaro (Eds.), Coordination Models and Languages. X, 347 pages. 2008.

Vol. 5051: G. Barthe, F.S. de Boer (Eds.), Formal Methods for Open Object-Based Distributed Systems. X, 259 pages. 2008.

Vol. 5048: K. Suzuki, T. Higashino, K. Yasumoto, K. El-Fakih (Eds.), Formal Techniques for Networked and Distributed Systems – FORTE 2008. XII, 341 pages. 2008.

Vol. 5047: K. Suzuki, T. Higashino, A. Ulrich, T. Hasegawa (Eds.), Testing of Software and Communicating Systems. XII, 303 pages. 2008.

Vol. 5030: H. Mei (Ed.), High Confidence Software Reuse in Large Systems. XII, 388 pages. 2008.

Vol. 5026: F. Kordon, T. Vardanega (Eds.), Reliable Software Technologies – Ada-Europe 2008. XIV, 283 pages. 2008.

Vol. 5025: B. Paech, C. Rolland (Eds.), Requirements Engineering: Foundation for Software Quality. X, 205 pages. 2008.

Vol. 5020: J. Barnes, Ada 2005 Rationale. IX, 267 pages. 2008.

Vol. 5016: M. Bernardo, P. Degano, G. Zavattaro (Eds.), Formal Methods for Computational Systems Biology. X, 538 pages. 2008.

Vol. 5014: J. Cuellar, T. Maibaum, K. Sere (Eds.), FM 2008: Formal Methods. XIII, 436 pages. 2008.

Vol. 5007: Q. Wang, D. Pfahl, D.M. Raffo (Eds.), Making Globally Distributed Software Development a Success Story. XIV, 422 pages. 2008.

Vol. 5002: H. Giese (Ed.), Models in Software Engineering. X, 322 pages. 2008.

Vol. 4989: J. Garrigue, M.V. Hermenegildo (Eds.), Functional and Logic Programming. XI, 337 pages. 2008.

Vol. 4970: M. Nagl, W. Marquardt (Eds.), Collaborative and Distributed Chemical Engineering. XII, 851 pages. 2008.

Vol. 4966: B. Beckert, R. Hähnle (Eds.), Tests and Proofs. X, 193 pages. 2008.

Vol. 4954: C. Pautasso, É. Tanter (Eds.), Software Composition. X, 263 pages. 2008.

Vol. 4951: M. Luck, L. Padgham (Eds.), Agent-Oriented Software Engineering VIII. XIV, 225 pages. 2008.

Vol. 4949: R.M. Hierons, J.P. Bowen, M. Harman (Eds.), Formal Methods and Testing. XIII, 367 pages. 2008.

Vol. 4937: M. Dumas, R. Heckel (Eds.), Web Services and Formal Methods. IX, 169 pages. 2008.

Vol. 4922: M. Broy, I.H. Krüger, M. Meisinger (Eds.), Model-Driven Development of Reliable Automotive Services. XVIII, 183 pages. 2008.

Vol. 4916: S. Leue, P. Merino (Eds.), Formal Methods for Industrial Critical Systems. X, 251 pages. 2008.

Vol. 4909: I. Eusgeld, F.C. Freiling, R. Reussner (Eds.), Dependability Metrics. XI, 305 pages. 2008.

Vol. 4906: M. Cebulla (Ed.), Object-Oriented Technology. VIII, 204 pages. 2008.

Vol. 4902: P. Hudak, D.S. Warren (Eds.), Practical Aspects of Declarative Languages. X, 333 pages. 2007.

Vol. 4899: K. Yorav (Ed.), Hardware and Software: Verification and Testing. XII, 267 pages. 2008.

Vol. 4895: J.J. Cuadrado-Gallego, R. Braungarten, R.R. Dumke, A. Abran (Eds.), Software Process and Product Measurement. X, 203 pages. 2008.

Vol. 4888: F. Kordon, O. Sokolsky (Eds.), Composition of Embedded Systems. XII, 221 pages. 2007.

Vol. 4880: S. Overhage, C. Szyperski, R. Reussner, J.A. Stafford (Eds.), Software Architectures, Components, and Applications. X, 249 pages. 2008.

Vol. 4849: M. Winckler, H. Johnson, P. Palanque (Eds.), Task Models and Diagrams for User Interface Design. XIII, 299 pages. 2007.

Vol. 4839: O. Sokolsky, S. Taşıran (Eds.), Runtime Verification. VI, 215 pages. 2007.

Vol. 4834: R. Cerqueira, R.H. Campbell (Eds.), Middleware 2007. XIII, 451 pages. 2007.

Vol. 4829: M. Lumpe, W. Vanderperren (Eds.), Software Composition. VIII, 281 pages. 2007.

Vol. 4824: A. Paschke, Y. Biletskiy (Eds.), Advances in Rule Interchange and Applications. XIII, 243 pages. 2007.

Vol. 4821: J. Bennedsen, M.E. Caspersen, M. Kölling (Eds.), Reflections on the Teaching of Programming. X, 261 pages. 2008.

Vol. 4807: Z. Shao (Ed.), Programming Languages and Systems. XI, 431 pages. 2007.

Vol. 4799: A. Holzinger (Ed.), HCI and Usability for Medicine and Health Care. XVI, 458 pages. 2007.

Vol. 4789: M. Butler, M.G. Hinchey, M.M. Larrondo-Petrie (Eds.), Formal Methods and Software Engineering. VIII, 387 pages. 2007.

Vol. 4767: F. Arbab, M. Sirjani (Eds.), International Symposium on Fundamentals of Software Engineering. XIII, 450 pages. 2007.

Vol. 4765: A. Moreira, J. Grundy (Eds.), Early Aspects: Current Challenges and Future Directions. X, 199 pages. 2007.

Vol. 4764: P. Abrahamsson, N. Baddoo, T. Margaria, R. Messnarz (Eds.), Software Process Improvement. XI, 225 pages. 2007.

Vol. 4762: K.S. Namjoshi, T. Yoneda, T. Higashino, Y. Okamura (Eds.), Automated Technology for Verification and Analysis. XIV, 566 pages. 2007.

Vol. 4758: F. Oquendo (Ed.), Software Architecture. XVI, 340 pages. 2007.

Vol. 4757: F. Cappello, T. Herault, J. Dongarra (Eds.), Recent Advances in Parallel Virtual Machine and Message Passing Interface. XVI, 396 pages. 2007.

Vol. 4753: E. Duval, R. Klamma, M. Wolpers (Eds.), Creating New Learning Experiences on a Global Scale. XII, 518 pages. 2007.

Vol. 4749: B.J. Krämer, K.-J. Lin, P. Narasimhan (Eds.), Service-Oriented Computing – ICSOC 2007. XIX, 629 pages. 2007.